THE DUAL BRAIN

UCLA FORUM IN MEDICAL SCIENCES

NUMBER 26

SERIES EDITOR: MARY A. B. BRAZIER

University of California, Los Angeles

THE DUAL BRAIN

HEMISPHERIC SPECIALIZATION IN HUMANS

Edited by

D. FRANK BENSON

DEPARTMENT OF NEUROLOGY
UNIVERSITY OF CALIFORNIA, LOS ANGELES

ERAN ZAIDEL

DEPARTMENT OF PSYCHOLOGY
UNIVERSITY OF CALIFORNIA, LOS ANGELES

THE GUILFORD PRESS

New York   London

© 1985 The Guilford Press
A Division of Guilford Publications, Inc.
200 Park Avenue South, New York, N.Y. 10003

Printed in the United States of America

Library of Congress Cataloging in Publication Data

Main entry under title:

The Dual brain.

    (UCLA forum in medical sciences ; no. 26)
    Includes bibliographies and indexes.
    1. Cerebral dominance.   2. Brain—Localization of
functions.   3. Split brain.   I. Benson, D. Frank
(David Frank), 1928–   .   II. Zaidel, Eran.
III. Series.
QP385.5.D83   1985   612′.825   85-24755
ISBN 0-89862-643-9

UCLA FORUM IN MEDICAL SCIENCES

MARY A. B. BRAZIER, Editor

1. *Brain Function: Cortical Excitability and Steady Potentials; Relations of Basic Research to Space Biology.* Ed. Mary A. B. Brazier, 1963.
2. *Brain Function: RNA and Brain Function. Memory Learning.* Ed. Mary A. B. Brazier, 1964.
3. *Brain and Behavior: The Brain and Gonadal Function.* Eds. Roger A. Gorski and Richard E. Whalen, 1966.
4. *Brain Function: Speech, Language, and Communication.* Ed. C. Carterette, 1966.
5. *Gastrin.* Ed. Morton I. Grossman, 1966.
6. *Brain Function: Brain Function and Learning.* Eds. Donald B. Lindsley and Arthur A. Lumsdaine, 1967.
7. *Brain Function: Aggression and Defense. Neural Mechanisms and Social Patterns.* Eds. Carmine D. Clemente and Donald B. Lindsley, 1967.
8. *The Retina: Morphology, Function, and Clinical Characteristics.* Eds. Bradley R. Straatsma, Raymond A. Allen, Frederick Crescitelli, and Michael O. Hall, 1969.
9. *Image Processing in Biological Science.* Ed. Diane M. Ramsey, 1969.
10. *Pathophysiology of Congenital Heart Disease.* Eds. Forrest H. Adams, H. J. C. Swan, and V. E. Hall, 1970.
11. *The Interneuron.* Ed. Mary A. B. Brazier, 1969.
12. *The History of Medical Education.* Ed. C. D. O'Malley, 1970.
13. *Cardiovascular Beta Adrenergic Responses.* Eds. Albert A. Kattus, Jr., Gordon Ross, and Rex N. MacAlpin, 1970.
14. *Cellular Aspects of Neural Growth and Differentiation.* Ed. Daniel C. Pease, 1971.
15. *Steroid Hormones and Brain Function.* Eds. Charles Sawyer and Roger A. Gorski, 1971.
16. *Multiple Sclerosis: Immunology, Virology, and Ultrastructure.* Eds. Frederick Wolfgram, George Ellison, Jack Stevens, and John Andrews, 1972.
17. *Epilepsy: Its Phenomena in Man.* Ed. Mary A. B. Brazier, 1973.
18. *Brain Mechanisms in Mental Retardation.* Eds. Nathaniel A. Buchwald and Mary A. B. Brazier, 1975.
19. *Amyotrophic Lateral Sclerosis: Recent Research Trends.* Eds. John M. Andrews, Richard T. Johnson, and Mary A. B. Brazier, 1976.

CONTRIBUTORS TO THIS VOLUME

D. FRANK BENSON, MD
Department of Neurology

JOSEPH E. BOGEN, MD
Department of Psychology

WARREN S. BROWN, PhD
Department of Psychiatry and
Graduate School of Psychology,
Fuller Theological Seminary,
Pasadena, California

PAUL H. CRANDALL, MD
Departments of Surgery and Neurology

JEFFREY L. CUMMINGS, MD
Department of Neurology

SUSAN CURTISS, PhD
Department of Linguistics

JEROME ENGEL, JR., MD, PhD
Department of Neurology

ALAN FORSYTHE, PhD
Department of Biomathematics

ITZHAK FRIED, PhD
Departments of Anatomy and
Psychiatry

VICTORIA A. FROMKIN, PhD
Department of Linguistics

ROGER A. GORSKI, PhD
Department of Anatomy

ROLANDO HENRY, PhD
Department of Psychiatry

MELISSA HINES, PhD
Department of Anatomy

ANN KAO
Department of Anatomy

JAMES T. MARSH, PhD
Department of Psychiatry

JOHN C. MAZZIOTTA, MD, PhD
Departments of Neurology and
Radiological Sciences

J. RICHARD MENDIUS, MD
Department of Neurology

DOUGLAS NOFFSINGER, PhD
Department of Head and Neck Surgery

DONNA L. ORSINI, PhD
Department of Psychiatry

LINDA PAUL, PhD
Department of Anatomy

MICHAEL E. PHELPS, PhD
Department of Radiological Sciences
and Laboratory of Biomedical and
Environmental Sciences

RONALD E. PONSFORD, PhD
Department of Psychiatry

REBECCA RAUSCH, PhD
Department of Psychiatry

ERIC SASLOW, MD
Department of Pediatrics

PAUL SATZ, PhD
Department of Psychiatry

ARNOLD B. SCHEIBEL, MD
Departments of Anatomy and
Psychiatry

AVRAHAM SCHWEIGER, PhD
Department of Psychology

JAMES SLOTNICK
Department of Anatomy

ROGER W. SPERRY, PhD
Division of Biology, California Institute
of Technology, Pasadena, California

PETER E. TANGUAY, MD
Department of Psychiatry

WARREN D. TENHOUTEN, PhD
Department of Sociology

UWAMIE TOMIYASU, MD
Department of Pathology

ADAM WECHSLER, MD
Department of Neurology

M. C. WITTROCK, PhD
Department of Education

DAHLIA W. ZAIDEL, PhD
Department of Psychology

ERAN ZAIDEL, PhD
Department of Psychology

PREFACE

This volume represents the 26th in a series founded by Dr. Sherman Mellinkoff in 1960, a series to which he gave the name UCLA Forum in Medical Sciences. In the past quarter century 26 symposia have been held at UCLA representing many diverse activities of its School of Medicine.

The goal of these conferences and of the volumes that follow from them cannot be expressed more eloquently than in the words of Dr. Mellinkoff in the Preface of Volume 1 of the series:

> The UCLA Forum in Medical Sciences has been created to review, to synthesize, and to analyze rather than to serve as another outlet for original papers. The Forum will be published irregularly as the spirit moves the Editorial Board and as those from our own school and from afar gather under its aegis for discussion.
>
> The topics will vary widely from the deep roots of medicine in biology, chemistry, and physics to the applied medical arts. It is our hope that each volume, whatever its subject, will in its sphere provide that broad view which stands between atomistic surfeit on the one hand and a formless void on the other.
>
> Even more we hope that the Forum will reflect among participants, auditors, and readers alike, a certain warmth felt by those whose labors are related by content and aspiration to works in distant lands and, indeed, related to life itself.

In its way, however, this present volume breaks new ground for it is the first in the series in which only one of the primary contributors is not affiliated with UCLA. It therefore reflects essentially the views of the workers here on this most fascinating topic of lateralization in the brain.

Mary A. B. Brazier
Editor-in-Chief
UCLA Forum in Medical Sciences

WELCOMING ADDRESS

SHERMAN MELLINKOFF, MD
Dean, UCLA School of Medicine

Forty-four years ago — as freshman medical students — our class was told that the left cerebral hemisphere was very important, as we could all see in right-handed patients with brain tumors or strokes. The other hemisphere was thought, in Roger Sperry's words much later, "to be typically lacking . . . in the cognitive faculties . . . [and] in higher cognitive function." So entrenched was that belief that in the early 1960s, when Roger Sperry and his colleagues, who were to be joined by Eran Zaidel, one of the editors of this volume, were publishing their initial papers on the great importance of the neglected half of the human split brain, the surgeon who had severed the two hemispheres as a treatment for intractable epilepsy asked that his name be removed from those revolutionary papers.

This sequence of discovery is a recurrent theme in the history of science. In the late eighteenth century the French physiologist Bichat had ventured to suspect that contrary to prevailing opinion it was unlikely that nature would have created an organ as large as the liver solely for the purpose of excreting a liquid less copious than urine.

Pioneers have repeatedly faced the truth expressed by Josh Billings, who said, "It ain't so much what we don't know that holds us back; it's more what we do know that ain't so."

How far we have been taken beyond the Billings handicap in understanding the hemispheric specialization of the human brain is the timely purpose of this volume, and I am cheered to know that all can now share this experience.

CONTENTS

CLINICAL STUDIES OF HEMISPHERIC SPECIALIZATION

CONTENTS

IMPLICATIONS

OVERVIEW

INTRODUCTION

D. FRANK BENSON, MD
Department of Neurology

That the human cerebral hemispheres are actually two separate brains, two potentially independent sources of mental activity, is a relatively recent idea and one that remains vague and controversial. A growing body of evidence indicates that each hemisphere alone is capable of sustaining mental life and that, even when working together, each carries out some activities that are unique to that hemisphere. Removal of an entire hemisphere, either right or left, has been carried out on both children and adults; while suffering significant residual defects, the subjects of hemispherectomy are able to react in a human manner. A single cerebral hemisphere, either right or left, is capable of carrying out a mental life. In addition, study of subjects following separation of the two hemispheres by section of the corpus callosum reveals that each hemisphere can carry out many responses independently. The two separated hemispheres may show quite different responses to the same stimulus. The demonstration of these individual hemispheric qualities in the 1950s and 1960s led to a variety of dual-brain theories. These hypotheses of independent hemispheric actions impinge on and, theoretically, influence many divergent fields of study. A number of the diverse but related approaches to hemispheric activity will be presented, and some of the implications this work has for future investigations of human mental function will be explored.

While the demonstration that the two hemispheres of the human brain could act as separate functional entities is of recent origin, there were suggestions, even in antiquity, that separate portions of the brain could carry out different functions. An anterior–posterior "localization" of perception, reasoning, and memory into anterior, middle, and posterior parts of the brain, respectively, was the prevalent theory for almost 2,000 years (6). In addition, crossed innervation of the hemispheres was clearly demonstrated in the days of Hippocrates but was not widely known or utilized. It was not until the early 18th century that definitive demonstrations of localized brain function were first presented, when Morgagni (5) demonstrated crossed innervation. A century later Meynert (4) demonstrated the anterior–posterior distribution of motor and sensory functions in the cerebral cortex. Along with the correlation of behavioral functions with neuroanatomical areas, suggestion was made that the two hemispheres could perform independently (8). Despite the suggestion of dual minds, it was not until 1865, following Broca's behavioral–anatomical correlation of language loss with focal brain damage, that a functional specialization for a single cerebral hemisphere was first proposed (1). The evidence accumulated by Broca and his contemporaries that the left hemisphere subserved the function of language in the vast majority of humans was so overwhelming that it was accepted as fact; left-hemisphere dominance for language has remained an accepted medical dictum. It was, however, a case of blind acceptance, recognition of an observed fact that was not understood, and remained in that status for almost a century. Thus, while physicians dealing with the brain were fully aware of the importance (dominance) of the left hemisphere in language functions, this was accepted as a clinically useful curiosity, not as an indication of differences in the hemispheres. It has taken many generations of investigators and a good deal of additional observation to discount the notion that the brain acts as a single functional unit, an idea that still remains popular.

Reluctance to accept a novel observation, even when strong proof has been produced, is not unusual in science; this situation is well recorded in neuroanatomy. The remarkable (and almost simultaneous) investigations of Golgi (3) and Ramón y Cajal (7), utilizing silver stains to demonstrate the morphology of neurons, were widely accepted, but many of the implications of these investigations for neural function were not even considered. It took a number of generations of newly trained neuroscientists, each aware of the early demonstrations and progressively less indoctrinated by academic dogma, to utilize the silver-staining techniques and the implications of these demonstrations to the understanding of cell physiology. Only recent generations of neuroanatomists have been able to put these techniques to the broad use they deserve.

The possibility of dual, separately functioning cerebral hemispheres has been even slower in development. Despite the clear demonstration of significant differences in the functions of the two hemispheres in the 1860s, it is only within the present generation of investigators that this information has been accepted and broadened in attempting to understand brain function. Why has there been such a reluctance to consider the cerebral hemispheres as functionally discrete entities? A number of pertinent reasons can be suggested, all of which appear partially responsible.

First, there has always been a strong religious/philosophical/academic tendency to speak of the mind rather than the brain when discussing human mental function. In this context the mind is considered a holistic entity, a responsive organism that is quite separate from the static concept of the brain pictured in neuroanatomy textbooks or seen as a specimen in a formaldehyde bucket. The concept of mind as a single functioning unit remains strong, actually prevalent, in the thinking of most who discuss and investigate mental activities, and the premise of a single mental activity continues to act as a strong damper on considerations of localized brain function. The mind, while sufficiently nonspecific as to approach the mythological, has remained more powerful than the brain in conjectures about mental life.

Actually, the differences between holistic and localizationist approaches came to be exaggerated as the topic of active debate for over a century. Since the time of Gall, the father of phrenology, whose major treatise on the localization of functions within portions of the brain was published in 1810 (2), there has been a schism between those brain scientists who seek cerebral localization for function and another group who consider that the most important brain functions reflect activity of the entire brain. At times the disagreement has been formal, such as the academic presentations to an Anthropological Society where Broca first demonstrated his cases of aphasia, but more often the presentations have been purely one-sided written discourses. The participants have tended to develop fixed and codified approaches, based on their stance in the continuing controversy. While most investigators admit that both approaches offer useful ideas, movement away from either the holistic or localizationist stances has proved difficult.

Finally, the greatest problem keeping all of us from readily accepting that a major mental function can be carried out by one human cerebral hemisphere but not the other concerns the uniqueness of this finding in biology. While some recent evidence suggests a degree of anatomical asymmetry in the human cerebral hemispheres, merely gazing at medical illustrations or even at the hemispheres themselves demonstrates that the degree of symmetry is far more striking than the subtle differences. To all but closely studied comparison, the right hemisphere appears to be the mirror image of the left hemisphere. In fact, there are many dual organs in the human body in which the degree of symmetry is considerably less. For instance, the right and left lungs are readily distinguished grossly and, in fact, do not even have the same number of major divisions. The two kidneys, two thyroids, two parathyroids, and even the two testicles are routinely asymmetrical. The differences between analogous areas of right and left cerebral hemispheres are far less striking than the similarities. Even more important, however, is the knowledge that throughout animal biology there are countless examples of bilateral organs that are mirror images of each other and carry out identical functions. Thus, the human body has two lungs, two kidneys, a pair of thyroid glands, paired reproductive glands, and multiple double appendages (including eyes, ears, arms, legs, etc.); and, almost without exception, the right- and left-sided paired organs perform identical functions. The demonstration by Broca and his contemporaries that language was a function of the left cerebral hemisphere alone was so totally unique and unexpected that for over a century it was accepted as a clinical fact without serious attempts to seek or understand other asymmetries of the human cerebral hemispheres. Even in more recent years, despite the evidence from hemispherectomy and split-brain surgery, the implications of these observations have not ranked high in discussions of mental function. Holistic approaches have held sway in academic approaches to mental activity. Nonetheless, it is now becoming clear that recognition of hemispheric asymmetry of function is essential to both present and future understanding of human mental function. Among milestones of thought, Broca's demonstration of hemispheric specialization may well rank with Darwin's theory of evolution and Freud's demonstration of the unconscious as the major intellectual discoveries of the 19th century.

Within the past several decades, a number of functions other than language have been demonstrated to function asymmetrically within the human cerebri. The continuing demonstration of such functional differences and the implications that these differences have to human mental function will be the topic of this presentation.

REFERENCES

1. Broca, P., Sur la faculté du langage articulé. *Bull. Soc. Anthr.* (Paris), 1865, 6: 337–393.
2. Gall, F., and Spurzheim, G., *The Anatomy and Physiology of the Nervous System in General and the Brain in Particular*. F. Schoell, Paris, 1810–1819 (4 volumes).
3. Golgi, C., *Il Sistema Nervoso Centrale*. Vallardi, Milano, 1883.
4. Meynert, T., The brain of mammals. In: *Manual of Human and Comparative Histology*, Vol. II (S. Stricker, Ed.). New Sydenham Society, London, 1872: 367–537.
5. Morgagni, J. B., *De sedibus et causis morborum per anatomen indagatis*. Padua, 1761.
6. Pagel, W., Medieval and Renaissance contributions to knowledge of the brain and its functions. In: *The History and Philosophy of the Brain and Its Functions* (F. N. L. Peyater, Ed.). Charles C Thomas, Springfield, Ill., 1958.
7. Ramón y Cajal, S. R., *Degeneration and Regeneration of the Nervous System* (R. M. May, Trans.). Oxford University Press, Oxford, 1928.
8. Wigan, A. L., *The Duality of the Mind*. Longmans, London, 1844.

ROGER W. SPERRY: AN APPRECIATION

ERAN ZAIDEL, PhD
Department of Psychology

Roger Wolcott Sperry was born in Hartford, Connecticut, on August 20, 1913. He received his BA in English and his MA in psychology from Oberlin College and his PhD in zoology from the University of Chicago. From 1954 until his retirement in July 1984, he was the Hixon Professor of Psychobiology at the California Institute of Technology. At the present time he is continuing his work at Cal Tech as Professor Emeritus.

In 1981, he was awarded the Nobel Prize in Physiology and Medicine, shared with David Hubel and Torsten Wiesel from Harvard, for his work on hemispheric specialization in the split brain (2). While his Pasadena office struggled to handle the deluge of calls and telegrams that poured in from well-wishers all over the world, Sperry and his wife snorkeled along the beaches of the Sea of Cortez off Baja California, returning only after the hoopla had subsided.

Dr. Sperry's contributions to the study of hemispheric specialization are of such obvious stature that we decided to dedicate this volume to him and preface it with a short review of his accomplishments, particularly in the field of hemispheric specialization, and an abstract of the philosophical directions he has developed from this material. These brief comments will serve to introduce Dr. Sperry's following chapter, an update of his last major public lecture delivered at the Smithsonian Institution in 1977.

Twice in his scientific career Sperry boldly overthrew existing scientific dogma: first in connection with his work on neurospecificity, and later with his work on the functions of the corpus callosum and the specialization of the two cerebral hemispheres. In both cases, his view was strongly connectionist, emphasizing the hardwired aspects of brain organization. But both also focused on very general questions: the development of behavioral networks in the central nervous system, and principles of brain integration for higher mental activity, especially consciousness.

Sperry's work in nerve transplantation and on the orderly regeneration of surgically scrambled central fiber systems directly challenged the anticonnectivity or "resonance" impulse-specificity ideas of his teacher, Paul Weiss. It also radically revised and extended the ideas of his mentor, Karl Lashley, who in accoreance with the prevailing views of the 1940s believed in wholesale plasticity of the brain.

In turn, his work on callosal mediation of information transfer between the two cerebral hemispheres directly opposed some earlier negative experiments on the effects of callosal section in humans. In his Nobel lecture, he noted that split-brain studies have led to a better appreciation of nonverbal forms of intelligence and increased understanding of "the inherent individuality in the structure of human intellect." He also feels his research has helped to underscore the need for educational tests and policies "to selectively identify, accommodate, and serve the differentially specialized forms of individual intellectual potentials" (1).

My strongest impression of Sperry comes from his style of doing science. One sunny afternoon in the fall of 1970, I went to Professor Sperry's office on the third floor of Church Building in the Biology Division at Cal Tech and proposed a new technique for presenting information to one visual half-field at a time while permitting continuous hemispheric ocular scanning. Others had tried different electronic techniques and failed, and Sperry was skeptical. One could foresee difficulties in getting these patients to accept and to wear during testing a large scleral contact lens. He was critical but not devastating. In fact, he provided money for developing the technique, as well as office space in his psychobiology lab. For 9 months I struggled with optical design and with the precision machinists in the Chemistry Instrument Shop.

Only later, when comparing notes with fellow and former students, did I realize that Sperry's skepticism was his usual "survival test." The question was whether students had enough commitment to persevere in spite of doubts. Did they have enough insight to follow their own hunches? If they did, they would gain Sperry's respect.

Mindful of the need for a sense of personal accomplishment, Sperry did not, as a rule, try to tell students directly what experiments to run. But he was always quick to reinforce good ideas and provide tough-minded, insightful, critical analysis when it was required. And he often reminded his students to keep the big picture in mind, to ask the critical question, run the critical experiment. He said, "If the man in the street will not be affected by the results, then the experiment needs a hard look."

While one may argue about this kind of criterion, there is no doubt that the "man-in-the-street" rule is a powerful antidote to becoming lost in the technicalities of one's own field, to losing sight of the overall goals of the research program. Sperry's students absorbed the rule by osmosis during a period of apprenticeship, but not everyone flourished in this laissez-faire environment. Some younger or perhaps less independent students did not enjoy or pass the "survival test."

As scientists we must ask ourselves when an unexpected observation is an aberration, an error to be attributed to random noise and ignored, and when it can be considered a clue to a new insight. In the throes of day-to-day research, without the benefit of hindsight, the answer is not always clear. Few scientists feel secure facing this ambiguity, and even fewer are skillful and gifted enough to resolve it.

Sperry searched out and faced this ambiguity, and on two separate and notable occasions he resolved it with critical experiments: those on neural plasticity and on hemispheric specialization. He is a master at designing dramatic experiments whose results are unencumbered by special cases or complex theoretical machinery. But it is not enough just to correct ongoing errors. He advised us always to ask, "What difference does it make?" Or, even better, "What difference is it going to make 10 years from now?"

In recent years Sperry has turned his inquiring mind to considerations of philosophical questions, as illustrated by the following interview (1):

> **Question**: It seems that many scientists turn their attention to global and philosophical problems as they get older.
>
> **Sperry**: As most scientists age, they see the end approaching and they no longer have the patience to waste their time on the kinds of things they thought they could once do forever. You raise your perspectives with age. I don't think this is something to be ridiculed, as many scientists are inclined to do in their younger years. It's something to be fostered and valued—put up rather than put down.

He now concentrates his remaining creative efforts on the so-called "big three": consciousness, free will, and values—"three long-standing thorns in the hide of science." According to Sperry, "Materialist science could not cope with any of them, even in principle. It's not just that they are difficult problems, they are in direct conflict with the basic premises and models. Physical science has had to renounce them, to deny their existence, or to say that they are beyond the domain of science."

As an alternative to materialist reductionism, Sperry offers his own concept of mentalism. One key realization is that the higher levels of brain activity control the lower. The higher cerebral properties of mind and consciousness are in command.

> **Question**: How do you define mentalism?
>
> **Sperry**: In psychology mentalism is contrasted to behaviorism and materialism. It's a doctrine holding that mental events, as consciously experienced in the mind, determine and explain behavior. The mental qualities used to be conceived in nonphysical, supernatural ("parallelist") terms, but we now view them as the emergent (interactive) properties of brain processes.
>
> **Question**: How does your shift to this mentalist view fit with your split-brain studies?
>
> **Sperry**: It was a matter of explaining the effects of split-brain surgery on conscious experience. We found that each disconnected hemisphere was capable of sustaining its own conscious awareness, each largely oblivious of experiences of the other. The separated hemispheres were able to carry on independently at a fairly high level. They could even perform mutually contradictory tasks at the same time, and each was able to exert its own volitional control and select its own differential preferences. Since each side of the surgically divided brain is able to sustain its own conscious volitional system in this manner, the question arises: Why, in the normal state, don't we perceive ourselves as a pair of separate left and right persons instead of the single, apparently unified mind and self that we all feel we are?

The answer Sperry favors goes something as follows: The normal bilateral consciousness can be viewed as a higher emergent entity that is more than just the sum of the awareness in the separate right and left hemispheres, and supersedes these as a directive force in our thought and actions. The two hemispheres normally function together as an integrated whole, and the mind as a bilateral unit then supervenes and integrates the activites within each hemisphere. Putting this together with some notions about emergence and causation, Sperry found he could see a way around the old behaviorist logic and the mind–brain paradox — a way to finally affirm the causal usefulness of consciousness without violating scientific principles.

Moreover, according to Sperry's new views of consciousness, ethical and moral values become a very legitimate part of science. In his new view they are no longer conceived as reducible to brain physiology. Instead, "we now see that subjective values themselves exert powerful causal influence in brain function and behavior. They are universal determinants in all human decision making, and they are actually the most powerful causal control forces now shaping world events. No other causal system with which science now concerns itself — earthquakes, chemical reactions, magnetic fields, you name it — is of more critical importance in determining our future."

In response to his lifetime of intellectual achievements, including major advances in the recognition of the separate capabilities of the two hemispheres, we dedicate this volume to Roger W. Sperry. Upon reading this, he would probably respond, as he did on another occasion, "The great pleasure and feeling in my right brain is more than my left brain can find the words to tell you."

REFERENCES

1. Baskin, Y., Interview with Roger Sperry. *Omni*, 1983, **5**: 68–75, 98–100.
2. Sperry, R. W., Some effects of disconnecting the cerebral hemispheres. *Science*, 1982, **217**: 1223–1226.

CONSCIOUSNESS, PERSONAL IDENTITY, AND THE DIVIDED BRAIN*

ROGER W. SPERRY, PhD
Division of Biology
California Institute of Technology

I

It has now become a familiar story in neuroscience that, when you divide the brain surgically by midline section of the cerebral commissures, the mind also is correspondingly divided. Each of the disconnected hemispheres continues to function at a high level, but most conscious experience generated within one hemisphere becomes inaccessible to the conscious awareness of the other. The parallel mental functions of the separated hemispheres are found to differ further in important ways, the most conspicuous being that the disconnected left hemisphere retains the ability to speak its mind, much as before, whereas the right hemisphere, for most practical purposes, is unable to express itself either in speech or in writing.

In turning to examine more closely these and related phenomena as they bear on our present topic, I shall be drawing on studies by a long line of associates and myself, conducted on a select group of about a dozen so-called "commissurotomy" or "split-brain" patients of Drs. Philip Vogel and Joseph Bogen, neurosurgeons at the White Memorial Medical Center in Los Angeles. This commissurotomy operation is performed in rare cases as a last-resort measure to help control severe, intractable epilepsy.

A few points about the surgery need to be kept in mind: First, it permanently divides in the brain nearly all direct connections mediating cross-talk between the left and right hemispheres (see Figure 1). This includes those fiber systems that normally interconnect left and right halves of the cortical field for vision. As a result, the visual perception of objects in each hemisphere becomes restricted to half the normal field of view, cut off sharply at the vertical midline and center of gaze. The left hemisphere sees things in the right half of the visual field, using either one or both eyes, while things to the left are perceived by the right hemisphere. Interconnections are severed also between the cerebral representations for the right and

*Public lecture presented at the Smithsonian Institution, December 1977, in the Frank Nelson Doubleday Lecture Series on "The Human Mind." Some editorial updating of recent references has been made in this chapter.

11

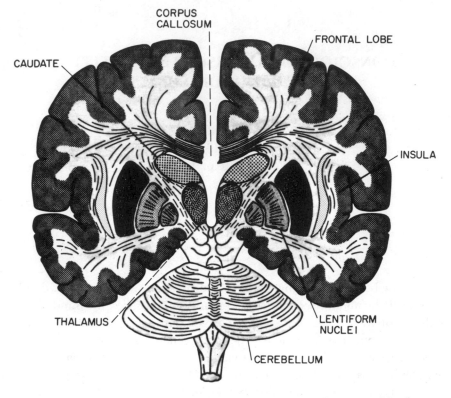

Figure 1. Nature of hemispheric separation effected by surgical section of forebrain commissures. Some indirect cross-communication remains possible through intact midbrain and associated brain stem structures.

left arms and legs, including both the primary sensory projections and also the main motor controls for skilled movement. Hence, things felt with the right hand are perceived mainly in the left hemisphere, which governs related motor adjustments of the same hand. Conversely, motor coordination and tactual perception for the left hand are mediated predominantly by the right hemisphere. In addition, the surgery cuts off the functions of the right hemisphere from speech and the main language centers, located (in approximately 95% of the population) in the left hemisphere (see Figure 2).

A leading question with which we shall be concerned can be stated as follows: Are there really in the brain thus divided, two separately conscious minds, in effect two co-conscious selves sharing the one cranium? And, if so, what does this signify regarding the nature and the substrate of mind and the unity of the conscious self in the normal intact brain?

The first point to be emphasized is that these patients following surgery appear in ordinary, everyday behavior to be very typical, single-minded, normally unified individuals. What prompted our studies in the beginning was a series of published reports supporting the conclusion that no definite symptoms are detected after surgery, even with extensive neurological and psychological testing. (For a review of the earlier literature, see 5.) Usually a year or so is required to fully recover from the extensive neural trauma caused by section of the cerebral commissures, which include the largest fiber systems of the brain, estimated to contain well over 200 million nerve fibers. After recovery, patients without other brain damage are able to return to school or to household duties, or to an undemanding job assignment.

Figure 2. Schematic representation of some of the main cerebral functions found to be lateralized following hemisphere disconnection.

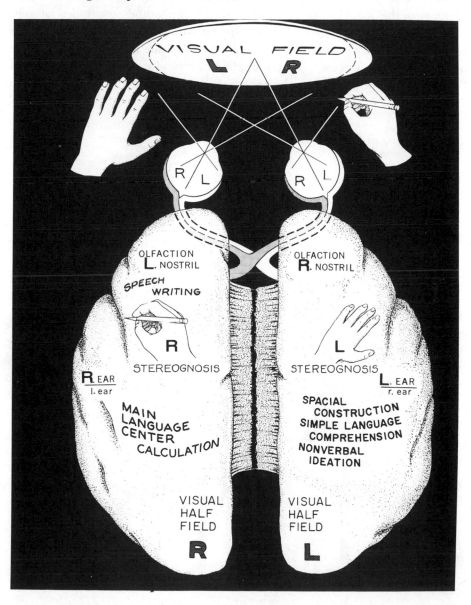

Two years after surgery, a typical commissurotomy patient without complicating disorders could easily go through a complete routine medical examination without revealing to an uninformed practitioner that anything is abnormal. Nor is there any marked change in the verbal scores on the standard IQ test. Complaints about short-term memory are common especially in the early years after surgery (35). However, the general behavior and conversation during the course of a casual social encounter without special tests typically reveals nothing to suggest that these people are not essentially the same persons that they were before the surgery, with the same inner selves and personalities.

Despite the outward seeming normality, however, and the apparent unity and coherence of the behavior and personality of these individuals, controlled lateralized testing for the function of each hemisphere independently (see Figure 3) indicates that in reality these people live with two largely separate left and right domains of inner conscious awareness. (The basic split-brain syndrome in man is reviewed in 24 and 30; the split-brain animal work is reviewed in 21 and 26.) Each hemisphere

Figure 3. Testing setup for determining laterality of mental functions in the surgically separated hemispheres.

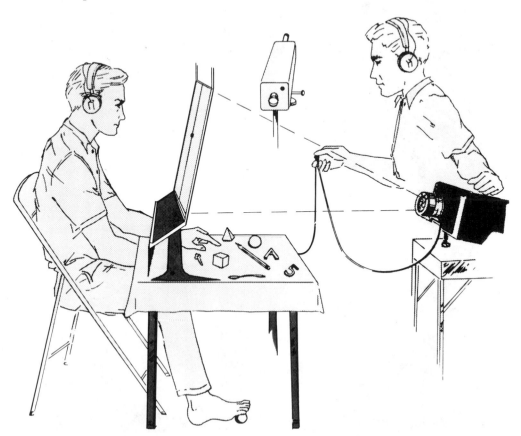

can be shown to experience its own private sensations, percepts, thoughts, and memories that are inaccessible to awareness in the other hemisphere. Introspective verbal accounts from the vocal left hemisphere report a striking lack of awareness in this hemisphere for mental functions that have just been performed immediately before in the right hemisphere. In this respect each surgically disconnected hemisphere appears to have a mind of its own, but each cut off from, and oblivious to, conscious events in the partner hemisphere.

Following the surgery, these people are unable to recognize by sight something they have just looked at in one visual half-field if it is then presented across the vertical meridian in the opposite half-field of view. Objects perceived and identified tactually with one hand out of sight cannot be recognized with the other hand. Such objects also can be recognized in the corresponding half-field of vision but not in the opposite half-field. Similarly, odors identified through one nostril are not recognized through the other. Split-brain subjects fail to identify by verbal report objects felt with the left hand, seen in the left visual field, or smelled through the right nostril—in other words, things experienced within the right hemisphere. Meantime, good perception and comprehension of these same test stimuli, of which the subject *verbally* disclaims any knowledge, is readily demonstrated *manually*—for example, by selective retrieval with the left hand, or by pointing to the correct picture in a choice array, or by appropriate hand signals or gestures (see Figure 4).

From the collective results of these and similar kinds of tests, it is inferred that both disconnected hemispheres retain mental function at a rather high level, but are no longer cognizant of most mental functions of the partner hemisphere. The two disconnected hemispheres can further be shown to function concurrently but independently in parallel, by presenting different stimulus items simultaneously to the two hands or to the two visual half-fields. Under these conditions, each of the two hemispheres is found to process concurrently its own separate perceptual–cognitive–mnemonic functions; these may be grossly incompatible or even mutually contradictory, without either hemisphere noticing that anything is wrong, so separate are the inner experiences of the disconnected hemispheres. The basic hemisphere disconnection syndrome is apparent as well in experiments with animals, as shown earlier in extensive studies on cats and subhuman primates during the 1950s (21, 26). As in humans, the surgically separated hemispheres were found to perceive, learn, and remember independently at a high level, apparently with equal proficiency on left and right sides.

Some authorities, concerned for the essential unity of the conscious self, have been reluctant to accept the conclusion that the mind is divided by commissurotomy, maintaining instead that the mind and self remain unified within the language hemisphere or centered in the intact brain stem or in the person as a whole, and that the nonspeaking, subordinate hemisphere operates only as a computer-like, unconscious automaton. (A recent treatment of this controversy may be found in 36. See also 16.) While these alternative interpretations may better conform with common concepts and traditions regarding the essential unity of the inner being, we have not been able to see any real justification in our test findings for denying consciousness

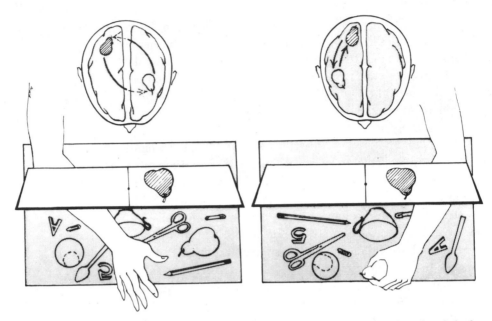

Figure 4. Visual–tactual associations function correctly within either hemisphere but fail when cross left–right or right–left combinations are involved. Shown an object in left visual field, commissurotomy subjects report verbally that they "did not see" the left field stimulus (projected to right hemisphere). However, the subject then has no difficulty in finding the same stimulus object using the left but not the right hand. In this same setup objects presented to the left hand for tactual identification cannot then be found with the right hand.

to the disconnected mute hemisphere. Everything we have observed in many kinds of task performances over many years of testing reinforces the conclusion that the mute hemisphere has an inner experience of much the same order as that of the speaking hemisphere, though differing in quality and cognitive faculties, as will be outlined later. Clearly the right hemisphere perceives, thinks, learns, and remembers, all at a very human level. It also reasons nonverbally, makes studied cognitive decisions, and carries out novel volitional actions. Further, it can be shown to generate typical human emotional responses when confronted with affect-laden stimuli and situations (31).

II

Contrary to prior neurological doctrine based on unilateral lesions, the disconnected mute hemisphere has been found to be neither "word-blind" nor "word-deaf." To our initial surprise, the comprehension of spoken instructions proved to be quite good in the right hemisphere, and the reading of printed words was performed moderately well. This comprehension in the minor hemisphere of spoken and written words was demonstrated by selective retrieval or pointing to corresponding objects or pictures. It was possible to go in the reverse direction also, that is, from objects or pictures to words, written or spoken, and to go from spoken to written words and vice versa (24, 30). The right hemisphere could also spell simple three- and four-letter words with cut-out letters and read such words presented tactually, in contrast to the strong earlier impressions in neurology that the right hemisphere ordinarily is lacking in this kind of language comprehension and higher cognition.

Our findings are in line with the earlier controversial views of Hughlings Jackson, but are counter to many other observations that unilateral lesions confined to the left hemisphere alone may cause total global aphasia, or leave a person word-deaf and/or word-blind despite the retention of an intact, undamaged right hemisphere. Although this disparity is still not fully resolved, the evidence seems to be settling out in favor of the conclusions drawn from commissurotomy. In particular, the language profile of the right hemisphere after commissure section conforms rather well to that seen after rare surgical removals of the speech hemisphere for malignancy (19). The vocabulary in the disconnected right hemisphere for comprehension of single spoken words about 10 years after surgery is found to have a mental age rating only slightly below that of the language hemisphere (33).

Earlier interpretations based on the symptoms produced by focal lesions, which pictured the minor or subordinate hemisphere as a comparative retardate in brain evolution, have had to be revised. The mental performance of this hemisphere after commissurotomy has been found repeatedly to be superior and dominant to that of the speaking hemisphere in a growing series of nonverbal, largely spatial tests. The tasks involved are of the kind where a single spatial image processed as a whole proves to be more effective than a detailed verbal or mathematical description. Examples include the copying of designs, reading faces, fitting forms into molds, discrimination and recall of nondescript tactual and visual forms, spatial transformations and transpositions, judging whole circle size from a small arc, grouping series of different-sized and -shaped blocks into categories, perceiving whole plane forms from a collection of parts, and intuitive apprehension of geometrical properties. (This literature is still scattered, but see reviews in 9, 21, 24, 26, and 30.)

Commissurotomy makes possible precise left–right comparisons for positive performance within the same brain, where most of the usual confusing background variables cancel out. Also, the deceptive interhemispheric interference effects that complicate inferences drawn from focal lesions are eliminated or greatly reduced. Earlier doubts regarding the presence of advanced mental function in the minor hemisphere are now largely dispelled, and the concept of a complementary evolution of both hemispheres has come to replace our older classic view of a single one-sided dominance.

In any case, after watching repeatedly the superior performance of the right hemisphere in tests like those mentioned above, one finds it most difficult to think of this half of the brain as being only an automaton lacking in conscious awareness. Especially, it is difficult to deny consciousness to the right hemisphere, where it proves to be superior in novel tasks that involve logical reasoning, and also when it generates typical facial expressions of satisfaction at tasks well done or of annoyance at its own errors or at those made by its uninformed partner hemisphere. Also difficult to reconcile with the concept of an automaton state is the clear ability of the right hemisphere to learn from experience, remembering test items it has seen or felt on prior testing sessions days or even weeks previously.

III

In many kinds of tests, it is found that both disconnected hemispheres, regardless of differential speech and proficiency, are able to come up with the correct answers. Further analysis indicates that the answers are arrived at, however, by different processing strategies or modes of thinking on left and right sides. Beyond the more obvious differences like those of speech, writing, and constructive visual–spatial manipulation, more subtle organizational differences are indicated that tend to be obscured by individual patient variation in ordinary brain lesion studies, where it is taken for granted that some individuals will be more talkative than others, or more inclined to use verbal logic or visual imagery, and so on. Under the conditions of commissurotomy, however, with the same subjects working the same test task with each hemisphere, even slight cognitive differences on left and right sides become meaningful. The same person is observed to consistently employ one or the other of two different kinds of mental strategy — much like two different people, depending on whether the right or the left hemisphere is in use. The first evidence for this was obtained by Levy in 1969 (12) and has been repeatedly confirmed many times since (24). The discovery of complementary cognitive-mode asymmetries following commissurotomy has prompted many further studies in normal, in brain-damaged, and in other select populations, helping to better pinpoint and delineate the left–right cognitive differences and their variations.

Correlations of cerebral laterality have been extended to handedness, sex, occupational preferences and ability, special innate talents, eye dominance, genetic variations like Turner syndrome, endocrine pathology, congenital dyslexia, autism, dreaming, hypnosis, inverted writing, and so on. (An introduction and references to this large and rapidly expanding literature can be found in 4 and 13.) This has become a rapidly developing and fascinating story in itself, of which I mention briefly a few summary points in passing. One important outcome is the increased insight and appreciation, in education and elsewhere, for the importance of nonverbal forms and components of learning, intellect, and communication. By the early 1970s it already had become evident, from the standpoint of brain research, that our educational system and modern urban society generally, with its heavy emphasis on linguistic communication and early training in the three R's, tends increasingly to discriminate against the nonverbal, nonmathematical half of the brain, which has its own perceptual–mechanical–spatial mode of apprehension and reasoning (3, 23, 27). The amount of formal training given to right-hemisphere functions in our public schools traditionally has been almost negligible, compared to that devoted to the specialties of the left hemisphere. The need for better methods by which to detect, measure, and develop the nonverbal components of intellect before their critical development periods have passed is becoming widely recognized.

These and related developments also help to bring an increased respect and regard for the inherent individuality in the structure of human intellect. Brains can no longer be assumed to be qualitatively similar at birth, with equal potentiality for becoming a Beethoven or a Shakespeare, an Edison or a Michaelangelo, and so on. Different mental disciplines employ qualitatively different forms of cognitive processing that require different patterns of neural circuitry, the basic cerebral requirements for which are largely prewired. Even the potentialities of the two hemispheres of the same brain with respect to verbal and spatial functions are already at birth found to be qualitatively different (6, 11, 14, 32). There is strong indication that cognitive spatial ability is partly genetic and correlated with a sex-linked recessive. Evidence is mounting for other genetic and innate developmental variations involved in congenital dyslexia, autism, Turner syndrome, androgenic females, and the like. Statistically, the hemispheres mature earlier and show less lateralization in females; this is thought to account in part for the significant sex differences obtained in large-scale tests for intellectual factors and special abilities — females scoring higher in verbal tests, and males in mathematics and tests that demand spatial processing. But many other variables are involved (13).

Actually, the more we learn, the more complex becomes the picture for predictions regarding any one individual, and the more it seems to reinforce the conclusion that the kind of unique individuality we each carry around in our inherent brain wiring makes that of fingerprints or facial features appear gross and simple by comparison. The need for educational tests and policy measures to selectively identify, accommodate, and serve the differentially specialized forms of intellectual potential becomes increasingly evident.

One must caution in this connection that the experimentally observed polarity in right–left cognitive style is an idea in general with which it is very easy to run wild. You can read today that things such as intuition, the seat of the subconscious, creativity, parapsychic sensitivity, the mind of the Orient, ethnocultural disposition, hypnotic susceptibility, the roots of the counterculture, altered states of consciousness, and what not, all reside predominantly in the right hemisphere. The extent to which extrapolations of this kind may eventually prove to be more fact or fancy will require many years to determine. Meanwhile, it is important to remember that the two hemispheres in the normal intact brain tend regularly to function closely together as a unit, and that different states of mind are apt to involve different hierarchical and organizational levels, or front–back and other differentiations, as well as differences in laterality.

IV

In face of the mounting evidence for higher cognitive faculties and a complementary specialization in the right hemisphere, earlier claims that this hemisphere is not conscious have given way to intermediate positions. A recent one concedes that the mute hemisphere may be conscious at some levels, but denies that the non-language hemisphere possesses the higher, reflective, and self-conscious type of awareness that characterizes the human mind and is needed, so it is said, to qualify a conscious system as a "person" (7, 17). Self-consciousness is said to be predominantly a human attribute, according to present thinking based on evidence drawn mainly from mirror tests for self-recognition (10). On these terms, self-awareness seems to be largely lacking in animals below the primates and appears only to a limited extent in the great apes. In human childhood, self-consciousness is reported to emerge relatively late, somewhere around 18 months of age. Thus, self-consciousness, by developmental as well as by evolutionary criteria, is rated as a relatively advanced phase of conscious awareness.

We accordingly devised some tasks specifically designed to test for self-consciousness and levels of social awareness in the disconnected minor hemisphere. Procedures were used in which the subject, working with the mute hemisphere, merely has to point manually, on request, to select items in a choice array in order to indicate recognition, identification, personal approval, dislike, or whatever, as requested. The test arrays consist of four to nine pictures, drawings, or photographs, among which key personal and affect-laden items are inserted irregularly among neutral unknowns. The subject's vision is lateralized throughout to one hemisphere (34), and audiotape and videotape recordings are used to analyze the more subtle aspects of emotional responses.

Under these conditions, we found that the right hemisphere can readily recognize and identify, with appropriate emotional reactions and social evaluations, pictures of the subject's self; his or her family, relatives, and acquaintances; pets and other belongings; familiar scenes; political, historical, and religious figures; and television and screen personalities. The general level of recognition and quality of reaction were quite comparable throughout to those obtained from the same subject using the left hemisphere or free vision. All results to date support the conclusion that the right hemisphere, despite its language deficits, harbors a well-developed, seemingly normal conscious self with a basic personality and social self-awareness that is in close accord with the presurgical character of the patient and also with that of the speaking hemisphere of the same subject (31). Similar procedures were used in exploring for a sense of time and concern for the future in the right hemisphere, with no evidence of abnormal deficit. The nonvocal hemisphere appears to be aware of daily and weekly schedules and important dates of the year, and to make appropriate discriminations with regard to possible future accidents and family losses; life, fire, and theft insurance; and the like.

V

Accepting the dual conscious state of the hemispheres following surgical separation, students of the problem of personal identity and the nature of the conscious self have used the split-brain findings, along with cases of fugue states or multiple personality, to support the argument that it is no longer correct to think of a "person" as being correlated one-to-one with a body — that we need now to sharpen and refine the concept in terms of the critical brain states and neural systems involved.

Such refinement becomes important in medical–legal decisions dealing, for example, with prolonged states of coma, stages in fetal development, vital organ transplants, and so on.

An extreme position in regard to selfhood and "personal identity" is held by Puccetti (18) and Bogen (2), who infer that each hemisphere must have a separate mind of its own, not only after brain bisection but also in the normal intact brain as well. The surgery, they argue, simply reveals what already is there — namely, that we are all of us actually a dual compound of right and left minds, or "persons" as Puccetti puts it, and that this bicameral condition normally goes undetected because the experiences of right and left hemispheres are kept in close synchrony when the commissures are intact. I myself have favored the view that the conscious mind is normally single and unified, mediated by brain activity that spans and involves both hemispheres. This assumes, first, that the fiber systems of the brain mediate conscious awareness in conjunction with switching mechanisms, synaptic interfaces, and other properties of the gray matter; and, second, that fiber cross-connections between the hemispheres are not different in this respect from fiber systems within each hemisphere. The bilateral process can be viewed as an integrated dynamic entity that, functionally and causally, is qualitatively different from, and more than, the mere sum of the left and right activities. In the normal state, the two hemispheres function together as a very closely integrated whole, not as a double, divided, or bicameral system. The two hemispheres normally perceive, think, emote, learn, and remember as a unit. They even speak as a unit, in that the right hemisphere during speech is not idling or diverted, but is actively focused to aid and sustain the cerebral processing involved in speech, to add tone and expression, and to inhibit unrelated activity.

Even in the bisected brain, the question of whether there exists a right–left division of conscious experience is not subject to an unqualified "yes" or "no" answer. While the right–left division of many perceptual, cognitive, and mnemonic processes is clearly evident in lateralized testing as already described, there are other aspects of consciousness that are not divided. Two principal ways are recognized in which the conscious mind remains undivided after commissurotomy (24). The first is attributed to the presence in the brain of bilateral wiring systems that ensure the representation of both left and right components of experience within each hemisphere. The cutaneous sensory system for the face is an example. Sensations from both left and right sides of the face mediated by the trigeminal nerves are each represented in both hemispheres. The kind of separation that applies for right and left halves of the field of vision and for right and left hands does not therefore hold with respect to the face. The same is true for audition and other systems like those mediating crude pain, temperature, pressure, and position sense, especially from the more axial parts of the body. Bilateral motor controls also are extensively present in both hemispheres. For lateralized testing, we must necessarily be highly selective and take considerable pains to avoid activity that cannot be reliably confined to a single hemisphere. We thus depend heavily on moderately sophisticated input from the hands and from the half-fields of vision.

Bilateral representation within each hemisphere is further achieved by factors of a more functional kind. Exploratory movements of the eyes, for example, can provide bilateral representation of a perceived scene or object in both disconnected hemispheres. Similarly, exploratory movements of the hands with interchange and overlap can provide for a bilateral unified percept of an object in both hemispheres. These kinds of factors must be routinely guarded against and excluded in our lateralized testing.

Another fundamental way in which the conscious mind is not divided by commissurotomy is illustrated in the tests for social and self-awareness mentioned above, in which mental–emotional ambience or semantic surround generated in one hemisphere promptly spreads also to the second hemisphere. These "deep-structure" components in conscious awareness, which appear to include attitudinal, orientational, emotional, contextual, semantic, and related cognitive factors, are presumably mediated through undivided deep components of cognition. I have described the structure of the conscious system in the divided brain as being Y-shaped, that is, divided in its upper, more structured levels but undivided below (26). Each of the separated hemispheric limbs of the"Y," it should be remembered, contains within itself extensive bilateral representation, providing bilateral corporeal and extracorporeal subsystems. Each disconnected hemisphere, for example, functions with much the usual sense of awareness of the positions and movements of all body parts on both sides, a sense of being able to initiate and direct motor commands for the whole body, and an awareness also of the environment on all sides. Visceral sensations and central states like those involved in hunger, fatigue, and so forth, also are bilateralized. Even where the ipsilateral representations are weak or absent, there is good reason to think that there is no direct awareness of the ipsilateral deficits. This accords with a general rule that in many respects brains tend to be oblivious of what they lack.

The brain process responsible for a unified conscious experience need not itself be unified, single, or localized. In addition to the recognized diversity and discontinuity or "graininess" of its neuronal firing patterns, the brain process also is subject to major subdivisions like the left–right and front–back fractionations and the vertical divisions into higher cognitive and lower emotional components already described. The brain process as such seems to have no counterpart to match the unity, continuity, quality, constancy, and other psychological properties that are experienced subjectively. A hypothesized correlation between mental and neural events based on isomorphic electric fields was suggested by Gestalt theory in the 1940s, but was largely abandoned when we found that the insertion of short-circuiting wires or current-distorting dielectric plates all through the visual cortex failed to correspondingly disrupt visual form perception (20, 22).

Some years ago we proposed that the answer must lie alternatively in thinking of conscious experience as a functional or operational interaction with the perceived object rather than as a spatial–temporal copy or transform (29). In other words, what counts for subjective unity may lie in the way the brain process functions as a unity or entity, regardless of the multilevel and multicomponent makeup of the neural events involved. The overall, holistic functional effect could thus determine the con-

scious experience. If the functional impact of the neural activity has a unitary effect in the upper-level conscious dynamics, the subjective experience is unified. On
these terms, the qualities of subjective experience need not correlate with the diverse
particulate components of the neuronal infrastructure, only with the function of the
active process as a whole. By these operational criteria for generation of subjective
meaning, the mind may be seen to be largely divided after commissurotomy, but
unified in the normal intact brain.

VI

Another thing to come out of these concerns for the unity and/or duality of
mind, with and without the commissures, is a modified concept of the nature of consciousness. A revised view of the conscious self is involved that includes a formula
for mind–brain interaction. For many decades science was traditionally careful to
explicitly exclude from its objective explanations any use of conscious or mental forces
or phenomena as causal constructs. Mind or subjective experience was accordingly
treated in science as an acausal epiphenomenon or as a passive parallel correlate of
brain activity, a semantic artifact, or most commonly as an inner aspect of the one
main physical brain process. On these terms the physiological brain process is assumed to be causally complete in itself, with no need, or any place, for the causal
intervention or operation of conscious or mental forces.

The more we learned about the neuronal circuitry and electromechanical
mechanisms of brain activity, the more incredible it became to think that the course
of these physiochemical events could be influenced in any way by the qualities of
conscious experience. As Eccles (8) phrased it in 1966, "We can, in principle, explain all our input–output performance in terms of activity of neuronal circuits; and
consequently, consciousness seems to be absolutely unnecessary," and again, " . . . as
neurophysiologists we simply have no use for consciousness in our attempt to explain
how the nervous system works." This was the kind of reasoning that had prevailed
widely for more than half a century and had led to the philosophy of scientific
materialism with its firm renunciation of consciousness and mentalism in science.

Since the mid-1960s, our thinking on these matters has undergone some revolutionary changes. In the course of wrestling with the problem of conscious unity in
the presence and absence of the cerebral commissures, I became convinced that consciousness is better conceived as being causal in brain activity rather than noncausal,
and that science had been wrong on this for more than half a century (28). Today,
many of us in behavioral and neuroscience accept the position that inner conscious
experience per se plays a top-level, causal role in brain function. Consciousness in
this revised view is defined rather simply to be a holistic or emergent, functional
property of high-order brain activity. Unlike emergent theory of the past, from Lloyd
Morgan (15) onward, our current view no longer interprets the emergent mental
properties as passive correlates of cerebral activity, but rather as integral working
components with causal potency.

We do not look for conscious awareness in the nerve cells of the brain, or in the molecules or atoms of brain processing. Along with the larger as well as lesser building blocks of brain function, these elements are common as well to unconscious, automatic, and reflex activity. For the subjective qualities, we look higher in the system at organizational properties that are select and special to operations at top levels of the brain hierarchy, and that are seen to supersede in brain causation the powers of their neuronal, molecular, atomic, and subatomic infrastructure. The subsidiary components embodied in the conscious processes, such as the timing of neuronal firing and flow patterns of impulse traffic, as well as the inner molecular and atomic "forces within forces," are all carried along in space and time, subject to the overriding higher level dynamics of the mental properties — just as the flow of electrons in a TV receiver is differentially determined by the program content on different channels.

Without going into further detail, it follows on this revised scheme that mind does actually move matter within the brain (28), and outside as well, indirectly through physical behavior. Further, it now becomes "mind over matter" in a very real sense. This is all within the brain hierarchy, of course. There is no implication that mind is separate from matter in the dualistic sense. Mentalism is no longer equivalent to dualism in the framework of today's modified paradigm. The revolution of the past decade toward increased scientific acceptance of consciousness does not do anything directly to bolster dualist beliefs in the mystical, the paranormal, or the supernatural. At the same time, the new position directly opposes prior materialist doctrine, which has been telling us for more than half a century that "Man is nothing but a material object, having none but physical properties" and that "Science can give a complete account of man in purely physio-chemical terms." These quotations are from the late 1960s by Armstrong (1), a founding father and leader of the materialist, so-called "mind–brain identity" theory, which still today finds support, though with major reinterpretations to bring it now into close concordance with the causal emergent views of mind outlined above.

Once science thus modifies its traditional materialist–behaviorist stance and begins to accept in theory, and to encompass in principle, within its causal domain the whole world of inner, conscious, subjective experience (the world of the humanities), then the very nature of science itself is changed. The change is not in the basic methodology or procedures, of course, but in the scope of science and in its limitations; in its relation to the humanities; and in its role as a cultural, intellectual, and moral force. The kinds of interpretations that science supports, as well as the world picture and attendant value perspectives and priorities and the concepts of physical reality that derive from science, all undergo substantial revisions on these new terms. The change is away from the mechanistic, deterministic, and reductionistic doctrines of pre-1965 science to the more humanistic interpretations of the 1970s. Our current views are more mentalistic, holistic, and subjectivist. They give more freedom, in that they reduce the restrictions of mechanistic determinism, and they are more rich in quality, value, and meaning.

The pervasive broad paradigm changes involved are particularly welcomed by all who look to science, not alone for objective knowledge and material advances, but also for world-view perspectives and criteria of ultimate value and meaning, those who see science as the best source of true understanding and the most valid route to an intimate comprehension of "the forces that made and move the universe and created man." Our new mind–brain paradigm qualifies science to assume a higher and more critical societal role that, I hope, future science will come increasingly to fulfill.

REFERENCES

1. Armstrong, D. M., *A Materialist Theory of the Mind*. Routledge & Kegan Paul, London, 1968.
2. Bogen, J. E., The other side of the brain: II. An appositional mind. *Bull. Los Angeles Neurol. Soc.*, 1969, **34**: 135–62.
3. Bogen, J. E., Some educational aspects of hemispheric specialization. *UCLA Educator*, 1975, **17**: 24–32. Reprinted in *The Human Brain* (M. C. Wittrock, Ed.). Prentice-Hall, Englewood Cliffs, N.J., 1977. Also in *Allos* (K. Gaburo, Ed.). Lingua Press, La Jolla, Cal., 1980. Also in *Dromenon*, 1979, **1**: 16–21.
4. Bradshaw, J. L., and Nettleton, N. C., *Human Cerebral Asymmetry*. Prentice-Hall, Englewood Cliffs, N.J., 1983.
5. Bremer, F., Brihaye, J., and Andre-Balliseaux, G., Physiologie et pathologie du corps calleux. *Schweiz. Arch. Neurol. Neurochir. Psychiatr.* 1956, **78**: 31–87.
6. Dennis, M., and Kohn, B., Comprehension of syntax in infantile hemiplegics after hemidecortication: Left hemisphere superiority. *Brain Lang.*, 1975, **2**: 272.
7. Dewitt, L., Conscious, mind and self. *Br. J. Phil. Sci.*, 1975, **26**: 41–7.
8. Eccles. J. C., Conscious experience and memory. In: *Brain and Conscious Experience* (J. C. Eccles, Ed.). Springer-Verlag, Berlin, 1966: 314–344.
9. Franco, L., and Sperry, R. W., Hemispheric lateralization for cognitive processing of geometry. *Neuropsychologia*, 1977, **15**:107–114.
10. Gallup, G. G., Self-recognition in primates. *Am. Psychol.*, 1977, **32**: 329–338.
11. Levy, J., Cerebral lateralization and spatial ability. *Behav. Genet.*, 1976, **6**: 171–188.
12. Levy, J., Information processing and higher psychological functions in the disconnected hemispheres of human commissurotomy patients. Doctoral dissertation, California Institute of Technology, 1969.
13. Levy, J., Psychobiological implications of bilateral asymmetry. In: *Hemisphere Function in the Human Brain* (S. Dimond and J. B. Beaumont, Eds.). Paul Elek, London, 1974: 121–183.
14. Levy, J., and Nagalaki, T., A model for the genetics of handedness. *Genetics*, 1972, **72**: 117–128.
15. Morgan, C. L., *Emergent Evolution*. Holt, New York, 1923.
16. Nagel, T., Brian bisection and unity of consciousness. *Synthese*, 1971, **22**: 396–413.
17. Popper, K., and Eccles, J. C., *The Self and Its Brain*. Springer International, New York, 1977.
18. Puccetti, R., Brain bisection and personal identity. *Br. J. Phil. Sci.*, 1973, **24**: 339–355.
19. Smith, A., Speech and other functions after left (dominant) hemispherectomy. *J. Neurol. Neurosurg. Psychiatry*, 1966, **29**: 467–471.
20. Sperry, R. W., Brain mechanisms in behavior. *Eng. Sci.*, 1957, **8**: 24–31.
21. Sperry, R. W., Cerebral organization and behavior. *Science*, 1961, **133**: 1749–1757.

22. Sperry, R. W., In search of psyche. In: *The Neurosciences: Paths of Discovery* (F. G. Worden, J. P. Swazey, and G. Adelman, Eds.). MIT Press, Cambridge, Mass., 1975: 425–434.

23. Sperry, R. W., Lateral specialization of cerebral function in the surgically separated hemispheres. In: *The Psychophysiology of Thinking* (F. J. McGuigan and R. A. Schoonover, Eds.). Academic Press, New York, 1973: 209–229.

24. Sperry, R. W., Lateral specialization in the surgically separated hemispheres. In: *The Neurosciences: Third Study Program* (F. O. Schmitt and F. G. Worden, Eds.). MIT Press, Cambridge, Mass., 1974: 5–19.

25. Sperry, R. W., Mental phenomena as causal determinants in brain function. In: *Consciousness and the Brain* (G. Globus, G. Maxwell, and I. Savodnik, Eds.). Reprinted in *Process Studies*, 1976, **5**: 247–256.

26. Sperry, R. W., Mental unity following surgical disconnection of the cerebral hemispheres. In: *The Harvey Lectures Series*, Vol. 62. Academic Press, New York, 1968: 293–323.

27. Sperry, R. W., Messages from the laboratory. *Eng. Sci.*, 1974, **37**: 29–32.

28. Sperry, R. W., Mind, brain and humanist values. In: *New Views of the Nature of Man* (J. R. Platt, Ed.). University of Chicago Press, Chicago, 1965: 71–92.

29. Sperry, R. W., Neurology and the mind–brain problem. *Am. Scient.*, 1952, **40**: 291–312.

30. Sperry, R. W., Gazzaniga, M. S., and Bogen, J. E., Interhemispheric relationships: The neocortical commissures. Syndromes of hemisphere disconnection. In: *Handbook of Clinical Neurology* (P. J. Vinken and G. Bruyn, Eds.). North-Holland, Amsterdam, 1969: 273–290.

31. Sperry, R. W., Zaidel, E., and Zaidel, D., Self-recognition and social awareness in the deconnected hemisphere. *Neuropsychologia*, 1979, **17**: 153–166.

32. Wada, J. A., Clarke, R., and Hamm, A., Cerebral hemispheric asymmetry in humans. Cortical speech zones in 100 adult and 100 infant brains. *Arch. Neurol.*, 1975, **32**: 239–246.

33. Zaidel, E., Auditory vocabulary of the right hemisphere following brain bisection or hemidecortication. *Cortex*, 1976, **12**: 191–211.

34. Zaidel, E., A technique for presenting lateralized visual input with prolonged exposure. *Vision Res.*, 1975, **15**: 283–289.

35. Zaidel, D., and Sperry, R. W., Memory impairment after commissurotomy in man. *Brain*, 1974, **97**: 263–272.

36. Zangwill, O. L., Consciousness and the cerebral hemispheres. In: *Hemisphere Function of the Human Brain* (S. Dimond and J. Beaumont, Eds.). Paul Elek, London, 1974: 264–278.

THE DUAL BRAIN: SOME HISTORICAL AND METHODOLOGICAL ASPECTS

JOSEPH E. BOGEN, MD
Department of Psychology

When we speak of the dual brain, we are not talking about duality of the brain stem, but rather of the cerebral hemispheres. Cerebral-hemisphere duality is our topic. There is an historical precedent for this usage of the word "brain." It was published in 1874 by John Hughlings Jackson.* He wrote, "I use the word brain to include the cerebral hemisphere and the subjacent motor and sensory tract. I use the word encephalon to include all parts of the nervous system within the skull." And he went on to ask that we restrict the use of the word "side" to a side of the body. Following that usage, then, an injury to the left half-brain (or "left brain") would produce a disability (for example, a paralysis) of the right side. He avoided using the word "side" for the brain and restricted it to the body.

One of the major discoveries from the study of the dual brain is that one can think effectively without language. On the other hand, the kind of language we use influences how we think; thus, being precise and consistent in our use of words has its virtues.

THE HOURGLASS METAPHOR

To help us consider the historical aspects, I would suggest a metaphor — actually, I have several metaphors to offer. The first has to do with tracing the origins of what we can call the right-brain–left-brain story, or, as some of us (12) prefer to call it, Neowiganism. Whatever it is called, the question remains: Where does the history of it begin? You may have heard that there are three villages in Minnesota, each of which claims to be the origin of the mighty Mississippi River, and another two in Canada, one in Manitoba, and one in Ontario. Moreover, the color and at least half the volume of the Mississippi below St. Louis is contributed by the Missouri River. The Missouri River is actually the longest river in the United States, and it rises at a place called Three Forks in Montana where three other rivers come together. Trying to be dogmatic about where something started is certain to elicit objections from many people who believe that they too were in at the beginning, someplace.

*It occurs, characteristically, in a footnote; he seems to have put many of his most memorable thoughts in footnotes.

27

Hughlings Jackson is probably as good a place to start as any. The article from which I just quoted was entitled, "On the Nature of the Duality of the Brain." This introductory chapter was expected to include a short list of key papers. This paper by Jackson (43) is one of them.

It is no small task to pick six or so papers out of the available thousands. Such choosing requires, among other things, that we have an opinion as to how best to summarize the immense amount of available data. In the ideal case, we could hope to arrive at some generalization as quantitatively concise as $e = mc^2$ or $f = ma$. But of course we're a long way from that in neuropsychology. The question is: What *can* we do? I have a suggestion to make, in the form of another metaphor—the hourglass metaphor. Think of an hourglass as made up of two cones, the bottom cone consisting of a mass of data of many different kinds, a huge base continually expanding at a rapid rate. What we're looking for are some generalizations or abstractions that, we hope, characterize the data. Suppose we place them at the constriction or waist of the hourglass; above we have the rising and ever-expanding upper cone of inference and speculation, as represented in the closing chapters of this book.

Well, what *are* the generalizations at the waist of this hourglass? I would suggest that there are two: One is the idea of cerebral duality, and the other is the idea of hemispheric specialization.

Cerebral Duality

By "cerebral duality," we mean that each hemisphere can function to a significant extent independently of the other. That's true of the cat or the monkey, of course, as well as the human. And it is probably true of the dolphin as well. It seems that the dolphin's optic chiasm is crossed, which helps us to understand why, when the dolphin's left hemisphere goes to sleep, it is the right eye that is closed, and vice versa. Perhaps you already know that dolphin hemispheres are capable of alternating sleep and wakefulness (68, 76, 80). And perhaps, like me, you have wondered why it was that one eye closed whenever the contralateral hemisphere was asleep (by EEG criteria); the answer apparently is that dolphin optic chiasms are very nearly 100% crossed, unlike humans and monkeys. This is perhaps to be expected, since the eyes are aimed laterally with relatively little visual-field overlap.

The principle of cerebral duality began with the idea that a single hemisphere is enough for a mind. You may be familiar with the story of Arthur Ladbroke Wigan, an English physician who had an acquaintance who died rather suddenly. At the man's postmortem, when the skull was opened, one hemisphere was completely missing. This not only astounded Wigan, but he had the wits to realize that it was meaningful. He looked for other cases and found a few. Over 20 years later (in 1844), he published a book called, *The Duality of the Mind* (95), in which he claimed that one hemisphere is clearly enough for, as he put it, the emotions, sentiments, and faculties which we call, in the aggregate, "mind."

Wigan went on to state that if one hemisphere is enough for one mind, then with two hemispheres we can have two minds. Of course, one plus one does not always equal two. For example, a quart of alcohol and a quart of water when added together do not make two quarts of liquid. Even more generally, one can be somewhat skeptical of the absolute reliability of rational argument. We have often seen it fail. Hence, with respect to the idea that with two hemispheres one can have two minds, some kind of empirical evidence would be desirable. It was over 100 years before such evidence appeared in the split-brain experiments of Myers and Sperry (69, 85). Split-brains were made first in cats, later in monkeys, and eventually in humans. A point deserving emphasis is that the duality of the brain was well established from a scientific point of view in laboratory animals before there were any split-brain humans (11). Similarly, the principle of hemispheric specialization was established in the minds of many people before we had the human split-brain evidence, because of the results from unilateral lesions.

HEMISPHERIC SPECIALIZATION

The first evidence for hemispheric specialization was that left-hemisphere lesions interfere with language, while right-hemisphere lesions hardly interfere with language at all (although if one looks hard enough one can usually find something). This fact was established by a number of 19th-century physicians, including Broca and Wernicke. The point is that we owe to studies of lateralized lesions (and subsequently hemispherectomies) the basic ideas of hemispheric specialization (13, 98).

With respect to split-brain humans, the foregoing raises an interesting question: That is, if duality of the brain was established before there was any human split brain, and if hemispheric specialization has been established independently of the human split brain, then what is the significance of the human split-brain studies? One consideration is that with the split-brain human, cerebral duality and hemispheric specialization are seen simultaneously (88, 97). One might have supposed — we can imagine someone saying *a priori* — that you could have one or the other, but that you can't have them simultaneously. In addition, the human split-brain studies made these two notions more dramatically evident; people do take greater interest in other humans than they do in split-brain monkeys or cats.

More recently, hemispheric specializations has been investigated by studies on so-called "normal" people. We often talk about tests on normal people: dichotic-listening tests, half-field studies, blood flow studies, and so forth. Hence, to tell you what I think "normal" means in this context is probably worthwhile. If you look for a description of the subjects of such studies, they often turn out to be medical students, or members of a sophomore psychology class; the normality of these people may be open to a certain amount of question. What I think "normal" in this context means depends upon the knowledge that most of us bear scars on the brain. When babies are born, their heads are often molded out of shape. They look funny, most of them. Some of them look a little blue, too. And we all fall on our heads when we're little. So it is easy to see why almost everybody has scars on the brain. For most of us it doesn't make too much difference — it depends on the size of the scar, the location, the orientation, and so on. What the word "normal" refers to is the fact that when we have a fairly sizable group (say, an *n* of 30 or so) the scars are in different places, so it all washes out in the statistics.

That is quite different from a situation in which one has only five or six people, all of whom have had a right temporal lobectomy. There, the lesion in the brain, in this case the temporal lobectomy, is the major variable in the equation. In contrast, with 30 people, all of whom have small scars in a variety of locations, the lesion effects, if any, make little difference. And that is what I think is involved in the idea of a group of "normal" controls.

One might say that there are three kinds of studies of hemisphere specialization. We can study it with lateralized lesions. We can study it with lateralized input. And we can study it with lateralized readout, in which the input is made available to both hemispheres, but the blood flow or electrical activity of whatever is read out in a lateralized fashion. All of these methods have contributed to the growing conviction — indeed, the almost unassailable view — that there is complementary hemispheric specialization in the human.

METHODOLOGICAL PROBLEMS

With all these different kinds of information, there are inevitably many problems. That is, *each* of these methods presents certain methodological difficulties. You may be aware of certain criticisms of the split-brain evidence. For example, one article (and I will be very careful not to mention the author's name) was entitled, "The Fallacy of the Split Brain." The gist of the article was that split-brain evidence doesn't tell us anything. The article was in large part erroneous because the person who wrote it was sadly misinformed. But he did say one thing that is clearly true: All the persons with split brains had antecedent brain lesions that caused the seizures for which the operation was eventually done. His argument was that therefore the results cannot be representative of the normal brain. We already understand that, because a brain has scars, this doesn't mean that it is in no way representative of the "normal" brain. But there is an important point here, which is that in interpreting the results of the split-brain studies, we must take into account the extracallosal lesions (9, 10, 16, 17).

Interpretive difficulties are present with every method, and I would like to discuss briefly the question of cerebral localization, which has a long history in neurology. Cerebral localization illustrates well the different problems associated with different methods.

Hughlings Jackson based some of his most important conclusions, still considered important, on cases of brain tumor. Yet everyone involved in behavioral neurology is familiar with the difficulties in the clinical localization of brain tumor. Tumors can be misleading because of pressure effects or because the tumor has a continuing diaschistic or shock effect. Indeed, there's an entire literature on the subject of "false localization," describing the problems of localization of brain tumors.

Because of such problems, there are some people who have claimed that cerebral localization should not be based on tumor cases; they prefer fixed deficits from thrombotic stroke, particularly those coming to autopsy, although in recent years the CT scan has tended to enlarge immensely the number of stroke patients available for psychoanatomical correlation. One school of behavioral neurology (currently having its spiritual center in Boston) emphasizes that one should only do cerebral localization studies with strokes with fixed deficit. Unfortunately, there are also problems with the stroke cases.

In the first place, strokes occur mostly in older folks. They are frequently preceded by a previous small stroke or two. A well-known example is persistent prosopagnosia. When a person shows a long-term persistent deficit in facial recognition following a right-hemisphere stroke, it is typically preceded by a previously silent stroke in the posterior half of the left hemisphere. In most stroke cases, the putatively critical infarct has usually been preceded by previous, silent lesions, which means that our interpretation from the standpoint of localization has to be quite sophisticated, even ingenious, as you will all remember having read some of these papers. Even if there were no prior strokes, in an older person with arteriosclerosis the effect of a lesion depends upon the compensatory reserve, even in people who have shown no symptoms, and most older folks *do* have some symptoms. In other words, the effect of a stroke is dependent in part of the overall status of the arteriosclerotic brain within which it occurs.

One way to get away from the arteriosclerotic context is to look at lesions in young people, such as youths wounded in war. War has been a boon for the behavioral neurologist. Luria's book on traumatic aphasia (57), which really made his reputation, was based on Russian soldiers from World War II. Marie and Foix (59, 25) described French soldiers from World War I. Sir Ritchie Russell (79), as well as Freda Newcombe (70), studied British soldiers from World War II. Some very important studies have been based on missile wounds in young people. Of course, these are not free of problems either. It's not altogether clear where the boundaries of a missile injury are. And what may be even more tricky is that the missile can cause vascular derangement — for example, spasm in a blood vessel — which then results in focal damage to brain tissue at a considerable distance from the missile track.

Perhaps all of this tumor, stroke, and missile evidence should be discounted, and we should depend on cases of surgical removal where the boundaries of the ablation have been precisely described. The work at the Montreal Neurological Institute by Brenda Milner (65) and her students and colleagues has utilized just that sort of material. However, we are not always persuaded of the total reliability of the surgeon's reports, especially now that we have experience with postoperative CT scans. Besides, no matter how precise or reliable the surgical removal, these studies concern cases of long-standing epilepsy; thus there are ambiguities attributable to the compensatory changes that occurred subsequent to the epileptogenic lesions.

The same sort of problem comes up with hemispherectomy, which is as anatomically clean as any removal can be. In such cases, anything in the form of behavior is attributable to the residual hemisphere. But most hemispherectomies have been done for infantile hemiplegia, which means that people who have had those operations have had a long disease history with opportunity for a lot of compensatory

change. Even when hemispherectomy has been done in adults of normal development, and that's quite rare, there is some delay between the operation and behavioral
testing during which compensation could occur. In fact, compensation has been documented with repeated testing (83).

Some of the difficulties of compensatory change can be avoided with the so-
called "temporary hemispherectomy" — the carotid amytal injection or Wada test.
But this has its problems, too. For example, the posterior cerebral artery does not
feed from the carotid artery on that side as often as two-thirds of the time. The exact figure doesn't matter; the point is that it is fairly frequent, which means that
often there is not a total narcotization of the entire hemisphere. Even more misleading, at times, is that carotid branches to the brain stem can seriously affect the results of the injection.

What does all this mean? Does it mean that the conclusions from all these different kinds of approaches and all these kinds of subjects should be ignored? Certainly not! The point is that *every* subject population and *every* experimental method
has its own peculiar problems. This is also true of the EEG approach to cerebral
localization, blood flow measures, PET scanning, stimulation mapping, split-brain
studies, or what have you.

CONVERGENCE

There are at least two lessons to be learned from the foregoing. First, one does
not summarily dismiss data because they have interpretive complications. One takes
the time to become familiar with the qualifications and ambiguities, and then interprets the data with appropriate reservations. The second point is that any conclusion based on any method or material must remain tentative until it is confirmed
by other methods having different methodological problems. If several different approaches point to the same conclusion, we can have increased confidence in the result. It is this convergence on a common conclusion through a variety of different
approaches that has given us a near-certainty in our conviction of complementary
hemispheric specialization in the human. Similarly, the convergence of a variety of
different data leaves little doubt as to the duality of the brain in the sense that I previously mentioned: Each hemisphere can function, to a significant extent, independently of the other.

Let us consider how different methods contribute to a common conclusion. We
are faced early on with the problem of how to weigh the evidence. Suppose there
are seven different authors reporting seven different investigations; this doesn't mean
that we give them each one-seventh the weight in our eventual conclusion. Consider
a specific example. It is the experience of most investigators that if you do dichotic
listening with normal people ("normal" as previously described), if you use consonant–vowel syllables or digits, and if you have a group of right-handers, you get
about 15% to 20% (some people claim as high as 30%) with a left-ear advantage.
How is it that so many right-handers are hearing verbal material better with the
left ear? What does that mean? According to some, it means that these subjects are
not so well lateralized for language. This may be a serious misconception.

Let's first be clear about what we mean when we talk about right-handers. Handedness indicates which hand the individual *prefers*. Thus, these are people who, if you ask, "Are you right-handed?" answer, "Yes." And when you then ask, "Do you do *anything* better with your left hand?" They answer, "No." Once in a while you get somebody who says, "Yeah, I fret the guitar better with my left hand." That's a right-hander's maneuver and doesn't mean that the person is left-handed. Handedness is not a matter of skill or of dexterity; the right-handed guitarist is surely as dexterous with the left hand as anybody else with either hand. Handedness is a matter of *preference for monomanual tasks which you act out on the world*, such as hammering a nail, throwing a ball, and the like.

Now, for a strongly right-handed person, we know that the left hemisphere is dominant for language in the sense that, if lateralized damage causes serious language trouble, we can be 99% sure it is a left-hemisphere lesion. That is, crossed aphasia occurs in perhaps 1% of right-handers (2, 3, 18, 40, 41, 44, 51).

But with dichotic listening, from 15% to 30% of right-handers show a left ear advantage for the verbal material! Why is that? At this point we can do one of two things: Either we can suppose that dichotic testing is a dubious indicator of degree of dominance, or we can redefine dominance. The latter would not necessarily be irresponsible. For example, diabetes mellitus has been redefined. The expression "diabetes mellitus" literally means "copious urine that tastes sweet." "Diabetes insipidus" was "copious urine that does not taste sweet," and so on. In other words, diabetes mellitus was originally defined in terms of the sugar content of the urine. But nowadays it is defined in terms of the sugar content of the blood. This is because we feel that the measurement of sugar in the blood is sufficiently reliable, maybe *more* reliable than other measures. Further, we know about elevated kidney thresholds for sugar. So there are several reasons that have led to a change in the definition. Similarly, the definition of what we mean by "cerebral dominance for language" could be changed *if* we had sufficient reason to do it. What I'm saying is that we do not.

Why is it that 15% or more of subjects (it depends on the particular test) show a left-ear advantage for the verbal material? The correct answer is that cerebral dominance for language is not the only factor which influences ear preference. For example, brain stem asymmetries are probably important. You understand that the entire dichotic-listening enterprise is an artificial manipulation of what a brain was never designed to hear. It probably takes advantage, for one thing, of sound localization mechanisms in the brain stem. Bob Efron has devoted a large part of his life to studying the various factors that produce ear advantages, including an ear advantage for verbal material. Efron himself occasionally takes the extreme view that dichotic-ear advantages do not "logically permit us to infer *anything* about hemispheric specialization" (30, 31, and many personal communications).

At any rate, there are two choices: Either we are going to change our idea about what dominance is, redefine it, or else we explain the results from dichotic listening on some other grounds — in this case, probably including brain stem influences. The same thing comes up with tachistoscopic studies in which we present material in one visual half-field or the other. The standard story is that the verbal material is either seen better or recognized faster in the right half-field. Other material, certain faces for example, are identified better or faster in the left half-field. And yet we know that if we juggle the familiarity of the faces, or juggle the exposure time, or give the subjects a different set of instructions, or change the lighting, or change the nature of the symbol on which they fixate, the half-field advantage can change. It turns out that the half-field effect depends on all these, as well as a host of other things, including learning and fatigue.

Suppose some tachistoscopic evidence suggests that people are not so unilaterally dominant for language as we thought on the basis of the crossed aphasia data; what then? In answer, I might mention next the method of carotid amytal injection or Wada test. At Montreal, where they've probably done more carotid amytal studies than anywhere else, they found that among right-handers, 4% are right-hemisphere-dominant for language (75). That really is a pretty good confirmation of our idea that right-handers are 99% left-dominant for language, because that 4% figure (different from the 1% for crossed aphasia) is based on a population being prepared for surgery. They would not have had amytal testing if they did not have a history of epilepsy, you understand. So that in a population where we can *expect* some deviance because of the early brain injuries and long epileptic history, there is still only 4% right-hemisphere speech dominance (see also 62, 89). And I might mention the split brain: *Every* right-hander with a split brain has turned out to be a left-hemisphere speaker. (This includes two cases where there is evidence that the right hemisphere also — not *instead of*, but *also* — acquired some speech [63, 82].*)

The results from the split brain converge with the crossed aphasia and the amytal data; thus it is unlikely that we will soon give up our conviction that any right-hander should be thought of as having a 98%-plus likelihood of left-hemisphere dominance for language. There is a short statement concerning the tachistoscopic results that is worth quoting. It is a recent restatement of the familiar Kinsbournian view that the half-field advantage one obtains depends on which hemisphere is more activated:

> When laterality findings are deviant, this is perhaps because underlying hemispheric specialization is deviant or because hemispheric activation has deviated from the norm . . . the latter more parsimonious hypothesis must be ruled out before the former is adopted. (46)

Facial Recognition

A good example of the convergence of different lines of evidence can be seen in the now general acceptance of right-cerebral-hemisphere dominance for facial recognition (5). This idea originally arose from the common association of prosopagnosia (an inability to recognize familiar faces) with posterior right-hemisphere lesions (1, 19, 39, 78, 90, 94). But prosopagnosics usually have other lesions, known or reasonably suspected. On the lesion evidence alone, therefore, the dominance of

---

*In both of those patients (called PS and POV) the anterior commissure was not cut, so that leaves a certain amount of ambiguity to the observations.

the right hemisphere for facial recognition was uncertain (4, 21, 24, 33, 56, 58, 64, 73). Furthermore, the residual hemisphere can recognize faces after either right or left hemispherectomy. This shows that each hemisphere has a capacity for facial recognition, although probably functioning differently (26).

There remain two questions:

    a. Why has prosopagnosia usually appeared when the right hemisphere lesion follows the left, rather than vice versa?

    b. Why does a non-paired, right hemisphere lesion occasionally produce prosopagnosia, even if only transient, whereas this is much less common with non-paired left hemisphere lesions? (47)

An explanation favored at one time was that prosopagnosia from left-hemisphere lesions was masked by an associated aphasia, but we now know that the lesions' loci are different; so we would not be happy with this explanation even in the absence of other lines of evidence for right-hemisphere "face dominance." A second explanation might be that, when a right-hemisphere lesion directly damages the right-hemisphere competence for facial recognition, it simultaneously disables the left-hemisphere competence for a time by transcallosal diaschisis. But why would this not work in reverse; in other words, why should there be a unidirectional diaschisis? A third possibility (which I favor) is that most of us tend to rely more upon the right-hemisphere mechanisms, so that a previous left-hemisphere lesion would be relatively nondisturbing (or even "silent") until the second (right) lesion appeared. In contrast, a right-hemisphere lesion would be disabling for a time, until the left-sided mechanisms (if still intact) became operative.

As prosopagnosia became more widely appreciated, various tests of facial recognition were devised. Although these tests sometimes give normal results in patients with overt prosopagnosia, they did show that deficits in facial recognition could be elicited even in patients who did not spontaneously complain of trouble recognizing faces. Again, the right hemisphere was implicated (6, 27, 28, 37, 38, 49, 52, 67, 71, 84, 91, 92, 93, 96).

Then, evidence came from testing of intact ("normal") subjects. Presentation of faces to the right hemisphere (via the left visual half-field) usually (but not always) resulted in better scores than presentation to the left hemisphere (7, 8, 20, 32, 42, 53, 74, 77). This led Overman and Doty (72) to assert " . . . the overwhelming evidence of right hemispheric specialization for the recognition of faces in normal human subjects."

Furthermore, chimeric (split-stimulus) tests of split-brain patients showed a greater reliability of right-hemisphere identification of faces and suggested that the association of names with faces was quite difficult when both hemispheres were present but disconnected (54). Similar results were obtained using chimeric stimuli in a naturally occurring case of hemisphere disconnection (55). And there is EEG evidence, as yet meager, that the right hemisphere is dominant for faces (22, 29).

Blood Flow

Let's consider next another specific example. Some of the really exciting evidence in hemispheric specialization comes from PET scanning and blood flow studies. What shall we conclude from the blood flow results, which show that, when the subject talks, not only does the left hemisphere light up in several different places, but the right-hemisphere homologue of Broca's area also lights up? With speech, one sees increased blood flow in the *right* hemisphere in the general region of the inferior frontal gyrus (50). Shall we change our views about hemispheric specialization for speech, or shall we try to explain the results with some other interpretation? I am not about to change my views. I don't believe that people talk with the right inferior frontal gyrus, for several reasons: If you take it out, or if you narcotize it with amytal, they keep right on talking just fine. And, if you leave the right hemisphere in and take out a few other parts, they don't talk so well. So what does it mean when the blood flow increases in the right-hemisphere homologue of Broca's area? One thing it means is that there is increased neuronal activity: The blood flow is presumably increased because there is dilatation of the blood vessels, due to increased carbon dioxide, due to increased metabolism. There is more right inferior frontal nerve cell activity when people talk then when they're not talking.

How is it that the right inferior frontal region becomes active? Probably via commissural fibers. That is, when the left hemisphere becomes active as people start talking, there is likely a collateral discharge across the corpus callosum, stimulating nerve cells in the mirror-image regions. Whether that is true or not could of course be settled: One could do the same blood flow studies (with the same task of speech) on people who have the commissures cut. If this hypothesis were correct, at least in its simplest form, then individuals with split brains would not have activation of the right hemisphere when they start talking.

Timbre Recognition

I should like to conclude by presenting another example of converging lines of evidence—namely, that the right hemisphere is dominant for the recognition of timbre.

Figure 1 shows a recording by Stuart Butler of a split-brain patient doing mental arithmetic; there is less alpha activity over the left hemisphere. In Figure 2 the same subject is listening to music (the adagio from Rodrigo's *Concerto for Guitar*, played by Narciso Yepes); note that there is less alpha emanating from the right hemisphere. This agrees with the familiar story that left-hemisphere lesions can leave some musical ability intact, whereas right-hemisphere lesions can cause musical deficits without interfering with language. It is also consistent with our carotid amytal results (15, 36) that right-hemisphere suppression interferes with singing more than speech, and vice versa for left-hemisphere suppression. It also fits the left-ear advantage during dichotic listening to musical passages (45, 81).

Brenda Milner's studies of temporal lobectomy patients included results hav-

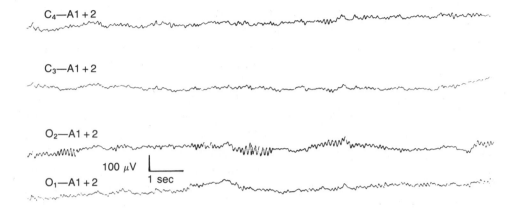

Figure 1. EEG tracings from the split-brain patient R. Y. while doing mental arithmetic. The electrode placements are standard 10–20 system from central (C_3 and C_4) and occipital (O_1 and O_2) locations to combined ears (so called "monopolar" derivations). Even-numbered electrodes are on the right side of the head.

ing particularly to do with timbre and tonal memory (66). She found that removal of the left temporal lobe didn't seem to make much difference in this respect, but that the right temporal lobe removals resulted in more errors in these two tests. There has been individual case evidence in this direction from the stroke data (61). But Milner's was really the first clear evidence for a right-hemisphere specialization specifically for timbre. That led to Harold Gordon's first dichotic-listening study: He showed that simple melodies without much in the way of timbre or harmonic con-

Figure 2. EEG tracings from R. Y. listening to music (see text); two separate epochs are shown, both from the occipital leads.

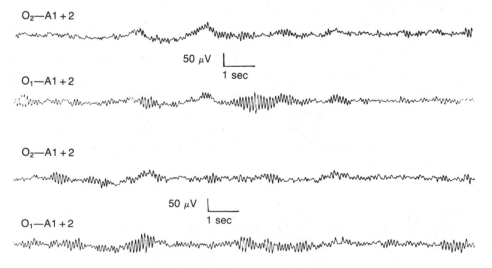

tent (played on a wooden flute) showed little if any left-ear advantage. However, organ chords produced a distinct left-ear advantage (34, 35).

We can again take note of some blood flow data work done with Ami Carmon in Israel (23). Blood flow increased more in the right hemisphere when the subjects were listening to a musical passage.*

The foregoing agrees with the PET scan data published by Mazziotta and colleagues (60). They found right-hemisphere activation with the same timbre subtest of the Seashore battery that Brenda Milner had used 20 years earlier. Their subjects differed (so there was what we call individual hemisphericity) with respect to the tonal-memory subtest; but on the timbre subtest the predominant glucose uptake was right-hemispheric (mainly right temporal) for essentially all subjects.

If the right hemisphere is more important for timbre recognition, this might be related to voice recognition. In fact, Van Lancker and Canter (91) found that people with right-hemisphere lesions are apt to have more trouble recognizing voices, as well as faces. So voice recognition (according to these data) fits the previous evidence that the right hemisphere is more concerned with timbre.

CONCLUDING STATEMENT

In conclusion, I should like to emphasize two crucial facts and underline what seems to me the really big question remaining. First, *it takes only one hemisphere to have a mind*. Second, *two hemispheres can sustain the activity of two separate spheres of consciousness following commissurotomy*. What remains in doubt is: Does the surgical splitting of the brain create a duality of consciousness or duality of mind (85, 86, 87)? Or is it an experimental maneuver that makes it possible to demonstrate a duality that was previously present (9, 48)? Similar questions apply to every experiment; that is, it can be argued that the outcome is produced by the technique, rather than actually revealing the underlying physiology. For example, in an experiment to measure blood pressure one could ask: Is the blood pressure high because it was high before, or did you raise the blood pressure when you stuck a needle in the artery? I believe the duality was present before cerebral commissurotomy, and that the operation does not create duality of mind so much as it makes it easier to demonstrate. I have reviewed elsewhere the considerable data supporting this conclusion (14). If this interpretation is correct, we can understand why ordinary self-consciousness is insufficient for the whole person, and why the full realization of human potential requires that each of us be devoted to a better understanding of our own dual brains.

---

*It was again the adagio from the *Concerto for Guitar* by Rodrigo, played by Narciso Yepes. I think Hal Gordon took three copies of this record with him when he went to Israel.

REFERENCES*

1. Assal, G., Regression des troubles de la reconnaissance des physionomies et de la mémoire topographique chez un malade opéré d'un hématome intracérébral pariéto-temporal droit. *Rev. Neurol.* (Paris), 1969, **121**: 184–185.

2. Assal, G., Perentes, E., and Deruaz, J. P., Crossed aphasia in a right-handed patient: Postmortem findings. *Arch. Neurol.*, 1981, **38**: 455–458.

3. Benson, D. F., *Aphasia, Alexia and Agraphia.* Churchill Livingstone, New York, 1979.

4. Benson, D. F., Segarra, J., and Albert, M. L., Visual agnosia–prosopagnosia. *Arch. Neurol.*, 1974, **30**: 307–310.

5. Benton, A. L., The neuropsychology of facial recognition. *Am. Psychol.*, 1980, **35**: 176–186.

6. Benton, A. L., and Van Allen, M. W., Prosopagnosia and facial discrimination. *J. Neurol. Sci.*, 1972, **15**: 167–72.

7. Berlucchi, G., Cerebral dominance and interhemispheric communication in normal man. In: *Neurosciences: Third Study Program* (F. O. Schmitt and F. G. Worden, Eds.). MIT Press, Cambridge, Mass., 1974: 65–69. (*)

8. Berlucchi, G., Brizzolara, D., Marzi, D. A., Rizzolatti, G., and Umilta, C., Can lateral asymmetries in attention explain interfield differences in visual perception? *Cortex*, 1974, **10**: 177–185.

9. Bogen, J. E., The callosal syndromes. In: *Clinical Neuropsychology*, 2nd Edition (K. M. Heilman and E. Valenstein, Eds.). Oxford University Press, New York, in press.

10. Bogen, J. E., Concluding overview. In: *Epilepsy and the Corpus Callosum* (A. Reeves, Ed.). Plenum, New York, 1985.

11. Bogen, J. E., Further discussion on split-brains and hemispheric capabilities. *Br. J. Phil. Sci.*, 1977, **28**: 281–286. (*)

12. Bogen, J. E., Neowiganism (concluding statement). In: *Drugs, Development and Cerebral Function* (W. L. Smith, Ed.). Charles C Thomas, Springfield, Ill., 1972: 358–361.

13. Bogen, J. E., The other side of the brain: II. An appositional mind. *Bull. Los Angeles Neurol. Soc.*, 1969, **34**: 135–162.

14. Bogen, J. E., Partial hemispheric independence with the neocommissures intact. In: *Brain Circuits and Theories of Mind* (C. Trevarthen, Ed.). Cambridge University Press, London, in press. (*)

15. Bogen, J. E., and Gordon, H. W., Musical tests for functional lateralization with intracarotid amobarbital. *Nature*, 1970, **230**: 524–552.

16. Bogen, J. E., and Vogel, P. J., Cerebral commissurotomy in man: Preliminary case report. *Bull. Los Angeles Neurol. Soc.*, 1962, **27**: 169–172.

17. Bogen, J. E., and Vogel, P. J., Neurologic status in the long term following cerebral commissurotomy. In: *Les Syndromes de Disconnexion Calleuse chez l'Homme* (F. Michel and B. Schott, Eds.). Hôpital Neurologique, Lyon, 1975: 227–251.

18. Boller, F., Destruction of Wernicke's area without language disturbance: A fresh look at crossed aphasia. *Neuropsychologia*, 1973, **11**: 243–246.

19. Bornstein, B., Sroka, H., and Munitz, H., Prosopagnosia with animal face agnosia. *Cortex*, 1969, **5**: 164–169.

---

*The eight references followed by an asterisk (*) are particularly recommended reviews related to the dual brain.

20. Broman, M., Reaction-time differences between the right and left hemisphere for face and letter discrimination in children and adults. *Cortex*, 1979, **14**: 578–591.
21. Bruyer, R., Laterre, C., Seron, X., Feyereisen, P., Strypstein, E., Peirrard, E., and Rectem, D., A case of prosopagnosia with some preserved covert remembrance of familiar faces. *Brain Cog.*, 1983, **2**: 257–284.
22. Butler, S. R., Glass, A., and Heffner, R., Asymmetries of the contingent negative variation (CNV) and its after positive wave (APW) related to differential hemispheric involvement in verbal and nonverbal tasks. *Biol. Psychol.*, 1981, **13**: 157–171.
23. Carmon, A., Lavy, S., Gordon, H., and Portnoy, Z., Hemispheric differences in rCBF during verbal and non-verbal tasks. In: *Brain Work* (D. H. Ingvar and N. A. Lassen, Eds.). Alfred Benzon Symposium VIII, Munksgaard, Copenhagen, 1975: 414–423.
24. Cohn, R., Neumann, M. A., and Wood, D. H., Prosopagnosia: A clinicopathological study. *Ann. Neurol.*, 1977, **1**: 177–182.
25. Cole, M. F., and Cole, M., *Pierre Marie's Papers on Speech Disorders*. Hafner, New York, 1971.
26. Damasio, A. R., Damasio, H., and Van Hoesen, G. W., Prosopagnosia: Anatomic basis and behavioral mechanisms. *Neurology*, 1982, **32**: 331–341.
27. De Renzi, E., Memory disorders following focal neocortical damage. *Philos. Trans. R. Soc. London (Biol.).*, 1982, **298**: 73–83.
28. De Renzi, E., Faglioni, P., and Spinnler, H., The performance of patients with unilateral brain damage on face recognition tasks. *Cortex*, 1968, **4**: 17–34.
29. Dumas, R., and Morgan, A., EEG asymmetry as a function of occupation, task, and task difficulty. *Neuropsychologia*, 1975, **13**: 219–228.
30. Efron, R., Experimental psychoacoustics of the central auditory system: Five myths. In: *Assessment of Central Auditory Dysfunction: Its Foundation and Clinical Correlates* (M. L. Pinheiro and F. E. Musiek, Eds.). Academic Press, New York, in press.
31. Efron, R., Koss, B., and Yund, E. W., Central auditory processing: IV. Ear dominance — spatial and temporal complexity. *Brain Lang.*, 1983, **19**: 264–282.
32. Geffen, G., Bradshaw, J., and Wallace, G., Interhemispheric effects on reaction time to verbal and non-verbal visual stimuli. *J. Exp. Psychol.*, 1971, **87**: 415–422.
33. Gloning, I., Gloning, K., Jellinger, K., and Quatember, R., A case of prosopagnosia with necropsy findings. *Neuropsychologia*, 1970, **8**: 199–204.
34. Gordon, H. W., Hemispheric asymmetries in the perception of musical chords. *Cortex*, 1970, **6**: 387–398.
35. Gordon, H. W., Music and the right hemisphere. In: *Functions of the Right Cerebral Hemisphere* (A. W. Young, Ed.). Academic Press, London, 1983: 65–86.
36. Gordon, H. W., and Bogen, J. E., Hemispheric lateralization of singing after intracarotid sodium amylobarbitone. *J. Neurol. Neurosurg. Psychiatry*, 1974, **37**(6): 727–738.
37. Hamsher, K., Levin, H. S., and Benton, A. L., Facial recognition in patients with focal brain lesions. *Arch. Neurol.*, 1979, **36**: 837–839.
38. Hécaen, H., The neuropsychology of face recognition. In: *Perceiving and Remembering Faces* (G. Davies, H. Ellis, and J. Shepherd, Eds.). Academic Press, New York, 1981: 39–54.
39. Hécaen, H., and Angelergues, R., Agnosia for faces (prosopagnosia). *Arch. Neurol.*, 1962, **7**: 92–100.
40. Henderson, V. W., Speech fluency in crossed aphasia. *Brain*, 1983, **106**: 837–857.
41. Henderson, V. W., Naeser, M. A., Weiner, J. M., Pieniadz, J. M., and Chui, H. C., CT criteria of hemisphere asymmetry fail to predict language laterality. *Neurology*, 1984, **34**: 1086–1089.
42. Hilliard, R. D., Hemispheric laterality effects on a facial recognition task in normal subjects. *Cortex*, 1973, **9**: 246–259.

43. Jackson, J. H., On the nature of the duality of the brain. *Med. Press Circular*, 1874, 1: 19, 41, 63. Reprinted in *Brain*, 1915, 38. (*)

44. Joanette, Y., Lecours, A. R., Lepage, Y., and Lamoureux, M., Language in right-handers with right-hemisphere lesions: A preliminary study including anatomical, genetic, and social factors. *Brain Lang.*, 1983, 20: 217–248.

45. Kimura, D., Left–right differences in the perception of melodies. *Q. J. Exp. Psychol.*, 1964, 16: 355–358.

46. Kinsbourne, M., and Bemporad, B., Lateralization of emotion: A model and the evidence. In: *The Psychobiology of Affective Development* (N. Fox and R. J. Davidson, Eds.). Erlbaum, Hillsdale, N.J., 1984: 259–291.

47. Landis, T., Cummings, J., Christen, L., Bogen, J., and Imhof, H., Are unilateral right posterior lesions sufficient to cause prosopagnosia? Clinical and radiological findings in six patients. *Cortex* (in press).

48. Landis, T., Graves, R., and Goodglass, H., Dissociated awareness of manual performance on two different visual associative tasks: A "split-brain" phenomenon in normal subjects? *Cortex*, 1981, 17: 435–440.

49. Lansdell, H., Effect of extent of temporal lobe ablations on two lateralized deficits. *Physiol. Behav.*, 1968, 3: 271–273.

50. Lassen, N. A., and Larsen, B., Cortical activity in the left and right hemispheres during language-related brain functions. *Phonetica*, 1980, 37: 27–37.

51. Lecours, A. R., Lhermitte, F., and Bryans, B., *Aphasiology*, Bailliere Tindall, London, 1983.

52. Levin, H. S., Hamsher, K. S., and Benton, A. L., A short form of the test of facial recognition for clinical use. *J. Psychol.*, 1975, 91: 223–228.

53. Levine, S. C., and Koch-Weser, M. P., Right hemisphere superiority in the recognition of famous faces. *Brain Cog.*, 1982, 1: 10–22.

54. Levy, J., Trevarthen, C., and Sperry, R. W., Perception of bilateral chimeric figures following hemispheric deconnexion. *Brain*, 1972, 95: 61–78.

55. Lhermitte, F., Chain, F., Chedru, F., and Penet, C., Syndrome de déconnexion interhémisphérique: Étude des performance visuelles. *Rev. Neurol.* (Paris), 1974, 130: 247–250.

56. Lhermitte, F., Chain, F., Escourolle, R., Ducarne, B., and Pillon, B., Étude anatomoclinique d'un cas de prosopagnosie. *Rev. Neurol.* (Paris)., 1972, 126: 329–346.

57. Luria, A. R., *Traumatic Aphasia*. Academy of Medical Science, Moscow. Reprinted in English by Mouton, The Hague, 1970.

58. Malone, D. R., Morris, H. H., Kay, M. C., and Levin, H. S., Prosopagnosia: A double dissociation between the recognition of familiar and unfamiliar faces. *J. Neurol. Neurosurg. Psychiatry*, 1982, 45: 820–822.

59. Marie, P., and Foix, C., Les aphasies de guerre. *Rev. Neurol.* (Paris), 1971, 31/32: 53–87. (English translation in 25.)

60. Mazziotta, J. C., Phelps, M. E., Carson, R. E., and Kuhl, D. E., Tomographic mapping of human cerebral metabolism: Auditory stimulation. *Neurology*, 1982, 32: 921–937.

61. Mazzucchi, A., Marchini, C., Budai, R., and Parma, M., A case of receptive amusia with prominent timbre preception defect. *J. Neurol. Neurosurg. Psychiatry*, 1982, 45: 644–647.

62. McGlone, J., Speech comprehension after unilateral injection of sodium amytal. *Brain Lang.*, 1984, 22: 150–157.

63. McKeever, W. F., Sullivan, D. F., Ferguson, S. M., and Rayport, M., Right hemisphere speech development in the anterior commissure-spared commissurotomy patient: A second case. *Clin. Neuropsychol.*, 1982, 4: 17–22.

64. Meadows, J. C., The anatomical basis of prosopagnosia. *J. Neurol. Neurosurg. Psychiatry*, 1974, 37: 489–501.

65. Milner, B., Interhemispheric differences in the localization of psychological processes in man. *Br. Med. Bull.*, 1971, **27**: 272–277. (*)
66. Milner, B., Laterality effects in audition. In: *Interhemispheric Relations and Cerebral Dominance* (V. B. Mountcastle, Ed.). Johns Hopkins University Press, Baltimore, 1962: 177–195.
67. Milner, B., Visual recognition and recall after right temporal lobe excision in man. *Neuropsychologia*, 1968, **6**: 199–209.
68. Mukhametov, L. M., Supin, A. Y., and Polyakova, I. G., Interhemispheric asymmetry of the electroencephalographic sleep patterns in dolphins. *Brain Res.*, 1977, **134**: 581–584.
69. Myers, R. E., and Sperry, R. W., Interocular transfer of visual form discrimination habit in cats after section of the optic chiasma and corpus callosum. *Anat. Rec.*, 1953, **115**: 351–352.
70. Newcombe, F., *Missile Wounds of the Brain: A Study of Psychological Deficits.* Oxford University Press, London, 1969.
71. Newcombe, F., and Russell, W. R., Dissociated visual perceptual and spatial deficits in focal lesions of the right hemisphere. *J. Neurol. Neurosurg. Psychiatry*, 1969, **32**: 73–81.
72. Overman, W. H., and Doty, R. W., Hemispheric specialization displayed by man but not by macaques for analysis of faces. *Neuropsychologia*, 1982, **20**: 113–1128.
73. Pevzner, S., Bornstein, B., and Loewenthal, M., Prosopagnosia. *J. Neurol. Neurosurg. Psychiatry*, 1962, **25**: 336–338.
74. Pirozzolo, F. J., and Rayner, K., Hemispheric specialization in reading and word recognition. *Brain Lang.*, 1977, **4**: 248–261.
75. Rasmussen, T., and Milner, B., The role of early left-brain injury in determining lateralization of cerebral speech functions. In: Evolution and lateralization of the brain (S. J. Dimond and D. A. Blizard, Eds.). *Ann. N.Y. Acad. Sci.*, 1977, **299**: 355–369.
76. Ridgway, S. H., and Flanigan, W. F., Electrophysiological observations during sleep in the bottlenosed porpoise (*Tursiops truncatus*). Forthcoming.
77. Rizzolatti, G., Umilta, C., and Berlucchi, G., Opposite superiorities of the right and left cerebral hemispheres in discriminative reaction time to physiognomical and alphabetical material. *Brain*, 1971, **94**: 431–442.
78. Rondet, P., and Tzavaras, A., La prosopagnosie, après vingt années d'études cliniques et neuropsychologiques. *J. Psychologie*, 1969, **2**: 133–165.
79. Russell, W. R., and Espir, M. L. E., *Traumatic Aphasia.* Oxford University Press, London, 1961.
80. Serafetinides, E. A., Shurley, J. T., and Brooks, R. E., Electroencephalogram of the pilot whale, *Globicephala scammoni*, in wakefulness and sleep: Lateralization aspects *Int. J. Psychobiol.*, 1972, **2**: 129–135.
81. Shankweiler, D., Effects of temporal lobe damage on perception of dichotically presented melodies. *J. Comp. Physiol. Psychol.*, 1966, **62**: 115–119.
82. Sidtis, J. J., Volpe, B. T., Wilson, D. H., Rayport, M., and Gazzaniga, M. S., Variability in right hemisphere language function after callosal section: Evidence for a continuum of generative capacity. *J. Neurosci.*, 1981, **1**: 323–331.
83. Smith, A., Dominant and nondominant hemispherectomy. In: *Hemispheric Disconnection and Cerebral Function* (M. Kinsbourne and W. L. Smith, Eds.). Charles C Thomas, Springfield, Ill., 1974: 5–33.
84. Speedie, L. J., and Heilman, K. M., Anterograde memory deficits for visuospatila material after infarction of the right thalamus. *Arch. Neurol.*, 1981, **40**: 183–186.
85. Sperry, R. W., Cerebral organization and behavior. *Science*, 1961, **133**: 1749–1757. (*)
86. Sperry, R. W., Lateral specialization in the surgically separated hemispheres. In: *Neurosciences: Third Study Program* (F. O. Schmitt and F. G. Worden, Eds.). MIT Press, Cambridge, Mass., 1974: 5–19. (*)

87. Sperry, R. W., Some effects of disconnecting the cerebral hemispheres. *Science*, 1982, **217**: 1223–1226.
88. Sperry, R. W., Gazzaniga, M. S., and Bogen, J. E., Interhemispheric relationships: The neocortical commissures; syndromes of hemisphere disconnection. In: *Handbook of Clinical Neurology*, Vol. 4 (P. J. Vinken and G. W. Bruyn, Eds.). Elsevier, Amsterdam, 1969: 273–290.
89. Strauss, E., and Wada, J. A., Lateral preferences and cerebral speech dominance. *Cortex*, 1983, **17**: 165–177.
90. Tzavaras, A., Hecaen, H., and Le Bras, H., Troubles de la reconnaissance du visage humain et latéralisation hémisphérique lésionnelle chez les sujets gauchers. *Neuropsychologia*, 1971, **9**: 475–477.
91. Van Lancker, D. R., and Canter, G. J., Impairment of voice and face recognition in patients with hemispheric damage. *Brain Cog.*, 1982, **1**: 185–195.
92. Vilkki, J., and Laitinen, L. V., Differential effects of left and right ventrolateral thalamotomy on receptive and expressive verbal performances and face-matching. *Neuropsychologia*, 1974, **12**: 11–19.
93. Warrington, E. K., and James, M., An experimental investigation of facial recognition in patients with unilateral cerebral lesions. *Cortex*, 1967, **3**: 317–326.
94. Whiteley, A. M., and Warrington, E. K., Prosopagnosia: A clinical, psychological, and anatomical study of three patients. *J. Neurol. Neurosurg. Psychiatry*, 1977, **40**: 395–403.
95. Wigan, A. L., *The Duality of the Mind*, Longmans, London, 1844. Reprinted 1985; J. Simon Press; Malibu, Calif.
96. Yin, R. K., Face recognition by brain-injured patients: A dissociable ability? *Neuropsychologia*, 1970, **8**: 395–402.
97. Zaidel, E., Concepts of cerebral dominance in the split-brain. In: *Cerebral Correlates of Conscious Experience* (P. Buser and A. Rougeul-Buser, Eds.). Elsevier, Amsterdam, 1978: 263–284.
98. Zangwill, O. L., Asymmetry of cerebral hemisphere function. In: *Scientific Aspects of Neurology* (H. Garland, Ed.). E. & S. Livingstone, London, 1961: 51–62. (*)

BIOLOGICAL AND PSYCHOLOGICAL
STUDIES OF
HEMISPHERIC SPECIALIZATION

INTRODUCTION

ERAN ZAIDEL, PhD
Department of Psychology

Human hemispheric specialization has a mysterious hold on the imagination of laypeople and scientists alike. On a subconscious level, the topic seems to capture everyone's favorite metaphysical dichotomy. This is undoubtedly due to the fact that hemispheric specialization is a paradigm case of mind–brain interaction. Hemispheric specialization contains at once a set of behavioral distinctions involving the highest mental functions, and specific anatomical references — namely, the two cerebral hemispheres and the neocortical commissures (corpus callosum, anterior commissure, and hippocampal commissure) that connect them. The resulting "dualism" is both the virtue and bane of modern neuropsychology.

On the one hand, the analysis of mind benefits from the analysis of brain by bringing to bear the neuroscientific method and anatomical–physiological constraints on a variety of functional accounts and models of higher mental functions. Moreover, hemispheric specialization is at the intersection of many domains of human knowledge, ranging from neuroanatomy and neurophysiology through psychology and linguistics to philosophy and art. Indeed, the study of hemispheric specialization is the study of mental life. Consequently, the field can benefit from interdisciplinary insight and in turn can catalyze research in adjoining domains.

On the other hand, the enormous scope of the field inevitably leads to frequent vagueness and bogus precision that encourage much misinterpretation and shoddy research. The purpose of this section of the book is to establish the scientific basis for dual-brain theory, to separate fact from hypothesis, and to distinguish hypothesis from fiction. What often emerges from reading the diverse publications in the field is a set of more or less detailed and fascinating local accounts of hemispheric specialization in separate domains, with little integration and no overall theoretical account. It is easy to formulate wrong generalizations, and it is misleading to state that a satisfactory unified model already exists. Nonetheless, an overall dual-brain theory is forthcoming, and the quickest road to it may be a set of converging, detailed interdisciplinary studies of the kind described in the following chapters.

In this section, the chapter by Scheibel *et al.* provides new anatomical findings. The chapters by D. W. Zaidel and by Noffsinger introduce the two most common behavioral techniques for studying hemispheric specialization in normal subjects — namely, hemifield tachistoscopy and dichotic listening. The rest of the chapters then discuss results obtained largely with these techniques. The chapter by Curtiss discusses the ontogenesis of hemispheric specialization, and the chapters by Hines and Gorski (sex differences) and by Satz *et al.* (handedness) discuss individual differences in patterns of cerebral dominance. These three chapters together introduce the concept of a natural gradient of degree of hemispheric specialization. More detailed and complementary recent discussions of these issues can be found in Bradshaw and Nettleton (5), Bryden (6), Beaumont (3), and Young (52).

COMPARATIVE ANALYSIS OF FUNCTIONAL SPECIALIZATION

Animal models of hemispheric specialization are important for two reasons. First, they provide opportunities for controlled experiments at molecular levels: anatomical, physiological, and neurochemical. Using animal preparations, we can apply surgical, electrical, and pharmacological interventions or behavioral deprivation techniques that are morally prohibitive in humans. Second, a comparative analysis of functional specialization may illuminate the evolution of hemispheric specialization in humans.

Songbirds

One of the few examples of hemispheric specialization in animals is bird song. In several species of perching songbirds (passerines), including the chaffinch, canary, white-crowned sparrow, and zebra finch, there is evidence for neural specialization in the left hemisphere (LH) for the control of song. This appears to be a promising model of LH specialization for language, since bird song is a system of communication that can be considered a primitive model of human phonology (sound systems). As in humans, LH specialization in bird song is sex-linked and hormone-dependent, and it is sensitive to a critical period in development. Most important, the analysis of cerebral lateralization in birds highlights two fundamental issues in the study of human lateralization: (1) the relative independence, complementarity, and interaction of the neural control centers in the two hemispheres; (2) the question of the level of neural control, from articulatory organs to cortical "song engrams," where lateralization emerges and predominates.

The following discussion parallels closely Arnold and Bottjer (2). The vocal organ of the bird is called the "syrinx." The syringeal muscles are bilaterally paired, innervated by the left and right hypoglossal nerves, respectively, and each side controls sound separately. The hypoglossal motor nucleus receives projections from several anatomically discrete and interconnected neural nuclei, the most prominent of which is the caudal nucleus of the hyperstriatum ventrale (HVc). The syringeal muscles and their neural control systems are separate and are apparently capable of producing two independent and simultaneous sounds.

In the chaffinch, canary, white-crowned sparrow, white-throated sparrow, and Java sparrow, sectioning the left hypoglossal nerve produces much greater deficits in vocal control than sectioning the right nerve. In these species, song is learned early, and the young male must hear his own species' song during this sensitive period to develop normal song as an adult. In both chaffinches and canaries, recovery of function after syringeal denervation is a function of age. Once song has crystallized, the bird cannot recover from hypoglossal section. Section of the left hypoglossos earlier, however, allows more or less complete recovery by the right syrinx; this is analogous to language recovery following dominant-hemisphere lesions causing childhood aphasia.

Although the left HVc seems to exert predominant control over the left-syringeal half and the right HVc controls only the right side, there must be rich interhemispheric interaction, since song elements sung on one side are rigidly coordinated with elements sung on the other. Indeed, in both zebra finches and canaries, there is a weak contralateral projection from HVc to the opposite syrinx. The system is analogous to ipsilateral motor systems in humans, and lesions of left HVc have a more devastating effect on song than lesions of right HVc. After left-sided HVc lesions, individual song elements are maintained, but phrasal structure is destroyed. In contrast, right-sided HVc lesions do not alter normal phrase organization, but abolish two-fifths to two-thirds of the repertoire of syllables. If true, then this analogy with LH specialization for syntactic organization and right-hemisphere (RH) competence for lexical analysis in human language is striking.

After early left-HVc lesions there is song recovery, apparently through right-HVc control. This suggested to Nottebohm (41) that the left HVc normally prevents the right HVc from acquiring a major role in song control, and that destruction of left HVc frees the right side from this constraint. A similar argument is invoked to explain RH takeover of some language functions in aphasia (see E. Zaidel, "Language in the Right Hemisphere," this volume).

To date, there is no evidence for anatomical asymmetry in HVc in any of the species that show asymmetric control of vocalization. Failures to find asymmetry are surprising, since size of HVc correlates with size of song repertoire in adult canaries and even with seasonal changes in song. Nottebohm attempted to resolve this paradox by hypothesizing that size of HVc correlates with capacity for vocal learning rather than with the size of the actual vocal repertoire.

A recent challenge to Nottebohm's lateralization hypothesis comes from McCasland (36) in Konishi's lab, where researchers recorded multiunit electrical activity in HVc of awake, singing canaries, correlating neuronal discharge patterns in HVc with sound function. No electrophysiological asymmetry was observed, suggesting interhemispheric interaction during song control. However, this does not prove functional equivalence. Indeed, active right-syringeal contraction may be necessary to prevent it from producing sound when the left syrinx controls the song.

Nottebohm (42) speculated that the asymmetric neural control of a behavior may evolve if the task is complex and learned. Yet if this is an evolutionary tendency, it is not always expressed (2). Several species of birds are capable of learning complex vocal sounds, yet show no syringeal asymmetry; where asymmetry occurs, as in canaries, it is not correlated with amount of vocal learning.

The avian model — especially the neural control of bird song — is instructive. It highlights three related concepts of hemispheric specialization. First, each hemisphere is to a large extent functionally independent of the other and can potentially control the sensory–motor repertoire by itself. Second, such independence creates ample opportunities for specialization through some asymmetry during development, and early developmental asymmetry could thereby be self-reinforcing. Third, asymmetry can lead to complementary specialization, and this may be a widespread vertebrate phenomenon (2).

In sum, the bird song is an appealing model for some aspects of human language and for interhemispheric interaction during language processing. LH dominance for song control is weaker than for human language; there is some bilateral HVc vocal control in the canary, and both hypoglossal and hemispheric dominance can be reversed in adult canaries. Humans can control the peripheral speech apparatus from either side but coordinate the speech function centrally from one hemisphere, whereas canaries, say, achieve dominance and "coordination" by simply dropping the whole control line on one side. Further, the use of human language has no sex specificity.

How can we interpret the evolutionary significance of hemispheric dominance in bird song? Is it a model for dominance in a vocal communication system, or more generally in a learned motor task? An evolutionary argument is needed to reconcile the avian–human analogy with the fact that hormone flow precipitates song learning in the male chaffinch, but seemingly inhibits new language learning in both male and female humans. Moreover, the distant evolutionary relationship between birds and humans, without known intervening examples of vocal lateralization, suggests that the respective mechanisms may not be homologous and that their parallel development is not the culmination of an evolutionary sequence, but merely one of many possible responses to local pressures.

Chicks

Rogers and colleagues (46) discovered that unilateral hemispheric injections of various pharmacological agents in young chicks produced differential effects on visual-discrimination learning, auditory habituation, attack, and copulatory behaviors. With one eye covered, injections of the LH disrupted visual learning no matter which hemisphere was active (i.e., which eye was exposed), whereas RH injections disrupted learning only if the right side was processing the information. The LH appeared necessary for visual search and could be said to be dominant for the task. Attack and copulatory behaviors were increased by drug injection into the LH but not the RH. Bilateral injections were ineffective, suggesting an interhemispheric balance, with the LH being inhibitory and the RH facilitatory.

These results are complemented by evidence for behavioral asymmetry in normal chicks. Andrew and Rainey (1) found that untreated chicks learned a visual discrimination faster and extinguished faster with the right eye alone than with the left eye alone, indicating LH specialization for this task. Conversely, they found that the RH showed greater fear response to emotionally charged stimuli. The establishment of neural asymmetry in chicks seems to depend on the orientation of the embryo in the egg and on exposure to light during a critical period. Hamilton (19) mentions the attractive if speculative hypothesis that a bird searches for food with its right eye, while it watches for predators with the left — as dramatic a proposal as any modern idea on complementary hemispheric specialization in humans.

There is even some evidence in chicks that the LH is necessary for the initial establishment of imprinting responses, but that the RH may be necessary for consolidating imprinting in neural circuits elsewhere (25).

Rodents

This discussion follows closely Hamilton (19). Much recent research with rats suggests that certain motoric, communicative, spatial, and emotional behaviors are lateralized, often in conjunction with asymmetrically distributed neurotransmitters. The RH is particularly implicated in complex behavioral tasks, novelty, emotionality, and aggression (9).

Robinson (45) found a strong but transient population effect of LH, but not RH, damage on overall activity levels of male rats, with correlated changes in noradrenalin levels. By contrast, Denenberg (9) reported no differential effect of unilateral hemispheric lesions on activity or directional preferences of normally reared male rats. Denenberg did, however, find differential effects of unilateral lesions on behavior, including spatial preference, taste aversion, and mouse killing, if they were handled shortly after birth. For example, handled rats were either made very active or virtually immobile by RH damage, depending on whether they were reared in groups or in isolation. They were unaffected by LH damage.

The data are complex, often conflicting, and their interpretation is ambiguous. It is rarely clear how the lateralized behaviors relate to functions that are specialized in humans. And results must be replicated and controlled for selection of subjects (sex, strain, handling), behavioral testing paradigm, and type of lesion. Systematic correlations with anatomical, physiological, and neurochemical differences seem especially promising for resolving some of these difficulties.

Old World Monkeys

Hamilton (19) argues that nonhuman primates are the most promising subjects of hemispheric specialization studies, because of their close phylogenetic relationship to humans and because of their similar behavioral repertoire. Both lesion studies (48) and split-brain studies (18) failed to find hemispheric differences in learning and memory when using pattern-discrimination tasks in monkeys. A few positive findings have been reported from experiments using stimuli such as orientation, movement, and facial features that would evoke lateralized processing in humans (19a). In general, spatial abilities are specialized in the LH and facial discrimination is in the RH. LH specialization for spatial discrimination in monkeys would be dissimilar to that in humans, but may reflect an analytic LH cognitive style that the monkeys apply to these stimuli. Two well-known positive findings are said to involve auditory functions. Dewson (10) found greater deficits following LH than RH auditory cortex lesions on a delayed conditional task involving auditory–visual sequences, but these results have been criticized for methodological reasons (47). Petersen *et al*. (44) showed a more robust right-ear (LH) dominance for discrimination of conspecific calls, but not of calls of other species in the Japanese macaque. This result is provocative because it resembles the right-ear advantage for dichotic listening in humans, thought to reflect LH specialization for the phonetic analysis of language. Most but not all positive results implicate LH specialization, but the effects are small, few subjects have been tested, and the studies remain to be replicated.

LeMay (32) found that 16 out of 17 great apes, including orangutan, chimpanzee, and gorilla, had sylvian fissure asymmetries in the same direction as those observed in humans (right fissure higher than the left one). However, anatomic asymmetries in the brains of nonhuman primates are not necessarily correlated with functional hemispheric asymmetries in lateralized tests, raising questions about the biological significance of left–right anatomical differences observed in the human brain. Further, the hypothesis that hemispheric asymmetry evolved to support advanced vocal communication in complex societies, where an individual must assume a variety of social roles and must convey subtle nuances of information, is undermined by the observation that relative asymmetries in monkeys and apes (51) fail to reflect the relative social use of vocal communication in these primates. The vocal communicative repertoire of apes and monkeys is used in conjunction with visual displays, including gestures, postures, and facial expressions, transmitting predominantly social/affective rather than perceptual/cognitive information as in humans. Furthermore, in contrast with the cortical locus of vocal motor control in humans, vocalization in primates appears to be subcortical, predominantly limbic. (For a critical view, however, see 35.) Thus, the hypothesis that possible hemispheric specialization for ape communication is a precursor of hemispheric specialization for language in humans has no *a priori* appeal.

Yeni-Komshian and Benson (51) also measured the length of the left and right sylvian fissures in brains of humans, chimpanzees, and rhesus macaques. A longer left sylvian fissure was seen in 84 % of the humans and in 80 % of the chimpanzees, but only in 44 % of the rhesus monkeys. The mean left–right differences were longer for humans (15 %) than for chimpanzees (5 %), and no overall differences were found for the rhesus. Since both rhesus monkeys and chimpanzees are highly sociable species with vocal repertoires of comparable complexity, Nottebohm (43) concluded that anatomical brain asymmetries in humans and apes bear no primary relation to complex forms of communication.

In conclusion, direct behavioral data on functional asymmetries in monkeys and apes are negative, inconclusive, preliminary, or lacking. There are no studies of hemispheric specialization in the great apes, particularly those trained in paralinguistic systems such as manual sign language or a visual-token lexicon. These animals are too precious to permit anatomical, physiological, or lesion studies, but it is less clear why benign indices of real-time cerebral activation such as EEG and event-related potentials have not been used on these subjects.

The Evolution of
Hemispheric Specialization in Humans

Theories about the Origin of Human Cerebral Dominance

Two main views about the origin of human cerebral dominance may be distinguished, each positing a different relationship between the origins of language and the evolution of other cognitive functions. Probably the most common view is that shared tool use in our hominid ancestry led in turn to the development of human dextrality and to LH specialization for fine motor control, hence to LH specialization for speech articulation, and finally to LH specialization for language (5). This view is supported by Liepmann's theory of LH dominance for motor control (praxis) and has a modern adherent in Kimura (29), who believes that the LH is specialized for control of motor sequencing, both manual and vocal. Implicit in these views is the vague concept of neural "spillover by proximity" from one system, such as manual control, to another, such as vocal communication. One difficulty with this view is that neither handedness nor hemispheric dominance for producing manual sequences correlates well with hemispheric control of speech (37). Nonetheless, it is possible that the evolution of manual dominance was a precursor of the evolution of cerebral dominance.

Jerison (27) posits a dramatically different view on the origin of human language. He argues that language evolved not merely to communicate, but to represent and "construct" reality. Language is primarily an adaptation of perceptual and cognitive functions in the human species and only secondarily adapted for communication. Animal communication features small repertoires of fixed action patterns conveying unambiguous social and affective information relevant to the immediate environment. By contrast, human language conveys perceptual and cognitive information, has a potentially infinite repertoire, and can reconstruct reality of a different time and place. Although Jerison rejects the argument that language has evolved cortically from the systems of communication of earlier primates, he nonetheless does accept the argument that the LH became specialized for vocal control by proximity to motor centers.

The Fossil Record

Bradshaw and Nettleton (5) suggest on the basis of recent paleoarcheological evidence that human brachiation, pedalism, and advanced tool use evolved in that order, and that all three preceded any dramatic increase in brain size or the development of speech-related brain structures. This would place the emergence of cerebral lateralization no earlier than 1.6 million years ago. Relevant evidence comes from endocasts that reflect the asymmetry of the sylvian fissure or the specific sulcal patterns in Broca's area of the left frontal lobe. LeMay and Culebras (33) reported asymmetry in the sylvian fissure of the Chapelle-aux-Saints Neanderthal endocast, based on the 1911 drawings by Boule and Anthony. The asymmetry is comparable to that in modern humans, which is believed to be related to language dominance (16). This evidence is weak — no other asymmetries of the sylvian fissure have been reported (24) — but Neanderthal artifacts have been recovered that suggest a linguistic culture (26).

Falk (11) has recently analyzed the fissural pattern of the frontal lobe of *Homo habilis*, which is about 2 million years old, and found a convolutional pattern in the LH that is consistent with Broca's area. This is also weak evidence for a language area, since similar convolutional patterns appear in both hemispheres of modern humans. An up-to-date review of hominid endocasts as evidence for the evolution of the human brain is presented in Blumenberg (4).

PSYCHOLOGICAL APPROACHES TO HEMISPHERIC SPECIALIZATION

Information-Processing Rationale

A feature of the neuropsychological approach to human cognition is the incorporation of structural brain considerations into the analysis of mental functions. Indeed, neuroscience and information-processing psychology share a core of cybernetic concepts that presuppose a fragmentation of component processes in space and time. Three concepts or assumptions are shared by neuroanatomy, neurophysiology, and information-processing psychology. The first is that of a functional unit, center, or stage with a definite spatial representation in the brain and designed to process discrete chunks of information at discrete moments in time. The second is that of connectivity or information flow between functional units through anatomical fiber tracts. The third concept concerns elaboration of information through a sequence of functional units, defining directionality of information flow in the system.

It is tempting to conceptualize a cognitive cerebral network with a finite number of basic perceptual or cognitive operations differentially localized in the brain. Each complex task has a temporal–spatial representation gradient in the cortex, describing its dependence on the primitive cognitive–cerebral network (31). Two tasks can interact (facilitate or interfere) with each other to the extent that they are functionally–anatomically interconnected — that is, to the extent that they share processing units or resources.

Such assumptions are oversimplified. Processing stages may be parallel and interactive rather than sequential and independent. Functional units may be distributed throughout the brain rather than localized. Nonetheless, a surprising amount of clinical data demonstrates modularity in the cognitive–cerebral system, both functional and structural. Hemispheric specialization probably represents the most general modular system in the brain. The LH and RH have sharp anatomical boundaries and some apparently sharp functional demarcations as well. The interaction between hemispheres thus becomes a paradigm case for information transfer within the cognitive–cerebral network. Even if oversimplified, the information-processing rationale is heuristically powerful and appropriate to our current state of ignorance.

Assumptions

The history of research in human hemispheric specialization is rooted in case studies of functional deficits due to localized cerebral lesions. Several assumptions are usually made in accepting such data as primary. The first assumption may be called the "transparency hypothesis." It states that cognitive deficit from focal brain damage exposes, or makes transparent, the structure of normal cognition, because the system must then operate in a simplified fashion. The system is slower and less elaborate, and in this view must follow regular and predictable rules for the substitution of deficient structures by functioning ones.

The second assumption may be called the "software hypothesis." Using a popular computer analogy, it states that a cognitive deficit due to a brain lesion is the result of a predictable loss of "software modules" from the complex cognitive program of the brain. Thus, specific functional units within each hemisphere correspond to specific hardware modules. This makes the common analogy between the brain and a computer more reasonable. Hemispheric functioning cannot be explained by purely abstract cognitive psychological concepts, nor exclusively in molecular neuroscientific terms. Even a complete input–output model in either description would be unsatisfactory, as it would fail to provide a phenomenological description of how the hemispheres actually operate and what experiences ensue.

The third assumption is the "simulation (convergence) hypothesis." It states that, under appropriate load and stress, it is possible in principle to simulate in the normal brain deficit conditions that are equivalent to lesion states. Thus, experiments on laterality effects in normal subjects may be interpreted as simulation of clinical callosal section by latency and accuracy differences in behavioral responses to lateralized stimulation near threshold levels (12). This would demand parallel research programs on hemispheric specialization in neurological patients with unilateral lesions, in commissurotomy patients, and in normal subjects (54). The assumption is important, as the normal brain remains the ultimate testing ground for any account of hemispheric specialization.

Methods

The psychological techniques used for studying hemispheric specialization in normal subjects involve the lateralization or restriction of sensory stimuli or motor responses to one half of space — that is, to one hemisphere. Performance in the two lateralized conditions, left and right, is then measured and compared, using either accuracy or latency as dependent variables. For example, LH output can be ensured by requiring response with speech or a right-hand manual button press. Another way to probe hemispheric involvement in a primary cognitive task is by the degree of interference with a concurrent secondary lateralized task, such as finger tapping (31), a technique that has some statistical validity and is becoming increasingly popular. Another technique monitors lateral gaze shifts during a cognitive task, under the assumption that such shifts reflect contralateral hemispheric activation (30), a relatively unreliable method that is sensitive to several confounding variables (55).

The most common technique for studying hemispheric specialization in normal subjects involves lateralization of the sensory stimuli to the left or right field. In the tactile modality, Witelson (50) introduced the method of dichaptic presentations: simultaneous presentation of competing stimuli to both hands out of view. Use of this technique has been limited, because it restricts the complexity of both stimuli and responses. In the visual modality, Franz (13, 14) and Mishkin and Forgays (38) introduced the hemifield tachistoscopic method that is commonly used today. Stimuli are projected briefly to either the left or right of fixation in order to involve first either the RH or LH (see chapter by D. W. Zaidel, this volume). In the auditory modality, Kimura (28) adapted Broadbent's dichotic-listening technique, in which two acoustically similar stimuli are presented simultaneously to the two ears. Under these conditions, the ipsilateral ear–hemisphere projections are masked so that each ear projects predominantly to the contralateral hemisphere (see chapter by Noffsinger, this volume).

Models

The split-brain preparation operationalizes the concept of "degree of hemispheric specialization" by allowing independent processing of the same task by each hemisphere. Thus, expressions like "hemisphere x obtained a score of y on task z," or "hemisphere x performed better than hemisphere y by amount z," become well defined and coherent. The disconnection syndrome can thus provide a criterial experiment for the concept of relative specialization in the normal brain (20). The disconnection syndrome also highlights the roles that hemispheric specialization and callosal connectivity play in the etiology of laterality effects. Once two independent hemispheric cognitive systems can be demonstrated in the normal brain, the concept of interhemispheric interaction becomes central. Little is known today about the dynamics of interhemispheric communication.

When a right-visual-field advantage (RVFA) is observed in a hemifield tachistoscopic task with manual responses, two interpretations are possible. First, it is possible that the LH is exclusively specialized for the task, and that when the stimuli are first flashed to the left visual field (LVF) they must be relayed from the RH to the LH through the corpus callosum for processing, at some cost in latency and accuracy. This is the "callosal-relay" or "exclusive-specialization" interpretation. Alternatively, it is possible that each hemisphere can process the sensory input it receives without need for callosal transfer. Then the RVFA would reflect the superiority of the LH processing style over RH strategies. This is the "direct-access" interpretation.

A "callosal-relay" task should show exclusive specialization with massive laterality effects in the split-brain or hemisphere-damaged subject, in contrast to a moderate laterality effect when the corpus callosum and the processing centers are intact. On the other hand, a "direct-access" task should point to bilateral competence in the lesioned or split brain and should yield a comparable laterality effect in the split and normal brains (54).

Another test for direct access is the "processing-dissociation" criterion. A significant interaction between hemifield of presentation and a stimulus dimension that should not affect callosal transfer (such as word abstraction but not length) suggests that each hemisphere uses a different strategy for the stimulus. In principle, it should also be possible to pair stimulus presentations in the left and right fields with responses by the left and right hands. Then direct-access tasks should show an interaction of response hand by sensory field, whereas callosal-relay tasks should show a main effect of response hand (54). Both would also show a main effect of sensory field, of course, if there is hemispheric specialization for the task. If there is no interference between central processing and response programming in a direct-access task, then the response hand × stimulus hemifield interaction should yield an ipsilateral advantage, whereas if there is interference, then the interaction should yield a contralateral advantage (56).

When a task combines a sequence of direct-access and callosal-relay components, the net resulting hand–field pattern is callosal relay, with the visual-field advantage determined by the first callosal-relay component, and the hand advantage determined by the last callosal-relay component. Direct-access components prior to the first callosal-relay component do affect the slope. Thus, a complex task that exhibits a callosal-relay pattern may conceal an intermediate direct-access component. However, a complex task that exhibits a direct-access pattern must reflect a purely direct-access sequence, and the slope reflects the net additive hemispheric processing differentials for all the component's processes. Both direct-access and callosal-relay tasks exist (54). For example, phonetic perception of dichotic stop consonant–vowel syllables is exclusively specialized in the LH and therefore requires callosal relay from the RH to the LH. Some lateralized visual lexical-decision tasks of concrete English words, on the other hand, can be processed by either hemisphere alone and do not require callosal relay. They are direct-access even in the normal brain (54).

Most cognitive tasks probably call for more or less complex interhemispheric interaction. Callosal relay and direct access represent the limits of complete or no transfer, respectively. As yet, little is known about the nature of normal cross-callosal interhemispheric communication, but certain experimental conditions can shift hemispheric control over a task. One example involves a shift from RH to LH control as the task becomes more familiar — that is, as the processing requirements change (17, 55). A second example involves shifts in hemispheric control over direct-access tasks resulting from hemispheric priming and overloading (23). Here dual-task priming is said to increase hemispheric activation, but overloading can eventually shift control to the other hemisphere (15, 22, 39). Dynamic shift models thus combine the direct-access assumption of bilateral competence and the callosal-relay emphasis on cross-callosal transfer.

Dual-task interference paradigms are easy to administer and can be applied to a variety of populations, but are ill-suited for teasing apart hemispheric specialization in component processes. Moreover, interference is always asymmetric in the sense that the primary cognitive task interferes with the second motor task; and it is not clear whether or how the technique can be applied to two cognitive tasks (but see 56). Dual-task experiments can determine whether a primary lateralized task is direct-access or callosal-relay by pairing it with a secondary task of known specialization.

Suppose the secondary task is exclusively specialized to the LH. Assume also that if the primary task is direct-access, then it shares no resources with the unstimulated hemisphere. The primary task interferes with the secondary task if the decrement in performance of the secondary task is sensitive to the difficulty of the primary task (40). Table 1 shows the possible combinations of interference patterns and their interpretations. Pattern 3 is indeterminate, since either the primary task is callosal-relay and specialized in the LH without sharing any resources with the secondary task in the same hemisphere, or else the primary task is direct-access and still shares no resources with the secondary task when processed in the LH. Patterns 1 and 2 distinguish callosal-relay from direct-access tasks. The interpretations can be confirmed by pairing the primary task with a secondary one that is callosal-relay, specialized in the RH.

The Laterality Index

There is still no definite rationale for choosing a laterality index to express data of perceptual asymmetry. A simple difference measure between left- and right-field scores is inadequate, because it confounds degree of laterality and accuracy in counterintuitive ways. For the same reason, an analysis of variance on the raw latency data is flawed. For accuracy data, the index f of Halwes and of Marshall *et al.* is currently the preferred solution (55), although there is no *a priori* reason to believe that laterality should always be independent of accuracy. For example, what if the RH is faster but less reliable than the LH (55)? Bryden and Sprott's lambda (7) is a continuous version of f and allows in addition direct tests of significance of the laterality effect for individual subjects.

TABLE 1

PATTERNS OF INTERFERENCE BETWEEN A CALLOSAL-RELAY
SECONDARY TASK SPECIALIZED IN THE LH AND A
PRIMARY TASK PRESENTED IN THE RVF AND,
IN TURN, IN THE LVF

Condition	RVF	LVF	Interpretation
1	I[a]	I	Primary task is callosal-relay, specialized in the LH
2	I	No I	Primary task is direct-access
3	No I	No I	? (Resource differentiation within hemispheres)
4	No I	I	Impossible

[a]I = Interference that is sensitive to difficulty of primary task.

Certainly, for a given task, we want to know not only the mean laterality effect for a given subject but also its variability. Thus, both population means and standard deviations need to be compared (34).

A more general approach to the measurement of behavioral laterality effects is the systematic use of psychophysical methods like signal detection theory. There the problem of accuracy–laterality tradeoffs is analyzed explicitly; a comparison between different laterality tests in different populations is made possible; and the data can provide criteria and procedures for determining the empirical adequacy of the laterality index d' (55).

Reliability and Validity

Problems of statistical reliability, validity, and inference continue to plague experiments on hemispheric specialization in normal subjects. Many common tests of perceptual asymmetries have low test–retest reliability. Reliability can be increased by using longer runs and paradigms that minimize strategy changes due to attentional shifts. There is evidence that systematic shifts in laterality effects occur as a function of familiarity with the test (55). Moreover, the observed perceptual asymmetries are highly sensitive to stimulus and task parameters, such as type of material, sensory modality, response mode, task instructions, attentional set, and stimulus quality.

Poor test–retest reliability or low cross-correlations among different tests for hemispheric specialization do not necessarily mean that the laterality tests are "noisy." They could also mean that laterality is a continuous variable in the general population with different perceptual, cognitive, and memory functions lateralized to different degrees within and across individuals. Indeed, individuals may differ in the degree of relative hemispheric specialization for a given function or differ in the degree of callosal connectivity for that function. In other words, the corpus callosum is conceptualized as a complex channel of communication with different parts transmitting different types of information, each with its own definite information capacity, rate of transmission, and measurable loss. Consequently, we may expect to find individual differences in the efficiency of collosal connectivity, as well as in sensitivity to experimental conditions that affect callosal transfer.

Visual information is known to be transferred through the posterior, splenial fibers of the corpus callosum, whereas auditory information seems to transfer through the posterior callosum just anterior to the splenium. Women and left-handers may show smaller behavioral laterality effects than men and right-handers, respectively, because of better callosal connectivity. Indeed, both women (8) and left-handers (49) are said to have larger corpus callosums. Continuing experiments in other laboratories fail to replicate the finding in women, but confirm the finding in left-handers (personal communication from Levy, Harshman, and Witelson, 1984). But this cannot be the whole story. Women show weaker laterality effects in direct-access tasks as well as in callosal-relay tasks (54), and thus must also differ from men in degree of hemispheric specialization.

The findings of weaker laterality effects in women (see chapter by Hines and

60 E. ZAIDEL

Gorski, this volume) and in sinistrals (see chapter by Satz *et al.*, this volume) have come to constitute evidence for the statistical validity of alleged tests of hemispheric specialization. This may be premature, as women may actually show increased laterality effects in some expressive language tasks (21). In general, the theoretical rationale for associating a higher degree of functional lateralization with a stronger laterality effect remains weak.

Another potential criterion for statistical validity of a laterality test is the alleged increase of cerebral lateralization with age. Actually, the evidence for an increase in relative degree of hemispheric specialization during ontogenesis is poor (see chapter by Curtiss, this volume). Interhemispheric connectivity may actually increase with age (15a), leading to progressively smaller laterality effects due to increasingly effective cross-callosal competition and transfer (53). In sum, much more theoretical and methodological work needs to be done on measures of hemispheric specialization in the normal brain before such measures can be used reliably to assess cerebral dominance for individual patients in the clinic.

Concluding Caveats

The anatomical connectionist models of laterality effects in the normal brain are oversimplified, but heuristically useful and theoretically illuminating. The distinction between direct-access and callosal-relay models potentially clarifies individual differences in behavioral laterality effects in terms of two independent factors: degree of relative hemispheric specialization and degree of callosal connectivity. Many experiments in the literature cannot be interpreted without prior model fitting. Thus, an experimental VFA need not mean that the other hemisphere cannot or does not process the task, and the absence of a VFA does not mean that there are no hemispheric differences in information-processing styles. Even worse are experiments that circumstantially "infer" hemispheric specialization on a task, simply because it seems to contain a component that is "known" by analogy to be performed in that hemisphere, such as LH specialization for sequential processing. Since small changes in a task can shift the pattern of hemispheric dominance, each task needs to be assessed independently and directly in some lateralized paradigm.

REFERENCES

1. Andrew, R. J., and Rainey, C., Right–left asymmetry of response to visual stimuli in the domestic chick. In: *Analysis of Visual Behavior* (D. J. Ingle, M. A. Goodale, and R. J. W. Mansfield, Eds.). MIT Press, Cambridge, Mass., 1982: 197–209.
2. Arnold, A. P., and Bottjer, S. W., Cerebral lateralization in birds. In: *Cerebral Lateralization in Subhuman Species* (S. Glick, Ed.). Academic Press, New York, in press.
3. Beaumont, J. G., *Divided Visual Field Studies of Cerebral Organization*. Academic Press, London, 1982.
4. Blumenberg, B., The evolution of the advanced hominid brain. *Curr. Anthropol.*, 1983, 24: 589–623.

5. Bradshaw, J. L., and Nettleton, N. C., *Human Cerebral Asymmetry*. Prentice-Hall, Englewood Cliffs, N.J., 1983.

6. Bryden, M. P., *Laterality: Functional Asymmetry in the Intact Brain*. Academic Press, New York, 1983.

7. Bryden, M. P., and Sprott, D. H., Statistical determination of degree of laterality. *Neuropsychologia*, 1981, **19**: 571–581.

8. De La Coste-Utamsing, C., and Holloway, R. L., Sexual dimorphism in the human corpus callosum. *Science*, 1982, **216**: 1431–1432.

9. Denenberg, V. H., Hemispheric laterality in animals and the effects of early experience. *Behav. Brain Sci.*, 1981, **11**: 1–49.

10. Dewson, J. H., III, Preliminary evidence of hemispheric asymmetry of auditory function in monkeys. In: *Lateralization in the Nervous System* (S. Harnad, R. W. Doty, L. Goldstein, J. Jaynes, and G. Krauthamer, Eds.). Academic Press, New York, 1977: 63–71.

11. Falk, D., Cerebral cortices of East African early hominids. *Science*, 1983, **221**: 1072–1074.

12. Filbey, R. A., and Gazzaniga, M. S., Splitting the normal brain with reaction time. *Psychonom. Sci.*, 1969, **17**: 335–336.

13. Franz, S. I., and Davis, E. F., Simultaneous reading with both cerebral hemispheres. In: *Studies in Cerebral Function, IV*. Publications of the University of California at Los Angeles in Education, Philosophy and Psychology, 1933, **1**: 99–106.

14. Franz, S. I., and Kilduff, S., Cerebral dominance as shown by segmental visual learning. *Studies in Cerebral Function, II*. Publications of the University of California at Los Angeles in Education, Philosophy and Psychology, 1933, **1**: 79–90.

15. Friedman, A., Polson, M. C., Dafoe, C. E., and Gaskill, S. J., Divided attention within and between hemispheres: Testing a multiple resources approach to limited-capacity information processing. *J. Exp. Psychol. H.P.&P.*, 1982, **8**: 625–650.

15a. Calin, D., Johnstone, J., Nakell, S., and Herron, J., Development of the capacity for tactile information transfer between hemispheres in normal children. *Science*, 1979, **204**: 1330–1332.

16. Geschwind, N., and Levitsky, W., Human brain: Left right asymmetries in temporal speech region. *Science*, 1968, **461**: 186–187.

17. Goldberg, E., and Costa, L. D., Hemispheric differences in the acquisition and use of descriptive systems. *Brain Lang.*, 1981, **14**: 144–173.

18. Hamilton, C. R., Investigations of perceptual and mnemonic lateralization in monkeys. In: *Lateralization in the Nervous System* (S. Harnad, R. W. Doty, L. Goldstein, J. Jaynes, and G. Krauthamer, Eds.). Academic Press, New York, 1977: 45–62.

19. Hamilton, C. R., Hemispheric specialization in monkeys. In: *Brain Circuits and Functions of the Mind* (C. B. Trevarthen, Ed.). Cambridge University Press, Cambridge, England, in press.

19a. Hamilton, C. R., and Vermiere, B. A., Complementary hemispheric superiorities in monkeys. *Soc. Neurosci. Abstr.*, in press.

20. Harshman, R., The meaning and measurement of differences in degree of lateralization. Paper presented in the Symposium on Methodological and Statistical Issues in Neuropsychological Research, chaired by S. A. Berenbaum, Eighth Annual Meeting, INS, San Francisco, January 29–February 2, 1980.

21. Healey, J. M., Waldstein, S., and Goodglass, H., Sex differences in the lateralization of language discrimination versus language production. *Brain Lang.*, in press.

22. Hellige, J. B., Visual laterality and cerebral hemisphere specialization: Methodological and theoretical considerations. In: *Conditioning, Cognition, and Methodology: Contemporary Issues in Experimental Psychology* (J. B. Sidowski, Ed.). Erlbaum, Hillsdale, N.J., in press.

23. Hellige, J. B., Cox, P. J., and Litvac, L., Information processing in the hemispheres:

Selective hemisphere activation and capacity limitations. *J. Exp. Psychol. (Gen)*, 1979, **108**: 251–279.

24. Holloway, R. L., and De La Coste-Lareymondie, M. C., Brain endocast asymmetry in pongids and hominids: Some preliminary findings on the paleontology of cerebral dominance. *Am. J. Phys. Anthropol.*, 1982, **58**: 101–110.

25. Horn, G., Neuromechanisms of learning: An analysis of inprinting in the domestic chick. *Proc. R. Soc. Lond. (Biol.)*, 1981, **213**: 101–137.

26. Jerison, H. J., Issues in brain evolution. In: *Oxford Survey in Evolutionary Biology*, Vol. 2 (R. Dawkins, Ed.). Oxford University Press, Oxford, in press.

27. Jerison, H. J., On the evolution of mind. In: *Brain and Mind* (D. Oakley, Ed.). Methuen, London, 1985: 1–31.

28. Kimura, D., Cerebral dominance and the perception of verbal stimuli, *Can. J. Psychol.*, 1961, **15**: 166–171.

29. Kimura, D., Neuromotor mechanisms in the evolution of human communication. Research Bulletin No. 454, Department of Psychology, The University of Western Ontario, London, Ontario, Canada, 1978. Also in *Neurobiology of Social Communication in Primates: An Evolutionary Perspective* (H. D. Steklis and M. J. Raleigh, Eds.). Academic Press, New York, 1979: 197–219.

30. Kinsbourne, M., Eye and head turning indicates cerebral lateralization. *Science*, 1972, **176**: 539–541.

31. Kinsbourne, M., and Hiscock, M., Asymmetries of dual-task performance. In: *Cerebral Hemisphere Asymmetry: Method, Theory and Application* (J. B. Hellige, Ed.). Praeger, New York, 1983: 255–334.

32. LeMay, M., Morphological cerebral asymmetries of modern man, fossil man, and nonhuman primate. *Ann. N.Y. Acad. Sci.*, 1976, **280**: 349–366.

33. LeMay, M., and Culebras, A., Human brain morphologic differences in the hemispheres demonstrable by carotid angiography. *N. Engl. J. Med.*, 1972, **287**: 168–170.

34. Levy, J., Is cerebral asymmetry of function a dynamic process? Implications for specifying degree of lateral differentiation. *Neuropsychologia*, 1983, **21**: 3–11.

35. Marin, O. S. M., Schwartz, M. F., and Saffran, E. M., Origins and distribution of language. In: *Handbook of Behavioral Neurobiology*, Vol. 2, *Neuropsychology* (M. S. Gazzaniga, Ed.). Plenum, New York, 1979: 179–213.

36. McCasland, J. S., Neuronal control of bird song production. Doctoral dissertation, Division of Biology, California Institute of Technology, Pasadena, 1983.

37. Milner, B., Invited address. Academy of Aphasia Annual Meeting, San Diego, 1979.

38. Mishkin, M., and Forgays, D. G., Word recognition as a function of retinal locus. *J. Exp. Psychol.*, 1952, **43**: 43–48.

39. Moscovitch, M., and Klein, D., Material-specific perceptual interference for visual words and faces: Implications for models of capacity limitations, attention, and laterality. *J. Exp. Psychol. H.P.&P.*, 1980, **6**: 590–604.

40. Navon, D., and Gopher, D., Task difficulty, resources, and dual-task performance. In: *Attention and Performance*, VIII (R. S. Nickerson, Ed.). Erlbaum, Hillsdale, N.J., 1980: 297–315.

41. Nottebohm, F., Asymmetries in neural control of vocalization in the canary. In: *Lateralization in the Nervous System* (S. Harnad, R. W. Doty, L. Goldstein, J. Jaynes, and G. Krauthamer, Eds.). Academic Press, New York, 1977: 23–44.

42. Nottebohm, F., Ontogeny of bird song. *Science*, 1970, **167**: 950–956.

43. Nottebohm, F., Origins and mechanisms in the establishment of cerebral dominance. In: *Handbook of Behavioral Neurobiology*, Vol. 2, *Neuropsychology* (M. S. Gazzaniga, Ed.). Plenum, New York, 1979: 295–344.

44. Petersen, M. R., Beecher, M. D., Zoloth, S. R., Moody, D. B., and Stebbins, W. C.,

Neural lateralization of species-specific vocalizations by Japanese macaques (*Macaca fuscata*). *Science*, 1978, **202**: 324–327.

45. Robinson, R. G., Differential behavioral and biochemical effects of right and left hemispheric cerebral infarction in the rat. *Science*, 1979, **205**: 707–710.

46. Rogers, L. J., Lateralization in the avian brain. *Bird Behav.*, 1980, **2**: 1–12.

47. Walker, S. F., Lateralization of functions in the vertebrate brain: A review. *Br. J. Psychol.*, 1980, **71**: 329–367.

48. Warren, J. M., and Nonneman, A. J., The search for cerebral dominance in monkeys. In: *Origins and Evolution of Language and Speech* (S. R. Harnad, H. D. Steklis, and J. Lancaster, Eds.). The New York Academy of Sciences, New York, 1976: 732–744.

49. Witelson, S. F., The corpus callosum is larger in left handers. *Soc. Neurosci. Abstr.*, 1983, **9**: 917.

50. Witelson, S. F., Hemisphere specialization for linguistic and nonlinguistic tactual perception using a dichotomous stimulation technique. *Cortex*, 1974, **10**: 3–17.

51. Yeni-Komshian, G. H., and Benson, D. A., Anatomical study of cerebral asymmetry in the temporal lobe of humans, chimpanzees, and rhesus monkeys. *Science*, 1976, **192**: 387–389.

52. Young, A. W., *Functions of the Right Cerebral Hemisphere*. Academic Press, London, 1983.

53. Zaidel, E., Auditory language comprehension in the right hemisphere following cerebral commissurotomy and hemispherectomy: A comparison with child language and aphasia. In: *Language Acquisition and Language Breakdown: Parallels and Divergencies* (A. Caramazza and E. B. Zurif, Eds.). Johns Hopkins University Press, Baltimore, 1978: 229–275.

54. Zaidel, E., Disconnection syndrome as a model for laterality effects in the normal brain. In: *Cerebral Hemisphere Asymmetry: Method, Theory and Application* (J. B. Hellige, Ed.). Praeger, New York, 1983: 95–151.

55. Zaidel, E., On measuring hemispheric specialization in man. In: *Advanced Technobiology* (B. Rybak, Ed.). Sijthoff & Noordhoff, Alphen aan den Rijn, 1979: 365–403.

56. Zaidel, E., Letai, D., and White, H., Modules of the brain: A dual task approach to hemispheric function. Manuscript, Department of Psychology, University of California at Los Angeles.

DIFFERENTIATING CHARACTERISTICS OF THE HUMAN SPEECH CORTEX: A QUANTITATIVE GOLGI STUDY

ARNOLD B. SCHEIBEL, MD,[1,2] ITZHAK FRIED, PhD,[1,2]
LINDA PAUL, PhD,[1] ALAN FORSYTHE, PhD,[3] UWAMIE TOMIYASU, MD,[4]
ADAM WECHSLER, MD,[5] ANN KAO,[1] and JAMES SLOTNICK[1]
Departments of [1]Anatomy, [2]Psychiatry, [3]Biomathematics,
[4]Pathology, and [5]Neurology

> *Le malade est mort le 17 avril 1861. A l'autopsie . . .*
> *le lobe frontal de l'hémisphère gauche est ramolli*
> *dans la plus grande partie de son étendue; les circon-*
> *volutions du lobule orbitaire, quoique atrophiées, ont*
> *conservé leur forme; la plupart des autres convolu-*
> *tions frontales sont entièrement détruites. Il est ré-*
> *sulté de cette destruction de la substance cérébrale,*
> *une grande cavité, capable du loger un oeuf de poule,*
> *et remplie de sériosité.* *
>
> —PAUL BROCA *(Sur le Siège de la Faculté de Langage)*

INTRODUCTION

In the mid-19th century, Dax (7) and Broca (2) first called attention to functional asymmetry between the two hemispheres, with particular reference to speech. With the recent studies of commissurotomized patients and the development of the split-brain preparation by Sperry and his colleagues (14, 22, 23), the investigation of lateralization of function has become one of the more robust areas of neuropsychology. Very much less is known about structural asymmetries, and, indeed, this area of research has followed a rocky road. Despite significant observations by Cunningham (6) and Eberstaller (10) on the unequal lengths of the two sylvian fissures, and subsequent qualitative descriptions of asymmetric parietal and temporal operculi between the hemispheres (5, 12, 20), Von Bonin (1) was still able to question the evidence for structural nonequivalence as recently as 1962. Six years later, Geschwind and Levitsky (15) presented quantitative data demonstrating increased area on the left planum temporale of 62% of the brains they studied, and thereby placed

---

*The patient died April 17, 1861. At the autopsy . . . the frontal lobe of the *left* hemisphere was softened in most of its extent; the circonvolutions of the orbital lobule, although atrophied, kept their form; the majority of the other frontal convolutions were entirely destroyed. The result of this destruction of the cerebral substance was a large cavity, capable of accommodating a hen's egg, and full of serous fluid.

the study of structural asymmetries between the hemispheres on a firmer footing. Despite the vigorous growth of anatomical studies of this sort, virtually nothing is known about related structural asymmetries in the substrate neurons. This study appears to be the first that addresses the problem; it is based on the thesis that functional differences between homologous areas of the two hemispheres should be reflected in differences in dendritic architecture and intercellular connections.

METHODOLOGY

Subjects and Materials

Initial attempts were made to analyze matched areas from left and right planum temporale where gross anatomical changes have been abundantly documented. Because of the complexity and variability in these cortical fields (11, 13), the anterior or motor speech zones of the frontal lobe seemed to provide better opportunity for rigorous quantitative study. Tissue was obtained at autopsy (within 6–28 hours after death) from eight male patients ranging in age from 58 to 77 years (mean age 65.9, $SD = 6.4$). All had been hospitalized at a Veterans Administration hospital, and all were free of known neurological disease. It was learned through family accounts that six of the eight patients were right-handed throughout life, while the other two were non-right-handed.

Tissue blocks were sampled bilaterally from areas triangularis and opercularis (Broca's area on the dominant side) (Figure 1) and from the foot of the precentral

Figure 1. Selection of the specimen. Tissue blocks were selected from the area triangularis–opercularis (a) of Broca (op) and from the orofacial area (b) of the precentral area (pc). Confirmatory blocks (c) were taken near the crest of the precentral area since the high proportion of giant pyramidal cells of Betz in this location served to validate our identification of the precentral gyrus (not mentioned in text). After tissue sections were mounted, cells were drawn and the basilar dendrite systems analyzed segment by segment (1, 2, 3, 4, 5). Coordinates of every dendritic branch point (x, y, z; x_2, y_2, z_2; x_3, y_3, z_3, etc.) were determined and entered into the computer for analysis.

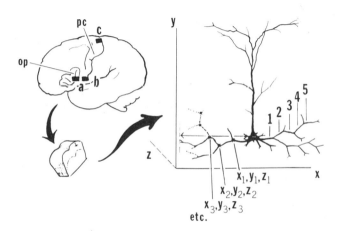

(motor strip) area just posterior. The latter provided material from the orofacial motor zone controlling movements of mouth, tongue and pharyngolaryngeal structures. Using cresyl-violet-stained sections as controls, each block was impregnated by the chrome–silver method of Golgi, sectioned at 120 μm, and mounted under cover slip. All slides were then coded to avoid investigator bias, and the study was performed blind.

For each of the eight brains, 24 cells were sampled, six from each of four regions: left and right opercularis–triangularis (abbreviated as LOP, ROP) and left and right precentral areas (abbreviated LPC, RPC). For each block, the cell sample consisted of the first six pyramidal neurons of cortical layer III that met predetermined criteria. These criteria included: (1) cell body depth below the pial surface ranging from 400–1300 μm (thereby including pyramidal cells of lower layer II and layer III); (2) the presence of at least three primary basilar dendrites with developed peripheral branching systems; and (3) location of the cell body approximately at the center of the 120-μm-thick section. Analysis was confined to the basilar dendrite system as seen in a single section.

Dendritic Analysis

Two methods of dendritic analysis were used. In the first, a series of concentric rings etched into the microscope eyepiece at regular intervals was centered over the cell body. The number of dendritic intersections with each ring was then counted following a method developed by the English mathematician–biologist, Donald Sholl, almost 30 years ago (21). This provides a surprisingly adequate first-order quantitative description of a dendrite arbor. In the second method, the sampled cells with their dendrite arbors were traced at 312.5 magnification using a drawing tube. Depth coordinates (z values) at the cell body, at each dendrite branch point, and at each dendrite tip were read off the calibrated fine focus of the microscope. The apparent status of the end point of each dendrite tip was noted (i.e., broken end, tip cut off at surface of the section, or tip intact). Planar coordinates for each branch point and terminal (x and y values) were subsequently measured with a TRS-80 microcomputer controlling a digitizing tablet, and the data were then transferred to a main frame computer for analysis.

RESULTS

The study was based on three *a priori* hypotheses: (1) Differences in dendritic architecture and dimensions should somehow reflect unique functional capacities of each cortical area; (2) the presumably more complex role of the left (dominant) motor speech area should result in neuronal dendritic trees that are more extensive and complex than those in the right homologous area; and (3) formulation of speech "strategies" in the left motor speech area should result in dendrite arbors that are more complex than those of the adjacent precentral orofacial zone concerned more with the motor "tactics" of speech.

Concentric Ring Analysis

The graphs in Figure 2 epitomize the type of data provided by concentric ring analysis of dendritic patterns. In brains 1, 3, and 4, the number of dendritic intersections for cells in Broca's area on the left was significantly greater than those for any other region. The zone of difference involved the dendritic field between rings 6 and 14 (ring interval = 28 μm), indicating that the differences become significant at and beyond 160 μm from the center of the soma. This represents an approximate transition area between third- and fourth-order dendrite branches. The unexpected reversal in the case of brain 5, where values for *right* Broca's area exceeded those of all other sites, became more reasonable when it was learned at the conclusion of the study that this patient was one of the two non-right-handers.

Analysis by Segment Order and Segment Length

Computer analysis of the digitized data from each dendrite tree provided several interesting bodies of information. The total (summed) dendrite length of a cell (TDL) can be taken as an index of the amount of dendritic surface potentially available for synaptic interaction. In the six right-handed patients, TDL in the opercular region exceeded that in precentral areas by about 10% ($F = 2.89$, $df = 1,134$, $p = .091$), but this difference was significant only in the left hemisphere ($t = 2.37$, $df = 1,134$, $p < .05$). More surprising was the lack of significant left–right differences in TDL. Significant differences emerged only when the proportion of TDL made up of lower-order (first plus second plus third) was compared with that made up of higher-order (fourth plus fifth plus sixth) dendrites. The fraction of TDL composed of higher-order dendrites was greater on the left than on the right ($F = 7.43$, $df = 1,134$, $p = .007$), and was also larger in the opercular than in the precentral areas ($F = 5.46$, $df = 1,134$, $p = .021$) (Figure 3). The higher-order dendrite branches of LOP neurons thus constituted a greater fraction of the total dendrite ensemble than did similarly situated branches in the ROP ($t = 2.25$) or in either LPC ($t = 1.95$) or RPC ($t = 3.67$).

Analysis of these data on a dendritic segment-by-segment basis is summarized in Tables 1 and 2. The average length of a dendritic segment of second or third order was significantly greater on the right than on the left. Differences in average dendritic number were noticeable primarily in higher-order dendrites, particularly for fourth-order segments, where those on the left side exceeded those on the right. The trend continued for fifth- and sixth-order branches, but the smaller number available for analysis prevented adequate statistical evaluation.

Of the two left–right asymmetries, longer secondary and tertiary segments on the right were primarily a feature of precentral cortex. The second asymmetry, characterized by more numerous higher-order (primarily fourth) segments on the left, was most obvious in opercular cortex. Partial or complete reversal of this pattern in the non-right-handed patients throws an interesting light on these data, suggesting that dendritic structural patterns have a more than trivial relationship to function. For instance, in one case, the mean length of secondary and tertiary dendrites was

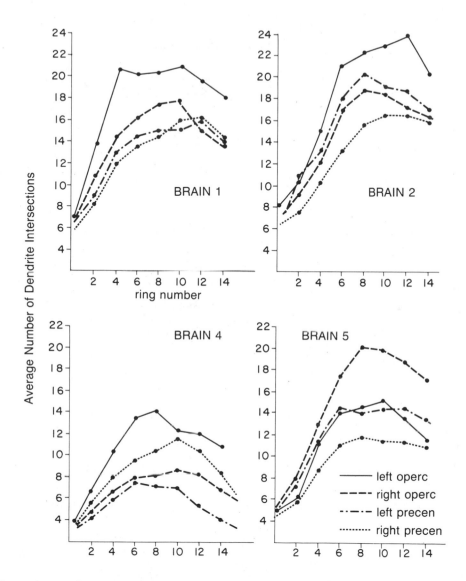

Figure 2. Graphs summarizing the average number of dendritic intersections per ring in a "Sholl-type" analysis of four cortical areas in cases 1, 3, 4, and 5. Dendrite ensembles from cells in the left opercular region (Broca's area) consistently provide a greater number of intersections with the target rings, especially beyond ring #6 (168 μm from center of the cell body) in all cases except that of brain 5. This patient, with a reversed ring–dendrite pattern, was found to have been a non-right-hander. Abbreviations: left operc, left opercularis–triangularis region of Broca; right operc, right opercularis–triangularis region; left and right precen, left and right precentral (motor) regions, respectively.

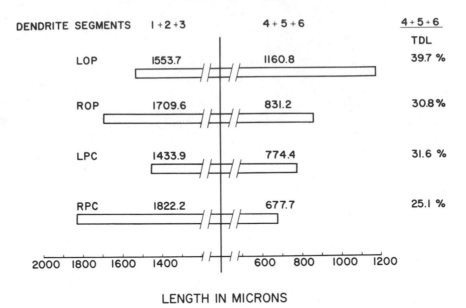

LENGTH IN MICRONS

Figure 3. Comparison of the contribution of the lower-order (1, 2, 3) and higher-order (4, 5, 6) dendrite segments to the length of the total neuronal dendritic tree in the four areas studied. Notice that total lengths of LOP and ROP are very similar, but higher-order dendrite branches make up almost 40 % of dendrite system in LOP and only 30 % in ROP. Note also the larger fractions made up of lower-order dendrites (1, 2, 3) on the right (ROP, RPC).

TABLE 1

ANALYSIS OF THE NUMBER OF DENDRITE SEGMENTS (MEAN ± *SE*) IN EACH OF THE FOUR AREAS STUDIED

	Order					
	1	2	3	4	5	6
LOP	5.20 ± 0.26	10.59 ± 0.56	12.57 ± 0.99	9.52 ± 1.38	$3.72 \pm .80$	0.74 ± 0.18
ROP	5.17 ± 0.26	10.80 ± 0.56	12.55 ± 0.99	6.89 ± 1.37	$2.58 \pm .80$	0.42 ± 0.18
LPC	4.95 ± 0.27	10.10 ± 0.58	12.18 ± 1.01	7.72 ± 1.39	$2.29 \pm .82$	0.09 ± 0.18
RPC	5.24 ± 0.26	10.56 ± 0.56	11.33 ± 1.00	6.36 ± 1.37	$1.49 \pm .81$	0.23 ± 0.18
Main effects[a]				$L > R$		$OP > PC$
				$F = 7.31$		$F = 4.24$
				$p < .01$		$p < .05$

[a]Adjusted for depth by analysis of covariance. Significant differences appear in fourth-order segments ($L > R$). Trend continues in fifth-order segments but does not achieve significance.

TABLE 2

Analysis of the Length of Dendrite Segments (Mean μm $\pm$ SE) in Each of the Four Areas Studied

	Order					
	1	2	3	4	5	6
LOP	23.71 ± 3.17	49.74 ± 4.82	71.53 ± 5.03	86.40 ± 7.25	79.38 ± 7.90	88.86 ± 14.48
ROP	28.41 ± 3.16	55.57 ± 4.80	74.82 ± 5.01	87.50 ± 7.35	82.82 ± 8.21	93.23 ± 29.11
LPC	28.51 ± 3.28	47.97 ± 5.03	62.13 ± 5.20	68.43 ± 7.60	86.87 ± 8.68	107.15 ± 24.53
RPC	29.78 ± 3.18	70.15 ± 4.84	82.52 ± 5.04	82.24 ± 7.52	83.90 ± 8.50	64.99 ± 12.68
Main effects[a]		$R > L$	$R > L$			
		$F = 8.21$	$F = 4.15$			
		$p < .005$	$p < .05$			

[a]Adjusted for depth by analysis of covariance. Significant differences appear in second- and third-order segments ($R > L$).

greater in the LPC (rather than the RPC). In the second non-right-hander, fourth-order dendrites were more numerous in the ROP (rather than the LOP). One reported right-handed patient also showed this pattern.

SOME REFLECTIONS ON THE DATA

These data underline differences in organization of the dendritic ensembles in four regions of human frontal cortex (Figure 4). These differences may have implications concerning both the physiology and the course of development of layer III pyramidal nerve cells in these regions. Dendritic spine distribution and density are known to vary with distance from the soma and with diameter (and presumably order) of the dendrite (16). The ultrastructural pattern of synaptic terminals (3), and perhaps their physiological role (18), vary as a function of their sites of termination on the postsynaptic surface — that is, soma and dendrite shaft versus dendrite spine. The recognized relationship between diameter of the dendrite shaft and resistance–impedance characteristics of the system (18) suggests that dendrite ensembles with a preponderance of higher-order (i.e., thinner) segments will have different functional properties from those with a larger proportion of lower-order (i.e., thicker) segments. Thus the LOP, with its greater number of higher-order dendrites and its shorter, lower-order segments, may have functional characteristics which differ from cells in the three other regions we studied.

Degree of "branchiness" may also serve as a powerful modifying variable. Each branch point represents a potential locus of enhancement or suppression of local electrical activity in the dendritic tree. The more extensive the branching pattern, the greater the number of degrees of freedom for the soma–dendrite complex with re-

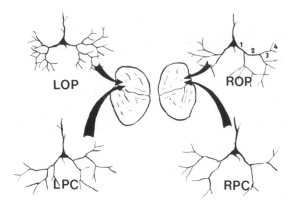

Figure 4. Semischematic drawing emphasizing differences among the dendritic trees in the four areas: left triangularis–opercularis (LOP), right triangularis–opercularis (ROP), left precentral (LPC), and right precentral (RPC).

spect to a given input. Accordingly, we view the contrasting organizational patterns of dendrite systems in left versus right anterior speech areas as functionally significant, despite their similarity in TDL.

Basilar dendrite systems develop from the cell body in stages, becoming progressively longer and more richly branched from the late prenatal era onward (4, 19). If the adult dendritic arbor is conceived of as a "fossilized" record of this dendritic development, we suggest that right–left differences in branching patterns represent differential sequences of growth peculiar to the two hemispheres and to the areas involved. Thus the greater dendritic length of lower-order branches suggests that portions of the right cortex may "lead" the left during the first year of life, when the infant depends extensively on sensory impressions of a highly concrete nature and is limited to relatively large-scale and undifferentiated motor acts (sensory–motor period of Piaget [17]). Somewhat later, with continuous maturation of the cortical systems, symbolic operations such as language and other "left-hemisphere tasks" emerge, and motor actions become more discrete. During this period the higher-order dendritic branches develop, and the LOP becomes anatomically more complex, coincident with its emerging functional dominance.

As a pilot study, this investigation has several limitations. The number of cases studied is small, providing only limited exposure to the range of dendritic structural patterns that may be present. All of the brain samples examined came from male patients — a potentially significant limitation in light of recent data indicating sexual dimorphism in cerebral cortical structure (8, 9). Both of these problems in research design will be addressed in more extensive follow-up work.

Speculations about the relationship of differential dendritic segment lengths to the time of their appearance and the nature of the functional load placed upon them necessitate further investigation. We are presently embarked on a study of the sequential development of dendrite systems in these cortical areas in the brains of a number of infants from time of birth to the sixth year. This may throw further light on selective patterning of dendrite development. The present work indicates the possibilities for identification of structural specificities among neurons of functionally disparate cortical areas and of the subtle nature of some of these structural variations.

REFERENCES

1. Bonin, G. Von, Anatomical asymmetries of the cerebral hemispheres. In: *Interhemispheric Relations and Cerebral Dominance* (V. Mountcastle, Ed.). Johns Hopkins University Press, Baltimore, 1962: 1–6.
2. Broca, P., Du siège de la faculté du langage articulé. *Bull. Mem. Soc. Anthropol.* (Paris), 1865, **6**: 377–393.
3. Colonnier, M., The fine structural arrangement of the cortex. *Arch. Neurol.* (Chicago), 1967, **16**: 651–657.
4. Conel, J., *The Postnatal Development of the Human Cortex* (Vols. 1–6). Harvard University Press, Cambridge, Mass., 1939–1959.
5. Connolly, G. J., *External Morphology of the Primate Brain*. Charles C Thomas, Springfield, Ill., 1950.
6. Cunningham, D. F., *Contributions to the Surface Anatomy of the Cerebral Hemispheres*. Royal Irish Academy, Dublin, 1892.
7. Dax, G., Lesions de la moitié gauche de l'encéphale coincidant avec trouble des signes de la pensée (lu à Montpellier en 1836). *Gaz. Hibd. Med. Chir .*, 2nd series, 1865, **2**: 259.
8. Diamond, M., Dowling, G. A., and Johnson, R. E., Morphological cerebral cortical asymmetry in male and female rats. *Exp. Neurol.*, 1980, **71**: 261–268.
9. Dowling, G. A., Diamond, M. C., Murphy, G. M., and Johnson, R. E., A morphological study of male rat cerebral cortical asymmetry. *Exp. Neurol.*, 1982, **75**: 51–67.
10. Eberstaller, O., *Das Stirnhirn*. Urban & Schwarzenberg, Vienna, 1890.
11. Economo, C. von, *The Cytoarchitectonics of the Human Cerebral Cortex*. Oxford University Press, New York, 1929.
12. Economo, C. von, and Horn, L., Ueber Windingsrelief, Masse und Rindenarchitektonik der Supratemporalflache, ihre individuellen und ihre Seitenunterschiede. *Zentralbl. Gesamte Neurologie Psychiatrie*, 1930, **130**: 687–757.
13. Galaburda, A. M., Sanides, F., and Geschwind, N., Human brain: Cytoarchitectonic left–right asymmetries in the temporal speech region. *Arch. Neurol.*, 1978, **35**: 812.
14. Gazzaniga, M. S., *The Bisected Brain*. Appleton-Century-Crofts, New York, 1970.
15. Geschwind, M., and Levitsky, W., Left–right asymmetries in temporal speech region. *Science*, 1969, **161**: 186–187.
16. Marin-Padilla, M., Number and distribution of the apical dendritic spines of the layer V pyramidal cells in man. *J. Comp. Neurol.*, 1967, **131**: 475–489.
17. Piaget, J., *The Construction of Reality in the Child*. Basic Books, New York, 1954.
18. Rall, W., Distinguishing theoretical synaptic potentials compiled for different soma–dendritic distributions of synaptic input. *J. Neurophysiol.*, 1967, **30**: 1138–1168.
19. Ramón y Cajal, S., *Histologie du Système Nerveux de l'Homme et des Vertébrés*. A. Maloine, Paris, 1911.
20. Shellshear, J. L., The brain of the aboriginal Australian: A study in cerebral morphology. *Philos. Trans. R. Soc. London (Biol.)*, 1937, **227**: 293–409.
21. Sholl, D. A., *The Organization of the Cerebral Cortex*. Methuen, London, 1956.

22. Sperry, R. W., Hemisphere deconnection and unity in conscious awareness. *Am. Psychol.*, 1968, **23**: 723–733.
23. Sperry, R. W., Lateral specialization in the surgically separated hemispheres. In: *The Neurosciences: Third Study Program* (F. O. Schmitt and F. G. Worden, Eds.). MIT Press, Cambridge, Mass., 1974: 5–19.
24. Uchizono, K., Characteristics of excitatory and inhibitory synapses in the central nervous system of the cat. *Nature* (London), 1965, **207**: 642–643.

HORMONAL INFLUENCES ON THE DEVELOPMENT OF NEURAL ASYMMETRIES

MELISSA HINES, PhD, and ROGER A. GORSKI, PhD
Department of Anatomy

In this chapter we will review evidence regarding hormonal influences on neural asymmetries.* The hypothesis that such influences exist is based on evidence that some neural asymmetries are sexually dimorphic, and that sexually dimorphic characteristics in laboratory animals are related to the gonadal hormone environment during early development. We will, therefore, begin our review with a brief summary of androgenic and estrogenic influences on development in nonhuman species. This summary will be followed by a discussion of sex differences in human asymmetries, and of evidence that gonadal hormones may be involved in their development. Finally, the chapter will conclude by describing asymmetries in laboratory animals and discussing the possibility of using such animal models to investigate neural mechanisms that could underlie lateralization of human function.

HORMONAL INFLUENCES ON NEURAL AND BEHAVIORAL DEVELOPMENT IN LABORATORY ANIMALS

The mammalian brain is inherently bipotential in regard to sex. Research in laboratory animals indicates that regardless of genetic factors, the nervous system is capable of developing in either a masculine or feminine direction (see, e.g., 42). The direction taken depends on the gonadal hormone environment during critical or sensitive periods of early life. For example, treatment of genetic female animals

---

*We will use the terms "neural asymmetry" and "lateralization" interchangeably to refer to asymmetry at any level of the nervous system, including, but not limited to, the hemispheres.

Acknowledgments: We thank Drs. Fred C. Davis and Robert J. Handa who collaborated with us on some of the research discussed in this chapter; Drs. Arthur P. Arnold, Glenn D. Rosen, and Sheri A. Berenbaum for helpful discussions of neural asymmetries in birds, rodents, and human beings, respectively; Jim Shryne for help with figure preparation; and Marian Schneider for typing the manuscript. Our work has been supported by a National Institutes of Health (NIH) postdoctoral fellowship (#NS-06594) and a Bank of America, Giannini Foundation Fellowship to Melissa Hines, and by an NIH grant (#HD-01182) to Roger A. Gorski.

with testosterone shortly after birth results in masculinization* of the genitalia, of behavior, and of certain neural regions that differ for male and female animals. The period when such treatment is effective is characterized by elevated testosterone levels in the developing male animal. In the rat, the species in which these influences have been studied most extensively, the sensitive period extends from approximately day 17 of a 21-day gestation to day 10 of postnatal life (28, 42, 58, 105).

Of course, hormone levels differ in male and female rats not only during early development, but also in adulthood. At the time of puberty (approximately 35–45 days of age in the female rat and 55–60 days of age in the male rat), males begin to show higher levels of testosterone than do females, and females begin to show cyclic changes in estrogen and progesterone that are not seen in males. These hormonal changes also influence behavior, but these influences later in development tend to be transient; the behavior is seen while the hormone is present to activate it, but generally wanes when hormone levels fall. In contrast to these activational influences, the behavioral outcomes of the early hormonal environment are almost always permanent and appear to result from hormone-induced changes in the fundamental organization of the brain (42, 107). It is these permanent or organizational influences on which we will focus in this chapter.

Several types of neural changes may underlie the behavioral changes. Sex differences have been documented in the type of synapses (83), the length and position of dendrites (4, 43, 45), the amount and distribution of neurochemicals (98), and even in the number of neurons (41) in various regions of the brain. These neural sex differences occur in areas implicated in the production of sexually dimorphic behavior. In addition, they are influenced by the same hormonal treatments that produce behavioral changes.

For example, a particularly dramatic sex difference has been identified in the preoptic area of the rodent brain (40). This region, which is called the sexually dimorphic nucleus of the preoptic area (SDN-POA), is severalfold larger in male than in female animals. In addition, its size may depend entirely on the early hormonal environment. Genetic female rats who have been treated from day 16 of gestation to day 10 of postnatal life with testosterone have an SDN-POA as large as that of a normal male rat (26). In contrast, treatment of adult rats with gonadal hormones has no influence on the volume of the nucleus (40).

Several additional aspects of hormonal influences will be relevant to our discussion. First, hormonal influences can be subtle. An animal is not simply male or

---

*Previous investigators of gonadal hormone influences on sexual differentiation have used the term "masculinization" to refer specifically to the development of male sexual behavior (e.g., mounting). Similarly, "feminization" has been used to refer to the development of female sexual behavior (e.g., lordosis) and cyclical control of gonadotropin secretion. Because sex differences in many other characteristics (e.g., lateralization) are more quantitative than qualitative, and because they probably result from changes in neural regions separate from those leading to changes in sexual behavior, it is not clear how this terminology can be extended to include them. We will, therefore, use the term "masculinization" to refer to development in a manner typical for male animals, and "feminization" to refer to development in a manner typical for female animals, regardless of the characteristic being discussed.

female, but can show varying amounts of behavior typical of one sex or the other. For instance, some normal female rats and mice will show male-typical behavior occasionally, and the likelihood that an individual animal will do so appears to be related to gradations in hormone levels during prenatal life. Rats and mice are born in mixed-sex litters of several animals, and the amount of masculine behavior shown by female animals is correlated with their intrauterine position (16, 68, 100). Female rats or mice in a position where they receive blood after it has been in contact with male siblings are most likely to show male characteristics. Presumably, the small amount of androgen they have received from their male littermates has masculinized them slightly. Hormonal influences may thus explain behavioral differences between individuals within a sex as well as differences between the sexes.

Second, estradiol has many of the same influences on neural and behavioral development, but not on physical development, that testosterone has. Although these masculinizing influences of estradiol were originally considered paradoxical, they are now thought to parallel the process of masculinization that occurs in the normal male animal. The two major active metabolites of testosterone are dihydro-testosterone (DHT) and estradiol. DHT appears to be responsible for genital masculinization, whereas estradiol appears to be responsible for most aspects of neural masculinization (e.g., 27, 42, 50, 63, 64, 84). For example, administration of DHT to developing female rats masculinizes the genitalia, but not sexual behavior. In contrast, similar administration of estradiol or certain synthetic estrogens masculinizes sexual behavior and the volume of the SDN-POA, but not the genitalia. The hypothesis that testosterone is converted to estradiol before exerting many of its neural and behavioral influences is supported also by evidence that behavioral masculinization can be prevented by exposing developing male rats to substances that block conversion of testosterone to estradiol or that block neural estrogen receptors (15, 29, 63, 64).

Interestingly, synthetic estrogens, such as diethylstilbestrol (DES), are even more potent masculinizers of neural structure and function than is estradiol (e.g., 39, 52). This increased potency probably results from the ability of synthetic estrogens to by-pass mechanisms that normally protect the developing female animal from masculinization by estrogen from her own ovaries or from the maternal circulation (65). The dramatic influence of DES on the SDN-POA is illustrated in Figure 1. Administration of DES to developing female animals during late prenatal and early postnatal life produced an SDN-POA equal in size to that of a normal male animal (27).

Third, the behavioral influences of gonadal hormones are not limited to reproductive activities. Rather, a variety of characteristics that are sexually dimorphic — that is, that differ for male and female animals — are influenced. In the rat these characteristics include social play behavior, activity levels, performance in mazes, active- and passive-avoidance learning, taste preferences, aggression, and, most important for the present discussion, neural and behavioral asymmetries. We will return to these sex differences in asymmetries in the rodent in the last section of the chapter. (Sex differences in other nonreproductive characteristics are reviewed in 7.)

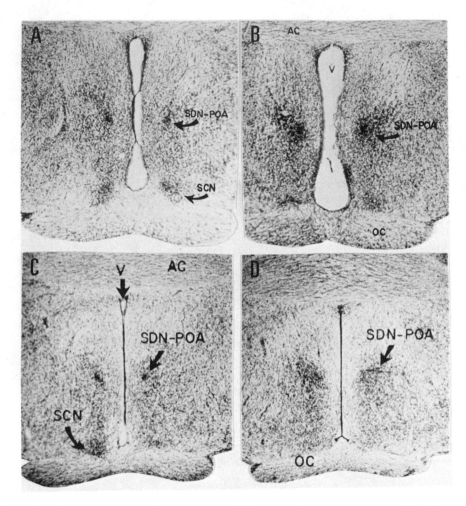

Figure 1. The influence of early exposure to DES on the development of the SDN-POA (arrows). (A) Normal female rat. (B) Normal male rat. (C) Female rat treated with oil perinatally (day 16 of gestation to day 10 of postnatal life). (D) Female rat treated with DES perinatally. Animals were sacrificed at 60 days of age. Illustrations are of 60-μm frozen sections taken in the coronal plane and stained with thionin. The volume of the SDN-POA in the DES-treated female is greater than that in the normal or oil-treated females ($p < .001$) and equivalent to that in the normal male. AC, anterior commissure; OC, optic chiasm; SC, suprachiasmatic nucleus. (From 27. Adapted by permission.)

Sexually Dimorphic Neural Asymmetries in Human Beings

Various approaches have been used to investigate asymmetries in the human brain. Particularly relevant to a discussion of sex differences are data regarding hand preferences (right vs. left) for writing and other tasks; cognitive processing (particularly of verbal stimuli) following unilateral neural injury; and performance on tasks in which stimuli (e.g., words, melodies or shapes) are presented preferentially to one hemisphere or the other. (For further discussion of such tasks, see chapters in this volume by D. W. Zaidel and Noffsinger.) Results of these studies suggest that in right-handed individuals the left hemisphere is dominant for processing verbal material, whereas the right hemisphere is dominant for processing spatial information and nonspeech sounds.

Although both men and women show the same types of asymmetries, there are some sex differences in their magnitude. For instance, men tend to show greater lateralization than do women for several aspects of verbal processing. This enhanced lateralization (i.e., increased language specialization to the left hemisphere) has been suggested, for example, by studies examining impairment in verbal intelligence following unilateral neural injury (66, 89). In these studies men have been found to show dramatic impairment in verbal ability following left-hemisphere damage and little impairment following right-hemisphere damage, whereas women have been found to show an intermediate degree of impairment following either left- or right-hemisphere damage. Studies of normal individuals also suggest increased lateralization for verbal stimuli in men. They show larger or more consistent left-hemisphere advantages than do women for verbal stimuli lateralized via either tachistoscopic visual presentation or dichotic auditory presentation (e.g., 12, 47, 54, 56, 57, 60, 93). There is also some evidence of clearer asymmetry in males than in females on tachistoscopic tasks composed of dots (right-hemisphere stimuli) (55, 57, 67), although such data are less extensive than those for verbal stimuli.

In contrast to the greater lateralization of men than women for verbal and perhaps spatial processing, numerous studies indicate that women and girls show greater asymmetries than men and boys in regard to handedness. Females are more likely than males to be right-handed and to show an extreme preference for use of the right hand (e.g., 1, 2, 6, 13, 49, 90). It has been suggested that the stronger female preference for the right hand may reflect a tendency for women to endorse extreme responses (see, e.g., 11, 66). This explanation cannot account for the increased incidence of right-handed females and left-handed males, however. In addition, as will be described in detail in the next section of this chapter, asymmetries in laboratory animals that may correspond to human handedness are greater in females than in males. Another type of asymmetry that has been reported to be enhanced in women as compared to men involves performance on dichotic-listening tasks composed of melodies or other nonspeech sounds (right-hemisphere stimuli) (9, 81), although data supporting these sex differences are less extensive than those supporting sex differences in hand preferences or verbal processing.

It should be mentioned that not all studies have reported the sex differences described above. As is true of most behavioral and neural sex differences in people, sex differences in asymmetries are small and thus are most likely to be seen in large samples. In addition, sex differences vary to some extent, depending on specific aspects of the technique used to assess them. In the case of verbal stimuli presented tachistoscopically, for example, sex differences may be stronger for unfamiliar than familiar material and when subjects respond manually rather than verbally (10, 48). Similarly, sex differences on verbal dichotic-listening tasks are seen more reliably with single consonant–vowel–consonant or consonant–vowel stimuli than with more complicated stimuli (47, 66). There is also some evidence that sex differences on certain tasks are influenced by the instructions given subjects or by attentional strategies (12).

Thus, sex differences in neural asymmetries appear to be very complex. One sex is not simply more lateralized than the other. Rather, males seem to be more lateralized than females in some respects; females seem to be more lateralized than males in other respects; and the sexes seem to be equally lateralized in still other respects. Although this complexity may seem disheartening, it is probably an accurate reflection of neural organization. Each type of task in which asymmetries have been documented can be expected to involve a somewhat different neural circuitry that may be differentially sensitive to factors determining sex differences. In addition, even small variations in specific methods of assessment, such as whether a response is manual or vocal, may involve other neural systems in a way that enhances or obscures sex differences.

Regardless of the complexity of sex differences in human neural asymmetries, the close relationship between gonadal hormones and neural sex differences in other species suggests the possibility of a relationship to the early hormonal environment (51). Data from at least one study support this suggestion (50, 53). In this study, women who had been exposed to DES for at least 5 months of prenatal life, including the presumed critical period for hormonal influences on human development, were found to differ from their unexposed sisters in performance on a verbal dichotic task composed of consonant–vowel stimuli. As would be expected, given the masculinizing influences of DES on neural and behavioral development in other species (see the first section of this chapter for a discussion of some of these influences), their pattern of performance was shifted in the masculine direction (see Figure 2). Like men in a pilot study using the same dichotic task, as well as in other studies using similar tasks, they showed an enhanced right-ear advantage and a strong negative correlation between right- and left-ear scores. These differences did not seem to be due to other factors, such as age, birth order, pregnancy complications, socioeconomic status, or educational background. Nor were they secondary to changes in personality, intelligence, or physical development, all of which were similar in the DES-exposed women and their unexposed sisters (53). Rather, the most likely explanation for the differences between the two groups in performance on the dichotic task seemed to be the early hormonal environment.

Although the study of DES-exposed women is, to our knowledge, the first study intended to test directly the influence of the early hormonal environment on the development of human neural asymmetries, data from other studies could also be interpreted to support such influences. For example, several studies of women with Turner syndrome have found reduced or reversed ear asymmetries on verbal dichotic tasks composed of syllables as well as those composed of digits (38, 72, 73, 101). One consequence of Turner syndrome is a failure of the ovary to develop fully, with a

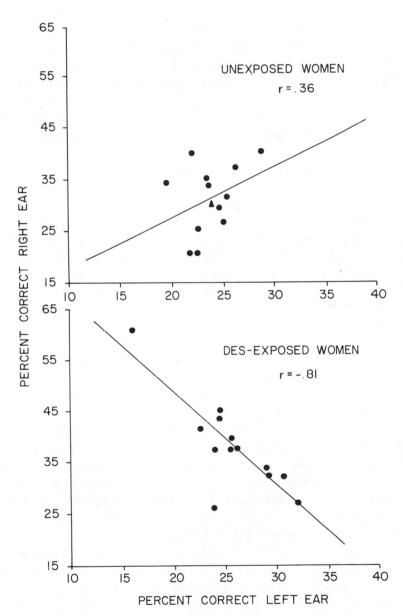

Figure 2. A relationship between exposure to DES during prenatal development and dichotic listening performance in adulthood. DES-exposed women show higher right-ear scores than their unexposed sisters ($p < .05$), and a negative correlation between right- and left-ear scores ($p < .001$). This pattern of performance resembles that of normal men. ▲ indicates left-handed subject. (From 53. Reprinted by permission.)

resultant deficit in estrogen and progesterone both pre- and postnatally (92, 99). Thus, the diminished asymmetry could be due to low levels of gonadal hormones during early development. It must be cautioned, however, that individuals with Turner syndrome have only one intact X chromosome. The second is absent or imperfect. The unusual lateralization patterns could, therefore, result directly from this genetic defect or from other problems associated with it, rather than from hormonal influences.

A study reporting a relationship between rate of maturation and neural asymmetry might also be interpreted to suggest hormonal influences. This study reported that performance on a verbal dichotic task varied with maturation rate, as reflected in the development of secondary sexual characteristics (102). Individuals with late maturation (i.e., reduced secondary sexual characteristics for their age) showed an enhanced right-ear advantage in comparison to those with early maturation (i.e., enhanced secondary sexual characteristics for their age). This relationship is often interpreted to suggest a causal relationship between the rate of neural maturation and the degree of lateralization. Because gonadal hormones determine the development of secondary sexual characteristics, however, the cause of the enhanced lateralization could be hormones rather than maturation rate.

A third relationship that has been interpreted to suggest gonadal hormone influences on the development of neural asymmetries involves left-handedness, immune disease, migraine, and developmental learning disorders. Geschwind and Behan (33) reported that individuals who were strongly left-handed were more likely to exhibit learning disorders (i.e., dyslexia and stuttering) and certain immune diseases (e.g., thyroid and bowel disorders) than those who were strongly right-handed. They also found that individuals who suffered from migraine or myasthenia gravis were more likely than controls to show some preference for use of the left hand. The authors suggest that the cause of the associations observed might be elevated testosterone levels during development. They speculate that high levels of testosterone produce left-handedness and learning disorders by delaying the growth of the left hemisphere *in utero*, and influence the maturation of the immune system by suppressing the thymus. Of interest to the present discussion is the suggestion that prenatal elevations in testosterone may be related to the development of left-handedness. This possibility is consistent with the increased incidence of left-handedness among men and boys (see discussion above), but not with the evidence available from studies of individuals exposed to high levels of testosterone or other gonadal hormones *in utero*. These individuals have been reported to show a normal incidence of left-handedness (50, 53, 85). Larger samples may be needed to detect a hormonal influence on handedness, however, since the associations reported by Geschwind and Behan were small. Alternatively, the relationship among left-handedness, learning disorders, and immune diseases could be caused by other factors (e.g., the genome or developmental trauma).

Another area of research that could help elucidate the relationship between gonadal hormones and the development of human neural asymmetries involves investigations of sex differences in the structure of the human brain. Several neural asymmetries that may underlie functional lateralization have been described (see, e.g., 30), and at least one of these has been reported to vary with sex. The planum temporale, an area related to language function, is larger on the left than on the right in most people (34, 103, 106). Some individuals have a larger right than left planum temporale, however, and this reversed asymmetry has been found to occur more often in women than in men (103). Surprisingly, a similar sex difference is not seen in fetuses or neonates, where development of the left planum temporale is, if anything, greater in the female than in the male (103, 106). This discrepancy between young brains and adult brains may be caused, however, by the great degree of postnatal development in the planum temporale, particularly the left side (103), coupled with more rapid early development in the female than in the male.

Sex differences have also been reported in the corpus callosum (19) and in the massa intermedia, a midline structure joining the two halves of the thalamus (69, 82). The cross-sectional surface area of the corpus callosum has been found to be larger relative to brain weight in the female brain than in the male brain, and the shape of the splenium has been reported to be rounder and more bulbous in women than in men. The massa intermedia is not always present in the human brain, and is more likely to be absent in men than in women. Both of these sex differences have been reported in infants or fetuses (5, 82) as well as in adults, suggesting that they result from genetic or hormonal influences. In addition, although the specific functional significance of these neural sex differences is not yet known, their location suggests a relationship to sexually dimorphic aspects of neural asymmetries.

It must be noted that very recent data suggest that sex differences in the corpus callosum may not be present in all samples. S. F. Witelson (personal communication) has been comparing the size of the corpus callosum in the brains of left- and right-handed individuals, and, because her sample includes male and female brains, has been investigating possible sex differences as well. Although marked differences have been noted in the size of the corpus callosum in the brains of the left- versus right-handed individuals, no evidence of sex differences has been found. As of this writing, these data are not ready for publication. We cannot, therefore, offer confident explanations for the discrepancy with previous reports. Perhaps a reasonable conclusion at this point is that the data on sex differences in the corpus callosum suggest interesting possibilities regarding the mechanisms underlying asymmetries, but that additional research is needed to determine the conditions under which sex differences can be seen and/or the groups in which they are present.

SEXUALLY DIMORPHIC NEURAL ASYMMETRIES IN LABORATORY ANIMALS

Until recently it was thought that neural asymmetries were uniquely human. We now know differently. Asymmetries have been demonstrated in nonhuman primates, in birds, and in rodents. The general topic of lateralization in animals has been reviewed elsewhere (e.g., 20, 35, 46). In this section, we will focus on animal models in which asymmetries have been found to relate to the sex of the animal or to the early hormonal environment.

In several avian species, including canaries and zebra finches, males but not females sing, and the neural regions controlling song are larger in male than in female birds (77). Like sexually dimorphic characteristics in mammals, the size of the nuclei and the production of song are both related to the early hormonal environment, at least in the zebra finch. Treatment of female chicks with estradiol enlarges the size of the sexually dimorphic neural regions, and allows the bird to respond to androgen, when an adult, with a song similar to that of a male (44).

In addition to being sexually dimorphic and sensitive to the early hormonal environment, the bird song system is lateralized. In the canary at least, lesions of song-system nuclei or their efferents on the left side of the brain produce dramatic impairments in song production, whereas the same manipulations on the right produce only minor deficits (see 75).

To discuss the possible mechanisms underlying this asymmetry, it is necessary to describe the bird song system in some detail. The sexually dimorphic neural regions involved in song include: (1) area X of the lobus parofactorius; (2) the hyperstriatum ventrale, pars caudale (HVc); (3) the robust nucleus of the archistriatum (RA); and (4) the hypoglossal nucleus of the medulla (nXII). These nuclei, as well as the vocal organ, the syrinx, are pairs of independent structures. There are unilateral efferent projections from the higher areas to nXII on each side, which in turn innervate the syrinx (75). Although there appears to be some interaction between the two sides (76, 78, 79), ipsilateral projections predominate. The bird, in a sense, thus appears to have two song systems, one on the left and one on the right.

The areas in which left-sided lesions have been found to impair song production are HVc, RA, and nXII (75). An asymmetry in the volume of nXII and in the syringeal musculature have been found in the canary (59, 77). Consistent with the lesion data, these regions are larger on the left than the right. However, asymmetries have not been found in the volume of HVc or RA (77), the dendritic organization of RA (24), or the electrical activity of HVc (62). Because efferent pathways from these regions to the syrinx are largely unilateral, it is thus possible that the asymmetries at the level of nXII or the syrinx itself account for the asymmetrical results of lesions at all levels (61). Alternatively, given the large number of neural characteristics that could underlie functional lateralization, it is possible that the neural substrate for asymmetries at higher levels remains to be identified. (These and other possibilities are discussed further in 3.)

Finally, although the bird song system presents a promising model for investigating the neural basis for lateralization, as well as the role of gonadal hormones in the development of asymmetries, it should be noted that sex-related asymmetries in this system differ to some extent from human asymmetries. For example, in regard to both handedness and verbal processing, men and women differ in the *extent* of lateralization, not in the presence of the lateralized function. In contrast, in songbirds the lateralized function, song, is present only in male birds.

The types of neural and behavioral asymmetries that have been documented to be sexually dimorphic in rats and other rodents are summarized in Table 1. This table also indicates the influence of the early hormonal environment on these asymmetries when such information is available.

Several studies suggest asymmetries in postural or movement biases in rodents that may resemble human handedness. For example, although rodents do not show a dramatic right-paw preference at the population level comparable to the human right-hand preference, individual animals do show asymmetries. In C56BL/6J mice, for instance, individual animals show strong paw preferences that can be reproduced reliably across different situations (17). Interestingly, like human hand preferences, these paw preferences are stronger in female mice than male mice (17).

Another type of asymmetry involves circling or rotating behavior. Laboratory rodents circle spontaneously, particularly at night. Circling can also be elicited by amphetamine administration. In all three situations (spontaneous, nocturnal, and amphetamine-induced rotation), individual animals show a bias to circle in a particular direction. Again, like the paw preference in mice, this bias is stronger in female than male animals (36, 37, 86). Additionally, neurochemical asymmetries in the nigrostriatial system that appear to underlie these rotational asymmetries are greater in female than in male animals (37).

This type of asymmetry, as well as its relationship to sex, appears to be present from birth. Female neonates show asymmetries in 2-deoxy-D-glucose (dGlc) uptake in the hippocampus, diencephalon, cortex, and medulla–pons, whereas no asymmetries are seen in males (88). Also, when neonatal rats are aligned symmetrically and then allowed to assume a preferred posture, they show a preference for deflecting the tail in a particular direction. This preference is stronger in females than in males (23, 87, 88), and the tail posture preferred as a neonate correlates significantly for individual animals with the direction of the adult rotational bias (88).

Our own research in this area has involved a somewhat different asymmetry, turning preferences in an open field or T-maze. In the open-field situation, an adult animal is placed in a standard position in the center of the field (a large box with an overhead light), and the direction in which the animal turns when it encounters the wall is noted. Our results using this paradigm are consistent with those from other studies of rotational and postural asymmetries. Female animals, but not male animals, show a significant tendency to turn right. Female rats turned right 62% of the time, whereas male rats did so only 48% of the time (unpublished observations of M. Hines and R. A. Gorski).

In the T-maze situation, adult animals are placed in the long arm of a T-maze, and the direction chosen when they reach the cross arm is noted. We tested hormonally manipulated as well as control animals in this situation (unpublished observations of M. Hines, F. C. Davis, and R. A. Gorski). Manipulations occurred on day 2 of life (day 1 is the day of birth) and involved injection of testosterone propionate (TP) into female neonates and castration of male neonates. Controls included untreated male and female animals as well as females injected with oil and males given sham castrations. Each of the animals was tested in the T-maze on four separate days when between 60 and 90 days old.

TABLE 1
HORMONE- OR SEX-RELATED NEURAL ASYMMETRIES IN RODENTS

Asymmetry	Sex Difference	Hormonal Influence	Species	Reference
Behavior				
Neonatal bias in tail position.	Female shows a bias toward the right; male does not.	Negative correlation between percentage of females in each litter with right bias and the number of males in the litter.	Sprague–Dawley rat.	Ross et al. (88)
Neonatal bias in tail position.	Female shows a larger bias toward the left than the male does, and more males than females show no bias.	No correlation between female's bias and the number of males in the litter.	Purdue–Wistar rat.	Denenberg et al. (23)
Neonatal bias in tail position.	Female shows a larger bias toward the left than the male does, and more males than females show no bias.	Prenatal treatment with TP, but not DHT, eliminates left bias in females.	Purdue–Wistar rat.	Rosen et al. (87)
Rotational bias.	Female shows greater asymmetry than the male does.	Not investigated.	Sprague–Dawley rat.	Glick et al. (36)
Rotational bias induced by amphetamine.	Female shows greater asymmetry than the male does.	Not investigated.	Sprague–Dawley rat.	Robinson et al. (86)
Spontaneous rotational bias.	Female shows greater rotational bias than male does.	Not investigated.	Gerbil.	Glick et al. (37)
Paw preference.	Female shows greater preference than male does.	Not investigated.	C57BL/6J mouse.	Collins (17)
Turning bias in open field.	Female shows a bias toward the right; males does not.	Not investigated.	Sprague–Dawley rat.	Hines and Gorski (unpublished)
Turning bias in T-maze.	Female shows stronger bias than males does.	Neonatal testosterone treatment abolishes female preference, but so does oil.	Sprague–Dawley rat.	Hines et al. (unpublished)
Neuroanatomy and Neurochemistry				
Neonatal dGlc incorporation in medulla–pons, hippocampus, cortex, and diencephalon.	Female shows asymmetries; male does not.	Not investigated.	Sprague–Dawley rat.	Ross et al. (88)
Striatal dopamine.	Female shows greater asymmetry than the male does.	Not investigated.	C57BL/6J mouse.	Glick et al. (36)

TABLE 1
(CONTINUED)

Asymmetry	Sex Difference	Hormonal Influence	Species	Reference
Thickness of certain cortical regions.	Male shows increase on right side; female does not.	Neonatal gonadectomy produces or increases bias in both males and females.	Long–Evans rat.	Diamond et al. (25)
Effect of hypothalamic deafferentation on compensation for removal of gonad on same side.	Compensation blocked by deafferentation on the right in males and on the left in females.	Not investigated.	Sprague–Dawley rat.	Nance et al. (70,71)

As in other studies, untreated females, but not untreated males, showed a significant directional bias. This bias was not seen in females treated with TP neonatally, suggesting that sex differences in rodent postural asymmetries may be related to the early hormonal environment. Oil-treated females also failed to show a bias, however. A great deal of evidence indicates that many types of stressful stimuli, if present during the perinatal period, can influence the development of sexually dimorphic characteristics, apparently by altering testosterone production and metabolism (e.g., see 104). Perhaps the stress of the neonatal injection procedure itself produced hormonal changes that altered the normal female bias. Others have reported that female rats bred in the laboratory but not those obtained from breeders show sex differences in rotational biases (36), and that female rats left unhandled in infancy, but not those experiencing daily handling, show directional biases (91). Assuming that animals bred in the laboratory and those left unhandled during infancy are relatively unstressed, these reports would be consistent with our results and the hypothesis that early stress can alter directional biases.

Neonatal castration did not produce a bias in genetic male animals in our study. Although this result was not consistent with our expectation, it is not surprising in light of other data. Rosen et al. (87) reported that prenatal exposure to TP abolished neonatal asymmetries in tail posture in genetic female rats. Thus, the testosterone present prenatally in our neonatally castrated males may have been sufficient to abolish a directional bias. The study of Rosen et al. (87) also suggested that the metabolite of testosterone responsible for masculinizing or defeminizing postural biases may be estradiol. Although prenatal exposure to TP abolished the bias in female rats, prenatal exposure to the propionate of DHT, the nonestrogenic metabolite of testosterone, did not.

The asymmetries described above may provide models for human handedness. They differ from human handedness, however, in the degree of the asymmetry as well as its direction. The human population is overwhelmingly right-handed. In contrast, postural and movement asymmetries in rodents are detectable only in large samples, and do not always favor the right side. Regardless of the direction of the asymmetry, however, when sex differences have been found they consistently have favored female animals. It has been suggested that the variability in the direction of biases is related to the strain of animal studied, Purdue–Wistar rats, for example, showing left biases, and Sprague–Dawley rats right biases (91). Our own research using Sprague–Dawley rats found evidence of a particularly pronounced right bias in female animals (unpublished observations of M. Hines and R. A. Gorski), as well as evidence of a particularly pronounced bias in females that could favor either the right or the left (unpublished observations of M. Hines, F. C. Davis, and R. A. Gorski). These data favor an interpretation previously proposed, at least in part, by Collins (17). The direction of asymmetry may be determined by the environment, whereas its strength is determined by genetic factors, or, we would like to add, other early influences, such as the hormonal environment.

What of other asymmetries, particularly those that might provide models for understanding lateralization of complex human capacities such as language, spatial abilities, or emotional responses? There are data suggesting lateralization of functions such as communication, spatial sense, and affect in rodents, as well as in non-human primates (see 20 for a review). Japanese macaques show a right-ear (left-hemisphere) advantage for identifying species-specific vocalizations (8, 80), and in rats the effects of hemispherectomy on open-field activity and taste aversion differ, depending on the hemisphere lesioned (21, 22). Although at least some of these relationships are affected by early experience (21), the role of gonadal hormones in their development is not known.

Another area in which sexually dimorphic asymmetries have been investigated in rodents is neuroanatomy. Diamond *et al.* (25) looked at the thickness of the left and right cortex in male and female rats and found enhanced thickness on the right in areas 17, 18a, and 39 of normal male animals. No significant differences were seen between right and left cortex in normal female animals. However, ovariectomy of female rats shortly after birth produced a pattern of cortical thickness similar to that seen in the normal male rats. Gonadectomy of neonatal male animals did not alter areas 17 or 30, but did increase the right-hemisphere advantage in the area 18a, and produce significant right-hemisphere advantages in areas 10 and 2.

These results suggest a role for gonadal hormones in the development of cortical asymmetries. The nature of the hormonal influence (promotion of masculine-typical development following early removal of gonadal steroids), however, is not typical of hormonal influences on other behavioral and neural characteristics. As described in the first section of this chapter, masculine-typical development is usually enhanced in the presence of high levels of testosterone or estradiol, and is impaired by removal of the testis. In addition, the ovary secretes only a small amount of hormone during the perinatal period. Although these secretions have been reported to influence the development of some aspects of feminine-typical behavior in the rat (31, 94), removal of the ovary does not influence the development of the majority of sex-typical characteristics.

It should be noted also that the general subject of cortical asymmetry in the rodent, regardless of its relationship to sex or gonadal hormones, appears to be very complex. For instance, J. Stewart (personal communication) and B. Kolb have recently completed a study in which they investigated cortical asymmetries in intact and neonatally gonadectomized male and female animals at 90 days of age. They studied 3 strains of animals and found no evidence of cortical asymmetry in either sex in any of the 3 strains. They did find, however, that neonatal gonadectomy of male rats increased cortical thickness on both sides of the brain in all 3 strains studied. In a second study they also found a right-over-left hemispheric asymmetry in 200-day-old male Long-Evans rats. In discussing their data, and that of others investigating cortical asymmetries in the rodent, they suggest that right–left asymmetries vary not only with sex but also with age, rearing condition, and the part of the cortex measured. The relationship of these factors, and their interactions, to cortical asymmetry is not clear yet. Until we understand the nature of these relationships, it may be difficult to understand hormonal influences on the development of cortical asymmetries.

We also have investigated the possibility of sex-related asymmetries in neural structure by comparing the volume of the right and left SDN-POA (unpublished observations of M. Hines, F. C. Davis, R. J. Handa, and R. A. Gorski). Despite seeing the usual dramatic sex difference in this nucleus, we saw no asymmetry. The values $(M \pm SD)$ for the volume of the right and left SDN-POA in the adult male were 20.8 ± 2.7 and 20.9 ± 5.1 mm$^3 \times 10^{-3}$, respectively. In the adult female, the same values were 9.3 ± 2.4 and 9.1 ± 1.9 mm$^3 \times 10^{-3}$. Of course, it is possible that more subtle asymmetries exist in this sexually differentiated structure. For example, there could be asymmetries in input from, or output to, other regions or in cellular ultrastructure.

Finally, there may be asymmetries in the function of sexually differentiated regions of the rodent brain. Nordeen and Yahr (74) reported asymmetries in the functional consequences of implanting estradiol in the preoptic area (a region including but not limited to the SDN-POA) and in the ventromedial nucleus of the hypothalamus of newborn female rats (24–48 hours old). Implants on the left were more likely than those on the right to impair normal feminine development of gonadotropin regulation and lordosis behavior, whereas implants on the right were more likely than those on the left to enhance the masculine behavior, mounting.

The period when gonadal steroids impair feminine-typical functions, such as gonadotropin regulation and lordosis, occurs a few days later than that when they enhance masculine-typical function, such as mounting (see, e.g., 14, 42). There is also some evidence that the left side of the mammalian brain develops earlier than the right (18). Nordeen and Yahr, therefore, suggest that the right and left sides of the hypothalamus, because they are developing at somewhat different rates, are undergoing sexual differentiation of different functions between 24 and 48 hours of age (the time when the animals received implants). Should this be the case, it would provide a potentially powerful mechanism for the development of asymmetries in sexually dimorphic functions. Because testosterone levels vary from day to day during the critical period (e.g., 28, 105) comparable regions of the two sides of the brain could develop in appreciably different hormonal environments.

There is also evidence of a functional asymmetry in the hypothalamus of the adult rat as reflected in control of gonadotropin release, and the direction of this asymmetry differs for the two sexes. In male animals, deafferentation of the hypothalamus on the right side of the brain, but not on the left, blocks facilitation of follicle-stimulating hormone (FSH) release that normally follows removal of the testis on the same side (71). In females, in contrast, deafferentation of the hypothalamus on the left side of the brain, but not on the right, blocks ovarian compensatory hypertrophy that normally follows removal of the ovary on the same side (70). Perhaps related to this functional asymmetry, there is an asymmetry in FSH releasing hormone in the hypothalamus of the female rat; levels on the right are higher than those on the left (32).

Summary and Conclusions

It seems likely that gonadal hormones influence the development of neural asymmetries in laboratory animals as well as in human beings. In people, the early hormonal environment is related to the degree of asymmetry shown in performance on verbal dichotic tasks. In rodents, a similar relationship exists between the early hormonal environment and the development of postural asymmetries. In both cases, the metabolite of testosterone responsible for the relationship appears to be estradiol.

The extent to which specific aspects of neural asymmetries in laboratory animals resemble those in people is not yet known. Questions regarding the relationship between the early hormonal environment and the development of asymmetries in communicative or affective systems in laboratory species, or hand preferences in the human being, remain to be answered. Nevertheless, even the limited information currently available provides insight into several issues related to the development of neural asymmetries.

First, previous research has failed to find consistent relationships among normal individuals between the degree of neural asymmetry and genetic factors (other than those inferred from associations with sex and handedness) or environmental factors such as educational background. The relationship between prenatal exposure to DES and enhanced asymmetry for processing verbal dichotic stimuli (50, 53) suggests a possible mechanism for the development of such individual differences in neural asymmetries. Although the performance of the DES-exposed women was shifted in the masculine direction in comparison to their unexposed sisters, it was still within the normal range of performance for women in general. Thus, it may be that normal variations in gonadal hormone levels, derived, for example, from the maternal system or the fetus's own gonads, contribute to variation among individuals in degree of neural asymmetry.

Second, the relationship between estrogenic hormones and lateralization may provide clues as to specific mechanisms underlying the development of neural asymmetries. For instance, in the SDN-POA, estrogen apparently acts early in development to increase the number of neurons present (27, 41), so estrogen could act to enhance lateralization by increasing the number of neurons in regions providing the substrate for lateralized functions. Of course, action through this mechanism would seem to require some other type of asymmetry. One possibility is the more rapid development of the left side than the right side of the brain (18), which was mentioned above in discussing the work of Nordeen and Yahr. Other possibilities include asymmetric hormone distribution or an inherent asymmetry in the function of comparable regions on the two sides of the brain. A second known influence of estrogen on neural development in rodents is enhancement of neurite (axonal and dendritic) growth (95, 96, 97). Via this mechanism, estrogen could affect neural asymmetries by enhancing excitatory or inhibitory pathways between the two hemispheres.

Finally, the relationship between the early gonadal hormone environment and the development of neural asymmetries provides a tool for manipulating this development. This tool, used in conjunction with viable animal models for lateralization and further studies of hormone-exposed human populations, could lead to substantial advances in our understanding of the neural basis of functional asymmetries and the factors involved in their development.

REFERENCES

1. Annett, M., The distribution of manual asymmetry. *Br. J. Psychol.*, 1972, 63: 343–358.
2. Annett, M., Handedness in families. *Ann. Hum. Genet.*, 1973, 37: 93–105.
3. Arnold, A. P., and Bottjer, S. W., Cerebral lateralization in birds. In: *Cerebral Lateralization in Non-human Species* (S. D. Glick, Ed.). Academic Press, New York, in press.
4. Ayoub, D. M., Greenough, W. T., and Juraska, J. M., Sex differences in dendritic structure in the preoptic area of the juvenile macaque monkey brain. *Science*, 1983, 219: 197–198.
5. Baack, J., and de LaCoste-Utamsing, C., Sexual dimorphism in fetal corpus callosum. *Soc. Neurosci. Abstr.*, 1982, 8: 213.
6. Bakan, P., Handedness and birth order. *Nature*, 1971, 229: 195.
7. Beatty, W. W., Gonadal hormones and sex differences in nonreproductive behaviors in rodents: Organizational and activational influences. *Horm. Behav.*, 1979, 12: 112–163.
8. Beecher, M. D., Petersen, M. R., Zoloth, S. R., Moody, D. B., and Stebbins, W. C., Perception of conspecific vocalizations by Japanese macaques. *Brain Behav. Evol.*, 1979, 16: 443–460.
9. Berenbaum, S. A., Harshman, R. A. and Hampson, E., Individual differences in cognitive abilities and brain organization, Part II: Sex and handedness differences in dichotic lateralization. Manuscript in preparation.
10. Bradshaw, J. L., and Gates, E. A., Visual field differences in verbal tasks: Effects of task familiarity and sex of subject. *Brain Lang.*, 1978, 5: 166–187.
11. Bradshaw, J. L., and Nettleton, N. C., *Human Cerebral Asymmetry*. Prentice-Hall, Englewood Cliffs, N.J., 1983.
12. Bryden, M., Evidence for sex differences in cerebral organization. In: *Determinants of Sex-Related Differences in Cognitive Functioning* (M. Wittig and A. Peterson, Eds.). Academic Press, New York, 1979: 121–143.

13. Bryden, M., Measuring handedness with questionnaires. *Neuropsychologia*, 1977, **15**: 617–624.
14. Christensen, L. W., and Gorski, R. A., Independent masculinization of neuroendocrine systems by intracerebral implants of testosterone or estradiol in the neonatal female rat. *Brain Res.*, 1973, **146**: 325–340.
15. Clemens, L. G., and Gladue, B. A., Feminine sexual behavior in rats enhanced by prenatal inhibition of androgen aromatization. *Horm. Behav.*, 1978, **11**: 190–201.
16. Clemens, L. G., Gladue, B. A., and Coniglio, L. P., Prenatal endogenous androgenic influences on masculine sexual behavior and genital morphology in male and female rats. *Horm. and Behav.*, 1978, **10**: 40–53.
17. Collins, R. L., Toward an admissible genetic model for the inheritance of the degree and direction of asymmetry. In: *Lateralization in the Nervous System* (S. Harnad, R. W. Doty, L. Goldstein, J. Jaynes, and G. Krauthamer, Eds.). Academic Press, New York, 1977: 137–150.
18. Corballis, M. C., and Morgan, M. J., On the biological basis of human laterality. I. Evidence for a naturational left–right gradient. *Behav. Brain Sci.*, 1978, **1**: 261–296.
19. de LaCoste-Utamsing, C., and Holloway, R. L., Sexual dimorphism in human corpus callosum. *Science*, 1982, **216**: 1431–1432.
20. Denenberg, V. H., Hemispheric laterality in animals and the effects of early experience. *Behav. Brain Sci.*, 1981, **4**: 1–49.
21. Denenberg, V. H., Garbanati, J., Sherman, G., Yutzey, D. A., and Kaplan, R., Infantile stimulation induces brain lateralization in rats. *Science*, 1978, **201**: 1150–1152.
22. Denenberg, V. H., Hoffman, M., Garbanati, J. A., Sherman, G. F., Rosen, G. D., and Yutzey, D. A., Handling in infancy, taste aversion, and brain laterality in rats. *Brain Res.*, 1980, **200**: 123–133.
23. Denenberg, V. H., Rosen, G. D., Hoffman, M., Gall, J., Stockler, J., and Yutzey, D. A., Neonatal postural asymmetry and sex differences in the rat. *Dev. Brain Res.*, 1982, **2**: 417–419.
24. deVoogd, T., and Nottebohm, F., Sex differences in dendritic morphology of a song control nucleus in the canary: A quantitative Golgi study. *J. Comp. Neurol.*, 1981, **196**: 309–316.
25. Diamond, M. C., Dowling, G. A., and Johnson, R. E., Morphologic cerebral cortical asymmetry in male and female rats. *Exp. Neurol.*, 1981, **71**: 261–268.
26. Döhler, K. D., Coquelin, A., Davis, F. C., Hines, M., Shryne, J. E., and Gorski, R. A., Differentiation of the sexually dimorphic nucleus in the preoptic area of the rat brain is determined by the perinatal hormone environment. *Neurosci. Lett.*, 1982, **33**: 295–298.
27. Döhler, K. D., Hines, M., Coquelin, A., Davis, F. C., Shryne, J. E., and Gorski, R. A., Pre- and postnatal influence of diethylstilbestrol on differentiation of the sexually dimorphic nucleus in the preoptic area of the female rat brain. *Neuroendocrinol. Lett.*, 1982, **4**: 361–365.
28. Döhler, K. D., and Wuttge, W., Changes with age in levels of serum gonadotropins, prolactin, and gonadal steroids in prepubertal male and female rats. *Endocrinology*, 1975, **97**: 898–907.
29. Doughty, C., Booth, J. E., McDonald, P. G., and Parrott, R. F., Inhibition by the anti-oestrogen MER-25, of defeminization induced by the synthetic oestrogen RU 2858. *J. Endocrinol.*, 1975, **67**: 459–460.
30. Galaburda, A. M., Le May, M., Kemper, T. L., and Geschwind, N., Right–left asymmetries in the brain. *Science*, 1978, **199**: 852–856.
31. Gerall, A. A., Dunlap, J. L., and Hendricks, S. E., Effect of ovarian secretions on female behavioral potentiality in the rat. *J. Comp. Physiol. Psychol.*, 1972, **82**: 449–465.
32. Gerendai, I., Rotsytein, B., Marchetti, B., and Scapagnini, U., LH-RH content changes in the mediobasal hypothalamus after unilateral ovariectomy. In: *Neuroendocri-*

nology: Biological and Clinical Aspects, Proceedings of Serano Symposium, Vol. 19 (A. Polleri and R. MacLeod, Eds.). Academic Press, New York, 1979: 97–102.

33. Geschwind, N., and Behan, P., Left-handedness: Association with immune disease, migraine, and developmental learning disorder. *Proc. Nat. Acad. Sci. U.S.A.*, 1982, **79**: 5097–5100.

34. Geschwind, N., and Levitsky, W., Left/right asymmetries in temporal speech region. *Science*, 1968, **161**: 186–187.

35. Glick, S. D. Ed., *Cerebral Lateralization in Non-human Species*. Academic Press, New York, in press.

36. Glick, S. D., Schonfeld, A. R., and Strumpf, A. J., Sex differences in brain asymmetry of the rodent. *Behav. Brain Sci.*, 1980, **3**: 236.

37. Glick, S. D., Zimmerberg, B., and Jerussi, T. P., Adaptive significance of laterality in the rodent. *Ann. N.Y. Acad. Sci.*, 1977, **299**: 180–185.

38. Gordon, H. W., and Galatzer, A., Cerebral organization in patients with gonadal dysgenesis. *Psychoneuroendocrinology*, 1980, **5**: 235–244.

39. Gorski, R. A., Localization and sexual differentiation of the nervous structures which regulate ovulation. *J. Reprod. Fertil.*, 1966, Suppl. 1: 67–68.

40. Gorski, R. A., Gordon, J. H., Shryne, J. E., and Southam, A. M., Evidence for a morphological sex difference within the medial preoptic area of the rat brain. *Brain Res.*, 1978, **143**: 333–346.

41. Gorski, R. A., Harlan, R. E., Jacobson, C. D., Shryne, J. E., and Southam, A. M., Evidence for the existence of a sexually dimorphic nucleus in the preoptic area of the rat. *J. Comp. Neurol.*, 1980, **193**: 529–539.

42. Goy, R. W., and McEwen, B. S., *Sexual Differentiation of the Brain*. MIT Press, Cambridge, Mass., 1980.

43. Greenough, W. T., Carter, C. S., Steerman, C., and deVoogd, T. J., Sex differences in dendritic patterns in hamster preoptic area. *Brain Res.*, 1977, **126**: 63–72.

44. Gurney, M. E., and Konishi, M., Hormone-induced sexual differentiation of brain and behavior in zebra finches. *Science*, 1980, **208**: 1380–1383.

45. Hammer, R. P., Jr., and Jacobson, C. D., Sex difference in dendrites during development of the sexually dimorphic nucleus in the preoptic area. *Soc. Neurosci. Abstr.*, 1982, **8**: 197.

46. Harnad, S., Doty, R. W., Goldstein, L., Jaynes, J., and Krauthamer, G. (Eds.), *Lateralization in the Nervous System*. Academic Press, New York, 1977.

47. Harshman, R., and Remington, R., Sex, language and the brain. Part I. A review of the literature on adult sex differences in lateralization. Paper presented at UCLA Conference on Human Brain Functions, Los Angeles, 1974.

48. Healey, J. M., Waldstein, S., and Goodglass, H., Lateralization of receptive and expressive language functions in normal males and females: Methodological considerations. Paper presented at the meeting of the American Psychological Association, Anaheim, California, 1983.

49. Hicks, R., and Kinsbourne, M., Human handedness: A partial cross-fostering study. *Science*, 1976, **192**: 908–910.

50. Hines, M., Prenatal diethylstilbestrol (DES) exposure, human sexually dimorphic behavior and cerebral lateralization (Doctoral dissertation, University of California, Los Angeles, 1981). *Diss. Abs. Int.*, 1981, **42**: 423B. (University Microfilms No. 81-13858)

51. Hines, M., Prenatal gonadal hormones and sex differences in human behavior. *Psychol. Bull.*, 1982, **92**: 56–80.

52. Hines, M., Alsum, P., Gorski, R. A., and Goy, R. W., Prenatal exposure to estrogen masculinizes and defeminizes behavior in the guinea pig. *Soc. Neurosci. Abstr.*, 1982, **8**: 196.

53. Hines, M., and Shipley, C., Prenatal exposure to diethylstilbestrol (DES) and the development of sexually dimorphic cognitive abilities and cerebral lateralization. *Dev. Psychol.*, 1984, **20**: 81–94.

54. Kail, R., and Siegel, A., Sex and hemispheric differences in the recall of verbal and spatial information. *Cortex*, 1978, **14**: 557–563.

55. Kimura, D., Spatial localization in left and right visual fields. *Can. J. Psychol.* 1969, **23**: 445–458.

56. Lake, D., and Bryden, M., Handedness and sex differences in hemispheric asymmetry. *Brain Lang.*, 1976, **3**: 266–282.

57. Levy, J., and Reid, M., Variations in cerebral organization as a function of handedness, hand posture in writing, and sex. *J. Exp. Psychol. (Gen.)*, 1978, **107**: 119–144.

58. Lieberburg, I., Krey, L. C., and McEwen, B. S., Sex differences in serum testosterone in exchangeable brain cell nuclear estradiol during the neonatal period in rats. *Brain Res.*, 1979, **178**: 207–212.

59. Luine, V., Nottebohm, F., Harding, C., and McEwen, B. S., Androgen effects cholinergic enzymes in syringeal motor neurons and muscle. *Brain Res.*, 1980, **192**: 89–107.

60. Marshall, J. C., and Holmes, J., Sex, handedness and differential hemispheric specialization for components of word perception. *International Research Communication System*, 1974, **2**: 1344.

61. McCasland, J. S., Neuronal control of bird song production. Doctoral dissertation, California Institute of Technoloy, 1983.

62. McCasland, J., and Konishi, M., Central control of avian vocalization: Neuronal recordings from song birds. *Soc. Neurosci. Abstr.*, 1981, **7**: 188.

63. McEwen, B. S., Lieberburg, I., Chaptal, C., and Krey, L. C., Aromatization: Important for sexual differentiation of the neonatal rat brain. *Horm. Behav.*, 1977, **9**: 429–463.

64. McEwen, B. S., Lieberburg, I., MacLusky, N., and Plapinger, L., Do estrogen receptors play a role in the sexual differentiation of the rat brain? *J. Steroid Biochem.*, 1977, **8**: 593–598.

65. McEwen, B. S., Plapinger, L., Chaptal, C., Gerlack, J., and Wallach, G., Role of fetoneonatal estrogen binding proteins in the association of estrogen with neonatal brain cell nuclear receptors. *Brain Res.*, 1975, **76**: 400–406.

66. McGlone, J., Sex differences in human brain asymmetry: A critical survey. *Behav. Brain Sci.*, 1980, **3**: 215–263.

67. McGlone, J., and Davidson, W., The relation between cerebral speech lateralization and spatial abilities with special reference to sex and hand preference. *Neuropsychologia*, 1973, **11**: 105–113.

68. Meisel, R. L., and Ward, I. L., Fetal femal rats are masculinized by male littermates located caudally in the uterus. *Science*, 1981, **213**: 239–242.

69. Morel, F., La massa intermedia ou commissure grise. *Acta Anat.*, 1948, **4**: 203–207.

70. Nance, D. M., Bhargava, M., and Myatt, G. A., Further evidence for hypothalamic asymmetry in neuroendocrine control. *Soc. Neurosci. Abstr.*, 1983, **9**: 415.

71. Nance, D. M., and Moger, W. H., Ipsilateral hypothalamic deafferentiation blocks the increase in serum FSH following hemi-castration. *Brain Res. Bull.*, 1982, **8**: 299–302.

72. Netley, C., Dichotic listening of callosal agenesis and Turner's syndrome patients. In: *Language Development and Neurological Theory* (S. J. Segalowitz and F. A. Gruber, Eds.). Academic Press, New York, 1977.

73. Netley, C., and Rovet, J., Atypical hemispheric lateralization in Turner syndrome subjects. *Cortex*, 1982, **18**: 377–384.

74. Nordeen, E. J., and Yahr, P., Hemispheric asymmetries in the behavioral and hormonal effects of sexually differentiating mammalian brain. *Science*, 1982, **213**: 391–394.

75. Nottebohm, F., Brain pathways for vocal learning in birds: A review of the first ten years. In: *Progress in Psychobiology and Physiological Psychology*, Vol. 9. Academic Press, New York, 1980: 85–125.

76. Nottebohm, F., Neural lateralization of vocal control in a passerine bird: I. Song. *J. Exp. Zool.*, 1971, **177**: 229–261.

77. Nottebohm, F., and Arnold, A. P., Sexual dimorphism in vocal control areas of the songbird brain. *Science*, 1976, **194**: 211–213.

78. Nottebohm, F., Stokes, T. M., and Leonard, C. M., Central control of song in the canary (*Serinus canarius*). *J. Comp. Neurol.*, 1976, **165**: 457–486.

79. Paton, J. A., and Manogue, K. R., Bilateral interactions within the vocal control pathway of birds: Two evolutionary alternatives. *J. Comp. Neurol.*, 1982, **212**: 329–335.

80. Petersen, M. R., Beecher, M. D., Zoloth, S. R., Moody, D. B., and Stebbins, W. C., Neural lateralization of species-specific vocalizations by Japanese macaques (*Macaca fuscata*). *Science*, 1978, **202**: 324–327.

81. Piazza, D. M., The influence of sex and handedness in the hemispheric specialization of verbal and nonverbal tasks. *Neuropsychologia*, 1980, **18**: 163–176.

82. Rabl, R., Strukturstudien an der massa intermedia des thalamus opticus. *J. Hirnforschung*, 1958, **4**: 78–112.

83. Raisman, G., and Field, P. M., Sexual dimorphism in the neuropil of the preoptic area of the rat and its dependence on neonatal androgen. *Brain Res.*, 1973, **54**: 1–29.

84. Reddy, V. V. R., Naftolin, F., and Ryan, K. J., Conversion of androstenedione to estrone by neural tissues from fetal and neonatal rats. *Endocrinology*, 1974, **94**: 117–121.

85. Resnick, S. M., Psychological functioning in individuals with congenital adrenal hyperplasia: Early hormonal influences on cognition and personality. Doctoral dissertation, University of Minnesota, 1982.

86. Robinson, T. E., Becker, J. B., and Ramirez, V. D., Sex differences in amphetamine-elicited rotational behavior and the lateralization of striatal dopamine in rats. *Brain Res. Bull.*, 1980, **5**: 539–545.

87. Rosen, G. D., Berrebi, A. S., Yutzey, D. A., and Denenberg, V. H., Prenatal testosterone causes shift of asymmetry in neonatal tail posture of the rat. *Dev. Brain Res.*, 1983, **9**: 99–101.

88. Ross, D. A., Glick, S. D., and Meibach, R. C., Sexually dimorphic brain and behavioral asymmetries in the neonatal rat. *Proc. Natl. Acad. Sci. U.S.A.*, 1981, **78**: 1958–1961.

89. Sasanuma, S., Do Japanese show sex differences in brain asymmetry?: Supplementary findings. *Behav. Brain Sci.*, 1980, **3**: 247.

90. Searleman, A., Tweedy, J., and Springer, S., Interrelationships among subject variables believed to predict cerebral organization. *Brain Lang.*, 1979, **7**: 267–276.

91. Sherman, G. F., Garbanati, J. A., Rosen, G. D., Hoffmann, M., Yutzey, D. A., and Denenberg, V. H., Lateralization of spatial preference in the female rat. *Life Sci.*, 1983, **33**: 189–193.

92. Singh, R. P., and Carr, D. H., The anatomy and histology of XO human embryos and fetuses. *Anat. Rec.*, 1966, **155**: 369–383.

93. Springer, S., and Searleman, A., The ontogeny of hemispheric specialization: Evidence from dichotic listening in twins. *Neuropsychologia*, 1978, **16**: 269–281.

94. Stewart, J., and Cygan, D., Ovarian hormones act early in development to feminize adult open-field behavior in the rat. *Horm. Behav.*, 1980, **14**: 20–32.

95. Toran-Allerand, C. D., Sex steroids and the development of the newborn mouse hypothalamus and preoptic area *in vitro*: Implications for sexual differentiation. *Brain Res.*, 1976, **106**: 407–412.

96. Toran-Allerand, C. D., Sex steroids and the development of the newborn mouse hypo-

thalamus and preoptic area *in vitro*: II. Morphological correlates and hormonal specificity. *Brain Res.*, 1980, **189**: 413–427.

97. Toran-Allerand, C. D., Hashimoto, K., Greenough, W. T., and Saltarelli, M., Sex steroids and the development of the newborn mouse hypothalamus and preoptic area *in vitro*: III. Effects of estrogen on dendritic differentiation. *Dev. Brain Res.*, 1983, **7**: 97–101.

98. Vaccari, A., Sexual differentiation of monoamine neurotransmitters. In: *Biogenic Amines in Development* (H. Parvey and S. Parvey, Eds.). Elsevier/North-Holland, Amsterdam, 1980: 327–352.

99. Villee, D. B., *Human Endocrinology: A Developmental Approach*. W. B. Saunders, Philadelphia, 1975.

100. vom Saal, F. S., and Bronson, F. H., *In utero* proximity of female mouse fetuses to males: Effect on reproductive performance during later life. *Biol. Reprod.*, 1978, **19**: 842–853.

101. Waber, D. P., Neuropsychological aspects of Turner's syndrome. *Dev. Med. Child Neurol.*, 1979, **21**: 58–70.

102. Waber, D. P., Sex differences in mental abilities, hemispheric lateralization, and rate of physical growth at adolescence. *Dev. Psychol.*, 1977, **13**: 29–38.

103. Wada, J. A., Clarke, R., and Hamm, A., Cerebral hemispheric asymmetry in humans. *Arch. Neurol.*, 1975, **32**: 239–246.

104. Ward, I. L., The prenatal stress syndrome: Current status. *Psychoneuroendocrinology*, 1984, **9**: 3–11.

105. Weisz, J., and Ward, I. L., Plasma testosterone and progesterone titers of pregnant rats, their male and female fetuses and neonatal offspring. *Endocrinology*, 1980, **106**: 306–316.

106. Witelson, S. F., and Pallie, W., Left hemisphere specialization for language in the newborn. *Brain*, 1973, **96**: 641–646.

107. Young, W. C., The hormones and mating behavior. In: *Sex and Internal Secretions*, Vol. 2, third edition (W. C. Young and G. W. Corner, Eds.). Williams & Wilkins, Baltimore, 1961: 1173–1239.

THE DEVELOPMENT OF
HUMAN CEREBRAL LATERALIZATION

SUSAN CURTISS, PhD
Department of Linguistics

INTRODUCTION

The fact that there are human cerebral lateral asymmetries has been recognized for over 120 years. These asymmetries were first observed with respect to the human language faculty, but have since been found for a variety of higher cognitive functions (e.g., visual closure, arithmetic calculations, face recognition). It is only within the last 20 years, however, that fundamental questions regarding the development of lateralization have been addressed. These are the questions I will consider here.

Structural asymmetries exist in almost all species, so it is no surprise that they exist in humans. The origin of such asymmetries is not yet known, although, in most if not all instances, the ultimate explanation will probably rest in genetics. Are human cerebral asymmetries of the same order as other physical asymmetries, however? After all, cerebral asymmetry is not a species-invariant trait; that is, different patterns of cerebral organization exist in different subpopulations of the species. While species-variable traits can also be under genetic control (14, 50), the causal mechanisms underlying human brain asymmetries are not at all understood, including the basic question of whether the pattern of asymmetry is established by genetic or environmental factors. I will therefore leave aside questions regarding the genetic origins of laterality (but see items 14, 50, 51, and 63 for discussion of these issues). I will instead concentrate on the following questions: When does cerebral dominance set in? Is it present at birth, or is it a developmental process? Is it subject to environmental influences during ontogenesis? What factors determine variations in lateralization?

THE SPECIAL ROLE OF LANGUAGE

Cerebral dominance in the human has been most extensively considered in relation to human language, so much so that the phrase "cerebral dominance" (or "lateralization") is often used to mean "cerebral dominance (or lateralization) for language." This association of lateralization with language lateralization is probably a by-product of the fact that language loss is the most obvious or noticeable behavioral consequent of brain damage, and is therefore easier to localize with regard to cerebral control. To that extent, then, it would seem an accident that language has played such a large role in exploring issues of lateralization. It seems to have been a well-designed accident, however, for there is now reason to believe that language plays a crucial role in both the development and character of cerebral organization.

Lenneberg's Hypothesis

Because of the special place language holds in understanding the development of lateralization, it is fitting that the first set of hypotheses regarding the establishment of cerebral laterality came from Lenneberg's treatise *Biological Foundations of Language* (49). A reanalysis of the data Lenneberg used and a consideration of data unavailable to Lenneberg in 1967 have since challenged his views on the development of lateralization; however, in Lenneberg's treatment of the topic, he raised and addressed so many of the issues still considered to be central ones that his position is useful not only as a starting point but as a framework for our larger discussion.

In his seminal work, Lenneberg argues that at birth the two cerebral hemispheres are unspecialized and have equal potential for subserving language. At about the age of 2, maturationally timed changes in neurochemistry and neurophysiology underlie both the onset of true language acquisition and the onset of the neurological process of language lateralization. These changes involve changes in brain weight, myelination of nerve fibers, the growth of individual neurons, changes in neurodensity, and changes in relative chemical composition of brain tissue. Lenneberg notes that these changes, which unfold along a maturational timetable, parallel milestones of linguistic development and patterns of recovery from brain damage. The establishment of cerebral dominance for language, Lenneberg argues, is therefore a continuing process, nontrivially tied to the process of language acquisition. As more language is acquired, the left hemisphere becomes increasingly dominant for the representation of language knowledge and for the control of its performance. The left hemisphere thus becomes specialized for language. At the same time, having started out participating equally in the early language functions of the child, the right hemisphere becomes less and less involved as the left hemisphere's dominance for language grows. This process continues until puberty, its completion corresponding to the loss of the ability to learn language naturally, which is in turn linked to the endpoint in the brain's organizational plasticity.

There are several theses central to Lenneberg's view: (1) The two hemispheres are equipotential at birth; (2) lateralization is a process of increasing specialization or control (of language) by the left hemisphere alongside a decreasing involvement of the right — a process lasting from age 2 to puberty; (3) recovery of (language) function after brain damage is determined by degree of lateralization (i.e., how well-established or complete cerebral dominance is); (4) cerebral dominance for language is the key brain–behavior relationship to consider in understanding lateralization, because brain lateralization is tied to language acquisition.

Each of these arguments touches on issues fundamental to an understanding of the development of lateralization, and I will consider them in turn. The first two are intimately interwoven and will be considered together.

EQUIPOTENTIALITY AND LATERALIZATION AS A
PROCESS OF INCREASING HEMISPHERIC SPECIALIZATION

Lenneberg's contention that at birth the two hemispheres are equipotential for language, and that lateralization for language is a process of increasing specialization of the left hemisphere alongside a decrease in the right hemisphere's role in language, rests on his interpretation of clinical data regarding the incidence of acquired aphasia in children. Relying largely on Basser's (4) study of the effects on language of unilateral lesions in childhood, Lenneberg concludes that, if language acquisition has already begun, children develop transient aphasia regardless of which hemisphere is lesioned, and before that point, they will acquire language regardless of which hemisphere is damaged.

Krashen (46, 47) was the first to reassess these arguments. In his reexamination of the data Lenneberg considered, Krashen notes that in all cases involving right-hemisphere lesions leading to aphasia, the lesion was sustained before age 5. Krashen then postulates a lateralization-by-5 hypothesis. Like Lenneberg, Krashen posits that lateralization is linked to language acquisition, but argues that both are essentially complete by age 5. Krashen also examines the results of dichotic-listening experiments with children. He argues that with the use of an appropriate metric that corrects for performance level, these data reveal that degree of lateralization does not change after 5 and thus support his lateralization-by-5 hypothesis. Krashen further argues that cerebral lateralization (complete by 5) is separate from organizational plasticity, which holds until close to puberty, approximately age 10.

Krashen's work challenges Lenneberg's notions that lateralization continues to puberty. However, Krashen's lateralization-by-5 hypothesis does not address the equipotentiality issue and still leaves us with the possibility that lateralization may be a continuing process from birth to 5 or from 2 to 5. It could be the case, in other words, that initially both hemispheres have equal potential to subserve language, and that the left hemisphere's specialization for language only gradually and progressively sets in sometime before 5. Considerable research argues against both of these logical possibilities.

Clinical Data

To begin with, reexamination of the clinical data Lenneberg used to support his arguments about equipotentiality and the lateralization of language as a progressively increasing phenomenon has shown these data to be unreliable, fragmentary, and difficult to interpret (45). More important, however, Woods and Teuber (87) point out that recent data contradict the early data and show no greater incidence of aphasia after right-sided lesions in children than in adults. They point out that conditions that may earlier have led to aphasia (e.g., systemic infections, unchecked, resulting in diffuse, bilateral encephalopathy) are now treated with antibiotics, restricting recent clinical series to cases that more accurately elucidate the relationship between lateralized lesions and consequent aphasia. The recent data do not

support either the equipotentiality hypothesis or the view that lateralization gradually sets in.

Other clinical data argue perhaps even more strongly against the equipotentiality view. Cases of infantile hemiplegia and hemidecortication demonstrate the unequal potential of the two hemispheres for mediating language (and visual and spatial
ability). Hood and Perlstein (42) and Bishop (7), comparing the consequences of left-
sided versus right-sided injury in cases of infantile hemiplegics sustaining early damage but not involving hemispherectomy, noted that right-hemisphere damage led
only to deficits in articulation and vocabulary acquisition, while left-hemisphere injury led to widespread deficits and delays in language acquisition. Annett (3), whose
cases of infantile hemiplegia also involved early damage (before 13 months) without hemispherectomy, demonstrated that subsequent language impairments were
far more frequently associated with left-hemisphere damage than with right-sided
damage.

These cases involve children whose damaged hemispheres may nonetheless continue to exert an inhibitory influence over their healthy hemisphere during development. Milner (59), for example, reports that early left-hemisphere lesions must be
situated in the classic language areas before the right hemisphere's potential for language can be released. Better test cases for true equipotentiality are cases where children develop language with only one extant hemisphere. Dennis and her colleagues
(21, 22, 25, 26, 27, 28) have studied three such cases. They are cases where one hemisphere was surgically removed in infancy, before language acquisition. In these cases
(and in a similar series of seven additional cases), the two hemispheres are revealed
to be unequal substrates for language acquisition, with the left hemisphere out-
performing the right across a broad range of linguistic tasks. The right hemisphere
is particularly deficient in acquiring what I will refer to as the computational aspects
of language (after Chomsky) — phonology, morphology, syntax, and the integration
of semantic and syntactic structure — that is, most of the grammar.

There is another aspect of Lenneberg's hypothesis that might yet hold, however.
Despite their unequal potential for language acquisition, a process that does not actively begin until 1 to 2 years of age, the two hemispheres may still be equally involved in perceiving and processing linguistic information before that point. There
are no clinical data that bear on this possibility, but experimental investigations have
produced relevant data.

Experimental Data

Consistent with the clinical data referred to above, experimental data demonstrate no change (increase) in the lateralized response to language and nonlanguage
stimuli between ages 2½ and 5. (See 85 for a review of many of these data.) Moreover, experiments on even younger children indicate that at birth, the two hemispheres already differ in their sensitivity and response to language and nonlanguage
stimuli. The left hemisphere appears to be preprimed for language stimuli; the right
hemisphere, for visual and certain nonlinguistic auditory stimuli. Entus (30) found

that infants aged from 22–140 days display the pattern of lateral asymmetry found in older children and adults for both speech and nonspeech (music) stimuli presented dichotically. Molfese, Freeman, and Palermo (62) demonstrated that infants as young as 1 week of age manifest strongly lateralized electrophysiological responses to speech and nonspeech stimuli. Davis and Wada (19) found a strongly lateralized right-hemisphere response to a visual stimulus in infants as young as 2 weeks. Newborns demonstrate strongly asymmetric motor reflexes and responses as well (e.g., head turning [80]; grasp reflex and grasp duration [9]; stepping reflex [57]; limb movements in response to speech and music [75]), although these responses may be subcortically, not cortically, mediated.

The evidence consistently indicates that the left hemisphere is prepotent for language. And contrary to Lenneberg's view, long before language acquisition has begun, the cortical response to language (and certain nonlanguage) stimulation is clearly lateralized. Functional specialization, then, does not appear to develop in tandem with language acquisition. Functional asymmetries (or their precursors) appear to be present at birth, and at no time from birth on do the two hemispheres appear to be equipotential for language on any interpretation of the term equipotential. Furthermore, neuroanatomical asymmetries that may be mapped onto the functional asymmetries demonstrable in infants and newborns are found in neonatal and fetal brains. With respect to the areas of the two hemispheres in which adult brains have been found to differ reliably—longer left-hemisphere sylvian fissure (in particular, length and area of the planum temporale), and sharper slope of the right-hemisphere sylvian fissure—infant and fetal brains have been found to differ in parallel fashion, and to the same extent, from at least the 29th gestational week (11, 16, 48, 83, 86). Although these neuroanatomical asymmetries do not correlate with functional asymmetries as well as might be expected (see 84 for discussion), lateral asymmetries are present at birth, and the neuroanatomical asymmetries may represent a prewired, neurobiological precursor of functional lateralization.

RECOVERY OF FUNCTION AS A REFLECTION OF LATERALIZATION

A third of Lenneberg's notions about lateralization is that recovery of function reflects the degree to which cerebral dominance has been established for that function. The data Lenneberg uses are the same clinical data he uses to support his other arguments.

There are several problems inherent in interpreting recovery data. Age is not the only factor that constrains or determines recovery. Size of lesion, depth of lesion, handedness, sex, and the extent and character of the deficit itself all play a role in recovery. In general terms, degree of recovery is greatest in the young child and decreases with age (but cf. 87). This decrease in recovery with age reflects degree of plasticity rather than degree of dominance, however, and both the resulting deficit and subsequent recovery reflect the functional maturity of the lesioned areas at the time the lesion is incurred. The important fact here regarding lateralization is that with damage to the left hemisphere, language is affected throughout life, even though differently at different ages. This suggests that the left hemisphere's specialization or specialized potential for language is preset at birth — a conclusion consistent with the findings discussed above.

This view of lateral specialization is not incompatible with cerebral plasticity, for, while each hemisphere may be preprogrammed to mediate certain functions, each may also hold the "prospective potency" (30) to subserve functions that are normally under the control of the opposite hemisphere. However, it appears that the degree of innate specification of the language areas, especially for the computational aspects of language, limits the interhemispheric transfer of these language functions such that there is always some residual consequence of the right hemisphere's taking over what was destined to be governed by the left hemisphere, with greater residual effects associated with postacquisition damage. Since plasticity appears to decrease with age, "prospective potency" may be inversely related to the knowledge state of the individual, and potentially to its automatization and degree of innate specification.

To review, I have looked at three of Lenneberg's four central theses about lateralization; it is apparent that each of them fails to be supported. The two hemispheres appear to be unequal substrates for language from birth; lateralization does not seem to set in via a process that gradually and progressively functionally differentiates the two hemispheres, but appears to be preset at birth; and finally, recovery from brain damage reflects brain plasticity, not cerebral lateralization.

What factors, then, affect lateralization? Is lateralization subject to environmental influences? Since lateralization is not a species-invariant trait — that is, different subgroups within the species evidence different patterns of brain organization — what factors influence or determine which pattern of lateralization develops? Two factors appear primary in their relationship to varying patterns of lateralization: sex and handedness.

SEX

Male–female differences in cerebral asymmetry in the human would not be surprising, given increasing data on the important role of sex hormones on brain organization in other species (29) and on the possible relationship between sex chromosomes and both cerebral asymmetry and neuropsychological function in humans (64, 65; but see 43). However, there is considerable controversy over the issue of sex differences in lateralization. Nonetheless, amidst the controversy over how valid and reliable the data are, and how in any event they should be interpreted, the body of clinical and experimental data pointing to sex differences in laterality patterns grows.

McGlone (55) and Sasanuma (73) report a significant sex difference in the incidence of aphasia following insult to the left hemisphere. Both researchers found a less frequent incidence of language breakdown in females than in males after quite similar damage. No incidence of aphasia resulted for either males or females after right-hemisphere damage. Sasanuma also found a significantly smaller incidence of severe aphasia in females than males. Kimura presents additional data that suggest a male–female difference in the intrahemispheric organization or representation of language (44). These findings, taken together, raise several possibilities: (1) that females have less lateralized, more bihemispheric linguistic function than males; (2) that females have less localized, more diffuse representation of language within the left hemisphere; (3) that females have otherwise different intrahemispheric organization; (4) that females have greater interhemispheric connectivity than males; and (5) that some combination of these holds. Clearly, far more data are needed before we can decide among these alternatives.

There are many more experimental than clinical data on sex differences in language lateralization, including a considerable number of developmental studies on the question (see 56 for review), but here, too, the data are controversial. With exceptions, experimental results generally indicate that males have greater lateralization of verbal, visual, and spatial abilities than females, once again suggesting either greater bihemisphericity of language represented in females, or greater interhemispheric connectivity in the female brain.

Developmental experimental data are at first glance in conflict with the adult data. Of 23 language dichotic-listening studies (see 52 and 81 for reviews), 16 have shown no sex differences, 5 showed sex differences only for children in particular age groups, and only 2 showed more pervasive sex differences (one study indicating a greater right-ear advantage for girls, the other for boys). Of 7 tachistoscopic studies investigating sex differences for language processing, 6 have found no sex differences, and 1 found a greater right-visual-field effect for boys. Of 17 studies looking at the development of motoric lateral asymmetries (i.e., handedness, footedness, etc.), 11 found no sex differences, and 6 found sex differences, in each case indicating greater lateral asymmetry for girls.

The developmental data look as if there is either no sex difference in lateralization or a tendency for females to show greater laterality at an earlier age. However, this apparent conflict with the adult data may be resolvable through consideration of maturational factors. Waber (81, 82) has shown that maturational rate figures critically in the laterality effects evidenced in experimental measures of hemispheric asymmetry. Early maturers show greater laterality effects that late maturers. Since females in general mature earlier than males (15, 67), equivalent laterality effects for girls and boys, or even greater laterality effects for girls, could be expected at least up to puberty.

These developmental data do not, then, contradict the adult data. Sex differences in laterality patterns may exist throughout life, but take different forms at different points in maturation. There is also increasing evidence that sex differences in brain organization do not appear to result from experiential factors. Within the first 2 years of life, male–female differences in hemispheric maturation rate and sensitivity to auditory and visual stimuli have been found (15, 79). In addition, studies of adults exposed prenatally to abnormal levels of sex hormones have been found to display atypical patterns of lateral asymmetries (40, 41). There is little likelihood that these male–female differences could be the result of gender-related differences in social/cultural experience.

Although the state of the art on sex differences in laterality does not warrant any firm conclusions (see 56 and peer commentary for a review), sex may well turn out to be an important factor governing the pattern of lateralization that develops. As sex is clearly a genetically determined phenomenon, the development of lateralization may be prefixed, at least partially, by genetic factors.

HANDEDNESS

There is a greater tendency for human beings to have language lateralized to the left hemisphere than to be right-handed, but the species is nonetheless predominantly right-handed. According to most estimates, only 8–12% of the population is non-right-handed. The hand–brain relationship is a complex matter, and many aspects of this relationship will not be considered here. I will consider only two issues: (1) that handedness is not the result of experience, and (2) that right-handers and non-right-handers have been shown to possess different patterns of cerebral organization.

Handedness is not fully expressed at birth. This fact has led some researchers to look for indices of growth or maturation of handedness. Some have found changes in handedness in the course of growth. Bingley (6), for example, found evidence of a decrease in mixed and left-handedness with age, such that non-right-handers become increasingly right-preferent. Different forms of mixed lateral preferences are common at all ages, but observations of uncertain, ill-defined, or changing preferences in young children have led some scholars to associate ambilaterality with immaturity. In this view, ambilaterality is related to functionally undifferentiated hemispheres (undifferentiated for motor as well as cognitive function). This view assumes an initial equipotentiality for control of handedness. While lateral preference is not fully expressed at birth, there are strong indications that handedness is genetically determined. First, there are clear precursors of handedness (e.g., tonic neck reflex position [36], orientation of the head at birth [12]); second, from early in childhood hand preference remains constant (2, 3, 35); and third, handedness is not the result of experience or social factors (1, 3, 10).

More immediately relevant is the fact that handedness is one of the key factors related to the pattern of lateralization that develops. Most studies report less lateralized representation of function in the non-right-handed. Clinical data reveal that a portion of left-handers have sufficient language governed by both hemispheres so as to be rendered aphasic after damage to either hemisphere (37, 60, 68, 71). These data suggest greater bihemispheric and less lateralized representation of language in the left-hander than in the right-hander. Clinical data also indicate that the initial aphasia in left-handers is generally less severe and recovery more rapid and complete than in right-handers. This fact raises the additional possibility of less inhibitory control of one hemisphere by the other in the left-handed. Experimental data are consistent with the clinical data in that left-handers as a group show consistently smaller laterality effects than right-handers on both language and visual–spatial tasks.

Left-handers are not a homogeneous group with respect to patterns of lateralization, however. Clinical and experimental data reveal an important difference between familial and nonfamilial left-handers. Nonfamilial left-handers appear to be more like male right-handers; the incidence of aphasia is consistently associated with lesions to only one side of the brain, the left hemisphere. Initial aphasia can be more severe and recovery from aphasia slow and limited as well (53). But familial left-handers and those right-handers with left-handedness in the family appear to have greater bilateral control of language and better prognosis for recovery. In experimental data as well, cerebral ambilaterality is more associated with familial sinistrality, while nonfamilial left-handers show more consistent unilateral left-sided dominance for language (39, 95).

As with sex, handedness is a genetically determined matter, probably preset at birth (but see 34). Thus the factors implicated in variations of cerebral laterality patterns are genetic factors, either preestablished or preprogrammed at birth. This picture is consistent with the neuroanatomical and electrophysiological data reported earlier, suggesting functional lateralization and its possible physiological basis to be prewired. If true, we are led to the view that lateralization is a biologically determined phenomenon wherein at the time of birth each hemisphere is dedicated to specific processes to a prespecified degree. At birth the hemispheres are not yet specialized, but are prepotent for their specialized functions. Their specialization potential is then actualized as specialization for particular knowledge domains, psychological abilities, or information-processing abilities, once they are functional.

LANGUAGE ACQUISITION AND LATERALIZATION

Lenneberg argued that language acquisition and lateralization go hand in hand, degree of lateralization reflecting degree of language mastery. While in detail his arguments do not hold up, here Lenneberg appears to have been at least partially right. His basic thesis that language acquisition and lateralization are tied does find support.

The specific lateralization pattern an individual is programmed to have is not related to the development of normal language abilities. Normal left-handers, right-handers, females, and males all develop normal ordinary language abilities. Interestingly, though, the development of normal language and the unfolding of an individual's preset laterality pattern do appear to be related. Only a very small body of relevant data exists, but these data suggest a critical tie between language acquisition and the instantiation of the preset pattern of lateralization for language, such that if either one is disrupted, the other will be affected.

The most common subpopulations with disorders of language acquisition— namely, developmentally aphasic children, dyslexics, and autistics—are consistently associated with atypical laterality patterns. Each of these populations comprises more than one subgroup, and the etiology of the disorders is unknown. Yet with each group, we find developmental language dysfunction accompanied by indications of abnormal or atypical cerebral organization. With both developmental aphasics and dyslexics, there is a higher than normal incidence of non-right-handedness; mixed laterality of handedness, footedness, eyedness, and "visual-fieldedness"; and a family history of mixed laterality and developmental language problems (see 88 for review).

Some research on developmental aphasia and dyslexia is most suggestive of a specific left-hemisphere deficit. Tallal (77) has demonstrated that a substantial portion of language-impaired children are deficient in processing rapidly changing acoustic information of the sort embodied in formant transitions between stop consonants and vowels. Such a deficit has also been demonstrated for aphasics with unilateral left-hemisphere damage and for the disconnected right but not the left hemisphere. In addition, language-impaired children and both the disconnected and isolated right hemisphere of adults evidence similar performance on the Token test (76, 94), implicating an impairment in short-term verbal memory, normally lateralized to the left hemisphere. Recent research on reading in the disconnected and isolated right hemisphere (93) elucidates provocative parallels between patterns of abilities and strategies evidenced by dyslexic children and the right hemisphere. These findings are supported by recent neuroanatomical studies (32, 32a) showing that developmental dyslexia is associated with structural abnormalities of the left hemisphere.

There is no consensus on the origin or cause of autism, a disorder involving pervasive and somewhat unique language-learning impairments, but again, recent research suggests a left-hemisphere dysfunction or abnormal hemispheric dominance and interaction. There is a higher than normal proportion of non-right-handedness (13, 72), an enlargement of the left lateral ventricle (38), a relative increase in the size of the left hemisphere's evoked potential during REM sleep compared to normals (78), and behavioral evidence of right-sided hemiattention or leftward sensory and sensory–motor bias (8, 48).

Direct experimental investigation of cerebral laterality in these groups has led to contradictory or inconclusive results. Thus, no specific conclusions can be drawn other than that each of these groups is associated with developmental language impairments coupled with an abnormality in cerebral dominance. Although which part of this relationship is cause and which effect cannot yet be determined, an intimate relationship between intact language acquisition and the establishment of a normal pattern of cerebral dominance is supported.

Other data provide more direct evidence for the idea that if lateralization is disrupted, language acquisition is adversely affected. This evidence comes from children with congenital or acquired brain disease—specifically, cases of unilateral lesions in childhood and of childhood hemidecortication or hemispherectomy. Unilateral lesions of the left hemisphere in childhood, whether acquired or congenital, interfere with the left hemisphere's prewired specialization for language, and they consistently result in language deficits. Studies of the effects of unilateral lesions in childhood (3, 7, 42) have found that left-hemisphere lesions produce speech delay and disorder. Rankin *et al.* (70), examining language performance in more detail, found that unilateral left-hemisphere lesions produce particular deficits in comprehension and production of syntax. Dennis (24) also found expressive and receptive deficits in structural linguistic knowledge in a case of left-hemisphere arteriopathy.

In cases of hemidecortication or hemispherectomy, a normal pattern of cerebral organization is prevented by disease and ensuing surgery. Here, too, the inability of the left hemisphere to subserve language (because of its removal) results in consistent and persistent linguistic deficits. Cases of damage and hemispherectomy in childhood *after* early stages of language acquisition reveal that, even before puberty, removal of the left hemisphere results not only in initial global aphasia, but in a preponderance of routinized social speech, inability to correct syntactic errors, and severe deficits in the comprehension and production of many syntactic and morphological structures (21, 93). Even in a female (symptoms at 7–8, hemispherectomy at 10), where we might have expected some residue of linguistic ability due to more bilateral control of language, we find severe, lasting linguistic impairment — telegrammatic speech, limited morphological elaboration, and limited syntactic comprehension (94, 95). These data suggest that once language has been acquired and hemispheric specialization for language established, removal of the language areas of the brain permanently disrupts language function and prevents language from developing normally again, even in childhood.

Hemispherectomy or hemidecortication of the left hemisphere with damage at or shortly after birth has also been shown to result in consistent, though less severe, linguistic deficits (20, 25, 27, 28, 70). In females and males alike, impairments in the processing and production of complex syntax are present in all the left hemispherectomies and hemidecorticates studied. Some of these infant left hemispherectomies have been shown to have semantic and more pervasive syntactic deficits as well. Dennis and her colleagues (22, 23, 25, 27, 28), for example, have found systematic linguistic deficits encompassing most of the computational aspects of the linguistic system — that is, syntax, morphology, phonological manipulations and recodings, and the integration of syntax with interpretive semantic elements.

In addition, in cases of agenesis of the corpus callosum, where the two hemispheres may be healthy but a preprogrammed pattern of cerebral asymmetry may not be established (64, 74), recent evidence suggests that deficits in linguistic function may result. What is more, these deficits seem to parallel in character the deficits found in cases of hemispherectomy and hemidecortication (23).

The kinds of studies that would document clearly the effects of early brain damage on language acquisition have only begun to be done, and the data are consequently sparse and limited. They all point to the same conclusion, however: Disruption of the preset specialization of the left hemisphere for language appears to permanently affect linguistic development, even if it occurs in infancy before the process of language acquisition has begun. Impaired linguistic function contrasts with the generally intact intellectual function of these same children (21, 27).

This part of the relationship between lateralization for language and language acquisition may seem somewhat unsurprising. After all, these cases all involve brain damage; it could be expected that language impairments might result. The uniformity and systematicity of the deficits would not be as predictable, however. What is also less expected is that the relationship should hold in reverse as well. There are even fewer data to consider here, but those that exist suggest that the tie between language acquisition and lateralization is a bidirectional one. Disrupt first language acquisition, and the establishment of a normal pattern of cerebral dominance will be affected. Cases of first language acquisition after the normal and perhaps critical period — that is, after childhood — raise the possibility that language acquisition itself may be the trigger or crucial factor in actualizing the preprogrammed pattern for functional specialization of the hemispheres.

The case of Genie, a case of first language acquisition in adolescence, is one such case (see 17, 18, and 31 for details). Social isolation prevented Genie from acquiring language in childhood, and her language development as a teenager and young adult has been limited primarily to lexical and propositional semantics, with little acquisition of structural (or computational) linguistic knowledge.

Experiments involving dichotic listening and event-related potentials (ERP) were conducted with Genie to assess laterality effects in her processing of language and nonlanguage stimuli. The two experimental techniques produced parallel results. They indicated that Genie uses her right hemisphere for both language and nonlanguage processing (she is strongly right-handed). As illustrated by her dichotic-listening performance presented in Table 1, both her failure to evidence a difference in the direction of laterality effect for language and nonlanguage stimuli and the degree of effect she displayed mark her performance as highly atypical. In terms of ear advantage, Genie's dichotic-listening performance parallels the dichotic-listening performance of subjects with only one hemisphere responding to the task, as illustrated in Table 2. This suggests unihemispheric control of both language and nonlanguage cognitive functions.

TABLE 1
DICHOTIC-LISTENING RESULTS WITH GENIE

Date	Number of Pairs Presented	Stimulus	Number Correct	
			RE	LE
3/27/72	29	Words[a]	6	29
5/10/72	15	Words[a]	1	15
8/16/72	30	Words[a]	5	30
6/3/73	28	Words[b]	0	28
8/2/72	20	Environmental sounds[a]	12	18
8/16/72	20	Environmental sounds[a]	14	19
6/3/73	20	Environmental sounds[a]	14	20
6/3/73	28	Environmental sounds[b]	15	27

[a]Single pair presented.
[b]Two pairs presented.

TABLE 2
GENIE COMPARED WITH SUBJECTS USING A SINGLE HEMISPHERE TO PERFORM THE TASK

| | | Percentage Correct | |
Subjects	Stimulus	Better Ear	Weaker Ear
Genie	Words	100 (L)	16.0
Right hemispherectomized[a]	Consonant–vowel syllables	99 (R)	24.3
Disconnected hemispheres[b]	Digits	90.7 (R)	22.2

[a]Berlin *et al.* (5).
[b]Milner *et al.* (61).

Behavioral data support this interpretation of the experimental data. In level of ability, number of errors, error types, and style of performance evidenced behaviorally, Genie's performance strongly resembles that of the adult disconnected right hemisphere of split-brain individuals on a wide range of tests, including tests of auditory short-term memory, visual short-term memory, visual reproduction, and disembedding (89, 90, 91, 92, D. Zaidel and E. Zaidel, personal communication; see 17 for details).

Genie's failure to learn language in childhood appears to have led not only to abnormal and restricted linguistic function, but to the absence of a normal pattern of cerebral specialization, marked in particular by the failure of the left hemisphere to specialize for language.

A second case of first language acquisition beyond childhood is the case of Chelsea, brought to light by P. Glusker. Chelsea is an individual attempting first language acquisition in adulthood (in her 30s), a severe and undiagnosed hearing impairment having prevented her from acquiring language as a child. Her language to date appears to consist solely of certain aspects of lexical knowledge and to be devoid of the constraints and principles of English grammar. It is thus agrammatic and ungrammatical, and is limited to the somewhat unconstrained concatenation of lexical items (Curtiss, unpublished data).

Preliminary data from Chelsea's performance on visual ERP and tachistoscopic language tasks indicate a lack of lateral specialization for language (H. Neville and N. Dronkers, personal communication and unpublished data). Here too, then, the possibility is raised that without first language acquisition in childhood, not only will language acquisition itself be affected, but a normal pattern of hemispheric specialization will not develop.

Data from congenitally deaf children and adults who are not linguistically proficient in any language (including sign) are consistent with these cases. Examining visual ERPs, Neville (66) found that those deaf individuals who lacked a formal language showed no evidence of hemispheric asymmetries for processing linguistic or nonlinguistic information, while those deaf individuals who had acquired a formal language in childhood showed asymmetries for both. Unexpectedly, Neville (65a) has also found that the acquisition of sign language as a native language in childhood (and its concomitant lateralization to the left hemisphere) is associated with a specialization of the left hemisphere for certain spatial functions, much as the specialization of the left hemisphere for spoken language may be associated with a specialization for temporal functions.

Neville's data are additionally important because they demonstrate that what is at issue is not the presence or absence of speech, but knowledge of language — spoken or signed. Recent data on the incidence and character of aphasia in fluent signers support Neville's findings (54, 69). The pattern of sign language deficits occurring after left-hemisphere damage or sodium amytal injection is quite parallel to those seen with spoken language. These data provide further evidence that the left hemisphere is specialized (in most individuals) for what linguists refer to as "the grammar," regardless of performance modality. What is most relevant here, however, is that current data indicate that when sign language is learned at the appropriate time (in childhood), signers show functional specialization of the hemispheres; but without language, signed or spoken, individuals show an absence of functional asymmetry.

One particularly striking fact about both the cases involving specific brain damage and those involving the acquisition of a first language past childhood is that the linguistic deficits involved fall within a circumscribed area of linguistic function: the computational modules of language, that is, the grammar minus the lexicon. Those with early left-hemisphere damage are limited in their capacity to acquire the computational modules. Those acquiring a first language after childhood appear even more severely limited in their capacity to acquire the computational component (see also 54a, 66a). Since the left hemisphere seems to be specialized for the computational component and not for all aspects of language knowledge and use, it may not be the entirety of language acquisition, but only the acquisition of the computational component of language that is critically tied to the establishment of a normal pattern of cerebral lateralization. Actualization of hemispheric specialization, either for grammar itself or for the particular abilities the processing and performance of grammar requires in addition to its representation, may be what triggers the establishment of cerebral lateralization. And all of this may depend on first language acquisition at the normal time, by the area of cortex prewired for the task.

SUMMARY AND QUESTIONS FOR THE FUTURE

In summary, the evidence points to certain conclusions that differ from Lenneberg's — namely, that lateralization is preprogrammed at birth; that lateralization is not a species-invariant trait; and that the particular pattern of lateralization an individual is prewired to develop depends in part on factors such as handedness and sex. But it looks as though Lenneberg may have been right in holding that language acquisition and lateralization are closely related. The data considered here suggest that language acquisition — more specifically, the acquisition of the computational component — may be a crucial trigger for the development of lateralization. If language acquisition is prevented, lateral asymmetries may never be established.

This hypothesis tying the development of lateralization to the acquisition of the computational component is most speculative at this point, and many questions remain. What is the picture regarding the development of cerebral asymmetries for lateralized abilities aside from language, such as facial recognition, arithmetic calculation, spatial operations, and so on? Since many of these abilities develop later than language, what role (if any) does their acquisition play in the establishment of the final pattern of cerebral dominance? Will systematic limitations or abnormalities in these other systems of knowledge be associated with missing or atypical lateral asymmetries, or will evidence continue to support a special role for language in the development of cerebral lateralization? Definitive answers await more data.

Other questions also remain unresolved and await future research. What is the biological basis of lateralization? Is the basic pattern set by genes or by unknown environmental events? What factors aside from handedness and sex might contribute to variations in lateralization?

What is the precise relationship between neuroanatomical asymmetries and the development of functional asymmetries? There are anatomical asymmetries involving several areas of cortex. Which, if any, lateralized abilities are these asymmetries connected with? Do morphological asymmetries in fact underlie functional asymmetries? The correlation is far from 1.0, so how should this imperfect correlation be interpreted? Perhaps the structures more relevant to understanding the neural basis of functional asymmetries will turn out not to be at the level of gross anatomy, but at a deeper level involving neurons, synapses, transmitter substances, and circuits.

Finally, although lateralization appears to be prewired, there are respects in which cerebral asymmetries may be a changing phenomenon in development. The ontogenetic development of interrelationships between different brain areas (especially between the frontal lobes and other areas) changes with age. This is true for both intrahemispheric and interhemispheric organization. Changes in knowledge states or performance may reflect reorganization of different subsystems of the developing brain and different levels of connectivity both within a single hemisphere and across hemispheres. Understanding the establishment of cerebral organization will require a better understanding of the development of intra- and interhemispheric communication and of the facilitative and inhibitory effects of one cerebral area on another. Since the right hemisphere appears to be dominant or at least indispensable for the performance of particular linguistic abilities (33, 58), the fullest instantiation of the human language capacity is an example of a cognitive system that involves, maybe even requires, an interaction of both the left and right hemispheres.

Only sophisticated studies of the specific cognitive and linguistic capacities of each hemisphere can reveal what it is that becomes lateralized. Only future neurological studies can determine the neural basis for lateralization. A true understanding of the development of lateralization will thus require a serious interdisciplinary effort in which cognitive theories and neurological theories are related to explain this fundamental aspect of the relationship between brain and behavior.

112   CURTISS

REFERENCES

1. Annett, M., Genetic and nongenetic influences on handedness. *Behavior*, 1978, **8**: 227–249.
2. Annett, M., The growth of manual preference and speed. *Br. J. Psychol.*, 1970, **61**, 4: 545–558.
3. Annett, M., Laterality of childhood hemiplegia and the growth of speech and intelligence. *Cortex*, 1973, **9**: 4–33.
4. Basser, L., Hemiplegia of early onset and the faculty of speech with special reference to the effects of hemispherectomy: Two case studies. *Brain*, 1962, **85**: 427–460.
5. Berlin, C., Porter, R., Lowe-Bell, S., Berlin, H., Thompson, C., and Hughes, L., *Dichotic signs of the recognition of speech elements in normals, temporal lobectomees, and hemispherectomees*. IEEE Group on Audio and Electroacoustics Transactions, 1972.
6. Bingley, T., Mental symptoms in temporal lobe epilepsy and temporal lobe gliomas. *Acta Psychiat. Neurol.*, 1958, **33**, Suppl. **120**: 1–151.
7. Bishop, N., Speech in the hemiplegic child. In: *Proceedings of the 8th Medical and Educational Conference of the Australian Cerebral Palsy Association*. Tooranga Press, Melbourne, 1967: 141–153.
8. Blackstock, E., Cerebral asymmetry and the development of early infantile autism. *J. Autism Child. Schizophr.* 1978, 8(3): 339–353.
9. Caplan, P., and Kinsbourne, M., Baby drops the rattle: Asymmetry of duration of grasp by infants. *Child Dev.*, 1976, **47**: 532–534.
10. Carter-Saltzman, L., Biological and structural effects on handedness: Comparison between biological and adoptive families. *Science*, 1980, **209**: 1263–1265.
11. Chi, J., Dooling, E., and Gilles, F., Left–right asymmetries of the temporal speech areas of the human fetus. *Arch. Neurol.*, 1977, **34**: 346–348.
12. Churchill, J., Igna, E., and Senf, R., The association of position at birth and handedness. *Pediatrics*, 1962, **22**: 307–309.
13. Colby, K., and Parkinson, C., Handedness in autistic children. *J. Autism Child. Schizophr.*, 1977, **7**: 3–9.
14. Collins, R., Toward an admissable genetic model for the inheritance of the degree and direction of asymmetry. In *Lateralization in the Nervous System* (S. Harnad, R. Doty, L. Goldstein, J. Jaynes, and G. Grauthamer, Eds.). Academic Press, New York, 1977: 137–150.
15. Conel, J., *The Postnatal Development of the Human Cerebral Cortex*, Vols. 1–6. Harvard University Press, Cambridge, Mass., 1939–1959.
16. Cunningham, D., *Contribution to the surface anatomy of the cerebral hemispheres*. Royal Irish Academy, Dublin, 1892.
17. Curtiss, S., Genie: Language and cognition. *UCLA Working Papers in Cognitive Linguistics*, 1979, **1**: 15–62.
18. Curtiss, S., *Genie: A Psycholinguistic Study of a Modern-Day "Wild Child."* Academic Press, New York, 1977.
19. Davis, A., and Wada, J., Hemispheric asymmetries in human infants: Spectral analysis of flash and click evoked potentials. *Brain Lang.*, 1977, **4**: 23–31.
20. Day, P., and Ulatowska, H., Perceptual, cognitive, and linguistic development after early hemispherectomy: Two case studies. *Brain Lang.*, 1979, **7**: 17–33.
21. Dennis, M., Capacity and strategy for syntactic comprehension after left or right hemidecortication. *Brain Lang.*, 1980, **10**: 287–317.
22. Dennis, M., Language acquisition in a single hemisphere: Semantic organization. In: *Biological Studies of Mental Processes* (D. Caplan, Ed.). MIT Press, Cambridge, Mass., 1980: 159–185.

23. Dennis, M., Language in a congenitally acallosal brain. *Brain Lang.*, 1981, **12**: 33–53.
24. Dennis, M., Strokes in childhood I: Communicative intent, expression, and comprehension after left-hemisphere arteriopathy in a right-handed nine-year-old. In: *Language Development and Aphasia in Children* (R. Rieber, Ed.). Academic Press, New York, 1980: 45–67.
25. Dennis, M., and Kohn, B., Comprehension of syntax in infantile hemiplegics after cerebral hemidecortication: Left hemisphere superiority. *Brain Lang.*, 1975, **2**: 475–486.
26. Dennis, M., Lovett, M., and Wiegel-Crump, C., Written language acquisition after left or right hemidecortication in infancy. *Brain Lang.*, 1981, **12**: 54–91.
27. Dennis, M., and Whitaker, H., Hemispheric equipotentiality and langauge acquisition. In: *Language Development and Neurological Theory* (S. Segalowitz and F. Gruber, Eds.). Academic Press, New York, 1977: 93–106.
28. Dennis, M., and Whitaker, H., Language acquisition following hemidecortication: Linguistic superiority of the left over the right hemisphere. *Brain Lang.*, 1976, **3**: 404–433.
29. Diamond, M., New data supporting cortical asymmetry differences in males and females. *Behav. Brain Sci.*, 1980, **3**: 233–234.
30. Entus, A., Hemispheric asymmetry in processing of dichotically presented speech and nonspeech stimuli by infants. In: *Language Development and Neurological Theory* (S. Segalowitz and F. Gruber, Eds.). Academic Press, New York, 1977: 64–73.
31. Fromkin, V., Krashen, S., Curtiss, S., Rigler, D., and Rigler, M., The development of language in Genie: A case of language acquisition beyond the "critical period." *Brain Lang.*, 1974, **1**: 81–107.
32. Galaburda, A. M., and Kemper, T. L., Cytoarchitectonic abnormalities in developmental dyslexia: A case study. *Ann. Neurol.*, 1979, **6**: 94–100.
32a. Galaburda, A. M., Sherman, G. F., and Geschwind, N., Developmental dyslexia: Third consecutive case with cortical anomalies. Poster presented at the Annual Meeting of the Society for Neuroscience, Boston, 1983.
33. Gardner, H., and Winner, E., Artistry and aphasia. In: *Acquired Aphasia* (M. Sarno, Ed.). Academic Press, New York, 1981: 361–384.
34. Geschwind, N., and Behan, P., Left-handedness: Association with immune disease, migraine, and developmental learning disorder. *Proc. Natl. Acad. Sci. U.S.A.*, 1982, **79**(16): 5097–5100.
35. Gesell, A., *The First Five Years of Life: A Guide to the Study of the Preschool Child*. Harper & Brothers, New York, 1940.
36. Gesell, A., and Ames, L., The development of handedness. *J. Genet. Psychol.*, 1947, **70**: 155–175.
37. Goodglass, H., and Quadfasel, F., Language and laterality in left-handed aphasics. *Brain*, 1954, **77**: 521–548.
38. Hauser, S., DeLong, G., and Rosman, N., Pneumographic findings in the infantile autism syndrome. *Brain*, 1975, **98**: 667–688.
39. Hécaen, H., and Sauguet, J., Cerebral dominance in left-handed subjects. *Cortex*, 1971, **7**: 19–48.
40. Hines, M., Prenatal diethylstilbestrol (DES) exposure, human sexually dimorphic behavior and cerebral lateralization. Doctoral dissertation, UCLA, 1981.
41. Hines, M., and Shipley, C., Prenatal exposure to diethylstilbestrol (DES) and the development of sexually dimorphic cognitive abilities and cerebral lateralization. *Dev. Psychol.*, 1984, **20**: 81–94.
42. Hood, P., and Perlstein, M., Infantile spastic hemiplegia: II. Laterality of involvement. *Am. J. Phys. Med.*, 1955, **34**: 457–466.
43. Kempler, D., and Curtiss, S., The changing neuropsychological profile of Turner's syndrome. Unpublished manuscript.

44. Kimura, D., Sex differences in intrahemispheric organization of speech. *Behav. Brain Sci.*, 1980, **3**: 240–241.

45. Kinsbourne, M., The ontogeny of cerebral dominance. In: *The Neuropsychology of Language* (R. Rieber, Ed.). Plenum Press, New York, 1976: 181–191.

46. Krashen, S., Language and the left hemisphere. *UCLA Working Papers in Phonetics*, 1972, **24**.

47. Krashen, S., Lateralization, language learning, and the critical period: Some new evidence. *Language Learning*, 1973, **23**(1): 63–74.

48. LeMay, M., and Culebras, A., Morphologic differences in the hemispheres demonstrable by carotid arteriography. *N. Engl. J. Med.*, 1972, **287**: 168–170.

49. Lenneberg, E., *Biological Foundations of Language*. Wiley, New York, 1967.

50. Levy, J., Lateralization and its implications for variation in development. In: *Developmental Plasticity* (E. Gollin, Ed.). Academic Press, New York, 1981: 175–228.

51. Levy, J., The origins of lateral asymmetry. In: *Lateralization in the Nervous System* (S. Harnad, R. Doty, L. Goldstein, J. Jaynes, and G. Grauthamer, Eds.). Academic Press, New York, 1977: 195–209.

52. Levy, J., Meck, B., and Staikoff, J., Dysfunction of the left cerebral hemisphere in autistic children. Unpublished manuscript, 1978.

53. Luria, A., *Traumatic Aphasia: Its Syndromes, Psychology, and Treatment*. Mouton, The Hague, 1970.

54. Mateer, C., Rapport, R., and Kettrick, C., Cerebral organization of oral signed language responses: Case study evidence from amytal and cortical stimulation studies. *Brain Lang.*, 1984, **21**: 123–135.

54a. Mayberry, R., Fischer, S., and Hatfield, N., Sentence repetition in American Sign Language. In: *Language in Sign: International Perspectives on Sign Language* (J. Kyle and B. Woll, Eds.). Groom Helm, London, 1983.

55. McGlone, J., Sex differences in functional brain asymmetry. *Cortex*, 1978, **14**: 122–128.

56. McGlone, J., Sex differences in human brain asymmetry: A critical survey. *Behav. Brain Sci.*, 1980, **3**: 215–263.

57. Melekian, B., Lateralization in the human newborn at birth: Asymmetry of the stepping reflex. *Neuropsychologia*, 1981, **19**: 707–711.

58. Millar, J., and Whitaker, H., The right hemisphere's contribution to language: A review of the evidence from brain-damaged subjects. In: *Language Functions and Brain Organization* (S. Segalowitz, Ed.). Academic Press, New York, 1983: 87–113.

59. Milner, B., Hemispheric specialization: Scope and limits. In: *The Neurosciences: Third Study Program* (F. O. Schmitt and F. G. Worden, Eds.). MIT Press, Cambridge, Mass., 1974: 75–89.

60. Milner, B., Branch, C., and Rasmussen, T., Observations on cerebral dominance. In: *Ciba Foundation Symposium on Disorders of Language* (A. de Reuck and M. O'Connor, Eds.). Churchill Livingstone, London, 1964: 200–214.

61. Milner, B., Taylor, L., and Sperry, R., Lateralized suppression of dichotically presented digits after commissural section in man. *Science*, 1968, **161**: 184–185.

62. Molfese, D., Freeman, R., and Palermo, D., The ontogeny of brain lateralization for speech and nonspeech stimuli. *Brain Lang.*, 1975, **2**: 356–368.

63. Morgan, M., Embryology and inheritance of asymmetry. In: *Lateralization in the Nervous System* (S. Harnad, R. Doty, L. Goldstein, J. Jaynes, and G. Krauthamer, Eds.). Academic Press, New York, 1977: 173–194.

64. Netley, C., Dichotic listening of callosal agenesis and Turner's syndrome patients. In: *Language Development and Neurological Theory* (S. J. Segalowitz and F. A. Gruber, Eds.). Academic Press, New York, 1977: 134–143.

65. Netley, C., and Rovet, J., Specific verbal deficits in children with abnormalities of sex

chromosome complement. Paper presented at the International Neuropsychological Society Annual Meeting, San Francisco, 1980.

65a. Neville, H., Effects of early sensory and language experience on the development of the human brain. In: *Neonate Cognition: Beyond the Blooming Buzzing Confusion* (J. Mehler and R. Fox, Eds.). Erlbaum, Hillsdale, N. J., 1984.

66. Neville, H., Electroencephalographic testing of cerebral specialization in normal and congenitally deaf children: A preliminary report. In: *Language Development and Neurological Theory* (S. J. Segalowitz and F. A. Gruber, Eds.). Academic Press, New York, 1977: 122–131.

66a. Newport, E., Constraints on learning: Studies in the acquisition of ASL. In: *Papers and Reports on Child Language Development* (Stanford), 1984, 23: 1–22.

67. Ounsted, C., and Taylor, D., *Gender Differences: Their Ontogeny and Significance*. Churchill Livingstone, London, 1972.

68. Penfield, W., and Roberts, C., *Speech and Brain Mechanisms*. Princeton University Press, Princeton, N.J., 1959.

69. Poizner, H., Bellugi, U., and Iragui, V., Apraxia and aphasia for a visual–gestural language. Unpublished manuscript, 1983.

70. Rankin, J., Aram, D., and Horwitz, S., A comparison of right and left hemiplegic children's language ability. Paper presented at the International Neuropsychological Society Annual Meeting, San Francisco, 1980.

71. Russell, W., and Espir, M., *Traumatic Aphasia*. Oxford University Press, London, 1961.

72. Rutter, M., and Folstein, S., Genetic influences and infantile autism. *Nature*, 1977, 265: 726–728.

73. Sasanuma, S., Do Japanese show sex differences in brain asymmetry?: Supplementary findings. *Behav. Brain Sci.*, 1980, 3: 247–248.

74. Saul, R., and Gott, P., Language and speech lateralization by amytal and dichotic listening tests in agenesis of the corpus callosum. In: *Conference on Human Brain Function* (D. O. Walter, L. Rogers, and J. M. Finze-Fried, Eds.). Brain Information Service, Los Angeles, 1976: 138–141.

75. Segalowitz, S., and Chapman, J., Cerebral asymmetry for speech in neonates: A behavioral measure. *Brain Lang.*, 1980, 9: 281–288.

76. Tallal, P., Perceptual and linguistic factors in the language impairment of developmental dysphasics: An experimental investigation with the Token Test. *Cortex*, 1975, 11: 196–205.

77. Tallal, P., Rapid auditory processing in normal and disordered language development. *J. Speech Hear. Res.*, 1976, 19: 561–571.

78. Tanguay, P. E., Clinical and electrophysiological research. In: *Autism: Diagnosis, Current Research and Management* (E. R. Ritvo, B. Freeman, E. M. Ornitz, and P. E. Tanguay, Eds.). Spectrum, New York, 1976: 75–84.

79. Taylor, D., Differential rates of cerebral maturation between sexes and between hemispheres. *Lancet*, 1969, 2: 140–142.

80. Turkewitz, G., Gordon, B., and Birch, M., Head turning in the human neonate: Effect of prandial condition and lateral preference. *J. Comp. Physiol. Psychol.*, 1968, 59: 189–192.

81. Waber, D., Sex differences in cognition: A function of maturation rate. *Science*, 1976, 192: 572–574.

82. Waber, D., Sex differences in mental abilities, hemisphere lateralization, and rate of physical growth at adolescence. *Dev. Psychol.*, 1977, 13: 29–38.

83. Wada, J., Clarke, R., and Hamm, A., Cerebral hemispheric asymmetry in humans. *Arch. Neurol.*, 1975, 32: 239–246.

84. Witelson, S., Bumps on the brain: Right–left asymmetry as a key to functional lateraliza-

tion. In: *Language Functions and Brain Organization* (S. Segalowitz, Ed.). Academic Press, New York, 1983: 117–144.

85. Witelson, S., Early hemisphere specialization and interhemispheric plasticity: An empirical and theoretical review. In: *Language Development and Neurological Theory* (S. J. Segalowitz and F. A. Gruber, Eds.). Academic Press, New York, 1977: 213–287.

86. Witelson, S., and Pallie, W., Left hemisphere specialization for language in the newborn. *Brain*, 1973, **96**: 641–646.

87. Woods, B., and Teuber, H., Changing patterns of childhood aphasia. *Ann. Neurol.*, 1978, **3**: 273–280.

88. Wyke, M., *Developmental Dysphasia*. Academic Press, New York, 1983.

89. Zaidel, D., and Sperry, R., Memory impairment after commissurotomy in man. *Brain*, 1974, **97**: 263–272.

90. Zaidel, E., Auditory vocabulary of the right hemisphere following brain bisection of hemidecortication. *Cortex*, 1976, **12**: 191–211.

91. Zaidel, E., Concepts of cerebral dominance in the split brain. In: *Cerebral Correlates of Conscious Experience* (P. Buser and A. Rougeul-Buser, Eds.). Elsevier, Amsterdam, 1978: 1263–1284.

92. Zaidel, E., Linguistic competence and related functions in the right cerebral hemisphere of man following commissurotomy and hemispherectomy. Doctoral dissertation, California Institute of Technology, Pasadena, 1973.

93. Zaidel, E., Reading in the disconnected right hemisphere: An aphasiological perspective. In: *Dyslexia* (Y. Zotterman, Ed.). Pergamon Press, Oxford, 1981: 67–91.

94. Zaidel, E., Unilateral auditory language comprehension on the Token Test following cerebral commissurotomy and hemispherectomy. *Neuropsychologia*, 1977, **15**: 1–18.

95. Zurif, E., and Bryden, M., Familial handedness and left–right differences in auditory and visual perception. *Neuropsychologia*, 1969, **7**: 179–188.

EARLY BRAIN INJURY AND PATHOLOGICAL LEFT-HANDEDNESS: CLUES TO A SYNDROME

PAUL SATZ, PhD,[1] **DONNA L. ORSINI, PhD,**[1] **ERIC SASLOW, MD,**[2]
and ROLANDO HENRY, PhD[1]

Departments of [1]Psychiatry and [2]Pediatrics

The conference title of "Dual Brain: Hemispheric Specialization in the Human" provides an interesting theme for the current chapter, which addresses a special situation in which the normal pattern of lateralization is altered. We will show that an early brain lesion to one cerebral hemisphere (mild or severe) may produce alterations not only in hemispheric specialization but in other domains of lateral development. These domains will be shown to include any or all of the following: shifts in manual dominance, trophic changes in the extremities, transfer of hemispheric speech specialization, and/or intrahemispheric reorganization of visual–spatial cognitive functions. (A detailed review including illustrative cases, can be found in 29.)

The associated changes in lateral development, which may affect motor, anthropometric, and/or cognitive structures, have escaped recognition as a clinical syndrome. It will be argued that this syndrome exists, and involves individuals with known or suspected brain injury, even if otherwise asymptomatic. It is caused by a hemispheric lesion that is predominately left-sided, with onset before age 6, and that encroaches upon the speech zones of the frontal–temporal–parietal cortex. Identification of these individuals, all with manifest left-handedness (MLH), will be shown to have implications for diagnosis and remediation and for models of recovery of function.

The primary clue to the syndrome, which we choose to refer to as "pathological left-handedness" (PLH), is the presence of MLH in an individual with known or suspected early brain injury. Why? The reason is that the incidence of MLH has long been known to be raised (approximately twofold) in individuals (e.g., epileptic) with verified early brain injury (1, 9, 24). This increase in MLH is due to a small proportion (approximately 20%) of individuals with natural right-handedness (NRH) who, because of early (mild or severe) injury to the left hemisphere, suffer a hypofunc-

Acknowledgments: Supported in part by funds from a National Institute of Health grant to Paul Satz (NS18462-03) and a National Institute of Mental Health grant to Rolando Henry (MH08865-02). We gratefully acknowledge the critical comments of Dr. Marcel Kinsbourne in the preparation of this chapter.

tion of the contralateral hand that causes a *shift* in manual preference to the left
(25, 26). The model of PLH (25, 26) also states that only a small proportion of NRH
individuals, with early left-sided damage, will shift handedness: this shift depends,
in part, on whether the lesion enroaches on the speech zones of the frontal–temporal–
parietal cortex, and possibly on genotypic variables that affect the manual transfer
threshold. Predictions from the model have been confirmed in studies of epileptics
(28, 30), mental retardates (32), and children with suspected brain injury (3, 19).
The model predicts at least two groups of MLH in the population. One is a "pathological" group (PLH) whose members would have developed as right-handers but
who, because of early left-sided brain injury (mild or severe), masquerade as left-
handers. The other group consists of natural left-handers whose handedness is determined by genetic and/or environmental factors.

Although the presence of left-handedness, especially in individuals with known
or suspected early brain injury, signals an increased likelihood of PLH, it does not
guarantee it. If the incidence of MLH is approximately twice as high (17–20%) in
populations with known early brain injury, then one might assume that half of these
patients are PLH.* The likelihood of PLH would be even lower in individuals with
suspected or unverified brain injury. Therefore, the expression of MLH provides,
at best, a necessary though insufficient condition for the presence of PLH.

The purpose of this chapter is to show that previous efforts to identify cases of
PLH have been limited by failure to recognize other correlative traits that are also
altered by the lesion that produces PLH. Although some of these correlates of PLH
have long been known, they have not been recognized as an interrelated pattern of
traits that constitute a clinical syndrome. (See 29 for a review of this literature.)

The PLH Syndrome

Altered Hemispheric Speech Specialization (Right or Bilateral)

One of the more commonly recognized correlates of *early* left-brain injury in
dextrals, apart from PLH, is a reduction in the incidence of left-hemisphere speech
dominance. It has long been known that lesions in the left perisylvian and/or peri-
rolandic regions, if occurring before age 6 years, may *displace* speech and language
representation to the right hemisphere or to both hemispheres (1, 6, 11, 23,24). This
capacity of the right hemisphere (in genetic right-handers) to subserve speech and
language functions after early injury to the left hemisphere is observed indirectly in the
rather dramatic *preservation* or *recovery* of speech and language skills in right hemiplegics (6), left hemidecorticates (2, 5, 33), childhood aphasics (4, 12, 16, 35), and left
temporal lobe epileptics (23). The strongest evidence to date rests on the presurgery assessment of hemispheric speech dominance (using the Wada technique) in epileptic patients at the Montreal Neurological Institute (23). Patients *without* early clinical

*The incidence of MLH in the Penfield and Roberts (21) study dropped from 17% to 8% after ex-
clusion of those epileptic patients who had early left-sided brain injury.

evidence of left-sided injury showed the well-established unilateral left-sided representation of speech in the right-handed (96%) and the more variable unilateral and/or bilateral representation of speech in the left-handed (left = 70%; right = 15%; bilateral = 15%) (10, 27). However, in those patients with *early* clinical evidence of left-sided injury, two major results emerged: (1) an increase in MLH and (2) three times as great an incidence of right-hemispheric speech dominance in the left-handers (53%). Although no reference to PLH was made, the raised incidence of patients with both MLH *and* right-sided speech strongly implicates this phenomenon, especially as " . . . an early lesion that does not modify hand preference is on the whole unlikely to change the side of speech representation" (23: 359).

Impaired Visual–Spatial–Constructional Ability

A putative link between *early* left-sided brain injury and impaired visual–spatial–constructional ability was first reported by Lansdell (15). He tested 18 left-brain-injured epileptics, 15 of whom sustained their lesions prior to age 5; interestingly, *all* of the latter patients were left-handed (MLH), most probably pathological (PLH), and *all* had right-hemisphere speech (including the 3 right-handers) as verified by sodium amytal testing. Lansdell then examined the association between age when initial neurological symptoms appeared and the difference between verbal (V) and nonverbal (P, N) factors on the Wechsler–Bellevue Scale. He noted that the earlier the lesion, the less the verbal factor suffered, whereas the later the lesion (i.e., > age 5 years), the less the nonverbal factors suffered. He concluded that the relative sparing of verbal cognitive functions in the group with early left-sided injury may have been due to commitment of right-hemisphere tissue to displaced verbal functions, which consequently interfered with the growth of nonverbal abilities normally subserved by this hemisphere. Lansdell's hypothesis, which essentially predicts a paradoxical event — namely, preservation of verbal cognitive functions at the expense of nonverbal spatial functions following early left-sided brain injury — has enjoyed little recognition or firm empirical support. In fact, Kohn and Dennis (13) failed to observe an impairment in visual–spatial ability in four left-hemidecorticate patients whose language *and* visual–spatial skills were unequivocally isolated in the right cerebral hemisphere. It should be noted, however, that this null finding rests on an exceedingly small number of individuals who lacked a comparable intact though dysfunctional hemisphere. Also, despite the early onset of hemiplegia in each case, the age of surgery ranged from 10–18 years. If language functions were still represented on the left at the time of operation, nonverbal spatial skills might have remained spared.

An early study of hemiplegic children by Tizard, Paine, and Crothers (34) provided some additional support, albeit indirect, for an association between early left-brain injury and visual–spatial deficit. The authors investigated disturbances of sensation in 106 hemiplegic patients (59 right and 45 left) and found impairment in half of the cases, regardless of age of lesion onset. Interestingly, 57 of the right hemiplegics (n = 59) were left-handed (presumably PLH), despite the fact that in 22 cases the motor disability was very mild or absent. The authors then reported four cases with right hemiplegia (all MLH), three of whom had disturbances of sensation (e.g., stereognosis, two-point discrimination). In each of the latter cases (all presumably PLH), there was evidence of preserved verbal abilities and impaired perceptual–motor ability, suggesting a link between early left-brain injury and indices of left-handedness (PLH), preserved language, and impaired visual–spatial ability. In the fourth case, cortical sensation was intact, and there was no impairment in perceptual–motor ability.

The authors may have overlooked an important connection between cortical sensation and perceptual–motor ability, their primary concern being the predictive role of cortical sensation for ultimate motor function in hemiplegics. They did note that " . . . a definite relationship seemed to exist between skeletal undergrowth (i.e., bony shortening as opposed to merely muscular underdevelopment) and sensory defects" (34: 630). They were unable to explain how these various factors interrelated, and whether they could be caused by a single underlying lesion. A clue in this study was the association between unilateral skeletal undergrowth (i.e., hemihypoplasia) and sensory defect, which should have suggested a parietal lobe lesion. In fact, the first report on this association was published a decade earlier in a seldom-referenced paper by Penfield and Robertson (22). The Tizard et al. study contributes what may be one of the primary biological markers of PLH — namely, trophic changes in the right upper and/or lower extremities.

Right Hemihypoplasia

The cases reported by Penfield and Robertson (22) comprised all operations performed between 1933 and 1943 on epileptics with focal lesions in whom evidence of bodily asymmetry was clearly established. The authors stated:

> It has long been obvious that decrease in growth of one half of the body, or of one member, may result from a lesion of the corresponding portion of the spinal cord at an early age or from a large birth injury of the opposite hemisphere of the brain. In the cases here described evidence will be presented to show that limitation of growth is produced by lesions of the cerebral cortex alone, but only if such lesions have a specific localization. (22: 405)

That specific localization, in each case, involved lesion of the *postcentral gyrus*. In each case, the lesions occurred *before age 2 years*. Although some of the patients had additional lesions (e.g., of the precentral gyrus), all had lesions common to the postcentral gyrus. The authors also noted that the often subtle smallness of the limbs (hands, fingers, and/or feet) associated with lesions of the postcentral gyrus is usually less than that produced by a lesion of the anterior horns of the spinal cord or by a deep cerebral lesion.

Whereas the Tizard et al. (34) study suggests an association between impaired cortical sensation and perceptual–motor deficit in right hemiplegics, and an association between skeletal undergrowth and sensory impairment, Penfield and Robertson (22) identified the age and locus of the lesion associated with unilateral skeletal undergrowth, which, incidentally, could also impair tactile sensory discrimination (i.e., a parietal lobe lesion). Each study focused on only separate parts of what probably constituted, in some patients, the PLH syndrome. Landauer (14) reviewed 22 literature cases of *congenital hemiatrophy* involving the arm and/or the leg. None were hemiplegic. He reported that of the 22 cases, 16 involved the left body side and 6 the right body side. Of particular interest, 5 of the 6 cases with right hemiatrophy (i.e., hemihypoplasia) were left-handed while only 2 of the 16 cases with left hemiatrophy were left-handed. Although the author was puzzled by this relationship, it suggests that right-sided skeletal undergrowth might represent a biological marker of PLH. This possibility was insightfully suggested by Schmidt and Wilder (31) in their discussion of soft signs in the neurological examination of epileptics.

> For instance, why is a certain patient left-handed? A family history of left-handedness was genetically predestined. On the other hand, he may have used the left hand preferentially because an early or minimal defect in the left cerebral hemisphere impaired the use of the right hand. Early acquired defects of one cerebral hemisphere may lead to a reduction in somatic growth on the opposite side of the body, resulting in shorter and smaller limbs. (31: 126)

This hypothesis was recently investigated in a large sample of epileptic patients and a matched sample of non-brain-injured psychiatric controls (30). The epileptic patients ($n = 230$) were divided into subgroups based on age of lesion onset (i.e., early: birth–age 2; middle: ages 2–17; and late: ages > 17) and side of lesion (left, right, bilateral). Results were as follows: (1) An increased incidence of MLH was observed, but only in epileptic patients with early onset and with focal EEG abnormalities ($8/36 = 22\%$). (2) A robust relationship between EEG focus (left or right) and manifest hand preference was also observed, but only in the epileptic patients with early or middle onset; approximately 90% of the patients with MLH with an EEG focus (early and middle onset) had a left-sided EEG abnormality, which fits predictions from the model of PLH (25, 26). (3) A significant relationship was observed between EEG focus and pedal asymmetry scores, but only for patients with early onset of seizures; patients with early-onset left-sided lesions (EEG) had a significantly shorter right foot ($\bar{x} = -0.26$ cm), whereas patients with early-onset right-sided lesions (EEG) had a shorter left foot ($\bar{x} = 0.18$ cm). (4) The pedal asymmetry scores were shown to be a *potential marker* of PLH. All of the MLH patients who were predicted to be highly *suspect* of PLH (i.e., lesion = focal, left-sided, and early onset) had a shorter right foot.

The unique demonstration in the study of Satz *et al.* (29) was the suggested relationship between MLH (probably PLH) and right-sided pedal asymmetry, both of which were associated with a lesion that was focal, left-sided, and of early onset. Unfortunately, as in most of the preceding studies, only components of the full PLH syndrome were assessed.

The coupling of MLH *and* right-sided pedal asymmetry with a lesion that was predominantly left-sided and of early onset signals the presence of three key signs of the PLH syndrome. What remains unknown, in these suspected PLH individuals, is the status of hemispheric speech specialization, language and visual–spatial competency, and familial sinistrality. While the other studies discussed have shown a relationship between some of these variables and MLH and/or early left-sided brain injury, no study to date has simultaneously demonstrated the full syndrome of PLH. Nor has any study identified the critical areas within the left hemisphere responsible for the alterations in lateral development that constitute this syndrome. This research awaits prosecution.

To date, we have studied 12 consecutive cases that illustrate some of the dominant features of the syndrome. With the exception of four cases drawn from other reports, these patients were referred for reasons other than PLH. We recently reported a description and analysis of these cases (29). For purposes of brevity, these cases are presented in tabular form in Table 1, which lists each element of the syndrome as follows:

1. MLH.
2. Right-sided or bilateral speech representation.
3. Relatively preserved verbal cognitive functions.
4. Impaired visual–spatial functions.
5. Hemihypoplasia of the right upper and/or lower extremity.
6. Low probability of familial sinistrality.

What is striking is the high frequency of positive signs within and between individual cases. At least four of the six symptoms were present in each case, despite a

TABLE 1

SUMMARY OF THE 12 CASES WITH REGARD TO THE PRESENCE OR ABSENCE
OF DOMINANT FEATURES OF THE PLH SYNDROME

Case	MLH or A	Familial Sinistrality	Relatively Intact Language	Visual–Spatial Deficits	Right-sided or Bilateral Speech Representation	Right-sided Trophic Changes	Early Trauma (Birth–Age 2)
1	+	U	+	+	+	U	+
2	+	+	+	+	+	+	+
3	+	U	+	+	U	+	+
4	+	+	+	+	+	+	+
5	+	+	+	+	U	+	+
6	+	+	+	+	U	+	+
7	+	+	+	+	−	+	+
8	+	U	+	+	+	+	+
9	+	+	+	+	−	+	U
10	+	+	+	+	+	+	U
11	+	+	+	+	U	+	+
12	+	+	+	+	−	−	+

Note. + = presence of traits; − = absence of traits; U = unknown; A = ambidextrous.

number of instances in which the presence of the sign was unknown. In fact, there were only four instances in all of the cases in which the expected sign was absent, suggesting that the presence of any two positive signs in an individual (e.g., MLH and visual–spatial impairment) increases the likelihood of additional signs of the PLH syndrome.

Perhaps the most remarkable features of these 12 individuals with MLH, none of whom reported a positive history of familial sinistrality, were the almost complete *dissociation* between verbal cognitive and visual–spatial–constructional functions. Reports of spared or preserved language were consistently contrasted by reports of impaired visual–spatial performance in the same individual, despite clear evidence of early left-sided brain injury in seven of the cases (1–6, 12) and indirect evidence in two additional cases (7, 8). Moreover, in two of the cases (1, 4), the Wada test confirmed right-sided or bilateral speech representation. In three other cases (2, 8, 10) the presence of visual–spatial impairment was associated with indirect signs of right-sided speech organization based on a verbal dichotic-listening task.

The dissociation between verbal and nonverbal cognitive functions was particularly evident on the WISC and WAIS scores. Significant discrepancies between verbal and performance IQ were found, with lower performance IQ scores observed in every case ($\bar{x}$ VIQ = 98.3, $\bar{x}$ PIQ = 78.3, $t = 7.87$, $p < .001$).

The relative sparing of speech and language functions, in individuals with known and/or suspected early left-hemisphere injury, suggests, albeit indirectly, that such sparing occurred primarily via displacement and/or reorganization of language functions in the right hemisphere. The dramatic impairment in visual–spatial and/or constructional ability in each of the cases lends indirect support for the displacement hypothesis; in five cases, this hypothesis was more directly supported by the Wada or dichotic-listening technique.

One might argue, on the other hand, that the impairment in visual–spatial ability is common to most left-handers, pathological or otherwise. Levy (17, 18) attributes the deficit to the effects of interference caused by an atypical bilateral mode of speech in the left-handed. This position, which postulates a "crowding" mechanism similar to that advanced by Lansdell (15), but without invoking a left-brain injury, has been unequivocally rejected in subsequent studies (7, 8, 20). We propose that the relationship between visual–spatial ability and MLH does exist, but only for a subset of the population — namely, those with PLH.

A final comment is necessary. Despite the consistency with which these signs appeared across cases, the reports provide only indirect support to date for the syndrome of PLH. More direct support must await the results of an empirical investigation that assesses all of the elements in a design that controls for the effects of lesion side, locus, and onset; that is based on more rigorous neuroradiological methods; and that uses a larger study sample. It is hoped that the present chapter will provide an heuristic framework for documenting the existence of a clinical syndrome with both diagnostic and theoretical implications, especially for models of recovery of function.

REFERENCES

1. Bingley, T., Mental symptoms in temporal lobe epilepsy and temporal lobe gliomas with reference to laterality of lesion and the relationship between handedness and brainedness. *Acta Psychiatr. Neurol.*, 1958, **33**, Suppl. **120**: 151–196.
2. Bishop, D., Linguistic impairment after left hemidecortication for infantile, hemiplegia? A reappraisal. *Q. J. Exp. Psychol.*, in press.
3. Bishop, D. V. M., Measuring familial sinsitrality. *Cortex*, 1980, **16**: 311–313.
4. Bullard-Bates, P. C., and Satz, P., A case of the pathological left-hander. *J. Clin. Neuropsychol.*, 1981, **5**: 128–129.
5. Dennis, M., Capacity and strategy for syntactic comprehension after left or right hemidecortication. *Brain Lang.*, 1980, **10**: 287–317.
6. Dennis, M., and Whitaker, H. A., Hemispheric equipotentiality and language acquisition. In: *Language Development and Neurological Theory* (S. J. Segalowitz and F. A. Gruber, Eds.). Academic Press, New York, 1977: 93–104.
7. Fennell, E., Satz, P., Van den Abell, T., Bowers, D., and Thomas, R., Visuo-spatial competence, handedness, and cerebral dominance. *Brain Lang.*, 1978, **5**: 206–214.
8. Hardyck, C., and Petrinovich, L. F., Left-handedness. *Psychol. Bull.*, 1977, **84**: 385–404.
9. Hécaen, H., and de Ajuriaguerra, J., *Left-Handedness: Manual Superiority and Cerebral Dominance*. Grune & Stratton, New York, 1964.
10. Hécaen, H., and Sauguet, J., Cerebral dominance in left-handed subjects. *Cortex*, 1971, **7**: 19–48.
11. Kinsbourne, M., The ontogeny of cerebral dominance. *Ann. N.Y. Acad. Sci.*, 1975, **263**: 244–250.
12. Kinsbourne, M., and Hiscock, M., Does cerebral dominance develop? In: *Language Development and Neurological Theory* (S. J. Segalowitz and F. A. Greuber, Eds.). Academic Press, New York, 1977.
13. Kohn, B., and Dennis, M., Selective impairments of visuo-spatial abilities in infantile hemiplegics after right cerebral hemi-decortication. *Neuropsychologia*, 1974, **12**: 505–512.
14. Landauer, W., Supermammary nipples, congenital hemihypertrophy and congenital hemiatrophy. *Hum. Biol.*, 1939, **11**: 447–472.
15. Lansdell, H., Verbal and nonverbal factors in right-hemisphere speech: Relation to early neurological history. *J. Comp. Physiol. Psychol.*, 1969, **69**: 734–738.
16. Lenneberg, E., *Biological Foundations of Language*. Wiley, New York, 1967.
17. Levy, J., Possible basis for the evolution of lateral specialization of the human brain. *Nature*, 1969, **224**: 614–615.
18. Levy, J., Psychobiological implications of bilateral asymmetry. In: *Hemispheric Function in the Human Brain*, (S. Diamond and J. Beaumont, Eds.). Halstead Press, New York, 1974: 121–183.
19. Liederman, J., and Coryell, J., The origin of left hand preference: Pathological and nonpathological influences. *Neuropsychologia*, 1982, **20**: 721–725.
20. Newcombe, F., and Ratcliff, G., Handedness, speech lateralization and ability. *Neuropsychologia*, 1973, **11**: 399–407.
21. Penfield, W., and Roberts, L., *Speech and Brain Mechanisms*. Princeton University Press, Princeton, N.J., 1959.
22. Penfield, W., and Robertson, J. S. M., Growth asymmetry due to lesion of the post-central cerebral cortex. *Arch. Neurol. Psychiatry*, 1943, **50**: 405–430.
23. Rasmussen, T., and Milner, B., The role of early left-brain injury in determining lateralization of cerebral speech functions. *Ann. N.Y. Acad. Sci.*, 1977, **299**: 355–369.

24. Roberts, L. H., Functional plasticity in cortical speech areas and integration of speech. *Arch. Neurol. Psychiatry*, 1958, **79**: 275–283.
25. Satz, P., Pathological left-handedness: An explanatory note. *Cortex*, 1972, **8**: 121–135.
26. Satz, P., Left-handedness and early brain insult: An explanation *Neuropsychologia*, 1973, **11**: 115–117.
27. Satz, P., A test of some models of hemispheric speech organization in the left- and right-handed. *Science*, 1979, **203**: 1131–1133.
28. Satz, P., Baymur, L., and Van der Vlugt, H., Pathological left-handedness: Cross-cultural tests of a model. *Neuropsychologia*, 1979, **17**: 77–81.
29. Satz, P., Orsini, D. L., Saslow, E., and Henry, R., The pathological left-handedness syndrome. *Brain Cog.*, 1985, **4**: 27–46.
30. Satz, P., Yanowitz, J., and Willmore, J., Early brain damage and lateral development. In: *Interfaces in Psychology*. (R. Bell, J. Elias, R. Green, and J. Harvey, Eds.). Austin, Texas University Press, 1984.
31. Schmidt, R., and Wilder, B. J., *Epilepsy*. F. A. Davis, Philadelphia, 1968.
32. Silva, D. A., and Satz, P., Pathological left-handedness: Evaluation of a model. *Brain Lang.*, 1979, **7**: 8–16.
33. Smith, A., Principles underlying human brain functions in neuropsychological sequelae of different neuropsychological processes. In: *Handbook of Clinical Neuropsychology* (S. B. Filskov and T. J. Boll, Eds.). Wiley, New York, 1981: 175–226.
34. Tizard, J. P. M., Paine, R. S., and Crothers, B., Disburbances of sensation in children with hemiplegia. *JAMA*, 1954, **155**: 628–632.
35. Woods, B. T., and Teuber, H. L., Changing patterns of childhood aphasia. *Ann. Neurol.*, 1978, **3**: 273–280.

DICHOTIC-LISTENING TECHNIQUES IN THE STUDY OF HEMISPHERIC ASYMMETRIES

DOUGLAS NOFFSINGER, PhD
Department of Head and Neck Surgery

Overview

This is the third decade of active interest and research in the use of dichotic-listening techniques for the study of hemispheric asymmetries in the normal and abnormal brain. A chapter of this text could easily be devoted entirely to lists of things that one hemisphere does better than the other as determined by use of dichotic-listening techniques. While most students of dichotic listening will agree that the right-ear–left-hemisphere system is adept at handling temporal patterns and other attributes of speech, and the left-ear–right-hemisphere network is skilled at handling nonverbal acoustic sequences such as melody and environmental sounds, this distinction is not thought free from question.

Instead of attempting an exhaustive review of the voluminous dichotic-listening literature, this chapter will concentrate on an explanation of dichotic-listening tasks and how difficult versions of such tests force the auditory system to process incoming signals in a way it would not ordinarily employ. Examples will be given of dichotic-listening behavior from normal listeners and from subjects with cortical damage, since the study of such behavior has contributed importantly to the formulation of a model of auditory function that explains dichotic listening. The model that best fits the data obtained from lesioned patients will be presented, along with implications of the model for the study of hemispheric asymmetries in the normal human. Data presented throughout the text that are not attributed to other sources were collected in my laboratory.

Normal Brain Studies

The term "dichotic listening," as used in this chapter, refers to a situation in which both ears receive signals in a roughly simultaneous fashion. In a laboratory setting, this usually is done by having a subject listen through earphones to signals

Acknowledgments: Previously unpublished data presented in this chapter were collected with the support of the National Institute of Neurological and Communicative Disorders and Stroke through the mechanism of grant No. NS 11859. This support is gratefully acknowledged. David Bellaire, MA, tested most of the subjects. Amy B. Schaefer, MA, designed and made the figures, and she, Charles D. Martinez, MA, and Bruce R. Gerratt, PhD did helpful critiques of the text.

127

that are different at the two ears, although they may be related to one another. The signals are delivered by totally independent channels, so that the events at each ear can be manipulated separately. One dichotic-listening task that will be used as an example throughout this chapter is dichotic nonsense syllables (3), in which a person listens to a pair of syllables, such as "pa" and "ta," and tries to identify each of them correctly. The syllables are never the same at the two ears, and the set of syllables from which the syllable pairs are drawn is small — example, the six syllables formed by combination of each of the stop plosives and the vowel "a." Over a series of trials, presentation of such syllable pairs allows the establishment of a percentage of correct responses for each ear, and thus the identification of the ear that is better at recognizing the syllables. This ear is said to have an advantage for the stimuli being utilized, and therefore the commonly occurring phrases in the dichotic-listening literature such as "The subject has a right-ear advantage for dichotic nonsense syllables," or "The subject has a left-ear advantage for dichotic musical chords."

The ear advantage established in this way is no inconsequential matter. If the ear advantage for a particular class of signals (see Table 1) is consistent in human beings, it is thought to represent the advantage of the opposite cortical hemisphere for perception of the materials. In this manner, dichotic listening furnishes a way to evaluate the asymmetry in function of the two hemispheres for various types of acoustic signals. Continuing with dichotic nonsense syllables as an example, most human beings show a right-ear advantage for these syllables, leading to the conclusion that the left hemisphere is dominant for their perception.

If this were all one could conclude from dichotic-listening experiments, it would be a small yield indeed. The ear advantages revealed by such tasks are often quite small; they require many stimulus presentations to establish; and the listening task required of the subject is quite demanding and not particularly pleasant. Additionally, if the only unusual quality found in one test session about a patient or subject is the absence of a right-ear advantage for dichotic nonsense syllables, one has learned nothing of importance about lateral dominance or anything else.

There is more to it, of course. Normative studies, and, more critically, studies of patients with lesions at specific parts of the central auditory nervous system have made apparent an important fact: Stringently controlled dichotic speech stimuli force the auditory system to work in ways that it would not ordinarily do, such that each ear has only one way to route signals to the cortex. Under routine listening circumstances, each ear has both ipsilateral and contralateral pathways available to transmit signals. A signal entering the left ear can move up pathways on the left side of the brain stem to the left hemisphere, the ipsilateral route, or can cross the brain stem to the right side and move up pathways there to the right hemisphere, the contralateral route. In fact, under ordinary circumstances, signals entering each ear move up both ipsilateral and contralateral pathways to the brain, assuring a widespread, duplicative representation of all signals in both halves of the brain.

Dichotic listening, under conditions of precise signal control, suppresses the

TABLE 1
EAR ADVANTAGES FOR VARIOUS DICHOTIC SIGNALS

Right-Ear Advantage	Left-Ear Advantage	No Ear Advantage	Variable Ear Advantage
Digits (20)	Melodies (21)	Vowels (6, 37)	Tone bursts (13, 14, 50)
Words (22)	Musical chords (16, 18)	Isolated fricatives (11)	
Nonsense syllables (consonant–vowel syllables, or CVs) (17, 22, 28, 30, 38)	Environmental sounds (9, 25)	Rhythms (18, 44)	
Formant transitions (26)	Emotional sounds and hummed melodies (24)	Hums (non-melodic) (49)	
Backward speech (23)	Intonational contour or emotional tone processed independent of their linguistic medium (51)		
Morse code (33)			
Pitch change in Thai words (by Thais) (49)	Complex pitch perception (39, 40)		
Difficult rhythms (31)			
Concrete word recall (15)			
Intonational contour or emotional tone used in linguistic decisions (51)			
Tonal sequences with frequency transitions (19)			
Processing and ordering temporal information (2, 12)			
Movement-related tonal signals (47, 48)			
Liquids in initial position (10)			
Reaction time to CVs (45)			
Voicing and place dimensions of CVs (35)			

ipsilateral route of access to the brain for each ear. A syllable presented to the right ear ascends to the cortex by way of the left brain stem route, the contralateral pathway, and is represented first in the left cortical hemisphere. A syllable directed to the left ear must travel the right brain stem pathways, its contralateral route, and is represented first in the right cortical hemisphere. In addition, lesion data discussed later suggest that after reaching the right hemisphere, left-ear signals must cross the corpus callosum to the left hemisphere, where they compete for processing with right-ear signals.

The ability of the dichotic-listening technique to force a signal presented to one ear to be initially represented only in the contralateral hemisphere's auditory field is what makes the procedure so important in the study of hemispheric asymmetries. This ability provides to audition a tool of similar importance to that of tachistoscopic techniques in vision.

Hemispheric Asymmetries

In Table 1, hemispheric asymmetries for various kinds of dichotic signals are listed. In particular, the table gives examples of dichotic signals that produce a right-ear advantage, a left-ear advantage, *no* ear advantage, or ear advantages that are divided among the three categories just described. Although the categories in Table 1 are designed only to give a representative summary of the stimulus sets that have been used to seek hemispheric asymmetry, they also allow insight into the kinds of signals to which one hemisphere or the other is most receptive. Speech (words, syllables) generates a right-ear–left-hemisphere advantage; music and less deliberately structured sounds produce a left-ear–right-hemisphere advantage; static sounds generate no ear advantage; and dichotic tone bursts yield ear advantages that are equally distributed across right-ear, left-ear, and no ear advantages.

Dominance Effects versus Lesion Effects

Two important effects can be demonstrated by dichotic-listening techniques. The "dominance effect" is the advantage in performance by one ear attributable to its location being contralateral to the hemisphere that is dominant for the signals being used. This advantage is usually small and is best elicited by dichotic stimuli that are brief and virtually simultaneous in time. Even under such strict conditions, the demonstration of a dominant ear requires many trials. A "lesion effect" describes the breakdown in one or both ear's performance on a dichotic-listening task, due to the location of brain damage. Such breakdown is often dramatic, sometimes producing near-chance performance by the ear on the side opposite the cortical damage (4).

Unfortunately, the distinction between the two effects is often blurred. For example, the devastating impact of a stroke on one ear's performance on a dichotic nonsense syllable task is often accompanied by a corresponding increase in the unaffected ear's performance. The real cause of the improved performance by the unaffected ear is a lesion effect that eliminates competition for processing. In effect, this turns the dichotic procedure into a monotic one and is often mistakenly described as an increase in hemispheric dominance, a conclusion that implies an assumption or takeover of responsibilities that the unaffected hemisphere did not previously possess. In adults, at least, this is seldom the case in any clinically meaningful way. Longitudinal studies of recovering stroke victims' dichotic-listening abilities are not consistent with such plasticity of the adult auditory cortex (32, 46).

Dominance Effect

Figure 1 illustrates the behavior of normal listeners when listening to dichotic nonsense syllables. The right ear has an advantage over the left ear when the syllables are simultaneous in onset (zero msec onset time difference), and maintains that advantage for most conditions in which the syllable onsets are not aligned. Across all time conditions displayed in Figure 1, the right-ear advantage for the syllables for

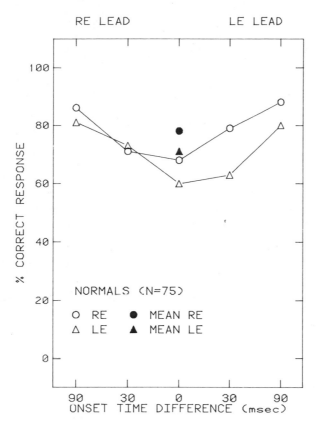

Figure 1. Dichotic nonsense syllable results obtained from 75 normal listeners. Correct response rate is shown on the vertical axis. The relationship between syllable onsets in the two ears is shown on the two horizontal axes. Open symbols represent each ear's scores for the five different onset time alignments. The filled symbols are the scores for each ear averaged across the five onset time differences. Open and filled circles represent the right ear. Open and filled triangles represent the left ear. Presentation was at 58-dB hearing level. The subjects were forced to give two responses to each pair of syllables. Stimuli were counterbalanced such that each ear received identical numbers and types of syllables. Sixty pairs of syllables were presented during the simultaneous condition (0-msec onset time difference) and 30 pairs were presented during each of the time-staggered conditions.

these listeners is 7%. Listening one ear at a time—that is, monotically—all of these listeners can correctly and consistently identify all of the nonsense syllables. It is the special nature of the dichotic competition that enables one to see the right-ear advantage.

Exactly what produces a right-ear advantage for these syllables and other ear advantages for other stimuli is unclear. For the syllables, it has become clear that the right-ear signal and the left-ear signal compete for final processing in the dominant left hemisphere (42). Speculation about why the left-ear signal operates at a slight disadvantage in such competition has produced confusion. Cullen *et al.* (8) attribute the left-ear disadvantage to the fact that the left-ear signal must traverse the corpus callosum and thus has a longer pathway and an increased number of synapses through which to pass. The longer-pathway–more-synapses problem produces a reduced signal–noise ratio for the left-ear signal, and thus it is processed slightly less efficiently. While this notion is appealing in its simplicity, it remains unproven.

It is important at this point to note that the size of the ear advantage usually elicited from normal listeners for dichotically presented speech and tonal signals is neither consistent across listeners nor overly robust (26, 27). For example, if one presents a complement of dichotic nonsense syllables to a single subject over a long series of test sessions, the size of the right-ear advantage will be nearly normally distributed over those sessions. Put another way, 25–30% of the sessions will result in no ear advantage or a left-ear advantage. A similar finding occurs if one administers only a single test session to a large number of subjects. Some 27% of them will show no ear advantage for that one session. However, over repeated trials, the overwhelming majority of these 27% will demonstrate a clear right-ear advantage. This distribution of the right-ear advantage over multiple trials or among a large population tested one time has been shown for both adults and children (34, 43).

Injured Brain Studies

Lesion Effect

HEMISPHERIC LESIONS

Figure 2 illustrates the behavior of the two ears when a lesion effect is present. These are data from the ears of 39 right- and 39 left-hemisphere stroke victims. All of these 78 patients had at least some involvement of the temporal lobe. All had normal hearing sensitivity and normal discrimination for meaningful speech presented monotically in both ears. The dichotic stimuli were the nonsense syllables discussed throughout this chapter. Note the virtually perfect ipsilateral right-ear performance and virtually chance left-ear performance for the right-hemisphere cases shown in Figure 2A. This is a good example of the classic contralateral ear effect (7), in which the ear on the side opposite the damaged hemisphere is at a marked disadvantage. The ipsilateral ear, however, is helped by the situation, since it now has little meaningful competition for dichotic processing, and performs better than even normal listeners' ears on the task (see Figure 1 for comparison).

The lesion effect is not so prominent for the left-hemisphere cases shown in Figure 2B. The ipsilateral left ear performs well, but neither as well as the right ear of right-hemisphere cases nor as well as the left ear of normal listeners. The contralateral right ear performs poorly, much like the left ear of the right-hemisphere subjects.

The apparent marked difference in lesion effects between right- and left-hemisphere lesions shown in Figures 2A and 2B is misleading. If one divides, on the basis of neurological, radiological, and aphasic test data, the 39 left-hemisphere cases into a group with primarily anterior lesions and a group with primarily posterior

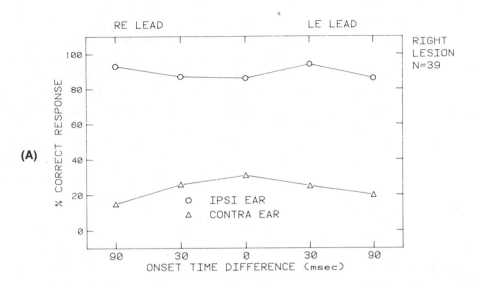

(A)

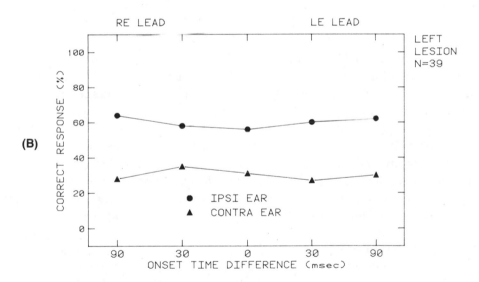

(B)

Figure 2. (A) Dichotic nonsense syllable results obtained from 39 subjects who had experienced right-hemisphere strokes involving at least the temporal lobe. Correct response rate and onset time differences are portrayed in the same fashion as shown in Figure 1. Ipsilateral (right-ear) results are represented by open circles and contralateral (left-ear) results are shown as open triangles. The other experimental variables explained in the legend to Figure 1 also apply here. (B) Dichotic nonsense syllable results obtained from 39 subjects who had experienced left-hemisphere strokes involving at least the temporal lobe. Correct response rate and onset time differences are portrayed as they were in previous figures. Ipsilateral (left-ear) results are represented by filled circles and contralateral (right-ear) results are shown as filled triangles. See Figure 1 for other experimental variables which also apply here.

lesions, a new picture emerges. As is shown in Figure 3, the apparent marked difference in lesion effects produced by right- and left-hemisphere damage really reflects the presence of two populations in the original left-hemisphere group: a left anterior temporal lobe population (Figure 3A) that shows the same marked contralateral ear effect as does the right temporal lobe group (Figure 2A), and a left posterior temporal lobe group (Figure 3B) that has deficits in dichotic nonsense syllable performance with *both* ears.

The realization that damage to the hemisphere dominant for the materials being used can reduce both ears' performance is an important finding (see 36). It implies that some kind of final processing of both ears' input is accomplished in the dominant hemisphere, and that for speech, the processing is accomplished in regions that include the posterior left temporal lobe.

Data such as these lead to one of the paramount conclusions derived from dichotic-listening experiments. Damage to certain areas of the left hemisphere not only impairs the contralateral right ear's understanding of speech, but similarly hinders left-ear performance. Taken together with other normative and lesion studies (4, 36, and see review in 5), they make defensible the position that the left hemisphere is dominant for certain acoustic properties and/or temporal sequences that human speech possesses.

CORPUS CALLOSUM LESIONS

Additional crucial knowledge necessary to lay the foundation of a model of how dichotic stimuli are processed was provided by Sparks and Geschwind (41) and Milner *et al*. (29). They demonstrated that without a corpus callosum pathway between the two hemispheres, left-ear performance during dichotic listening wilted dramatically, often to virtual extinction of correct performance. This gave impetus to the notion that during dichotic speech stimulation, the left-ear signal ascends via the contralateral right brain stem pathway to the right hemisphere, and then must cross to the left hemisphere through at least the corpus callosum for final processing. This realization was also compatible with the finding that damage to the posterior temporal lobe in the left hemisphere could reduce both ears' performance on a dichotic speech task.

Although the patients in the studies just mentioned had surgically disconnected hemispheres, similar findings have been made in nonsurgical patients. Shown in Figure 4 are the dichotic nonsense syllable scores for 18 multiple sclerosis subjects with excellent hearing. The striking decrement in left-ear performance shown in the figures is seen in about 55% of all multiple sclerosis patients who have other than purely spinal cord symptoms. Note in Panels 1–6 of Figure 4A that both the mean scores across conditions for the left ear and the ranges of scores for the left ear are markedly worse than their right-ear counterparts. Test–retest sessions for nine of these subjects are shown in Panels 1–6 of Figure 4B. These sessions were separated by 2–4 weeks and were done to confirm the earlier findings, which they did. Although the results are fair game for speculative explanation, the most obvious conclusion seems the most compelling. These results represent an insidious, partial hemispheric disconnection syndrome caused by partial demyelination of the corpus callosum.

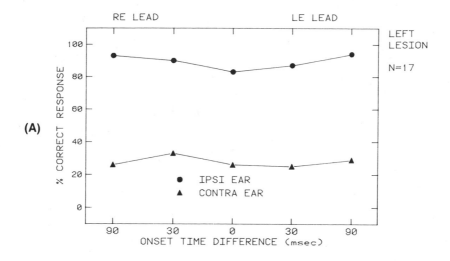

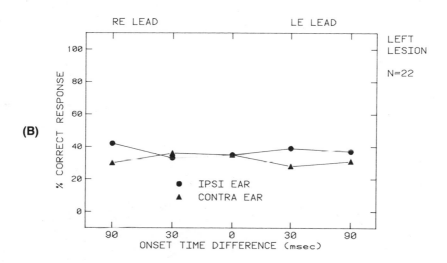

Figure 3. (A) Dichotic nonsense syllable results obtained from 17 subjects who had experienced left-hemisphere strokes involving at least the temporal lobe. These 17 subjects are drawn from the 39 subjects depicted in Figure 2B and are grouped here because radiologic, neurologic, and aphasic test data suggested primarily *anterior* temporal lobe damage. Correct response rate and onset time differences are shown as in previous figures. Ipsilateral (left-ear) data are shown as filled circles and contralateral (right-ear) data are shown as filled triangles. See Figure 1 for other experimental variables which also apply here. (B) Dichotic nonsense syllable results obtained from 22 subjects who had experienced left-hemisphere strokes involving at least the temporal lobe. These 22 subjects are drawn from the 39 subjects depicted in Figure 2B and are grouped here because radiologic, neurologic, and aphasic test data suggested primarily *posterior* temporal–parietal area damage. Correct response rate and onset time differences are shown as in previous figures. Ipsilateral (left-ear) data are shown as filled circles and contralateral (right-ear) data are shown as filled triangles. See Figure 1 for other experimental variables which also apply here.

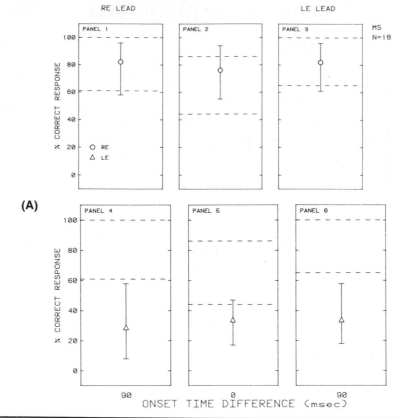

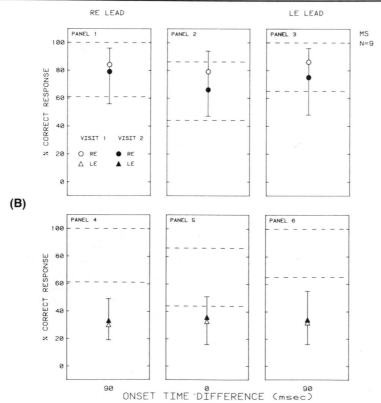

136

Subjects like the multiple sclerosis patients are potentially valuable in the study of hemispheric asymmetry, since they represent a class of subject with gradual rather than congenital or sudden isolation of the right hemisphere from the left. What remains to be seen is whether such gradual isolation produces different behaviors from those often seen in sudden hemispheric disconnection.

THEORETICAL CONSIDERATIONS

In Table 2, much of the work discussed in this chapter is capsulized. Although the section labeled "Explanation" is a means of accounting for the lesion effects observed by many scientists, it is also a model that explains dichotic speech perception, based on the work of Sparks *et al.* (42) and Sparks and Geschwind (41).

Unaddressed in the model are how and why the auditory system responds in the way it does when confronted with dichotic auditory signals like speech. Cullen *et al.* (8) confronted some of these issues. One of their concerns was the mechanism that separates and controls routing of contralateral and ipsilateral signals coming from the ears. They hypothesized, based on animal studies by Aitken and Webster (1), that cells in the medial geniculate bodies give preferential passage to contralateral signals when both ears are stimulated. Aitken and Webster (1) observed cells in the cat's medial geniculate that not only responded better to contralateral stimulation than to ipsilateral stimulation, but actually enhanced the contralateral response at the expense of the ipsilateral response during stimulation of both ears. Such a gating mechanism could be responsible for the suppression of ipsilateral route transmission, although there is no definitive evidence that this is the case.

It is unknown why the human auditory system would develop in a way that forces dichotic speech signals to compete for the attention of a final processor in the left posterior temporo-parietal area (42), and that allows a single lesion in that area to disrupt dichotic processing of signals from both ears. One would think that having the capability for processing information in each hemisphere, not an unusual arrangement in the human brain, would be more efficient and advantageous, since it would allow a person to hear correctly twice as much during dichotic-listening situations as during monotic-listening ones and to be more immune to the effects of unilateral brain lesion. However, that certainly is not the case for humans. When

---

Figure 4. (A) Dichotic nonsense syllable results obtained from 18 subjects with medically diagnosed multiple sclerosis. Correct response rate and onset time differences are shown as in previous figures. Panels 1–3 show right-ear results (open circles) and ranges (vertical bars), and panels 4–6 show left-ear results (open triangles) and ranges. The horizontal dashed lines encompass the range of performance of the right and left ears of 80 normal listeners on these same conditions. See Figure 1 for other experimental variables which also apply here. (B) Dichotic nonsense syllable results obtained from nine subjects with medically diagnosed multiple sclerosis. Correct response rate and onset time differences are shown as in previous figures. Panels 1–3 show right-ear findings and ranges (vertical bars) at test (open circles) and retest (filled circles) sessions, and panels 4–6 give similar findings for the left ear (open and filled triangles). The horizontal dashed lines encompass the range of performance of the right and left ears of 80 normal listeners on these same conditions. See Figure 1 for other experimental variables which also apply here.

TABLE 2
DICHOTIC LISTENING TO SPEECH: CONDITIONS AND EXPLANATION

Conditions
   Stimuli are brief, simultaneous speech units whose onsets, offsets, and durations are carefully controlled.
Commonly used
   Dichotic nonsense syllables: "pa," "ta," "ka," "ba," "da," "ga."
Expected results — normal listeners
   Over repeated trials, a right-ear advantage is seen. Usually ranges from 6–12%. Right ear typically scores from 65–75% and left ear from 55–65% if listeners are unsophisticated.
Expected results — brain lesions
   Ear contralateral to temporal lobe lesion shows breakdown. When posterior left temporal lobe is damaged, both ears show breakdown. When corpus callosum is damaged, left ear shows breakdown.
Explanation
   1. In dichotic format, posterior left temporal lobe does final processing of signals from both ears.
   2. Ipsilateral routes of access from ear to cortex are suppressed.
   3. Left-ear signal must cross to right brain stem, ascend to right temporal lobe, then cross corpus callosum to receive processing by left posterior temporal lobe.
   4. Right-ear signal crosses to left brain stem, and then has relatively direct access to processing by the left posterior temporal lobe.

trying to identify dichotic nonsense syllables, the accurate processing capacity of the human auditory system is only 30–50% greater for dichotic listening than it is for monotic listening. This is a far cry from the 100% improvement one could expect if dichotic listening produced a processing capability that was twice the monotic one. In addition, a single lesion in the left posterior temporo-parietal area can ruin perception of speech presented dichotically for both ears.

When confronted with a conclusion about the organization of the human brain that does not seem particularly logical or practical, such as the monotic versus dichotic issue in auditory processing, it is usually wise to reexamine the premises on which the conclusion is based. Dichotic listening of the sort usually foisted on subjects in research laboratories is rarely encountered in nature. People almost never listen that way. To assume that examination of the peculiarities of processing artificial dichotic speech tokens gives any clue to why the auditory system is organized and works as it does is not sensible.

Dichotic listening is a useful tool with which to study auditory system organization, hemispheric asymmetries, and the effects of brain damage. However, it will probably never provide much insight into why the system works as it does. In fact, it is worth remembering that even the basic assumption that the left hemisphere is dominant for speech ignores the fact that it may very well be dominant for many attributes that speech only happens to possess, or more likely, that speech possesses *because* of the way the brain hemispheres are organized in humans. This cause-and-effect question may never be resolved. Despite that, within some overall grand scheme, the way the hemispheres are organized and asymmetric may be sensible, efficient, and as yet not quite comprehensible to their hosts.

REFERENCES

1. Aitken, L., and Webster, W., Medial geniculate body of the cat: Organization and responses to tonal stimuli of neurons in ventral division. *J. Neurophysiol.*, 1972, **35**: 365.

2. Berlin, C., and Cullen, J., Dichotic signs of speech mode listening. In: *Structures and Process in Speech Perception* (A. Cohen and S. Nooteboom, Eds.). Springer-Verlag, Berlin, 1975: 296–311.

3. Berlin, C., Lowe-Bell, S., Cullen, J., Thompson, C., and Loovis, C., Dichotic speech perception: An interpretation of right ear advantage and temporal offset effects. *J. Acous. Soc. Am.*, 1973, **53**: 699–709.

4. Berlin, C., Lowe-Bell, S., Jannetta, P., and Kline, D., Central auditory deficits after temporal lobectomy. *Arch. Otolaryngol.*, 1972, **96**: 4–10.

5. Berlin, C., and McNeill, M., Dichotic listening. In: *Contemporary Issues in Experimental Phonetics* (N. Lass, Ed.). Academic Press, New York, 1976: 327–387.

6. Blumstein, S., Tartter, V., Michel, D., Hirsch, B., and Leiter, E., The role of distinctive features in the dichotic perception of vowels. *Brain Lang.*, 1977, **4**: 508–520.

7. Bocca, E., Calearo, C., Cassinari, V., and Migliavacca, F., Testing "cortical" hearing in temporal lobe tumors. *Acta Otolaryngol.*, 1955, **45**: 289–304.

8. Cullen, J., Berlin, C., Hughes, L., Thompson, C., and Samson, D., Speech information flow: A model. In: *Proceedings of a Symposium on Central Auditory Processing Disorders* (M. Sullivan, Ed.). University of Nebraska Press, Lincoln, 1975: 108–127.

9. Curry, F., A comparison of left-handed and right-handed subjects on verbal and non-verbal dichotic listening tasks. *Cortex*, 1967, **3**: 343–352.

10. Cutting, J., Ear advantage for stops and liquids in initial and final position. *J. Acous. Soc. Am.*, 1973, **54**: 285.

11. Darwin, C., Ear differences and hemispheric specialization. In: *Hemispheric Specialization and Interaction* (B. Milner, Ed.). MIT Press, Cambridge, Mass., 1975: 57–63.

12. Divenyi, P., and Efron, R., Spectral versus temporal features in dichotic listening. *Brain Lang.*, 1979, **7**: 375–386.

13. Divenyi, P., Efron, R., and Yund, E., Ear dominance in dichotic chords and ear superiority in frequency discrimination. *J. Acous. Soc. Am.*, 1977, **62**: 624–632.

14. Efron, R., and Yund, E., Dichotic competition of simultaneous tone bursts of different frequency: I. Dissociation of pitch from lateralization and loudness. *Neuropsychologia*, 1974, **12**: 249–256.

15. Fennell, E., Bowers, D., and Satz, P., Within-modal and cross-modal reliabilities of two laterality tasks. *Brain Lang.*, 1977, **4**: 63–69.

16. Friedrich, B., Perception of dichotic simultaneous and time-staggered synthetic musical chords. Doctoral dissertation, Northwestern University, 1975.

17. Gelfand, S., Hoffmand, S., Waltzman, S., and Piper, N., Dichotic CV recognition at various interaural temporal onset asynchronies: Effect of age. *J. Acous. Soc. Am.*, 1980, **68**: 1258–1261.

18. Gordon, H., Hemispheric asymmetries in the perception of musical chords. *Cortex*, 1970, **6**: 387–398.

19. Halpernin, Y., Nachson, I., and Carmon, A., Shift of ear superiority in dichotic listening to temporally patterned nonverbal stimuli. *J. Acous. Soc. Am.*, 1973, **53**: 46–50.

20. Kimura, D., Some effects of temporal-lobe damage on auditory perception. *J. Psychol.* (Canada), 1961, **15**: 156–165.

21. Kimura, D., Left–right differences in the perception of melodies. *Q. J. Exp. Psychol.*, 1964, **16**: 355–358.

22. Kimura, D., Functional asymmetry of the brain in dichotic listening. *Cortex*, 1967, **3**: 163–178.

23. Kimura, D., and Folb, S. Neural processing of background sounds. *Science*, 1968, **161**: 395–396.

24. King, F., and Kimura, D., Left-ear superiority in dichotic perception of vocal, non-verbal sounds. *J. Psychol.* (Canada), 1972, **26**: 111–116.

25. Knox, C., and Kimura, D., Cerebral processing of non-verbal sounds in boys and girls. *Neuropsychologia*, 1970, **8**: 227–237.

26. Lauter, J., Dichotic identification of complex sounds: Absolute and relative ear advantages. *J. Acous. Soc. Am.*, 1982, **71**: 701–707.

27. Lauter, J., Stimulus characteristics and relative ear advantages: A new look at old data. *J. Acous. Soc. Am.*, 1983, **74**: 1–17.

28. Lowe, S., Cullen, J., Berlin, C., Thompson, C., and Willett, M., Perception of simultaneous dichotic and monotic monosyllables. *J. Speech Hear. Res.*, 1970, **13**: 812–822.

29. Milner, B., Taylor, S., and Sperry, R., Lateralized suppression of dichotically presented digits after commissural section in man. *Science*, 1968, **161**: 184–185.

30. Morais, J., and Landercy, M., Listening to speech while retaining music: What happens to the right ear advantage? *Brain Lang.*, 1977, **4**: 63–69.

31. Natale, M., Perception of nonlinguistic auditory rhythms by the speech hemisphere. *Brain Lang.*, 1977, **4**: 32–44.

32. Noffsinger, D., Dichotic auditory behavior following cortical lesion. *NIH Progress Report*, *NS 11859-03*, 1979: 1–11.

33. Papcun, G., Krashen, S., Terbeek, D., Remington, R., and Harshman, R., Is the left hemisphere organized for speech, language and/or something else? *J. Acous. Soc. Am.*, 1974, **55**: 319–327.

34. Proctor-Loser, C., Reliability of the right ear advantage in 6-year old children. Master's thesis, Northwestern University, 1978.

35. Repp, B., Dichotic competition of speech sounds: The role of acoustic stimulus structure. *J. Exp. Psychol.*, 1977, **3**: 37–50.

36. Schulhoff, C., and Goodglass, H., Dichotic listening, side of brain injury and cerebral dominance. *Neuropsychologia*, 1969, **7**, 149–160.

37. Shankweiler, D., and Studdert-Kennedy, M., Lateral differences in perception of dichotically presented synthetic consonant–vowel syllables and steady-state vowels. *J. Acous. Soc. Am.*, 1966, **39**: 1256.

38. Shankweiler, D., and Studdert-Kennedy, M., Identification of consonants and vowels presented to left and right ears. *Q. J. Exp. Psychol.*, 1967, **19**: 59–63.

39. Sidtis, J., Predicting brain organization from dichotic listening performance: Cortical and subcortical functional asymmetries contribute to perceptual asymmetries. *Brain Lang.*, 1982, **17**: 287–300.

40. Sidtis, J., and Gazzaniga, M. Complex pitch perception after callosal section: Further evidence for a right hemisphere mechanism. *J. Acous. Soc. Am.*, 1981, **69**: S199.

41. Sparks, R., and Geschwind, N., Dichotic listening in man after section of neocortical commissures. *Cortex*, 1968, **4**: 3–16.

42. Sparks, R., Goodglass, H., and Nickel, B., Ipsilateral versus contralateral extinction in dichotic listening resulting from hemisphere lesions. *Cortex*, 1970, **6**: 249–260.

43. Speaks, C., and Niccum, N., Variability of the ear advantage in dichotic listening. *J. Am. Audiol. Soc.*, 1977, **3**: 52–57.

44. Spellacy, F., Lateral preference in the identification of patterned stimuli. *J. Acous. Soc. Am.*, 1970, **47**: 574–584.

45. Springer, S., Reaction-time measures of ear advantage in dichotic listening. *J. Acous. Soc. Am.*, 1973, **54**: 286.

46. Strauss, E., and Wada, J., Lateral references and cerebral speech dominance. *Cortex*, 1983, **19**: 165–177.
47. Sussman, H., Evidence for left hemisphere superiority in processing movement-related tonal signals. *J. Speech Hear. Disord.*, 1979, **22**: 224–235.
48. Sussman, H., MacNeilage, P., and Lumbley, J., Sensorimotor dominance and the right ear advantage in mandibular–auditory tracking. *J. Acous. Soc. Am.*, 1974, **56**: 214–216.
49. Van Lancker, D., and Fromkin, V., Hemispheric specialization for pitch and "tone": Evidence from Thai. *J. Phonetics*, 1973, 1, 101–109.
50. Yund, E., and Efron, R., Dichotic competition of simultaneous tone bursts of different frequency: II. Suppression and dominance functions. *Neuropsychologia*, 1975, **13**: 137–150.
51. Zurif, E., Auditory lateralization: Prosodic and syntactic factors. *Brain Lang.*, 1974, **1**: 391–404.

HEMIFIELD TACHISTOSCOPIC PRESENTATIONS AND HEMISPHERIC SPECIALIZATION IN NORMAL SUBJECTS

DAHLIA W. ZAIDEL, PhD

Department of Psychology

INTRODUCTION

Functional asymmetries in the two cerebral hemispheres are well established from over a century of clinical research into the behavioral effects of unilateral cortical lesions (22), as well as from over 30 years of experiments examining visual half-fields and dichotic listening in normal subjects (9, 31). Some of the characterizations of hemispheric specialization that have emerged from these studies include the views that the left hemisphere is specialized for verbal, detailed analysis, and logical or propositional thinking, whereas the right hemisphere is specialized for nonverbal, overall closure, and holistic or appositional thinking (3, 34, 43).

The purpose of the first part of this chapter is to provide a selective overview, rather than an exhaustive review, of the basic findings in hemifield tachistoscopic testing that have led to current conceptualizations of cerebral functional asymmetry. The standard topics in hemifield tachistoscopic research have been thoroughly treated elsewhere, and it is recommended that interested readers refer to those works for additional details (1, 7, 9). In the second part, a description will be given of a new line of research in which long-term semantic memory is explored in the two hemispheres. In all of the studies described here, the focus has been on normal right-handed subjects; left-handers paint a somewhat different picture, and a review of that literature is beyond the scope of this paper (see chapter by Satz *et al.*, this volume).

GENERAL BACKGROUND

Functional cerebral asymmetry in the normal brain has been the subject of countless investigations in the past two decades. Much of what was known prior to that time was based on studies in patients with unilateral, focal lesions. Such preparations provided investigators with fragmented behavior, the units of which could be studied systematically because some were selectively missing. In comparison, in the normal intact brain, hemispheric asymmetries cannot easily be teased apart, since the functional units are all interconnected. However, since the normal brain is what we wish to ultimately understand, it is important to devise effective experimental tools that will further the understanding of hemispheric specialization by highlighting the components of normal processing rather than infer them from deficit. Tachistoscopic hemifield stimulus presentations, more than dichotic-listening techniques,* provide an excellent tool for studying this problem.

In the 1960s, the work of Roger Sperry at Cal Tech and his coworkers on the commissurotomy patients operated on by P. J. Vogel and J. E. Bogen spurred interest in the tachistoscopic hemifield technique developed earlier in studies by the McGill group (40, 51).

It is important to recognize in detail the logic of alternative methods for studying hemispheric specialization. In studying the behavior of patients with unilateral brain damage, the assumption made is that functions or abilities that have become impaired are normally subserved by the impaired tissue. This, in essence, is a negative inference, and the evidence is indirect. Further, it is not always clear whether the observed functions are subserved by the damaged hemisphere or by the intact hemisphere on the opposite side. It is therefore important to find convergent evidence where the information for observed function is obtained with relatively healthy tissue. This is accomplished in tachistoscopic presentations to normal subjects.

The hemifield tachistoscopic technique capitalizes on known anatomical arrangements of sensory optic tracts and motor control pathways in the brain. Through partial decussation of optic neural pathways at the optic chiasma, sensory visual input occurring in one visual half-field reaches the hemisphere contralateral to the stimulated field (see Figure 1). Thus, complex visual input arising in the right visual half-field (RVF) is processed initially in the primary visual area of the left hemisphere, while stimuli in the left visual half-field (LVF) are processed first in the right hemisphere. Communication between the two hemispheres about highly patterned information processed in the two cortical visual areas is accomplished through interhemispheric cortical connections.

When a visual stimulus and a motor response are processed in the same hemisphere, a direct cortical route between visual and motor areas results in fast, efficient execution. On the other hand, when the stimulus reaches one hemisphere and the response originates in the other hemisphere, a time delay occurs, due to transfer of information through the corpus callosum or other forebrain commissures. The additional synaptic traffic and translation typically result in slower reaction time and less accurate responses.

Historically, Poffenberger (45) was the first to investigate systematically the latency of motor responses to tachistoscopic presentations falling on the different halves of the retina. His results showed that faster visual–motor responses were given

---

*"Dichotic listening" refers to the experimental condition where two competing messages, one in each ear, are heard simultaneously. Under these conditions, each ear projects predominantly to the contralateral hemisphere and with the proper response mode, say verbal or nonverbal, functional hemispheric asymmetries can be studied. This is the standard way of restricting auditory information to one hemisphere (see chapter by Noffsinger, this volume). The technique, however, is fraught with methodological and theoretical problems: It is technically more cumbersome, and the interpretation of the behavioral laterality effects is more speculative than results based on hemifield tachistoscopic presentations.

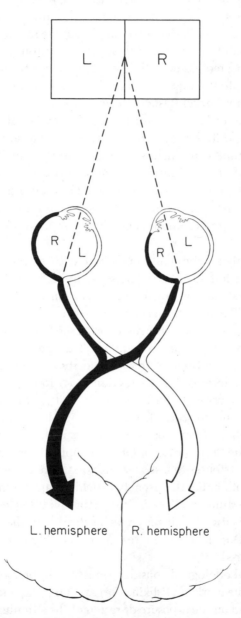

Figure 1. Schematic diagram of the classical visual system. On the top is a projection screen with a central point for gaze fixation. Images flashed on the left (L) project to the right hemisphere while images flashed on the right (R) project to the left hemisphere. The nasal part of the right eye and the temporal part of the left eye (black) transmit visual information to the left hemisphere; the nasal part of the left eye and the temporal part of the right eye (white) transmit visual information to the right hemisphere.

when controlled within the same hemisphere rather than across the two hemispheres. The long latency differentials were attributed to transmission time across commissural fibers. More specifically, Poffenberger used a simple manual reaction-time task in which the subject had to decide, and then press a button as fast as possible, if a brief flash of light projected either in the ipsilateral or contralateral hemifield had occurred. Poffenberger found that reaction times to contralateral light stimuli were 3 msec slower than to ipsilateral flashes. He concluded that the extra time was due to cross-callosal transfer of the motor (or visual) signal when stimulus and response were controlled by opposite hemispheres in the contralateral condition.

Choice reaction-time experiments typically show a much longer interhemispheric transfer time of about 30 msec. This may be due to psychological "translation" before and after transfer and can be expected to vary as a function of stimulus complexity. But interhemispheric transfer need not occur until a hemisphere is ready to send the results of a complex and independent computation. This can last up to 300 msec in some cases.

It is now commonly accepted that in order to ensure that the lateralized visual stimulus does reach the intended hemisphere, several standard procedures must be followed. The first is a steady gaze on a specific fixation point positioned on a screen in front of the subject. Then, quick tachistoscopic presentations of less than the 180 msec it takes to initiate a saccade in the direction of the flash must be used. The brief exposure duration is crucial in order to minimize "leakage" of information about the stimulus to the "wrong" hemisphere. In the majority of experiments, however, exposure durations of 100 msec or less are used in order to make the task harder and to observe the resulting error pattern. However, within the acceptable exposure range, it is often difficult to assess from the available data the significance for hemispheric specialization of long versus short exposures. An additional crucial control procedure is random alternation of tachistoscopic presentations to the LVF or RVF. This method contributes to a steady gaze on the fixation point, since on any one trial subjects cannot predict the visual half-field of input. Finally, it is important to define the size of the stimulated visual fields: Stimuli falling less than half a degree to either side of the fixation point may reach both hemispheres, due to bilateral macular projections. One degree or more — up to possibly nine degrees — on either side is usually considered "safe."

Several other methodological considerations should be mentioned. It became known early on from the work of Mishkin, Forgays, Orbach, and Heron that visual-laterality effects depend on the exposure duration of the stimulus, its horizontal and vertical eccentricity, its subtended visual angle, and, of course, the nature of the stimulus and of the task (52). Simultaneous bilateral presentation of two different stimuli, such as words set apart horizontally, often together with a neutral central stimulus between them which must be reported or identified first to ensure fixation, are said to yield stronger laterality effects than unilateral presentations (25). On the other hand, words presented as a continuous string across the central fixation point or even split apart to the left and right of fixation tend to evoke a left-to-right scanning bias that confounds the laterality effect. Such confounds can be minimized with unilateral, horizontal presentations of words in one hemifield at a time, but then the beginning edge of the word in the LVF is much farther away from fixation and maximum acuity than the beginning edge of the word in the RVF. This may not be serious if, in fact, when we read a word we actually focus our attention somewhere in the middle of it (48). Alternatively, words can be flashed vertically rather than horizontally. This would overcome the alleged asymmetry in eccentricity, but at the same time would introduce some unnaturalness and possibly some hemispheric bias in performing the requisite transformation.

RVF Superiority for Letters and Words

There is by now ample evidence for RVF superiority in tachistoscopic reading of single letters or words. With previous evidence for left-hemisphere specialization in language functions based on the damaged brain, this evidence is not surprising. Historically, however, when early workers in this field used hemifield presentations of letters or words, they concluded that RVF superiority for these stimuli must be due to scanning habits. Franz and Davis in 1933 (19) and Mishkin and Forgays in 1952 (40) published the first reports (2).

Franz and Davis obtained a LVF superiority because they divided four-letter words into LVF and RVF halves. Subjects "read" the material in their mind's eye from left to right, so that when attention finally focused on the RVF half, some stimulus decay must have occurred. On the other hand, Mishkin and Forgays described visual experiments in which English words were identified more accurately in the RVF. However, they too were misled by a confound with reading scanning habits. In their view, since in reading we scan from left to right, words situated to the right of each fixation draw particular attention, and a bias develops in favor of events occurring to the right of fixation. Mishkin and Forgays proved their point by presenting lateralized words in Yiddish, which, unlike English, is written from right to left. The scanning-habits hypothesis was confirmed when bilingual subjects reported more accurately Yiddish words appearing in the LVF than in the RVF, though this effect was not statistically significant. Although the LVF superiority over the RVF was smaller with the Yiddish words than that of the RVF with the English words, Mishkin and Forgays, in keeping with their interest in learning and experience, concluded that the results reflect reading habits.

However, subsequent hemifield studies in which great care was taken to control exposure duration, and in which sensitive measures such as reaction time were adopted, gaze fixation procedures undertaken, and handedness of subject considered, all proved — together with the early reports in the 1960s from Cal Tech — that these earlier results could be interpreted differently.

Thus, in 1961, Kimura published a report in which she suggested that RVF recognition superiority for English letters or words in normal subjects may be related to left-hemisphere specialization for linguistic material (27). Subsequently, in 1972, Carmon *et al.* reported shorter latencies for Hebrew letters in the RVF, not in the LVF (10). In sum, it is by now commonly agreed that letters, words, or digits are better recognized in the RVF than in the LVF (see 7, for review).

LVF Superiority in "Nonverbal" Material

While investigators in the late 1950s and early 1960s were preoccupied with verbal material, which, as expected, generally showed left-hemisphere specialization, it remained to be determined what functions were lateralized to the right cerebral hemisphere of normal subjects. Again, much of the work that followed was influenced by the work reported by Roger Sperry and his coworkers. In the 1960s, it became evident that the right hemisphere of patients whose two hemispheres had been disconnected surgically was superior to the left in visual–spatial tasks (4, 33). Although this by itself was not a new discovery, the knowledge having been gained earlier from work with patients suffering unilateral, localized cortical lesions (8, 23, 43, 44, and see 22 for review), the evidence was "direct" rather than inferred from negative results. It had a dramatic and immediate effect.

One of the earliest reports describing LVF superiority in normal subjects was published by Kimura (28, 30). The tasks consisted of enumerating and localizing in space tachistoscopically presented dots. The results were consistent with previous work reported about patients suffering from right or left temporal lobe lesions (29) and right or left parietal lesions (37, 54).

Other studies using tachistoscopic presentations confirmed LVF superiority for recognition of complex forms (14, 15, 16, 24), recognition of dot figures (38), recognition of overlapping figures (26), face recognition (46, 47), and line orientation (17, 20).

However, unlike consistent RVF recognition superiority for verbal material such as letters and words, LVF for nonverbal stimuli is smaller in comparison and, in general, less consistent. For example, subjects in Kimura's study (28) failed to demonstrate LVF superiority for nonsense shapes such as inkblots. Similarly, Hines (25) failed to demonstrate LVF superiority for complex Vanderplass figures, and Hatta and Dimond (21) found LVF superiority for complex shapes only with European subjects and not with Japanese (for additional examples, see 13). The important conclusion is that it is more difficult to demonstrate right- than left-hemisphere superiority. One possible explanation is that left-hemisphere interference occurs in most tasks, interference stemming from pervasive dominance of verbal-type reasoning in attentive tasks. Another explanation is lack of adequate experimental control for sex of subject; there are suggestive reports that women are particularly poor in right-hemisphere tasks.

An Example of Individual Differences: Sex of Subject

There is much controversy about the existence of sex differences in hemispheric specialization. Fairweather (18) estimates that in 103 out of 129 experiments using hemifield presentations, evidence does not support the view that men and women differ in degree of functional lateralization. However, given that the relatively few positive results have received much attention, it is important to outline the main findings.

The lability of the right hemisphere is commonplace in laterality research, as stated above, with both normal and clinical populations, but it is also most apparent in the area of gender differences. For instance, Kimura (30) found significant differences between the LVF and RVF on the dot localization task only in men, not in women. Similar results for dot localization tasks were reported by Davidoff (12).

This trend of weak or no field effects in women but not in men reportedly extends to a number of other tasks, such as perception of faces, perception of line orientation, or line detection (50).

In verbal tasks, there is general agreement that men show a greater magnitude of RVF advantage over their LVF than do women (6, 35, 39). However, in tasks that are not linguistically complex, or where an expressive component is lacking, the sex-related RVF advantage in men is reportedly diminished (5, 6).

Long-Term Semantic Memory in the Left and Right Hemispheres

In order to understand the basis for individual differences in hemispheric specialization, it is necessary to know the range and extent of such differences. Are they restricted to sensory processing or perceptual analysis, or do they also emerge in problem-solving strategies and the internal storage of experience?

Whether the material presented to normal subjects and patients with unilateral, focal lesions is linguistic or nonlinguistic, the visual sensory information must be sorted out and organized to form perception. It is logical to assume that the transformation of sensations into perceptions and higher cognitive constructs does not occur in a void. Visual sensations are meaningless patches of light, shade, or color unless they are processed by reference to a preexisting memory store of experiences. Cognitive psychologists have described such a system of internal representation and labeled it "long-term memory" (LTM) or "long-term semantic memory."

Within the information-processing approach to the study of memory, the theoretical framework adopted in my own research, semantic knowledge is considered an important component of LTM that is derived from past experience and is said to represent world knowledge (32). It is conceived by some as providing the basis for a range of functions from crossing the street on a green light to solving problems, making inferences, anticipating common events, and, importantly, accumulating new facts (53). By virtue of LTM, a person is said to be able to function within the environment in a meaningful way (42). The interaction with the environment involves a search through the multiple levels of information storage in LTM, a process that is facilitated by coherently structured internal organization of the information in the brain (36). Sensory input is processed in several stores or stages: LTM is conceptualized as the last store in a multiple-staged system (information processing) made up of several structural components (e.g., iconic store, short-term memory, and LTM). The duration of each store is variable. Iconic store lasts 250 msec, short-term memory lasts 20–30 sec, and LTM lasts from 30 sec to hours to years (11).

The question now occurs: Which of these information-processing stages reveals hemispheric specialization? If there are hemispheric differences, can those be demon-

strated separately for the iconic store, short-term store, or LTM? Many hemifield
studies have shown hemispheric differences in perceptual recognition and identification, but do these differences extend to the long-term representation of experience,
and thus to the cognitive styles that the two hemispheres apply to both affective and
cognitive problem solving? At the same time, do hemispheric differences occur in
the early stages of perception? Views diverge sharply on these issues (41).

The work of Sperry and his colleagues suggested that each hemisphere is an independent cognitive system with its own perceptions, memories, and characteristic
problem-solving styles. Thus, work with commissurotomy patients would lead us
to predict that hemispheric differences in hemifield testing should occur at any stage
of information processing. I will show that laterality effects extend to long-term
storage of experience in each hemisphere—that is, to LTM. Such differences in long-
term semantic memory in turn may underlie hemispheric differences in perception
and problem solving alike.

Fortunately for scientists of the mind, mental associations stored in LTM are
highly organized, and this organization lends itself to psychological analysis by using
reaction-time paradigms. For example, verification latency to the question "Is a robin
a bird?" can be compared to that for "Is a penguin a bird?" Since it takes longer to
respond to the second than to the first question, it is commonly considered by
cognitive psychologists that the mental distance between the concept "bird" and
"robin" is shorter than between "bird" and "penguin" (possibly because "bird" is
associated with flying, which robins are often seen to do, while penguins are not).
Through the use of verification or semantic-relatedness tasks, it is possible to construct a theoretical map of LTM.

In my own work I have attempted to do just that—namely, begin to construct
a map of semantic relationships among concepts stored in LTM in the left or right
cerebral hemisphere (55). The hope was to provide new clues about the mechanisms of functional asymmetries in humans, leaving the traditional emphasis on the
verbal–nonverbal dichotomy and on perceptual asymmetries during early stages of
information processing. In undertaking the task, the following assumptions were
made: (1) The two cerebral hemispheres are exposed to the same experiences, but
either LTM or retrieval from it is specialized; (2) "semantic" refers to "meaning"
in general and not to linguistic meaning alone; and (3) pictures denote meaning and
thus can be used as stimuli to test the right, nonlanguage hemisphere.

I chose a task that required making decisions about category membership—
that is, knowing whether or not specific instances are representations of specific
categories. Five natural superordinate categories, "furniture," "fruit," "vehicle,"
"weapon," and "vegetable," were chosen. Two types of instances, one highly typical
and one atypical, were selected to represent each of the five superordinate categories
(see Figure 2 for examples). Simple line drawings were prepared for each instance
according to norms provided in Rosch (49). Rosch had already tested normal subjects in the center of vision and found that those category instances that were previously rated as highly typical were verified with much shorter latencies than those

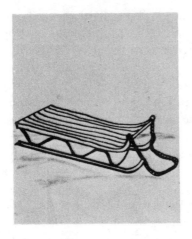 

Figure 2. Examples of pictures flashed on the left or right visual half-fields. These items are pictorial instances of natural superordinate categories. The two items on the top row are both members of the category of "vehicle." The sled has a low level of typicality whereas the car has a high level of typicality. The bottom two represent the category of "furniture," with the stove having a low level of typicality and the bed a high level of typicality.

that were rated atypical. The question, then, was whether this pattern is true in both visual half-fields or not.

The procedure consisted of flashing pairs of pictures on each trial. One member of a pair of instances appeared in the center of vision for 500 msec, while a second member appeared 700 msec later in either the LVF or RVF for 150 msec. The task was to decide whether or not the two simple pictures, together as a pair, belonged to the category named by the experimenter ahead of time. There were 80 subjects, with gender balanced, and responses were manual rather than verbal.

The results revealed a dramatically different pattern of latency responses for each hemisphere (55, 56, 57). Only performance in the LVF matched the pattern predicted from Rosch's results — that is, faster positive responses to highly typical instances than to atypical ones. Under the testing conditions adopted here, no difference was found in the RVF for these two levels of typicality. Furthermore, the interaction between visual half-field and typicality was significant. The important finding here was that it appeared that different selective emphases were given to specific concepts stored in LTM by each hemisphere. Since there were no significant differences in accuracy scores, it is logical to assume that the task was within the capacity of both hemispheres or that long-term storage was available in both. Thus, these results could be interpreted to reflect selective storage/retrieval from LTM in each hemisphere.

It is important to emphasize that these results extended beyond the mere demonstration of hemispheric specialization to a demonstration of relative hemispheric independence. In other words, the principal result was that each hemisphere treated typicality in a different way. Each hemisphere when probed directly revealed its own LTM. In short, the two hemispheres process information concurrently and independently even in the normal brain.

One potential implication of the finding is a hemispheric division of labor in the perception and analysis of visual events, not only in laboratory settings, as was the case here, but in daily experience as well. Clearly, we cannot expect a random registration of all events that impinge on our senses. Pickup of informatiom must be selective, and selection may be hemisphere-dependent. Thus, our reaction to the environment and our actions in the world may differ, depending on which hemisphere is in control. Future research will undoubtedly tell us which factors determine hemispheric control and how we can modulate these factors.

SUMMARY AND CONCLUSION

Past hemifield tachistoscopic studies with normal subjects have by and large verified characterizations of the dual mind that had originally been formulated in studies with the damaged brain. This convergent evidence is important, if only because damage cannot be perfectly localized and the contributing brain processes that become active following damage are not completely understood. At the same time, from the point of view of research in normal subjects, the studies on verbal and nonverbal stimulus material reviewed above have by and large extended rather than generated new knowledge about the dual mind. It has been suggested that this trend may have occurred because typical experiments on laterality effects, in both normal and clinical populations, have neglected the underlying issue of hemispheric semantic structure in LTM from which other asymmetries may follow. Since understanding, inferring, and recognizing are all processes that depend on the repository of accumulated knowledge in LTM, it is both theoretically and empirically important to chart the differential organization of long-term semantic memory in each hemisphere. The results of the study reported herein revealed hemispheric LTM asymmetry in storage/retrieval.

REFERENCES

1. Beaumont, J. G., Ed., *Divided Visual Field Studies of Cerebral Organization*. Academic Press, London, 1982.
2. Bertelson, P., Lateral differences in normal man and lateralization of brain function. *Int. J. Psychol.*, 1982, **17**: 173–210.
3. Bogen, J. E., The other side of the brain: II. An oppositional mind. *Bull. Los Angeles Neurol. Soc.*, 1969, **34**: 135–162.
4. Bogen, J. E., and Gazzaniga, M. S., Cerebral commissurotomy in man: Minor hemisphere dominance for certain visuospatial functions. *J. Neurosurg.*, 1965, **23**: 394–399.
5. Bradshaw, J. C., Bradley, D., and Patterson, K., The perception and identification of mirror reversed patterns. *Q. J. Exp. Psychol.*, 1976, **28**: 221–246.
6. Bradshaw, J. C., and Gates, E. A., Visual field differences in verbal tasks: Effects of task familiarity and sex of subject. *Brain Lang.*, 1978, **5**: 166–187.
7. Bradshaw, J. C., and Nettleton, N. C., *Human Cerebral Asymmetry*. Prentice-Hall, Englewood Cliffs, N.J., 1983.
8. Brain, R., Visual disorientation with special reference to the lesions of the right hemisphere. *Brain*, 1941, **64**: 43–62.
9. Bryden, M. P., *Laterality: Functional Asymmetry in the Intact Brain*. Academic Press, New York, 1982.
10. Carmon, A., Nachshon, I., Isseroff, A., and Kleiner, M., Visual field differences in reaction times to Hebrew letters. *Psychonom. Sci.*, 1972, **28**: 222–224.
11. Crowder, R. G., *Principles of Learning and Memory*. Erlbaum, Hillsdale, N.J., 1976.
12. Davidoff, J. B., Hemispheric differences in dot detection. *Cortex*, 1977, **13**: 434–444.
13. Davidoff, J. B., Studies with non-verbal stimuli. In: *Divided Visual Field Studies of Cerebral Organization* (J. G. Beaumont, Ed.). Academic Press, London, 1982: 29–55.
14. Dee, H. L., and Fontenot, D. J., Cerebral dominance and lateral differences in perception and memory. *Neuropsychologia*, 1973, **11**: 167–173.
15. Dee, H. C., and Hannay, H. J., Asymmetry in perception: Attention versus other determinants. *Acta Psychol.*, 1973, **37**: 241–247.
16. Fontenot, D. J., Visual field differences in the recognition of verbal and non-verbal stimuli in man. *J. Comp. Physiol. Psychol.*, 1973, **85**: 564–569.
17. Fontenot, D. J., and Benton, A. L., Perception direction in the right and left visual fields. *Neuropsychologia*, 1972, **10**: 447–452.
18. Fairweather, H., Sex differences: Little reason for females to play midfield. In: *Divided Visual Field Studies of Cerebral Organization* (J. G. Beaumont, Ed.). Academic Press, London, 1982: 147–194.
19. Franz, S. I., and Davis, E. F., *Simultaneous Reading with Both Cerebral Hemispheres: Studies in Cerebral Function*. Publications of UCLA in Education, Philosophy and Psychology, Vol. 1, Los Angeles, 1933: 99–106.
20. Hatta, T., Visual field differences in a mental transformation task. *Neuropsychologia*, 1978, **16**: 637–641.
21. Hatta, T., and Dimond, S. J., Comparison of lateral differences for digit and random forms recognition in Japanese and Westerners. *J. Exp. Psychol. (Hum. Percept.)*, 1980, **6**: 368–374.
22. Hécaen, H., and Albert, M. L., *Human Neuropsychology*. Wiley, New York, 1978.
23. Hécaen, H., de Ajuriaguerra, J., and Massonet, J., Les troubles visuo-constructifs par lésions pariéto-occipitales droites: Rôle des perturbations vestibulaires. *L'Encephale*, 1951, **1**: 122–179.

24. Hellige, J. B., and Cox, P. J., Effects of concurrent verbal memory on recognition of stimuli from left and right visual fields. *J. Exp. Psychol. (Hum. Percept.)*, 1976, **2**: 210–221.
25. Hines, D., Visual information processing in the left and right hemispheres. *Neuropsychologia*, 1978, **16**: 593–600.
26. Kershner, J. R., and Jeng, A., Dual functional asymmetry in visual perception: Effects of ocular dominance and postexposural processes. *Neuropsychologia*, 1972, **10**: 437–446.
27. Kimura, D., Cerebral dominance and the perception of verbal stimuli. *Can. J. Psychol.*, 1961, **15**: 166–171.
28. Kimura, D., Dual functional asymmetry of the brain in visual perception. *Neuropsychologia*, 1966, **4**: 275–285.
29. Kimura, D., Right temporal lobe damage: Perception of unfamiliar stimuli after damage. *Arch. Neurol.*, 1963, **8**: 264–271.
30. Kimura, D., Spatial localization in left and right visual fields. *Can. J. Psychol.*, 1969, **23**: 445–458.
31. Kimura, D., and Durnford, M., Normal studies on the function of the right hemisphere in vision. In: *Hemisphere Function in the Human Brain* (S. J. Dimond and J. G. Beaumont, Eds.). Elek, London, 1974: 25–47.
32. Klatzky, R. L., *Human Memory: Structures and Processes.* W. H. Freeman, San Francisco, 1975.
33. Levy-Agresti, J., and Sperry, R. W., Differential perceptual capacities in major and minor hemispheres. *Proc. Natl. Acad. Sci. U.S.A.*, 1968, **61**: 1151.
34. Levy, J., Possible basis for the evolution of lateral specialization of the human brain. *Nature*, 1969, **224**: 614–615.
35. Levy, J., and Reid, M., Variations in writing postures and cerebral organization. *Science*, 1976, **194**: 337–339.
36. Mandler, G., *Organization and Memory: The Psychology of Learning and Motivation*, Vol. 1. Academic Press, New York, 1967: 327–372.
37. Mcfie, J., Piercy, M. F., and Zangwill, O. L., Visual spatial agnosia associated with lesions of the right cerebral hemisphere. *Brain*, 1950, **73**: 167–190.
38. McKeever, W. F., and Huling, M. D., Right hemispheric superiority in graphic reproduction of briefly viewed dot figures. *Percept. Mot. Skills*, 1970, **31**: 201–202.
39. McKeever, W. F., and Jackson, T. L., Cerebral dominance assessed by object and color naming latencies: Sex and familial sinistrality. *Brain Lang.*, 1979, **7**: 175–190.
40. Mishkin, M., and Forgays, D. G., Word recognition as a function of retinal locus. *J. Exp. Psychol.*, 1952, **43**: 43–48.
41. Moscovitch, M., Information processing and the cerebral hemispheres. In: *Handbook of Behavioral Neurobiology*, Vol. 2 (M. S. Gazzaniga, Ed.). Plenum Press, New York, 1979: 379–446.
42. Norman, D. A., and Bobrow, D. G., On the role of active memory process in perception and cognition. In: *The Structure of Human Memory* (C. N. Cofer, Ed.). W. H. Freeman, San Francisco, 1976: 114–132.
43. Paterson, A., and Zangwill, O. L., Disorders of visual space perception associated with lesions of the right hemisphere. *Brain*, 1944, **67**: 331–338.
44. Piercy, M., Hécaen, H., and de Ajuriaguerra, Constructional apraxia associated with unilateral cerebral lesion: Left and right cases compared. *Brain*, 1960, **83**: 225–242.
45. Poffenberger, A. T., Reaction time to retinal stimulation with special reference to the time lost in conduction through nerve centers. *Arch. Psychol.*, 1912, **23**: 1–73.
46. Pollatsek, A., Bolozky, S., Well, A. D., Rayner, K., Asymmetries in the perceptual span for Israeli readers. *Brain Lang.*, 1981, **14**: 174–180.

47. Rizzolatti, G., and Buchtel, H. A., Hemispheric superiority in reaction time to faces: A sex difference. *Cortex*, 1977, **13**: 300–305.

48. Rizzolatti, G., Umilta, C., and Berlucchi, G., Opposite superiorities of the right and left cerebral hemispheres on discriminative reaction time to physiognomical and alphabetical material. *Brain*, 1971, **94**: 431–442.

49. Rosch, E., Cognitive representation of semantic categories. *J. Exp. Psychol. (Gen.)*, 1975, **104**: 192–233.

50. Sasanuma, S., and Kobayashi, Y., Tachistoscopic recognition of line orientation. *Neuropsychologia*, 1978, **16**: 239–242.

51. Sperry, R. W., Hemisphere deconnection and unity in conscious awareness. *Am. Psychol.*, 1968, **23**: 723–733.

52. Springer, S., *Left Brain, Right Brain*. W. H. Freeman, San Francisco, 1981.

53. Tulving, E., Episodic and semantic memory. In: *Organization of Memory* (E. Tulving and W. Donaldson, Eds.). Academic Press, New York, 1972: 382–403.

54. Warrington, E. K., and James, M., Disorders of visual perception in patients with localized cerebral lesions. *Neuropsychologia*, 1967, **5**: 253–266.

55. Zaidel, D. W., Long-term semantic memory in the two cerebral hemispheres. In: *Brain Circuits and Functions of the Mind: Festchrift for R. W. Sperry* (C. B. Trevarthen, Ed.). Cambridge Univeristy Press, Cambridge, England, in press.

56. Zaidel, D. W., Long-term storage of semantic relations in the left or right cerebral hemisphere. Paper presented at the International Neuropsychological Society meeting, Mexico City, 1983.

57. Zaidel, D. W., Long- versus short-term effects on semantic decisions in each cerebral hemisphere. Paper presented at the 6th Annual European International Neuropsychological Society meeting, Lisbon, 1983.

CLINICAL STUDIES OF
HEMISPHERIC SPECIALIZATION

INTRODUCTION

D. FRANK BENSON, MD
Department of Neurology

The topics to be discussed under the heading of clinical studies truly represent a continuum with the biological and psychological studies discussed thus far. The differences, while relatively subtle in the first presentations, reflect the increased amount of observation and categorization of clinical phenomena — an approach that becomes paramount in the later presentations. The clinical patient, a subject with behavioral abnormality based on brain alteration, replaces the normal human or the laboratory animal as the object of investigation. The initial reports in this section, while utilizing clinical information, remain strongly attached to hard-nosed, replicable laboratory techniques. As such, they act as a link between the behavior of the living patient and the procedures studied in the laboratory; nature's experiments, pathologically derived variations from the normal, are investigated by laboratory methods.

Following in sequence, the more clinically oriented observations, particularly those that suggest differences in the function of the two cerebral hemispheres, will then be presented. These studies utilize observations and investigations of disease states as the primary research tools, often using highly refined laboratory techniques as adjuncts. While the multiple differences in individual patients make this a less exacting approach and one that appears less promising for research, history shows that the observations of disease states made by properly trained clinicians have produced many important discoveries. Experience from clinical research centers clearly demonstrates that both types of investigations — laboratory and clinical — are of value, and that the accomplishments of combined efforts may be far greater than the sum of efforts limited to a single approach. The clinician–observer and the clinician–investigator may be the same individual, but, not infrequently, these tasks are better performed by two individuals working in cooperation.

With the exception of psychological studies, which have a long history, the laboratory study of abnormal behavior is a relatively new field. Electrophysiological studies are the best-established investigations of this type, and modern refinements are constantly increasing the usefulness of electrical studies. The electroencephalogram (EEG) was the brainchild of a psychiatrist, developed in the hope that severe mental disorders would show a diagnostic electrical pattern. This dream did not materialize, but the EEG did prove useful for the demonstration of serious brain disorders, particularly epilepsy. Following considerable technical innovation and improvement, sophisticated variations of the EEG technique now show promise in the study of a broad variety of conditions, including behavior disorders.

A second clinical laboratory approach, the correlation of altered cerebral metabolism with both health and disease states, has been difficult to study in the living human. Abnormalities of systemic metabolism have long been known to affect nervous function (e.g., hyperthyroidism, inappropriate ADH secretion, subacute combined sclerosis), but the behavioral concomitants of altered metabolic milieu of the brain have proved difficult to measure. The chemical concomitants of specific brain areas in postmortem specimens have been investigated for a number of years, but such investigations give only a static picture; studies of the dynamic alterations of metabolic constituents that underlie mental activity in the living, functioning human brain have remained crude. Even the exciting new neuroimaging techniques (CT and MRI scans) provide only a static, structural view of the brain. The recent introduction of a technique to image radioactive metabolites appears to have opened a new field, one with considerable promise for a better understanding of the chemical–metabolic alterations that occur with changing behavior in the active human brain. Human studies with these techniques can be augmented by appropriate animal investigations, the combination greatly enhancing current knowledge of brain activities.

Both the electrophysiological and the metabolic studies provide useful information for clinical investigations; they are technically complex, sophisticated laboratory studies capable of directly probing clinical states. As one side effect, these techniques are capable of providing previously unavailable information concerning asymmetrical functions in the cerebral hemispheres. The ability to investigate differences in individual hemisphere activation that may occur during behavioral responses provides an exciting new dimension.

In contrast to the recent flowering of the clinical laboratory approach, pure clinical research has a long and important history. Based on their own clinical observations, the ancients noted the importance of the brain for mental functioning and attempted to divide the brain into functional compartments. As far back as 400 B.C., Greek clinicians had noted that damage to one side of the skull produced motor paralysis on the opposite side of the body (3). Physical explanations of human behavior were not popular during the religious excesses of the Dark Ages, but with the Renaissance came an escape from religious dogma as a universal explanation and a return to the observation of human disease states. The clinical observation of crossed innervation was confirmed by the animal work of Morgagni (8), an early example of the clinician investigator. The basic split into an anterior/motor and a posterior/sensory organization of the cerebral hemispheres was clearly demonstrated by the work of Meynert (7). These basic observations provided important foundations for the flowering of clinical–anatomical investigations in the late 19th century, the Golden Era of the clinical–pathological correlations that provided much of the basis for modern medicine.

Language, particularly as exemplified by the language disturbance caused by brain damage (aphasia), was among the earliest topics in which separate hemispheric function was demonstrated by the clinical–anatomical method. Correlations of aphasic behaviors with the sites of brain damage have provided an approach to the understanding of mental behavior; these studies continue to evolve. While many excellent laboratory techniques for the study of language have become available, particularly in the past two decades (see chapters by D. F. Benson and E. Zaidel in this section), the fact that language is a uniquely human function has maintained an important position for the study of the clinical defect (aphasia) in language investigations. Not only was the study of aphasia important as a starting point for the correlation of focal brain function with language, but other abnormal behaviors could also be correlated with these anatomical observations. The study of aphasia and related disorders was, and continues to be, a major source of information concerning hemispheric asymmetry.

The study of epilepsy has offered another excellent avenue for probing human cerebral function. Epileptic seizures, particularly when focal, produce a variety of striking behavioral alterations (4), allowing correlation of behavior with the discharge sites. Both the clinical and the electrical findings are transient, however, and demand sophisticated sampling techniques and educated interpretation. The simple correlation of a behavior with an EEG abnormality has proved useful but not entirely adequate; similar correlations are now possible with many related studies, the aggregate providing valuable localizing information. For instance, the long-term residua following surgical removal of a single temporal lobe as an attempt to control seizures have offered an opportunity to investigate the relationship of mental behaviors such as memory, emotion, and appetite to both specific neuroanatomy (portions of the temporal lobe) and unilateral hemispheric function. Focal seizure problems, studied by both clinical and electrical techniques, offer a potentially rich source of behavior localizing information.

In recent years, it has become apparent that the right hemisphere has a relatively greater importance than the left hemisphere in many visual–spatial functions. While it has long been suspected that some visually oriented activities are primarily performed by the right hemisphere, work by many clinical investigators (1, 2, 5, 6) has clearly demonstrated the dominant status of the right hemisphere for a number of visual–spatial activities. Clinical correlation studies also suggest, however, that each hemisphere participates in most complex visual functions (e.g., construction), but in different manners; it has been suggested that the right hemisphere subserves visual–spatial discrimination, while the left carries out a more executive function (9). Newer localizing techniques such as the x-ray CT scan, coupled with observations of the behavior of brain-damaged patients, have allowed anatomical correlation with a number of visual defect syndromes, some of which appear to be localized to a single hemisphere. In this same manner, nonvisual behavioral abnormalities, coupled with the improved localizing techniques, are providing considerable additional information concerning the intricate functions of the human brain in cognitive and behavioral activities.

Of a great many new clinical laboratory techniques currently used for brain investigation, only two will be presented in this volume. One approach will out-

line some of the new techniques using stimulus-evoked responses and the results of
these studies as they pertain to cortical activation, particularly as they reflect hemispheric asymmetry. A second approach will discuss the current state and potential
uses of isotope metabolic studies in the demonstration of cortical asymmetry in
human disease processes. While far from a total exposition of the many clinical
laboratory approaches to hemispheric asymmetry currently under investigation, these
presentations will provide a picture of the diverse approaches now becoming available within the scope of clinical laboratory studies. Four clinical approaches will
be presented in the following pages, starting with a review of the functions of both
the left and the right hemisphere in language. Next will be a review of current
knowledge concerning visual disturbances based on damage to a single cerebral
hemisphere. Two presentations will provide insight into the usefulness and pitfalls
of investigations that use surgically treated epileptic patients for determining unilateral hemisphere function. Finally, the operative techniques and major behavioral
residua of two surgical procedures that allow study of individual hemisphere activity — hemispherectomy and callosal section — will be reviewed.

REFERENCES

1. Benton, A. L., Constructional apraxia and the minor hemisphere. *Confinia Neurologica*,
   1967, **29**: 1–16.
2. Benton, A. L., and Fogel, M. L., Three dimensional constructional praxis. *Arch. Neurol*,
   1962, **7**: 347–354.
3. Chadwick, J., and Mann, W. W., *The Medieval Works of Hippocrates*. Blackwell Scientific Publications, Oxford, 1950.
4. Daly, D. D., Ictal clinical manifestations of complex partial seizures. In: *Advances in
   Neurology*, Vol. 11. (J. K. Perry and D. D. Daly, Eds.). Raven Press, New York,
   1975: 57–83.
5. Kleist, K., Konstructive (optische) apraxia. In: *Handbuch der artzlichen erfahrungen in
   weltkriege 1914/1918* (K. Bonhoeffer, Ed.). Barth, Leipzig, 1934.
6. McFie, J., and Zangwill, O. L., Visual constructive disabilities associated with lesions of
   the left cerebral hemisphere. *Brain*, 1960, 83: 243–260.
7. Meynert, T., The brain of mammals. In: *Manual of Human and Comparative Biology*
   (S. Stricker, Ed.). New Sydenham Society, London, 1872.
8. Morgagni, J. B., *De sedibus et causis morborum per anatomen indagatis*. Padua, 1761.
9. Warrington, E. K., Constructional apraxia. In: *Handbook of Clinical Neurology*, Vol.
   4 (P. J. Vinken and G. W. Bruyn, Eds.). North-Holland, Amsterdam, 1969: 67–83.

HEMISPHERIC DIFFERENCES IN
EVENT-RELATED BRAIN POTENTIALS

WARREN S. BROWN, PhD, JAMES T. MARSH, PhD,
and RONALD E. PONSFORD, PhD
Department of Psychiatry

From the time of Hans Berger's (3) remarkable demonstration that electrical activity of the brain could be recorded from the human scalp, much interest has focused on relations between various aspects of the EEG and mental activity. This has resulted in the accumulation of a considerable data base relating various parameters of the EEG to levels of arousal and elements of cognitive functioning. The pioneering work of Sperry and his colleagues (57) in elucidating some fundamental features of functional cerebral asymmetry has stimulated the application of electrophysiological methods to the study of functional asymmetries of the brain. Over the past two or three decades, much has been learned about the relationship between EEG measures and functional cerebral asymmetries.

For the most part, electrophysiological studies of hemispheric differences have used two general methodologies. The first involves the study of the predominant frequencies of the ongoing EEG, comparing the spectral power in recordings from the two hemispheres during tasks that involve language or visual–spatial processes. Most studies of this kind have been based on the long-held assumption (15) of an inverse relationship between mental effort and the presence or amplitude of alpha waves (i.e., 8- to 10-Hz EEG waves), such that engagement of a hemisphere will result in suppression of alpha in that hemisphere. The majority of these studies have found reduced levels of alpha activity from the hemisphere most heavily engaged in the performance of the task (15). Thus, for example, alpha activity is reduced in left-hemisphere recordings as compared to right- while the subject is mentally composing a letter. The opposite situation obtains while the subject is putting together blocks to match a pictured design (22).

The second general approach has utilized event-related potentials (ERPs) — that is, the series of positive and negative voltage waves that follow in time-locked fashion the presentation of a stimulus to be processed by the subject. It is this latter ERP approach to the study of hemispheric specialization in humans that will be briefly discussed in this chapter.

Reviews of ERP studies have been published by Donchin *et al.* (14, 15), Hillyard and Woods (27), and Molfese (43). This chapter will present a selective review of the literature illustrating various ERP approaches to the study of cerebral asymmetries, including a number of studies done in our laboratory. We first review work from the late 1960s and the 1970s that addressed primarily the question of processing asymmetries observed in ERPs to language versus nonlanguage stimuli. We then illustrate research that focuses on lateralized ERP correlates of the processing of specific dimensions within language. Our own research on ERP correlates of perception of the meaning of noun–verb homophone words is discussed as an example of a paradigm that attempts to demonstrate lateralized correlates of specific aspects of language processing. Finally, we survey some recent work using ERPs to explore lateralization in clinical populations.

ERP Methodology

The development of ERP research has been closely linked to the availability and power of laboratory computers. The ERP method involves computerized digitizing and averaging of the EEG waveforms for a short time epoch (e.g., 1 sec) following the onset of multiple presentations of a stimulus — a process that enhances the very small (5–25 μV) signal embedded in the higher-amplitude continuing EEG. Because the waves of the ERP are closely time-locked to the stimulus while the ongoing EEG is not, the ERP sums with each repetition of the stimulus, while the EEG in which the ERP is embedded cancels.

Once an ERP is averaged, its waves, or components, are measured in terms of both latency and amplitude. Such measures are used to compare ERPs across experimental conditions or populations. ERP component amplitudes may also be used in comparisons between scalp recording sites to prepare topographic maps of relative voltages over the scalp for each time sample of the ERP. Such scalp field maps can be graphically displayed in the same manner as CT or PET images and used in the study of lateralized hemispheric functions.

We emphasize these procedural points because, while they permit us to see what would otherwise be invisible in scalp EEG recordings, they also impose constraints on the design of experiments that are sometimes difficult to circumvent. For example, averaging may require as many as 50 repetitions of the same stimulus or stimulus class. Such redundancy may create an artificial information-processing situation for the subject, particularly in ERP studies of language functions. Natural language, of course, almost never involves such repeated presentation of the same stimulus word or phrase. A number of approaches have recently been developed to address this problem. These are discussed later in this chapter.

Summary of ERP Components

ERP components can be distinguished in terms of their latency following stimulus onset (16). Early components, occurring within the first 50 msec following stimulus onset, reflect activity in afferent sensory systems as information is conducted through the brain stem and thalamus and received at the cortex. Later ERP components, occurring up to 1 sec or more following the onset of the stimulus, reflect higher levels of cortical information processing. The later ERP components are of particular interest in studies of hemispheric lateralization, because they vary as a function of information-processing parameters — that is, what the subject does about a stimulus.

Two of the later ERP components, the N1 and the P3 (the first negative and third positive wave of the ERP), have been given particular attention in research on higher cognitive functions. The N1 component has been associated with selective attention, in that it has been shown to increase in amplitude in response to degree of attention to the response-evoking stimulus (26, 48). The P3 has been shown to correlate with perceptual discrimination and the recognition of the occurrence of target events in a continuing series of stimuli. The amplitude of P3 is related to the degree to which a stimulus is surprising (i.e., has a low probability of occurrence) and task-relevant (i.e., attended and processed) (13). P3 latency is related to cognitive processing time (18). A recently identified component, the N400 (a negative wave peaking at 400 msec), occurs in response to words which are semantically incongruous within the context of a sentence (30).

Another form of ERP that has been examined in laterality studies is the very slow negative shift that may occur over several seconds. There are two similar forms of slow potentials: those that follow a warning signal and are associated with the preparation for cognitive processing (the contingent negative variation, or CNV), and those preceding some kind of voluntary action, including speech (the *Bereitschaft* potential or motor readiness potential, abbreviated as RP) (16).

Comparison of ERPs with Other Brain Function Indices

Much of the research on hemispheric differences has involved the study of individuals with lateralized cerebral lesions or patients with commissurotomies. While such studies have been very productive, they have been conducted on individuals with damaged brains and therefore involve some limitations. They are instructive concerning the capacities of an undamaged hemisphere where the other has been damaged or surgically removed, or where the hemispheres have been disconnected. However, such studies may offer little direct evidence regarding the relative participation of normal hemispheres in a given cognitive function.

Behavioral methods, such as dichotic listening (see chapter by Noffsinger, this volume) and hemifield tachistoscopy (see chapter by D. W. Zaidel, this volume), have been used ingeniously in studies of functional lateralization in normal subjects. While these methods address the issue of relative laterality, they do so largely by inference from behavior rather than from direct physiological measurement.

Techniques for imaging the physiology of the brain (i.e., PET) offer great promise for the direct observation of functional hemispheric asymmetry in the normal brain (see chapter by Mazziotta and Phelps, this volume). Currently, however, the time frame of cognitive processing that can be represented in an image encompasses the period of time necessary for uptake of radioactively labeled substances (usually longer than 5 min).

ERP methods, in contrast to other imaging techniques, can track rapid fluctuations in brain electrical fields related to cognitive processing occurring within a second or less. However, there are a number of limitations imposed by ERP methods. Previously mentioned is the problem created by the necessity of averaging over multiple trials of the same stimulus condition. Another problem is the uncertainty regarding the anatomical loci of the generators of ERP components, such that the sources of scalp-recorded ERPs can only be roughly specified. There is also some temporal uncertainty, in that components are not always distinctly separated in time; they often overlie one another in ways that make clear measurement of amplitudes and latencies difficult.

SUMMARY OF ERP RESULTS IN STUDIES OF LATERALIZATION

Asymmetric ERPs in Sensory and Motor Processing

It would be unlikely for one to find ERP correlates of the somewhat subtle lateralization of higher cognitive functions if it were not first possible to demonstrate the more obvious lateralization of sensory and motor processing in relation to right and left sensory–motor fields. Lateralization of sensory processing has, in fact, been demonstrated or visual (25), auditory (53), and somatosensory (23) stimuli. For example, Perronet *et al.* (53), using a coronal array of electrodes, demonstrated that the N1 component of the auditory ERP is larger in amplitude over the hemisphere contralateral to the ear being stimulated. They also reported a polarity inversion of the N1 at the sylvian fissure. Individuals with lesions of the auditory cortex resulting in extinction of the contralateral ear during dichotic listening do not show this polarity inversion over the damaged hemisphere. Similarly, visual stimulation of the right and left fields produces greatest amplitude of the positive wave at 100 msec over the occipital cortex contralateral to the visual field being stimulated (25). Comparable results have also been found for somatosensory stimulation (23).

Slow negative potentials that precede the onset of motor activity (the RPs) are largest not only over the frontal motor areas, but also over the hemisphere contralateral to the limb that is to be moved. Kutas and Donchin (29), for example, have published data on the lateralization of premotor potentials when subjects are squeezing a dynamometer with the right or left hand.

Asymmetries in N1 Amplitude in Language and Nonlanguage Tasks

In the case of both visual and auditory ERPs, the most easily detectable waveform is the N1 component (a negative wave occurring at about 100–150 msec). This component is detectable in some form over most of the scalp and is affected by attention, increasing in amplitude in response to stimuli more at the center of the individual's attentional focus (26, 48).

A number of studies (10, 37, 45, 49) have demonstrated that the N1 (or in some cases the N1–P2) amplitude to language stimuli is largest over the left, language hemisphere, and is equal in amplitude or oppositely lateralized for nonlanguage stimuli. For example, Molfese *et al.* (45) found larger N1–P2 amplitudes over the left hemisphere for speech stimuli, but larger right-hemisphere amplitudes for non-speech stimuli. This asymmetry, interestingly enough, was present in infants, and the asymmetry actually decreased from infancy to adulthood. Neville (49) was able to demonstrate N1 amplitude asymmetries during a verbal dichotic-listening task.

Application of a somewhat more complex paradigm to this area of research is exemplified by the work of Wood and his associates (64, 65). In this case, ERPs were compared to the same potentially linguistic stimulus (e.g., "ba") when subjects were asked to make either phonetic (e.g., "ba" vs. "da") or pitch (high or low voice) discriminations. Wood has consistently found ERP differences for the phonetic (language) versus pitch (nonlanguage) tasks only over the left hemisphere; that is, responses were larger for the phonetic-discrimination task than the pitch task.

In a similar kind of study, although not specifically related to the N1 component, Buchsbaum and Fedio (9) demonstrated that visual ERPs to words and non-sense patterns produced ERPs that varied in waveform for these two categories of stimuli when recorded over the left hemisphere, but not the right. This effect was greatest for the direct left hemiretina–hemisphere visual pathway.

Shucard (56) took a different and somewhat novel approach by observing changes in the amplitude of the N1 component to task-irrelevant stimuli during continuing right- or left-hemisphere processing tasks. Thus, responses to irrelevant clicks were found to decrease over the left hemisphere during reading and over the right hemisphere while listening to music. It is important to note that this unique ERP paradigm avoids the necessity of many presentations of the same stimulus for averaging. Since the response-evoking stimulus is irrelevant, the subject can be engaged in a nonpaced, nonredundant, continuous task while the irrelevant probes are presented in order to detect which hemisphere is most heavily involved in the processing of the particular task.

The study of Shucard and his colleagues (56) is noteworthy for having devised a paradigm that allowed them to observe ERP correlates of lateralized cognitive processing in a more natural language-processing setting. Hillyard and Woods (27) were similarly able to develop an ERP paradigm that allowed for the observation of ERP laterality during natural language processing (i.e., listening to poetry). ERPs were averaged across each word of the passage and compared to ERPs from a series of tones matched in intensity, duration, and rise time to the words of the poetry passage. Word ERPs had larger N1s and sustained negative potentials than nonwords over both hemispheres, but the effect was greatest over the left hemisphere.

Lateralization of Late Endogenous Components

Although the P3 usually has a symmetrical distribution over the parietal areas, it does show lateral asymmetries during certain language-processing and nonlanguage-processing tasks. Friedman *et al.* (21) have demonstrated that both the N1 and P3 waves of the ERP to signal words were larger over the left hemisphere when subjects were trying to detect the signal word in a list of words. No lateralization was found when human nonspeech sounds were used as stimuli in a similar detection task. Desmedt (12) has demonstrated that subjects involved in a tactile processing task (form and orientation discrimination) manifest a large P3 over the right hemisphere, but not the left, regardless of the hand stimulated.

Kutas and Hillyard (30), in a study of the effects of semantic incongruity in the final word of a seven-word sentence, also observed P3s to occur to each word in the sentence. P3 amplitude was larger over the left hemisphere for each of the seven words in the sentence, again confirming the lateralization of P3 amplitude in language-processing tasks. Semantically anomalous words at the end of the sentence elicited a large negative wave at about 400 msec poststimulus (N400), which was slightly larger and more prolonged over the right hemisphere.

A similar N400 ERP component was observed by Neville *et al.* (50) in a study utilizing single four-letter nouns presented to the left and right visual fields. In all normal subjects this N400 was lateralized to the left hemisphere, regardless of the visual field stimulated. In this study semantic anomaly was not a factor, which may explain the apparent discrepancy in N400 laterality compared to that described by Kutas and Hillyard (30). Neville *et al.* (51) applied their paradigm to a group of congenitally deaf adults and found no lateralization of the N400 component in these subjects.

Asymmetry of CNV and Premotor Potentials

As described above, the slow potentials preceding movement of the left or right hand are largest over the hemisphere contralateral to the hand being moved. Similarly, McAdam and Whitaker (38) have shown that the epoch preceding the onset of speech is marked by a slow negative potential that is lateralized to the left side of the head. The motor potentials that precede nonspeech vocal acts (coughing, spitting, etc.) were not found to be left-lateralized. At least two other studies have produced comparable results (34, 47). Indeed, overt motor activity is not necessary for the demonstration of left-lateralized slow negative potentials. Marsh *et al.* (36) have demonstrated a left-hemisphere-predominant CNV in the interval between a warning signal and a linguistic analysis task. No such laterality was evident in an analogous nonlinguistic task.

Lateralized ERP Correlates of Specific Language Dimensions

The research discussed so far shares as a basic paradigm the comparison of ERP responses from the two hemispheres in language-processing versus nonlanguage-processing tasks. Much additional research has been done attempting to determine if ERP waveforms are affected by variation of stimuli and tasks along several linguistic dimensions such as phonetic, semantic, syntactic, and lexical categories, and to determine if such correlates are most evident in recordings taken over one or the other hemisphere.

Molfese and his colleagues have published a series of papers reporting attempts to determine the ERP correlates of linguistic parameters (40, 41, 42, 44, 46). For example, Molfese and Hess (46) studied the effect of voice-onset time (VOT) on ERPs of preschool children. VOT is the relatively silent interval between laryngeal pulsing and consonant release and is the phonetic property of voicing that partially underlies the distinction between a "b" and a "p." VOT can be continuously varied by a computer over a range of acoustically different values. However, listeners will only distinguish two different sounds (a "b" or "p" sound in the example above). In other words, VOT as a phonetic cue is perceived categorically (as a "b" or a "p," but not both), with a relatively stable boundary between the categories. Molfese and Hess (46) argued that an ERP correlate of phonetic discrimination, as opposed to merely acoustic processing, would be represented by an ERP change that mirrored the categorical nature of the phonetic perception. Using principal-component factor analysis to break up the ERP waveform into different components, they found a late component in the ERPs of preschool children that varied in amplitude in a categorical manner with the stimulus VOT. Of particular note is the fact that these effects were found only for right-hemisphere records. A later replication with adults by Molfese (40) showed a similar categorical effect lateralized to the right hemisphere for the amplitude of this same late wave, and an additional categorical amplitude effect on the earlier N1–P2 complex occurring over both hemispheres. While Molfese indicates that there may be mechanisms involved in the processing of VOT that are in the right hemisphere, it may also be that the task of discriminating "b" and "p" sounds in isolation is somewhat remote from natural language processing.

Other parameters of speech process that have been studied by Molfese include place of articulation and vowel contrasts (41, 42, 44). The work of Molfese represents a particularly outstanding example of the use of ERPs to ask specific questions regarding the lateral distribution of the processing of various parameters of language, and the course of development of this lateralization.

HIGHLIGHTS OF CONTINUING RESEARCH

Contextual Meaning Effects on Speech ERPs

Over the past 10 years, our laboratory has conducted a number of studies of the effects of contextually determined meaning on words that have the same sound (homonyms or homophones). Depending on the context of the sentence in which they appear, homophones can be interpreted as either nouns or verbs, with different semantic referents in each case. A straightforward example of such a paradigm is our original study using the words "fire" and "duck" (6). Responses to the word "fire" in the phrases "sit by the fire" versus "ready, aim, fire" were found to be more different in waveform when recorded from left- than from right-hemisphere electrodes; that is, the different contexts affected left- but not right-hemisphere responses. An example of comparable results can be seen in Figure 1. This effect was particularly marked for left anterior electrodes (located approximately over Broca's area). Similar results were found for the word "duck" in the phrases "he'd better duck" and "a fly-

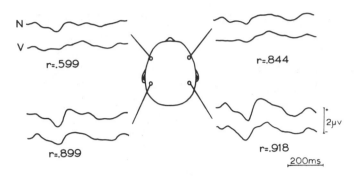

Figure 1. Across subject average ($N = 15$) of averaged ERPs ($N = 100$) to the word "led" ("lead") in the phrase "It was led (lead)" presented through earphones. Correlations represent the degree of waveform similarity of responses to the noun (N) and (V) forms of the stimulus word.

ing duck." Using the phrases "fire the gun" and "fire is hot" randomly intermixed, left-lateralized waveform differences could be made to disappear, since subjects did not know the context of "fire" when they heard the word (35).

Similar results were obtained with auditory presentations of the single ambiguous phrase "it was led" (or "it was lead") (7, 8). Again, response to the words "led" and "lead" differed most at the left anterior recording site (Figure 1). Use of stepwise discriminant analysis (7) and principal-component factor analysis (8) of ERP waveforms demonstrated that while the major differences occurred at the left anterior electrode, statistically reliable effects also existed at the left posterior site. It was shown that responses to the noun and verb meanings of "led" ("lead") were sufficiently similar for different subjects so that a discriminant function reliably differentiated the noun and verb responses in the different subjects.

Another series of experiments was conducted in order to compare the contextual meaning effects of different noun–verb homophones in different subject groups and different languages (4). In this study, a group of native English speakers listened to the phrases "a pretty rose" and "the boatman rows." Another group of native Swiss speakers listened to the phrases "i schoni clini fluuge" and "en vogel cunnt z'fluuge" ("a pretty little fly" or "the bird comes flying"). A third group of native Swiss speakers listened to a degraded version of one of the Swiss phrases, while imagining it to be one Swiss phrase or the other on alternate blocks of trials. Although some lateralized effects were evident in each paradigm analyzed separately, the major effect common to the three paradigms was a difference in the anterior–posterior distribution of the scalp topography of the responses to nouns and verbs. In all three experiments, ERP fields for verbs were more positive anteriorly than noun fields. Thus, in this paradigm, while right–left differences were found, effects common to the three paradigms were primarily anterior–posterior differences. It is possible that this may reflect the contribution of frontal areas to syntactic aspects of the understanding of verbs. Recent evidence suggests that frontal areas participate not only in the formulation, but also in the understanding of syntax (59).

Lateralization, Sex, and Stuttering

The research described above related to ERP correlates of the perception of meaning in language. These correlates have been found to be left-lateralized in right-handed individuals. Therefore, the degree of difference in ERP waveforms elicited by the two meanings of a homophone word can form the basis for a measure of hemispheric asymmetry of language processing. Thus, a ratio of the correlations at left and right homologous recording points provides an index of lateralization (R/L + R). We have utilized such a measure in the study of sex differences in lateralization of language, and in the investigation of language lateralization in stutterers.

With respect to sex differences, there is increasing support for the idea that females have a lower margin of hemispheric asymmetry for the processing of language than males (31). Data supporting this assertion come from studies using dichotic listening (28), hemifield tachistoscopy (33), and EEG (55, 63). McGlone, in a series of studies of stroke patients, reaches a similar conclusion (39).

Similarly, Orton (52) and Travis (61, 62) postulated that stuttering results from a failure to develop adequate hemispheric asymmetry for language functions. While the results on experiments bearing on this theory have not always been consistent, it has received support from studies using dichotic listening (11, 54), articulatory tracking (60), and CNV measures (66, 67).

Using the asymmetry of noun–verb ERP correlation as a measure of lateralization for language processing, we (5) conducted a study of language dominance in three groups: right-handed male nonstutterers, right-handed female nonstutterers, and right-handed male stutterers. To assure a reasonably homogeneous group relative to etiology of stuttering, only subjects whose stuttering began before the age of 6 took part in this study. ERPs were recorded to visual presentations of the word "fire" in the phrases "fire is hot" and "fire the gun"; the subjects were informed before each block of trials as to which phrase they would see, so that the meaning of the word "fire" was known by the subject beforehand. Recording loci were over Broca's and Wernicke's areas of the left hemisphere, and homologous points on the right. Two average ERPs, one for each meaning of the stimulus word, were obtained for each electrode (Figure 2). A correlation was computed between the ERP waveforms to the two meanings at each electrode. Hemisphere asymmetry was expressed in a laterality index (R/L + R) of Z-transformed correlations. Separate indices were calculated for the anterior and posterior electrode pairs. Since a relatively low correlation reflects greater noun–verb ERP difference, a laterality index greater than 0.5 indicates left lateralization of noun–verb ERP difference. The results are illustrated in Figure 3.

For the male reference group, 9 of 10 subjects had lateralization scores greater than 0.5 for the anterior electrode pair (anterior mean index greater than 0.5, $p < .05$), but only 6 of the 10 for the posterior pair (n.s.). While females also showed relative left lateralization, the pattern was different, such that the greatest margin of lateralization was at the posterior leads. Eight of 10 female subjects had laterality scores greater than 0.5 at posterior leads ($p < .05$), but only 6 of 10 for the anterior

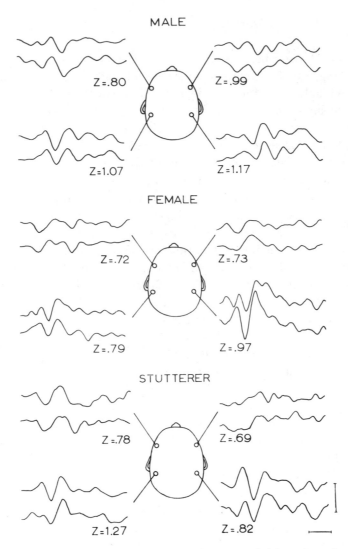

Figure 2. Average potentials evoked by the word "fire" recorded from four electrode loci in three individual subjects: a male nonstutterer, a female nonstutterer, and a male stutterer. The upper trace of each pair is related to the noun meaning of "fire" and the bottom trace is related to the verb meaning. Z-transformed correlations between the 64 digital values representing the noun and verb waveforms appear below each waveform pair. Vertical scale is 4 μV, positive up. Horizontal scale is 100 msec.

electrode pair (n.s.). For the stutterer group, neither the anterior nor the posterior lateralization scores differed significantly from 0.5.

As Figure 3 clearly indicates, differences in the variance of laterality scores between groups were more striking than differences in mean laterality. The reference male group showed left lateralization only at the anterior leads, and little variance in either anterior or posterior laterality scores. Females showed a significant left laterality and small variance for posterior derivations, but a wide range of laterality scores for anterior leads. Stutterers showed an inconsistent pattern, and a wide range of laterality scores at both anterior and posterior loci.

The great variability of laterality scores in the stutterer group, and to a lesser extent in the female group, raises the question of within-subject consistency of anterior and posterior laterality measures. As expected, the male reference group showed a high level of consistency in laterality scores (anterior–posterior correlation, rho = .73, $p < .05$). Female subjects were less consistent (rho = .46, n.s.) and stutterers were inconsistent (rho = .18, n.s.). Taken together, these results suggest that the three groups represented in this study are distinguished not so much by the magnitude of laterality scores, but by their consistency within and between subjects. Individual right-handed females or male stutterers may manifest greater laterality for any particular measurement than right-handed males.

The correlation of this ERP index of laterality with a behavioral measure of laterality, dichotic listening, is of interest. Both the male stutterers and nonstutterers were administered a dichotic-listening task using consonant–vowel combinations (e.g. "da," "ba," "ka"). For the nonstutterers the rank-order correlation between dichotic-listening scores (percentage of error) and the ERP lateralization was significant (anterior, rho = .75, $p < .05$; posterior, rho = .64, $p < .05$). In contrast, the male stutterers showed no correlation between dichotic-listening scores and either anterior (rho = .08, n.s.) or posterior (rho = .06, n.s.) ERP laterality indices. These results

Figure 3. Laterality scores (R/L + R) for male and female nonstutterers and male stutterers computed from the noun–verb ERP waveform correlations. Values greater than 0.5 indicate left laterality of greatest ERP waveform difference. Distribution means are indicated by the arrow below each graph. Upper graphs are from the anterior homologous electrode pair, and the lower, from the posterior homologous pair.

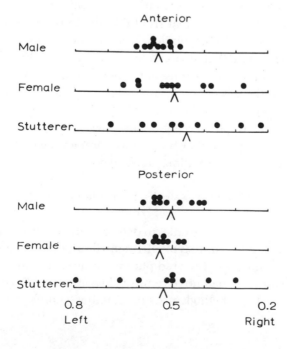

suggest that in the male nonstutterers, both the dichotic listening scores and ERP laterality indices were anchored by, and reflected, left-hemisphere dominance for language. In the stutterers, the wide variance and lack of correlation between various measures of lateralization suggest that the statistical indices of lateralization were not influenced by a common underlying determinant such as hemispheric dominance.

ERP Laterality and Information Processing in Schizophrenia

The issue of whether schizophrenia involves aberrant cerebral functional asymmetry has been raised by a number of investigators (20, 24). An ERP study conducted in our laboratory bears on this question (58). ERPs were recorded from normal and schizophrenic children during the performance of a complex information-processing task, the Span of Apprehension (19). The task involves the rapid search and discrimination of a target letter within a matrix of distractor letters. It has been shown to be particularly sensitive to individuals at risk for schizophrenia, actively schizophrenic, or in remission (1). Impaired performance reflects poor mobilization of attentional resources and discriminative capacities. ERPs are of interest in such a paradigm, since the capacity for selective attention has been related to amplitude variations in the N1 component.

In our study, normal children showed increases in the amplitude of the N1 component with increasing task difficulty, while schizophrenic children did not. Moreover, normal children showed larger N1 component amplitudes at right posterior leads than at left posterior leads. This finding is likely a reflection of the fact that the task involved pattern recognition, rather than verbal–symbolic processing. Schizophrenic children showed no such N1 amplitude lateralization. These findings are illustrated in Figure 4 (bottom).

Also evident in Figure 4 (top) are marked differences in ERP laterality between normal and schizophrenic children at frontal leads. In this case, however, normal children showed clear symmetry, while schizophrenic children had a marked and prolonged negativity (CNV) that prevaded most of the ERP epoch in the right hemisphere only. At present the nature of the relationship between the frontal right lateralized CNV and the lack of posterior asymmetry of the N1 in schizophrenic children is not clear. However, it is known that attentional processes which might be manifest in N1 asymmetry are largely regulated by frontal lobe mechanisms (28). Thus, the data support the notion that schizophrenics have abnormalities in the lateralization of complex information processing.

SUMMARY AND FUTURE PROSPECTS

The paradigms used in ERP studies to date are sufficiently diverse as to preclude a conclusive summary and synthesis of ERP contributions to the study of laterality. Moreover, new and more sophisticated paradigms are constantly being developed that yield promise for more definitive results. The various studies described here indicate, at least, that ERP methods provide a unique complement to clinical, be-

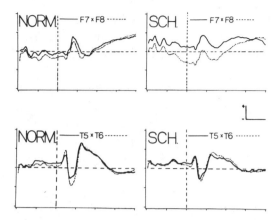

Figure 4. Group mean ERPs at anterior, left (F7) and right (F8), and posterior, left (T5) and right (T6), recording sites for normal and schizophrenic children during performance of the Span of Apprehension task. Solid lines represent left-hemisphere activity, and dashed lines, the right hemisphere. Traces begin with the onset of the auditory warning stimulus, and the vertical line which intersects the traces 500 msec later marks the onset of the visual Span stimuli. The dashed horizontal line represents the zero-voltage baseline with respect to the linked earlobe reference. (From 58. Reprinted by permission.)

havioral, and brain-imaging methods in studying the lateralization of human cortical function. In general, research with ERPs thus far has consistently confirmed what other methods have indicated—that is, left dominance for language functions and right for visual–spatial functions in right-handed subjects.

The ERP studies we have described (including our own) emphasize the point that laterality is relative and that each hemisphere may make contributions to a given mental operation or psychological process at different stages in information processing. Specifically, the data of Molfese (40), as well as others, suggest that there may be shifts in lateralization during the course of language processing, such that some elements may be handled primarily by the right hemisphere.

What are the future prospects for the application of ERP methods to the study of hemispheric specialization? One area of research in which ERPs should provide a major source of new information is the study of laterality in clinical populations. Our results from studies of ERPs in stutterers and schizophrenic children, as well as the studies of Knight *et al.* (28) involving brain-damaged patients with lateralized lesions, suggest the potential of this approach.

A second area of promise is the application of topographic methods in lateralization studies as a means of greatly increasing the spatial resolution and localization of ERP components (17, 32). These methods require the use of a large number of recording electrodes closely spaced on the scalp, rather than the few bilateral pairs characteristic of work to date. The work of Lehmann (32), Duffy (17), and others has demonstrated the value of this approach.

The increasing power and availability of large-capacity data storage in laboratory computers, as well as the development of new methods for the measurement of ERP components in single trials, have opened the way for the analysis of un-averaged single ERPs throughout an experiment. Single-trial methodologies may allow for the design of more natural, less redundant information-processing tasks in the study of hemispheric asymmetry.

Finally, the newly developed magnetoencephalogram (MEG) offers a potentially valuable technique in lateralization studies. Since the MEG measures magnetic fields, which are more circumscribed than voltage fields, greater precision of localization of lateralized generators should be possible (2). However, at the present stage of its development, the cost per channel places limitations on the number of loci that can be simultaneously recorded.

The temporal resolution implicit in ERP measurement, along with continuing improvements in paradigms and methodologies, suggest that ERPs can form the basis for fine-grained analysis of hemispheric asymmetries in various language and visual–spatial cognitive functions.

REFERENCES

1. Asarnow, R. F., and MacCrimmon, D. J., Residual performance deficit in clinically remitted schizophrenics: A marker of schizophrenia? *J. Abnorm. Psychol.*, 1978, **87**: 597–608.
2. Barth, D. S., Sutherling, W., Engle, J., and Beatty, J., Neuromagnetic evidence of spatially distributed sources underlying epileptiform spikes in the human brain. *Science*, 1984, **223**: 293–296.
3. Berger, H., Uber das Elektrenkephalogramm des Menschen. Zweite Mitteilung. *J. Psychologie Neurologie*, 1930, **40**: 160–179.
4. Brown, W. S., Lehmann, D., and Marsh, J. T., Linguistic meaning related differences in evoked potential topography: English, Swiss-German, and imagined. *Brain Lang.*, 1980, **11**: 340–353.
5. Brown, W. S., Marsh, J. T., Ponsford, R. E., Travis, L. E., and Smith, J. C., Language, laterality, sex and stuttering: ERPs to contextual meaning. Unpublished paper.
6. Brown, W. S., Marsh, J. T., and Smith, J. C., Contextual meaning effects on speech evoked potentials. *Behav. Biol.*, 1973, **9**: 755–761.
7. Brown, W. S., Marsh, J. T., and Smith, J. C., Evoked potential waveform differences produced by the perception of different meanings of an ambiguous phrase. *Electroencephalogr. Clin. Neurophysiol.*, 1976, **41**: 113–123.
8. Brown, W. S., Marsh, J. T., and Smith, J. C., Principal component analysis of ERP differences related to the meaning of an ambiguous word. *Electroencephalogr. Clin. Neurophysiol.*, 1979, **46**: 706–714.
9. Buchsbaum, M., and Fedio, P., Hemispheric differences in evoked potentials to verbal and nonverbal stimuli in the left and right visual fields. *Physiol. Behav.*, 1970, **5**: 207–210.
10. Cohn, R., Differential cerebral processing of noise and verbal stimuli. *Science*, 1971, **172**: 599–601.
11. Curry, F. K. W., and Gregory, H. R., The performance of stutterers on dichotic listening tasks thought to reflect cerebral dominance. *J. Speech Hear. Res.*, 1969, **12**: 73–82.
12. Desmedt, J. E., and Robertson, D., Search for right hemisphere asymmetries in event-related potentials to somatosensory cueing signals. In: *Language and Hemispheric Specialization in Man: Cerebral ERPs.* Vol. 3, *Progress in Clinical Neurophysiology*

(J. E. Desmedt, Ed.). Karger, Basel, 1977: 172–178.

13. Donchin, E., Surprise! . . . Surprise? *Psychophysiology*, 1981, **18**: 493–513.

14. Donchin, E., Kutas, M., and McCarthy, G., Electrocortical indices of hemispheric utilization. In: *Lateralization in the Nervous System* (S. Harnad, R. W. Doty, L. Goldstein, J. Jaynes, and G. Krauthamer, Eds.). Academic Press, New York, 1976: 339–384.

15. Donchin, E., McCarthy, G., and Kutas, M., Electroencephalographic investigations of hemispheric specialization. In: *Language and Hemispheric Specialization in Man: Cerebral ERPs*. Vol. 3, *Progress in Clinical Neurophysiology* (J. E. Desmedt, Ed.). Karger, Basel, 1977: 212–242.

16. Donchin, E., Ritter, W., and McCallum, C., Cognitive psychophysiology: The endogeneous components of the ERP. In: *Event-Related Brain Potentials in Man* (E. Callaway, P. Tueting, and S. Koslow, Eds.). Academic Press, New York, 1978: 349–442.

17. Duffy, F. H., Burchfield, J. L., and Lombroso, C. T., Brain electrical activity mapping (BEAM): A new method for extending the clinical utility of EEG and evoked potential data. *Ann. Neurol.*, 1979, **5**: 309–321.

18. Duncan-Johnson, C., P300 latency: A new metric of information processing. *Psychophysiology*, 1981, **18**: 207–215.

19. Estes, W. K., and Taylor, H. A., A detection method and probabilistic models for assessing information processing from brief visual displays. *Proc. Natl. Acad. Sci. U.S.A.*, 1964, **52**: 446–454.

20. Flor-Henry, P., Lateralized temporal–limbic dysfunction and psychopathology. *Ann. N.Y. Acad. Sci.*, 1976, **280**: 777–797.

21. Friedman, D., Simson, R., Ritter, W., and Rapin, I., Cortical evoked potentials elicited by real speech words and human sounds. *Electroencephalogr. Clin. Neurophysiol.*, 1975, **38**: 13–19.

22. Galin, D., and Ornstein, R., Lateral specialization of cognitive mode: An EEG study. *Psychophysiology*, 1972, **9**: 412–418.

23. Goff, W. R., Rosner, B. S., and Allison, T., Distribution of cerebral somatosensory evoked responses in normal man. *Electroencephalogr. Clin. Neurophysiol.*, 1962, **14**: 697–713.

24. Gruzeller, J. H., and Hammond, N. V., Schizophrenia: A dominant hemisphere temporal-lobe disorder? *Res. Commun. Psychol. Psychiatry Behav.*, 1976, **1**: 33–72.

25. Halliday, A. M., and Michael, W. F., Changes in pattern-evoked responses in man associated with the vertical and horizontal meridians of the visual field. *J. Physiol.*, 1970, **208**: 499–513.

26. Hansen, J., and Hillyard, S. A., Endogenous brain potentials associated with selective attention. *Electroencephalogr. Clin. Neurophysiol.*, 1980, **49**: 277–290.

27. Hillyard, S. A., and Wood, D. L., Electrophysiological analysis of human brain function. In: *Handbook of Behavioral Neurobiology* (M. S. Gazzaniga, Ed.). Plenum, New York, 1979: 345–378.

28. Knight, R. T., Hillyard, S. A., Woods, D. L., and Neville, H. J., The effects of frontal cortex lesions on event-related potentials during auditory selective attention. *Electroencephalogr. Clin. Neurophysiol.*, 1981, **52**: 571–582.

29. Kutas, M., and Donchin, E., Studies of squeezing: Handedness, responding hand, response force, and asymmetry of readiness potential. *Science*, 1974, **186**: 545–548.

30. Kutas, M., and Hillyard, S. A., Lateral distribution of event-related potentials during sentence processing. *Neuropsychologia*, 1982, **20**: 579–590.

31. Lake, D. A., and Bryden, M. P., Handedness and sex differences in hemispheric asymmetry. *Brain Lang.*, 1976, **3**: 266–283.

32. Lehmann, D., The EEG as scalp field distribution. In: *EEG Informatics* (A. Remond, Ed.). Elsevier/North-Holland, Amsterdam, 1977: pp. 365–384.

33. Levy, J., and Reid, M., Variations in writing posture and cerebral organization. *Science*, 1976, **194**: 337–339.

34. Low, M. D., Wada, J. A., and Fox, M., Electroencephalographic localization of the conative aspects of language production in the human brain. In: *The Responsive Brain* (C. McCallum and J. R. Knott, Eds.). John Wright & Sons, Bristol, England, 1976: 165–168.

35. Marsh, J. T., and Brown, W. S., Evoked potential correlates of meaning in the perception of language. In: *Language and Hemispheric Specialization in Man: Cerebral ERPs*. Vol. 3, *Progress in Clinical Neurophysiology* (J. E. Desmedt, Ed.). Karger, Basel, 1977: 60–72.

36. Marsh, G. R., and Thompson, L. W., Effct of verbal and non-verbal psychological set on hemispheric asymmetries in the CNV. In: *Event-Related Slow Potentials of the Brain* (C. McCallum and J. R. Knott, Eds.). Elsevier, New York, 1973: 195–200.

37. Matsumiya, Y., Tagliasco, V., Lombroso, C., and Goodglass, H., Auditory evoked response: Meaningfulness of stimuli and interhemispheric asymmetry. *Science*, 1972, **175**: 790–792.

38. McAdam, D. W., and Whitaker, H. A., Language production: Electroencephalographic localization in the normal human brain. *Science*, 1971, **172**: 499–502.

39. McGlone, J., Sex differences in the cerebral organization of verbal functions in patients with unilateral brain lesions. *Brain*, 1977, **100**: 775–793.

40. Molfese, D. L., Electrophysiological correlates of categorical speech perception in adults. *Brain Lang*, 1978, **5**: 25–35.

41. Molfese, D. L., Hemispheric specialization for temporal information: Implications for the processing of voicing cues during speech perception. *Brain Lang.*, 1980, **11**: 285–299.

42. Molfese, D. L., The phoneme and the engram: Electrophysiological evidence for the acoustic invariant in stop consonants. *Brain Lang.*, 1980, **9**: 372–376.

43. Molfese, D. L., Event related potentials and language processing. In: *Tutorial in ERP Research: Endogenous Components* (A. W. K. Gaillard and W. Ritter, Eds.). Elsevier, Amsterdam, 1983: 345–368.

44. Molfese, D. L., and Erwin, R. J., Intrahemispheric differentiation of vowels: Principal component analysis of auditory evoked responses to computer synthesized vowel sounds. *Brain Lang.*, 1981, **13**: 333–344.

45. Molfese, D. L., Freeman, R. B., Jr., and Palermo, D. S., The ontogeny of lateralization for speech and nonspeech stimuli. *Brain Lang.*, 1975, **2**: 356–368.

46. Molfese, D. L., and Hess, T. M., Speech perception in nursery school age children's sex and hemisphere differences. *J. Exp. Child Psychol.*, 1978, **26**: 71–84.

47. Morrell, L. K., and Huntington, D. A., Cortical potentials time-locked to speech production: Evidence for probable cerebral origin. *Life Sci.*, 1972, **11**: 921–929.

48. Naatanen, R., An evoked potential reflection of selective attention. *Psychol. Bull.*, 1982, **92**: 605–640.

49. Neville, H., Event-related potentials in neuropsychological studies of language. *Brain Lang.*, 1980, **11**: 300–318.

50. Neville, H., Kutas, M., and Schmidt, A., Event-related potential studies of cerebral specialization during reading: I. Studies of normal adults. *Brain Lang.*, 1982, **16**: 300–315.

51. Neville, H., Kutas, M., and Schmidt, A., Event-related potential studies of cerebral specialization during reading: II. Studies of congenitally deaf adults. *Brain Lang.*, 1982, **16**: 316–337.

52. Orton, S. T., Studies in stuttering. *Arch. Neurol. Psychiatry*, 1927, **18**: 671–672.

53. Peronnet, F., Michel, F., Echallier, J. F., and Girod, J., Coronal topography of human auditory evoked responses. *Electroencephalogr. Clin. Neurophysiol.*, 1974, **37**: 225–230.

54. Quinn, P., Stuttering, cerebral dominance and the Dichotic Word Test. *Med. J. Aust.*, 1972, **2**: 639–643.
55. Ray, W. J., Morrell, M., Frediani, A. W., and Tucker, D., Sex differences and lateral specialization of hemispheric functioning. *Neuropsychologia*, 1976, **14**: 391–394.
56. Shucard, D. W., Shucard, J. L., and Thomas, D. G., Auditory evoked potential as probes of hemispheric differences in cognitive processing. *Science*, 1977, **64**: 1358–1368.
57. Sperry, R. W., Lateral specialization in the surgically separated hemispheres. In: *The Neurosciences: Third Study Program* (F. O. Schmitt and F. G. Worden, Eds.). MIT Press, Cambridge, Mass., 1974: 5–19.
58. Strandburg, R., Marsh, J. T., Brown, W. S., Asarnow, R. F., and Guthrie, D., Event-related potential concomitants of information processing dysfunction in schizophrenic children. *Electroencephalogr. Clin. Neurophysiol.*, 1984, **57**: 236–253.
59. Stuss, D. T., and Benson, D. F., Neurological studies of the frontal lobe. *Psychol. Bull.*, 1984, **95**: 3–28.
60. Sussman, H., and MacNeilage, P., Hemispheric specialization for speech production and perception in stutterers. *Neuropsychologia*, 1975, **13**: 19–26.
61. Travis, L. E., *Speech Pathology*. Appleton-Century, New York, 1931.
62. Travis, L. E., and Knott, J. R., Bilaterally recorded brain potentials from normal speakers and stutterers. *J. Speech Disord.*, 1937, **2**: 239–241.
63. Tucker, D. M., Sex differences in hemispheric specialization for synthetic visuospatial functions. *Neuropsychologia*, 1976, **14**: 447–454.
64. Wood, C. C., Auditory and phonetic levels of processing in speech perception: Neurophysiological and information processing analyses. *J. Exp. Psychol. (Hum. Percept.)*, 1975, **104**: 3–20.
65. Wood, C. C., Goff, W., and Day, R., Auditory evoked potential during speech perception. *Science*, 1971, **173**: 1248–1251.
66. Zimmerman, G. N., and Knott, J. R. CNVs related to spoken words in stutterers and non-stutterers. *Electroencephalogr. Clin. Neurophysiol.*, 1974, **36**: 216.
67. Zimmerman, G. N., and Knott, J. R. Slow potentials of the brain related to speech processing in normal speakers and stutterers. *Electroencephalogr. Clin. Neurophysiol.*, 1974, **37**: 599–607.

METABOLIC EVIDENCE OF LATERALIZED CEREBRAL FUNCTION DEMONSTRATED BY POSITRON EMISSION TOMOGRAPHY IN PATIENTS WITH NEUROPSYCHIATRIC DISORDERS AND NORMAL INDIVIDUALS

JOHN C. MAZZIOTTA, MD, PhD,[1] and MICHAEL E. PHELPS, PhD[2]

Departments of [1]Neurology and [1,2]Radiological Sciences, and
[2]Laboratory of Biomedical and Environmental Sciences

Positron emission tomography (PET) is a technique that allows for the analytic, non-invasive measurement of local tissue physiology in humans. PET is able to provide information about local cerebral blood flow (LCBF), oxygen (LCMRO$_2$), and glucose (LCMRGlc) metabolic rates and extraction fractions, as well as blood volume (33, 49). These physiological measurements are made possible by using biologically active compounds labeled with positron-emitting isotopes of carbon, nitrogen, oxygen, fluorine, and others. Since the radioisotopes employed are those of the natural elements of the body (fluorine-18 is substituted for hydrogen), it is possible to label biochemical substrates, substrate analogues, and drugs. These agents may then be used *in vivo* without disturbing their biochemical properties (49).

An effective combination of PET instrumentation and mathematical models based on tracer kinetic principles is required to make accurate local tissue radioactivity measurements with PET. PET is able to measure functional biochemical changes in the early stages of disease before anatomical alterations are detected by more conventional diagnostic imaging techniques (e.g., x-ray CT) (16, 28). In this fashion, information derived from PET can improve our knowledge and understanding of the underlying biochemical mechanisms associated with normal cerebral function as well as with human neuropathology. This chapter will describe the methodology involved in making PET measurements, as well as data obtained with PET

Acknowledgments: We thank the various investigators in positron emission tomography who generously contributed their time and data. Gratitude is expressed to Maureen Kinney for preparing the manuscript and to Patrick Welton for his editorial assistance. This work was partially supported by DOE Contract No. AM03 76 SF00012; NIH Grants No. R01 6M 248389 and No. P01 NS 15654; and NIMH Grant No. R01-MH-37916-01. John C. Mazziotta is the recipient of Teacher Investigator Award 1K07 0058801 NSPA.

that are relevant to human cerebral hemispheric specialization in health and disease. (For more detailed discussions of the methods and results of PET studies, see 49 and 51.)

Methodology

Three basic components constitute the major methodological elements of PET: (1) analytic PET instrumentation, (2) positron-labeled compounds, and (3) tracer kinetic methods.

The unique physical properties of positron decay make possible the accurate and quantifiable imaging of PET (45, 49, 59). Positrons are positively charged electrons that are emitted from certain unstable nuclei as they decay to more stable nuclei. When a positron combines with an electron, they annihilate (i.e., the masses of the electrons and positrons are converted to electromagnetic radiation) and produce a pair of high-energy (511 keV) annihilation photons. The detection of these events utilizes the fact that the annihilation photons are emitted in essentially opposite directions. PET devices use rings or banks of opposed detectors to identify this emitted radioactivity. The detectors are electronically linked in opposition to accept only those events that are recorded simultaneously (within 10–20 nsec) at opposing detectors (45, 49, 59). This approach provides an electronic form of collimation and establishes the origin of the recorded radiation to well-defined regions between the opposing detectors. Using these methods, only a thin (1–2 cm) slice of tissue is sampled, with relatively uniform resolution across the slice. The data from each set of detectors are collected at many linear positions and angles around the cross-section of the brain. The collected profiles of tissue count rates resemble data collected using x-ray CT systems and are mathematically processed in a similar fashion to produce a two-dimensional map of the tissue radioactivity concentrations in the brain slice. The image is corrected for the attenuation of emitted radioactivity that occurs as it passes through the cranial structures. Final image resolution is presently in the range of 5 to 18 mm. The NeuroECAT PET device (Figure 1) (23, 24) achieves a spatial resolution of 8 mm. The theoretical limit of resolution is on the order of a few millimeters.

PET is a technique analogous to tissue autoradiography for quantitatively measuring local tissue radioisotope concentrations. The PET method is, however, noninvasive. This measurement capability provides the means to implement tracer kinetic studies in humans and to estimate local rates of physiological variables such as metabolism and blood flow. The instrument therefore, is not simply a cross-sectional imaging device, but, more importantly, an analytic measurement tool for examining local biochemical reaction rates within the body.

Positron-emitting isotopes have to be selected so as to provide acceptable radiation dose properties, physical half-lives, and chemical syntheses in order to study biological systems. Many labeled compounds are available for measuring physiological variables (49). However, the problem of actually achieving these measurements is much more complex. Such measurements require careful selection of labeled compounds and the process to study, and the use of tracer kinetic models within the limitations imposed by PET studies in humans (49). Thus far, radioisotopes have been incorporated into compounds capable of measuring cerebral blood flow, blood volume, amino acid incorporations, and brain receptor–ligand binding, as well as oxygen and glucose transport, metabolism, and extraction fractions (49).

The combined use of the PET triad, which includes instrumentation, labeled compounds, and tracer kinetic models, is a complex and multidisciplined technique. It is, however, now becoming more routine in centers throughout the world. It has been used to study normal cerebral function as well as human neuropathology from a physiological and biochemical perspective. PET is uniquely suited to the investigation of issues such as hemispheric specialization, since, for the first time, one is able to examine with high spatial resolution the functional response of cerebral substructures to specific physiological stimuli and to pathological damage. Thus, much in the way Penfield and his colleagues (44) investigated human cortical phenomena through intraoperative stimulation, PET studies in normal subjects provide similar information in a more physiological and noninvasive manner.

Studies in Normals

Normal individuals have been studied using PET techniques in "resting" states as well as during sensory, motor, and neurobehavioral stimulation. The effects of visual (20, 29, 39, 47, 50, 52, 53), auditory (20, 35, 36, 38, 53), somatosensory (3, 20), and motor tasks (56, 57) have already been reported in normal individuals. Most of these studies have used [^{18}F]fluorodeoxyglucose (FDG) and PET to measure local cerebral glucose utilization (25, 46, 55, 58).

There are a number of reasons for performing activation studies in normals with PET. First, sensory, motor, and cognitive studies will map the cortical and subcortical extent of specific cerebral processes and hemispheric lateralization using truly physiological tasks and appropriate stimulation paradigms (34, 35, 38). Second, through the comprehensive investigation of such tasks in normal populations with PET, sets of paradigms will be developed that predictably activate specific cortical and subcortical brain regions (34–39). These paradigms can then be used in patient populations where subtle alterations in metabolism, flow, or other physiological parameters may go undetected in simple "resting" PET imaging sessions (34).

Sensory Deprivation

Left–right metabolic hemispheric symmetry for glucose utilization has been reported in most normal subjects who were scanned with eyes and ears open (27, 37, 40). Some subjects, however, have demonstrated a relative left-sided hypermetabolism (13), and studies of sensory deprivation have resulted in left > right asymmetries of glucose utilization (37). Mazziotta *et al.* found that left–right LCMRGlc symmetry was consistently found in subjects with minimal sensory deprivation (e.g., eyes and ears open or either eyes or ears selectively occluded) but that left > right metabolic asymmetries occurred when both the eyes and ears were occluded (37). This right-sided relative hypometabolism was most significant in the inferior prefrontal, posterior superior temporal, and lateral occipital cortex. The absolute metabolic values for LCMRGlc revealed that this asymmetry was caused by significantly greater metabolic depressions for these regions in the right hemisphere with progressive sensory deprivation. These asymmetries are in contrast with the left–right metabolic symmetries found in less sensory-deprived states when LCMRGlc was measured (left–right = 1.01 ± 0.03) (Figure 2) (27, 37, 40).

The left > right metabolic asymmetries with more complete sensory deprivation may reflect basic anatomical and functional differences between the two cerebral hemispheres, particularly in the region of the perisylvian cortex. Both anatomical and functional explanations are possible. Anatomical causes would include the finding that perisylvian cortical areas are larger in the left hemisphere of right-handed individuals (19); therefore, at low overall metabolic rates, this anatomical asymmetry may be measured as a side-to-side difference in cerebral metabolism, with the higher value being found in the dominant hemisphere. However, no consistent cortical anatomical asymmetries have been demonstrated for the lateral occipital cortex, while the above-described metabolic asymmetries have been reported for these zones (37). It is also possible that microscopic or ultrastructural anatomic asymmetries (i.e., higher density of neurons, cell processes, or synapses) will be identified in the left hemisphere relative to the right and will correlate with the higher glucose utilization rates found in these regions with PET.

Functional explanations are certainly possible; however, the limited data thus far available do not allow for selection among possible hypotheses. Some of these functional explanations would include (1) selective tuning of cortical language areas in the dominant hemisphere for potential verbal auditory input; (2) verbal-based cognitive processes (i.e., inner language) unmasked with diminished sensory inputs; and (3) reduced vigilance and monitoring of sensory inputs by the right hemisphere with progressive decreases in sensory access to the environment (22, 37). The exact cause of these metabolic findings remains to be determined, but the results do emphasize the fact that in sensory-deprived states metabolic hemispheric asymmetries can be consistently observed. It is also of importance to realize that such asymmetries need to be accounted for when ambient test conditions are designed for PET studies of stimulation of normal individuals, as well as of patients with neuropathology.

Auditory Stimulation

Studies of the human auditory system's response to verbal and nonverbal stimuli has resulted in data demonstrating hemispheric specialization that is dependent on the content of the stimulus and the analysis strategy of the subject, rather than the side of presentation of the stimulus (35, 36, 39). This is in contrast to PET studies of the occipital cortex, which has a symmetric functional response to full-field visual stimulation (47, 50). That is, LCMRGlc values for the left and right visual cortices in all states (monocular and binocular stimulation and deprivation) were

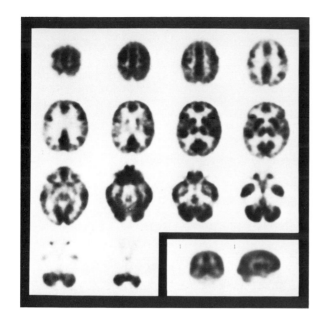

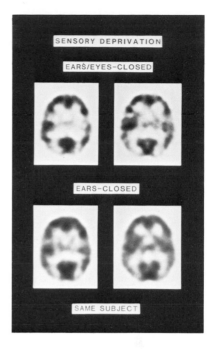

SENSORY DEPRIVATION

EARS/EYES-CLOSED

EARS-CLOSED

SAME SUBJECT

CONTROL

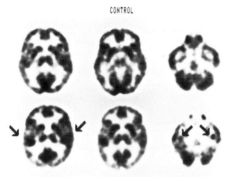

AUDITORY STIMULATION : FORMED LANGUAGE AND MEMORY

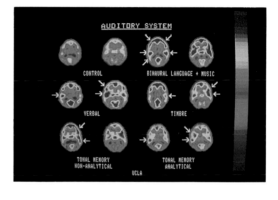

AUDITORY SYSTEM

CONTROL   BINAURAL LANGUAGE + MUSIC

VERBAL   TIMBRE

TONAL MEMORY   TONAL MEMORY
NON-ANALYTICAL   ANALYTICAL

UCLA

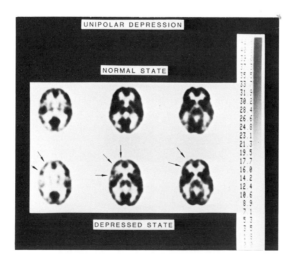

UNIPOLAR DEPRESSION

NORMAL STATE

DEPRESSED STATE

Figure 1 (upper left). Cerebral glucose metabolism. PET images of a normal subject studied with [^{18}F]fluorodeoxyglucose (FDG) to measure glucose metabolism using the NeuroECAT positron computed tomograph. Both tomographic and two-dimensional rectilinear images (lower right corner) are obtainable with this device. Note the details of the cerebral anatomy: top row, cerebral cortical gyri and sulci; second row, basal ganglia, thalamus, and visual cortex (two right-most images); third row, temporal lobe, brain stem, and cerebellum, including cerebellar cortex, vermis, and dentate nuclei (two right-most images). Gray scale of images is in proportion to the glucose metabolic rate with black being the highest. Left hemisphere is shown at the left of this and all image sets. (From 49. Reprinted by permission.)

Figure 2 (upper right). Two sets of images from a normal individual studied with FDG to measure local cerebral glucose metabolic rates in two states of sensory deprivation. The upper row of images was obtained from a subject studied with both auditory input occlusion (ear plugs and soundproof headphones) and light-excluding eye patches. Metabolic asymmetry is seen in this state, with the right side being relatively hypometabolic compared to the left. The site of maximal asymmetry is in the perisylvian cortical regions and the lateral occipital cortex. Lower set of images was obtained in the same subject with his ears occluded but with eyes open. This set of images demonstrates left–right symmetry for glucose metabolism in all cortical and subcortical zones. Studies such as these demonstrate that ambient conditions can affect the magnitude and pattern of the distribution of metabolic activity in PET images and reveal hemispheric asymmetries not seen in less-sensory-deprived states. (From 49. Reprinted by permission.)

Figure 3 (middle left). Two sets of images from two different normal subjects studied with FDG to determine LCMRGlc in a control (top row) and auditory-stimulated state (bottom row). Images were obtained with the NeuroECAT PET device (23, 24). The top row of images was obtained from a subject with no auditory stimulation. The bottom row was obtained from a subject listening to a factual story monaurally. Note the activation of the primary auditory cortex situated bilaterally in the posterior transverse temporal cortical zone. Left–right asymmetries closely parallel known anatomical asymmetries for these areas of the human brain (i.e., the region on the left is larger, wedge-shaped, and more posterior than its counterpart on the right) (19). Note also in the lowest plane (bottom right image) activation of the mesial temporal lobe during the verbal task. Subject was instructed to remember specific phrases of the auditory stimulus material and told that he would be paid in proportion to his performance on an examination following the stimulation task. (From 36. Reprinted by permission.)

Figure 4 (middle right). Cerebral glucose metabolism measured with PET and FDG in a variety of states of auditory stimulation. Color scale is proportional to LCMRGlc with red being the highest. Upper-left image set represents the control state with ears closed by rubber stoppers and covered with soundproof headphones (eyes open). Upper-right images were obtained during bilateral stimulation with language (Sherlock Holmes story) and music (Brandenburg concerto). In this state subjects demonstrated diffuse activation of both posterior temporal and frontal lobes. The verbal stimulation consisted of a monaurally presented Sherlock Holmes story and resulted in diffuse left-sided activity with frontal lobe metabolism greater on the left and bilateral posterior temporal and left temporal occipital activations. The responses to nonverbal stimuli are also shown. The timbre test consisted of subjects identifying chord pairs that differed in harmonic composition. All subjects had diffuse right-sided activations and asymmetries and bilateral inferior parietal activations. Nonverbal stimulation with tone sequences resulted in activations dependent on the subject's analysis strategy. Musical sophistication and/or use of stereotyped visual imagery strategies (analytic) produced left-sided asymmetries, whereas subjects who were musically naive or who used nonanalytic, nonvisual imagery strategies had diffuse right-sided activations (nonanalytic) similar to subjects examined while performing the timbre test. (From 36. Reprinted by permission.)

Figure 5 (bottom). Cerebral glucose metabolism in patients with unipolar depression. Top row is a set of PET images of glucose metabolism in the normal age-matched individual. Bottom row was obtained from a subject with a diagnosis of unipolar depression who was studied in the depressed state. Note the metabolic asymmetries in these images. There is less metabolic activity in the posterior inferior frontal cortex and superior temporal cortex on the left side relative to the right. Not all patients with this diagnosis demonstrated metabolic asymmetries; and correlations with clinical state, trait, and ambient test conditions are presently being investigated. In patients treated with methylphenidate who had a positive clinical response (i.e., a change toward euthymic state) the metabolic asymmetries were reduced. (From 48. Reprinted by permission.)

symmetric, confirming a 50% functional input from each eye to both visual cortices (47, 50).

In studies of the auditory system using PET and FDG to measure glucose utilization, various types of verbal and nonverbal stimuli have been employed (20, 30, 35, 38, 53). Initial studies of the auditory system performed by Rievich *et al.* (53) used monaurally presented factual stories. This stimulus produced 20–25% increases in metabolic rate in the entire right temporal lobe, regardless of the ear stimulated. This was true whether the story was meaningful or nonmeaningful (foreign language). In six subjects who listened monaurally (three left, three right) to the factual story, Greenberg *et al.* (20) found a $7.0 \pm 2.5\%$ LCMRGlc asymmetry for the temporal cortex, with the higher value consistently contralateral to the stimulated ear.

In contrast to these studies, Mazziotta *et al.* (35, 36) demonstrated that the stimulus content rather than the side of stimulation determined the site of greatest functional activation. Strongly right-handed subjects were monaurally presented with either a factual story or one of two types of nonverbal stimuli. The verbal material was a Sherlock Holmes story, while the nonverbal material was obtained from the Seashore Battery of Musical Aptitude tests. All studies were paired, such that a control PET study was obtained with the subject's ears plugged and covered with soundproof headphones, and a stimulation study, performed on a subsequent day, was obtained using one of the above-mentioned stimulus sets.

Regardless of the stimulus employed, bilateral activations of the superior transverse temporal cortex were identified (36). The magnitude of the metabolic response in these cortical zones was symmetric, although there was a trend toward a greater response in the transverse temporal cortex contralateral to the stimulated ear. The distribution of the increased metabolic activity in the transverse temporal cortex was, however, asymmetric. This asymmetry conformed to known anatomical asymmetries of the primary auditory cortex and the planum temporale (Figure 3) (19).

Verbal stimuli produced consistent left > right (frontal and temporal) metabolic asymmetries, left thalamic activation, and bilateral transverse and posterior temporal cortical activations (35, 36). Relative to the verbal stimuli, nonverbal stimuli with pairs of chords produced mirror-image, right-sided activations and asymmetries, as well as bilateral inferior parietal activations. Nonverbal stimuli consisting of tone sequences produced metabolic responses that correlated with the analysis strategy employed by the subjects. Individuals who used stereotyped visual-imagery approaches (e.g., "I saw bar graphs of the frequencies in my mind") or who were musically sophisticated had left > right temporal metabolic asymmetries. Conversely, subjects who used less stereotyped strategies, those who used no visual-imagery approaches, or those who were musically naive had diffuse right-sided activations and metabolic asymmetries. Thus, in a paradigm where the stimulus set and the task were identical, two quite different sets of results emerged that seemed to correlate with the analysis strategy employed by the subjects and/or their past musical experiences. In summary, this study demonstrates that while metabolic responses were seen in both hemispheres in complex patterns (Figure 4), a predominant and consistently reproducible distribution of asymmetric cortical responses was reported for each type of stimulus set.

Cognitive Tasks

Cerebral glucose metabolic asymmetries have been reported for tasks with purported hemispheric specialization properties (21, 54). In subjects who were asked to perform Miller Analogies, the superior temporal, inferior parietal, and frontal eye fields had higher metabolic rates in the left hemisphere when compared with a group of subjects performing a spatial task (Benton's Line Orientation Task), in whom the nondominant right hemisphere was more active. Gur *et al.* (21, 54) used PET to examine a group of subjects performing various stimulation tasks and compared these studies with those obtained with a different group of subjects who were scanned in a "resting" (no-task) state. It was noted that the subjects who were performing the stimulation tasks consistently had right inferior parietal metabolic activations when compared to the control population, regardless of the task to which they were assigned. The investigators interpreted this data to be indicative of the right parietal area's role as a center for sensory attention to environmental processes.

STUDIES IN PATIENTS WITH NEUROPATHOLOGY

A large number of studies have been performed with PET to examine all of the major categories of neuropathological processes (33, 49). In a few instances, specific attention has been paid to hemispheric specialization and the impact of cerebral pathology on these lateralized functions.

Patients with Aphasia

Glucose metabolic studies were performed by Metter *et al.* (41, 42) to examine clinical–metabolic correlations in aphasic stroke patients. These studies demonstrated that defects in metabolic activity were typically larger than those seen by x-ray CT. In addition, metabolic depression of the dominant parietal and/or posterior temporal cortex was consistently associated with difficulties in auditory comprehension, oral reading, naming, and repetition. These investigators examined patients with subcortical versus cortical metabolic lesions as well. They found a consistent correlation between abnormal verbal memory and hypometabolism of the left thalamus. They concluded that these data were indicative of a functional relationship between dominant thalamic function and verbal memory.

In metabolic studies of aphasic patients, examples have been found of metabolic lesions that could explain clinical symptoms despite normal x-ray CT studies (42). However, cases were also reported having similar PET results but quite different clinical syndromes. Careful correlation of ambient test conditions (i.e., language activations), timing of the study following the stroke ictus, and the degree of poststroke–prescan speech therapy are needed to characterize such disorders further.

It may be possible to use knowledge gained via PET about hemispheric specialization to provide more pathophysiologically relevant approaches to speech therapy in patients with brain injuries producing aphasia. Such studies would be aimed at the development of stimulation paradigms that could be used to study recovery of brain function following just this sort of cerebral injury (34). For example, consider the following situation: First, a task is selected that produces a focal activation in a given brain region as determined with PET. Second, a patient population is identified in which individuals can perform this task (perhaps with less efficiency than normal individuals), but have clear evidence (from x-ray CT or "resting" PET studies) of abnormalities within the structure identified as participating in this task in a normal population. Last, a set of PET images is obtained while these patients are performing the specific task. Resultant data should provide clues as to how the brain functionally reorganizes or adapts to perform a task, even though the system identified in normals that performs the task has been compromised by cerebral pathology. Such studies should not only provide insights into the fundamental process of cerebral reorganization after injury, but can also potentially provide guidelines for the pathophysiologically oriented rehabilitation of such brain-injured individuals. If, for instance, significant regions of the nondominant hemisphere are seen to be activated concomitant with clinical recovery of language functions, rehabilitation could be aimed at processes that, through other PET stimulation paradigms, have been shown to activate these same right-hemispheric zones in normal individuals.

PET studies in patients with tumors and stroke that measured blood flow and glucose and oxygen metabolism have demonstrated physiological abnormalities at sites distant from the primary structural lesion seen by x-ray CT (1, 8, 9, 11, 17, 27, 31, 32, 43). These distant lesions occurred in a distribution that seems to correspond to the efferent projection systems emanating from the region of structural damage. These distant zones of reduced flow and metabolism have taken a number of patterns, which include (1) reduced metabolism in the thalamus ipsilateral to a cortical structural lesion; (2) reduced metabolism in the cortex overlying a thalamic structural lesion; (3) reduced metabolism in the cortex contralateral to a cortical structural lesion (these have been either focal, mirror-image, or diffuse); (4) reduced metabolism in the cortex overlying a structural lesion in the white matter of the ipsilateral hemisphere; and (5) hypometabolism in the cerebellar hemisphere contralateral to a supratentorial (carotid artery distribution) structural lesion.

Since these distant effects of structural brain lesions have thus far only been demonstrated by PET, they not only confound but provide a means of investigating prior clinical–pathological interpretations of neurobehavioral abnormalities in patients with brain injury. It can no longer be assumed that a patient with a structural lesion at a specific site has symptoms related only to that anatomical zone. These new data demonstrate that far-reaching and widespread effects can occur in the opposite hemisphere, in subcortical structures, and even in the posterior fossa as a result of a structural lesion localized to one hemisphere. The extent, severity, and position of the lesions that result in these various types of distant effects are presently under investigation. The further PET characterization of these effects should result in a more complete understanding of cerebral dysfunction resulting from acute structural lesions and should provide important clues in the understanding of cerebral hemispheric specialization as it relates to brain-damaged individuals.

Demented Patients

A large number of studies have already been performed to examine blood flow and oxygen and glucose metabolism in patients with Alzheimer disease (2, 10, 14, 15, 16, 18, 26). These studies demonstrate no consistent lateralized abnormalities, but rather broad reductions in blood flow and metabolism in neocortical areas. In patients with early disease, more focal abnormalities have been reported (6, 10, 14, 15, 26).

A number of studies have looked at specific features of cortical dysfunction that were particularly prominent in subgroups of subjects with Alzheimer disease. Frackowiak *et al.* (16) found no specific regional differences in flow or oxygen metabolism in patients with more profound symptoms of aphasia or apraxia. Foster *et al.* and Chase *et al.* (6, 7, 14, 15) found a different result, however. These investigators also examined patients that had specific predominant symptoms of cortical dysfunction and the diagnosis of Alzheimer disease. Subgroups included patients with specific constructional abnormalities, language disorders, and pure memory syndromes. In the group with abnormal spatial and constructional test scores, a 32% decrease in glucose utilization was found in the right parietal cortex, whereas those with specific language abnormalities had metabolic decrements of 18% in the left frontal–temporal–parietal region relative to the contralateral sides. Patients with predominant memory abnormalities had no left–right metabolic asymmetries. In these patients, who had little evidence of cerebrovascular disease and who were not on medication, it was concluded that focal abnormalities could be identified in metabolic images that correlated with the predominant clinical symptoms and revealed lateralized metabolic lesions associated with cognitive disabilities.

Patients with Psychiatric Disorders

Only a limited number of studies in psychiatric populations have thus far been performed with PET. Results, however, provide some interesting information about asymmetric hemispheric abnormalities in this heterogeneous group of disorders. While by no means consistent, some studies have reported hypometabolism of the frontal cortex in patients with schizophrenia (4, 12, 60). A similar though preliminary finding has been reported for reductions in frontal amino acid incorporation in hebephrenic, schizophrenic patients (5).

Preliminary studies in patients with affective disorders have demonstrated metabolic asymmetries in a select subgroup. In patients with unipolar depression, glucose metabolism was determined using FDG and PET (Figure 5) (48). Some, but not all, of these patients had relative hypometabolism of the left posterior, inferior frontal cortex. All these patients were young (20–40), strongly right-handed, not medicated, and suffering from endogenous depression. As yet, no clinical or biochemical features have been identified that correlate with the left < right metabolic subgrouping of these depressed patients, although there is preliminary evidence that these patients also have an obsessive–compulsive behavioral disorder in addition to their depression. In this same study, depressed patients were studied in a resting, baseline state and then on a subsequent day after the administration of 15 mg of methylphenidate (48). In those patients with left < right metabolic asymmetries who had a positive clinical response to the drug (change toward euthymia), a reduction in the metabolic asymmetries occurred. In a single patient who had worsening of symptoms following the administration of the drug, the metabolic asymmetry was exaggerated. In normal subjects studied on and off methylphenidate (administered in the same way as for the depressed patients), no drug-induced metabolic left–right differences have been detected thus far.

FUTURE PROSPECTS

Since PET provides the opportunity to look at functional brain responses in health and disease with a high degree of anatomical detail, it is extremely well suited to the study of hemispheric specialization. Thus far, studies in normal individuals have demonstrated that these techniques have the ability to show the complex patterns of asymmetric cerebral responses to physiological types of stimuli. More detailed experiments, which will be more physiologically interpretable, are now under way to look at basic principles of language, memory, and cognitive tasks using these techniques. By progressively building data obtained from increasingly complex studies of these cerebral processes, it is hoped that a picture will emerge of how these complex tasks are performed in the normal brain and following brain injury. The examples provided of studies in patients with cerebral pathology demonstrate that lateralized hemispheric effects may be extremely important in the expression of neuropsychiatric disease. The use of PET to study such patients, particularly in the recovery phase of their illness, may allow for the pathophysiologically oriented rehabilitation of patients with brain injury. It seems certain that despite the complexity and cost of PET studies, PET will play an important role in the understanding of cerebral function and hemispheric specialization, both in normal individuals and in patients with neuropsychiatric disorders.

REFERENCES

1. Baron, J. C., Bousser, M. G., Comar, D., *et al.*, "Crossed cerebellar diaschisis" in human supratentorial brain infarction. *Trans. Am. Neurol. Assoc.*, 1980, **105**: 459–461.
2. Benson, D. F., The use of positron emission scanning techniques in the diagnosis of Alzheimer's disease. In: *Alzheimer's Disease: A Review of Progress* (S. Corkin, K. L. Davis, J. H. Growdan, *et al.*, Eds.). Raven Press, New York, 1982: 79–82.
3. Buchsbaum, M. S., Holcomb, H. H., Johnson, J., King, A. C., and Kessler, R., Cerebral metabolic consequences of electrical cutaneous stimulation in normal individuals. *Hum. Neurobiol.*, 1983, **2**: 35–38.
4. Buchsbaum, M. S., Ingvar, D. H., Kessler, R., *et al.*, Cerebral glucography with positron tomography: Use in normal subjects and in patients with schizophrenia. *Arch. Gen. Psychol.*, 1982, **39**: 251–259.

5. Bustany, P., Henry, J. F., deRotrou, J., *et al.*, Local cerebral metabolic rate of ^{11}C-L-methionine in early stages of dementia, schizophrenia, and Parkinson's disease. *J. Cereb. Blood Flow Metab.*, 1983, 3(Suppl. 1): S492–S493.

6. Chase, T. N., Brooks, R. A., DiChiro, G., *et al.*, Focal cortical abnormalities in Alzheimer's disease. In: *The Metabolism of the Human Brain Studied with Positron Emission Tomography* (T. Greitz, D. H. Ingvar, and L. Widen, Eds.). Raven Press, New York, 1985: 433–440.

7. Chase, T. N., Foster, N. L., Fedio, P., *et al.*, Alzheimer's disease: Local cerebral metabolism studies using ^{18}F-fluorodeoxyglucose positron emission tomography techniques. In: *Aging of the Brain* (D. Samuel, *et al.*, Eds.). Raven Press, New York, 1983: 143–154.

8. DeLaPaz, R. L., Patronas, N. J., Brooks, R. A., *et al.*, A PET study of suppression of glucose utilization in cerebral gray matter associated with brain tumor. *J. Cereb. Blood Flow Metab.*, 1983, 3(Suppl. 1): S21–S22.

9. DeLaPaz, R. L., Patronas, N. J., Brooks, R. A., *et al.*, Positron emission tomographic study of suppression of gray matter glucose utilization by brain tumors. *AJNR*, 1983, 4: 826–829.

10. deLeon, M. J., Ferris, S. H., George, A. E., *et al.*, Regional correlation of PET and CT in senile dementia of the Alzheimer type. *AJNR*, 1983, 4: 553–556.

11. DiChiro, G., DeLaPaz, R. L., Brooks, R. A., *et al.*, Glucose utilization of cerebral gliomas measured by [^{18}F]fluorodeoxyglucose and positron emission tomography. *Neurology* (NY), 1982, **32**: 1323–1329.

12. Farkas, T., Reivich, M., Alavi, A., *et al.*, The application of [^{18}F]-2-deoxy-2-fluoro-D-glucose and positron emission tomography in the study of psychiatric conditions. In: *Cerebral Metabolism and Neural Function* (J. V. Passonneau, R. Hawkins, W. D. Lust, *et al.*, Eds.). Williams & Wilkins, Baltimore, 1980: 403–408.

13. Finklestein, S., Alpert, N. M., Ackerman, R. H., *et al.*, Positron imaging of the normal brain — Regional patterns of cerebral blood flow and metabolism. *Trans. Am. Neurol. Assoc.*, 1980, **105**: 8–10.

14. Foster, N. L., Chase, T. N., Fedio, P., *et al.*, Alzheimer's disease: Focal cortical changes shown by positron emission tomography. *Neurology*, 1983, **33**: 961–965.

15. Foster, N. L., Chase, T. N., Patronas, N. J., *et al.*, Cerebral mapping of apraxia by positron emission tomography of Alzheimer's disease. *Ann. Neurol.*, 1982, **12**: 89.

16. Frackowiak, R. S., Pozzilli, C., Legg, N. J., *et al.*, Regional cerebral oxygen supply and utilization in dementia. *Brain*, 1981, **104**: 753–778.

17. Frackowiak, R. S., and Wise, R. J., Positron tomography in ischemic cerebrovascular disease. *Neurol. Clin.*, 1983, 1: 183–200.

18. Friedland, R. P., Budinger, T. F., Ganz, E., *et al.*, Regional cerebral metabolic alterations in dementia of the Alzheimer type: Positron emission tomography with [^{18}F]-fluorodeoxyglucose. *J. Comput. Assist. Tomogr.*, 1983, 7: 590–598.

19. Geschwind, N., and Levitsky, W., Human brain: Left-right asymmetries in temporal speech region. *Science*, 1968, **161**: 186–187.

20. Greenberg, J., Reivich, M., Alavi, A., *et al.*, Metabolic mapping of functional activity in human subjects with the [^{18}F]fluorodeoxyglucose technique. *Science*, 1981, **212**: 678–680.

21. Gur, R. C., Gur, R. E., Rosen, A. D., *et al.*, A cognitive-motor network demonstrated by positron emission tomography. *Neuropsychologia*, 1983, **21**: 601–606.

22. Heilman, K. M., and Van Den Abell, T., Right hemisphere dominance for mediating cerebral activity. *Neuropsychologia*, 1979, **17**: 315–321.

23. Hoffman, E. J., Phelps, M. E., Huang, S. C., *et al.*, A new tomograph for quantitative positron computed tomography of the brain. *IEEE Trans. Nucl. Sci.*, 1981, **NS-28**: 99–103.

24. Hoffman, E. J., Phelps, M. E., and Huang, S. C., Performance evaluation of a positron

tomograph designed for brain imaging. *J. Nucl. Med.*, 1983, **24**: 245–257.

25. Huang, S. C., Phelps, M. E., Hoffman, E. J., *et al.*, Noninvasive determination of local cerebral metabolic rate of glucose in man. *Am. J. Physiol.*, 1980, **238**: E69–E82.
26. Kuhl, D. E., Metter, E. J., Riege, W. H., *et al.*, Local cerebral glucose utilization in elderly patients with depression, multiple infarct dementia and Alzheimer's disease. *J. Cereb. Blood Flow Metab.*, 1983, 3(Suppl. 1): S494–S495.
27. Kuhl, D. E., Phelps, M. E., Kowell, A. P., Metter, E. J., Selin, C., and Winter, J., Mapping local metabolism and perfusion in normal and ischemic brain by emission computed tomography of ^{18}FDG and ^{13}NH$_3$. *Ann. Neurol.*, 1980, **8**: 47–60.
28. Kuhl, D. E., Phelps, M. E., Markham, C. H., *et al.*, Cerebral metabolism and atrophy in Huntington's disease determined by ^{18}FDG and computed tomographic scan. *Ann. Neurol.*, 1982, **12**: 425–434.
29. Kusher, M., Rosenquist, A., Alavi, A., *et al.*, Macular and peripheral visual field representation in the striate cortex demonstrated by positron emission tomography. *Ann. Neurol.*, 1982, **12**: 89.
30. Lauter, J. L., Formby, C., Fox, P., Herscovitch, P., and Raichle, M. E., Tonotopic organization in human auditory cortex as revealed by regional changes in cerebral blood flow. *J. Cereb. Blood Flow Metab.*, 1983, 3(Suppl. 1): S248–S249.
31. Lenzi, G. L., Frackowiak, R. S., and Jones, T., Regional cerebral blood flow (CBF), oxygen utilization (CMRO$_2$) and oxygen extraction ratio (OER) in acute hemispheric stroke. *J. Cereb. Blood Flow Metab.*, 1981, 1(Suppl. 1): S504–S505.
32. Lenzi, G. L., Frackowiak, R. S., and Jones, T., Cerebral oxygen metabolism and blood flow in human cerebral ischemic infarction. *J. Cereb. Blood Flow Metab.*, 1982, **2**: 321–335.
33. Mazziotta, J. C., Studies of cerebral function and dysfunction. In: Positron computed tomography for studies of myocardial and cerebral function (M. E. Phelps, Moderator). *Ann. Intern. Med.*, 1983, **9**: 339–359.
34. Mazziotta, J. C., and Phelps, M. E., Human sensory stimulation and deprivation. PET results and strategies. *Ann. Neurol.*, 1984, (Suppl.): 550–560.
35. Mazziotta, J. C., Phelps, M. E., and Carson, R. E., Tomographic mapping of human cerebral metabolism: Subcortical responses to auditory and visual stimulation. *Neurology*, 1984, **34**: 825–828.
36. Mazziotta, J. C., Phelps, M. E., Carson, R. E., *et al.*, Tomographic mapping of human cerebral metabolism: Auditory stimulation. *Neurology*, 1982, **32**: 921–937.
37. Mazziotta, J. C., Phelps, M. E., Carson, R. E., *et al.*, Tomographic mapping of human cerebral metabolism: Sensory deprivation. *Ann. Neurol.*, 1982, **12**: 435–444.
38. Mazziotta, J. C., Phelps, M. E., and Halgren, E., Local cerebral glucose metabolic responses to audio-visual stimulation and deprivation: Studies in human subjects with positron CT. *Hum. Neurobiol.*, 1983, **2**: 11–23.
39. Mazziotta, J. C., Phelps, M. E., Halgren, E., Carson, R. E., Huang, S. C., and Bayer, J., Hemispheric lateralization and local cerebral metabolic and blood flow responses to physiologic stimuli. *J. Cereb. Blood Flow Metab.*, 1983, 3(Suppl. 1): S246–S247.
40. Mazziotta, J. C., Phelps, M. E., Miller, J., *et al.*, Tomographic mapping of human cerebral metabolism: Normal unstimulated state. *Neurology*, 1981, **31**: 503–516.
41. Metter, E. J., Riege, W. H., Hanson, W. R., *et al.*, Comparison of metabolic rates, language and memory in subcortical aphasia. *Brain Lang.*, 1983, **19**: 33–47.
42. Metter, E. J., Waterlain, C. G., Kuhl, D. E., *et al.*, ^{18}FDG positron emission computed tomography: A study of aphasia. *Ann. Neurol.*, 1981, **10**: 173–183.
43. Patronas, N. J., DiChiro, G., Smith, B. H., *et al.*, Depressed cerebellar glucose metabolism in supratentorial tumors. *Brain Res.*, 1984, **291**: 93–101.
44. Penfield, W., and Rasmussen, T., *The Cerebral Cortex of Man*. Macmillan, New York, 1950.

45. Phelps, M. E., Positron computed tomography studies of cerebral glucose metabolism: Theory and application in nuclear medicine. *Semin. Nucl. Med.*, 1981, **11**: 32–49.

46. Phelps, M. E., Huang, S. C., Hoffman, E. J., Selin, C., Sokoloff, L., and Kuhl, D. E., Tomographic measurement of local cerebral glucose metabolic rate in humans with (F-18)2-fluoro-2-deoxyglucose: Validation of method. *Ann. Neurol.*, 1979, **6**: 371–388.

47. Phelps, M. E., Kuhl, D. E., and Mazziotta, J. C., Metabolic mapping of the brain's response to visual stimulation: Studies in man. *Science*, 1981, **211**: 1445–1448.

48. Phelps, M. E., Mazziotta, J. C., Gerner, R., *et al.*, Human cerebral glucose metabolism in affective disorders: Drug-free states and pharmacologic effects. *J. Cereb. Blood Flow Metab.*, 1983, **3**(Suppl. 1): S7–S8.

49. Phelps, M. E., Mazziotta, J. C., and Huang, S. C., Study of cerebral function with positron computed tomography. *J. Cereb. Blood Flow Metab.*, 1982, **2**: 113–162.

50. Phelps, M. E., Mazziotta, J. C., Kuhl, D. E., *et al.*, Tomographic mapping of human cerebral metabolism: Visual stimulation and deprivation. *Neurology*, 1981, **31**: 517–529.

51. Phelps, M. E., Schelbert, H. R., and Mazziotta, J. C., Positron computed tomography for studies of myocardial and cerebral function. *Ann. Intern. Med.*, 1983, **98**: 339–459.

52. Reivich, M., Cobbs, W., Rosenquist, A., *et al.*, Abnormalities in local cerebral glucose metabolism in patients with visual field defects. *J. Cereb. Blood Flow Metab.*, 1981, **1**(Suppl. 1): S471–S472.

53. Reivich, M., Greenberg, J., Alavi, A., *et al.*, The use of the ^{18}F-fluorodeoxyglucose technique for mapping functional neural pathways in man. *Acta Neurol. Scand.*, 1979, **60**(Suppl. 72): 198–199.

54. Reivich, M., Gur, R., and Alavi, A., Positron emission tomographic studies of sensory stimuli, cognitive processes and anxiety. *Hum. Neurobiol.*, 1983, **2**: 25–33.

55. Reivich, M., Kuhl, D., Wolf, A., Greenberg, J., Phelps, M., Ido, T., Casella, V., Hoffman, E., Alavi, A., and Sokoloff, L., The [^{18}F]fluorodeoxyglucose method for the measurement of local cerebral glucose utilization in man. *Circ. Res.*, 1979, **44**: 127–137.

56. Roland, P. E., Meyer, E., Shibaski, T., *et al.*, Regional cerebral blood flow changes in cortex and basal ganglia during voluntary movements in normal volunteers. *J. Neurophysiol.*, 1982, **48**: 467–480.

57. Roland, P., Meyer, E., Yamamoto, Y., *et al.*, Dynamic positron emission tomography as a tool in neuroscience: Functional brain-mapping in normal human volunteers. *J. Cereb. Blood Flow Metab.*, 1981, **1**(Suppl. 1): S463–S464.

58. Sokoloff, L., Reivich, M., Kennedy, C., DesRosiers, M. H., Patlak, C. S., Pettigrew, K. D., Sakurada, O., and Shinohara, M., The [^{14}C]deoxyglucose method for the measurement of local cerebral glucose utilization: Theory, procedure and normal values in the conscious and anesthetized albino rat. *J. Neurochem.*, 1977, **28**: 897–916.

59. Ter-Pogossian, N. M., Physical aspects of emission CT. In: *Radiology of the Skull and Brain: Technical Aspects of Computed Tomography* (T. H. Newton and D. G. Potts, Eds.). C. V. Mosby, St. Louis, 1981: 4372–4388.

60. Widen, L., Bergstrom, M., Bromqvist, G., *et al.*, Glucose metabolism in patients with schizophrenia: Emission computed tomography measurements with 11-C-glucose. *J. Cereb. Blood Flow Metab.*, 1981, **1**(Suppl. 1): S455–S456.

LANGUAGE IN THE LEFT HEMISPHERE

D. FRANK BENSON, MD
Department of Neurology

Discussing the importance of the left hemisphere for language is somewhat akin to discussing the good qualities of motherhood. Everyone with knowledge of the field recognizes that the left hemisphere is of paramount importance for language function in the vast majority of humans. In fact, this statement is so fully accepted that it remains basically unchallenged; instead, the reasons for discussing the localization of language functions anywhere other than in the left hemisphere are questioned. When one examines the functions attributed to the left hemisphere in language activities over the past several centuries, a continuing alteration of opinions is easily discerned. The left hemisphere's position in language function has been neither static nor fixed; significant and meaningful changes concerning postulated functions of the two hemispheres in language continue to occur. To understand the shifts of position that are occurring today, some realization of prior positions is needed.

"In the beginning there was Broca." While excessively dramatic, this statement is not far from the truth. Learned, sometimes furious, debates concerning whether mental functions were carried out by the brain as a whole or were the product of individual portions of the brain had been carried on for over half a century. Gall's localization postulations had been thoroughly challenged by the studies of Flourens; Bouillad's outspoken belief that "speech" was a focal activity of the brain was thoroughly discounted by his contemporaries (17). The demonstration by Broca in 1861 (6) of the brain of a patient who had lost the ability to use language opened new vistas; it did not settle the argument. Although Broca's patient had suffered an almost total loss of expressive language, the brain was not totally damaged; rather, there was a relatively localized disturbance that involved the inferior frontal cortex and underlying tissues. While the focal nature and frontal location were the aspects that were stressed and debated, it was the technique—the correlation of an abnormal behavior observed during lifetime with the location of damage to the brain demonstrated at postmortem—that was the momentous innovation. Here was a major new research tool, one that could be utilized in many institutions. And many investigators, from many parts of the world, were soon providing similar evidence, either supportive or contradictory to Broca's language localization hypothesis. The behavioral–anatomical correlation process used by Broca produced one of the great forward leaps in the knowledge of brain function.

With the study of additional patients, Broca and his contemporaries were able to confirm the importance of the frontal lobe for speaking. Thus, in 1863, Broca (7) reported eight cases with language output (speech) disturbance who had left frontal damage at postmortem. He also reported one case with right frontal damage who had no speaking disturbance. The novelty of these findings warranted caution, and Broca stated: "Here are eight cases where the lesion is situated in the posterior portion of the third frontal convolution . . . and a most remarkable thing, in all of these patients the lesion is on the left side. I do not dare make a conclusion and I await new findings." He did not take long in evaluating additional cases, quite possibly pushed by the publication in 1863 of a paper that had been written many years earlier by a physician named Dax but never previously published (13, 21). Primarily on the basis of observations that right hemiplegia was far more common than left in those patients with an acquired speech disturbance, Dax suggested that the left hemisphere subserved language functions. In an 1865 paper, Broca (8) stated this position clearly: "We speak with the left hemisphere."

Based on the new methodology introduced by Broca, clinicians soon outlined a number of syndromes of abnormal language behavior, each correlated, more or less exactly, with specific areas of left-brain involvement (14, 15, 20, 23, 25, 33). While many of these early syndromes were incompletely described and a number of the early postulates of language function have not survived, a nidus of consistency was present, and the basic observations outlined in this period have remained in use for over a century. The currently accepted neurological presentation of aphasia is based on the syndromes originally devised in the nineteenth century, updated and modified to correlate with more modern psychological and linguistic terminology and improved by use of modern brain imaging devices. Table 1 presents a listing of the better-accepted aphasic syndromes, outlining the major language and basic neurological features. Figure 1 presents the location of the area of cortex in the left hemisphere most likely to be involved when one of these syndromes is present. All of these syndromes indicate abnormality in the left hemisphere, and, with little exception, all localizations fall within the territory of the middle cerebral artery.

The collection of additional types of aphasia in the ensuing several decades did not detract from Broca's original statement that humans speak with the left hemisphere. In fact, the accumulated case material gave considerable additional strength to his statement. The frequent combination of language impairment and paralytic changes in the preferred hand was recognized and compared to the relative intactness of language when the nonpreferred hand was paralyzed. An opposite state for non-left-handers was proposed. Thus, two rules concerning language dominance became widely accepted in the late 19th century:

1. The left hemisphere is crucial (dominant) for language in the right-handed individual.

2. The right hemisphere is similarly important for the left-handed individual.

The dictum of the crucial status of the left hemisphere for language was so totally accepted that a number of terms were developed to demarcate this importance. The most commonly used were "dominant" and "nondominant" for the left and right hemispheres, respectively. Even more descriptive was the use of "major" and "minor"

TABLE 1
SYNDROMES OF APHASIA

Type of Aphasia	Spontaneous Speech	Paraphasia	Comprehension	Repetition	Naming	Motor Function	Sensory Function	Visual Field
Broca	Nonfluent	Uncommon	Good	Poor	Poor	Poor	Good	Normal
Wernicke	Fluent	Common (verbal)	Poor	Poor	Poor	Good	Variable	Superior quadrantopsia
Conduction	Fluent	Common (literal)	Good	Poor	Poor	Good	Variable	Normal
Global	Nonfluent	Variable	Poor	Poor	Poor	Poor	Poor	Hemianopsia
Mixed transcortical	Nonfluent	Uncommon	Poor	Good (echolalia)	Poor	Poor	Poor	Hemianopsia
Transcortical motor	Nonfluent	Uncommon	Good	Good (echolalia)	Poor	Poor	Good	Normal
Transcortical sensory	Fluent	Common	Poor	Good (echolalia)	Poor	Good	Poor	Hemianopsia
Anomic	Fluent	Absent	Good	Good	Poor	Good	Good	Normal

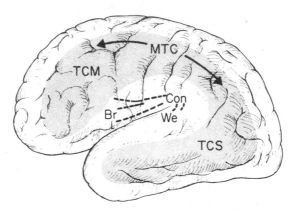

Figure 1. Lateral surface of left cerebral hemisphere indicating areas in which damage most often produces specific aphasia syndromes. The entire area enclosed by stippling is in the distribution of the left middle cerebral artery and represents the language area. The outer stippled area can be considered border zone and the inner white is the perisylvian area. Abbreviations: BR, Broca; Con, conduction; We, Wernicke; TCM, transcortical motor; TCS, transcortical sensory; MTC, mixed transcortical.

to describe the two hemispheres. While noting the separate functional capability of the two hemispheres for many activities, these terms implied that for higher-level functions such as language the right hemisphere acted as a spare, an area of brain held in reserve in case a problem developed in the more important hemisphere.

The question of handedness took on considerable importance at this stage. The correlation between patients who apparently spoke with their left hemisphere and right-handedness, and the converse, those who preferred the left hand and spoke with their right hemisphere, became a subject for investigation. The basic rule was only partially confirmed. The best data concerning this topic in the early years came from study of brain-injured individuals, particularly the injuries to the brain incurred in wartime or as a result of neurosurgical treatment. A number of studies were published, all presenting the same general figures (11, 19, 26, 30). Among right-handed individuals who suffered left-hemisphere damage, approximately 60% became aphasic, while only a third of those individuals who claimed to be left-handed and suffered left-hemisphere damage were rendered aphasic. On the other hand, of right-handers who had damage to their right hemisphere, only a handful (usually 1–2%) became aphasic, while only about 25% of those said to be left-handed developed a long lasting aphasia following a right-hemisphere lesion (see Table 2). It became accepted that a majority of so-called left-handed individuals would become aphasic following left-hemisphere lesions, and that dominance for language was also in the left hemisphere for them. As a sizable number of humans (over 90%) prefer the right hand, and even those who do not also appear to have language dominance on the left, this hemisphere was totally accepted as the brain area dominant for language in the human.

Studies attempting to correlate handedness and language are open to errors, however, and through much of the 20th century, refinements of these studies have further confused the problem. The possibility that many individuals have mixed hemispheric dominance for language has become increasingly evident and further confounds the issue. Many now agree with Annett (1), who insists that two conditions be noted: first, that right-handedness and non-right-handedness (not left-handedness) are the appropriate divisions; second, that language function is likely to be subserved primarily by the left hemisphere in the former, whereas a mixture of right- and left-hemisphere locus of language function is the rule in the latter. The proposition that mixed dominance was prevalent in non-right-handers was strongly supported by the investigation of Karl Gloning (18), who selected all "left-handed" individuals who had presented to the neurological wards in Vienna with structural brain abnormality and who had eventually come to autopsy. He matched these individuals for age, socioeconomic status, education, and location and type of pathology with right-handed subjects who had come to postmortem. While approximately 80% of the right-handed individuals with left-hemisphere lesions had shown aphasic symptomatology, none with lesions of the right hemisphere had become aphasic; in contrast, in the left-handed individuals the presence of aphasia was reported during the clinical course in approximately 80%, regardless of whether the right or the left hemisphere was involved. These and similar findings strongly support a thesis of bilaterality of language function in the non-right-handed individual. On the basis of these observations, a new general rule could be suggested in the 1970s:

1. The left hemisphere is crucial (dominant) for language in the right-handed individual.

2. Non-right-handers are much less definite in the cerebral locus of language; some may have language dominance in the right hemisphere, some in the left, but most have mixed hemispheric dominance.

As broad and loose as the handedness–language correlation has now become, it still cannot be accepted as entirely true. A number of important clinical findings further confound the dichotomy. One notable and frequently quoted exception concerns crossed aphasia, usually defined as the onset of aphasia in a right-handed individual following right-hemisphere damage. Crossed aphasia has been reported through

TABLE 2
INCIDENCE OF APHASIA WITH UNILATERAL HEMISPHERIC LESIONS

Reference	Left-hemisphere Damage		Right-hemisphere Damage	
	Right-handed	Left-handed	Right-handed	Left-handed
Conrad (11)	175/338	10/19	11/249	7/18
Penfield and Roberts (26)	121/175	10/48	1/252	2/12
Russell and Espir (30)	186/288	9/24	3/221	4/24
Total	482/801	29/91	15/722	13/54
%	60%	32%	2%	24%

the years (5, 10), but in a review of the early published cases, Boller (4) was impressed that an inordinately large number of those reported suffered aphasia following either brain trauma or treatment for an intracranial mass lesion. The tendency for bilateral damage to the brain in these conditions is considerably greater than in cases of cerebrovascular accident. It is at least possible that the aphasia found in a sizable portion (quite possibly a majority) of cases of crossed aphasia reported in the literature reflects bilateral brain damage, not right-hemisphere damage alone. Nonetheless, some apparently true crossed aphasias are reported and demand consideration. An example will be presented.

A 46-year-old male with no previous history of cardiac disease noted the sudden occurrence of a jumbled verbal output one evening. His friends thought he had consumed too much liquor, but when the same problem was present the next day, he drove over 40 miles to be seen by his physician. He was found to have a fluent, paraphasic verbal output, excellent comprehension of auditory language, but severe breakdown into paraphasic jargon when he attempted to repeat language. Reading for comprehension was within normal limits, whereas reading aloud was contaminated by numerous paraphasias. In addition, he showed left unilateral inattention (neglect) and some degree of left somesthetic impairment. A diagnosis of conduction aphasia and left sensory disturbance was made. Intense interest was given to the questions of handedness and lesion location. The patient insisted that he was totally right-handed in all activities and denied any blood relatives who were not right-handed. An x-ray CT scan demonstrated a sizable parieto-temporal radiolucency in the right hemisphere, and repeated scans failed to show any left-hemisphere abnormality. From the standpoint of clinical examination, this right-handed patient appeared to develop a clear-cut aphasic syndrome on the basis of right-hemisphere damage, a crossed aphasia.

Another set of incompletely documented clinical findings, the transfer of language function from one hemisphere to another following unilateral brain damage, further clouds the hemispheric dominance picture. It has long been recognized that left-hemisphere damage in children does not produce a lasting aphasia; this phenomenon has been interpreted as an "equipotentiality" of the two hemispheres to subserve the function of language during the early, developmental years (35). It has also been recognized that the ability of the right hemisphere to take over the function of language decreases with advancing age (22), and it is generally agreed that transfer of language capability from one hemisphere to the other does not take place in the adult. This is not entirely true, as another clinical case will attest.

A 58-year-old male was in normal health. Approximately 1 year prior to the onset of aphasia he had undergone cardiac surgery for mitral valve repair. He recovered well and returned to an executive position. Anticoagulant medication, given as a prophylactic treatment, was discontinued 1 year after the surgery; 2 days later he suffered a massive cerebrovascular accident (CVA), demonstrated to be caused by total occlusion at the bifurcation of the left middle cerebral artery. Clinically, this was manifested by a right hemiplegia, right hemisensory loss, right homonymous hemianopsia, and a global aphasia. Despite intense aphasia therapy administered in a number of courses in several institutions over a period of several years, there was no real improvement. However, when a reevaluation was performed about 4 years after the cerebrovascular accident, a significant return of language comprehension and some ability to name, to repeat, and to express himself with language in a meaningful manner was present. X-ray CT at that time demonstrated total destruction of cerebral tissues in the middle cerebral artery territory of the left hemisphere. Again, intense investigation of this patient's background revealed nothing to suggest anything but total right-handedness in himself or in any relative. It was interpreted that this patient suffered only the single cerebral lesion, and, based on the demonstrated destruction of the entire left-hemisphere language area, that the right hemisphere had taken over much of the language function previously subserved by the left hemisphere.

Yet another complication to the simplified handedness–language dominance correlation appears to depend upon the degree of education of the patient prior to the brain injury. In a report of a single well-studied case, Wechsler (32) reported aphasia in a right-handed illiterate secondary to right-hemisphere CVA. Cameron *et al.* (9) studied 65 patients with known left-hemisphere CVAs, divided into three groups based on their premorbid ability to handle written language: literate, semiliterate, and illiterate. Of the literate group, 78% were aphasic and 22% nonaphasic; 64% of the semiliterate group became aphasic, while 36% did not. In the totally illiterate group, on the other hand, the findings were reversed — 36% became aphasic and 64% did not. Both studies suggest that formal education, even at a minimum level of semiliteracy, may influence the lateralization or at least the degree of hemispheric dominance for language. Damasio *et al.* (12), on the other hand, based on aphasic studies of an illiterate, did not support this view. Too few studies of language disturbance in the illiterate are available to adequately evaluate the postulation that literacy affects dominance for language, but the continuation of the nature–nurture controversy is obvious. The relationship of motor preference (handedness) and hemispheric dominance for language appears real but not exact.

Even more disturbing, these problems demonstrate that one of the greatest weaknesses plaguing studies of language impairment concerns the definitions used for the function of verbal communication over the past century. Originally, "speech" was the term used; then "verbal images" and later "language" referred to the function in question. None has been used with precision. "Language" is a commonly used word that has attained a variety of meanings through broad use. When used to define a brain function, "language" should be carefully separated from "speech," the neuromechanical aspect of communication, and also from "thought," the integration of perceptions and knowledge into ideas. Language can be considered the ability to use a communication system, common to a group of individuals, in order to express one's ideas. Neither separation is easy to define or to demonstrate in clinical practice. Nonetheless, it is now widely agreed that it is the loss or impairment of some portion of the ability to use a common communication system that should be called "aphasia" (2).

Language can be subdivided into a number of separate activities that are quite different (28); some appear to be uniquely human functions, but others are definitely present in animals. As an elementary division, four types of language can be presented:

1. Motor (gestural) language.
2. Vocal (prosodic) language.
3. Meaning (semantic) language.
4. Relational (syntactic) language.

The first two types, gestural and prosodic language, appear to be present through much of the higher animal kingdom. Thus, a dog readily communicates its feelings through the appearance of its body (wagging tail, raising of neck hairs) or the sound of its barking. Semantic and syntactic language, on the other hand, are almost exclusively human functions; it is impairment of one or both of these that is routinely referred to as the language impairment called "aphasia."

In attempting to demonstrate a separate role for each of the hemispheres in these four language functions, some guidelines can be presented. First, the portions of language in which the right hemisphere appears to function significantly can be outlined. A number of recent studies suggest that the right hemisphere is far more important (dominant) for that part of vocal (prosodic) language that depends on melody (16, 29). The right hemisphere also appears to be important (quite probably, dominant) for that part of semantic language function that deals with the verbal images produced by words (3, 34). In addition, the right hemisphere appears to participate (but not to the extent to be considered dominant) in the concepts formed from words, a semantic attribute, and in the inflection and timbre (prosodic) qualities of vocal language. In fact, the comprehension of these qualities appears to depend more on the right than the left hemisphere. Finally, the right hemisphere participates significantly in gestural language (27).

Against this background, we come then to the stated purpose of this presentation — an outline of those language functions subserved by the left hemisphere, both as the dominant member and as a participant. First, the left hemisphere appears to be dominant for all forms of syntactic language — the relationships between words, except those based on melody, and even this appears shared with the right hemisphere (31). In addition, the left hemisphere appears to be dominant for the verbal meaning (dictionary definition) of words (semantic language); the ability to provide a name for a visualized (or otherwise sensed) object appears to be strongly left-hemisphere-oriented. Attempts by the right hemisphere to enter this task often lead to substitutions (semantic paraphasias) (24), the production of a basically correct but specifically inaccurate term (e.g., calling a tomato a "red fruit"). Because of this highly specialized attribute, the left hemisphere has an important, but not exclusive, function in the formation of concepts (another semantic quality). The left hemisphere is important for the timing, inflection, and timbre of vocal output (prosody) and participates in gestural language, attributes shared with the right hemisphere. Table 3 outlines the current conceptions of the activities subsumed by each hemisphere in the many different functions called "language." No attempt has been made to separate the functions that are primarily cortical from those primarily based on subcortical activity; those functions that are shared by the two hemispheres may turn out to be primarily dependent on subcortical activity.

Evidence suggesting that each of the two hemispheres functions in several dif-

TABLE 3
LANGUAGE-RELATED FUNCTIONS OF EACH HEMISPHERE

Function	Left Hemisphere	Right Hemisphere
Gestural language	Participates	Participates
Prosodic language		
Timing	Participates	Participates
Inflection	Participates	Participates
Timbre	Participates	Participates
Melody	—	Dominant
Semantic language		
Verbal meaning	Dominant	—
Concepts	Participates	Participates
Visual image	—	Dominant
Syntactic language		
Sequencing	Dominant	—
Relationships	Dominant	—

ferent language activities deserves additional comment. Future observation and investigation may well reveal that the input of each hemisphere is different and may provide further support of the concept of hemispheric specialization. For instance, it has been suggested that both hemispheres are active in the formation of concepts based on language. That the input of the two hemispheres to the overall concept may be quite different appears probable. In crude terms, the right hemisphere is more likely to provide a visual image and the left hemisphere a semantic relationship, with the combination producing the total concept. Concept formation thus appears to be a bihemispheric function with specialized input from each of the hemispheres. In a related manner, prosody also appears to be a product of both hemispheres. The right hemisphere appears to be most important for the melody of verbal output, both for the comprehension and the production of melody and for the comprehension of the timbre, inflection, and timing qualities of vocal output. On the other hand, it is well recognized that production qualities, particularly timbre, timing, and inflection, become abnormal after damage to certain left-hemisphere areas. Whether the latter qualities are primarily dependent upon subcortical or cortical anatomical areas remains to be demonstrated.

When we speak of "dominance for language" by one cerebral hemisphere, it is essential that the term "language" be carefully defined. Concepts of language function are fluid and will change in the future. What can be stated with absolute certainty is that the two hemispheres of the human perform different functions in the use of communication symbols. Not only are semantic and syntatic language almost unique for the human, but they appear to be strongly correlated with left-hemisphere function in most humans. While the function of the left hemisphere remains far more obvious, and apparently more important, not all of the functions important for human communication are the product of left-hemisphere activity. Whether the non-left-hemisphere functions should be excluded from future definitions of language, should be addressed as exceptions to the general rule, or should be accepted as important but separate communication functions is a matter for scholastic controversy. The exceptions to left-hemispheric dominance in language may well prove crucial to a full understanding of brain function.

REFERENCES

1. Annett, M., Genetic and non-genetic influence on handedness. *Behav. Genet.*, 1978, **8**: 227–249.
2. Benson, D. F., *Aphasia, Alexia, and Agraphia*. Churchill Livingstone, New York, 1979.
3. Benson, D. F., The alexias: A guide to the neural basis of reading. In: *The Neurology of Aphasia* (H. S. Kirshner, Ed.). Swets, Amsterdam, 1982: 139–162.
4. Boller, F., Destruction of Wernicke's area without language disturbance: A fresh look at crossed aphasia. *Neuropsychologia*, 1973, **11**: 243–246.
5. Bramwell, B., On crossed aphasia and the factors which go to determine whether the "leading" or "driving" speech centers shall be located in the left or in the right hemisphere of the brain. *Lancet*, 1899, **1**: 1473–1479.
6. Broca, P., Remarques sur le siège de la faculté du langage articulé, suivés d'une observation d'aphémie. *Bulletin Société Anatomique de Paris*, 1861, **2**: 330–357.
7. Broca, P., Localisation des functions cérébrales: Siège du langage articulé. *Bulletin Société Anthropologie*, 1863, **4**: 200.
8. Broca, P., Sur la faculté du langage articulé. *Bulletin Société Anthropologie*, 1865, **6**: 337–393.
9. Cameron, R. F., Currier, R. D., and Haerer, A. F., Aphasia and literacy. *Br. J. Disord. Commun.*, 1971, **6**: 161–163.
10. Clarke, B., and Zangwill, O., A case of "crossed aphasia" in a dextral. *Neuropsychologia*, 1965, **3**: 81–86.
11. Conrad, K., Über aphasische Sprachstorüngen hirnverletzten Linkshander. *Nervenarzt*, 1949, **20**: 148.
12. Damasio, A. R., Castro-Caldes, A., and Grosso, J. T., Brain specialization for language does not depend on literacy. *Arch. Neurol.*, 1976, **33**: 300–301.
13. Dax, M., Lésions de la moitié gauche de l'encéphale coincidant avec l'oubli des signes de la pensée. Paper presented in Montpelier, France, 1836.
14. Dejerine, J., Sur un cas de cécité verbale avec agraphie, suivi d'autopsie. *Memoires Société Biologique*, 1891, **3**: 197–201.
15. Dejerine, J., Contribution à l'étude anatomoclinique et clinique des différentes variétés de cécité verbale. *Mémoires Société Biologique*, 1892, **4**: 61–90.
16. Dordain, M., Degos, J. D., and Dordain, G., Troubles de la voix dans les hémiplégies gauches. *Rev. Laryngol. Otol. Rhinol. (Bord.)*, 1971, **92**: 178–188.
17. Gardner, H., *Frames of Mind*. Basic Books, New York, 1983.
18. Gloning, K., Handedness and aphasia. *Neuropsychologia*, 1977, **15**: 355 358.
19. Goodglass, H., and Quadfasel, F. A., Language laterality in left-handed aphasics. *Brain*, 1954, **77**: 521–548.
20. Henschen, S. E., *Klinische und anatomische beitrage zur pathologie der gehirns*. Almquist & Wiksell, Stockholm, 1922.
21. Joynt, R. J., and Benton, A. L., The memoir of Marc Dax on aphasia. *Neurology*, 1964, **14**: 851–854.
22. Lenneberg, E., *Biological Foundations of Language*. Wiley, New York, 1967.
23. Lichtheim, L., On aphasia. *Brain*, 1885, **7**: 433–484.

24. Marshall, J. C., and Newcombe, F., Syntactic and semantic errors in paralexia. *Neuropsychologia*, 1966, **4**: 169–176.
25. Nielsen, J. M., *Agnosia, Apraxia and Aphasia: Their Value in Cerebral Localization*, 2nd ed. Hafner, New York, 1936.
26. Penfield, W., and Roberts, L., *Speech and Brain-Mechanisms*. Princeton University Press, Princeton, N.J., 1959.
27. Ross, E. D., The aprosodias: Functional–anatomic organization of the affective components of language in the right hemisphere. *Arch. Neurol.*, 1981, **38**: 561–569.
28. Ross, E. D., Harner, J. H., and de LaCoste-Utamsing, C., How the brain integrates affective and propositional language into a unified behavioral pattern. *Arch. Neurol.*, 1981, **38**: 745–748.
29. Ross, E. D., and Mesulam, M.-M., Dominant language functions of the right hemisphere? Prosody and emotional gesturing. *Arch. Neurol.*, 1979, **36**: 144–148.
30. Russell, W. R., and Espir, M. L. E., *Traumatic Aphasia — A Study of Aphasia in War Wounds of the Brain*. Oxford University Press, London, 1961.
31. Van Lancker, D., and Fromkin, V. A., Hemispheric specialization for pitch and "tone": Evidence from Thai. *Phonetics*, 1973, **1**: 101–109.
32. Wechsler, A., Crossed aphasia in an illiterate dextral. *Brain Lang.*, 1976, **3**: 164–172.
33. Wernicke, C., *Das Aphasiche Symptomenkomplex*. Cohn & Weigart, Breslau, 1874.
34. Zaidel, E., and Peters, A. M., Phonological encoding and ideographic reading by the disconnected right hemisphere: Two case studies. *Brain Lang.*, 1981, **14**: 205–234.
35. Zangwill, O. L., *Cerebral Dominance and Its Relation to Psychological Function*. Charles C Thomas, Springfield, Ill., 1960.

LANGUAGE IN THE RIGHT HEMISPHERE

ERAN ZAIDEL, PhD
Department of Psychology

Introduction: The Importance of Right-Hemisphere Language

Why study right-hemisphere (RH) language? One answer is that it illuminates the structure of natural language. In this chapter I will argue that the normal RH has a unique linguistic profile that can be regarded as a nonstandard model of natural language. It illuminates standard, normal language by laying bare those limit cases and partial, simplified linguistic structures that are more transparent to analysis. I will argue that the RH has impoverished syntax and phonology. Therefore, it exemplifies human communication without the special linguistic apparatus of the left hemisphere (LH). It shows how much language functioning can be accomplished with a general cognitive apparatus designed to subserve other human functions.

I will argue that the old view that language is exclusively specialized in the LH is no longer tenable. The RH has considerable competence for comprehending both spoken and written language, and it may well be specialized for certain pragmatic and paralinguistic functions of human communication. It has a unique cognitive style involving perceptual closure and template pattern matching that applies to both linguistic and nonlinguistic material alike.

If the RH has some language competence, then it becomes clinically important to determine under what conditions it can be used to compensate for language deficit in aphasia due to a lesion restricted to the LH. Experimental control over these conditions, together with knowledge of the learning and processing style of the RH and the range of its linguistic competence, could then guide speech therapy programs in brain-damaged patients.

Acknowledgments: Thanks to D. Frank Benson, L. Menn, and A. Schweiger for helpful comments on the manuscript. This work was supported by NIH Grant No. NS 20187 and NIMH Grant No. RSDA MH-00179 to Eran Zaidel.

CLINICAL NEUROLOGICAL TRADITION

History

Until the mid-19th century, the common view based on extrapolation from animal studies was that the two hemispheres are structurally and functionally identical. When Paul Broca first published the doctrine of LH specialization for language (see the chapter on LH language by Benson, this volume), he also believed that both hemispheres can decode speech and that the RH can take over speech following an aphasiogenic lesion to the LH. The view at the time was that LH dominance for speech holds for right-handers only; in left-handers the RH was supposed to be dominant for language, in mirror-image fashion. By the 1930s the prevailing view was that the LH is dominant for all higher mental functions.

Some prophetic exceptions to the dominant view existed. As early as 1874, Hughlings Jackson believed that the RH can support automatic language in nonfluent aphasics (including interjections, oaths, clichés, and recurring utterances, because these are often preserved in aphasia). Jackson believed in a phylogenetically and ontogenetically motivated hierarchical organization of brain functions. For him, brain damage leads to a retreat from a primary to a secondary system of representation of the affected function. Jackson believed that the RH has a secondary representation system for language (it is the hemisphere for the automatic use of words) and could therefore support residual language in aphasia.

The first empirically based claim that the RH may be involved in recovery from aphasia was made by Gowers (40), who observed that, when an aphasic patient who recovered some speech following LH damage sustained a second lesion to the RH, speech was again disrupted. Henschen (42) repeatedly argued for RH function in a variety of aphasic disorders in cases where the LH lesions were large or strategically placed or where a subsequent RH lesion abolished residual language. Similar observations by the Los Angeles neurosurgeon Nielsen (69) led him to conclude that the RH is much more likely to recover auditory comprehension than speech and other functions. Furthermore, he believed that auditory, motor, or visual language functions can transfer to the RH to different degrees. Thus, Nielsen in effect ascribed a unique and consistent linguistic profile to the RH, although he also believed that general RH capacity for takeover of language functions is highly variable across individuals. At any rate, there was little question in traditional clinical neurology but that in right-handers the RH has little or no role in language.

Perhaps the best example of the traditional view on RH language is the classical account of alexia without agraphia, a dramatic acquired syndrome consequent to a posterior LH lesion in a right-handed patient, where reading is much more impaired than writing, either spontaneously or to dictation. The disconnection account of alexia without agraphia (or pure alexia) posits two component lesions in the LH. The first is to the left visual area (usually with blindness in the right visual field [RVF], or right homonymous hemianopsia), preventing visual stimuli entering the LH from reaching the left angular gyrus, which is presumed to be the "center" for visual images of words and therefore important for reading. The second is in the splenium of the corpus callosum, preventing visual stimuli that enter the intact RH from again reaching the left angular gyrus. Thus, although the "reading apparatus" in the LH remains intact, it has no access to visual input.

The disconnection account of pure alexia therefore explicitly denies that the RH can read. Otherwise, the patient should have been able to read some words in spite of disconnection. However, the disconnection argument for the claim that the RH is word-blind is not watertight. Frequently, pure alexics can name letters and digits as well as some objects in the left visual field (LVF), on rare occasions even with semantic errors, suggesting that the disconnection is not complete and that it is not the only factor in the etiology of the syndrome. Moreover, with certain reading-comprehension paradigms using brief targets and pointing responses to multiple-choice pictures, it is possible to show some residual reading in pure alexia, believed to be controlled by the intact RH (51). I will say more about this below.

Damage to the Right (Minor) Hemisphere, circa 1960

Occasional reports in the literature suggested a variety of selective deficits in language functions following RH lesions in dextrals. Eisenson (27) found evidence for a slight impairment on vocabulary and sentence completion tasks, especially those involving abstract concepts and words. Critchley (22) noted some problems in articulation, verbal creativity, word finding, and learning new linguistic material. Weinstein (87) argued that denial of illness, disorientation and confabulation, and a variety of naming difficulties following RH lesions reflect RH involvement in the relationship between language and perceptual and emotional processes on which metaphorical speech is dependent. Marcie et al. (61) found a tendency toward vocal perseveration, repetition of syllables, disorders of articulation, dysprosody in spontaneous expression, and disorders of syntactic transformations and vocabulary selection, with lengthening of sentences following right-brain damage (RBD). Archibald and Wepman (1) described eight RBD patients with language difficulties as well as general cognitive deficits. Many of these reports foreshadow more recent and systematic clinical neurological evidence for a special role for the RH in providing perceptual–cognitive support for complex linguistic constructions, as well as in processing lexical semantics, in language acquisition, in the relationship of language to experience, in emotion, and in prosody (see below).

Lateralized Tests of Hemisphere-Damaged Patients

In principle, we should be able to use hemifield tachistoscopy or dichotic listening with aphasic patients to determine whether particular language components reflect residual LH processing or RH takeover. In practice, however, left-brain-damaged (LBD) aphasics may be too impaired to perform these difficult diagnostic tasks. Moreover, the presence of a "lesion effect" (77), which deflates performance in the visual field or ear contralateral to the lesion due to a sensory or an agnosic deficit, confounds the observed laterality effect. Thus, an LVF advantage (LVFA) or a left-ear advantage (LEA) does not guarantee RH takeover. Instead, we may be able to track down a posttraumatic shift in lateral dominance and correlate it with degree of recovery. For example, an increasing LEA due to a progressive increase in left-ear (LE) score, a decrease in right-ear (RE) score, and associated recovery suggest RH takeover (44).

Alternatively, we may be able to uniquely characterize LH and RH language processing by particular patterns of dissociation or errors on specific direct-access tests that are processed in the receiving hemisphere, either left or right. For example, the RH may be selectively unable to process abstract nouns (24); selectively unable to benefit from pronounceability of nonwords in identification (89); or selectively sensitive to semantic facilitation and insensitive to semantic inhibition in a lexical-decision task (92). This kind of argument was applied by Landis *et al.* (51), who showed that aphasics elicited the same rank order of error types during free-field reading as did normal subjects reading words flashed to the LVF but not to the RVF. The underlying assumption here is that when the intact RH compensates for an aphasic LH, it retains its characteristic linguistic profile rather than, say, adopting LH characteristics.

The Split-Brain Challenge

Disconnection Syndrome

In the 1950s, in an elegant series of experiments on cats and monkeys, R. Meyers and R. W. Sperry demonstrated that callosal section in animals largely abolishes interhemispheric transfer of sensory and learned information. So in 1960, when a young neurosurgeon, Joseph E. Bogen, considered complete cerebral commissurotomy to manage intractable epilepsy, he naturally turned to R. W. Sperry in the Biology Division at Cal Tech for an experimental study of its effects. Together with graduate student Michael S. Gazzaniga, they embarked on a systematic pre- and postoperative testing program capitalizing on the animal paradigms and data. In 1961 Geschwind and Kaplan also observed the first modern case of disconnection syndrome in a stroke patient. This patient had anomia for stimuli palpated out of view with the left hand, and also had a left-hand apraxia. The syndrome was interpreted in the connectionist–associationist tradition of Wernicke, Dejerine, and Liepmann, but the study was motivated by the animal studies of Meyers and Sperry.

Initial testing of commissurotomy patients in the California series, operated on by Phillip Vogel and Joseph Bogen at White Memorial Hospital, quickly demonstrated a dramatic disconnection syndrome (10). Those patients who had complete cerebral commissurotomy, including the corpus callosum, anterior commissure, and hippocampal commissure, were unable to name objects which were palpated by the left hand out of view (left-hand anomia) or whose pictures were flashed briefly to the LVF. At the same time, these patients could retrieve with the left hand objects whose picture was flashed in the LVF without being able to name them. More surprisingly, they could retrieve with the left hand an object named or described verbally by the experimenter. It was concluded that the disconnected RH is mute but not word-deaf.

Similar "first-generation" experiments, where part of the stimulus (not necessarily the linguistic target itself) was lateralized either somesthetically or visually, led to the conclusion that the disconnected RH is not word-blind either. As long as responses were signaled nonverbally, the RH was seen to have at least a modest receptive vocabulary and functional associations among the lexical items (32, 82). It could understand some phrases and obey some simple commands, and it seemed able to understand verbal task instructions. Initial reports that the RH can understand nouns, but not verbs or nouns derived from verbs, and that it cannot carry out spoken commands (30) were challenged by Levy (55), who showed that the RH understood the meaning of the command (and was able to point to a corresponding picture or to select a corresponding object) even when unable to execute it. Syntactically, it was initially believed that the disconnected RH could understand simple active or negative sentences, but not tense, plural inflections, or the relationship among subject, verb, and object (31). This belief was also challenged later (see below).

These experiments focused largely on two patients with complete commissurotomy, L. B. and N. C.,* who had the least amount of extracallosal damage relative to the group as a whole. Neither one of them had the kind of massive LH damage to the language area expected to result in an unusual language reorganization in the RH. Indeed, neither of them had a history of language deficit either in childhood or as adults. Thus these two patients were believed to be most representative of the true disconnection syndrome. Occasional "second-generation" studies reported some language competence in the disconnected RHs of other patients as well. Those studies include auditory comprehension by A. A. (67, 68), RH execution of verbal commands by R. Y. (37), phonological encoding in the RH of C. C. (58), and auditory comprehension by the RH in N. W. and R. M. (9).

Systematic Analyses of RH Language

Both tachistoscopic and somesthetic stimulus lateralization severely restrict the complexity of the linguistic input or of the experimental paradigm used, introduce short-term memory effects that may be lateralized in their own right, and create increased opportunities for interhemispheric cross-cueing. Consequently, in 1970, a contact-lens technique for continuous hemispheric ocular scanning of complex visual arrays was developed, allowing visual guidance of manual control by one hemisphere (102). Standardized visual tests could now be administered to each hemisphere separately.

*Initials identify commissurotomy patients (see 10, for details of clinical background).

LINGUISTIC ANALYSIS

Initial testing of the disconnected RHs of the two selected complete commissurotomy patients, L. B. and N. G., who were fitted with contact lenses, disclosed little or no speech, much auditory comprehension, some reading, and little writing. Language comprehension, both aural and visual, became the focus of study. Auditory language comprehension was studied by lateralizing visual multiple-choice arrays for left-hand pointing responses rather than by lateralizing the auditory messages themselves. It is more difficult to lateralize auditory stimuli to one hemisphere, since both ears are represented in both hemispheres (see chapter by Noffsinger, this volume).

Sound (Phonology). The disconnected RHs have large auditory vocabularies and smaller visual vocabularies. Thus the RH has acoustic access routes to the lexicon, but we know little about the abstract phonological structure available to it. There is indirect evidence that the acoustic representation of words in the RH is auditory rather than phonetic (see 59), where "phonetic" refers to the coding of sounds by reference to the articulatory apparatus. Also, standardized auditory-comprehension tests with multiple-choice pictures that include both semantic and phonological decoys usually lead to semantic errors. We would interpret this to mean that the RH does not use phonological analysis.

The RHs performed poorly on an auditory-discrimination test where the names of the decoy pictures differ from the monosyllabic consonant–vowel–consonant or consonant–vowel names of the targets in only one phoneme, including a difference of one to three phonetic features. When background noise was added to the stimuli, reducing the signal-to-noise ratio, the disconnected RHs suffered more than the disconnected LHs (95). It would seem that the noise that lacks specific phonetic information interferes much more with the hypothesized auditory analysis of the RH, which would depend on general acoustic cues, than with phonetic analysis in the LH. If we take the RH to represent a nonphonetic or nonlinguistic processor, then the rank ordering of phonetic confusions in the RH can be taken to rank the linguistic codedness of these features. These confusion data do not support the view that place of articulation is linguistically more coded than voicing (cf. 65). The disconnected RHs are especially poor in decoding nonsense consonant–vowel syllables with initial stop consonants ("ba," "da," "ga," "pa," "ta," "ka") by matching them with lateralized visual probes (the letters "b," "d," "g," "p," "t," or "k") (94). The stop consonants with their fast formant transitions are taken to be highly coded phonetic stimuli that require the specialized linguistic processing of the LH.

The argument that the RH is phonetically deficient because it has no access to a constructive speech mechanism has other circumstantial support in the apparent impairment of its short-term verbal memory (STVM). For example, the disconnected RH is poor at decoding Token Test instructions, which depend on memory more than on grammar (103). It would seem that the RH has an STVM with a capacity of 3 ± 1 items, whereas the LH has the normal capacity of 7 ± 2 items (cf. 36).

The disconnected RH is poor at evoking the phonological image of an object name by pointing to two of four pictures "whose names sound alike, but which mean different things" — for example, a (finger)nail and a carpenter's nail (104). The RH of patient L. B. could occasionally point to the homonyms even though it could not name them. But no disconnected RH in the California series can construct the phonological image of a printed word; that is, the RH has no grapheme–phoneme conversion. This is illustrated by the inability of these RHs to match rhyming words that have different end-spellings or to point to the correct regular spelling of a spoken nonsense word. It thus appears that the RH can access meaning directly from print, using perhaps some visual orthographic rules, but without intermediate phonological recoding.

Grammar (Syntax). The Token Test contains a part that introduces grammatical and syntactic complexity (verbs, prepositions, conjunctions, dependent clauses, etc.). The RHs were more sensitive to memory load than to these linguistic variables (103). L. B. and N. G. were also given several tests designed expressly for comprehension of grammatical structures, where the responses consist of pointing to multiple-choice pictures. The tests included Lee's Northwestern Syntax Screening Test; Carrow's Test for Auditory Comprehension of Language; Shewan's Sentence Comprehension Test; and Fraser, Bellugi, and Brown's Test (96).

The results may be summarized as follows:

1. The disconnected RH can comprehend not only nouns, verbs, and adjectives, but also a variety of grammatical and syntactic structures extending from functors to tense markers and to simple syntactic transformations such as the passive or negative.

2. Despite a large variability across subjects and linguistic structure, uninflected morphological constructions (free morphemes) are easier for the RHs than inflected ones (bound morphemes). There is a relatively high error rate in the RH on lexical items involving numbers, adjectives of relative quantity, and quantifiers (such as "four," "many," "middle"). By contrast, the RHs are adept at understanding spatial prepositions (such as "on," "in," "under"). The RHs scored least well on constructions requiring the coordination of subject–object and direct-object–indirect-object relations, which place a premium on order and a load on memory.

3. The RH is selectively affected by the length of the message more than by its syntactic complexity or difficulty of vocabulary (Shewan's Test; 90).

4. The RH finds syntactic structures (predication, complementation, etc.) more difficult than grammatical categories (case, number, gender, tense, etc.), which are in turn more difficult for the RH than morphological constructions (suffixes), with lexical items (nouns, verbs, adjectives, adverbs, and prepositions) being relatively easiest (Carrow's Test; 90, 95).

Lexical Semantics. The disconnected RH has a rich auditory lexicon that extends over diverse semantic fields and parts of speech. It recognizes some abstract nouns, many verbs, and spatial prepositions. It is facile in handling a variety of semantic relations, including synonymy, hoponymy (class membership), and antonymy. It is sensitive to word frequency and thus, presumably, to linguistic or communicative experience. It is sensitive to word associations (there is auditory semantic facilitation in a visual lexical-decision task lateralized to the LVF; 92), and it recognizes linguistic and nonlinguistic references to significant events and people. It shows linguistic access to both what the cognitive psychologist calls "episodic" (personal) and "semantic" information (knowledge about the world; 83). In picture vocabulary tests, the RHs of L. B. and N. G. scored at the level of normal children of ages 16 and 12, respectively. But, when the picture decoys in the multiple-choice arrays were all semantically associated with the target, these RHs made many errors (e.g., on Lesser's Test; 54), more syntagmatic than paradigmatic. It would seem that the RH lexicon is characteristically connotative rather than denotative.

Both disconnected hemispheres of five commissurotomy patients of the California series can perform lexical decisions on orthographically regular English strings ("is this a word or not?"). The RHs showed facilitation of decision when the targets were preceded by semantically related *auditory* primes, but not when preceded by the same *printed* primes. This is because the visual vocabularies of the RHs seem to be proper subsets of the corresponding auditory vocabularies, reaching equivalent mental ages of only 10 and 7 as compared with 16 and 12, respectively (101). Moreover, the visual vocabulary of the RH seems to be organized differently from the auditory vocabulary in the same hemisphere, in the sense of showing a different pattern of deficits as a function of part of speech. For example, the RH visual vocabulary has selectively weaker representation for prepositions and verb forms in "-ing" as compared with nouns or adjectives (99).

The disconnected RH does not seem to have a selective inability to decode actions or verbs, as claimed earlier (30). It often fails to execute a printed action flashed in the LVF, but can point to a picture depicting the action among multiple choices and can imitate manual actions when vision and feedback are restricted exclusively to the RH (100). It is suggested that under these circumstances LH dominance and usurping of control over the motor system can be minimized or bypassed (56). A similar "release" of RH action is claimed to occur under conditions of simultaneous hemispheric activation and divided attention, as in dichotic listening (37).

Pragmatics and the Relation of Cognition to Language. The testing paradigms used to elicit language ability in the disconnected RH are artificial. Although they are geared to allow the RH to respond by eliminating speech output, they also incorporate some biases against the RH. The multiple-choice pointing paradigm is metalinguistic and context independent; the decoys often provide unnatural "temptations," and the recognition of the correct target requires a selection strategy and a memory load that may tax the short-term verbal capacity of the RH. Nonetheless, these disconnected RHs, even when they err by pointing to the wrong target, show appropriate test behavior and considerable communicative competence in interacting with the examiner. Usually the RH "understands" the instructions; it takes appropriate turns in responding; and it occasionally shows that it "knows" that it is unable to answer. Moreover, when the LH confabulates in attempting to respond to LVF or left-hand stimuli, the RH sometimes shows overt awareness without words of the error and may even attempt to correct it nonverbally. The result may be an emotional response signifying dissatisfaction or even temporary dominance over motor pathways (manual but not verbal) in an attempt to countermand the LH response (cf. 57).

There is considerable circumstantial evidence that RH language is more labile over time, less deterministic across stimuli, and more variable across individuals than LH language, even when restricted to subsystems for which the hemispheres appear to have roughly equal competence. Thus, there are large interindividual differences in the absolute levels of competence of the disconnected RHs, even though they all respect the same general pattern. Moreover, RH scores show a consistent short-term variability — that is, weak uniformity or concordance between subsequent administrations — even when the average long-term performance remains stable. This variability applies both to superior (e.g., auditory-picture vocabulary) and inferior (e.g., decoding nonredundant phrases, such as in the Token Test) component RH language functions (97). It also applies to problem-solving strategies (such as in the Raven Progressive Matrices; 93). Similarly, the disconnected RH benefits less than the LH from error correction or a second chance in solving both linguistic (96) and nonlinguistic problems (93). This suggests that RH learning from experience is quite different from our standard conception of a partial, stepwise progression.

Little has been learned of the contribution of the disconnected RH to the pragmatics of natural language, because so little spontaneous overt linguistic behavior is observed in these patients when communication is restricted to the RH. Benowitz (4) administered parts of a standardized test for nonverbal communication (PONS — Profile of Nonverbal Sensitivity; 75) separately to the RH and LH of L. B. and in free vision with verbal responses to N. G., R. Y., and N. W. Forty video items showed 2-second emotional scenes, portrayed either by the facial expression alone or by conventional body movements alone. L. B.'s RH performed normally on the facial expressions but poorly on the body movements, whereas his LH was more impaired in facial expressions. All three other split-brain subjects scored extremely poorly on the face channel when verbally identifying freely viewed test items, presumably reflecting LH processing. Responses to body movements and intonational qualities of voices varied from one patient to another (4). This result is consistent with findings in hemisphere-damaged patients and argues for a critical role of the RH in evaluating the significance of social interactions through nonverbal cues, particularly facial expressions.

Can the role of the RH in communication be explained by its more general cognitive profile? For example, does its linguistic competence correlate with its intelligence ("g") measured nonverbally? Can its syntactic deficits be explained by absence of allegedly underlying cognitive operations, such as reversibility and coordination? The answers seem to be "no." The two disconnected hemispheres have similar IQs on Raven's Progressive Matrices (mean RH = 83, mean LH = 87), a nonverbal intelligence test (106). Similarly, there is no correlation between the linguistic competence of either hemisphere and its developmental stage in the acquisition of reversibility, coordination, and conservation (91).

One characterization of the cognitive styles of the two hemispheres does seem to capture the information-processing strategies that each hemisphere brings to bear on linguistic and visual–spatial problems alike. This is the characterization in terms of Thurstone's two visual-closure factors (91). The RH seems to specialize in the first closure factor: the synthetic ability to integrate unrelated parts into a meaningful whole, as in figure completion. The LH seems to specialize in the second closure factor: the analytic ability to detect component features in more complex and distracting Gestalts, as in figure disembedding. From a linguistic point of view, the RH has the ability to label linguistic concepts by arbitrary, conventional linguistic Gestalts (words), but it does not seem to have the rich combinatorial capacity of the LH to operate on and combine these linguistic structures and to appreciate the resulting "grammars."

DEVELOPMENTAL ANALYSIS

In order to compare linguistic performance across hemispheres, tests, and patients, we measured performance in terms of equivalent mental age scores on standardized developmental tests for first language acquisition. Although an identical total score does not guarantee identical solution strategies or error patterns, the resulting developmental profile of RH language could be relevant to the debate on the ontogenesis of language lateralization in the brain (cf. 79). Furthermore, to the extent that the RH supports language in some aphasics, our data would also be relevant to the "regression hypothesis" in aphasia — that is, whether the sequence of language dissolution is the reverse of the sequence of normal language acquisition.

Lenneberg (53) hypothesized that the two cerebral hemispheres are equipotential for language processing, but that during ontogenesis RH competence is progressively inhibited as the LH becomes dominant for language by age 10 (see chapter by Curtiss, this volume). Such inhibition can only be removed with interference or malfunction in the LH, permitting RH compensation. In this view, latent RH competence for language should remain arrested at some uniform level of language development. However, this would not be required by an hypothesis of selective inhibition of specific RH functions such as speech in the adult brain. Curiously, the latter notion never seems to have been entertained in print.

A systematic sampling of the developmental status of the disconnected RH on diverse linguistic, paralinguistic, and allegedly underlying cognitive tasks reveals three facts. First, RH competence is locally "developmentally coherent," in the sense that it often corresponds to a well-defined developmental stage in terms of total score on specific tasks. Second, RH strategies and error patterns often diverge from those of normal children even when the total score is the same. Third, the profiles of wider RH language systems do not correspond uniformly to any stage in first language acquisition. Thus, the RH pattern of muteness with substantial auditory language comprehension is "abnormal." Similarly, no normal child who has learned how to read has a much smaller visual vocabulary than auditory vocabulary. Even for auditory language comprehension alone, the developmental profile of the disconnected RH is abnormal, with a rich auditory picture vocabulary but poor receptive grammar and poor comprehension of long, nonredundant phrases (91).

Those local language functions that do show developmental coherence probably reflect "processing modules" that are functionally relatively independent and are structurally separable or localizable. In general, the disconnected and (isolated) RHs tend to parallel the developmental pattern more in the semantic and acoustic analysis of single spoken words with well-specified denotations; the RHs tend to resemble the developmental pattern less well for auditory compehension of grammatical structures and least for reading.

In sum, the level of competence of most components of RH language falls between that of 3- to 6-year-old normal children. It is likely that up to that age both hemispheres participate in and interact during language development. Thereafter, some RH components, such as speech, are functionally suppressed, whereas others, like comprehension of lexical items, continue to develop in the RH into adulthood. Thus, different components of language lateralize to or specialize in the LH to different degrees and have different neurological histories. Since RH language does not correspond to a stage in first language acquisition, neither does an aphasic who relies on RH recovery of language. For such aphasics, the "regression hypothesis" is therefore false (90).

APHASIOLOGICAL ANALYSIS

A second metric for comparing RH language performance across hemispheres, patients, and functions is in terms of percentile ranks relative to patients with acquired aphasia due to LH lesions. This again provides an independent measure in terms of another model of partial language structure — namely, language dissolution. Moreover, the comparison should help determine to what extent different aphasic syndromes represent compensatory language recovery by the intact RH. Does, then, the RH language profile parallel any known aphasic syndrome?

Reading. Impressionistically, the total language profile of the disconnected RH comes closest perhaps to aphasic alexia associated with an anterior speech deficit. RH muteness really parallels global aphasia, but it may be said to approximate nonfluent aphasia. Anterior aphasics also resemble the disconnected RHs in their grammatical and phonological deficits and in their reliance on lexical semantics for decoding more complex phrases (7). The RH reading deficit resembles sentence alexia, but this is not a powerful localizing symptom (45). Even more, RH reading resembles acquired deep dyslexia (21). Both syndromes show semantic errors in reading comprehension, as well as better reading of concrete content words than of abstract function words, and both lack grapheme-to-phoneme conversion. On the other hand, deep dyslexics are much less impaired linguistically than the disconnected RHs. Deep dyslexics can speak and can read aloud, and their auditory vocabularies and sentence comprehension are superior to those of the disconnected RH, even though this is the best language component in the disconnected RH. We now believe that deep dyslexics frequently resort to lexical semantic access by the RH during reading when LH mechanisms fail (see the case study below).

Auditory Comprehension. Neither aphasics nor the RH show the normal shared features advantage in dichotic listening (benefiting from shared phonetic features between the sounds in the two ears). Tests of phonemic discrimination using common words disclose good RH scores, again comparable to the mean of a heterogeneous aphasic population (ranging from the 36th to the 72nd percentiles). On the other hand, some studies of LBD aphasics show an increased LEA correlated with language recovery that surpasses the competence of the disconnected RH. For example, Berlin et al.'s (6) patient who had left temporal lobectomy was tested sequentially after the surgery and showed a fixed RE score but a progressively increasing LE score. The LEA scores of aphasics with presumed RH language takeover (44) are consistent only with the upper level of RH competence, elicited under favorable conditions (pointing responses to picture probes, etc.). Thus the presence of the disconnected LH seems to prevent the disconnected RH from exhibiting its full phonetic potential.

On tests of auditory comprehension of single words, the disconnected and isolated RHs score around or below the mean of an unselected group of aphasics and show the same pattern of deficits for specific semantic word categories (objects, geometric shapes, actions, colors, numbers, letters in decreasing order of competence) as fluent and nonfluent aphasics (35).

Grammar. Tasks of auditory comprehension of grammar (96) disclose that the disconnected RHs are more sensitive to length than to difficulty of vocabulary or to syntactic complexity, whereas mixed, unselected aphasics are most sensitive to syntactic complexity. On Carrow's Test the RHs are superior to receptive aphasics in morphology but inferior in syntax (Carrow, unpublished data, 1975). Interestingly, rank-order correlation of item difficulty on this test between the RHs and the receptive aphasics is higher with moderate than with severe aphasics and higher after speech therapy than before therapy, suggesting RH language compensation in the milder, chronic aphasics (90). Other syntax tests suggest a higher correlation between the RH and Wernicke's aphasics than between the RH and Broca's aphasics (96). In general, aphasics seem more sensitive to linguistic variables of the task, whereas the RHs seem more sensitive to paralinguistic and perceptual constraints.

In sum, although the psychometric language competence of the disconnected RH is often comparable to that of a group of aphasics, the RH profile does not correspond to any classic syndrome. Actually, classic syndromes may apply to less than half of an unselected group of aphasics (5). The RH contribution to language in aphasia appears selective: It applies to some tasks, some of the time. The total aphasic syndrome more often than not reflects a complex, dynamic interhemispheric interaction with a frequently shifting locus of hemispheric control.

THE NORMAL BRAIN

There are two general classes of techniques commonly used for studying the linguistic role of the RH in the normal brain. The first relies on restricting the sensory stimuli or motor responses to one hemisphere and measuring latency or accuracy of responses to brief stimuli. The second consists in real-time monitoring of cerebral activation during various linguistic tasks. Both methods are somewhat artificial and lose some ecological validity. Each also has its peculiar difficulties.

Lateralization of Sensory–Motor Processing

HEMIFIELD TACHISTOSCOPY

In the normal brain, we can make a distinction among three classes of lateralized tasks: "direct-access" tasks, "callosal-relay" tasks, and those requiring interhemispheric interaction (see Introduction to section on Biological and Psychological Studies of Hemispheric Specialization, this volume). Direct-access tasks are those processed by the hemisphere directly receiving the sensory stimulus via crossed projections, without resort to callosal transfer. Callosal-relay tasks are those where the input is relayed through the corpus callosum to the specialized hemisphere at some cost in latency and accuracy if the stimuli are first projected to the incompetent hemisphere. Most complex tasks probably involve some degree of interhemispheric interaction.

Unfortunately, few experiments provide adequate data for determining whether an observed laterality effect reflects the direct-access or callosal-relay models. Thus a simple report of an RVF advantage (RVFA) for some hemifield tachistoscopic linguistic task does not necessarily mean that the RH is incompetent—only that it is inferior to the LH. By the same token, an observed LVFA in such an experiment suggests a special role for the RH during some stage of processing, but that stage may involve perceptual rather than linguistic analysis. Since it is statistically very unlikely that a linguistic task will yield an LVFA, the experimental literature most likely underestimates the linguistic competence of the RH, which is masked by an overall RVFA. Similarly, those who dismiss normal behavioral lateralization data in some linguistic dichotic-listening or hemifield tachistoscopic tasks because a substantial percentage of dextrals show an LFVA may be premature or are prejudging the issue. Those critics argue that 20% of right-handers could not have RH specialization for the linguistic task, since clinical neurological estimates for LH speech dominance from unilateral brain damage are about 1%. However, language is not all of a kind, and different components may be lateralized to different degrees. Thus, bilateral representation of a particular language module may include both duplicate components, which accomplish similar computations, and complementary processes, which supply different necessary inputs to a more general processor. In particular, receptive language, which is always involved in visual presentation, may have greater RH representation than speech, and there is no reason to suppose that all hemifield tachistoscopic tasks index speech lateralization.

Hemifield tachistoscopic studies in normal subjects suggest that the RH is superior or equal to the LH in physical-identity matches of letters (33), in recognizing unusual scripts (16), or in recognizing cursive script (13). Many workers found evidence consistent with a selective RH ability to understand concrete, imageable nouns, as against abstract, nonimageable words (cf. 14: 152–154). Patterson and Besner (71) have criticized these data; and Zaidel and Schweiger (105), in turn, have challenged part of Patterson and Besner's critique (72).

There is now considerable evidence that the normal RH can perform lexical and semantic decisions of concrete nouns. Day (24) has evidence for direct access in semantic categorization, although he does not report separately the effects of concreteness on visual field. Day (25) used a lexical-decision task and found processing dissociation as a function of concreteness and thus evidence for direct access. Zaidel, Radant, and Temple (unpublished) also found evidence for direct access in lexical decision of concrete nouns, and indeed for RH superiority in sensitivity to semantic relatedness of such nouns. Semantically associated lateralized primes facilitated decision predominantly in the LVF, whereas unassociated primes inhibited decision predominantly in the RVF (92). Underwood (84, 85), too, studied the effect of semantic relatedness of unattended word stimuli on a lateralized picture-naming task. He found greater interference by related words in the RVF, but greater LVF interference for semantically related words that enter awareness. For lexical decision, Lieber (52), who used manual responses, reported no visual-field advantage for "no" responses but an RVFA for the quicker "yes" responses, suggesting direct access by the processing dissociation criterion (see Introduction to section on Biological and Psychological Studies of Hemispheric Specialization, this volume). On this view, RH ability to decode nonwords can equal that of the LH even if the RH has a smaller lexicon than the LH. For example, the RH may recognize the "ideographs" of some words without knowing their meanings.

Several experiments converge on the conclusion that unlike the LH, the normal RH reads words "ideographically" — that is, by accessing meaning directly from the orthography, without an intermediate translation into a phonological code. Krueger (47) found a superiority effect for words (better detection of letters in words than in nonwords, believed by some to reflect the effect of a phonological code) in the RVF but not in the LVF of normal subjects. Cohen and Freeman (18) found a pseudohomophone effect (slowing down of lexical decisions for nonwords that sound like real words, presumably due to the conflict with the valid phonological code) in the RVF but not in the LVF of normal subjects (but see 3 for a failure to replicate). Bradshaw and Gates (12) in turn found a larger RVF advantage for *naming* homophonic than nonhomophonic nonwords. Similarly, Axelrod *et al.* (2) found no visual-field asymmetry in accuracy for naming unpronounceable nonwords, but an RVFA for pronounceable nonwords, although the low performance level for unpronounceable nonwords suggests a floor effect (49, 50). All these results suggest that the normal RH is not as sensitive to phonological parameters as the normal LH.

DICHOTIC LISTENING

The same model considerations that apply to hemifield tachistoscopic tasks also apply to dichotic-listening tasks. Thus dichotic listening to stop consonant–vowel nonsense syllables demonstrates a significant REA in normal dextrals, a massive REA in the disconnected LH, and no competence in the disconnected RH. It is therefore a callosal-relay task, and the LE of normal subjects is reported less accurately due to some information loss in callosal transfer from the RH to the LH.

Whereas dichotic listening to initial stop consonants yields an REA reflecting LH specialization for rapidly changing format transition frequencies, a smaller REA is observed for liquids, semivowels, and fricatives, and no REA occurs for steady-state vowels (14). Other paralinguistic aspects of speech, such as intonation contours and pitch processing, often show an LEA, reflecting predominant processing in the RH (cf. 14: 152). Spellacy and Blumstein (81) found that vowels in a linguistic context gave rise to an REA, whereas vowels in a nonlinguistic context gave rise to an LEA. Consonants produced a consistent REA regardless of context. McFarland *et al.* (60) paired words with competing speech stimuli and found an REA for abstract words in a running-memory-span task but no ear asymmetry for concrete words, suggesting RH ability to decide concrete but not abstract words (conflicting data exist; see 66).

Real-Time Indices of Cerebral Activation

In general, regional cerebral blood flow (rCBF) studies as well as glucose utilization (PET) studies show bilateral hemispheric activation during most language tasks, including speaking and reading aloud, although most tasks show greater LH activation. These studies are generally too preliminary to exclude the possibility that RH participation is restricted to some sensory–motor aspects of performance, such as low-level prosodic control in speech or the programming of ocular scanning patterns in reading. Also, it is not clear when activation signals facilitation and when it signals inhibition.

Studies of event-related potentials (ERPs) are somewhat more advanced and often disagree with behavioral studies. Measuring auditory evoked potentials, Molfese studied hemispheric asymmetries in responses to voice-onset time and to place of articulation contrasts. Surprisingly, both hemispheres showed evidence for categorical perception (65). These results suggest that the RH processes phonetic information, contrary to some results from the commissurotomy syndrome.

Findings of ERP asymmetries in lexical analysis differ with task. Brown *et al.* (this volume) found differential ERP responses to noun and verb homophones, with the largest waveform difference localized to the anterior LH. Hillyard and Kutas (43) reported differences in scalp distribution between the ERPs elicited by "open-class" (content words, names, etc.) and "closed-class" words (functors). But in contrast with behavioral studies (11), the open-class items showed greater left–right ERP asymmetry than did closed-class items.

More recently, the ERP correlates of semantic context and expectancy were studied by Kutas and Hillyard (48). First, they found an enhanced central parietal (roughly Wernicke's area but not Broca's area) negativity (N400) in response to semantically unexpected words at the ends of otherwise meaningful sentences. The amplitude of the N400 correlated highly and negatively with the "cloze" probability of the word for the sentence (how likely it is to be given as a completion to the open-ended sentence), and it was asymmetric, with larger amplitude over the RH. Second, a letter-detection task using word pairs that were related or unrelated gave rise to an asymmetric N400 (larger RH response) whose amplitude was proportional to the degree of unrelatedness of the word pair. If we take this response to reflect the same process as the inhibition effect by an unrelated prime in a lexical-decision task, then this result is in conflict with findings of greater inhibition (by unrelated primes) in the LH and greater facilitation (by related primes) in the normal RH (92). Posner and McLeod (73) regard inhibition as conscious, whereas the effect of Kutas and Hillyard seems to be automatic.

Thus, ERP indices, even if not always in agreement with behavioral experiments, do implicate the RH in certain aspects of phonetic and semantic processing in lexical analysis.

Novelty, Familiarity, and Experience

Several lines of recent research on normal subjects converge on the conclusion that the RH may play a special role in processing new, unfamiliar, or difficult linguistic material. This RH specialization for novel information has been interpreted in terms of (1) stimulus parameters, such as familiarity or degradation; (2) task parameters, such as stage of processing or practice effects in an experimental session; and (3) subject parameters, such as inexperienced versus expert.

Hemifield tachistoscopic presentations of unusual, unfamiliar, difficult, or perceptually degraded letter or word stimuli may result in an LVFA instead of the usual RVFA (14: 132, 153). Silverberg *et al.* (80) showed that native Israeli children with the usual REA in dichotic listening to linguistic stimuli show an LVFA for Hebrew script when they first learn how to read, but this shifts to an RVFA by the fifth grade.

Practice in an experimental task often reverses an initial LVFA or LEA or increases an RVFA or an REA in hemifield or dichotic-listening tasks with linguistic stimuli (14). Such shifts in laterality effects most likely represent a change of strategy. The LH seems superior in interpreting events with preexisting representations and well-delineated codes, and until such representations are established or recognized, the RH may be superior in processing the linguistic stimuli (34, 98). Thus Gordon and Carmon (38) showed an initial LVFA for naming lateralized visual instances of a new symbolic alphabet, which shifted to an RVFA with increased familiarity and competence during the experimental session.

In turn, expert users of various language-recoding systems, such as Braille (88: 266) and Morse Code (70), often show LH specialization, whereas inexperienced users show an RH dominance (98). One interpretation of the shift from RH to LH superiority in the long-term acquisition of such complex skills is that they become more languagelike with experience — that is, that linguistic strategies become optimal for processing them (cf. 34).

UNILATERAL BRAIN DAMAGE REEXAMINED

The dramatic demonstration of higher cognition and some language in the disconnected RH has led to a reexamination of communication deficits following RH lesions, with surprising and novel results.

RH Lesions: Paralinguistics and
Pragmatics

THE APROSODIAS

It is now generally acknowledged that patients with RBD can show selective deficits in the production and comprehension of intonational information in conversation. Ross (76) even believes that the anterior RH controls production and that the posterior RH controls comprehension of intonation contours, in a mirror-image fashion to the alleged respective speech functions of Broca's and Wernicke's areas of the LH. The questions remain whether impaired intonation carries over to impaired communication, and whether impaired comprehension of intonation is due to an inability to dissociate tonal patterns or to recognize emotions (28).

HUMOR, METAPHOR, THEME

The role of the RH in broader aspects of linguistic and paralinguistic communication is highlighted in the work of Gardner and associates (29). They found that RBD patients had difficulty in understanding cartoons, preferred *non sequitor* endings to jokes, and in general exhibited an inappropriate sense of humor. There is also a corresponding deficit in interpreting metaphors, figures of speech, and idiomatic expressions. Here the literal meaning is preserved, but the use of contextual pragmatic features seems impaired. Similarly, RBD patients are impaired in their comprehension of the overall structure or theme of connected text or discourse: They misinterpret emotions and motivations, fail to get the point of a story, misjudge the plausibility of isolated events, confabulate in retelling the story, and inject irrelevant personal elements.

PRAGMATICS

The pragmatic analysis of speech acts distinguishes different possible "illocutionary forces" of an utterance, that is, its intended consequences (e.g., a command, a request, or a promise). Thus, intention can be expressed explicity in the form of the utterance (a direct speech act) or implicitly through situational cues (e.g., the declarative sentence "That hurts" may be a request for stopping an action). Heeschen and Reiches (41) studied the ability of aphasics and RBD patients to understand the last sentence of a story with or without the use of context (i.e., using indirect or direct speech acts, respectively). All subjects found indirect acts harder, but, unlike the aphasics, the RBD patients failed to take into account the contextual information of the indirect acts and consistently chose the literal but incorrect interpretation of the indirect requests. Foldi *et al.* (28) suggest that the RH is needed to integrate the various subtle cues into a single concept and to organize the whole situation in an appropriate way.

Limits of RH Language

HEMISPHERECTOMY

Brain plasticity permits language reorganization in the isolated RH when the LH is lost perinatally. Any linguistic deficits following such early RH takeover of language must reflect inherent limitations in RH language, and the resulting language profile may be said to represent an upper limit on RH language competence. By same token, language in the isolated RH following LH removal in adulthood is unlikely to represent a lower limit on RH language, since such competence is apparently above that exhibited by some aphasics. This phenomenological observation leaves aside possible LH interference with RH competence in some aphasics.

Perinatal Lesions. Dennis and associates (26) studied children who had infantile hemiplegia and underwent complete hemispherectomy (removal of one hemisphere) for alleviating epilepsy in Sturge–Weber–Dimitri syndrome. The crucial variable in this case is the perinatal lesion leading to complete atrophy of one hemisphere. The age of removal of the diseased hemisphere is less important, since the diseased tissue does not support any functions and serves only to spread the epileptic seizures. Dennis found that left- but not right-hemispherectomy patients had selective deficits in linguistic and metalinguistic syntactic tasks, such as detecting and correcting errors of surface syntactic structure, comprehending complex syntactic transformations, or producing tag questions to match the grammatical features of a heard statement. Conversely, she found that semantic space was both more lawful and more tightly organized in left-hemispherectomy patients. Similarly, while left hemidecorticates had phonological deficits and were inferior on morphophonemic processing, they were superior in logographic or ideographic processing.

Dennis believes that these RH deficits reflect unique RH strategies rather than mere capacity limitations. In this view, RH strategies are limited to lexical sampling of the meaning and the grammatical function–structure of single morphemes; the strategies exclude the integration of interpretative rules with surface syntax to derive thematic meaning. Thus, Dennis believes that RH strategies are characterized by strong lexical semantics and ideographic reading and by impoverished syntax and phonology, but not by limited STVM. Her view is consistent with the principle of a unique RH language profile based on commissurotomy studies. However, it should be remembered that perinatal hemispheric atrophy results in grossly normal language on either side, regardless of the laterality of the lesion. These patients often develop clinically normal language repertoires, and the deficits are fairly subtle and require special testing. Bishop (8) pointed out methodological difficulties with Dennis's cases, arguing that the allegedly impaired syntactic skills in left hemidecorticates were actually within the normal range and reflected difficult tests.

Adult Lesions. Adult hemispherectomies for lesions occurring in adulthood present a dramatically different pattern. The few right-handed cases without early brain damage that have been reported have showed severe deficits in expressive speech, but regained considerable auditory comprehension. There is some ability to use expletives, recite automatisms, or sing, but poor ability to produce voluntary propositional speech. Reading is severely limited and writing usually absent (17). When left hemidecorticates were given tests of auditory language comprehension that had been also administered to disconnected RHs, they showed equal or better picture vocabularies (101). In general, then, left-hemispherectomy patients show the same RH language profile as commissurotomy patients.

Childhood Lesions. Children who have incurred LH lesions between ages 5 and 13 with subsequent hemidecortication show an intermediate pattern between infantile hemiplegics and adult hemidecorticates. Gott (39) and Zaidel (96) described a girl with dominant hemispherectomy for a tumor at age 10 who subsequently had severe and persistent expressive language deficits but better auditory comprehension, similar to that of the disconnected RHs. While her telegraphic expressive speech was far superior to the mute disconnected RH, her reading was inferior. By contrast, another patient who lost his nondominant RH due to encephalitis at age 6½ subsequently had fluent speech and good auditory comprehension but persistent dyslexia, dysgraphia, and dyscalculia. Like an acquired "surface dyslexic" with a LH lesion, this patient used simplified phonetic rules in his misspellings, and he also had severe visual–spatial and musical deficits. Together, these cases suggest that the RH may be important for reading acquisition as a complement to the LH. The RH will not acquire reading by itself, and it is not necessary for functional (if not speed) reading once the skill is acquired.

In sum, evidence from dominant hemispherectomy supports the existence of a unique RH language profile, which is characterized by adequate auditory comprehension and inferior speech, by competence in lexical semantics and pragmatics, but not by competence in phonology and syntax. However, there is a very wide range of competence for this profile, depending especially on the age of LH insult or removal.

HEMISPHERIC ANESTHESIA WITH SODIUM AMYTAL

Wada's test (86) is used to create temporary hemispherectomy by a barbiturate injected into the carotid artery in order to determine speech dominance prior to neurosurgery. The technique has limitations: Usually the diffusion of the anesthetic is not precisely known, the duration is short, and most subjects have preexisting brain pathology. In a large series of temporal lobe epileptics, Milner found that in most right-handed patients with LH speech, the LH anesthesia abolished speech but not auditory language comprehension (74), permitting the execution of simple verbal commands (86). Usually only naming is reported, and the full abilities of the RH remain to be assessed with this technique.

Milner (64) found word-finding errors with left-sided injection and errors in serial speech and in counting following right-sided injection to left-handed subjects, suggesting a hemispheric "division of labor" for bilateral speech. Brown (15), in turn, believes that residual language following left-sided injection in aphasics depends on type of aphasia. He found amytal evidence for RH language participation in a case of phonemic or conduction aphasia with good comprehension, but not in a case of neologistic jargon with poor comprehension. On the other hand, Kinsbourne (46) and Czopf (23) reported complete RH takeover in a substantial number of aphasics, regardless of aphasia type and of language function involved. Thus, amytal testing in aphasia provides rather mixed evidence for a unique RH language profile.

Dynamics of RH Language in Aphasia:
A Case Study of Deep Dyslexia

The syndrome of acquired deep dyslexia was first described almost two decades ago by Marshall and Newcombe (62, 63). The original description was purely behavioral, with reference to a theoretical information-processing or psycholinguistic model of the reading process. Anatomical localization of the syndrome remained unspecified. Some apparent similarities between the main symptoms and the characteristics of reading in the disconnected RH emerged in the 1970s and gave rise to the hypothesis that the intact RH is responsible for the symptoms by taking over lexical semantic access in the deep dyslexic (19, 20, 104). The "obligatory symptoms" of the syndrome include (1) semantic errors in reading aloud, (2) better reading of concrete nouns than of abstract function words, and (3) no grapheme–phoneme conversion. Some make semantic errors in reading comprehension, pointing to semantic decoys in multiple-choice pictures. Absence of grapheme–phoneme conversion can be measured by inability to read aloud nonsense words or inability to recognize rhyming between meaningful or nonsense words. Thus all three symptoms can be tested without speech responses and can be studied in the disconnected RH.

As noted, the disconnected RH indeed makes semantic errors in reading comprehension (101), reads nouns better than function words (99), and cannot match words for rhyming (104). Will a deep dyslexic patient show the same symptoms on these same speech-free tests? The answer for at least some patients is "yes." Recently, Schweiger studied a 38-year-old woman (R. W.) with Broca's aphasia due to an occlusion of the left middle cerebral artery (78). R. W. had intact fields and showed the three symptoms of deep dyslexia, including semantic errors in writing and in reading comprehension, tested by pointing to multiple-choice pictures. Although this patient resembles the disconnected RHs with respect to the symptoms of deep dyslexia, her reading competence is far superior. Thus, her RH apparently takes over lexical semantic access selectively when LH reading fails. Even when the RH succeeds in retrieving the meaning of a printed word, the LH is still necessary to retrieve the "phonological address" and articulate the name aloud. But do we have any direct evidence that lexical semantic access is carried out in the RH of R. W.? Two experiments provide just such evidence.

Since the patient has intact fields, both experiments used tachistoscopic presentations of lateralized words. The first experiment was a lexical decision task and showed a strong LVFA, whereas a control test of length decisions using the same stimuli showed no visual-field advantage. Thus, the patient showed evidence for a selective RH involvement in processing printed words. In the second experiment, the patient had to read aloud briefly lateralized words. She read more words correctly in the RVF and made many more semantic errors in the LVF. Visual and derivational errors predominated in the RVF. It thus appears that semantic errors in reading aloud by R. W. do in fact reflect a selective and major RH contribution, even if articulation is still controlled by the LH. Furthermore, it seems that control of lexical access is released to the RH on a trial-by-trial basis as LH competence is challenged.

Conclusions and Prospects

Is there a unique language profile in the RH? The overwhelming neuropsychological evidence suggests so. But different experimental populations paint somewhat different profiles. When the LH is separated from the RH, either through complete commissurotomy, through surgical removal of the LH, or through temporary anesthesia of the LH, there emerges a consistent profile of language in the remaining RH. This profile is characterized by better language comprehension than expression and better auditory comprehension than reading. Reading proceeds "ideographically," without intermediate phonological representation. The profile includes a rich lexical semantic organization and supports some conventional aspects of nonverbal communication, but it has limited syntax and phonology. Cognitively, it is characterized by a limited STVM. This profile does not correspond to any stage in natural language acquisition or to any classical aphasic syndrome.

The language profile emerging from deficits of dextral patients with RBD emphasizes the semantic, pragmatic, and integrative roles of the RH in natural language processing. This profile, like that in the disconnected or isolated RH, suggests a supportive role, complementing the dominant LH. But whereas the disconnection profile suggests RH involvement in relatively early and elementary langauge operations, such as lexical access, the unilateral damage profile emphasizes relatively late, holistic operations, such as the appreciation of theme in discourse. It is likely that this "damage" profile reflects the net effect of pathological inhibition of some RH operations by diseased tissue in homologous regions of the LH, as well as residual RH competence and some interaction between RH structures and intact structures in the LH.

The model of RH language emerging from the normal brain is least explored and understood. This is where the important future discoveries are likely to be made. Language in the RH of left-handers or of women does not seem to provide illuminating models of "standard" RH language competence—that is, as represented in right-handed males. Studies with lateralized stimuli and responses and of evoked responses during language processing in the normal brain suggest a selective RH contribution to lexical semantic and acoustic processing, but this may merely reflect limitations of the techniques preventing experimenters from presenting more complex language stimuli and tasks. There are clues that the normal RH may even be dominant for certain lexical semantic operations, such as the connotation of lexical meaning in response to linguistic and paralinguistic context. Thus, the disconnection profile seems to underestimate the normal profile of RH language when in cooperation with the intact LH.

The question of interhemispheric interaction is likely to be the next focus for profitable and important research. The findings will have profound implications for our understanding of the dynamics of interaction between anatomically separable processing modules that subserve highly complex functions in the brain.

These advances will require a deeper theoretical mathematical analysis of models of interaction between processing modules. This will in turn be aided by new technological advances that permit reversible intervention (both facilitory and inhibitory) with processing modules and with their intercommunication, as well as provide new *in vivo* imaging techniques of brain functioning that have new orders of spatial and temporal resolution.

With the growth in our understanding and control of human communication resulting from those advances, the RH is likely to assume an increasingly important role in interpersonal interaction, as spoken and written languages will be supplemented by direct communication of brain states.

REFERENCES

1. Archibald, Y. M., and Wepman, J. M., Language disturbance and nonverbal cognitive performance in eight patients following injury to the right hemisphere. *Brain*, 1968, **91**: 117–127.
2. Axelrod, S., Haryadi, T., and Leiber, L., Oral report of words and word approximations presented to the left and right visual fields. *Brain Lang.*, 1977, **4**: 550–558.
3. Barry, C., Hemispheric asymmetry in lexical access and phonological encoding. *Neuropsychologia*, 1981, **19**: 473–478.
4. Benowitz, L. I., Bear, D. M., Rosenthal, R., Mesulam, M., Zaidel, E., and Sperry, R. W., Hemispheric specialization in nonverbal communication. *Cortex*, 1983, **19**: 5–11.
5. Benson, D. F., *Aphasia, Alexia, and Agraphia*. Churchill Livingstone, New York, 1979.
6. Berlin, C. I., Cullen, J. K., Lowe-Bell, S. S., and Berlin, H. L., Speech perception after hemispherectomy and temporal lobectomy. Paper presented at the Speech Communication Seminar, Stockholm, August 1–4, 1974.
7. Berndt, R. S., Caramazza, A., and Zurif, E., Language functions: Syntax and semantics. In: *Language Functions and Brain Organization* (S. J. Segalowitz, Ed.). Academic Press, New York, 1983: 5–28.
8. Bishop, D. V. M., Linguistic impairment after left hemidecortication for infantile hemiplegia? A reappraisal. *Q. J. Exp. Psychol.*, 1983, **35A**: 199–208.
9. Bogen, J. E., A systematic quantitative study of anomia, tactile cross-retrieval and verbal cross-clueing in the long term following complete cerebral commissurotomy. Invited address, Academy of Aphasia, San Diego, 1979.
10. Bogen, J. E., and Vogel, P. J., Neurologic status in the long term following complete cerebral commissurotomy. In: *Les Syndromes de Disconnexion Calleuse chez l'Homme* (F. Michel and B. Schott, Eds.). Hôpital Neurologique, Lyon, 1975: 227–251.
11. Bradley, D. C., Computational distinctions of vocabulary type. Doctoral dissertation, Department of Psychology, MIT, Cambridge, Mass., 1978.
12. Bradshaw, J. L., and Gates, A., Visual field differences in verbal tasks: Effects of task familiarity and sex of subject. *Brain Lang.*, 1978, **5**: 166–187.

13. Bradshaw, J. L., and Mapp, A., Laterally presented words: Orthographic analysis and serial, parallel or holistic modes of processing. *Aust. J. Psychol.*, 1982, **34**: 71–90.
14. Bradshaw, J. L., and Nettleton, N. C., *Human Cerebral Asymmetry*. Prentice-Hall, Englewood Cliffs, N.J., 1983.
15. Brown, J. W., *Mind, Brain and Consciousness*. Academic Press, New York, 1977.
16. Bryden, M. P., and Allard, F., Visual hemifield differences depend on typeface. *Brain Lang.*, 1976, **3**: 191–200.
17. Burklund, C. W., and Smith, A., Language and the cerebral hemispheres: Observations of verbal and nonverbal responses during 18 months following left ("dominant") hemispherectomy. *Neurology*, 1977, **27**: 627–633.
18. Cohen, G., and Freeman, R., Individual differences in reading strategies in relation to cerebral asymmetry. In: *Attention and Performance, VII* (J. Requin, Ed.). Erlbaum, Hillsdale, N.J., 1978: 411–426.
19. Coltheart, M., Deep dyslexia: A right hemisphere hypothesis. In: *Deep Dyslexia* (M. Coltheart, K. Patterson, and J. Marshall, Eds.). Routledge & Kegan Paul, London, 1980: 326–380.
20. Coltheart, M., The right hemisphere and disorders of reading. In: *Functions of the Right Cerebral Hemisphere* (A. W. Young, Ed.). Academic Press, London, 1983: 171–201.
21. Coltheart, M., Patterson, K., and Marshall, J. C. (Eds.), *Deep Dyslexia*. Routledge & Kegan Paul, London, 1980.
22. Critchley, M., Speech and speech loss in relation to the duality of the brain. In: *Inter-Hemispheric Relations and Cerebral Dominance* (V. B. Mountcastle, Ed.). Johns Hopkins University Press, Baltimore, 1962: 208–213.
23. Czopf, J., Uber die Rolle der nicht dominanten Hemisphare in der Restitution der Sprache der Aphasischen. *Archiv für Psychiatrie und Nervenkrankheiten*, **216**: 162–171.
24. Day, J., Right hemisphere language processing in normal right handers. *J. Exp. Psychol. (Hum. Percept. Perform.)*, 1977, **3**: 518–528.
25. Day, J., Visual half-field word recognition as a function of syntactic class and imageability. *Neuropsychologia*, 1979, **17**: 515–519.
26. Dennis, M., Capacity and strategy for syntactic comprehension after left or right hemidecortication. *Brain Lang.*, 1980, **10**: 287–317.
27. Eisenson, J., Language and intellectual modifications associated with right cerebral damage. *Lang. Speech*, 1962, **5**: 49–53.
28. Foldi, N. S., Cicone, M., and Gardner, H., Pragmatic aspects of communication in brain-damaged patients. In: *Language Functions and Brain Organization* (S. J. Segalowitz, Ed.). Academic Press, New York, 1983: 51–86.
29. Gardner, H., Brownell, H. H., Wapner, W., and Michelow, D., Missing the point: The role of the right hemisphere in the processing of complex linguistic material. In: *Cognitive Processing in the Right Hemisphere* (E. Perecman, Ed.). Academic Press, New York, 1983: 169–191.
30. Gazzaniga, M. S., *The Bisected Brain*. Appleton-Century-Crofts, New York, 1970.
31. Gazzaniga, M. S., and Hillyard, S., Language and speech capacity of the right hemisphere. *Neuropsychologia*, 1971, **9**: 273–280.
32. Gazzaniga, M. S., and Sperry, R., Language after section of the cerebral commissures. *Brain*, 1967, **90**: 131–148.
33. Geffen, G., Bradshaw, J. L., and Nettleton, N., Hemispheric asymmetry: Verbal and spatial encoding of visual stimuli. *J. Exp. Psychol.*, 1972, **95**: 23–31.
34. Goldberg, E., and Costa, L. D., Hemisphere differences in the acquisition and use of descriptive systems. *Brain Lang.*, 1981, **14**: 144–173.
35. Goodglass, H., Disorders of naming following brain injury. *Am. Scientist*, 1982, **63**: 647–655.
36. Goodglass, H., Berko-Gleason, J., and Hyde, M. R., Some dimensions of auditory lan-

guage comprehension in aphasia. *J. Speech Hear. Res.*, 1970, **13**: 124–143.

37. Gordon, H. W., Right hemisphere comprehension of verbs in patients with complete forebrain commissurotomy: Use of the dichotic method and manual performance. *Brain Lang.*, 1980, **11**: 76–86.

38. Gordon, H. W., and Carmon, A., Transfer of dominance in speed of verbal response to visually presented stimuli from right to left hemisphere. *Percept. Mot. Skills*, 1976, **42**: 1091–1100.

39. Gott, P., Language after dominant hemispherectomy. *J. Neurol. Neurosurg. Psychiatry*, 1973, **36**: 1082–1088.

40. Gowers, W. R., *Lectures on the Diagnosis of Diseases of the Brain* (2nd Ed.). J. & A. Churchill, London, 1887.

41. Heeschen, C., and Reiches, F., On the ability of brain-damaged patients to understand indirect speech acts. Unpublished manuscript, 1979.

42. Henschen, S. E., On the function of the right hemisphere of the brain in relation to the left in speech, music, and calculation. *Brain*, 1926, **49**: 110–123.

43. Hillyard, S. A., and Kutas, M., Electrophysiology of cognitive processing. *Annu. Rev. Psychol.*, 1983, **34**: 33–61.

44. Johnson, J. P., Sommers, R. K., and Weidner, W. E., Dichotic ear preference in aphasia. *J. Speech Hear. Res.*, 1977, **20**: 116–129.

45. Kertesz, A., *Aphasia and Associated Disorders: Taxonomy, Localization and Recovery*. Grune & Stratton, New York, 1979.

46. Kinsbourne, M., The minor hemisphere as a source of aphasic speech. *Trans. Am. Neurol. Assoc.*, 1971, **96**: 141–145.

47. Krueger, L. E., The word-superiority effect: Is its locus visual spatial or verbal? *Bull. Psychonom. Soc.*, 1975, **6**: 465–468.

48. Kutas, M., and Hillyard, S. A., Event-related potentials to grammatical errors and semantic anomalies. *Memory Cognition*, 1983, **11**: 539–550.

49. Lambert, A. J., Right hemisphere language ability: 1. Clinical evidence. *Curr. Psychol. Rev.*, 1982, **2**: 77–94.

50. Lambert, A. J., Right hemisphere language ability: 2. Evidence from normal subjects. *Curr. Psychol. Rev.*, 1982, **2**: 139–152.

51. Landis, T., Regard, M., and Serrat, A., Iconic reading in a case of alexia without agraphia caused by a train tumour: A tachistoscopic study. *Brain Lang.*, 1980, **11**: 45–53.

52. Leiber, L., Lexical decisions in the right and left cerebral hemispheres. *Brain Lang.*, 1976, **3**: 443–450.

53. Lenneberg, E. H., *Biological Foundations of Language*. Wiley, New York, 1967.

54. Lesser, R., Verbal comprehension in aphasia: An English version of three Italian tests. *Cortex*, 1974, **10**: 247–263.

55. Levy, J., Information processing and higher psychological functions in the disconnected hemispheres of human commissurotomy patients. Doctoral dissertation, Division of Biology, California Institute of Technology, 1969.

56. Levy, J., Psychobiological implications of bilateral asymmetry. In: *Hemisphere Functions in the Human Brain* (S. J. Dimond and J. G. Beaumont, Eds.). Elek, London, 1974: 121–183.

57. Levy, J., Nebes, R., and Sperry, R., Expressive language in the surgically separated minor hemisphere. *Cortex*, 1971, **7**: 49–58.

58. Levy, J., and Trevarthen, C., Perceptual, semantic and phonetic aspects of elementary language processes in split-brain patients. *Brain*, 1977, **100**: 105–118.

59. Liberman, A. M., The specialization of the language hemisphere. In: *The Neurosciences: Third Study Program* (F. O. Schmitt and F. G. Worden, Eds.). MIT Press, Cambridge, Mass., 1974: 43–56.

60. MacFarland, F., MacFarland, M. L., Bain, F. D., and Ashton, R., Ear differences of abstract and concrete word recognition. *Neuropsychologia*, 1978, **16**: 555–561.

61. Marcie, P., Hécaen, H., Dubois, J., and Angelergues, R., Les troubles de la réalisation de la parole au cours des lésions de l'hémisphere droit. *Neuropsychologia*, 1965, **3**: 217–247.

62. Marshall, J. C., and Newcombe, F., Patterns of paralexia: A psycholinguistic approach. *J. Psycholingist. Res.*, 1973, **2**: 175–199.

63. Marshall, J. C., and Newcombe, F., Syntactic and semantic errors in paralexia. *Neuropsychologia*, 1966, **4**: 169–176.

64. Milner, B., Hemispheric specialization: Scope and limits. In: *The Neurosciences: Third Study Program* (F. O. Schmitt and F. G. Worden, Eds.). MIT Press, Cambridge, Mass., 1974: 698–717.

65. Molfese, V. J., Molfese, D. L., and Parsons, C., Hemisphere processing of phonological information. In: *Language Functions and Brain Organization* (S. J. Segalowitz, Ed.). Academic Press, New York, 1983: 29–49.

66. Moscovitch, M., Right hemisphere language. *Top. Lang. Disord.*, 1981, **1**: 41–61.

67. Nebes, R. D., Investigations on lateralization of function in the disconnected hemispheres of man. Doctoral dissertation, Division of Biology, California Institute of Technology, 1971.

68. Nebes, R. D., and Sperry, R. W., Hemispheric deconnection syndrome with cerebral birth injury in the dominant arm area. *Neuropsychologia*, 1971, **9**: 247–259.

69. Nielsen, J., *Agnosia, Apraxia, Aphasia: Their Value in Cerebral Localization*. Hoeber, New York, 1946.

70. Papcun, G., Krashen, S., Terbeck, D., Remington, R., and Marshman, R., Is the left hemisphere specialized for speech, language and/or something else? *J. Acoust. Soc. Am.*, 1974, **55**: 319–327.

71. Patterson, K., and Besner, D., Is the right hemisphere literate? *Cog. Neuropsychol.*, 1984, **1**: 315–341.

72. Patterson, K., and Besner, D., Reading from the left: A reply to Rabinowicz and Moscovitch and to Zaidel and Schweiger. *Cog. Neuropsychol.*, 1984, **1**: 365–380.

73. Posner, M. I., and McLeod, P., Information processing models — in search of elementary operations. *Ann. Rev. Psychol.*, 1983, **33**: 477–514.

74. Rassmussen, T., and Milner, B., The role of early left-brain injury in determining lateralization of cerebral speech functions. In: Evolution and lateralization of the brain (S. J. Dimond and B. A. Blizard, Eds.). *Ann. N.Y. Acad. Sci.*, 1977, **299**: 355–369.

75. Rosenthal, R., Hall, J. A., DiMatteo, M. R., Rogers, P. L., and Archer, D., *Sensitivity to Nonverbal Communications: The PONS Test*. Johns Hopkins University Press, Baltimore, 1979.

76. Ross, E. D., The aprosodias. *Arch. Neurol.*, 1981, **38**: 561–569.

77. Schuloff, C., and Goodglass, H., Dichotic listening, side of brain injury, and cerebral dominance. *Neuropsychologia*, 1969, **7**: 149–160.

78. Schweiger, A., Zaidel, E., Field, T., and Dobkin, B., Intermittent right hemisphere dominance for reading in an aphasic with deep dyslexia. Submitted for publication.

79. Segalowitz, S. J., and Gruber, F. A., *Language Development and Neurological Theory*. Academic Press, New York, 1977.

80. Silverberg, R., Gordon, H. W., Pollack, S., and Bentin, S., Shift of visual field preference for Hebrew words in native speakers learning to read. *Brain Lang.*, 1980, **11**: 99–105.

81. Spellacy, F., and Blumstein, S., The influence of language set on ear preference in phoneme recognition. *Cortex*, 1970, **6**: 430–439.

82. Sperry, R. W., and Gazzaniga, M. S., Language following surgical disconnection of the hemispheres. In: *Brain Mechanisms Underlying Speech and Language* (F. L.

Darley, Ed.). Grune and Stratton, New York, 1967: 108–121.

83. Tulving, E., Precis of elements of episodic memory. *Behav. Brain Sci.*, 1984, **7**: 223–238.

84. Underwood, G., Attention, awareness and hemispheric differences in word recognition. *Neuropsychologia*, 1977, **15**: 61–67.

85. Underwood, G., Semantic interference from unattended printed words. *Br. J. Psychol.*, 1976, **67**: 327–338.

86. Wada, J., and Rasmussen, T., Intracarotid injection of sodium amytal for the lateralization of cerebral speech dominance: Experimental and clinical observations. *J. Neurosurg.*, 1960, **17**: 266–282.

87. Weinstein, E., Affections of speech with lesions of the non-dominant hemisphere. *Research Publications of the Association for Research in Nervous and Mental Diseases*, 1964, **5**: 220–225.

88. Witelson, S. F., Early hemisphere specialization and interhemisphere plasticity: An empirical and theoretical review. In: *Language and Development and Neurological Theory* (S. J. Segalowitz and F. A. Gruber, Eds.). Academic Press, New York, 1977: 213–287.

89. Young, A. W., Ellis, A. W., and Bion, P. J., Left hemisphere superiority for pronounceable nonwords, but not for unpronounceable letter strings. *Brain Lang.*, 1984, **22**: 14–25.

90. Zaidel, E., Auditory language comprehension in the right hemisphere following cerebral commissurotomy and hemispherectomy: A comparison with child language and aphasia. In: *Language Acquisition and Language Breakdown: Parallels and Divergencies* (A. Caramazza and E. B. Zurif, Eds.). Johns Hopkins University Press, Baltimore, 1978: 229–275.

91. Zaidel, E., Concepts of cerebral dominance in the split brain. In: *Cerebral Correlates of Conscious Experience* (P. A. Buser and A. Rougeul-Buser, Eds.). Elsevier, Amsterdam, 1978, 263–284.

92. Zaidel, E., Disconnection syndrome as a model for laterality effects in the normal brain. In: *Cerebral Hemisphere Asymmetry: Method, Theory and Application* (J. Hellige, Ed.). Praeger, New York, 1983: 95–151.

93. Zaidel, E., Hemispheric intelligence: The case of the Raven Progressive Matrices. In: *Intelligence and Learning* (M. P. Friedman, J. P. Das, and N. O'Connor, Eds.). Proceedings of the NATO Conference, York, England, July 16–20, 1979. Plenum Press, New York, 1981: 531–552.

94. Zaidel, E., Language, dichotic listening, and the disconnected hemispheres. In: *Conference on Human Brain Function* (D. O. Walter, L. Rogers, and J. M. Finzi-Fried, Eds.). University of California, Brain Information Service, BRI Publications Office, Los Angeles, 1976: 103–110.

95. Zaidel, E., Lexical organization in the right hemisphere. In: *Cerebral Correlates of Conscious Experience* (P. A. Buser and A. Rougeul-Buser, Eds.). Elsevier, Amsterdam, 1978: 177–197.

96. Zaidel, E., Linguistic competence and related functions in the right cerebral hemisphere of man following commissurotomy and hemispherectomy (Doctoral dissertation, California Institute of Technology). *Diss. Abs. Int.*, 1973, **34**: 2350B. (University Microfilms No. 73-26, 481)

97. Zaidel, E., Long term stability of hemispheric Token Test scores following brain bisection and hemidecortication. In: *Auditory Comprehension with the Token Test* (F. Boller and M. Dennis, Eds.). Academic Press, New York, 1979: 135–159.

98. Zaidel, E., On measuring hemispheric specialization in man. In: *Advanced Technobiology* (B. Rybak, Ed.). Sijthoff & Noordhoff, Alphen aan den Rejn, 1979: 365–404.

99. Zaidel, E., On multiple representations of the lexicon in the brain: The case of the two hemispheres. In: *Psychobiology of Language* (M. Studdert-Kennedy, Ed.). MIT

Press, Cambridge, Mass., 1983: 105–125.

100. Zaidel, E., Reading in the disconnected right hemisphere: An aphasiological perspective. In: *Dyslexia: Neuronal, Cognitive and Linguistic Aspects* (Y. Zotterman, Ed.). Wenner-Gren Symposium Series, Vol. 35. Proceedings of an International Symposium held at the Wenner-Gren Center, Stockholm, June 3–4, 1980. Pergamon Press, Oxford, 1982: 67–91.

101. Zaidel, E., The split and half brains as models of congenital language disability. In: *The Neurological Bases of Language Disorders in Children: Methods and Directions for Research* (C. L. Ludlow and M. E. Doran-Quine, Eds.). NINCDS Monograph 22. U.S. Government Printing Office, Washington, D.C., 1979: 55–89.

102. Zaidel, E., A technique for presenting lateralized visual input with prolonged exposure. *Vision Res.*, 1975, **15**: 283–289.

103. Zaidel, E., Unilateral auditory language comprehension on the Token Test following cerebral commissurotomy and hemispherectomy. *Neuropsychologia*, 1977, **15**: 1–18.

104. Zaidel, E., and Peters, A. M., Phonological encoding and ideographic reading by the disconnected right hemisphere: Two case studies. *Brain Lang.*, 1981, **14**: 205–234.

105. Zaidel, E., and Schweiger, A., On wrong hypotheses about the right hemisphere: Commentary on K. Patterson and D. Besner, Is the right hemisphere literate? *Cog. Neuropsychol.*, 1984, **1**: 351–364.

106. Zaidel, E., Zaidel, D. W., and Sperry, R. W., Left and right intelligence: Case studies of Raven's Progressive Matrices following brain bisection and hemidecortication. *Cortex*, 1981, **17**: 167–186.

HEMISPHERIC ASYMMETRIES IN VISUAL–PERCEPTUAL AND VISUAL–SPATIAL FUNCION

JEFFREY L. CUMMINGS, MD
Department of Neurology

The two cerebral hemispheres are differentially specialized, each performing a variety of tasks of which the other is either incapable or able to accomplish with only marginal facility. The left hemisphere is specialized for language comprehension and execution, verbal memory, and the numerical aspects of calculation, whereas the right hemisphere is specialized for visual–spatial and visual–perceptual function, nonverbal memory and comprehension, and execution of speech prosody (12, 60, 70). The two hemispheres are also asymmetrical anatomically, with differences in hemispheric shape, ventricular size, and cytoarchitectonic arrangement (30). These differences in hemispheric function and structure are reflected in the different clinical syndromes produced by lesions in the two cerebral members. Injuries to the left hemisphere are associated primarily with language deficits, whereas the principal abnormalities following right-hemispheric injury involve visual–spatial and visual–perceptual functions. Despite the dominance of the right hemisphere for spatially relevant functions, however, the left hemisphere is not devoid of such functions, and for some activities both hemispheres must participate. This chapter will present the anatomical differences between the two hemispheres and will contrast the visual–spatial and visual–perceptual disturbances that are produced by lateralized lesions of the hemispheres.

ANATOMICAL DIFFERENCES BETWEEN THE HEMISPHERES

Functional asymmetries between the hemispheres had been known since Broca's original observation in 1865 that left-sided lesions give rise to aphasia, whereas no similar linguistic deficits follow right-hemispheric injury. An anatomical counterpart of the functional specialization, however, was not widely recognized until Geschwind and Levitsky's demonstration in 1968 that the planum temporale (the posterior superior surface of the temporal lobe) is significantly larger on the left than on the right (32, 34). This anatomical region corresponds to the auditory association cortex or Wernicke's area, and the larger volume on the left suggested a relation to the

Acknowledgments: This project was supported by the Veterans Administration. Norene Hiekel prepared the manuscript.

dominant language function of this region. Since this seminal discovery, many additional hemispheric asymmetries have been demonstrated (Table 1). The cytoarchitectonic characteristics of left and right planum temporale have been compared, and asymmetries corresponding to the gross observations have been confirmed (31). Anterior hemispheric regions corresponding to anterior language areas have also been investigated, and differences have been found between the left and right hemispheres. When both intra- and extrasulcal portions of cortex are considered, the frontal region on the left — corresponding to Broca's area — is found to be larger than the equivalent right-sided region (28). Similarly, the nuclei of the right and left thalamus are of unequal size. The lateral posterior nucleus, projecting to left inferior parietal lobule, is larger on the left, whereas the specific sensory nuclei are slightly larger on the right (27).

These volumetric asymmetries are reflected in configurational changes in the two hemispheres. The left hemisphere tends to be longer and wider posteriorly than the right, whereas the right hemisphere tends to be wider anteriorly than the left (50, 85). Similarly, in most cases the occipital and temporal horns of the lateral ventricles are larger on the left than on the right (49). The sylvian fissures also reflect the temporal lobe asymmetries: The fissure on the left is longer and extends directly posteriorly, whereas the right fissure bends abruptly superiorly in its posterior aspect (51, 74). This creates a larger temporal lobe volume on the left and a larger temporal–parietal–occipital junction region on the right. Descending tracts from the hemispheres are also asymmetrical. The pyramidal tract descending from the left hemisphere is larger and decussates first at the level of the medulla in most patients (46).

These asymmetries have long phylogenetic and ontogenetic histories. The anatomic differences between left and right sylvian fissures are evident on endocranial casts of the skulls of Neanderthal man, 40,000 years old (49, 51), and asymmetries

TABLE 1
ANATOMICAL DIFFERENCES BETWEEN THE LEFT AND RIGHT HEMISPHERES

Anatomical Region	Hemispheric Asymmetry
Planum temporale (Wernicke's area)	Larger on the left; cytoarchitectonic boundaries larger on the left; gyral pattern appears earlier on the right.
Inferior frontal area (Broca's area)	Larger on the left.
Posterior thalamus	Larger on the left
Hemispheric shape	Longer and wider in the left posterior and right anterior areas.
Sylvian fissures	Extends more posteriorly on the left and more superiorly on the right.
Lateral ventricles	Occipital horn larger on the left.
Pyramidal decussation	Pyramidal tract on the left is larger and decussates above the tract descending from the right hemisphere.

of the left and right planum temporale are evident in fetuses between the 29th and 31st gestational weeks (15, 80, 90).

Differences in the distribution of neurotransmitters between the hemispheres have also been identified. The left temporal lobe has a more dense concentration of choline acetyltransferase than the right, suggesting a richer concentration of acetylcholine, and norepinephrine is asymmetrically distributed in the thalamus, with the left posterior and right anterior nuclei having the greater concentrations (5, 63). The significance of these biochemical differences has not been determined: however, considering the role of norepinephrine in depression, the latter might explain the tendency for mood disturbances to occur with unequal frequency following unilateral hemispheric insults. These anatomical and biochemical asymmetries underlie the functional hemispheric specialization and determine the different clinical syndromes observed after unilateral hemispheric injury.

Visual–Spatial and Visual–Perceptual Syndromes

The visual–spatial and visual–perceptual syndromes that follow damage to the cerebral hemispheres are shown in Table 2. Some disorders are associated primarily with right-hemispheric lesions and some predominantly with left-hemispheric lesions. Others occur with lesions of either hemisphere, and some require bilateral lesions. These differences reflect an asymmetrical division of labor for some skills, relatively equal division for others, and interhemispheric cooperation for still others.

Syndromes Associated with Right-Hemispheric Lesions

The right cerebral hemisphere is the nondominant or minor hemisphere only insofar as linguistic functions are concerned. It is specialized for many aspects of spatially relevant activity, and lesions in this hemisphere produce a diverse array of spatial disabilities, including difficulty in recognizing familiar environments (environmental agnosia), impairment of discrimination of faces, dressing disturbances, visual hallucinations, and palinopsia.

ENVIRONMENTAL AGNOSIA

"Environmental agnosia" refers to an unusual clinical syndrome in which the afflicted individual is unable to recognize a familiar environment (19, 38, 55, 65, 88). Such patients can see and describe what they see accurately, but have no feeling of familiarity and, therefore, cannot identify their location. The patients are not suffering from dementia, acute confusional states, amnesia, severe unilateral neglect, or complete visual agnosia. The syndrome meets the classic definition of agnosia as a percept stripped of its meaning (61). The individual is able to recognize the class of the object (e.g., house), but is unable to distinguish among members of the class (i.e., to differentiate his or her house from all other houses).

The neuropsychological basis of environmental agnosia has only recently been clarified. Often the patients can describe familiar settings from memory and can even

TABLE 2

HEMISPHERIC BASIS OF VISUAL–SPATIAL AND
VISUAL–PERCEPTUAL SYNDROMES

Syndromes occurring primarily with right-hemispheric damage
   Environmental agnosia
   Facial-discrimination impairment
   Dressing disturbances
   Visual hallucinations
   Palinopsia

Syndrome occurring with left-hemispheric damage
   Alexia

Syndromes present when either hemisphere is damaged
   Constructional disturbances
   Hemispatial neglect
   Achromatopsia (hemifield)

Syndromes present when both hemispheres are damaged
   Visual object agnosia
   Prosopagnosia
   Balint syndrome

---

draw maps of areas well known to them, but experience no sense of familiarity or recognition when confronted with the actual environment. This suggests that nonverbal memory for the environment is intact, but the recognition process that depends on being able to compare current perceptions with stored perceptual memories is disrupted. The deficit is, thus, a class-specific agnosia for environmental stimuli produced by a disconnection between occipital–perceptual processes and temporal–mnemonic processes subserving visual recognition.

The lesion producing environmental agnosia is located in the medial occipito-temporal junction area of the right hemisphere. The frequency of superior quadrantanopies in affected individuals suggests that the lesion may be confined to below the calcarine fissure. Many patients with environmental agnosia have bilateral posteromedial lesions, but a right-sided unilateral lesion is sufficient to produce the recognition deficit (19). In most cases, the underlying lesion is an infarction in the distribution of the right posterior cerebral artery; however, tumors, cysts, and traumatic insults to the same region have also produced the syndrome.

ABNORMALITIES IN FACIAL DISCRIMINATION

Several varieties of face-identification tests have been administered to patients with either right- or left-hemispheric damage. Subjects with left-sided injuries perform the tests normally, whereas patients with right-sided damage have difficulty matching the front view of a face with the same face in profile or choosing a previously seen face from a collection of faces (25, 26). The disability appears to be particularly marked for emotional facial expressions (16, 41).

The deficits in recognizing and matching unfamiliar faces exhibited by patients with right-hemispheric damage suggest that right-hemispheric dysfunction may also explain the clinical syndrome of prosopagnosia. Thus far, all autopsied cases of prosopagnosia have had bilateral posterior hemisphere lesions; but three studies have reported patients with clinical and radiological evidence of unilateral right-sided lesions and prosopagnosia (19, 79, 87).

DRESSING DISTURBANCES

Two types of dressing disturbances have been identified: One variety is associated with unilateral neglect and is manifested by failing to dress, bathe, shave, comb, or make up one half of the body; the other is a unique form of body–garment disorientation, in which the visual–spatial disorder makes it impossible for the patient to orient a garment correctly with regard to his or her own body. The patient may turn the garment backward, inside out, or upside down and is able to dress only with great difficulty if at all (13, 43, 55). Essentially all reported patients with body–garment disorientation have had lesions in the right parietal lobe.

VISUAL HALLUCINATIONS

The incidence of visual hallucinations is dramatically different following lesions of the right and left cerebral hemispheres, being much more common following right-sided than left-sided insults (52). The hallucinations either may be of ictal origin, occurring as a manifestation of an epileptic discharge, or they may be "release" hallucinations, occurring with destructive lesions of the hemisphere. Ictal hallucinations are usually brief, stereotyped visual experiences that are not lateralized in the visual field and frequently consist of visual memories (35, 44, 62, 70). Release hallucinations, on the other hand, may persist for several hours or longer, are variable in content, are often lateralized, occur in the area of an existing visual-field defect, and are not usually remembered events (14, 47, 48). Ictal hallucinations associated with occipital lesions are more likely to be unformed flashes and colors, whereas temporal lesions more often produce organized complex hallucinations (75).

PALINOPSIA

"Palinopsia" refers to the abnormal persistence or late recurrence of visual images after the provocative stimulus has been removed (7, 20). After directing visual attention to a particular stimulus object, the image persists for up to several minutes after the patient looks away, and the image may spontaneously recur hours later. Like visual hallucinations, palinopsia is much more common after right-sided than left-sided injuries, and most lesions have been in the posterior occipital–parietal–temporal region (20, 58, 59). Most patients have a visual-field defect, but the palinopic images are not confined to the defective field. Although palinopsia was originally considered to be the result of seizure activity, recent EEG studies obtained in palinopic patients reveal no aberrant rhythms, and the phenomenon does not respond to anticonvulsant medication. Palinopsia is best considered as a unique type of release hallucination (20).

Syndromes Occurring with Left-Hemisphere Damage

Although the left hemisphere is clearly dominant in terms of verbal skills and the right in terms of visual–spatial abilities, each hemisphere shares some of its partner's specialized skills. Thus, the right hemisphere has limited verbal faculties (see chapter on the right hemisphere by E. Zaidel, this volume), and the left hemisphere is not bereft of visual–spatial abilities. Indeed, one language skill, reading, is dependent on visual-discrimination functions. Visual–spatial syndromes associated with left-hemisphere damage include alexia and the constructional disturbance commonly accompanying the Gerstmann syndrome.

ALEXIA

Alexia is usually conceived as a language-related deficit. The loss of ability to ascribe meaning to letter symbols, however, meets the definition of agnosia given above (61). Perception of the letters is intact and in many cases they can be copied correctly, but their meaning cannot be deciphered. Thus, alexia may be viewed as the left-hemisphere counterpart of environmental agnosia. Both represent specific agnosic syndromes in which stimuli that are dependent on one hemisphere for analysis are bereft of meaning when the hemisphere is lesioned.

Syndromes Present with Damage to Either Hemisphere

Constructional disturbances, hemispatial neglect, and contralateral achromatopsia can occur with damage to both the right and the left hemisphere. The occurrence of these syndromes with damage to either hemisphere suggests that the function is normally mediated by simultaneous participation of both hemispheres, and that when one is damaged the other cannot compensate sufficiently to restore the function. The syndromes are not necessarily identical when produced by the right and the left hemisphere.

CONSTRUCTIONAL DISTURBANCES

"Constructional disability" refers to performance on any of a variety of tests (copying drawings, reproduction of geometric patterns with match sticks, assembling blocks to imitate a model design) in which there is a disturbance in assembling or articulating the parts that cannot be accounted for on the basis of elementary sensory or motor deficits. Though often called "constructional apraxia," the constructional disability does not correlate with the existence of other types of apraxia and does not meet the definition of an apraxia as the inability to execute on command an act that can be performed spontaneously (33, 69).

The specific anatomical correlates and neurophysiological mechanisms of constructional disability remain obscure. Kleist originally proposed that constructional deficits reflect a disconnection between hemispheric perceptual and motor processes; other early investigators, noting the association of Gerstmann syndrome with constructional abnormalities, ascribed the deficits to executive performance deficits reflecting dominant-hemisphere dysfunction (8, 24, 81). As cases with right-hemispheric damage with constructional disorders were observed, new concepts evolved. Duensing proposed that lesions in either hemisphere could give rise to constructional problems, but by different mechanisms. He suggested that left-hemisphere injury leads to executive–apractic deficts and that right-hemisphere lesions lead to perceptual–agnosic deficits (8, 29, 68). More recently, some investigators have emphasized that constructional disturbances are more frequent and more severe with right-sided than with left-sided lesions (11, 68, 69), whereas others have found no differences in the prevalence or severity of constructional deficits with left- and right-sided injuries (6, 24, 29, 82). Most authors agree that posterior hemispheric lesions are more likely to produce constructional disturbances than anterior lesions, regardless of the laterality of the damage.

Attempts to find qualitative differences in constructions following lateralized hemispheric differences have also yielded equivocal results. In general, it has been found that patients with right-sided lesions produce constructions that are more complex and more asymmetrical, with a distorted orientation; they are also less likely to profit from use of a model. Patients with left-sided lesions, on the other hand, produce simplified structures lacking in detail and are more likely to benefit from a model (64, 81, 82). Despite these observations, however, the qualitative differences are difficult to measure; moreover, unless clear-cut lateralized neglect is noted, the productions are not sufficiently distinctive to differentiate left- and right-sided lesions (45).

Thus, constructional deficits can occur with lesions in either hemisphere, and, though there may be qualitative differences in constructions following left- and right-hemisphere injury, these are not sufficiently distinctive to allow clinical differentiation on the basis of the productions.

HEMISPATIAL NEGLECT

"Unilateral neglect" refers to the failure of the patient to report, respond to, or orient to stimuli presented on one side (39, 42). Visual neglect is one aspect of the syndrome, in which the patient fails to see stimuli on one side or extinguishes one of a pair of simultaneously presented visual stimuli. Unilateral visual neglect is accompanied by unilateral neglect of other sensory modalities as well as hemi-inattention and hemiakinesia (39, 42). In addition, patients may display allesthesia, wherein when touched on the side opposite their lesion, they report being touched on the ipsilateral side. Patients with neglect also frequently manifest anosognosia — a bizarre clinical syndrome characterized by denial of any neurological disability and occasionally by denial of ownership of the hemiparetic limbs (21, 86).

Visual neglect can be elicited or observed by a variety of techniques. In conversation, the patient may not orient to one side, and may even turn away from the examiner if the clinician approaches from the neglected hemifield. When copying figures, only one side of the figure will be reproduced; in the line-drawing test, only the lines on one side of a page with many randomly distributed lines will be crossed (2). Only half of words or sentences will be read (hemialexia), and only half of a vertical list of numbers will be summed. Only half of the visual environment will be perceived, and patients frequently get lost because they ignore turns into the neglected field (13). The occurrence of visual neglect is independent of a visual-field defect: Patients with hemianopias may not exhibit neglect, and patients manifesting neglect may have no field defect (89).

Visual neglect can occur with lesions of either the right or left hemisphere, but is more common, more severe, and more enduring with right-sided lesions (18, 21, 39, 41). Within the hemisphere, a variety of lesions have been associated with hemispatial (including visual) neglect. Lesions of the parietal lobe, dorsolateral frontal lobe, and medial fronto-cingulate regions have all produced contralateral neglect and have been associated with hemi-inattention, hemiakinesia, and hemi-in-intention, respectively (39, 40, 41). In addition, lesions in subcortical thalamic and basal ganglia nuclei — structures with prominent connections with frontal, cingulate, and parietal regions — can also produce neglect syndromes indistinguishable from those associated with cortical lesions (36, 41, 67, 77, 83, 84). Thus, hemispatial attention is comprised of many elements, including arousal, sensory attention, emotional motivation, and motor responsiveness. Each of these functions is mediated by different structures within an integrated anatomical system, and a lesion within any of these structures results in a similar neglect syndrome.

ACHROMATOPSIA

"Central achromatopsia" refers to acquired color blindness produced by central nervous system lesions. The lesion producing achromatopsia is located in the medial anterior region of the occipital cortex inferior to the calcarine fissure. The color blindness involves the contralateral visual field, but in many cases the lesions and the achromatopsia are bilateral (23, 57, 66). The lesions are usually located in the distribution of the posterior cerebral artery, and the syndrome is commonly associated with environmental agnosia and prosopagnosia.

Syndromes Requiring Bilateral Hemispheric Damage

A few visual–spatial syndromes — visual object agnosia, prosopagnosia, Balint syndrome — occur with bilateral hemispheric damage. The requirement of bilateral injury suggests that one hemisphere is able to compensate for dysfunction of the other; however, when bilateral damage is present, compensation becomes impossible.

VISUAL OBJECT AGNOSIA

The syndrome of visual agnosia is characterized by an inability to recognize objects in the visual environment, despite an adequate ability to perceive. Two varieties of visual agnosia have been identified: an apperceptive form, in which perception is limited to elemental components such as brightness, direction, and width; and an associative form, in which perception is intact and patients can even draw the stimulus adequately, but they cannot recognize the perceived object (9, 72, 73).

Visual agnosia requires bilateral hemispheric dysfunction. Patients with the apperceptive form have hade diffuse anoxic insults to the brain (1, 9), whereas patients with associative visual agnosia have had bilateral posterior cerebral artery occlusions with infarctions in the medial temporal regions (3, 10).

PROSOPAGNOSIA

Prosopagnosia is a clinical syndrome whose principal deficit is an inability to recognize familiar faces. The patient is unable to recognize friends, relatives, or even a spouse from visual clues alone, but recognizes them readily by the sound of their voices. In most cases perception is intact, though a few patients describe perceptual distortions that disturb the recognition process. As in environmental agnosia, primary perceptual and cognitive skills are preserved, and the patient's facial memory is intact (17, 22, 56).

The anatomical basis of prosopagnosia remains controversial. Meadows (56) and Damasio and colleagues (22) have pointed out that all autopsied cases of prosopagnosia have had bilateral posterior hemispheric lesions. The right-sided lesion involves the medial occipito-temporal region, whereas the left-sided lesion has been more variable in location but involves medial or lateral occipito-parietal areas. These authors suggest that bilateral lesions are necessary to disrupt the facial-recognition process. Whiteley and Warrington (87), on the other hand, described two patients with prosopagnosia and unilateral right-sided lesions on CT scans; they argued that unilateral right-sided lesions are sufficient to produce the syndrome. This position was supported by Cummings et al. (19), who found that six patients with environmental agnosia and unilateral right-sided lesions on CT scan also had prosopagnosia. Van Lancker and Canter (79) described an additional four patients with unilateral lesions and prosopagnosia. No autopsied cases of prosopagnosia with unilateral lesions have been described, and proof of the ability of a unilateral lesion to produce the syndrome must await confirmation from pathology. The radiological studies, however, suggest that appropriately placed right-sided lesions may be sufficient to disrupt recognition of familiar faces; this is consistent with the established superiority of the right hemisphere in tasks of facial discrimination, as discussed above (25, 26, 53, 76).

BALINT SYNDROME

Balint syndrome is an unusual, complex visual–spatial disorder manifested as "psychic paralysis of gaze," in which the patient cannot voluntarily redirect his or her gaze from one target to another; optic ataxia, characterized by an inability to visually guide hand movements; and a disorder of visual attention, in which simultaneous visual synthesis is deranged (4, 37, 54, 78). Balint syndrome occurs when there are bilateral parietal lesions, and some cases have had both biparietal and bifrontal lesions. The elements of the syndrome are frequently combined with other manifestations of parietal lobe dysfunction.

SUMMARY AND CONCLUSIONS

The two cerebral hemispheres are anatomically asymmetrical and functionally differentiated. The anatomic differences between the hemispheres are evident in ontogenetic history by the 29th gestational week and are manifest phylogenetically in the 40,000-year-old skulls of Neanderthal man. In the left hemisphere, the planum temporale containing Wernicke's area and subserving language is larger; in the right hemisphere, the parieto-occipital area subserving visual–spatial function is larger.

The division of labor between the cerebral members is reflected in the neurological syndromes that occur following injury to the hemispheres. Syndromes that occur primarily with lesions of the right hemisphere include environmental agnosia, impaired facial matching, dressing disturbances, visual hallucinations, and palinopsia. Alexia is the principal visual syndrome seen primarily with left-hemisphere damage. Constructional disturbances, hemispatial neglect, and contrafield achromatopsia can occur with lesions of either hemisphere, though neglect is usually more profound and more enduring with right-sided lesions. A few syndromes — visual object agnosia, prosopagnosia, Balint syndrome — appear to require bilateral lesions.

REFERENCES

1. Adler, A., Disintegration and restoration of optic recognition in visual agnosia. *Arch. Neurol. Psychiatry*, 1944, **51**: 243–259.
2. Albert, M. L., A simple test of visual neglect. *Neurology*, 1973, **23**: 658–664.
3. Albert, M. L., Soffer, D., Silverberg, R., and Reches, A., The anatomic basis of visual agnosia. *Neurology*, 1979, **29**: 876–879.
4. Allison, R. S., Hurwitz, L. J., White, J. G., and Wilmot, T. J., A follow-up study of a patient with Balint's syndrome. *Neuropsychologia*, 1969, **7**: 319–333.
5. Amaducci, L., Sorbi, S., Albanese, A., and Gainotti, G., Choline acetyltransferase (ChAT) activity differs in right and left human temporal lobes. *Neurology*, 1981, **31**: 799–805.
6. Arena, R., and Gainotti, G., Constructional apraxia and visuo-perceptive disabilities in relation to laterality of cerebral lesions. *Cortex*, 1978, **14**: 463–473.
7. Bender, M. B., Feldman, M., and Sobin, A. J., Palinopsia. *Brain*, 1968, **91**: 321–338.
8. Benson, D. F., and Barton, M. I., Disturbances in constructional ability. *Cortex*, 1970, **6**: 19–46.
9. Benson, D. F., and Greenberg, J. P., Visual form agnosia. *Arch. Neurol.*, 1969, **20**: 82–89.
10. Benson, D. F., Segarra, J., and Albert, M. L., Visual agnosia–prosopagnosia. *Arch. Neurol.*, 1974, **30**: 307–310.
11. Benton, A. L., and Fogel, M. L., Three-dimensional constructional praxis. *Arch. Neurol.*, 1962, **7**: 347–354.
12. Bradshaw, J. L., and Nettleton, N. C., The nature of hemispheric specialization in man. *Behav. Brain. Sci.*, 1981, **4**: 51–91.
13. Brain, W. R., Visual disorientation with special reference to lesions of the right cerebral hemisphere. *Brain*, 1941, **64**: 244–272.

14. Brust, J. C. M., and Behrens, M. M., "Release hallucinations" as the major symptom of posterior cerebral artery occlusion: A report of 2 cases. *Ann. Neurol.*, 1977, 2: 432–436.
15. Chi Je, G., Dooling, E. C., and Gilles, F. H., Left–right asymmetries of the temporal speech areas of the human fetus. *Arch. Neurol.*, 1977, 34: 346–348.
16. Cicone, M., Wapner, W., and Garnder, H., Sensitivity to emotional expressions and situations in organic patients. *Cortex*, 1980, 16: 145–158.
17. Cohn, R., Neumann, M. A., and Wood, D. H., Prosopagnosia: A clinicopathological study. *Ann. Neurol.*, 1977, 1: 177–182.
18. Colombo, A., De Renzi, E., and Gentilini, M., The time course of visual hemi-inattention. *Arch. Psychiat. Nervenkr.*, 1982, 231: 539–546.
19. Cummings, J. L., Landis, T., and Benson, D. F., Environmental disorientation: Clinical and radiologic findings. *Neurology*, 1983, 33(Suppl. 12): 103–104.
20. Cummings, J. L., Syndulko, K., Goldberg, Z., and Treiman, D. M., Palinopsia reconsidered. *Neurology*, 1982, 32: 444–447.
21. Cutting, J., Study of anosognosia. *J. Neurol. Neurosurg. Psychiatry*, 1978; 41: 548–555.
22. Damasio, A. R., Damasio, H., and Van Hoesen, G. W., Prosopagnosia: Anatomic basis and behavioral mechanisms. *Neurology*, 1982, 32: 331–341.
23. Damasio, A., Yamada, T., Damasio, H., Corbett, J., and McKee, J., Central achromatopsia: Behavioral, anatomic, and physiologic aspects. *Neurology*, 1980, 30: 1064–1071.
24. De Renzi, E., Hemispheric asymmetry as evidenced by spatial disorders. In: *Asymmetrical Functions of the Brain* (M. Kinsbourne, Ed.). Cambridge University Press, New York, 1978: 49–85.
25. De Renzi, E., Scotti, G., and Spinnler, H., Perceptual and associative disorders in visual recognition. *Neurology*, 1969: 19: 634–642.
26. De Renzi, E., and Spinnler, H., Facial recognition in brain-damaged patients. *Neurology*, 1966, 16: 145–152.
27. Eidelberg, D., and Galaburda, A. M., Symmetry and asymmetry in the human posterior thalamus. *Arch. Neurol.*, 1982, 39: 325–332.
28. Falzi, G., Perrone, P., and Vignolo, L. A., Right–left asymmetries in anterior speech region. *Arch. Neurol.*, 1982, 39: 239–240.
29. Gainotti, G., Miceli, G., and Caltagirone, C., Constructional apraxia in left brain-damaged patients: A planning disorder? *Cortex*, 1977, 13: 119–130.
30. Galaburda, A. M., LeMay, M., Kemper, T. L., and Geschwind, N., Right–left asymmetries in the brain. *Science*, 1978, 199: 852–856.
31. Galaburda, A. M., Sanides, F., and Geschwind, N., Human brain: Cytoarchitectonic left–right asymmetries in the temporal speech region. *Arch. Neurol.*, 1978, 35: 812–817.
32. Geschwind, N., The anatomic basis of hemispheric differentiation. In: *Hemispheric Function in the Human Brain* (S. J. Dimond and J. B. Beaumont, Eds.). Elek Science, London, 1974: 7–24.
33. Geschwind, N., The apraxias: Neural mechanisms of disorders of learned movement. *Am. Sci.*, 1975, 63: 188–195.
34. Geschwind, N., and Levitsky, W., Human brain: Left–right asymmetries in temporal speech region. *Science*, 1968: 161: 186–187.
35. Gloor, P., Oliver, A., Quesney, F., Anderdmann, F., and Horowitz, S., The role of the limbic system in experential phenomena of temporal lobe epilepsy. *Ann. Neurol.*, 1982, 12: 129–144.
36. Healton, E. B., Navarro, C., Bressman, S., and Brust, J. C. M., Subcortical neglect. *Neurology*, 1982, 32: 776–778.

244 CUMMINGS

37. Hécaen, H., and de Ajuriaguerra, J., Balint's syndrome (psychic paralysis of visual fixation) and its minor forms. *Brain*, 1954, **77**: 373–400.
38. Hécaen, H., Tzortzis, C., and Rondot, P., Loss of topographic memory with learning deficits. *Cortex*, 1980, **16**: 525–542.
39. Heilman, K. M., Neglect and related disorders. In: *Clinical Neuropsychology* (K. M. Heilman and E. Valenstein, Eds.). Oxford University Press, New York, 1979: 268–307.
40. Heilman, K. M., and Valenstein, E., Frontal lobe neglect in man. *Neurology*, 1972, **22**: 660–664.
41. Heilman, K. M., Watson, R. T., and Bowers, D., Affective disorders associated with hemispheric disease. In: *Neuropsychology of Human Emotion* (K. M. Heilman and P. Satz, Eds.). Guilford Press, New York, 1983: 45–64.
42. Heilman, K. M., Watson, R. T., Valenstein, E., and Damasio, A. R., Localization of lesions in neglect. In: *Localization in Neuropsychology* (A. Kertesz, Ed.). Academic Press, New York, 1983: 471–492.
43. Hemphill, R. E., and Klein, R., Contribution to the dressing disability as a focal sign and to the imperception phenomena. *J. Ment. Sci.*, 1948, **94**: 611–622.
44. Karagulla, S., and Robertson, E. E., Psychical phenomena in temporal lobe epilepsy and psychoses. *Brit. Med. J.*, 1955, **1**: 748–752.
45. Kertesz, A., Right-hemisphere lesions in constructional apraxia and visuospatial deficit. In *Localization in Neuropsychology* (A. Kertesz, Ed.). Academic Press, New York, 1983: 455–470.
46. Kertesz, A., and Geschwind, N., Patterns of pyramidal decussation and their relationship to handedness. *Arch. Neurol.*, 1971, **24**: 326–332.
47. Lance, J. W., Simple formed hallucinations confined to the area of a specific visual field defect. *Brain*, 1976, **99**: 719–734.
48. Lance, J. W., Cooper, B., and Misbach, J., Visual hallucinations as a symptom of right parieto-occipital lesions. *Proc. Aust. Assn. Neurol.*, 1974, **11**: 209–217.
49. LeMay, M., Morphological cerebral asymmetries of modern man, fossil man, and non-human primate. *Ann. N.Y. Acad. Sci.*, 1976, **280**: 349–366.
50. LeMay, M., Asymmetries of the skull and handedness: Phrenology revisited. *J. Neurol. Sci.*, 1977, **32**: 243–253.
51. LeMay, M., and Culebras, A., Human brain–morphologic differences in the hemispheres demonstrable by carotid arteriography. *New Eng. J. Med.*, 1972, **287**: 168–170.
52. Lessell, S., Higher disorders of visual function: positive phenomena. In: *Neuro-Ophthalmology*, Vol. 8. (J. S. Glaser and J. L. Smith, Eds.). C. V. Mosby, St. Louis, 1975: 27–44.
53. Levy, J., Trevarthen, C., and Sperry, R. W., Perception of bilateral chimeric figures following hemispheric deconnexion. *Brain*, 1972, **95**: 61–78.
54. Luria, A. R., Disorders of "simultaneous perception" in a case of bilateral occipito-parietal brain injury. *Brain*, 1959, **82**: 437–449.
55. McFie, J., Piercy, M. F., and Zangwill, O. L., Visual–spatial agnosia associated with lesions of the right crebral hemisphere. *Brain*, 1950, **73**: 167–190.
56. Meadows, J. C., Disturbed perception of colours associated with localized cerebral lesions. *Brain*, 1974, **97**: 615–632.
57. Meadows, J. C., The anatomical basis of prosopagnosia. *J. Neurol. Neurosurg. Psychiatry*, 1974, **37**: 489–501.
58. Meadows, J. C., and Munro, S. S. F., Palinopsia. *J. Neurol. Neurosurg. Psychiatry*, 1977, **40**: 5–8.
59. Michel, E. M., and Troost, B. T., Palinopsia: Cerebral localization with computed tomography. *Neurology*, 1980, **30**: 887–889.
60. Milner, B., Interhemispheric differences in the localization of psychological processes in man. *Brit. Med. Bull.*, 1971, **27**: 272–277.

61. Mundy-Castle, A. C., A case in which visual hallucinations related to past experience were evoked by photic stimulation. *Electroenceph. Clin. Neurophysiol.*, 1951, 3: 353–356.

62. Oke, A., Keller, R., Mefford, I., and Adams, R. N., Lateralization of norepinephrine in human thalamus. *Science*, 1978: **200**: 1411–1413.

63. Paterson, A., and Zangwill, O. L., Disorders of visual space perception associated with lesions of the right cerebral hemisphere. *Brain*, 1944, **67**: 331–358.

64. Paterson, A., and Zangwill, O. L., A case of topographical disorientation associated with a unilateral cerebral lesion. *Brain*, 1945, **68**: 188–212.

65. Pearlman, A. L., Birch, J., and Meadows, J. C., Cerebral color blindness: An acquired defect in hue discrimination. *Ann. Neurol.*, 1979, **5**: 253–261.

66. Perani, D., Nardocci, N., and Broggi, G., Neglect after right unilateral thalamotomy: A case report. *Ital. J. Neurol. Sci.*, 1982, 1: 61–64.

67. Piercy, M., Hécaen, H., and de Ajuriaguerra, J., Constructional apraxia associated with unilateral cerebral lesions — left and right sided cases compared. *Brain*, 1960, **83**: 225–242.

68. Piercy, M., and Smyth, V. O. G., Right hemisphere dominance for certain non-verbal intellectual skills. *Brain*, 1962, **85**: 775–790.

69. Robinson, P. K., and Watt, A. C., Hallucinations of remembered scenes as an epileptic aura. *Brain*, 1947, **70**: 440–448.

70. Ross, E. D., The aprosodias. *Arch. Neurol.*, 1981, **38**: 561–569.

71. Rubens, A. B., Agnosia. In: *Clinical Neuropsychology* (K. M. Heilman and E. Valenstein, Eds.). Oxford University Press, New York, 1979: 233–267.

72. Rubens, A. B., and Benson, D. F., Associative visual agnosia. *Arch. Neurol.*, 1971, **24**: 305–316.

73. Rubens, A. B., Mahowald, M. W., and Hutton, J. T., Asymmetry of the lateral (sylvian) fissures in man. *Neurology*, 1976, **26**: 620–624.

74. Russell, W. R., and Whitty, C. W. M., Studies in traumatic epilepsy: 3. Visual fits. *J. Neurol. Neurosurg. Psychiatry*, 1955, **18**: 79–96.

75. Schwartz, M., and Smith, M. L., Visual asymmetries with chimeric faces. *Neuropsychologia*, 1980, **18**: 103–106.

76. Stein, S., and Volpe, B. T., Classical "parietal" neglect syndrome after subcortical right frontal lobe infarction. *Neurology*, 1983, **33**: 797–799.

77. Teuber, H. L., Alteration of perception and memory in man. In: *Analysis of Behavioral Change* (L. Weiskrantz, Ed.). Harper & Row, New York, 1968: 274–328.

78. Tyler, H. R., Abnormalities of perception with defective eye movements (Balint's syndrome). *Cortex*, 1968, 4: 154–171.

79. Van Lancker, D. R., and Canter, G. J., Impairment of voice and face recognition in patients with hemispheric damage. *Brain Cog.*, 1982, 1: 185–195.

80. Wada, J. H., Clarke, R., and Hamm, A., Cerebral hemispheric asymmetry in humans. *Arch. Neurol.*, 1975, **32**: 239–246.

81. Warrington, E. K., Constructional apraxia. In: *Disorders of Speech, Perception and Symbolic Behavior*, Vol. 4, *Handbook of Clinical Neurology* (P. J. Vinken and G. W. Bruyn, Eds.). American Elsevier, New York, 1969: 67–83.

82. Warrington, E. K., James, M., and Kinsbourne, M., Drawing disability in relation to laterality of cerebral lesion. *Brain*, 1966, **83**: 53–82.

83. Watson, R. T., and Heilman, K. M., Thalamic neglect. *Neurology*, 1979, **29**: 690–694.

84. Watson, R. T., Valenstein, E., and Heilman, K. M., Thalamic neglect. *Arch. Neurol.*, 1981, **38**: 501–506.

85. Weinberger, D. R., Luchins, D. J., Morihisa, J., and Wyatt, R. J., Asymmetrical volumes of the right and left frontal and occipital regions of the human brain. *Ann. Neurol.*, 1982, **11**: 97–100.

86. Weinstein, E. A., and Kahn, R. L., The syndrome of anosognosia. *Arch. Neurol. Psychiatry*, 1950, **64**: 772–791.
87. Whiteley, A. M., and Warrington, E. K., Prosopagnosia: A clinical, psychological, and anatomical study of three patients. *J. Neurol. Neurosurg. Psychiatry*, 1977, **40**: 395–403.
88. Whiteley, A. M., and Warrington, E. K., Selective impairment of topographical memory: A single case study. *J. Neurol. Neurosurg. Psychiatry*, 1978, **41**: 575–578.
89. Willanger, R., Danielsen, U. T., and Ankerhus, J., Visual neglect in right-sided apoplectic lesions. *Acta Neurol. Scand.*, 1981, **64**: 327–336.
90. Witelson, S. F., and Pallie, W., Left hemisphere specialization for language in the newborn. *Brain*, 1973, **96**: 641–647.

DIFFERENCES IN COGNITIVE FUNCTION WITH LEFT AND RIGHT TEMPORAL LOBE DYSFUNCTION

REBECCA RAUSCH, PhD
Department of Psychiatry

Surgical treatment for control of intractable complex partial seizures produces potential candidates for study of hemispheric specialization. In particular, for seizures originating from a temporal lobe (the typical complex partial seizures), one treatment is removal of the entire anterior section of the involved temporal lobe, an area of the brain known to play a significant role in memory processing. Bilateral temporal lobe removal was formerly attempted as treatment for psychiatric or epileptic disorders, but the procedure resulted in a severe memory disturbance in which learning and/or conscious retrieval of newly learned information was severely impaired (45, 46); it has consequently been abandoned.

Unlike the bilateral surgical approach, unilateral temporal lobe resection continues to be a viable treatment for otherwise uncontrollable temporal lobe seizures (8, 12). Global memory disturbance does not result, unless there is damage of the contralateral, nonoperated temporal lobe (36, 37). Selective cognitive deficits do occur with unilateral temporal lobe resection, however, and study of these impairments has advanced knowledge of hemispheric specialization for behavior.

Early studies of subjects with unilateral temporal lobe resection reported material-specific memory deficits based on the hemisphere resected. Surgery to the speech-dominant (usually left) temporal lobe impaired verbal memory, whether the material was spoken or written or whether recall or recognition was tested (2, 25, 26, 28). Conversely, nondominant (right) temporal lobe resection impaired memory for material not easily verbalized, presented either visually or auditorily (20, 29, 47).

The present chapter presents a number of tests selectively affected by temporal lobe dysfunction, presents data on other cognitive information processes disrupted, and addresses current and future prospects of further delineating behavioral significance of temporal lobe structures.

FACTORS AFFECTING COGNITIVE PERFORMANCE OF PATIENTS WITH TEMPORAL LOBE SURGERY

Before the behavioral effects of unilateral temporal lobe surgery are described, a review of factors other than hemispheric side of surgery that are capable of affecting test performance is warranted. These factors, for the most part, are well known and are controlled experimentally (e.g., by matching patient groups) or statistically (e.g., covarying their effects), or are at least recognized for their potential contributions.

1. Age at testing, age at surgery, age at onset of seizures, gender, and presence of other seizure typologies. Variations in the neuropsychological effects of central nervous system damage due to age factors (21, 41, 49), gender (22), and seizure characteristics (21, 41) are well recognized.

2. Time since surgery. The pattern and extent of neuropsychological deficits following temporal lobectomy may vary as a function of time since surgical intervention. Some behavioral changes, such as aphasia, may be present after surgery but may disappear within the first year. In contrast, some neuropsychological changes, such as reduced performance IQ (24), may not be noted until later.

3. Medication levels. Recent studies show that cognitive changes in epileptics vary as a function of type and dosage of anticonvulsant medications (cf. 9). Most patients continue on an anticonvulsant regimen postoperatively.

4. Surgery size. The size of the surgical excision may be a function both of the estimated extent of the epileptogenic lesion and of the neurosurgeon's approach. In some centers, the surgeon attempts to remove only the epileptic focus. In others, a standard *en bloc* removal of the anterior temporal lobe is preferred (8, 16). The surgical resection is routinely 0.5 cm shorter on the dominant side to avoid temporal language area. The bloc routinely resects 5.5–6.0 cm of the anterior tip and includes the hippocampal pes, hippocampal gyrus, uncus, about two-thirds of the amygdala, and lateral neocortex.

5. Extratemporal lobe damage. Extratemporal lobe damage should be carefully considered and routinely sought. IQs lower than 80, diffuse EEG abnormalities, or any other evidence of a nonfocal disorder are thought to indicate extratemporal lobe dysfunction, patients with such indicators are not usually considered for standard surgical treatment (8, 12).

6. Surgical results. Patients who continue to have seizures postoperatively are suspected to have extratemporal lobe epileptic lesions, and their neuropsychological test results differ from those of patients who benefit from surgery (41). Cessation of seizures, on the other hand, can be accepted as indication that the epileptogenic tissue has been resected.

7. Hemispheric reorganization. Intracarotid sodium amytal injection to determine hemispheric dominance for language (51) and memory (12, 38) is used routinely at many surgical centers. This procedure has been especially valuable in detecting pathological shift of language to the right hemisphere (38, 43). The testing technique, however, has not been refined sufficiently to demonstrate hemispheric reorganization of nonverbal functions.

General Memory Deficits Associated with Unilateral Temporal Lobe Dysfunction

The most striking deficiency following left or right* temporal lobe resection is the reduced ability to remember verbal or nonverbal material, respectively. Except for subtle cognitive changes to be discussed below, the memory deficit is thought to occur without other neuropsychological deficiencies. Attention, concentration, intellectual level, and immediate memory span, as traditionally tested, are not impaired following anterior temporal lobe excisions. Detailed studies of postoperative patients indicate that some of these cognitive areas may improve in selected patients after surgery if seizures are controlled (33, 41). When examined at least 1 year postoperatively, these patients show no difficulties with traditional aphasia testing. Transient aphasia, however, may occur in the early postoperative period in patients with *dominant* temporal lobe resections and may be manifested as difficulty in naming, reading, and spelling. These symptoms usually resolve by 3 months after surgery; at 1 year, only a mild dysnomia may remain, correlated with the degree of verbal-memory deficit. The primary neurological deficit associated with surgery is a quadrantopsia in the visual field contralateral to the surgery. This occurs in about two-thirds of the patients, while hemianopsia may result in less than 5% (12). Patients with quadrantopsia compensate well and report no major disability.

Batteries of tests used to elicit the verbal-memory deficit in patients with left-sided surgery generally include the Logical Prose and Word Pairs Subtests of the Wechsler Memory Scale (WMS) (52). A 45-minute delay containing distraction intervening between immediate recall and an unexpected recall task enhances the deficit. Tasks consisting of visually presented verbal material also consistently demonstrate deficiencies in left-sided surgical patients (cf. 28). The deficiency may be elicited by use of stimuli containing either simple verbal material, such as consonant trigrams or unrelated words, or more organized material, such as stories from the WMS (52). Verbal recall, both immediately and following a delay, is worse if seizures are not controlled following the surgery (cf. 41), thus apparently reflecting the inability of the contralateral temporal lobe and/or extratemporal lobe areas to compensate for the impaired function.

The following are examples of a 45-minute delayed recall of a WMS (52) Logical Prose story from patients with either language-dominant, left (LTL) or nondominant, right (RTL) temporal lobe surgery. In addition, patients whose seizures were controlled by surgery are contrasted with those whose seizures persisted. Patients are matched for age, IQ, and time since surgery.

PATIENT 135 (RTL — seizures controlled): "Anna Thompson lives in Boston as a scrub-woman for a building. She got robbed of $15. The rent was due, she had four children who hadn't been fed. The police felt bad for her so they started to collect a purse."

PATIENT 158 (LTL — seizures controlled): "About a lady who lived in Boston. Worked as a floor scrubber. She got robbed of $50. The policeman felt sorry for her and did something for her. The office was located on . . . "

PATIENT 109 (RTL — seizures persisted): "A scrub lady named Mary from Boston lost her purse. She had 4 children. The police were going to make her a purse. She had $15 in it. I'm not sure."

PATIENT 103 (LTL — seizures persisted): "About a lady who I believe got robbed. She has 19 kids and the police helped her with money. I can't remember the term use."

---

*"Left temporal lobe resection" refers to surgery of the language-dominant, left hemisphere, while "right temporal lobe resection" refer to surgery of the nondominant, right hemisphere.

The memory deficits associated with nondominant temporal lobe resections are primarily manifested as difficulty in remembering nonverbal visual material. The Rey–Osterrieth Draw and Recall Test (34) (and Taylor's alternate form [48]), the WMS Visual Reproduction Subtest (using immediate and delayed testing; cf. 26), and Kimura's Unfamiliar Design Test (20) have consistently shown sensitivity to anterior nondominant temporal lobe dysfunction (see Figure 1 for examples). Modalities other than vision have also been used to show deficiencies in nonverbal memory. For example, olfactory memory has been reported to be selectively depressed following nondominant temporal lobe surgery (42; however, cf. 15). Perception of nonverbal sounds (i.e., discrimination of rhythms) has been reported from the Montreal group to be impaired with nondominant temporal lobe surgery (27), although we have failed to find a similar deficiency. The different results may reflect a number of parameters including sample size (the UCLA population is smaller) and patient characteristics (variations in surgical procedures).

OTHER OR RELATED COGNITIVE CHANGES ASSOCIATED WITH TEMPORAL LOBECTOMY

Studies attempting to delineate the nature of the deficits occurring in patients with anterior temporal lobe dysfunction have identified subtle cognitive changes, in addition to the more obvious memory problems. For example, we have found defective problem-solving strategies following both left and right temporal lobectomy, although the nature of the deficit varied, depending upon the side of the lobectomy (39). The task chosen was a visual-discrimination task in which a subject's set of hypotheses or problem-solving strategies could be determined by the responses (10, 23) (see Figures 2 and 3). In the normal subject population, if the hypothesis being tested is positively reinforced, the individual generally maintains the hypothesis, while if the hypothesis is indicated to be incorrect, the person changes it.

Two matched patient groups who had undergone either a left ($n = 7$) or right ($n = 9$) standard anterior temporal lobectomy (8) to relieve intractable seizures, and a matched control group ($n = 9$), were examined with the above-described hypothesis test (23), both with and without memory assistance (10). Overall performance levels on the hypothesis test (e.g., the number of problems solved correctly) were not significantly different between the two groups of temporal lobectomy patients, although both groups performed worse than controls (cf. Figure 4). Prominent differences between the patient groups emerged from analyses of cognitive strategies, and such patterns were found to occur whether or not memory was involved. Left temporal lobectomy patients utilized *fewer* hypotheses than normal subjects and tended to shift from a hypothesis even when told it was correct. They tended to shift more from a hypothesis containing *verbal* information (i.e., a letter) as opposed to those containing less overt verbal cues (i.e., color, position, size). In contrast, right temporal lobectomy patients showed a tendency to stay with a hypothesis, even when told the hypothesis was *wrong*. For the latter patient group, perseveration of a hypothesis was not related to any specific stimulus cue.

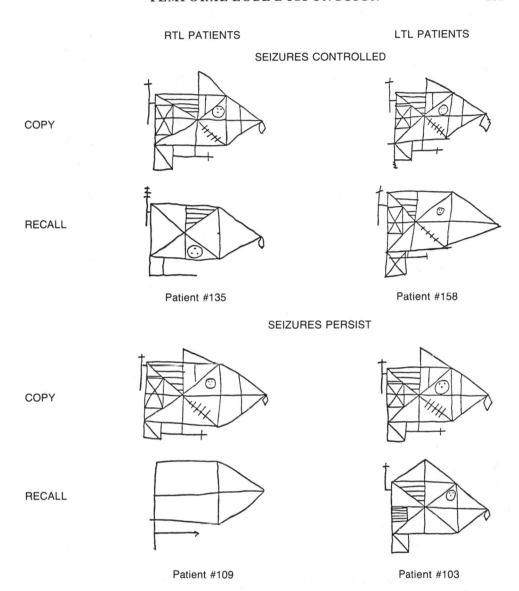

Figure 1. Examples of responses on the Rey–Osterrieth Copy and 45-minute Recall Test of patients with left (LTL) or right (RTL) temporal lobe resections. As a group RTL patients perform significantly worse on the recall component of the task than LTL patients. At least for the RTL patients, if seizures persist following surgery, performance is worse than if seizures were surgically controlled. Examples of the verbal memory performance of these same patients are given in the text.

The results suggest that left temporal lobe dysfunction affects the formulation of hypotheses and the maintenance of such conceptualizations, once established. And the stability of hypotheses directly related to verbal material appears more vulnerable than nonverbal hypotheses. On the other hand, dysfunction of the right temporal lobe appears to affect the ability to reevaluate a conceptualization or hypothesis once developed, even in light of negative information. Since these selective deficiencies

TRIAL

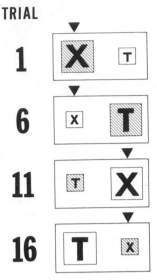

Figure 2. An example of a reinforced internally orthogonal set from one of the 16 problems presented in the hypothesis test. The slanted line and open squares signify the colors red and green, respectively. Four consecutive unreinforced trials are interspersed between each of these cards (see Figure 3). During the Memory-Assistant presentation, the correct stimuli are marked as shown in the figure and these reinforced cards are left in view after the response and reinforcement. Except for Trial 16, the nature of reinforcement, positive or negative, was predetermined and independent of the subject's choice. After reinforcement on Trial 1, only four logically correct hypotheses remain; after reinforcement on Trial 6, two logically correct hypotheses remain; and after Trial 11, only one hypothesis can be logically correct, and this consequently determines the solution to the problem. A different set of internally orthogonal cards (not shown) was obtained by reversing the left and right positions of the stimuli on each of the reinforced cards. This second set was used in the unreinforced trials. (From 31. Reprinted by permission.)

occurred with or without reliance upon memory, they most likely represent cognitive changes not attributable to gross memory disturbances.

The perseverative tendency of patients following right temporal lobectomy has also been reported to occur when they are asked to generate abstract (meaningless) designs with a fixed number of lines (19). This task of design fluency also elicited perseveration in patients with dysfunction of other anatomical areas within the right hemisphere; nevertheless, the results provide confirmation that patients with right

TRIAL

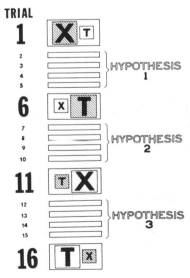

Figure 3. A schematic diagram of a sample hypothesis test problem. The reinforced set of cards, Trials 1, 6, 11, and 16, are interspersed with three sets of four consecutive cards. The hypothesis of the subject can be determined by the pattern of his responses on these latter unreinforced trials as described in the text. Hypotheses 1, 2, and 3 are deduced from subject responses on Trials 2–5, 7–10, and 12–15, respectively. If Hypothesis 3 of the subject corresponds to the only remaining cue which could be logically correct, the problem was considered to have been solved correctly. (From 31. Reprinted by permission.)

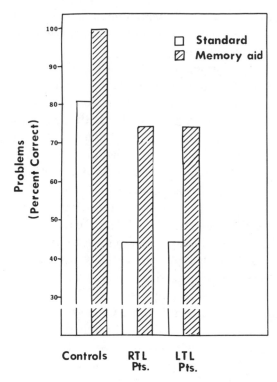

Figure 4. Percentage of hypothesis test problems solved correctly by subjects with either left (LTL) or right (RTL) temporal lobectomies and controls.

temporal lobe lesions have difficulty in using feedback to monitor continuing action, image, or thought. Since both the design fluency task and the hypothesis test have been shown to be sensitive to frontal lobe as well as to right temporal lobe dysfunction (4, 19, 39), it remains to be determined whether or not the perseverative tendencies induced by damage to these different brain regions are qualitatively as well as quantitatively distinguishable.

Other cognitive deficiencies have been reported with dominant or left temporal lobe dysfunction, with the data strongly indicating that a deficiency exists in the semantic organization of memory. For example, following left temporal lobe resection, patients often fail to organize or cluster words in a free-recall test of lists of associated words (53). They have also been reported to have real but subtle deficiencies in the semantic classification of drawings or words (54).

The false-recognition paradigm of Underwood (50) was used to evaluate the encoding strategies of lobectomized patients with verbal-memory deficits (40). Cermak *et al.* (3) had reported that Korsakoff patients with gross memory impairments have a reduced capacity or totally fail to encode verbal information in terms of semantic properties. Hence, it seems plausible that patients with left temporal lobe resection (and related verbal memory deficits) may have a similar deficit and thus may also fail to encode or utilize the semantic qualities of verbal material. Such a deficiency would be consistent with studies suggesting semantic organization deficiencies in this latter patient group.

Subjects were matched groups of patients with either left ($n = 9$) or right ($n = 11$) temporal lobectomy, and a matched control group ($n = 10$). The behavior tasks, administered in either visual or auditory modalities, consisted of a serial presentation of 60 words, some of which were presented earlier in the list. Words were presented at a rate of one every 5 seconds. The subject's response was to indicate by pressing a button whether or not the word appeared earlier in the list. For the auditory presentation, the word list contained words with the following relationship to previously presented words in the list: six words that represented a category of a previously presented word (1) (e.g., "doll"–"toy"); six words highly associated (35) (e.g., "black"–"white"); and six words acoustically related or rhyming (e.g., "coat"–"boat"). In addition, there were six words that had no obvious relationship to previously presented words (neutral words) and six words that were actually repeated. The visual task was similarly designed, except that instead of six words acoustically related, there were six words which were homonyms (e.g., "see"–"sea").

Figures 5 and 6 show the main findings. On both the visual and auditory tasks, left temporal lobe surgical patients made significantly more false-recognition errors — that is, falsely recognizing more unrepeated words as previously occurring — than either right temporal lobe surgical patients or normal controls. The errors made by

Figure 5. (a) Mean ($\pm SD$) of auditory false-recognition errors made by patients with left temporal lobectomies (LTL), patients with right temporal lobectomies (RTL), and normal controls (NC). Errors were calculated from words which were related to previously presented words in a serially presented word list (see text). (b) Mean ($\pm SD$) "yes" responses on the auditory false-recognition task by patients with left temporal lobectomies (LTL), patients with right temporal lobectomies (RTL), and normal controls (NC). A "yes" response on categories, associatives, rhymes, or neutral words indicates a false-recognition error. A "yes" response on a repeated word is a correct identification. (From 39. Reprinted by permission.)

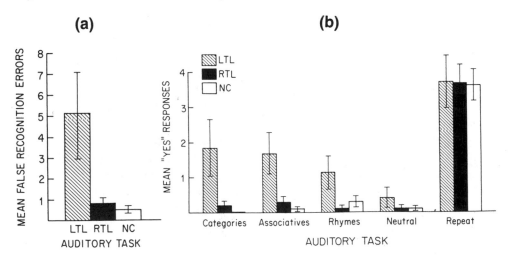

(a) (b)

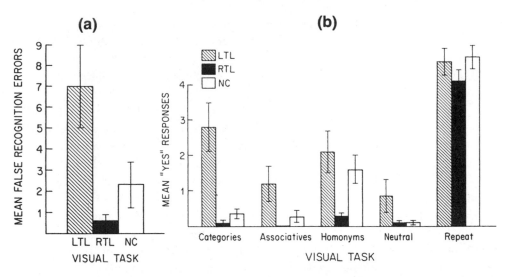

Figure 6. (a) Mean (±SD) of visual false-recognition errors made by patients with left temporal lobectomies (LTL), patients with right temporal lobectomies (RTL), and normal controls (NC). Errors were calculated in the manner described in Figure 5. (b) Mean (±SD) responses on the visual false-recognition task by patients with left temporal lobectomies (LTL), patients with right temporal lobectomies (RTL), and normal controls (NC). A "yes" response on categories, associatives, homonyms, or neutral words indicates a false-recognition error. A "yes" response on a repeated word is a correct identification. (From 39. Reprinted by permission.)

the left temporal lobectomy patients occurred only on words related in some way to previously presented words. On the other hand, these patients correctly identified those words actually repeated and did not falsely recognize as being previously presented words that had no relationship to other words in the list. This type of pattern indicates that the false-recognition errors on related words were more a function of the overlapping attributes of the words than simply a response pattern. While the left-sided patients made errors on all types of related words, they consistently made more errors in "falsely recognizing words as being repeated" on those words that represented the same taxonomic category of a previous word. Thus, the semantic association of the words within the list produced the most confusion.

Unlike the performance of the left temporal lobectomy patients, the performance of right surgical patients differed for the two tasks. The performance of the right temporal lobectomy patients was not different from controls on the auditory task, but was significantly different from that of both normals and left temporal lobe patients when the words were presented visually. When using the visual modality, the right temporal lobectomy patients, in marked contrast to the left-sided patients, made *fewer* false-recognition errors. Since they also correctly identified the words actually repeated, their unusual performance was a function of the stimulus characteristics rather than a gross response or attentional pattern.

These findings support the aforementioned conclusion that left temporal lobectomy patients have impairment in verbal semantic memory. From these studies, it can be postulated that the deficit is not a failure to utilize the semantic attributes of words (as in Korsakoff syndrome), but rather a failure to discriminate individual words from the semantic context. Somewhat unexpectedly, the right temporal lobectomy patients showed a reduced capability to process or utilize the multiple attributes of visual, but not auditory, verbal information.

The deficiency in semantic organization associated with left temporal lobe dysfunction is not limited to isolated linguistic stimuli (i.e., words or written prose), but generalizes to real-life schemas. Using pictorial scenes that represent typical situations, Zaidel and Rausch (56) found that memory for the semantic content of pictures was affected by left temporal lobe resections, but not right temporal resections. Patients with either left ($n = 8$) or right ($n = 11$) temporal lobectomies and a matched control group were shown "organized" and "disorganized" pictorial scenes (see Figure 7); they were then examined with a probe for details in the whole scene. Patients with left temporal lobe dysfunction performed worse than controls in remembering the details of the organized pictures but not of the disorganized pictures (cf. Figure 8). It is important to note that the alternatives in the probes were related to the actual target detail and reflected logical, realistic changes with respect to the

Figure 7. Examples of types of stimuli and probes used in the Zaidel and Rausch experiment. (a) An organized scene. (b) A disorganized scene. (c) A probe for a single detail. (d) A probe for a whole scene. (From 43. Reprinted by permission.)

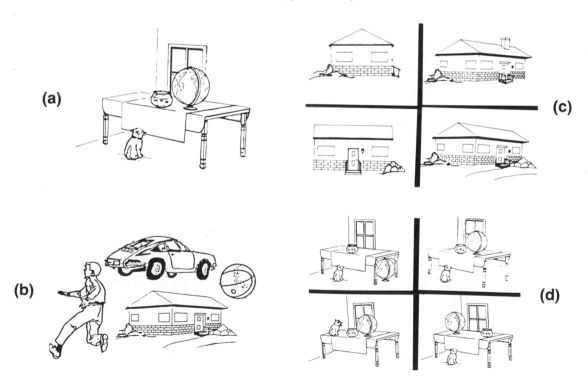

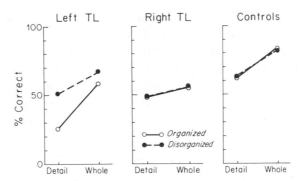

Figure 8. Mean percentage of correct responses in each of the main conditions for patients with either left temporal lobectomy (Left TL) or right temporal lobectomy (Right TL) and controls. (From 43. Reprinted by permission.)

correct answer. Thus, left temporal lobe patients, unless forced to attend to the details carefully in the disorganized pictures, lost the discriminatory information to correctly identify the target detail. The results are consistent with our findings that on false-recognition tasks, patients with left temporal resection have impaired ability to isolate particular information from its semantic context. Collectively, these studies show how a relatively specific deficit may be detected in aspects of a person's life.

CURRENT AND FUTURE PROSPECTS

It has been proposed that dysfunction of anatomically different areas within a temporal lobe may result in different types of memory deficits. The extent of removal of the mesial versus the lateral temporal lobe area is purported to be related to the learning of simplistic versus intrinsically organized material, respectively (31, 32). Nevertheless, the nature of the material affected, verbal or nonverbal, is still thought to be determined by the side of damage. For example, the extent of mesial removal of the *right* temporal lobe correlates with deficits in learning an unfamiliar sequence — for example, a series of turns in a maze (6) — or with recalling the position of a spot on a line (7), while the extent of mesial removal of the *left* temporal lobe correlates with deficits in learning unrelated consonants (44) or learning recurring supraspan digit sequences (7, 30). In contrast, the lateral temporal lobe neocortex appears to be more involved with learning of more complex (but not necessarily more difficult) material. Lateral neocortical damage of the *right* temporal lobe is reportedly sufficient to account for difficulties in recalling abstract, complex visual patterns (20, 48). Evidence of correlation of specific verbal deficits with the left lateral temporal lobe is less clear-cut (cf. 18).

The above findings, while not conclusive, are quite provocative in suggesting different roles of anatomical regions within the temporal lobe in various memory processes. Recently, experimental evidence has indicated that the human brain "honors" another dual memory system: declarative or data-based information, and procedural or rule-based information (5). Simplistic or rote memory, postulated to be associated with mesial temporal lobe structures, may be similar to declarative memory, in which the memory for specific items is emphasized. Conversely, the recall of material with intrinsic organization, a proposed lateral temporal lobe function, may be more compatible with recall of procedural or rule-governing operations. If one follows this line of thought in speculating that procedural memory processes are related to the lateral temporal neocortex, then the changes in cognitive strategies follow temporal lobe resection, clearly a conceptual procedural approach, should also be sensitive to lateral neocortex dysfunction. This hypothesis remains to be tested.

Another interpretation of proposed functional differentiations of temporal lobe regions is that damage to the mesial temporal lobe impairs the utilization or access of higher-order memory units necessary to encode new information, while damage to the lateral neocortical areas impairs the organizational structure of the memory units themselves. Thus, the proposed difficulty related to mesial structural damage, in learning simplistic or unrelated items, may be due to an inability to attach new data to existing memory systems. Similarly, the proposed deficits, associated with the lateral neocortical damage, in "organizational memory" may reflect disruption of the organizational aspect of hierarchical memory units. Human memory research utilizing conceptual categories has psychological tools available to examine this explanation.

The constraints, however, in further specifying the functional significance of areas within the temporal lobe lie more in the inability to clearly define the anatomical boundaries than in the lack of psychological theories. To date, most data delineating temporal lobe areas have been based on studies of epileptic patients with varying degrees of excision of mesial versus lateral neocortical temporal lobe areas. While these studies are obviously valuable, their imprecision may reflect inexact anatomical correlates. In these latter studies, patients have been classified on the extent of tissue removed. The amount and area of tissue removed in these patients were determined by the limits of suspected epileptogenesis and surgical approach of the neurosurgeon. It cannot be assumed that because an area was not removed, it was normal. Hippocampal tissue may escape resection if there are no EEG spikes from this area, but this may actually be because of the presence of severe mesial temporal lobe sclerosis (13).

Thus, while studies of epileptic patients with varying extents of surgical excision are valuable, there are inherent limitations and restrictions. Complementing these studies with other approaches, albeit with other particular restrictions, will increase the research potential of this unique population. For example, correlating the type and extent of memory deficits *prior to* surgery with the underlying neuroanatomical pathology and dysfunction will provide another approach. Subsequent microscopic and biochemical analyses can provide detailed evidence of preoperative intactness of surgically removed tissue. Other *in vivo* studies of the anatomical basis of memory in epileptic patients can be undertaken with the aid of positron computed tomography (17, 55). Patterns of memory deficits may be related to anatomically localized functional deficiencies, or to reduced local glucose metabolism, a frequent finding in this patient population (cf. 14). This latter technique, although offering less exact spatial resolution than the pathological analyses, has the advantage of identifying extratemporal lobe dysfunction and of identifying dysfunctional temporal lobe areas that may not show obvious gross or microscopic pathology (11). Such investigations can be complemented by studies of normal subjects, using similar paradigms to activate selective anatomical areas.

Studies of epileptic patients and the effects of surgical treatment on their behavior will continue to enhance understanding of temporal lobe functioning; these studies require the correlation of knowledge from diverse research approaches.

REFERENCES

1. Battig, W. F., and Montague, W. E., Category norms for verbal items in 56 categories: A replication and extension of the Connecticut category norms. *J. Exp. Psychol.*, *Monograph*, 1969, **80**: 1–46.
2. Blakemore, C. B., and Falconer, M. A., Long-term effects of anterior temporal lobectomy on certain cognitive functions. *J. Neurol. Neurosurg. Psychiatry*, 1967, **30**: 364–367.
3. Cermak, L. S., Butters, N., and Jerrein, J., The extent of the verbal encoding ability of Korsakoff patients. *Neuropsychologia*, 1973, **11**: 85–94.
4. Cicerone, K. D., and Lazar, R. M., Effects of frontal lobe lesions on hypothesis sampling during concept formation. *Neuropsychologia*, 1983, **21**: 513–524.
5. Cohen, N. J., and Squire, L. R., Preserved learning and retention of pattern-analyzing skill in amnesia: Dissociation of knowing and knowing that. *Science*, 1980, **210**: 207–210.
6. Corkin, S., Tactually guided maze-learning in man: Effects of unilateral cortical excisions and bilateral hippocampal lesions. *Neuropsychologia*, 1965, **3**: 339–351.
7. Corsi, P., Human memory and the medial temporal region of the brain. Doctoral dissertation, McGill University.
8. Crandall, P. H., Engel, J., Jr., and Rausch, R., Indications for depth electrode recordings in complex partial epilepsy and subsequent surgical results. In: *Progress in Epilepsy* (F. C. Rose, Ed.). Pitman Medical Publishing, London, 1983: 507–526.
9. Dodrill, C. B., Neuropsychology of epilepsy. In: *Handbook of Clinical Neuropsychology* (S. B. Filskov and T. J. Boll, Eds.). Wiley, New York, 1981: 366–395.
10. Eimas, P. D., Effects of memory aids on hypothesis behavior and focusing in young children and adults. *J. Exp. Child Psychol.*, 1970, **10**: 319–336.
11. Engel, J., Jr., Brown, W. J., Kuhl, D. E., Phelps, M. E., Mazziotta, J. C., and Crandall, P. H., Pathological findings underlying focal temporal lobe hypometabolism in partial epilepsy. *Ann. Neurol.*, 1982, **12**: 518–528.
12. Engel, J., Jr., Crandall, P. H., and Rausch, R., The partial epilepsies. In: *The Clinical Neurosciences*, Vol. 2 (R. N. Rosenberg, R. G. Grossman, S. Schochet, E. R. Heinz, and W. D. WIllis, Eds.). Churchill Livingstone, New York, 1983: 1349–1380.
13. Engel, J., Jr., Driver, M. V., and Falconer, M. A., Electrophysiological correlates of pathology and surgical results in temporal lobe epilepsy. *Brain*, 1975, **98**: 129–156.
14. Engel, J., Jr., Rausch, R., Lieb, J. P., Kuhl, D. E., and Crandall, P. H., Correlation of criteria used for localizing epileptic foci in patients considered for surgical therapy for epilepsy. *Ann. Neurol.*, 1981, **9**: 215–244.

15. Eskenazi, B., Cain, W. S., Novelly, R. A., and Friend, K. B., Olfactory functioning in temporal lobectomy patients. *Neuropsychologia*, 1983, **21**: 365–374.
16. Falconer, M. A., Anterior temporal lobectomy for epilepsy. In: *Operative Surgery*, Vol. 13 (C. Rob and R. Smith, Eds.). Butterworths, London, 1976: 315–322.
17. Hoffman, E. J., Phelps, M. E., Huang, S. C., Kuhl, D. E., Crabtree, M., Burke, M., Burgiss, S., Keyser, R., Highfill, R., and William C., A new tomograph for quantitative positron emission computed tomography of the brain. *IEEE Trans. Nucl. Sci. N.S.*, 1981, **28**: 99–103.
18. Jaccarino-Hiatt, G., Impairment of cognitive organization in patients with temporal lobe lesions. Doctoral dissertation, McGill University, 1978.
19. Jones-Gotman, M., and Milner, B., Design fluency: The invention of nonsense drawings after focal cortical lesions. *Neuropsychologia*, 1977, **15**: 653–674.
20. Kimura, D., Right temporal-lobe damage. *Arch. Neurol.*, 1963, 8: 264–271.
21. Kløve, H., and Matthews, C. G., Neuropsychological studies of patients with epilepsy. In: *Clinical Neuropsychology: Current Status and Applications* (R. M. Reitan and L. A. Davison, Eds.). V. H. Winston & Sons, Washington, D.C., 1974: 247–266.
22. Lansdell, H., A sex difference in effect of temporal lobe neurosurgery on design preference. *Nature*, 1962, **194**: 852–854.
23. Levin, M., Hypothesis behavior by humans during discrimination learning. *J. Exp. Psychol.*, 1966, **71**: 331–338.
24. Meier, M. J., and French, L. A., Longitudinal assessment of intellectual functioning following unilateral temporal lobectomy. *J. Clin. Psychol.*, 1966, **22**: 22–27.
25. Meyer, J., and Yates, A. J., Intellectual changes following temporal lobectomy for psychomotor epilepsy. *J. Neurol. Neurosurg. Psychiatry*, 1955, **18**: 44–52.
26. Milner, B., Psychological defects produced by temporal-lobe excision. *Research Publications of the Association for Research on Nervous and Mental Disease*, 1958, **36**: 244–257.
27. Milner, B., Laterality effects in audition. In: *Interhemispheric Relations and Cerebral Dominance* (V. B. Mountcastle, Ed.). John Hopkins University Press, Baltimore, 1962: 177–195.
28. Milner, B., Brain mechanisms suggested by studies of the temporal lobes. In: *Brain Mechanisms Underlying Speech and Language* (F. L. Darley, Ed.). Grune & Stratton, New York, 1967: 122–132.
29. Milner, B., Visual recognition and recall after right temporal excision in man. *Neuropsychologia*, 1968, **6**: 191–210.
30. Milner, B., Hemispheric specialization: Scope and limits. In: *The Neurosciences: Third Study Program* (F. O. Schmitt and F. G. Worden, Eds.). MIT Press, Cambridge, Mass., 1974: 75–89.
31. Milner, B., Clues to the cerebral organization of memory. In: *Cerebral Correlates of Conscious Experience* (P. A. Buser and A. Rougeul-Buser, Eds.). Elsevier/North-Holland Biomedical Press, Amsterdam, 1978.
32. Milner, B., Complementary functional specialization of the human cerebral hemispheres. In: *Nerve Cells, Transmitters and Behavior* (R. Levi-Montalcini, Ed.). Elsevier/North-Holland Biomedical Press, Amsterdam, 1980: 601–625.
33. Novelly, R. A., Augustine, E. A., Mattson, R. H., Glaser, G. H., Williamson, P.D., Spencer, D. D., and Spenser, S. S., Selective memory improvement and impairment in temporal lobectomy for epilepsy. *Ann. Neurol.*, 1984, **15**: 64–67.
34. Osterrieth, P., Le test de copie d'une figure complexe. *Arch. Psychol.*, 1944, **30**: 206–356.
35. Palermo, D. S., and Jenkins, J. J., *Word Association Norms, Grade School through College*. University of Minn. Press, Minneapolis, 1964.
36. Penfield, W., and Mathieson, M. D., Memory: Autopsy findings and comments on the

role of hippocampus in experiential recall. *Arch. Neurol.*, 1974, **31**: 145–154.

37. Penfield, W., and Milner, B., Memory deficit produced by bilateral lesions in the hippo-campal zone. *AMA Arch. Neurol. Psychiatry*, 1958, **79**: 475–497.

38. Rasmussen, T., and Milner, B., The role of early left brain injury in determining lateraliza-tion of cerebral speech functions. *Ann. N.Y. Acad. Sci.*, 1977, **29**: 355–369.

39. Rausch, R., Cognitive strategies in patients with unilateral temporal lobe excisions. *Neuro-psychologia*, 1977, **15**: 385–395.

40. Rausch, R., Lateralization of temporal lobe dysfunction and verbal encoding. *Brain Lang.*, 1981, **12**: 92–100.

41. Rausch, R., and Crandall, P. H., Psychological status related to surgical control of temporal lobe seizures. *Epilepsia*, 1982, **23**: 191–202.

42. Rausch, R., Serafetinides, E. A., and Crandall, P. H., Olfactory memory in patients with anterior temporal lobectomy. *Cortex*, 1977, **13**: 445–453.

43. Rausch, R., and Walsh, G. O., Right hemisphere language dominance in right-handed epileptic patients. *Arch. Neurol.*, 1984, **41**: 1077–1080.

44. Samuels, I., Butters, N., and Fedio, P., Short-term memory disorders following temporal lobe removals in humans. *Cortex*, 1972, **8**: 283–298.

45. Scoville, W. B., Dunsmore, R. H., Liberson, W. T., Henry, C. E., and Pepe, A., Ob-servations on medical temporal lobectomy and uncotomy in the treatment of psy-chotic states. *Res. Nerv. Ment. Dis., Proc.*, 1963, **31**: 347–368.

46. Scoville, W. B., and Milner, B., Loss of recent memory after bilateral hippocampal lesions. *J. Neurol. Neurosurg. Psychiatry.*, 1957, **20**: 11–21.

47. Shankweiler, D., Effects of temporal lobe damage on perception of dichotically presented melodies. *J. Comp. Physiol. Psychol.*, 1966, **62**: 115–119.

48. Taylor, L. B., Localization of cerebral lesions by psychological testing. *Clin. Neurosurg.*, 1969, **16**: 269–287.

49. Teuber, H. L., and Rudel, R. G., Behavior after cerebral lesions in children and adults. *Child Neurol.*, 1962, **4**: 3–20.

50. Underwood, B. J., False recognition by implicit verbal responses. *J. Exp. Psychol.*, 1965, **70**: 122–129.

51. Wada, J., and Rasmussen, T., Intracarotid injection of Sodium Amytal for the lateraliza-tion of cerebral speech dominance: Experimental and clinical observations. *J. Neurosurg.*, 1960, **17**: 266–282.

52. Wechsler, D., and Stone, C. P., *Wechsler Memory Scale*. Psychological Corporation, New York, 1945.

53. Weingartner, H., Verbal learning in patients with temporal lobe lesions. *J. Verb. Learn. Verb. Behav.*, 1968, **7**: 520–526.

54. Wilkins, A., and Moscovitch, M., Selective impairment in semantic memory after tem-poral lobectomy. *Neuropsychologia*, 1978, **16**: 73–79.

55. Williams, C. W., Crabtree, M. C., Burke, M. R., Keyser, R. M., Burgiss, S. G., Hoff-man, E. J., and Phelps, M. E., Design of the NeuroECAT: A high resolution, high efficiency positron tomography for imaging the adult head and infant torso. *IEEE Trans. Nucl. Sci. N.S.*, 1981, **28**: 1736–1740.

56. Zaidel, D. W., and Rausch, R., Effects of semantic organization on the recognition of pictures following temporal lobectomy. *Neuropsychologia*, 1981, **19**: 813–817.

STUDIES OF HEMISPHERIC LATERALIZATION
IN PATIENTS WITH PARTIAL EPILEPSY

J. RICHARD MENDIUS, MD, and JEROME ENGEL, JR., MD, PhD
Department of Anatomy

Basic neuroscientists traditionally utilize lesion and stimulation studies in animals when attempting to localize function within the brain. Clinical neuroscientists, for the most part, rely upon disease-induced pathological changes for such studies. Clinical pathological studies include both focal destructive lesions such as strokes or tumors and presumed focal stimulation processes as in epilepsy. In this chapter, we will discuss some of the methodological problems and sources of potential error encountered when using epileptic discharges for localization of higher cerebral functions in humans. Although studies of epileptic patients during direct brain stimulation (26, 28) and following surgical resection (38, 43, 48) have contributed greatly to understanding of human brain function, this discussion will be concerned with functional information derived from observations of spontaneous epileptic events.

The International League against Epilepsy's current classification of epileptic seizures divides them into "partial" or "generalized," based on behavioral and electrophysiological phenomena (11). Partial seizures appear to have a localized onset limited to one hemisphere, while generalized seizures apparently begin in both hemispheres simultaneously. Partial seizures are further divided into "simple" or "complex," the latter involving an alteration of consciousness.

Partial seizures might be assumed to reveal the behavioral effects of stimulation of specific cerebral structures if the exact site of ictal onset and pathways of propagation were known and temporally correlated with observed ictal behavior. Furthermore, partial seizures are often followed by transient postictal symptomatology resulting from decreased function in the areas involved in the seizure — for example, Todd's paralysis (12). Specific pathological lesions exist in the partial epilepsies and may be associated with fixed focal deficits in function, in addition to transient disturbances associated with ictal events. Ideally, patients with partial seizures should

Acknowledgments: This work was sponsored in part by a Merritt–Putnam Fellowship grant from the Epilepsy Foundation of America to J. Richard Mendius; Grants NS 02808, NS 15654, and CA 32855 from the U.S. Public Health Service; and Contract DE-ACO 3-76-SF00012 from the Department of Energy. We gratefully acknowledge the assistance of Ms. Edith Barsky in typing and editing the manuscript. We are also indebted to D. Frank Benson, MD, and Rebecca Rausch, PhD, for many helpful suggestions and discussions.

provide neuroscientists with opportunities to create experimental paradigms similar to animal studies that combine selective lesions and focal stimulation.

The initial work on localization of cerebral function based on studies with epileptic patients by Jackson (30), Penfield and Jasper (41), and other early investigators involved careful documentation of ictal events correlated with structural changes observed in the postmortem brain. Relatively reliable conclusions regarding primary motor, sensory, and language functions were drawn from these studies. More recently, however, as investigators have attempted to characterize the structural substrates of less well-defined uniquely human behaviors, the reliability of their conclusions has decreased. In part this can be attributed to the complexity of the behaviors studied, and in part to the use of localizing techniques that are somewhat less precise than postmortem observations of structural lesions. Specifically, behavioral–anatomical correlations are now often made *in vivo*, based on EEG localization of the site of epileptiform excitability — a localization that can be misleading (15, 20, 24, 34). Furthermore, the cerebral organization of higher cognitive processes may be quite diffuse and variable, particularly in epileptic patients (1, 44). These processes often apparently involve limbic structures on the mesial and basal surfaces of the hemisphere, areas that are difficult to probe with available electrophysiological and radiological techniques. Finally, many current studies now suggest localization or at least lateralization of emotional experiences (36, 47, 53), personality traits (5, 7, 42), and psychoses (7, 23, 31, 49, 54, 55), based on observations of interictal behavioral disturbances in epileptic patients. Such behaviors are not necessarily directly related to the location of the epileptogenic lesion, but may be correlated with other variables associated with the underlying disease process. Prominent examples of the contradictory results obtained from this approach can be cited from the literature.

Alterations in mood often occur during seizures; fear and terror are the most common mood alterations, followed in frequency by depression and joy (57). Sackheim (47) reviewed published case reports and EEG data from interictal and ictal recordings and determined that the epileptic focus in 91 cases of gelastic epilepsy (forced laughter) was predominately left-sided. The focus in four of the six cases of dacrystic epilepsy (forced crying) was right-sided. A different conclusion as to lateralization of mood alterations in epileptic patients was reached by Strauss *et al.* (53), who found that ictal fear was equally present in patients with left- and right-sided temporal lobe epileptic foci. They noted, however, that patients with left-sided foci demonstrated more social and sexual fearfulness than patients with right-sided foci or nonepileptic patients. In a series of patients at UCLA, those with left-sided epileptic foci reported more depression and anxiety than those with right-sided epileptic foci (36).

Differences in interictal personality changes in patients with complex partial epilepsy, based on the hemisphere involved, have been widely debated. In a study published by Bear and Fedio (5), patients with left-sided foci were more circumstantial and hyperphilosophical and displayed an overall "tarnishing" or "catastrophic" outlook. Patients with right temporal foci were more prone to alterations in drive, were overconcerned with orderliness, and tended toward a "polishing" or "denial" response. A division into a reflective cognitive style with a left-sided focus as opposed to an impulsive cognitive style with a right-sided focus was reported by Pritchard *et al.* (42). Other investigators, however, strongly deny any specific personality changes associated with temporal lobe epilepsy, at least as differentiable from generalized epilepsy, and have not been able to document any effects of lesion laterality (29, 45, 51).

Psychotic behavior in patients with psychomotor seizures has been studied by numerous authors, and both the presence of epilepsy-related psychosis and any lateralized differences in psychotic phenomenology based on the location of the epileptic focus remain controversial topics. Slater and Beard found an increased association between psychosis and temporal lobe epilepsy, but reported no significant differences between dominant and nondominant temporal lobe foci in a study of patients admitted to the Maudsley Hospital between 1948 and 1959 (50). Flor-Henry, in a controlled case comparison study, found schizophrenic psychosis lateralized to the dominant hemisphere whereas manic–depressive psychosis appeared more often when the seizure affected the nondominant hemisphere (23). Taylor, studying the same patient population, concluded that psychosis was more likely in left-handed women with left temporal hamartomas, and postulated that a developmental disturbance in thought processes was important for the production of a schizophreniform psychosis (54, 55). More recently, Sherwin estimated that 10–15% of patients with severe temporal lobe epilepsy demonstrated a schizophrenic-like psychosis, and this was more prevalent in patients with left-sided lesions (49). In contrast, Stevens has suggested that the association between partial complex seizures and psychosis merely reflects patterns of patient referral to tertiary care centers (51, 52). Kristensen and Sindrup did not find any consistent EEG lateralization, but did find more bilateral or multiple-spike foci in their 96 patients with psychosis (33).

Thus, studies on lateralization and localization of higher mental function and dysfunction in epileptic patients have produced conflicting, contradictory conclusions. The remainder of this chapter will examine tests currently available to localize epileptogenic lesions, point out possible sources of error in their interpretation, and illustrate these points with a small study of our patient population.

TECHNIQUES FOR LOCALIZATION OF THE EPILEPTOGENIC LESION

The most sophisticated localizing techniques for epileptic foci are utilized in centers performing resective surgery for partial epilepsy, since success of treatment depends upon accurate identification of the site of the lesion to be removed. When resective surgical therapy is considered in patients with medically refractory partial seizures who have no definable structural lesions on radiographic studies, a number of electrographic, clinical, structural, and metabolic variables must be examined to localize the epileptogenic lesion (13). A presurgical evaluation protocol currently used at UCLA has been divided into tests of epileptiform excitability and tests of focal functional deficit (16) (Table 1). The protocol can be subdivided further into

TABLE 1
STANDARD TESTS USED IN THE UCLA PROTOCOL FOR PRESURGICAL
EVALUATION OF PATIENTS FOR ANTERIOR TEMPORAL LOBECTOMY

Structural studies
  1. X-ray CT scan
  2. Nuclear magnetic resonance tomography
  3. Angiography
  4. Pneumoencephalography
Phase I studies — carried out without stereotaxic depth electrodes
  1. Tests of epileptic excitability
     a. Spontaneous EEG interictal spikes
     b. EEG ictal onset
  2. Tests of focal functional deficit
     a. Focal EEG slowing
     b. Visual field cut
     c. Neuropsychological testing
     d. Focal attenuation of thiopental-induced beta activity
     e. PET scan hypometabolic region
     f. Intracarotid amytal (Wada) language lateralization
     g. Intracarotid amytal (Wada) lateralization of memory dysfunction
Phase II studies — carried out with stereotaxic depth electrodes
  1. Tests of epileptic excitability
     a. Spontaneous SEEG interictal spikes
     b. SEEG ictal onset
  2. Tests of focal functional deficit
     a. Focal SEEG baseline slowing or attenuation
     b. Focal attenuation of thiopental-induced beta activity
     c. Elevated afterdischarge threshold to electrical stimulation

tests using noninvasive techniques and tests requiring EEG recording from stereo-taxically placed depth electrodes (SEEG).

Evidence of epileptiform excitability is derived from (1) spontaneous interictal EEG spike activity; (2) ictal onset from scalp and sphenoidal electrodes; (3) spontaneous interictal SEEG spike activity; and (4) SEEG-recorded ictal onsets. Evidence of functional deficit is derived from (1) focal attenuation of thiopental-induced fast activity recorded from sphenoidal and surface electrodes (17); (2) focal attenuation or slowing of baseline EEG rhythms; (3) focal attenuation of thiopental-induced SEEG-recorded fast activity (20); (4) focal attenuation or slowing of baseline SEEG-recorded rhythms; (5) elevated afterdischarge thresholds determined by stimulation of depth electrodes (9, 37); (6) global memory deficit following contralateral intra-carotid amytal injection (6, 20, 32, 39, 56); (7) shift of hemispheric language dominance demonstrated by intracarotid amytal injection (44); and (8) focal hypometabolism detected by positron emission tomography using [18F]fluorodeoxyglucose (FDG-PET) (14, 18, 19, 20, 21).

A composite picture of the seizure focus is formed, surgical candidates chosen, and the site of surgery selected on the basis of concordance of the findings from these studies. The greatest confidence may be placed on preoperative localization when

tests of focal epileptiform excitability and focal functional deficit indicate abnormalities in the same cerebral structures. Such concordance most often occurs when
the epileptogenic lesion is located in one temporal lobe, particularly in mesial structures, as most of the tests of focal functional deficit in Table 1 are particularly sensitive to mesial temporal function. In some patients, concordance is sufficiently great
from the noninvasive studies to recommend surgical resection without depth electrode evaluation (16). A more critical point for the present discussion, however, concerns the variability of lateralizing findings between tests. Most patients will have
some studies that are equivocal or falsely localizing (Table 2). While the yield of positive results is generally highest for tests of focal epileptiform excitability, these tests
have higher rates of false localization than tests of focal functional deficit. A variety of independent but complementary tests are essential for determining the temporal lobe primarily involved.

Sources of Error in Localization of the Epileptogenic Lesion

False localization of an epileptogenic lesion may occur for many reasons. It is
hypothesized that chronic epileptogenic lesions consist of at least three components:
a central region of structural damage, surrounded by dysfunctional tissue containing abnormally excitable neurons, which in turn are connected to normal tissue re-

TABLE 2

Variability in the Lateralization of the Epileptogenic Lesion among Tests of Epileptic Excitability and Focal Functional Deficit[a]

Tests	Ipsilateral	Contralateral	Nondiagnostic	Total
EEG interictal spike	37 (77%)	6 (13%)	5 (10%)	48
EEG ictal onset	28 (58%)	7 (15%)	13 (27%)	48
SEEG interictal spike	21 (62%)	6 (18%)	7 (21%)	34
SEEG ictal onset	33 (97%)	1 (3%)	0	34
EEG thiopental fast	13 (29%)	0	32 (71%)	45
SEEG baseline rhythms	21 (62%)	0	13 (38%)	34
SEEG thiopental fast	19 (63%)	1 (3%)	10 (33%)	30
PET scan	34 (72%)	1 (2%)	12 (26%)	47
Wada—language[b]	9 (35%)	—	17 (65%)	26[b]
Wada—memory	26 (54%)	0	22 (46%)	48

[a]Data from 48 patients who benefited from surgery, postoperative surgical outcomes
Classes 1 (seizure-free since surgery or 2 years postop), 2 (rare seizures, less than 2 per year
or nocturnal), and 3 (worthwhile improvement, less than 1 per month).

[b]Data shown for 26 patients with left-sided lesions, as no shift in hemispheric dominance for language was seen in the 22 patients with right-sided lesions.

cruited into the seizure. Results of recent studies correlating site of actual pathology
with localization of SEEG-recorded ictal onset in human mesial temporal epileptogenic lesions agree with this view (2). In addition, secondary foci of abnormal hyperexcitability may be seen, initially dependent on the primary focus but perhaps becoming independent over time (40). Accurate localization of an epileptogenic lesion
demands differentiating the epileptic excitability of the primary focus from that of
secondary foci.

Localization based only on EEG-recorded interictal spikes is hazardous. These
spikes may reflect secondary areas of hyperexcitability, may be orthodromically projected from primary lesions distant from the recording electrode sites, or may even
result from antidromic excitation from a primary focus (3, 10, 27). Our own data
suggest that EEG-recorded interictal spikes are falsely lateralizing (e.g., the predominant interictal spike focus is contralateral to the epileptogenic lesion) in approximately 10–20% of patients (see Table 2).

SEEG-recorded interictal spikes may be falsely localizing for reasons similar
to those above. In addition, normal tissue and areas of hyperexcitability that do not
ordinarily give rise to clinical seizures may become irritable as a result of insertion
of depth electrodes and/or drug withdrawal (15). Furthermore, depth electrodes are
sensitive to neuronal activity only within a few millimeters of their tips, and sampling errors may occur if the electrodes are not placed in or immediately adjacent
to the seizure focus. An additional theoretical possibility is that cancellation of electrical fields between multicontact electrodes passing through infolded temporal cortex
may result in failure to detect meaningful interictal spike activity or a true focal
seizure onset (25).

Both interictal and ictal EEG activity may be equivocal or may yield falsely
lateralizing information when muscle and movement artifacts obscure the tracing.
This problem is less common for SEEG recordings, since muscle artifact does not
occur and movement artifact is usually much reduced. Other specific artifacts unique
to SEEG and telemetry recording techniques do occur, however; these make it necessary that experienced individuals interpret these records.

Studies of functional deficit may also be inaccurate. In the present series, 30%
of patients with partial epilepsy did not show a zone of hypometabolism on FDG-
PET scan, even though electrophysiological evidence had indicated an epileptic
focus. Some of these patients with normal FDG-PET scans who have undergone
surgical resection have had a lesion confirmed by pathological evaluation of resected
tissue, and most have benefited from the procedure (21). At the present time, there
is no explanation for the variable sensitivity of FDG-PET scans for localizing an epileptogenic lesion. When hypometabolism is seen, particularly when the lesion involves mesial temporal structures, the zone of metabolic abnormality is invariably
much larger than the structural lesion (14). This suggests that functional alterations
can also occur at a distance from the primary epileptic focus. With the present resolution limitations of FDG-PET scanning, this phenomenon has tended to improve
recognition of the focal abnormality; conceivably, it could lead to false localization
in future scans with finer resolution and greater differentiation of small focal hypo-

metabolic zones. Two patients in our series had transient zones of hypometabolism believed to be induced by depth electrode placement (14, 19). FDG studies are no longer performed with depth electrodes in place, and there have been no known additional false localizations with FDG-PET scans since.

Neuropsychological test results can be very helpful in lateralizing epileptic foci, but results of these tests can be altered by drugs and seizure frequency. Localizing with psychometric methods is further confounded in many patients with partial seizures because of shifts from the normal location of higher cortical functions (44). Plasticity of the central nervous system is particularly prominent early in development, a time when many of the lesions responsible for partial seizures are thought to occur.

PROBLEMS WITH POSTOPERATIVE VERIFICATION OF THE LOCALIZATION OF AN EPILEPTOGENIC LESION

In some patients who undergo anterior temporal lobectomy, no demonstrable pathological lesion appears to be present in the resected specimen on gross or microscopic examination. Nonetheless, many of these patients become seizure-free or benefit substantially from the surgery (17, 20). Perhaps an epileptogenic lesion did exist within the resected specimen, but consisted only of an abnormality that was not apparent on routine microscopic examination. The resection may also have interrupted a pathway for seizure propagation and thereby disrupted expression of the ictal behavior, even though the primary epileptogenic lesion remained. If this were the case, features of the ictal behavior could not be attributed to functions of the tissue removed, even though the removal resulted in relief from seizures.

When a structural abnormality is identified within the resected temporal lobe, the clinician may be more confident that this was the true epileptic focus, but it should not be concluded automatically that this was the lesion responsible for the behavior exhibited by the patient, for several reasons. First, removal of a structural lesion in some cases does not result in relief or even reduction of habitual seizures, suggesting that some structural abnormalities such as hippocampal sclerosis may be the effect rather than the cause of epileptic seizures (8, 35). Second, even if a lesion is present and seizures disappear after its removal, it may not have been the only lesion present in the brain. Resection may have reduced the "critical mass" of the remaining epileptogenic tissue to a level insufficient to generate ictal behavior. The ictal behavior observed prior to surgery may have reflected activation of the abnormal tissue still remaining after surgery, rather than activation of the abnormal tissue removed. Third, because epileptiform activity propagates, ictal behavior may have reflected activation of normal structures efferent to the site of resection, or activation of normal structures afferent to the resected tissue by antidromic "backfiring" (3, 10, 27). Chronic disruption of efferent and afferent pathways to the same or the opposite hemisphere could conceivably account for interictal disturbances. In the absence of data addressing these issures, it is impossible to conclude definitively that an observed behavior is a direct consequence of epileptiform excitability in structures at the site of a resected lesion.

Surgical resection of an epileptic focus does create a defined lesion that can be utilized for studies of functional deficit. However, great care must be exercised in attempting to use observation of functional deficit in postsurgical epileptic patients to extrapolate lateralization or localization of cerebral function. Most partial epileptic seizures result from lesions acquired early in life or present even before birth (22). While lesions are often small and may not be sufficient in themselves to produce shifts in functional localization, repeated epileptiform discharges may disrupt function sufficiently to produce full or partial shifts of localization that are confounding when viewed in the light of the traditional concepts based on ablative lesions. For instance, some patients with epileptogenic lesions in the left temporal lobe prefer the right hand for motor activity, but have right-hemisphere (crossed) dominance for language (44). Apparently, the temporal lobe lesion does not alter dominance for motor activity (handedness), but does cause a shift of language function.

An Example of the Variability of Results of Lateralization Studies on Epileptic Patients

To demonstrate how easily erroneous conclusions of lateralization of cerebral function can be drawn on the basis of epileptic phenomena, a retrospective study was carried out on our patient population. Based on recent data suggesting that emotional expression is a function of the nondominant cerebral hemisphere (4, 46, 47), we hypothesized that patients with complex partial seizures and an emotional aura such as fear, anger, or euphoria would have nondominant-hemisphere epileptic foci. Conversely, patients with nonemotional auras were hypothesized to have dominant-hemispheric epileptic foci. Epileptic patients with no auras would presumably have their epileptic foci equally divided between the hemispheres, assuming that they often suffer ictal retrograde amnesia that prevented their recalling the aura. This hypothesis was tested with a retrospective study of 20 consecutive patients who were treated by anterior temporal lobectomy at UCLA for intractable complex partial seizures, and who were subsequently seizure- and aura-free for more than 2 years. The total absence of both seizures and auras allowed us to conclude that the epileptogenic lesion had been removed in these patients and that true localization of the focus had been confirmed. The character of the auras was then correlated with lateralization of (1) the predominant interictal EEG spike focus; (2) the EEG-recorded ictal onset; (3) the SEEG-recorded ictal onset; (4) the temporal lobe removed (reflecting the final "best guess" for localization of the lesion based on the results of all tests of epileptiform excitability and functional deficit); and (5) the presence of a structural lesion in the resected specimen. Lateralization of the hemisphere dominant for language was determined by intracarotid amytal examination. The demonstration on the intracarotid amytal test of bilateral language function or of language lateralization ipsilateral to the dominant hand was taken as evidence for some shift of language function. For each comparison, the lateralization of emotional and nonemotional auras only was compared using Fischer's exact test. The results are shown in Table 3.

Although the sample was small, the difference between lateralization of emotional and nonemotional auras based on EEG interictal spike data alone was statistically significant, while the absence of auras was not lateralized as expected. Interestingly, both emotional and nonemotional auras lateralized to the hemisphere opposite to that predicted by the hypothesis. The reversal might be explained as impaired emotional expression due to structural damage of the nondominant hemisphere in patients with right-sided foci, while patients with left temporal lesions developed emotional auras due to propagation of the ictal discharge to the intact nondominant hemisphere. Conversely, one could conclude that emotional auras actually arise from the left hemisphere. Significant results in either direction could be explained logically. More importantly, lateralization of emotional auras to the left or right hemisphere, or within the dominant or nondominant hemisphere (determined by the intracarotid amytal test), was not statistically significant when correlated with other more reliable indicators of localization of the epileptogenic lesion.

TABLE 3
LATERALIZATION OF EMOTIONAL AND NONEMOTIONAL AURAS USING DIFFERENT EEG,
FUNCTIONAL, AND PATHOLOGICAL TECHNIQUES

	Side of Interictal Spike Focus				Side of Surface Ictal Onset				Side of Depth Ictal Onset		
	L	R	T		L	R	T		L	R	T
E	4	0	4	E	2	2	4	E	3	1	4
NE	2	6	8	NE	4	6	10	NE	6	6	12
0	2	2	4	0	1	1	2	0	3	1	4
T	8	8	16	T	7	9	16	T	12	8	20

Fischer's exact (two-tailed)
for E/NE versus L/R
$p = .03$ $p > .10$ $p > .10$

	Side of Surgery				Side of Surgery with Lesion				Side of Surgery with Lesion Based on Language Dominance		
	L	R	T		L	R	T		D	ND	T
E	3	1	4	E	3	1	4	E	2	1	3
NE	5	7	12	NE	3	5	8	NE	3	5	8
0	3	1	4	0	2	1	3	0	1	1	2
T	11	9	20	T	8	7	15	T	6	7	13

$p > .10$ $p > .10$ $p > .10$

Note. Based on a total *n* of 20 patients. Not all patients had specific data in each category. An apparently significant difference between left- and right-hemisphere localization of emotional and nonemotional auras, based on identical spike localization, does not hold up when more reliable criteria for identifying the focus are used, and when dominant- versus nondominant-hemisphere effects are taken into account. E = emotional aura, NE = nonemotional aura, 0 = no aura, L = left hemisphere, R = right hemisphere, D = dominant hemisphere, ND = nondominant hemisphere, T = total.

The results of this study do not support any specific theory regarding lateralization of emotional expression in the human brain. Even though small, this study does provide considerable insight into the reasons for the contradictory nature of reports in the literature that suggest lateralization of specific cerebral functions on the basis of incomplete analysis of the pathophysiology.

Conclusions

Patients with partial seizures provide unique opportunities for the study of the effects of focal stimulation on the human brain. Much understanding of the localization of cerebral function in the human brain is based on studies of patients with epilepsy, and research involving this patient population should continue to produce useful information. This is especially true when data are gathered in clinical centers that perform resective surgery for epilepsy, since invasive studies are possible and resected tissue ultimately becomes available for pathological and biochemical evaluation. Conclusions regarding localization of cerebral function based on epileptic lesions must, however, consider a number of confounding factors that can lead to erroneous conclusions:

1. Standard tests for localizing the site of the epileptogenic lesion may be inaccurate. This is particularly true for EEG-recorded interictal spikes, often the sole criterion used in behavioral studies. Ideally, localization should be based on a variety of independent studies that demonstrate the site of predominant focal epileptiform excitability, with confirmation of this localization by demonstration of focal functional deficit in the same area. For further validation, the patient should then have had resective surgery, with a structural lesion found in the resected tissue, and should have been free of seizures and auras for at least 2 years. These criteria represent the most reliable means currently available for localizing the epileptogenic lesion underlying an observed behavior.

2. A distinction must be made between assumptions about localization of function drawn from studies of ictal behavior and those drawn from studies of postictal or interictal behavior. It can be assumed that ictal behavior results from abnormal excitation of specific brain areas, but that postictal disturbances may reflect either focal functional deficits or consequent inhibitory release of other regions. Interictal behavior may result from chronic epileptic disruption of normal function, facilitated transmission along specific pathways, hyperexcitability, unrelated structural changes induced by the underlying lesion or disease process, or situational–psychosocial factors. Caution must be exercised when attempting to derive information concerning lateralization or localization of cerebral function from studies of interictal behavioral disturbances.

3. Ictal, postictal, and interictal behavioral disturbances in patients with partial epilepsy may reflect transient or chronic abnormalities at a distance from the site of the epileptic focus, due to orthodromic efferent or even antidromic afferent propagation to cerebral structures connected to the ictal focus. The cerebral structure responsible for generating the ictal, postictal, or interictal behavior may be far from the epileptic focus, even located in the contralateral hemisphere. Since the number of efferent and afferent sites involved in propagation of epileptiform discharges are limited for any given epileptogenic lesion, cerebral localization based on studies of patients with partial seizures is not completely negated, but does require critical evaluation of all possible explanations for observed results.

4. The most difficult problem to deal with when attempting study of the localization of cerebral function using patients with partial seizures is that shifts in functional localization may occur early in life. Some investigative techniques, such as the intracarotid amytal test, may provide information about the degree of functional relocalization between the hemispheres.

Ideally, conclusions concerning localization of function drawn from the study of epileptic patients should be confirmed by studies carried out on normal healthy volunteers, using noninvasive techniques such as topographic functional mapping of EEG, evoked potential, and magnetoencephalographic activity, as well as positron emission tomography. Studies should be designed to use all relevant techniques in a complementary fashion in order to reach the most reliable conclusions.

REFERENCES

1. Ajmone Marsan, C., Clinical–electrographic correlations of partial seizures. In: *Modern Perspectives in Epilepsy, Proceedings of the Inaugural Symposium of the Canadian League against Epilepsy* (J. Wada, Ed.). Eden Press, Montreal, 1978: 76–98.
2. Babb, T. L., Lieb, J. P., Brown, W. J., Pretorius, J., and Crandall, P. H., Distribution of pyramidal cell density and hyperexcitability in the epileptic human hippocampal formation. *Epilepsia*, 1984, **25**: 721–728.
3. Baumbach, H. D. and Chow, K. L., Visuocortical epileptiform discharges in rabbits. Differential effects on neuronal development in the lateral geniculate nucleus and superior colliculus. *Brain Res.*, 1981, **209**: 61–75.
4. Bear, D. M., Hemispheric specialization and the neurology of emotion. *Arch. Neurol.*, 1983, **40**: 195–202.
5. Bear, D. M., and Fedio, P., Quantitative analysis of interictal behavior in temporal lobe epilepsy. *Arch. Neurol.*, 1977, **34**: 454–467.
6. Blume, W. T., Grabow, J. D., Darley, F. L., and Aronson, A. E., Intracarotid amobarbital test of language and memory before temporal lobectomy for seizure control. *Neurology (Minneap.)*, 1973, **23**: 812–819.
7. Blumer, D., and Benson, D. F., Psychiatric manifestations of epilepsy. In: *Psychiatric Aspects of Neurologic Disease*, Vol. 2 (D. F. Benson and D. Blumer, Eds.). Grune & Stratton, New York, 1982: 25–48.
8. Brown, W. J., Structural substrates of seizure foci in the human temporal lobe. In: *Epilepsy: Its Phenomena in Man* (M. A. B. Brazier, Ed.). Academic Press, New York, 1973: 339–374.
9. Cherlow, D. G., Dymond, A. M., Crandall, P. H., *et al.*, Evoked response and afterdischarge thresholds to electrical stimulation in temporal lobe epileptics. *Arch. Neurol.*, 1977, **34**: 527–531.
10. Chow, K. L., Baumbach, H. D., and Glanzman, D. L., Abnormal development of lateral geniculate neurons in rabbits subjected to either eyelid closure or corticofugal paroxysmal discharges. *Brain Res.*, 1978, **146**: 151–158.

11. Commission on Classification and Terminology of the International League against Epilepsy, Proposal for revised clinical and electroencephalographic classification of epileptic seizures. *Epilepsia*, 1981, **22**: 489–501.
12. Efron, R., Post-epileptic paralysis: Theoretical critique and report of a case. *Brain*, 1961, **84**: 381–394.
13. Engel, J., Jr., Functional localization of epileptogenic lesions. *Trends in Neurosci.*, 1983, **6**: 60–65.
14. Engel, J., Jr., Brown, W. J., Kuhl, D. E., Phelps, M. E., Mazziotta, J. C., and Crandall, P. H., Pathological findings underlying focal temporal lobe hypometabolism in partial epilepsy. *Ann. Neurol.*, 1982, **12**: 518–528.
15. Engel, J., Jr., and Crandall, P. H., Falsely localizing ictal onsets with depth EEG telemetry during anticonvulsant withdrawal. *Epilepsia*, 1983, **24**: 344–355.
16. Engel, J., Jr., Crandall, P. H., and Rausch, R., The partial epilepsies. In: *The Clinical Neurosciences*, Vol. 2 (R. N. Rosenberg, R. G. Grossman, S. Schochet, E. R. Heinz, and W. D. Willis, Eds.). Churchill Livingstone, New York, 1983: 1349–1380.
17. Engel, J., Jr., Driver, M. V., and Falconer, M. A., Electrophysiological correlates of pathology and surgical results in temporal lobe epilepsy. *Brain*, 1975, **98**: 129–156.
18. Engel, J., Jr., Kuhl, D. E., Phelps, M. E., and Crandall, P. H., Comparative localization of epileptic foci in partial epilepsy by PCT and EEG. *Ann. Neurol.*, 1982, **12**: 529–537.
19. Engel, J., Jr., Kuhl, D. E., Phelps, M. E., and Mazziotta, J. C., Interictal cerebral glucose metabolism in partial epilepsy and its relation to EEG changes. *Ann. Neurol.*, 1982, **12**: 510–517.
20. Engel, J., Jr., Rausch, R., Lieb, J. P., Kuhl, D. E., and Crandall, P. H., Correlation of criteria used for localizing epileptic foci in patients considered for surgical therapy of epilepsy. *Ann. Neurol.*, 1981, **9**: 215–224.
21. Engel, J., Jr., Sutherling, W. W., Cahan, L., Crandall, P. H., Kuhl, D. E., and Phelps, M. E., The role of positron emission tomography in the surgical therapy of epilepsy. In: *Advances in Epileptology*, XVth Epilepsy International Symposium (R. J. Porter, R. H. Mattson, A. A. Ward, Jr., and M. Dam, Eds.). Raven Press, New York, 1984: 427–432.
22. Epilepsy Foundation of America. *Basic Statistics on the Epilepsies*. F. A. Davis, Philadelphia, 1975.
23. Flor-Henry, P., Psychosis and temporal lobe epilepsy. *Epilepsia*, 1969, **10**: 363–395.
24. Gloor, P., Contributions of electroencephalography and electrocorticography to the neurosurgical treatment of the epilepsies. *Adv. Neurol.*, 1975, **8**: 59–106.
25. Gloor, P., Electroencephalography and the role of intracerebral depth electrode recording in the selection of patients for surgical treatment of epilepsy. In: *Advances in Epileptology*, XVth Epilepsy International Symposium (R. J. Porter, R. H. Mattson, A. A. Ward, Jr., and M. Dam, Eds.). Raven Press, New York, 1984: 433–437.
26. Gloor, P., Olivier, A., Quesney, L. F., Andermann, F., and Horowitz, S., The role of the limbic system in experiential phenomena of temporal lobe epilepsy. *Ann. Neurol.*, 1982, **12**: 129–144.
27. Gutnick, M. J., and Prince, D. A., Spontaneous antidromic spikes from axons in cortical penicillin foci. *Epilepsia*, 1973, **13**: 354–355.
28. Halgren, E., Walter, R. D., Cherlow, D. G., and Crandall, P. H., Mental phenomena evoked by electrical stimulation of the human hippocampal formation and amygdala. *Brain*, 1978, **101**: 83–117.
29. Hermann, B. P., Dikmen, S., and Wilensky, A. J., Increased psychopathology associated with multiple seizure types: Fact or artifact? *Epilepsia*, 1982, **23**: 587–596.
30. Jackson, J. H., *Selected Writings of John Hughlings Jackson on Epilepsy and Epileptiform Convulsions* (J. Taylor, Ed.). Hodder & Stoughton, London, 1931.

31. Jensen, I., and Larsen, J. K., Psychoses in drug-resistant temporal lobe epilepsy. *J. Neurol. Neurosurg. Psychiatry*, 1979, **42**: 948–954.

32. Klove, H., Grabow, J. D., and Trites, R. L., Evaluation of memory functions with intracarotid sodium amytal. *Trans. Am. Neurol. Assoc.*, 1969, **94**: 76–80.

33. Kristensen, O., and Sindrup, E. H., Psychomotor epilepsy and psychosis: I. Physical aspects. II. Electroencephalographic findings (sphenoidal electrode recordings). *Acta Neurol. Scand.*, 1978, **57**: 361–379.

34. Lieb, J. P., Engel, J., Jr., Gevins, A. S., and Crandall, P. H., Surface and deep EEG correlates of surgical outcome in temporal lobe epilepsy. *Epilepsia*, 1981, **22**: 515–538.

35. Meldrum, B. S., and Brierly, J. B. Prolonged epileptic seizures in primates: Ischemics cell change and its relation to ictal physiologic events. *Arch. Neurol.*, 1973, **28**: 10–17.

36. Mendius, J. R., and Perini, G. I., Interictal profiles of emotion, depression, and anxiety in patients with temporal lobe epilepsy. In: *Abstracts, XVth International Epilepsy Symposium*, 1983: 158.

37. Mendius, J. R., Rausch, R., Nuwer, M., Lucia, M., and Crandall, P. H., Intrastimulatory discharges and afterdischarges in patients with temporal lobe seizures. In: *Abstracts, American Electroencephalographic Society–American Epilepsy Society, Joint Annual Meeting*, 1982: 68–69.

38. Milner, B., Psychological aspects of focal epilepsy and its neurosurgical management. In: *Advances in Neurology*, Vol. 8, *Neurosurgical Management of the Epilepsies* (D. P. Purpura and R. D. Walter, Eds). Raven Press, New York, 1975: 299–321.

39. Milner, B., Branch, C., and Rasmussen, T., Study of short-term memory after intracarotid injection of sodium amytal. *Trans. Am. Neurol. Assoc.*, 1962, **84**: 224–226.

40. Morrell, F., Secondary epileptogenesis in man. *Arch. Neurol.*, 1985, **42**: 318–335.

41. Penfield, W., and Jasper, H., *Epilepsy and the Functional Anatomy of the Human Brain*. Little, Brown, Boston, 1954.

42. Pritchard, P. B., Lombroso, C. T., and McIntyre, M., Psychological implications of temporal lobe epilepsy. *Neurology*, 1980, **30**: 227–232.

43. Rausch, R., and Crandall, P. H., Psychological status related to surgical control of temporal lobe seizures. *Epilepsia*, 1982, **23**: 191–202.

44. Rausch, R., and Walsh, G. O., Right hemisphere language dominance in right handed epileptic patients. *Arch. Neurol.*, 1984, **14**: 1077–1080.

45. Rodin, E. A., Schmaltz, S., and Twitty, G., What does the Bear–Fedio personality inventory measure? In: *Abstracts, XVth International Epilepsy Symposium*, 1983: 156.

46. Ross, E. D., Functional–anatomic organization of the affective components of language in the right hemisphere. *Arch. Neurol.*, 1981, **38**: 561–569.

47. Sackheim, H. A., *et al.*, Hemispheric asymmetry in the expression of positive and negative emotions. *Arch. Neurol.*, 1982, **39**: 210–218.

48. Scoville, W. B., and Milner, B., Loss of memory after bilateral hippocampal lesions. *J. Neurol. Neurosurg. Psychiatry*, 1957, **20**: 11–21.

49. Sherwin, I., *et al.*, Prevalence of psychosis in epilepsy as a function of the laterality of the epileptogenic lesion. *Arch. Neurol.*, 1982, **39**: 621–625.

50. Slater, E., and Beard, A. W., The schizophrenia-like psychoses of epilepsy. *Br. J. Psychiatry*, 1963, **109**: 95–150.

51. Stevens, J. R., Interictal clinical manifestations of complex partial seizures. In: *Advances in Neurology*, Vol. 11, *Complex Partial Seizures and Their Treatment* (J. K. Penry and D. D. Daly, Eds.). Raven Press, New York, 1975: 85–112.

52. Stevens, J. R., and Hermann, B. P., Temporal lobe epilepsy, psychopathology and violence: The state of the evidence. *Neurology*, 1981, **31**: 1127–1132.

53. Strauss, E., Risser, A., and Jones, M. W., Fear responses in patients with epilepsy. *Arch. Neurol.*, 1982, **39**: 626–630.

54. Taylor, D. C., Ontogenesis of chronic epileptic psychoses: A reanalysis. *Psychol. Med.*, 1971, **1**: 247–253.
55. Taylor, D. C., Factors influencing the occurrence of schizophrenia-like psychoses of epilepsy. *Br. J. Psychiatry*, 1975, **5**: 249–254.
56. Wada, J., and Rasmussen, T., Intracarotid injection of sodium amytal for the lateralization of cerebral speech dominance: Experimental and clinical observations. *J. Neurosurg.*, 1960, **17**: 266–282.
57. Williams, D., The structure of emotions reflected in epileptic experiences. *Brain*, 1956, **79**: 29–67.

CLINICAL PHENOMENOLOGY FOLLOWING HEMISPHERECTOMY AND THE SYNDROMES OF HEMISPHERIC DISCONNECTION

PAUL H. CRANDALL, MD
Departments of Surgery and Neurology

INTRODUCTION

In modern-day neurosurgery, removal of cerebral cortex is very unusual. The introduction of microsurgery with surgical microscopes and miniature instruments allows lesions of the brain to be removed through limited-access routes and under greater illumination. It is in surgery for epilepsy that the responsibility for cortical removal lies. This is because all types of partial elementary, partial complex, and secondary generalized seizures originate from the cerebral cortex; and the epileptogenic cortex, if possible, must be completely removed if the operation is to be effective. Yet the question always is, "Is it safe?"

The early operations for epilepsy were guided by the presence of gross macroscopic pathological lesions, such as missile injuries, brain abscess scars, depressed skull fractures, or cysts. In addition, electrical stimulations were used to elicit auras or seizures from the patient, and structures essential for sensory–motor and language functions could be spared. The surgeons knew that if cortical removals were restricted to the neighborhood of the lesion, there would not be additional neurological deficit after the operation. These circumstances particularly applied to supratemporal forms of epilepsy.

When temporal lobe epilepsy, which is the most common partial epilepsy, came to be defined, I was fortunate to witness the early operations take place on what appeared to be normal temporal lobe. Percival Bailey (3) was persuaded by Frederic Gibbs to be guided by electroencephalography alone. Although it was the prevailing view at that time that there were "silent areas" of cerebral cortex including the anterior temporal lobe, as an assistant to Dr. Bailey I observed his caution and conservative approach. He realized that every area of the cortex must have a function which was yet to be determined. Today there are no "silent areas" of cortex.

The extent of cortical resection for temporal lobe epilepsy was determined empirically. First there were anterior temporal gyrectomies, then topectomies (a slab

Acknowledgments: This research was supported by U.S. Public Health grant NS 02808. I am grateful to Sasha Biletsky for preparing the manuscript.

including several gyri), then anterior temporal lobectomies of the pole of the lobe. He was of the opinion that the hippocampal formation should never be removed, yet the amygdala could be safely removed. The posterior limit in the dominant hemisphere was determined by the limits of Wernicke's zone for language (4.5 cm behind the tip of the temporal pole as measured along the middle temporal gyrus). In the nondominant lobe, the limit was restricted because of resultant visual-field defects. Beyond 6 cm, there was a significant risk of postoperative homonymous hemianopsia. Contralateral quadrantanopsia became an acceptable and common postsurgical effect because it was not functionally disabling.

Later it was shown that the hippocampal formation should be included in the resection, with improved results in the control of seizures. After Falconer developed *en bloc* resections of the temporal lobe, it was found that there was a pathological substrate to complex partial epilepsy, with about 50% mesial temporal sclerosis and 25% small tumors involving the same areas. Recently preoperative detection has become possible with the introduction of positron emission scanning. Histopathological studies were carried out on temporal lobe tissue in 25 patients of the UCLA series (11) who were studied by interictal positron emission tomography (PET) with [18F]fluorodeoxyglucose and subsequently underwent anterior temporal lobe resection. Hypometabolic zones were observed on PET scans of 22 patients and corresponded to focal pathological abnormalities in 19 (15 mesial temporal sclerosis, 2 small neoplasms, 1 angioma, 1 heterotopia). The degree of relative hypometabolism measured by PET correlated well with the severity of the pathological lesion, but the size of the hypometabolic zone was generally much larger than the area of pathological involvement as seen by light microscopy. It is interesting that the hypometabolic zone correlates well with the extent of anterior temporal lobectomy as practiced today.

Importance of Tests of Cognitive Function
in the Surgery of Epilepsy

Information concerning the effects on cognitive function of surgical operations for epilepsy has followed at some distance in time. Although the tissue removed has a pathological substrate, it is not necessarily without function. A comparison of the effects of left and right anterior temporal lobectomy in epileptic patients has revealed certain specific memory defects that vary with the side of the lesion and are restricted to a particular kind of stimulus material (19).

Left temporal lobectomy, in the dominant hemisphere for speech, selectively impairs the learning retention of verbal material, whether heard or read, and regardless of whether a recall or recognition procedure is used. Yet left temporal lesions do not affect memory for perceptual material, such as faces, melodies, or nonsense patterns. Right, nondominant temporal lobectomy leaves verbal memory intact, but impairs the recognition and recall of visual and auditory patterns that do not lend themselves easily to verbal coding. Right temporal lobectomy retards the learning of mazes.

Further subtle deficits have been demonstrated from time to time. The most recently demonstrated deficit appears to be in the mechanism of central auditory processing. The capacity to selectively attend to only one of multiple spatially separated, simultaneous sound sources — the "cocktail party" effect — was evaluated in normal subjects and in those with anterior temporal lobectomy, using common environmental sounds (10). A significant deficit in this capacity was observed for those stimuli located on the side of space, when other sound sources were present on that side. Damage to this mechanism also appears to be associated with a deficit of spatial localization for sounds contralateral to the lesion.

Hemispherectomy for Seizures Associated with Infantile Hemiplegia

Complete hemispherectomy as a treatment for intractable seizures associated with infantile hemiplegia and hemianopsia was introduced by a South African neurosurgeon (17) in 1950. The last complete hemispherectomy, to my knowledge, was done in 1968. In these patients the affected hemisphere is reduced to an atrophic shell. Usually it is a small sclerosed hemisphere due to prior vascular occlusions, porencephalic cysts, or dysgenetic malformations. Porencephalic cysts are now known to be the result of intracerebral and intraventricular hemorrhages in premature infants of subnormal weight. It is believed that these hemorrhages are due to rupture of vascular germinal matrix. As a result, these patients are often handicapped by hemiplegia or spastic athetosis. It was also observed that there was frequently a behavioral abnormality described as episodic outbursts of violent "temper tantrums." Krynauw's operation was removal of the hemisphere except the thalamus and caudate nucleus, including its tail. The choroid plexus, putamen, and globus pallidus were removed.

The results were quite striking in relief of seizures and improved behavior. Although the hemiparesis was increased at first, the return to preoperative power occurred within days and there was a lessening of spasticity over many months and years. In addition to relief from seizures, there was considerable improvement in the EEG patterns. Rasmussen reported the results in 29 patients at the Montreal Neurological Institute from 1952 through 1968 (20). Two patients died during the first postoperative year of a progressive encephalopathy. The median time of follow-up was 11 years. Thirteen patients (48%) were seizure-free and another three (11%) became seizure-free after a few postoperative attacks. Six patients (22%) had recurrence of rare or occasional attacks after being seizure-free for 3 to 17 years. A total of 23 patients (85%) had complete or nearly complete reduction of seizure tendency following the hemispherectomy. This is an outstanding record for surgery for epilepsy.

French and Johnson (12) examined the sensory system in patients after hemispherectomy. Preoperative examination usually revealed diminished response on the involved side to all modalities of sensory stimulation (light touch, superficial pain, temperature, position sense, vibration, deep pain, and stereognosis). It was felt that this diminished response was not a lessened sensitivity to stimuli, but rather a slowness in perception or recognition of the stimulus. Postoperative sensory examination revealed a relatively minimal change from the preoperative status, even in the early postoperative period. There seemed to be a diminution of the finer discriminative powers of touch perception rather than any actual lack of perception. Over several months to a year, this ability improved. Identifying digits was lost until 7–10 days. Griffith and Davidson (15) observed the long-term changes in 12 surviving patients at 10 years. The tests used were the Revised Stanford-Binet tests, Wechsler Intelligence Scale for Children, Wechsler Adult Intelligence Scale, and a 5-point scale for behavior (0, normal limits; 1, mild changes, e.g., poor concentration; 2, temper tantrums; 3, hyperactive behavior; 4, institutionalized for uncontrollable behavior). They concluded that there were worthwhile and significant long-term gains in intelligence in 5 of 12 patients, while 6 showed slight but insignificant gains. No patient lost ground. Changes in behavior were subjectively striking and have been maintained over the years.

The operation was abandoned because of complications related to delayed hemorrhage after hemispherectomy. In patients who have been studied with computed tomography (CT) scans, there is a shifting of brain structures after hemispherectomy. Postmortem studies have shown multiple hemorrhagic spots in the cavity membrane and the walls of the remaining lateral ventricle (16). Severe granular ependymitis, with closure of the third or fourth ventricles and hydrocephalus, was often present.

Rasmussen subsequently proposed a modification of the operation (21). He noted that the serious, late complication of superficial cerebral hemosiderosis, which appears after several years in one-quarter to one-third of patients who have undergone hemispherectomy, has resulted in recent years in a considerable reluctance to carry out this procedure. By preserving the frontal and occipital poles but disconnecting them from the rest of the brain, resulting in a functional complete but anatomical subtotal hemispherectomy, the operation retains the therapeutic effectiveness of a complete hemispherectomy while still protecting adequately against the serious late postoperative complication of superficial cerebral hemosiderosis and its associated neurological deterioration, hydrocephalus, and sometimes death.

CEREBRAL COMMISSUROTOMY

There are several types of operation to surgically separate the cerebral hemispheres. A brief summary of the anatomy and physiology of the cerebral commissures may be helpful in this discussion.

The corpus callosum is the main commissural connection between the two cortical hemisphere fields of the human being. The corpus callosum develops in proportion to the neocortex and, therefore, reaches its greatest size in humans, in whom it contains about 180 million axons (25). Although the majority of fibers connect homotopic regions of the two hemispheres, heterotopic connections also exist

(8). Callosal afferents connecting the frontal lobes occupy the rostral half of the corpus callosum. The frontal lobes comprise 60% of the volume of the brain. The order of interhemispheric connections in the caudal half is, in rostral–caudal order: parietal, temporal, and occipital. The anterior commissure interconnects the amygdala, olfactory bulbs, the piriform cortex, the entorhinal area, and portions of the temporal neocortex.

The hippocampal commissure is assumed to be divided whenever the corpus callosum is divided, because it is attached to the undersurface of the corpus callosum. However, cross-connections between the hippocampal formations via the hippocampal commissures have failed to be demonstrated by electrical stimulations. The "regression" of hippocampal commissural fibers in humans is concordant with their "regression" in monkeys, where only a small uncal region of hippocampus interconnects (22), and where there are only remnant fibers between the presubiculum and posterior parahippocampal gyrus that are homologously monosynaptic (2).

Previous studies in our series of patients with complex partial epilepsy with stereotaxically implanted electrodes in the medial temporal lobes bilaterally failed to disclose contralateral evoked responses to electrical stimulation (7). In the past 4 years, 196 stimulation sites in pes hippocampi (anterior, middle, and posterior) and parahippocampal gyrus (anterior, middle, and posterior) and in basolateral amygdala have resulted in 43% ipsilateral and 0% contralateral responses in a total of 354 recording sites ($n = 16$ patients). Hence, it appears from our data that the phylogenetic "need" for connected hippocampi has been replaced by the benefits of isolated hippocampi that have specialized functions (e.g., left hippocampus more important for verbal memory because of auditory and language cortico-hippocampal connections on the left side).

An excellent review of experimental and clinical data to provide a rationale for corpus callosum section for seizure control has been prepared by Warren Blume (4). According to him, the conceptual grounds for considering corpus callosum sectioning as a useful treatment for uncontrolled epileptic seizures, particularly primary or secondary generalized seizures, rest on several prerequisites:

1. Bilateral synchrony or near synchrony of cortical epileptiform discharges augments the seizure tendency, particularly for generalized attacks.

2. The corpus callosum serves as a major pathway for propagation of epileptiform discharges and must not play a significant role in inhibition of such discharges.

3. Sectioning of the corpus callosum must decrease or abolish the synchrony of epileptiform events and should inhibit the generation of generalized seizures.

4. Sectioning must not augment the quantity or propagation of cortically originating epileptiform discharges.

5. Previous, well-documented clinical experience gives promise for success of the procedure.

6. Any neuropsychological dysfunction consequent to corpus callosum sectioning must be imperceptible in the activities of daily life for the individual patient.

"Complete" Cerebral Commissurotomy

Although the operation of sectioning the cerebral commissures was introduced in 1940 by Van Wagenen and Herren (26), in 26 adult and adolescent patients between 1939 and 1943, only in one did the surgery include the entire corpus callosum and anterior commissure. Further evidence that these operations were probably incomplete was the fact that careful examinations by a qualified neuropsychologist failed to disclose either the acute disconnection syndrome or the long-term effects now known (1). The operation was not uniformly effective for seizure control, though in some patients the recurrent seizures were restricted to one side.

Bogen, Sperry, and Vogel (5, 6) undertook the first "complete" commissurotomies. They were done in patients with intractable seizures, usually of a mixed type. The seizures were very disabling, many of them involving serious falls and head injuries as well as status epilepticus. My observations are based on interviews with 10 patients in their series in company with Murray Falconer, FRCS, several years ago. The opportunity was provided by Drs. Bogen, Sperry, and Vogel to examine several long-term patients as well as one patient recently operated on who had the acute disconnection syndrome. These observations are based also on a review of the literature. A "complete" commissurotomy includes complete section of the large corpus callosum, the smaller anterior commissure, and the thin hippocampal commissure, which is not visualized but presumed to be severed along with the corpus callosum. The massa intermedia is included, when found. It involves opening the ventricular system. In some cases the fornix was divided on one side. In dividing the anterior commissure, the pillars of the fornix necessarily may be partially affected.

Acute Disconnection Syndrome

The acute disconnection syndrome is one of the most dramatic syndromes found in neurology. It occurs immediately after complete commissurotomy, frontal commissurotomy (anterior two-thirds corpus callosum, anterior commissure, and one fornix), and one-stage central commissurotomy (corpus callosum and hippocampal commissure). It occurs to a greater or lesser degree in all of the above and lasts days to weeks.

These patients appear to be mute, uncommunicative except by body language. Their left-sided apraxia is often severe and may be mistaken for hemiplegia. Similarly, their disregard for the left fields of vision may be mistaken for a hemianopsia. Their bodily movements appear strange because intermittently there may be competitive movements between the left and right hands. This is also complicated to interpret, in that some patients have had focal motor seizures on alternating sides without loss of consciousness (30).

On formal neurological examination, their mental status seems to be one of confusion and lack of concentration. There are bilateral grasp reflexes and bilateral Babinski signs. There may be left-sided weakness in the early phases, possibly due to retraction edema in the right hemisphere.

Further details are gained from the physical therapist at the Dartmouth–Hitch-cock Medical Center (27):

All patients demonstrated an early change in their speech habits. Speech was essentially absent for the first 10 to 14 postoperative days in the patients with complete sections. The patients who had undergone anterior (frontal) sections answered questions more readily than the first group but did not engage in spontaneous conversation. All responses were slow, but the patients demonstrated no difficulty with the actual production of speech.

Left-sided apraxia in the extremities was observed in the patients with complete sections. These patients responded more readily to verbal stimuli with the right hand and to visual stimuli with the left hand; for example, the response to the command "pick up the glass of water" was performed with the right hand. When confronted silently with a glass of water, however, these patients responded with the left hand even though they may have been right-handed.

Lateral trunk instability (truncal ataxia) was noted in all patients, being most severe in those patients with complete sections. The severity ranged from a "rag doll" appearance to a barely perceivable deviation.

In addition to truncal ataxia, the patients showed extremity incoordination as well as an unsteady gait characterized by a wide base of support, flat-footed pattern, and lack of rhythm. Other common problems included diminished attention to the left visual field, perseveration, masturbation, low endurance, and apathy.

Throughout the treatment, the patients' apathetic attitude was a constant frustration to the therapist, making it difficult to achieve the established goals.

Follow-up testing two to four months later generally demonstrated that the patients had improved in muscle strength, position sense and coordination. No long-standing motor problems were evident other than lack of ability to carry out rapid highly coordinated activities.

LATE DISCONNECTION SYNDROME

Sperry described very well the effects of complete commissurotomy in the patients of the Los Angeles series in a review article for *The Neurosciences* (24). To the casual observer of a patient more than 2 years after surgery, there might not seem to be any abnormal behavior.

Speech, verbal intelligence, calculation, motor coordination, verbal reasoning and recall, personality and temperament are all preserved to a surprising degree in the absence of hemispheric interconnection. Most of the deficits are easily compensated or concealed under ordinary conditions by exploratory movements of the eyes, shifting of the hands, and through auditory and other cues that bilateralize the sensory information. Their demonstration thus requires controlled lateralized testing procedures.

The most completely bisected system of the brain is the visual system. There is no component with bilateral representation. When visual images can be restricted to the left fields of vision there is no question that the individual cannot name the object. Yet in everyday life the two retinal half-fields of the eyeball move as one and eye movements are conjugate, so that when one hemisphere detects the gaze to a given target the other hemisphere is automatically locked in at all times on the same target. (24)

Similarly, these people are unable to name objects felt with the left hand or foot, sounds heard by the right hemisphere, and odors restricted to the right nostril. However, odors or sounds are seldom restricted in everyday life.

Central processing of sensory input leading to motor output in these patients is permanently impaired. Surgery separates the entire right hemisphere, and all that goes on in that hemisphere from the motor control centers in the left hemisphere. Simple tests such as localization of light touch, temperature discrimination, pain sensibility, and position sense showed that there was a marked separation of somesthetic effects from right and left extremities and from right and left sides of the trunk (13). However, the areas of the head and neck appear to have ipsilateral representation in the hemispheres, so these sensations are not disconnected.

The lack of transcallosal interaction between sensory information and motor output accounts for the slow bimanual motor coordination in speed and timing in tasks that require interdependent regulation between right and left hands. However, automatic early motor patterns such as tying shoelaces or neckties are completely unchanged.

It has been noted that these patients have an inability to keep track of more than three patterns perceived sequentially by touch. They give up easily in tasks that require prolonged concentration.

There have been certain exceptions to these effects of the disconnection syndrome. The youngest patient, operated on at age 13, had the usual deficits at 2 years after surgery; however, by the age of 20 he could report verbally symbols flashed onto the left fields, could do mathematics with numbers flashed onto both fields, and by blind tactual recognition could retrieve with the left hand an object identified by the right (24). A young college student with congenital absence of the corpus callosum but with an enlarged anterior commissure easily went through the entire battery of cross-integration tests (23). However, she was found to be selectively subnormal on a variety of perceptual–motor, spatial, and nonverbal reasoning tasks.

Patients with frontal commissurotomies (anterior two-thirds corpus callosum and anterior commissure) were free of the basic disconnection symptoms that involve cross-integration between the hands, visual half-fields, and the language centers. However, there was definite impairment in the learning of bimanual motor coordinations that require mutually dependent timing of movements of the two hands (14).

Relatives of the patients in the Los Angeles series remarked on postoperative changes related to memory. Many of these patients did not become fully independent, because they were unable to remember appointments or telephone messages, where they had put things or how to get back to a parked car, and the like. The husband of one patient said that he was unable to allow her to go marketing. Also, it was their custom for a summer vacation to park a van in a beach park: he always had to make special arrangements so that he could have the space next to the restroom facilities, because if his wife had to leave during the night she would surely get lost. This led Zaidel and Sperry (31) to administer standardized tests for memory with no attempt to restrict for hemispheric lateralization (Wechsler Memory Scale, Benton's Revised Visual Retention Test, Memory for Designs, Knox Cube Test, Visual Sequential Memory, and Memory Span for Objects). These tests were administered to eight patients with complete sections and two patients with partial sections. Although those with partial commissurotomy obtained on the average somewhat higher scores on four of the tests, all patients had findings with marked impairment in short-term memory. It was recognized that there was an additional factor — that extracallosal damage not associated with the surgery (some actually seen at surgery) was present in all cases, varying widely in nature and extent.

Subsequently, Bogen arranged for further testing using the Michigan Neuropsychological Test Battery to study 10 patients with complete commissurotomy and 2 with frontal commissurotomy in 1967 and again in 1976 (9). Following complete commissurotomy, four patients who were known preoperatively to have gross structural lesions in the right hemisphere revealed a unique pattern of marked, selective impairment of nonverbal cognitive functions. The remaining patients showed systematic patterns of greater impairment in verbal or nonverbal cognitive and contralateral sensory–motor functions, depending on the laterality of extracallosal damage. Other confounding factors were presence of severe and frequent seizures for years before surgery; the effects of postoperative complications; changes in anticonvulsant medications; differences in the operative procedures; elimination, reduction, or no change in seizure status; and lastly, differences due to age.

STAGED CENTRAL COMMISSUROTOMY

The late Donald Wilson took up commissurotomy for intractable seizures in 1972 (28). Although there were good effects with respect to seizures, there were unacceptable morbidity and mortality after complete or partial commissurotomies in eight patients. The postoperative complications included hydrocephalus, aseptic and bacterial meningitis, persistent neurological deficits, and one postoperative death. The surgical technique was then significantly modified: A microsurgical extraventricular division of only the corpus callosum was undertaken. Division of only the corpus callosum appeared to be as effective as complete commissurotomy in controlling multifocal attacks, including complex partial attacks arising from the temporal lobe (29). The operation was less debilitating, and the patients had fewer complications. Special split-brain neuropsychological tests were of immediate and practical value in detecting the extent of division of the corpus callosum after operation. The acute disconnection syndrome still persisted, but later there was observed to be an improvement in personality, due to diminished number of seizures and reduced medications.

Still later, six patients had this central commissurotomy performed in two stages separated by several months. This "ameliorated" the acute disconnection syndrome, which was seen in the six single-stage operations. Of the 12 patients who have had single- and double-staged central commissurotomy, 10 have had good or excellent results for seizure control. It has also been noted that patients with obvious unilateral hemispheric damage preoperatively have had good or excellent results, whereas severely retarded patients have benefited least. Atonic seizures responded dramatically.

The question of the short-term memory loss was addressed by LeDoux (18) in a single case report of one of these patients with central commissurotomy. This patient was 15 years of age, with atrophy of the right hemisphere from previous herpes encephalitis. The patient was tested preoperatively and postoperatively with the Wechsler Memory Scale, Memory for Designs, Visual Sequential Memory, Memory for Letters, Digit Span Memory, and Selective Reminding in Free Recall. No postoperative deficits were obtained. In fact, this patient showed marked improvement in almost every measure utilized. It was concluded that the cognitive processing of complex information is not necessarily dependent on the integrity of the corpus callosum, but rather suggests that cognitive functioning is largely an intrahemispheric process.

Conclusion

The various disconnection syndromes after commissurotomy have been described in terms of the deficits found in impairment of daily functional activities of these patients. I have traced the evolution of a method to control multifocal partial epilepsies, which represents one of the most difficult fields of surgical treatment for epilepsy. It is encouraging that the risk–benefit ratio has been improved by the development of two-stage "central commissurotomy." It appears that a permanent deficit of slow, bimanual motor coordination may be unavoidable. Also, it will be necessary to study more patients for short-term memory deficits.

REFERENCES

1. Akelaitis, A. J., A study of gnosis, praxis and language following section of the corpus callosum and anterior commissure. *J. Neurosurg.*, 1944, 1: 94–102.
2. Amaral, D. G., Insausti, R., and Cowan, W. M., The commissural connections of the monkey hippocampal formation. *J. Comp. Neurol.*, 1984, **224**: 307–336.
3. Bailey, P., and Gibbs, F. A., The surgical treatment of psychomotor epilepsy. *JAMA*, 1951, **145**: 365–370.
4. Blume, W. T., Corpus callosum section for seizure control: Rationale and review of experimental and clinical data. *Q. Rev., Cleveland Clinic*, in press.
5. Bogen, J. E., Sperry, R. W., and Vogel, P. J., Addendum: Commissural section and propagation of seizures. In: *Basic Mechanisms of the Epilepsies* (H. H. Hasper, A. A. Ward, and A. Pope, Eds.). Little, Brown, Boston, 1969: 439–440.
6. Bogen, J. E., and Vogel, P. J., Treatment of generalized seizures by cerebral commissurotomy. *Surg. Forum*, 1963, **14**: 431.
7. Brazier, M. A. B., Evoked responses from the depths of the human brain. *Ann. N.Y. Acad. Sci.*, 1964, **112**: 33–59.
8. Brodal, A., *Neurological Anatomy in Relation to Clinical Medicine*. Oxford University Press, New York, 1981.
9. Campbell, A. L., Bogen, J. E., and Smith, A., Disorganization and reorganization of cognitive and sensorimotor functions in cerebral commissurotomy. *Brain*, 1981, **104**: 493–511.

10. Efron, R., Crandall, P. H., Koss, B., Divenyi, P. L., and Yund, E. W., Central auditory processing: III. The "cocktail party" effect and anterior temporal lobectomy. *Brain Lang.*, 1983, **19**: 254–263.

11. Engel, J., Jr., Brown, W. J., Kuhl, D. E., Phelps, M. E., Mazziotta, J. C., and Crandall, P. H., Pathological findings underlying focal temporal lobe hypometabolism in partial epilepsy. *Ann. Neurol.*, 1982, **12**: 518–528.

12. French, L. A., and Johnson, D. R., Examination of the sensory system in patients after hemispherectomy. *Neurology*, 1955, **5**: 390.

13. Gazzaniga, M. S., Bogen, J. E., and Sperry, R. W., Laterality effects in somesthesis following cerebral commissurotomy in man. *Neuropsychologia*, 1963, **1**: 209–215.

14. Gordon, H. W., Bogen, J. E., and Sperry, R. W., Absence of deconnection syndrome in two patients with partial section of the neocommissures. *Brain*, 1971, **94**: 327–336.

15. Griffith, H., and Davidson, M., Long-term changes in intellect and behavior after hemispherectomy. *J. Neurol. Neurosurg. Psychiatry*, 1966, **29**: 571–576.

16. Hughes, J. T., and Oppenheimer, D. R., Superficial siderosis of the central nervous system. *Acta Neuropathol. (Berl.)*, 1969, **13**: 56–74.

17. Krynauw, R. A., Infantile hemiplegia treated by removing one cerebral hemisphere. *J. Neurol. Neurosurg. Psychiatry*, 1950, **13**: 243–267.

18. LeDoux, J. E., Risse, G. L., Springer, S. P., Wilson, D. H., and Gazzaniga, M. S., Cognition and commissurotomy. *Brain*, 1977, **100**: 87–104.

19. Milner, B., Functional recovery after lesions of the nervous system: 3. Developmental processes in neural plasticity. Sparing of language functions after early unilateral brain damage. *Neurosci. Res. Program Bull.*, 1974, **12**(2): 213–217.

20. Rasmussen, T., Cortical resection in the treatment of focal epilepsy. *Adv. Neurol.*, 1975, **8**: 139–154.

21. Rasmussen, T., Hemispherectomy for seizures revisited. *Can. J. Neurol. Sci.*, 1983, **10**(2): 71–78.

22. Rosene, D. L., and Van Hoesen, G. W., Commissural connections of the hippocampal formation in the rhesus monkey. *Soc. Neurosci. Abstr.*, 1981, **7**: 257.

23. Saul, R., and Sperry, R. W., Absence of commissurotomy symptoms with agenesis of the corpus callosum. *Neurology*, 1968, **18**: 307.

24. Sperry, R., Lateral specialization in the surgically separated hemispheres. In: *The Neurosciences: Third Study Program* (F. O. Schmitt and F. G. Worden, Eds.). MIT Press, Cambridge, Mass., 1974: 5–19.

25. Tomasch, J., Size, distribution and number of fibres in the human corpus callosum. *Anat. Rec.*, 1954, **119**: 119–135.

26. Van Wagenen, W. P., and Herren, R. Y., Surgical division of commissural pathways in the corpus callosum: Relationship to spread of an epileptic attack. *Arch. Neurol. Psychiatry*, 1940, **44**: 740–759.

27. Walter, J. M., Physical therapy following disconnection of the cerebral hemispheres. *Phys. Ther.*, 1976, **56**(4): 422–442.

28. Wilson, D. H., Culver, C., Waddington, M., and Gazzaniga, M., Disconnection of the cerebral hemispheres. An alternative to hemispherectomy for the control of intractable seizures. *Neurology*, 1975, **25**(12): 1149–1153.

29. Wilson, D. H., Reeves, A., and Gazzaniga, M., Division of the corpus callosum for uncontrolled epilepsy. *Neurology*, 1978, **28**: 649–653.

30. Wilson, D. H., Reeves, A., Gazzaniga, M., *et al.*, Cerebral commissurotomy for control of intractable seizures. *Neurology*, 1977, **27**(8): 708–715.

31. Zaidel, D., and Sperry, R. W., Memory impairment after commissurotomy in man. *Brain*, 1974, **97**: 263–272.

THE STABILIZED SYNDROME
OF HEMISPHERE DISCONNECTION

JOSEPH E. BOGEN, MD
Department of Psychology

When the cerebral commissures have been surgically divided (the "split-brain" operation) and the patient has recovered from the acute effects of the operation, a variety of stable long-term deficits in interhemispheric communication can be demonstrated (61, 69). It is an interesting fact of clinical neurology that many of these same deficits can appear, at least for a time, with only a partial interruption of the commissures (e.g., a portion of the corpus callosum) when the partial disconnection occurs in a setting of acute, naturally occurring disease such as a thrombosis (31). Earlier cases were often described as examples of "the anterior cerebral artery syndrome."

Callosal lesions are often accompanied by damage to or pressure on neighboring structures, resulting in several distinct types of signs: (1) signs of hemisphere disconnection, (2) neighborhood signs, and (3) nonlocalizing signs, such as signs of increased intracranial pressure when the callosal lesion is a tumor. In this chapter, attention will be given only to signs of types 1 and 2. A recent history of studies of the corpus callosum explains how the disconnection signs have come to be emphasized (4). Other extensive reviews are available (3, 8, 15, 16, 22, 27, 49, 57, 71).

Following hemisphere disconnection in the human, unilateral tactile anomia, left hemialexia, and unilateral apraxia are common. That is, a right-hander with complete cerebral commissurotomy cannot name aloud objects felt with the left hand, read aloud written material presented solely to the left half-field of vision, or execute with the left hand actions verbally named or described by the examiner. The apraxia usually recedes in a few months, whereas the hemialexia and unilateral anomia persist for years.

The relationship of apraxia to the corpus callosum was emphasized by Liepman (50). He considered the corpus callosum instrumental in left-hand responses to verbal command: The verbal instruction was comprehended only by the left hemisphere, and the left hand followed instructions delivered by a route involving callosal interhemispheric transfer from left to right and then by "contralateral control" (i.e., by right-hemisphere control of the left hand). Necessarily, then, callosal interruption would result in an inability to follow verbal commands with the left hand,

Acknowledgment: I am grateful for library assistance from S. Zeind and staff, including P. Logan and V. Caullay of the Huntington Memorial Hospital, and for word processing by Sally Johnstone.

although there would be no loss of comprehension (as expected from a left-hemi-sphere lesion) and there would be no weakness or incoordination of the left hand (as expected from a right-hemisphere lesion). We now recognize the notion that spa-tial or pictorial instructions understood by the right hemisphere require callosally mediated interhemispheric communication for correct right-hand execution. This right-to-left aspect of callosal function was not part of Liepmann's original callosal concept, although, in retrospect, it seems a natural corollary. Liepman himself con-sidered the left hemisphere to be the organizer of complex (particularly learned) motor behavior. Whether, and in what way, the left hemisphere is dominant for skilled movements generally (and not just those linguistically related) is currently a matter of active controversy (38, 40, 42, 45, 76).

NEIGHBORHOOD SIGNS

The relation of unilateral apraxia to the corpus callosum was doubted for many years; certain neighborhood signs, common with naturally occurring lesions, were emphasized. For example, patients with anterior callosal lesions often show a cer-tain apathy, akinesia, or "imperviousness." We now attribute this symptom not to involvement of the genu of the corpus callosum, but rather to involvement of the medial aspects of the frontal lobes. It resembles a milder form of the akinesia often seen in patients with "the subfrontal syndrome" consequent to bleeding from an an-terior cerebral artery aneurysm, or with an anterior third ventricle tumor.

Neighborhood signs have also been noted with posterior callosal lesions with involvement of the hippocampi. Translating Escourolle *et al.* (26):

> A certain number of our tumors of the splenium [twice as common as genu gliomas] were accompanied by memory dysfunction, whereas the anterior tumors were more often manifested by akinetic states with mutism, probably because of bilateral anterior cingulate involvement. (26: 48)

ABSENCE OF DISCONNECTION SIGNS

In numerous cases of callosal disease, the expected disconnection signs have not been elicited. This includes cases of toxic degeneration of the corpus callosum (such as Marchiafava–Bignami disease), as well as the far more common cases of callosal tumor or callosal infarction.

In retrospect, these negative findings can often be attributed to a lack of look-ing. It is not everyone's routine to look for dysgraphia in the left hand, or even for an anomia; and hemialexia in the left half-field can be elusive, particularly if no precautions are taken to prevent shift of gaze (such as using a tachistoscope so that stimuli appear in one visual half-field or the other for only a fraction of a second). In some instances, disconnection signs may not be demonstrable, because patients with callosal tumors or toxic degeneration are too obtunded for appropriate testing.

The Callosal Agenesis Puzzle

Lévy-Valensi (49) was an ardent admirer of Liepmann, gave him credit for the concept of apraxia, and said, " . . . apraxia is part of the callosal syndrome." But he, like so many others, was particularly troubled by callosal agenesis (CA) and admitted, "The physiologist is no less embarrassed than the anatomist by these disconcerting cases." When CA patients are examined, a few deficits in interhemispheric transfer may be present (54), but not the disconnection syndrome typical of the split-brain patients. This is true even with the most extensive, systematic testing (36, 43).

The interhemispheric transfer clearly present in CA patients seems attributable mainly to the anterior commissure. There may also be a duplication of function (such as speech in each hemisphere) or the compensatory development of unusually effective ipsilateral fiber tracts. The available postmortem evidence indicates that individuals with CA (if they reach an age sufficient for psychological testing) all have anterior commissures, sometimes larger than normal; and the anterior commissure has been shown in animal experiments to serve visual transfer nearly as well as the splenium. Furthermore, it is now known that in the chronic, stabilized state, splenial remnants can effect sufficient interhemispheric exchange to avoid the usual signs of disconnection (2, 30, 35, 60).

Three points are important:

1. An apparent lack of disconnection symptoms in cases of long-standing partial lesion (or of CA) is largely due to the remarkable compensatory capabilities of the remaining fibers.

2. Partial lesions are not usually compensated immediately. Hence, disconnection symptoms are more likely to occur after a sudden partial lesion (such as a stroke), or in the presence of progressive lesions (such as tumors) where the deficit is increasing faster than it can be compensated.

3. Negative findings often result from the use of inappropriate or insensitive testing techniques. What one finds depends on what one looks for; Dandy (20) said that callosal section produces no observable deficits, but among his own patients was the case of hemialexia reported by Trescher and Ford (70).

The paucity of disconnection deficits in patients with CA is not wholly explained by the presence of the anterior commissure. Compensation by the anterior commissure for loss of the splenium is not 100% in animal experiments (39). Nor does the anterior commissure compensate completely for splenial loss in the human, since hemialexia usually is present after splenial section.

Interhemispheric transfer via the anterior commissure seems to be incomplete in callosotomy cases (33, 62). Indeed, most of the syndrome seen after a complete cerebral commissurotomy is also seen (i.e., has *not* been compensated) after a callosotomy sparing the anterior commissure (29, 52). This is perhaps not surprising, since the anterior commissure is only 1/100 the size of the corpus callosum. On the other hand, we can appreciate how significant it might be when we consider the wealth of information which is conveyed over one optic nerve — the diameter of which is about the same as that of the anterior commissure. This question is complicated by the fact that the size of the anterior commissure is among the most variable of brain structures; a diameter difference of three or four times has been reported (74). The discrepancy between monkeys (transfer of learning by the anterior commissure) and humans (inability of the anterior commissure to compensate for callosotomy) may reflect differences between recently acquired memories as opposed to long-standing ones. Current evidence suggests that memory deficits can occur after frontal commissurotomy, including the anterior commissure, even when the splenium is spared (18, 55, 76).

DEVELOPMENT OF THE
SPLIT-BRAIN CONCEPTS

Current views on callosal function are largely attributable to studies of patients with surgical section of the cerebral commissures. These patients are indeed without, in Dandy's words, "any deficits" in the ordinary social situation, or even as determined by most of a routine neurological examination (12, 13). With specially devised testing situations, however, a wide variety of deficits in interhemispheric communication can be demonstrated (69, 78).

The split-brain patients confirmed in a dramatic way the importance of commissural fibers for interhemispheric communication. But the essential facts had already been described in animal experiments during the 1950s, initiated by Myers and Sperry (58). It was found that each hemisphere of a cat or monkey could learn solutions to a problem different from (even conflicting with) the solutions learned by the other hemisphere. This made it clear that effective functioning could occur independently in the two hemispheres. As Sperry put it:

> Callosum-sectioned cats and monkeys are virtually indistinguishable from their normal cagemates under most tests and training conditions. [But] if one studies such a "split-brain" monkey more carefully, under special training and testing conditions where the inflow of sensory information to the divided hemispheres can be separately restricted and controlled, one finds that each of the divided hemispheres now has its own independent mental sphere or cognitive system — that is, its own independent perceptual, learning, memory, and other mental processes . . . it is as if the animals had two separate brains. (67: 1749)

A striking example of mental duality occurs when *only one* hemisphere of a split-brain monkey has had a temporal lobectomy. When the intact hemisphere can see, the split-brain rhesus monkey behaves in the usual rhesus manner, manifesting a fierce fear of humans. But if only the temporal lobectomized hemisphere receives the visual information, the split-brain animal acts like a Klüver–Bucy monkey, particularly as regards its relative tameness (23, 24).

The Hemisphere-Disconnection
Syndrome in the Human

It was knowledge of the split-brain experiments in laboratory animals that alerted Geschwind and Kaplan (32) to the possibility of a hemisphere-disconnection syndrome in the human. This led them, when a suitable patient appeared, to search in a deliberate way for the disconnection effects. In their words, " . . . he behaved as if his two cerebral hemispheres were functioning nearly autonomously. Thus, we found that so long as we confined stimulation and response within the same hemisphere, the patient showed correct performance." In contrast, the patient performed incorrectly when the stimulus was provided to one hemisphere and the response required from the other. They concluded that his hemispheres were disconnected by a lesion of the corpus callosum; this was later confirmed by autopsy.

Widespread recognition of the human split-brain syndrome followed observations on patients whose forebrain commissures were sectioned to control severe intractable epilepsy. Results were favorable in the early patients (9, 11), which led to continued application of the operation. The increased number of patients exhibited a wide spectrum of disconnection deficits. In general, the older the patient at operation or the more extensive the extracallosal damage, the more pronounced and enduring the left-sided apraxia and related symptoms. Following a similar operation in other centers (73), further variation has been encountered, but the crucial observations remain. The following briefly outlines some of the typical findings (left-handers are excluded; for references to such cases, see 4).

Intermanual Conflict

Immediately after brain bisection (or some other acute callosal lesion such as a stroke), a transient state appears with left-sided apraxia or flaccidity, some degree of mutism, and (usually) bilateral Babinski signs. This has been termed "the acute disconnection syndrome" (see chapter by Crandall, this volume). As the severity subsides in a week or so, a phenomenon variously called "intermanual conflict" or "the alien hand" appears. Almost all complete commissurotomy patients manifest some degree of intermanual conflict in the early postoperative period. For example, a few weeks after surgery, one patient was seen buttoning his shirt with one hand while the other hand was following along undoing the buttons.

Similar phenomena were observed after commissurotomy by Wilson *et al.* (73) and by Akelaitis (1), who called it "diagnostic dyspraxia." And the phenomenon has been described in case reports of callosal infarcts or tumors (4). Even our youngest patient (L. B.), with no appreciable apraxia to verbal command in the long term, manifested this alienation 3 weeks after surgery: While doing the Block Design Test unimanually with his right hand, his left hand came up from beneath the table and was reaching for the blocks when he slapped it with his right hand and said, "That will keep it quiet for a while." Such behavior progressively subsides after callosotomy, probably because of other integrative mechanisms supplementing or replacing commissural function.

Most naturally occurring cases of hemisphere disconnection are in a process of recovery (as with a stroke), or worsening (as with a tumor), or fluctuating (as with remitting vascular disease or fluctuating edema). Findings that are quite clear on one occasion may be doubtful later (or earlier). Hence, repeated examinations at different times are most informative.

Various neighborhood signs can prevent the demonstration of disconnection signs. The imperviousness of medial bifrontal lesions or the deviation of gaze of unilateral hemispheric involvement can interfere. The anterior cerebral artery syndrome classically includes a unilateral crural (leg) weakness of the "pyramidal" type and/or a strong grasp reflex, unilateral or bilateral, which make testing for disconnection difficult. Most neighborhood signs subside after a stroke, leaving a period during which disconnection signs can be demonstrated before compensation supervenes.

Overall Effects in the Chronic, Stabilized State

Within a few months after operation, the symptoms of hemisphere disconnection become compensated to a remarkable degree. In personality and social situations, the patient appears much as before. With appropriate tests, however, the disconnected hemispheres can be shown to operate independently to a large extent. Each hemisphere appears to have its own learning processes and its own separate memories.

Split-brain patients soon accept the idea that they have capacities of which they are not conscious, such as left-hand retrieval of objects not namable. They may quickly rationalize such acts, sometimes in a transparently erroneous way (29). But even many years after operation, the patients will occasionally be quite surprised when some well-coordinated or obviously well-informed act has just been carried out by the left hand. This is particularly common under conditions of continuously lateralized input (78, 80).

Visual Effects

Visual material can be presented selectively to a single hemisphere by having the patient fix his or her gaze on a projection screen onto which pictures of objects or symbols are backprojected to either right, left, or both visual half-fields, using exposure times of 1/10 second or less. The patients can read and describe material of various kinds in the right half-field essentially as before surgery. When stimuli are presented to the left half-field, however, the patients usually report that they see "nothing" or at most "a flash of light." The disconnection (if it includes the splenium) can sometimes be demonstrated with simple confrontation testing. The patient is allowed to have both eyes open but does not speak, and is allowed to use only one hand (sitting on the other hand, for example). Using the free hand, the subject indicates the onset of a stimulus, such as the wiggling of the examiner's fingers. With such testing, there may appear to be an homonymous hemianopia in the half-field contralateral to the indicating hand. When the patient is tested with the *other* hand, there seems to be an homonymous hemianopia in the *other* half-field. Occasionally a stimulus in the apparently blind half-field (on the left when the right hand is being used) will produce turning of the head and eyes toward the stimulus, and *then* the hand will point.

This situation must be distinguished from the much more commonly occurring extinction or hemi-inattention deficits from a hemispheric lesion, such that the patient tends to indicate only one stimulus when the stimuli are in fact bilateral (72). An observable difference is that the double hemianopia is a symmetrical phenomenon (the deficit occurs on each side) whereas extinction or hemi-inattention is typically one-sided, more commonly for the left side.

Auditory Suppression

Following cerebral commissurotomy, the patient readily identifies single words (and other sounds) if they are presented to one ear at a time. But, if *different* words are presented to the two ears simultaneously ("dichotic listening"), only the words presented to the right ear will be reliably reported (25, 56, 65).

This large right-ear advantage is usually considered the result of two concurrent circumstances: (1) The ipsilateral pathway (from the left ear to the left hemisphere) is suppressed by the presence of simultaneous but differing inputs, as it is in intact individuals during dichotic listening (44); (2) the contralateral pathway from the left ear to the right hemisphere conveys information that ordinarily reaches the left (speaking) hemisphere by the callosal pathway, which has now been severed. Although left-ear words are rarely reported, their perception by the right hemisphere is occasionally evidenced by appropriate actions of the left hand (34).

Left-ear suppression also appears after right hemispherectomy or other right-hemisphere lesion. Since there is usually suppression of the right ear by left-hemisphere lesions, the suppression of the left ear by a left-hemisphere lesion has been called "paradoxical ipsilateral extinction." Further observations have led to the conclusion that, whether the lesion is in the left or the right hemisphere, if it is close to the midline the suppression of left-ear stimuli is probably attributable to interruption of interhemispheric pathways (19, 53, 66).

Unilateral Apraxia

The degree of left-hand dyspraxia is subject to large individual differences. Immediately after surgery, all of our patients showed some left-sided apraxia to verbal commands such as "Wiggle your left toes," or "Make a fist with your left hand." Left-limb dyspraxia can be attributed to the simultaneous presence of two deficits: poor comprehension by the right hemisphere (which has good control of the left hand), and poor ipsilateral control by the left hemisphere (which understands the commands). Subsidence of the dyspraxia, therefore, can result from two compensatory mechanisms: increased right-hemisphere comprehension of words, and/or increased left-hemisphere control of the left hand. The extent of ipsilateral motor control can be tested by flashing to the right or left visual half-field sketches of thumb and fingers in different postures, for the subject to mimic with one or the other hand. Responses are poor with the hand on the side opposite the visual input, simple postures such as closed fist or open hand being attainable after further recovery. As recovery proceeds, good ipsilateral control is first attained for responses carried out by the more proximal musculature. After several months, most of the patients can form a variety of hand and finger postures with either hand to verbal instructions, such as, "Make a circle with your thumb and little finger," and the like. Even many years later, some degree of apraxia can be demonstrated (77).

Somesthetic Effects

The lack of interhemispheric transfer following hemisphere disconnection can be demonstrated with respect to somesthesis (including touch, pressure, and proprioception) in a variety of ways.

CROSS-RETRIEVAL OF SMALL TEST OBJECTS

Unseen objects in the right hand are handled, named, and described in normal fashion. In contrast, attempts to name or describe the same objects held out of sight in the left consistently fail. In spite of the patient's inability to name an unseen object in the left hand, identification of the object by the right hemisphere is evident from appropriate manipulation of the item showing how it is used, or by retrieval of the same object with the left hand from among a collection of other objects screened from sight. What distinguishes the split-brain patients from normal is that their excellent same-hand retrieval (with either hand) is *not* accompanied by ability to retrieve with one hand objects felt with the other.

CROSS-REPLICATION OF HAND POSTURES

Specific postures impressed on one (unseen) hand by the examiner cannot be mimicked in the opposite hand. Also, if a hand posture in outline form is flashed by tachistoscope to one visual half-field, it can be copied easily by the hand on that side, but usually not by the other hand.

A convenient way to test for lack of interhemispheric transfer of proprioceptive information is as follows: The patient extends both hands beneath the opaque screen (or vision is otherwise excluded), and the examiner impresses a particular posture on one hand. For example, one can put the tip of the thumb against the tip of the little finger and have the other three fingers fully extended and separated. The split-brain patient cannot mimic with the other hand a posture being held by the first hand. This procedure should be repeated with various postures and in both directions.

CROSS-LOCALIZATION OF FINGERTIPS

After complete cerebral commissurotomy, there is a partial loss of the ability to name exact points stimulated on the left side of the body. This defect is least apparent, if at all, on the face; it is most apparent on the distal parts, especially the fingertips. This deficit is not dependent upon language, since it can be done in a nonverbal (picture-identification) fashion and in both directions (right to left and vice versa).

An easy way to demonstrate the defect is to have the subject's hands extended, palms up (with vision excluded). One touches the tip of one of the four fingers with the point of a pencil, asking the patient to then touch the same point with the tip of the thumb of the same hand. Repeating this maneuver many times produces a numerical score, about 100% in normals for either hand. In the absence of a parietal lesion, identification of any of the four fingertips by putting the tip of the thumb upon the particular finger can be done at nearly 100% level by the split-brain patient. One then changes the task so that the fingertip is to be indicated, not by touching it with the thumb of the same hand but by touching the *corresponding* fingertip of the other hand with the thumb of that (other) hand. Sometimes the procedure should be demonstrated with the patient's hand in full vision until the patient understands what is required. This cross-localization cannot be done by the split-brain patient at much better than chance level (25%), while most normal adults do better than 90%.

An incompetence to cross-localize or cross-match has been found in young children (28), possibly because their commissures are not yet fully functioning (75).

Verbal Comprehension by the Right Hemisphere

Auditory comprehension of words by the disconnected right hemisphere is suggested by the subject's ability to retrieve with the left hand various objects if they are named aloud by the examiner. Visual comprehension of printed words by the right hemisphere is often present; after a printed word is flashed to the left visual half-field, the subjects are often able to retrieve with the left hand the designated item from among an array of hidden objects. Control by the left hemisphere in these tests is excluded, because incorrect verbal descriptions given immediately after a correct response by the left hand show that only the right hemisphere knows the answer.

While the disconnected right hemisphere's receptive vocabulary can increase considerably over the years, this single-word comprehension is rarely accompanied by speech. The most extreme cases (to date) of right-hemisphere language ability in right-handed (and left-hemisphere-speaking) split-brain subjects are two with right-hemisphere speech, both with anterior commissure uncut (51, 64). Right-hemisphere language in the split-brain subject has other limitations, with syntactic ability being rudimentary at best. After studying a few cases in great depth for over 10 years, Zaidel concluded:

Whereas phonetic and syntactic analysis seem to specialize heavily in the left hemisphere, there is a rich lexical structure in the right hemisphere. The structure of the right hemisphere lexicon appears to be unique in that it has access to a severely limited short term verbal memory, and it has neither phonetic encoding nor grapheme-to-phoneme correspondence rules. . . . (79: 195)

Right-Hemisphere Dominance

Following commissurotomy, each hemisphere can be tested separately, demonstrating in a positive way those things that each hemisphere can do better than the other, rather than inferring what a hemisphere does from the loss of function when it is injured. Representative reviews are included in the bibliography (8, 48, 59, 68, 78). The rapidly growing literature on hemispheric specialization is well summarized by Bradshaw and Nettleton (14).

Unilateral (Left) Agraphia

Right-handers can write legibly, if not fluently, with the left hand. This ability is commonly lost with callosal lesions, especially those that cause unilateral apraxia. An inability to write to dictation is common with left-hemisphere lesions, almost always affecting both hands. The left hand may be dysgraphic if affected by a right-hemispheric lesion, such as a frontal lesion causing forced grasping. That the left dysgraphia following callosal sectioning is not simply attributable to an incoordination or paresis can be established if one can demonstrate some *other* ability in the left hand requiring as much control as would be required for writing. The left hand may spontaneously doodle or copy various designs or diagrams. It is not so much the presence of a deficit, but rather the *contrast* between certain deficits and certain retained abilities that is most informative. Simple or even complex geometric figures can often be copied by a left hand that cannot write or even copy writing previously made with the patient's own right hand (7, 10, 46, 77).

Unilateral (Left) Tactile Anomia

One of the most convincing ways to demonstrate hemisphere disconnection is to ask the patient to feel with one hand and then name various small, common objects such as a button, coins, safety pin, paper clip, pencil stub, rubber band, key, and so forth. Vision must be occluded. A blindfold is notoriously unreliable; it is better to hold the patient's eyelids closed, put a pillowcase over the patient's head, or use an opaque screen.

The patient with a hemisphere disconnection is generally unable to name or describe an object in the left hand, although he or she readily names objects in the right hand. Sometimes the patient will give a vague description of the object although unable to name it; but a contrast with the ability to readily name the object when it is placed into the right hand remains.

To establish hemisphere disconnection, other causes of unilateral anomia, particularly astereognosis (or a gross sensory deficit), must be excluded. The most certain proof that the object has been identified is for the subject to retrieve it correctly from a collection of similar objects. Such a collection is most conveniently placed in a paper plate about 12–15 cm in diameter, around which the subject can shuffle the objects with one hand while exploring for the test object. Even without evidence of correct retrieval, astereognosis can be reasonably excluded by observing the rapid, facile, and appropriate manipulation of an object, despite inability to name or verbally describe it.

In testing for unilateral anomia, the examiner must be aware of strategies for circumventing the defect. For example, the patient may manipulate it to produce a characteristic noise, or identify a pipe or some other object by a characteristic smell, and thus circumvent the inability of the left hemisphere to identify, by palpation alone, an object placed in the left hand.

Postcommissurotomy Mutism

Following complete section of the cerebral commissures, a mutism, of variable duration, often occurs. The patient does not talk even when he is quite cooperative and able to write. This was originally considered a simple neighborhood sign, a partial akinetic mutism from retraction affecting the anterior end of the third ventricle during section of the anterior commissure (17, 63). However, a number of patients have now been seen with similar retraction, but spared splenium, who did *not* become mute. We now favor the view that mutism results from either hemispheric conflict (possibly at a brain stem level) or a bilateral diaschisis that affects speech more than writing (5, 6). Whatever the explanation for these postsurgical observations, clinical experience indicates that when mutism occurs with naturally occurring callosal lesions, the disease process probably involves the anterior cingulate regions bilaterally (above the callosum) or the septal area (below the callosum).

Alexia without Agraphia

Stroke patients who can write but are unable to read, even what they have just written correctly to dictation, are not extremely rare. This remarkable dissociation of reading from writing has been known for nearly a century (21). One explanation is as follows: Since such a patient usually has a right homonymous hemianopia resulting from a left occipital lobe lesion, nothing can be seen, much less read, in the right half-field. Hence, visual information can reach the left-hemisphere language zone only from the left half-field via the right occipital cortex and transfer via the splenium. In stroke cases, another (or confluent) splenial lesion has disconnected the right occipital cortex from the left hemisphere. The left hemisphere retains competence to write to dictation, but no longer has access to information arriving in the right occipital lobe from the left visual half-field.

As its proponents have recognized, there are some difficulties with this explanation. These patients can often name objects, or pictures of objects, visualized in the left half-field, showing that information *can* reach the language zone from the left half-field. Moreover, alexia without agraphia can occur without an accompanying loss of the right visual half-field (37). And alexia without agraphia can occur in cases with the splenium largely intact. Reading appears to be a multistage process that can be disturbed in a variety of ways (37, 41, 47).

In the past 25 years, our understanding of commissural function has been greatly enriched and clarified. But many issues remain unresolved, including, to name only a few, the causes of postcommissurotomy mutism, the functions of the anterior commissure, and the extent and mechanisms of the compensatory capacities so characteristic of the injured brain (18).

REFERENCES

1. Akelaitis, A. J., Studies on the corpus callosum: I. Diagnostic dyspraxia in epileptics following partial and complete section of the corpus callosum. *Am. J. Psychiat.*, 1944, **101**: 594–599.

2. Apuzzo, M. L. J., Chikovani, O. K., Gott, P. S., Teng, E. L., Zee, C. S., Giannotta, S. L., and Weiss, M. H., Transcallosal, interfornicial approaches for lesions affecting the third ventricle: Surgical considerations and consequences. *Neurosurgery*, 1982, **10**: 547–554.

3. Berlucchi, G., Anatomical and physiological aspects of visual functions of corpus callosum. *Brain Res.*, 1972, **37**: 371–392.

4. Bogen, J. E., The callosal syndromes. In: *Clinical Neuropsychology*, 2nd Ed. (K. M. Heilman and E. Valenstein, Eds.). Oxford University Press, New York, 1985.

5. Bogen, J. E., Concluding overview. In: *Epilepsy and the Corpus Callosum* (A. Reeves, Ed.). Plenum, New York, 1984.

6. Bogen, J. E., Linguistic performance in the short term following cerebral commissurotomy. In: *Studies in Neurolinguistics* (H. Avakian-Whitaker and H. A. Whitaker, Eds.). Academic Press, New York, 1976: 193–224.

7. Bogen, J. E., The other side of the brain: I. Dysgraphia and dyscopia following cerebral commissurotomy. *Bull. Los Angeles Neurol. Soc.*, 1969, **34**: 73–105.

8. Bogen, J. E., and Bogen, G. M., The other side of the brain: III. The corpus callosum and creativity. *Bull. Los Angeles Neurol. Soc.*, 1969, **34**: 191–220.

9. Bogen, J. E., Fisher, E. D., and Vogel, P. J., Cerebral commissurotomy: A second case report. *JAMA*, 1965, **194**: 1328–1329.

10. Bogen, J. E., and Gazzaniga, M. S., Cerebral commissurotomy in man: Minor hemisphere dominance for certain visuospatial functions. *J. Neurosurg.*, 1965, **23**: 394–399.

11. Bogen, J. E., and Vogel, P. J., Cerebral commissurotomy in man. *Bull. Los Angeles Neurol. Soc.*, 1962, **27**: 169–172.

12. Bogen, J. E., and Vogel, P. J., Neurologic status in the long term following cerebral commissurotomy. In: *Les Syndromes de Disconnexion Calleuse chez l'Homme* (F. Michel and B. Schott, Eds.). Hôpital Neurologique, Lyon, 1975: 227–251.

13. Botez, M. I., and Bogen, J. E., The grasp reflex of the foot and related phenomena in the absence of other reflex abnormalities following cerebral commissurotomy. *Acta Neurol. Scand.*, 1976, **54**: 453–463.

14. Bradshaw, J. L., and Nettleton, N. C., *Human Cerebral Asymmetry*. Prentice-Hall, Englewood Cliffs, N.J., 1983.

15. Bremer, F., Brihaye, J., and Andre-Balisaux, G., Physiologie et pathologie du corps calleux. *Arch. Suisses Neurol. Psychiatrie*, 1956, **78**: 31–87.

16. Brion, S., and Jedynak, C. P., *Les Troubles du Transfert Interhémisphérique*. Masson, Paris, 1975.

17. Cairns, H. R., Disturbances of consciousness with lesions of the brainstem and diencephalon. *Brain*, 1952, **75**: 109–146.

18. Campbell, A. L., Bogen, J. E., and Smith, A., Disorganization and reorganization of cognitive and sensorimotor functions in cerebral commissurotomy: Compensatory roles of the forebrain commissures. *Brain*, 1981, **104**: 493–511.

19. Damasio, H., and Damasio, A. R., "Paradoxic" ear extinction in dichotic listening: Possible anatomic significance. *Neurology*, 1979, **29**: 644–653.

20. Dandy, W. E., Operative experience in cases of pineal tumor. *Arch. Surg.*, 1936, **33**: 19–46.

21. Dejerine, J., Contribution à l'étude anatomo-pathologique et clinique des différentes variétés de cécité verbale. *Comptes Rendus des Séances et Mémoires de la Soc. de Biol.*, 1892, **44**: 61–90.

22. Doty, R. W., and Negrão, N., Forebrain commissures and vision. In: *Handbook of Sensory Physiology VII/3* (R. Jung, Ed.). Springer-Verlag, Berlin, 1972: 543–582.

23. Doty, R. W., and Overman, W. H., Mnemonic role of forebrain commissures in macaques. In: *Lateralization in the Nervous System* (S. Harnad *et al.*, Eds.). Academic Press, New York, 1977: 75 88.

24. Downer, J. L. de C., Changes in visual gnostic functions and emotional behavior following unilateral temporal pole damage in the split-brain monkey. *Nature*, 1961, **191**: 50–51.

25. Efron, R., Bogen, J. E., and Yund, E. W., Perception of dichotic chords by normal and commissurotomized human subjects. *Cortex*, 1977, **13**: 137–149.

26. Escourolle, R., Hauw, J. J., Gray, F., and Henin, D., Aspects neuropathologiques des lésions due corps calleux. In: *Les Syndromes de Disconnexion Calleuse chez l'Homme*, (F. Michel and B. Schott, Eds.). Hôpital Neurologique, Lyon, 1975: 41–51.

27. Ethelberg, S., Changes in circulation through the anterior cerebral artery. *Acta Psychiat. Neurol. Suppl.*, 1975, **75**: 3–211.

28. Galin, D., Johnstone, J., Nakell, L., and Herron, J., Development of the capacity for tactile information transfer between hemispheres in normal children. *Science*, 1979, **204**: 1330–1332.

29. Gazzaniga, M. S., and LeDoux, J. E., *The Integrated Mind*. Plenum, New York, 1978.

30. Gazzaniga, M. S., Risse, G. L., Springer, S. P., Clark, E., and Wilson, D. H., Psychologic and neurologic consequences of partial and complete cerebral commissurotomy. *Neurology*, 1975, **25**: 10–15.

31. Geschwind, N., Disconnexion syndromes in animals and man. *Brain*, 1965, **88**: 237–294, 585–644.

32. Geschwind, N., and Kaplan, E., A human cerebral deconnection syndrome: A preliminary report. *Neurology*, 1962, **12**: 675–685.

33. Goldstein, M., Joynt, R., and Hartley, R., The long-term effects of callosal sectioning. *Arch. Neurol.*, 1975, **32**: 52–53.

34. Gordon, H. W., Verbal and nonverbal cerebral processing in man for audition. Unpublished doctoral dissertation, California Institute of Technology, 1973.

35. Gordon, H. W., Bogen, J. E., and Sperry, R. W., Absence of deconnexion syndrome in two patients with partial section of the neocommissures. *Brain*, 1971, **94**: 327–336.

36. Gott, P. S., and Saul, R. E., Agenesis of the corpus callosum: Limits of functional compensation. *Neurology*, 1978, **28**: 1272–1279.

37. Greenblatt, S. H., Neurosurgery and the anatomy of reading: A practical review. *Neurosurgery*, 1977, **1**: 6–15.

38. Haaland, K. Y., and Delaney, H. D., Motor deficits after left or right hemisphere damage due to stroke or tumor. *Neuropsychologia*, 1981, **19**: 17–27.

39. Hamilton, C. R., Mechanisms of interocular equivalence. In: *Advances in the Analysis of Visual Behavior* (D. Ingle, M. Goodale, and R. Mansfield, Eds.). MIT Press, Cambridge, Mass., 1982: 693–717.

40. Hampson, E., and Kimura, D., Hand movement asymmetries during verbal and nonverbal tasks. *Can. J. Psychol.*, 1984, **38**: 102–125.

41. Hécaen, H., and Kremin, H., Neurolinguistic research on reading disorders resulting from left hemisphere lesions: aphasic and pure alexias. In: *Studies in Neurolinguistics* (H. Avakian-Whitaker and H. A. Whitaker, Eds.). Academic Press, New York, 1976: 861–872.

42. Jason, G. W., Hemispheric asymmetries in motor function: I. Left-hemisphere specialization for memory but not performance. *Neuropsychologia*, 1983, **21**: 35–45.

43. Jeeves, M. A., Some limits to interhemispheric integration in cases of callosal agenesis and partial commissurotomy. In: *Structure and Function of Cerebral Commissures* (I. S. Russel, M. W. van Hof, and G. Berlucchi, Eds.). University Park Press, Baltimore, 1979: 449–474.

44. Kimura, D., Functional asymmetry of the brain in dichotic listening. *Cortex*, 1967, **3**: 163–178.

45. Kimura, D., and Archibald, Y., Motor functions of the left hemisphere. *Brain*, 1974, **97**: 337–350.

46. Kumar, S., Short-term memory for a nonverbal tactual task after cerebral commissurotomy. *Cortex*, 1977, **13**: 55–61.

47. Landis, T., Regard, M., and Serrat, A., Iconic reading in a case of alexia without agraphia caused by brain tumor: A tachistoscopic study. *Brain Lang.*, 1980, **11**: 45–53.

48. Levy, J., Cerebral asymmetries as manifested in split-brain man. In: *Hemispheric Disconnection and Cerebral Function* (M. Kinsbourne and W. L. Smith, Eds.). Charles C Thomas, Springfield, Ill., 1974: 165–183.

49. Lévy-Valensi, J., *Le Corps Calleux* (Paris Theses 448). G. Steinheil, Paris, 1910.

50. Liepmann, H., and Mass, O., Fall von linksseitiger Agraphie und Apraxie bei rechtsseitiger Lahmung. *Journal für Psychologie und Neurologie*, 1908, **10**: 214–227.

51. McKeever, W. F., Sullivan, K. F., Ferguson, S. M., and Rayport, M., Right hemisphere speech development in the anterior commissure-spared commissurotomy patient: A second case. *Clin. Neuropsychol.*, 1982, **4**: 17–22.

52. McKeever, W. F., Sullivan, K. F., Ferguson, S. M., and Rayport, M., Typical cerebral hemisphere disconnection deficits following corpus callosum section despite sparing of the anterior commissure. *Neuropsychologia*, 1981, **19**: 745–755.

53. Michel, F., and Peronnet, F., Extinction gauche au test dichotique: Lésion hémisphérique ou lesion commissurale? In: *Les Syndromes de Disconnexion Calleuse chez l'Homme* (F. Michel and B. Schott, Eds.). Hôpital Neurologique, Lyon, 1975: 85–117.

54. Milner, A. D., and Jeeves, M. A., A review of behavioral studies of agenesis of the corpus callosum. In: *Structure and Function of Cerebral Commissures* (I. S. Russell, M. W. van Hof, and G. Berlucchi, Eds.). University Park Press, Baltimore, 1979: 428–448.

55. Milner, B., Analysis of memory disorder after cerebral commissurotomy. In: *Essays in Honour of R. W. Sperry* (C. Trevarthen, Ed.). Cambridge University Press, Cambridge, England, in press.

56. Milner, B., Taylor, L., and Sperry, R. W., Lateralized suppression of dichotically presented digits after commissural section in man. *Science*, 1968, **161**: 184–186.

57. Mingazzini, G., *Der Balken*. Springer, Berlin, 1922.
58. Myers, R. E., Function of the corpus callosum in interocular transfer. *Brain*, 1956, **79**: 358–363.
59. Nebes, R. D., Hemispheric specialization in commissurotomized man. *Psychol. Bull.*, 1974, **81**: 1–14.
60. Ozgur, M. H., Johnson, T., Smith, A., and Bogen, J. E., Transcallosal approach to third ventricle tumor: case report. *Bull. Los Angeles Neurol. Soc.*, 1977, **42**: 57–62.
61. Reeves, A., Ed., *Epilepsy and the Corpus Callosum*. Plenum, New York, 1984.
62. Risse, G. L., LeDoux, J., Springer, S. P., Wilson, D. H., and Gazzaniga, M. S., The anterior commissure in man: Functional variation in a multisensory system. *Neuropsychologia*, 1978, **16**: 23–31.
63. Ross, E. D., and Stewart, R. M., Akinetic mutism from hypothalamic damage: Successful treatment with dopamine agonists. *Neurology*, 1981, **31**: 1435–1439.
64. Sidtis, J. J., Volpe, B. T., Wilson, D. H., Rayport, M., and Gazzaniga, M. S., Variability in right hemisphere language function after callosal section: Evidence for a continuum of generative capacity. *J. Neurosci.*, 1981, **1**: 323–331.
65. Sparks, R., and Geschwind, N., Dichotic listening in man after section of neocortical commissures. *Cortex*, 1968, **4**: 3–16.
66. Sparks, R., Goodglass, H., and Nickel, B., Ipsilateral versus contralateral extinction in dichotic listening from hemispheric lesions. *Cortex*, 1970, **6**: 249–260.
67. Sperry, R. W., Cerebral organization and behavior. *Science*, 1961, **133**: 1749–1757.
68. Sperry, R. W., Lateral specialization in the surgically separated hemispheres. In: *The Neurosciences, 3rd Study Program* (F. O. Schmitt and F. G. Worden, Eds.). MIT Press, Cambridge, Mass., 1974: 5–19.
69. Sperry. R. W., Gazzaniga, M. S., and Bogen, J. E., Interhemispheric relationships: The neocortical commissures; syndromes of hemisphere disconnection. In: *Handbook of Clinical Neurology*, Vol. 4 (P. J. Vinken and G. W. Bruyn, Eds.). Elsevier, Amsterdam, 1969: 273–290.
70. Trescher, H. H., and Ford, F. R., Colloid cyst of the third ventricle. Report of a case; operative removal with section of posterior half of corpus callosum. *Arch. Neurol. Psychiat.*, 1937, **37**: 959–973.
71. Unterharnscheidt, F., Jalnik, D., and Gott, H. Dei balkenmangel. In: *Monographien an die gesamtgebiete Neurologie und Psychiatrie*, No. 128. Springer, New York, 1968: 1–232.
72. Weinstein, E. A., and Friedland, R. P., (1977). *Hemi-Inattention and Hemisphere Specialization*. Raven Press, New York, 1977.
73. Wilson, D. H., Reeves, A., Gazzaniga, M., and Culver, C., Cerebral commissurotomy for control of intractable seizures. *Neurology*, 1977, **27**: 708–715.
74. Yamamoto, I., Rhoton, A. L., and Peace, D. A., Microsurgery of the third ventricle: Part 1. *Neurosurgery*, 1981, **8**: 334–356.
75. Yakovlev, P. I., and Lecours, A. R., The myelogenetic cycles of regional maturation of the brain. In: *Regional Development of the Brain in Early Life*, (A. Minkowski, Ed.). Blackwell, Edinburgh, 1967, 3–70.
76. Zaidel, D., Sperry, R. W., Memory impairment after commissurotomy in man. *Brain*, 1974, **97**: 262–272.
77. Zaidel, D., Sperry, R. W., Some long-term motor effects of cerebral commissurotomy in man. *Neuropsychologia*, 1977, **15**: 193–204.
78. Zaidel, E., Disconnection syndrome as a model for laterality effects in the normal brain. In: *Cerebral Hemisphere Asymmetry: Method, Theory and Application* (J. Hellige, Ed.). Praeger, New York, 1983: 95–151.
79. Zaidel, E., Lexical organization in the right hemisphere. In: *Cerebral Correlates of Con-*

scious Experience (P. Buser and A. Rougeul-Buser, Eds.). Elsevier, Amsterdam, 1978: 177–197.

80. Zaidel, E., Linguistic competence and related functions in the right hemisphere of man following cerebral commissurotomy and hemispherectomy (Doctoral dissertation, California Institute of Technology). *Dissertation Abstracts International*, 1973, 34: 2350B. (University Microfilms 73–26, 481).

IMPLICATIONS

INTRODUCTION

ERAN ZAIDEL, PhD
Department of Psychology

Recently, one of us received a phone call from a well-known Hollywood actress who related an argument with a friend concerning left-hemisphere–right-hemisphere differences. She had read that left–right brain differences are real, pervasive, and the subject of intense scientific studies. Her companion said they were pseudoscientific, popularized stuff, the fad of the decade. Who was right?

Probably both! True, the study of human hemispheric specialization has a long and respected history, starting over 150 years ago as a branch of clinical neurology. Today it is the subject of many scientific and scholastic fields and has recently become a proper part of experimental cognitive psychology. But it has also become part of our cultural background, an interpretative approach to human existence and the human condition. It is in this interpretative capacity that hemispheric-specialization theory has most often been abused.

One recent advance in studies of human hemispheric specialization is the recognition that each hemisphere represents a relatively complete and independent cognitive system with its own characteristic information-processing style. This insight is the main lesson of the split-brain syndrome and could not have been gained either from hemisphere-damaged patients or from normal subjects. Each hemisphere apparently embodies a separate, different representation of reality and of the self. Human behavior is then the result of complementary interaction between the two hemispheres, both facilitory and inhibitory. Nonetheless, hemispheric conflict can be demonstrated experimentally (22) and clinically (6) and serves as a favorite model of the duality of human nature. Unfortunately, there are many different notions of duality, and hemispheric-specialization theory cannot accommodate them all.

What criteria can be used to judge whether an application of hemispheric specialization theory to an interpretation of a humanistic or social-scientific issue is adequate? First and foremost, of course, the interpretation should satisfy internal standards of coherence and insight within the applied domain. Second, it should presuppose a scientifically conservative or empirical version of the theory. Third, it needs to develop an account of hemispheric-specialization theory that extends the concept of a differential hemispheric problem-solving style on a given task to the concept of predominant hemisphericity in a given individual (individual differences) or in a group of individuals (see chapter by TenHouten, this volume).

Thus, three main sorts of applications of hemispheric-specialization theory to other academic fields can be cited. The first, an "outward-directed" or "missionary" application, involves the use of techniques and results of hemispheric-specialization studies to probe problems in another field. An example is the hemispheric-dysfunction model of schizophrenia in psychiatry (e.g., see chapter by Tanguay, this volume). The second, an "inward-directed" or "egotistic" application, involves the use of techniques and results from another field to explore the nature of hemispheric special- ization itself. An example is the search for hemispheric specialization in long-term memory, a stage concept borrowed from cognitive psychology (see chapter by D. W. Zaidel, this volume). The third, an "interpretative" application, involves the explica- tion of theoretical constructs in another field by using results and concepts from hemispheric-specialization theory. An example is the hemispheric analysis of historical views on the sociology of knowledge (see chapter by TenHouten, this volume). Application of hemispheric specialization to the humanities and social sciences tends to be of the interpretative or missionary variety, whereas application to the life sciences tends to be of both missionary and egotistic varieties. Against this background, the implications of hemispheric specialization to a number of scholarly fields can be reviewed. These include not only linguistics, education, sociology, psychiatry, and the arts, but also philosophy, computer science, and anthropology.

PSYCHOLOGY

Many chapters in this book report applications of hemispheric-specialization theory to branches of psychology. Curtiss has covered developmental psycholin- guistics; Satz *et al.* have discussed individual differences as a function of handedness; Hines and Gorski have described sex differences; and D. W. Zaidel has introduced cognitive psychological considerations. Actually, since each hemisphere can be con- ceptualized as an independent cognitive system with its own perceptions, cognitions, memories, problem-solving strategies, affects, and personality, much of human ex- perimental psychology can be recast in the framework of hemispheric-specialization theory. Pertinent questions range from "Do the two hemispheres have the same visual-contrast sensitivity?" to "Are the two hemispheres equally anxious during tests?" and include "Do the two hemispheres solve the same problem by different means?" Hemispheric specialization potentially affects most aspects of human psy- chological research.

Perception and Cognition

With a few exceptions (e.g., 9), there has been an appalling lack of systematic psychophysical assessment of hemispheric differences, and this remains an area for fruitful future research. Some attention has been paid to the information-processing, or stage-of-processing, locus of hemispheric specialization (28). The stage-of-process- ing formulation was borrowed from cognitive psychology, the field that most influ- enced experimental studies of hemispheric specialization in humans. The shared information-processing rationale of both neuroscience and cognitive psychology suggests hemispheric differences in sensory store (cf. 27), in short-term memory (cf. my chapter on the right hemisphere, this volume), and long-term memory (cf. chapter by D. W. Zaidel, this volume). And of course, the recognized specialization of the left hemisphere for language and of the right hemisphere for visual–spatial analysis borrows from psycholinguistics and from the psychology of visual perception, respectively.

Developmental Psychology

A second major interface with a psychological approach is between hemispheric specialization and developmental psychology. This is natural in view of the interest in the ontogenesis of hemispheric specialization and in the role that hemispheric development plays in the acquisition of perceptual, cognitive, and linguistic skills (see chapter by Curtiss, this volume). Methodologically, it is possible to administer hemispheric-specialization tests to children to test the status of hemispheric development at different growth stages, or to administer developmental tests to the two hemispheres separately to determine the developmental status of each hemisphere. Neither approach has been explored systematically to date (but see 14, 31, 37, 38). This is somewhat surprising, since much of the staging in perceptual–cognitive development in the Piagetian tradition divides naturally into domains with clear hemispheric significance (e.g., the child's concept of language, space, time, etc.) and contains experimental paradigms appropriate to hemispheric testing, such as speech-free multiple-choice pointing tests, perceptual/construction tests, and so on.

Individual Differences

A third growing interface is between hemispheric specialization and the psychology of individual differences. The original impetus came from the realization that patterns of hemispheric organization depend on handedness and, to a smaller extent, on sex. It was natural to propose that hemispheric specialization, and perhaps callosal connectivity, are continuous variables in the population at large. Recently, there has been a growing emphasis on alternative hemispheric strategies for processing the same stimulus. The choice of a strategy may vary in an individual over time as a function of asymmetric hemispheric activation, or it may characterize the stable cognitive style of the person. This new emphasis on strategies represents a retrenchment from the universal application of a single pattern of hemispheric organization to all subjects—a shift based in part on the poor statistical validity of common laterality tests.

Factorial theories of individual differences in intelligence can also receive natural neuropsychological interpretations. Thus it is possible to seek cerebral localization of primary factors in a multivariate theory of human intelligence, such as the verbal and spatial abilities in Spearman's model, the two visual closure factors in Thurston's Primary Mental Abilities model, the semantic versus figural abilities in Guilford's Structure of the Intellect, or even "g" (39). With the possible exception of the Wechsler Intelligence Scale (e.g., 21, 23, 26), surprisingly little systematic exploration has been made in this direction, despite the early work of Halstead (15) (but see 32). This is particularly unfortunate, because neuropsychological evidence could be used to establish the validity of observed factors. Furthermore, neuropsychological data can relate primary factors that are not directly correlated, such as the prediction of increased degree of lateralization with increased field independence (43).

Personality and Social Psychology

Recent claims of hemispheric specialization for the regulation of affect remain inconsistent or speculative (7), but there is no doubt that the right hemisphere plays a special role in nonverbal communication, particularly in processing conventional facial expressions (cf. 3). There is little doubt that hemispheric specialization plays a role in the normal functioning as well as in the disintegration of the personality, but it is not clear whether this is a primary role or whether it is more an effect than a cause.

While attempts to find differences in the personal and aesthetic preferences of the disconnected hemispheres have generally failed (34, 41), nonverbal tests of social values suggest that, contrary to expectation, the disconnected right hemisphere professes more traditional, socially accepted norms: It behaves more like the seat of the superego than the seat of the id (40).

LINGUISTICS

The Chomskian position on theoretical linguistics argues that human language is biologically unique and innate. And yet many theoretical linguists ignore consideration of biological brain processes underlying natural linguistic performance, dismissing them as irrelevant or at least unnecessary for understanding the structure of linguistic competence as embodied in syntax. But the structure of syntax is a part of the structure of the human brain, and it is misleading to argue that the structure of the hardware (the brain) is opaque to the structure of the software (language). This may be true of some digital computers; it is not true of our modular brain, where spatially localized damage results in sharply demarcated behavioral deficits.

Anatomical modularity is particularly dramatic in the case of language. Thus, we associate phonological and syntactic disorders with anterior left-hemisphere lesions and semantic disorders with posterior left-hemisphere lesions. The left hemisphere seems specialized for language computation, whereas the right hemisphere has only linguistic–conceptual labeling, a limited lexical semantic system, and certain extralinguistic roles — all distinctions recognized by theoretical linguists. Neurolinguistic data also distinguish sharply between language performance modules that focus on specific modalities (e.g., auditory language comprehension vs. reading) — distinctions not recognized by theoretical linguists. Reading, in particular, seems to be a more recent evolutionary brain development; it is largely an overlaid structure that is partly parasitic on spoken language, and its neuroanatomical substrates seem particularly labile and subject to environmental and genetic perturbations, as in congenital dyslexia. None of these facts are reflected by or predicted by theoretical linguistic models of the native speaker–hearer–writer–reader.

Is there neurolinguistic evidence for the theoretical linguistic position that human language is innate, biologically unique, and psychologically autonomous — that is, special? We may identify linguistic specialness with language specialization in the left hemisphere and ask whether variations of language form, especially those with different sensory–motor frames (e.g., ordinary speech as against American Sign Language [ASL]), show the same left-hemisphere specialization. In ASL, expression is gestural and reception is visual, whereas in ordinary speech expression is vocal and reception is auditory. Speech is temporal, and manual signs more visual–spatial. Nonetheless, evidence to date indicates that ordinary speech and sign language have similar left-hemisphere specialization and similar forms of disintegration in aphasia (2).

Indeed, language seems to be predominant in its claim to cerebral territory in at least two different senses. First, as Hellen Neville's work on ASL demonstrates, language can "attract" to it subordinate cerebral machinery. Another example is left-hemisphere dominance (demonstrated by a right-ear advantage in dichotic listening) for intonational structures that subserve language, such as certain vowels in Japanese (35), pitch in Thai (36), and stress in English (12). Second, language can "crowd out" other cognitive functions when cerebral territory is limited, as following perinatal left-hemisphere atrophy (10).

It has been conjectured that different languages may differ in their cortical representation, depending on whether they are learned first or second, whether they are read from right to left or from left to right, or whether they are ideographic or phonotactic (as in the Japanese Kanji and Kana). Such cross-linguistic differences in cortical organization and patterns of hemispheric specialization, if they can be proved, would argue against the neurological specialness and unity of human language and would emphasize performance in addition to competence considerations in the analysis of language.

But neurolinguistic evidence need not involve localization data. Perturbation by lesion of separable behavioral systems, such as certain syntactic rules, can have important theoretical implications regardless of where they are localized. Evidence of this sort has been scant to date, but may improve when more linguists accept neurolinguistic data as primary and engage in neuropsychological research.

EDUCATION

Potential applications of hemispheric-specialization theory to education account for much of the enormous attraction that the field holds for the public (cf. 8). Four separate educational applications can be distinguished. First, the psychological characterization of the cognitive styles of the two hemispheres may help identify individual differences in perceptual and cognitive abilities in terms of predominant hemispheric function in persons (5), if this concept turns out to be scientifically valuable (1, 16). Moreover, since each style is best adapted to solving specific problems, "hemispheric typing" of an individual could become useful in personnel selection. For example, it is said that the Boole rule-learning and the Garcia experiential-immersion methods for teaching a second language correspond to left-hemisphere and right-hemisphere strategies, respectively, and are best suited for specific individuals (17).

Second, hemispheric characterization of certain learning disorders of neurological origin, such as specific developmental language disability, may help identify individuals at risk and prescribe remedial strategies. For example, so-called dysphonetic dyslexic children who have selective deficits in phonological reading may represent a selective left-hemisphere dysfunction and may benefit from learning to use alternative hemispheric strategies (4).

Third, to the extent that hemispheric organization is under experimental control, the cognitive repertoire of an individual may be dynamically changed to best fit the task at hand. Many questionable promises have been made for changes in well-established individual behavioral patterns through alleged selective hemispheric activation, usually promoting the "good" right hemisphere, whose powers have hitherto been suppressed. For example, right-hemisphere activation is now claimed to lead to creativity, withdrawal from addiction, and improved drawing ability. Neither the purported association of these behaviors with the right hemisphere nor the alleged methods for hemispheric activation have a scientific basis. Nonetheless, hemispheric independence and hemispheric specialization promise to have dramatic future educational significance in tailoring learning environments to individual cognitive–cerebral organization and in optimizing individual performance on specific tasks through controlled shifts in cerebral balance. In short, criticisms of existing educational innovations on the basis of the tenuous alleged relationship to dual-brain theory are usually justified, but, in-principle-objections to such advances (16) are not.

A fourth application is the interpretative effect that concepts of brain give to educational research (see chapter by Wittrock, this volume). Here neuropsychological concepts, such as hemispheric strategies, or domain-specific (linguistic vs. visual-spatial) knowledge, or hemispheric modulation of attention, are borrowed and used in educational research by analogy.

The controlled modulation of hemispheric activation does promise considerable educational benefits. Evidence for such modulation is becoming increasingly prominent as our view of the origins of hemispheric specialization is shifting in emphasis from nature to nurture. Not only can early brain damage shift hemispheric dominance, but relatively late experiences, such as exposure to reading instruction, may do so as well. Indeed, hemispheric control over a task is now believed to shift with the novelty of the stimuli and the experience of the performer.

Most exciting, perhaps, are experiments that show hemispheric priming and overloading effects in dual-task paradigms. New evidence suggests increased hemispheric superiority on a task with concurrent or prior priming by a secondary task. Such activation may in turn decrease cross-callosal inhibition of the competence of the other hemisphere, thus improving the performance of tasks that are optimally performed by one hemisphere alone. An alternative approach to removing cross-callosal inhibition is through interruption or reduction of callosal connectivity. Anxiety may play such a role, and function-specific neurochemical agents are probably not too far off in the future (13).

Our ability to use shifts in hemispheric control to an educational advantage depends on our understanding of the differences in the learning styles of the two hemispheres, as distinct from their cognitive repertoires. There is virtually no systematic work in the experimental neuropsychological literature on hemispheric differences in the formal parameters of a laboratory learning task. Yet tantalizing clues abound. For example, there is evidence that the learning style of the disconnected right hemisphere is nonalgorithmic and cannot be fractionated into stepwise components. It does not respond to trial and error, does not seem to benefit from partial solutions, and appears to have a different concept of error from that of the left hemisphere. Much more work needs to be done on the learning styles of the two hemispheres in different experimental populations.

COMPUTER SCIENCE

It is difficult to describe how the right hemisphere solves problems. Perhaps because right-hemisphere strategies are not logical, analytical, or stepwise, it may be difficult to describe them logically and analytically. This merely reflects our state of ignorance. A nonlogical solution can, indeed must, have a logical description. An attempted logical analysis of right-hemisphere-like strategies comes from Earl Hunt (18), who devised two very different computer models for solving Raven Matrices problems. One program depended on logical feature analysis and can be regarded as a left-hemisphere strategy. The other depended on pattern-recognition operations and can be regarded as a right-hemisphere strategy. Unfortunately, the performance and error patterns of the two models were never compared to the strategies used by hemisphere-damaged patients or the disconnected hemispheres in solving Colored or Standard Raven Progressive Matrices (39, 42). The right hemisphere may provide a useful empirical model for heuristic problem solving, where analogy and intuition (i.e., prior experience) play an important role (29). Nonstandard concepts of causality and of error may be embodied in such a model (39), and these concepts may in turn be clarified by computer modeling.

Concepts of artificial intelligence can explicate some theoretical problems in hemispheric-specialization theory. For example, the left hemisphere is usually characterized as "sequential." But what does this alleged capacity for processing order really refer to? Does it refer to temporal discrimination between two isolated sounds, retrieval of order information from context-dependent phonetic codes, distinction of meanings conveyed by different word orders, or detection of rapid changes in formant transition frequencies in the acoustic stream? There is no reason to believe that the same mechanism underlies all these functions. In particular, a different class of mechanisms may be involved in storing temporal order information about perceived psychological units and about smaller unconsciously processed units.

Computability theory shows that order information is equivalent to short-term memory, so that limitation in one can be compensated for by the other. Thus, computer models of hemispheric processing may elucidate alleged right-hemisphere deficits in sequential analysis and the possible relation of such deficits to the short-term verbal-memory deficit of the right hemisphere.

PHILOSOPHY

The experience of two separate and simultaneous streams of consciousness in the same individual, easily demonstrated in the disconnected brain, poses interesting philosophical challenges. What are the implications to concepts of consciousness and to the philosophy of mind? Is consciousness unified? Can it exist without language? The answers have a major bearing on the mind–body problem and on the question of other minds (11, 25, 30, 33).

If we accept that the two hemispheres represent two independent cognitive systems, each with a different representation of reality and with a different set of competencies, strategies, and preferences, then the two hemispheres may exhibit mutually incompatible behavior, an internal conflict. If each hemisphere is fully conscious, does each also have a free will? In that case, could the individual as a whole be considered to have a free will? If the mental conflict is thus seen to be biologically determined, is the individual ever morally responsible?

MacKay and MacKay (24) tried and failed to show simultaneous conflict behavior in the two disconnected hemispheres of a commissurotomy patient. They concluded that the available data support a monistic view of unified consciousness. But dramatic conflict behavior has been described in neurological patients with disconnection syndrome due to natural callosal lesions (6), and patients with complete commissurotomy routinely exhibit ignorance and denial by one hemisphere of experiences by the other. Indeed, these are common experiences as internal states in all of us; as such, they are compatible with our everyday notions of a unified consciousness, a free will, and individual moral responsibility. In that cast, the split brain provides no challenge for our ethics.

The recognition that the disconnected right hemisphere is conscious has highlighted the implausibility of the insistence that consciousness presupposes language. Rather, consciousness may be regarded as presupposing a certain degree of cognitive complexity. For a fully conscious human, this degree of cognitive complexity includes an ability to use abstract reasoning, an internal model of the self and of the environment, a sense of past and future, and the usual range of affective responses including the capacity for modulating the cognitive system itself. Since all these qualities are continuous (i.e., admit of degrees), this concept of consciousness also admits of degrees and applies to a greater extent to some humans than others, more to humans than to monkeys, and more to monkeys than to dogs. According to this definition, the evidence to date certainly suggests that each hemisphere is independently conscious.

Finally, incompatible hemispheric concepts of causality, error, meaning, and proof may lead to different and nonstandard concepts of truth, a challenge to the philosophy of language and of logic. For example, the right hemisphere may have a coherence sense of truth, and the left hemisphere a correspondence sense of truth. Moreover, since the representation of the world may differ radically between the two hemispheres, the same event may elicit conflicting estimates of veridicality, even though both are equally valid in relation to their own frame of reference.

Sociology

TenHouten's chapter (this volume) illustrates both the substantive and interpretative applications of hemispheric-specialization theory to sociology. The experimental part analyzes a systemic extension of the notion of predominant hemisphericity from superiority on a task, to a predominant cognitive style in an individual, and then to a style of a group of individuals. Specifically, TenHouten studies the effects of urbanization and cultural milieu on patterns of hemispheric organization in the population. The larger part of his chapter, however, is devoted to tracing analogies to the duality of hemispheric styles in the history of the dialectic of the sociology of knowledge. The implication, though never stated explicitly, is that theories of the sociology of knowledge are colored by a preconscious concept of duality that is attributable to our dual brain.

Art

Artistic abilities, like linguistic abilities, are biologically innate and neuroanatomically modular. Evidence for this comes from selective artistic deficits following circumscribed brain damage. For example, patients may retain the ability to read music while losing the ability to read words. Or they may lose the ability to read music but not the ability to play an instrument (see chapter by Schweiger, this volume). Is there hemispheric specialization for various forms of art? If so, experimental data from normal subjects as well as clinical experience suggest that it is different from that for language. Yet specific art systems, such as music or painting, can be described as abstract systems of representation. It is possible to model such a system by an abstract syntax, complete with rules of grammar and semantic interpretation. This grammar would not be localized in the left hemisphere and would thus provide a counterexample to the generalization that the left hemisphere is specialized for handling abstract syntax. Alternatively, the theory of an abstract syntax for art may be wrong. It is not sufficient to point out that no adequate grammar for music has been described, or that available art grammars differ in some fundamental way from linguistic grammars. To defend the Chomskian argument, one needs to show that all *possible* art grammars are different in principle from linguistic grammars. It is difficult to conceive of such a demonstration. Certainly, none has been forthcoming.

Schweiger restricts himself to a discussion of the cortical representation of the production of art. But dual-brain theory would seem to have just as much to say about brain representation of the appreciation of art. Art, like other cultural products, can be analyzed in terms of binary dimensions such as unitary–wholistic or abstract–concrete (19), which may have natural hemispheric interpretations. Then predominant styles in art may correspond to cultural cycles of shifting hemispheric dominance. Moreover, suppose we could show not only that one hemisphere is more astute in art appreciation (20), but also that each hemisphere has different artistic preferences, although two attempted empirical demonstrations of this in the split brain came up with negative results (E. Zaidel, W. T. Jones, and D. Faust, unpublished data; 34). Then dual-brain theory would become a proper part of aesthetics. The next step would undoubtedly be the spawning of a new field of knowledge — neuroaesthetics — with many subfields, including neurocomparative literature and neuroarchitecture.

REFERENCES

1. Beaumont, J. G., Young, A. W., and McManus, I. C., Hemisphericity: A critical review. *Cognitive Neuropsychol.*, 1984, 1: 191–212.
2. Bellugi, U., Poizner, H., and Klima, E. S., Brain organization for language: Clues from sign aphasia. *Human Dev.* (special issue, D. Kimura, Ed.), 1983, 2: 155–170.
3. Benowitz, L. I., Bear, D. M., Rosenthal, R., Mesulam, M. M., Zaidel, E., and Sperry, R. W., Hemispheric specialization in nonverbal communication. *Cortex*, 1983, 19: 5–11.
4. Boder, E., Developmental dyslexia: Prevailing diagnostic concepts and a new diagnostic approach. In: *Progress in Learning Disabilities*, Vol. 2 (H. R. Myklebust, Ed.). Grune & Stratton, New York, 1971: 293–321.
5. Bogen, J. E., Some educational implications of hemispheric specialization. In: *The Human Brain* (M. C. Wittrock, Ed.). Prentice-Hall, Englewood Cliffs, N.J., 1977: 133–152.
6. Brion, S., and Jedynak, C. P., Semeiologie calleuse dans les tumeurs et les malformations vasculaires. In: *Les Syndromes de Disconnexion Calleuse chez l'Homme* (F. Michel and B. Schott, Eds.). Hôpital Neurologique, Lyon, 1975: 253–264.
7. Bryden, M. P., *Laterality: Functional Asymmetry in the Intact Brain*. Academic Press, New York, 1982.
8. Chall, S. J., and Mirsky, A. F., *Education and the Brain*. University of Chicago Press, Chicago, 1978.
9. Davidoff, J. B., Studies with nonverbal stimuli. In: *Divided Visual Field Studies of Cerebral Organization* (J. G. Beaumont, Ed.). Academic Press, London, 1982: 30–55.
10. Dennis, M., Capacity and strategy for syntactic comprehension after left or right hemidecortication. *Brain Lang.*, 1980, 10: 287–317.
11. Eccles, J. C., Mental dualism and commissurotomy. *Behav. Brain Sci.*, 1981, 4: 105.
12. Emmorey, K., Linguistic prosodic abilities of left and right hemisphere damaged adults. Paper presented at the 22nd Annual Meeting of the Academy of Aphasia, Los Angeles, October 30, 1984.
13. Giurgea, C. E., and Moyersoons, F., Contribution à l'étude électrophysiologique et pharmacologique de la transmission calleuse. In: *Les Syndromes de Disconnexion Calleuse chez l'Homme* (F. Michel and B. Schott, Eds.). Hôpital Neurologique, Lyon, 1975: 53–72.

14. Grossman, M., Reversal operations after brain damage. *Brain and Cognition*, 1982, **1**: 331–359.

15. Halstead, W. C., *Brain and Intelligence*. University of Chicago Press, Chicago, 1947.

16. Hardyck, C., and Haapanen, R., Educating both halves of the brain: Educational breakthrough or neuromythology? *J. School Psychol.*, 1979, **17**: 219–230.

17. Hartnett, D., The relation of cognitive style and hemisphere preference to deductive and inductive second language learning. Paper presented at the UCLA Conference on Human Brain Function, Los Angeles, September 27, 1974.

18. Hunt, E., Quote the raven? Nevermore! In: *Knowledge and Cognition* (L. W. Gregg, Ed.). Erlbaum, Hillsdale, N.J., 1974: 129–157.

19. Jones, W. T., World views: Their nature and their function. *Curr. Anthro.*, 1972, **13**: 79–109.

20. Lansdell, H., Intellectual factors and asymmetry of cerebral function. *Catalog of Selected Documents in Psychology*, 1971, **1**: 7.

21. Lansdell, H., A sex difference in effect of temporal lobe neurosurgery on design preference. *Nature*, 1962, **194**: 852–854.

22. Levy, J., Trevarthen, C. B., and Sperry, R. W., Perception of bilateral chimeric figures following hemispheric deconnexion. *Brain*, 1972, **95**: 61–78.

23. Lezak, M. D., *Neuropsychological Assessment*, 2nd ed. Oxford University Press, New York, 1983.

24. MacKay, D. M., and MacKay, V., Explicit dialogue between left and right half-systems of split brains. *Nature*, 1982, **295**: 690–691.

25. Marks, C. E., *Commissurotomy, Consciousness and Unity of Mind*. MIT Press, Cambridge, Mass., 1981.

26. McFie, J., *Assessment of Organic Intellectual Impairment*. Academic Press, London, 1975.

27. McKeever, W. F., and Suberi, M., Parallel but temporally displaced visual half-field metacontrast functions. *Q. J. Exp. Psychol.*, 1974, **26**: 258–265.

28. Moscovitch, M., Information processing and the cerebral hemispheres. In: *Handbook of Behavioral Neurobiology*, Vol. 2, *Neuropsychology* (M. S. Gazzaniga, Ed.). Plenum, New York, 1979. 379–446.

29. Pearl, J., *Heuristics: Intelligent Search Strategies for Computer Problem Solving*. Addison-Wesley, Reading, Mass., 1984.

30. Puccetti, R., The case for mental duality: Evidence from split-brain data and other considerations. *Behav. Brain Sci.*, 1981, **4**: 93–123.

31. Risse, G. L., Cognitive structure in aphasic disorders. Doctoral dissertation, Department of Psychology, State University of New York at Stony Brook, 1976.

32. Royce, J. R., Yendall, L. T., and Bock, C., Factor analytic studies of human brain damage: I. First- and second-order factors and their brain correlates. *Multivariate Behavioral Research*, 1976, **4**: 381–418.

33. Sperry, R. W., *Science and Moral Priority*. Columbia University Press, New York, 1983.

34. Sperry, R. W., Zaidel, E., and Zaidel, D., Self recognition and social awareness in the disconnected minor hemisphere. *Neuropsychologia*, 1979, **17**: 153–166.

35. Tsunoda, T., Functional differences between right- and left-cerebral hemispheres detected by the key-tapping method. *Brain Lang.*, 1975, **2**: 152–170.

36. Van Lancker, D., and Fromkin, V., Hemispheric specialization for pitch and "tone": Evidence from Thai. *J. Phonetics*, 1973, **1**: 101–109.

37. Zaidel, E., Auditory language comprehension in the right hemisphere following cerebral commissurotomy and hemispherectomy: A comparison with child language and aphasia. In: *Language Acquisition and Language Breakdown: Parallels and Divergencies* (A. Caramazza and E. B. Zurif, Eds.). Johns Hopkins University Press, Baltimore, 1978: 229–275.

38. Zaidel, E., Concepts of cerebral dominance in the split brain. In: *Cerebral Correlates of Conscious Experience* (P. A. Buser and A. Rougeul-Buser, Eds.). Elsevier, Amsterdam, 1978: 263–284.

39. Zaidel, E., Hemispheric intelligence: The case of the Raven Progressive Matrices. In: *Intelligence and Learning* (J. P. Das and N. O'Connor, Eds.). Plenum, New York, 1981: 531–551.

40. Zaidel, E., How to live with a double standard. *Caltech Biology Annual Report*, 1977: 212.

41. Zaidel, E., Is the right hemisphere more artistic than the left? *Caltech Biology Annual Report*, 1974: 128.

42. Zaidel, E., Zaidel, D. W., and Sperry, R. W., Left and right intelligence: Case studies of Raven's Progressive Matrices following brain bisection and hemidecortication. *Cortex*, 1981, **17**: 167–186.

43. Zoccolotti, P., and Oltman, P. K., Field dependence and lateralization of verbal and configurational processing. *Cortex*, 1978, **14**: 155–163.

IMPLICATIONS OF HEMISPHERIC DIFFERENCES
FOR LINGUISTICS

VICTORIA A. FROMKIN, PhD
Department of Linguistics

Three long-standing problems of science and philosophy concern the nature of the brain, the nature of human language, and the relationship between the two. This relationship has been assumed for over 2,000 years as is shown in an excellent historical survey by Arbib, Caplan, and Marshall (1). Although platonic and Aristotelian wisdom did not extend to a recognition that the brain was the seat of all cognition and knowledge (1, 5, 24), one of the Hippocratic treatises suggests this basic connection. Gall's support for this view was first violently rejected (19), but he finally "convinced the scientific community that 'the brain is the organ of the mind'" (30). A pervasive reason, then, for studying language has been the historic assumption that language is a "mirror of the mind" or that "Speech is the only window through which the physiologist can view the cerebral life," as was suggested by Fournier in 1887.

In more recent years, a reason parallel to the aim of studying language as a means to increase our understanding of the mind or brain is that a study of the brain may provide insights into the nature of human language. The human brain seems to be uniquely suited for the acquisition and use of language. As noted by Geschwind (10), "The nervous systems of all animals have a number of basic functions in common, most notably the control of movement and the analysis of sensation. What distinguishes the human brain is the variety of more specialized activities it is capable of learning. *The preeminent example is language*" (my italics). Thus, it is hoped that further knowledge of the functional anatomy and neurology of the brain may provide new knowledge on the structure, acquisition, and use of language.

UNIVERSALS OF LANGUAGE

The quotation from Fournier refers to "speech," since there has been a persistent, though incorrect, view that equates speech with language. Speech (production and perception) is behavior, the use or performance of those who know a *spoken* language. Language is the abstract mental cognitive system that permits one to speak and understand. Language also underlies the ability of a deaf person to "sign" and to visually perceive and understand the gestures of a signing person. To equate speech with language is to obscure the nature of the linguistic systems that form the bases for all spoken languages and for all the sign languages used by communities of deaf persons throughout the world. As long as researchers concerned themselves only with spoken languages, there was no way to separate what is essential to the linguistic cognitive system from the constraints imposed, productively and perceptually, by the auditory–vocal modality; that is, to discover the genetically, biologically determined linguistic ability of the human brain. We now know, through the work of linguists conducting research on these sign languages (15), that their basic similarities to spoken languages are greater than their differences; that they are subject to the same constraints on their structures; and that they relate forms and meanings by means of the same kinds of rules. These findings therefore suggest that the human brain is organically equipped for language in any modality, and that the kinds of languages that can be acquired are not determined by the motor or perceptual systems but by higher-order brain mechanisms.

If this is so, then one can seek and find language universals that pertain to all human languages — a view accepted by Roger Bacon in the 13th century, when he wrote: "He that understands grammar in one language, understands it in another as far as the essential properties of grammar are concerned. The fact that he can't speak, nor comprehend, another language is due to . . . the accidental properties of grammar." While these accidental properties may prevent a speaker of Xhosa from understanding a speaker of Potowatamie, or a user of American Sign Language (ASL) from understanding a signer of Chinese Sign Language, Bacon was correct in that the more we look at all human languages the more they appear to be governed by the same universal principles and constraints, thereby supporting the view that the human brain seems to be uniquely suited for the acquisition and use of any language to which the child is exposed. Both sighted hearing and deaf children can learn sign language; the reason deaf children cannot learn spoken languages with ease is because they receive no auditory input. It is not the language ability that is lacking, since deaf children have intact brains. It is therefore not surprising that deaf signers with damage to the left hemisphere show aphasia for sign language similar to the language breakdown in hearing aphasics (2, 16, 21, 22). What is equally interesting is that the language impairments of these patients contrast markedly with their relatively intact capacities to process nonlanguage visual–spatial relationships, further enforcing the fact that the left hemisphere has an innate predisposition for language (not speech or the physical ways in which language is expressed).

THE UNIQUENESS OF HUMAN LANGUAGE

The view that the human brain is uniquely suited for the acquisition and use of language has been reinforced by the many attempts to teach language to other primates (25, 26, 27). While these studies seem to show that chimps and gorillas have greater nonlinguistic cognitive abilities than previously thought, their nonhuman brains appear unable to acquire even the vocabulary of signs, let alone the complexities of other parts of language equal to that of a 3-year-old child.

There are a number of empirical facts supporting the notion that the human brain is prewired for language.

All "Natural" Languages Can Be Learned

A child, regardless of race, economic status, geographical location, climate, religion, or size, can acquire any language to which he or she is exposed. No language — spoken or signed — used in the community in which the child is born and raised is too difficult for the child to learn. No special talents or skills are needed. Highly intelligent children (even geniuses) do not acquire language earlier or more completely or more easily than do children on the lower scale of intelligence (however measured). In fact, children diagnosed at birth as mentally retarded acquire language in the same way (see below) as those with normal intelligence (7, 8, 29). The human brain, as a language device, is very robust.

Children Do Not Need to Be Taught Language

Not only can a child learn any of the thousands of languages that exist in the world, he or she does so without being overtly taught.

No one teaches a child learning English, or ASL, or Swedish, or Yoruba, or Twi the specific rules by which an infinite set of sentences never previously spoken or signed or heard can be produced and understood. Yet by the age of 3 or 4 a child has this ability. For example, no one teaches a child learning English that to form the plural of words like "cow," "bee," "dog," or "head" one adds a "z" sound at the end of the singular form (not an "s," which is the way the regular plural form is spelled).* Nor does anyone overtly teach the child to add an /s/ to form plurals of "cat," "tack," or "nap." The child's brain is equipped to permit him or her to "construct" these rules — to group the sounds that are followed by a plural /z/, those that are followed by the plural /s/, and those that end the words "box," "match," or "judge," which require a short vowel followed by /z/ to form "boxes," "matches," or "judges." When children make mistakes on these plurals — e.g., "mouses," "childs" — the process of rule construction is clearly revealed, since the children cannot be simply imitating what they hear; children produce such errors even if they receive only the correct or standard forms as input. Similarly, no one teaches the child the rules which tell him or her that the following sentences have multiple meanings (i.e., are ambiguous).

1. Ronnie wanted the presidency more than Nancy.
2. Mr. Magoo made his wife turn on the barbecue spit.
3. The police were ordered to stop drinking after midnight.

Furthermore, a child hearing sentences 4 and 5 knows that in 4 it is John who would be going, whereas in 5 Bill would be the one to go (if he did what he was told).

4. John promised Bill to go.
5. John told Bill to go.

---

*To distinguish the sound from the letter, I will put the sound unit between slashes (e.g., /z/).

No theory of learning by imitation or reinforcement can account for the child's learning the rules to account for this. The child, at a very young age, appears to have the ability to construct the rules of the grammar in addition to learning the forms and meanings of words, since the meaning of such sentences depends on more than the meaning of the words. This ability is not simply due to a knowledge of serial order. Such knowledge of serial-order constraints might explain how we know that in 6 it was Arthur who did the loving, whereas in 7 it was Guinevere.

6. Arthur loved Guinevere.
7. Guinevere loved Lancelot.

Simple knowledge of serial order, however, cannot account for the fact that in sentence 8 Guinevere was not the loving one.

8. It is Guinevere who was loved by Arthur.

The brain is equipped to deal with serial order, and it appears to be the left cerebral cortex that is responsible for this ability, but this in itself cannot account for the kind of knowledge required to acquire and process the complex syntactic rules that are used to decode sentences such as those above, or the infinite set of sentences our knowledge permits us to produce and understand.

The brain appears to be specifically equipped for this task, rather than for abilities that language may share with other cognitive systems.

Universal Stages of Language Acquisition

Further evidence illustrating the particular language-learning characteristics of the brain is provided by the more or less universal stages of language acquisition. That is, the complexity of the grammar acquired at different stages, the sequence of sounds that are learned, the kinds of word order rules, or the morphological endings in languages as different as Turkish, English, and Russian are shown to be amazingly similar (13, 14, 17, 23). As the brain matures, so does the complexity of the language.

Language as Independent of Other Cognitive Systems

As stated above, these prewired language learning abilities of the human brain appear to be independent of other cerebral abilities. This is not to deny that when we use our knowledge of language in speaking and understanding, we also depend on nonlinguistic systems and general knowledge of the world. But language can be learned independently of other cognitive systems. Thus, for example, children who have no difficulty in learning to speak and understand may have serious developmental dyslexia preventing them from learning to read and write, or learning simple rules of arithmetic. The same child who knows that in sentence 9, John did not necessarily show a baby anything, whereas in 10 he did, may be unable to learn that if $x = 2y$, then $y = \frac{1}{2}x$.

    9. John showed the baby picture.
  10. John showed the baby the picture.

Yet it may well be that this algebraic rule is simpler than the syntactic rules that are used to decode the two sentences.

There are a number of case studies of children and adults severely mentally retarded from birth who display complex linguistic ability but are unable to learn other cognitive systems (6, 7, 8, 9, 29). Marta, a young woman described by Yamada (29), produces utterances like the following:

  11. "She does paintings, this really good friend of the kids who I went to school with last year and really loved."
  12. "Last year at [name of school] when I first went there, three tickets werc gave out by a police last year."

These utterances were spoken by someone who cannot add 2 + 2. Marta is not quite sure of when "last year" is or how many tickets were "gave" out and does not know whether 3 is larger or smaller than 2, but the structure of her sentences reveal a sophistication in syntax far greater than one would expect from someone with her deficient general cognitive knowledge.

Thus, the human brain appears to be organized in a modular fashion, with specific cognitive systems that can be acquired and disturbed independently of one another.

LINGUISTICS AND THE NEUROSCIENCES

We have come a long way in the past several decades in understanding the brain; similarly, we have come a long way in understanding the structure of human language. Of course, we are still far from reaching our goals. This is hardly surprising, given the complexities of both phenomena. A question of interest is whether the increased understanding of these two phenomena has led to a greater understanding of their relationship. Marshall (18) has stated the problem extremely well:

Biologists . . . have accumulated a vast body of knowledge concerning the gross anatomy of those parts of the central and peripheral nervous system which seem to be implicated in the acquisition and exercise of linguistic abilities. Some knowledge is even available about the slightly less gross physiology of the relevant brain areas. . . . [In addition] developmental psycholinguists . . . have amassed alarming amounts of data of the progression from the birth cry to the multiply embedded relative clause. The problem is . . . found in the simple fact that no one . . . has the slightest idea how to relate these two domains of inquiry to each other. . . . We have so far failed . . . to construct functional process models (that is, psychological [or linguistic] theories) that could mediate between noun phrases and neurones.

Why, then, should studies of the brain be of interest to linguists and studies of language be of interest to neurologists, biologists, neuropsychologists, or neuroanatomists?

Linguists are increasingly interested in the converging evidence that focal damage to the left cerebral hemisphere does not lead to an across-the-board reduction in language ability, and that lesions in different locations in the left hemisphere are selective in the language disorders that result. The chapters in this volume reveal a remarkable consistency in how such brain damage affects language or language processing. It is, however, an empirical question as to whether the parts of the language system that are impaired parallel the separate components of grammars posited by linguistic theories. If this is shown to be the case, such findings are important as further support for theories of language, and as a first step in bridging the gap between brain and linguistic mechanisms.

Linguistic knowledge, like all knowledge, is represented in the mind and brain. Linguists are concerned with the nature of this representation, including answers to questions such as: How is the grammar organized? What features of the grammar are universal and relate to all human languages? What are the basic units of language and the basic components of the grammar? Are these independent of each other? Are, for example, syntactic rules of sentence formation independent of rules of semantics, which provide the meanings of these sentences? How do the phonological representations and rules (pronunciation specification) of vocabulary or lexical items relate to their orthographical representations (i.e., their spelling)?

Since Broca, there has accumulated, through studies of aphasia and by means of new technologies and experimental methods (such as dichotic listening, EEGs, ERPs, tachistoscopic studies, blood flow studies, etc.), increasing evidence to support models and theories of generative grammar developed by linguists on the basis of their studies of languages themselves. The linguists argue that knowledge of a language is represented by an autonomous formal grammar, finite in size and capable of generating an infinite set of sentences. This grammar consists of various components—that is, the phonology (sound system), the syntax (rules of sentence formation), the morphology (word structure), the vocabulary or lexicon, and those aspects of meaning determined by syntactic configuration. These components "form a structural system whose primitive terms are not artifacts of a system that encompasses both human language and other human facilities or abilities" (19).

The differential and selective breakdown of different parts of language as seen in aphasia studies, as well as data that show, for example, differential recruitment of localized brain areas depending on the kinds of linguistic input or tasks, provide independent evidence for the autonomy of the components in linguists' grammars.

The fact that it is not the perceptual or motor system per se that is affected, but only the linguistic aspects of these systems, further supports the separation of linguistic knowledge from general behavior, and from other cognitive systems. Over 20 years ago, Tissot, Lhermitte, and Ducarne (28) and Zangwill (31) reported on cases of aphasia patients who appeared to have retained general cognitive ability despite severe language loss. Similarly, Gleason et al. (12) discuss the ability of some patients to use alternative syntactic means that preserve the meanings of sentences, but that avoid the structures that are difficult for them. A particularly cogent example of the asymmetry of cognitive loss is provided by Zurif (32): Two Broca's aphasics were unable to use the definite article correctly, but showed no loss of the concept of definiteness.

Newmeyer (20), in arguing for the independence of specifically *grammatical* abilities from other mental systems, summarizes the results of many studies. Curtiss (6) summarizes supporting evidence particularly in relation to child development.

There is also support from many studies to show that linguistic prosody (e.g., intonation and stress contrasts), which distinguishes sentence 13 from 14, 15 from 16, and 17 from 18, can be destroyed, while the ability to comprehend nonlinguistic or affective prosody can be retained, and vice versa.

13. John loved Mary.
14. John loved Mary?
15. John hit Bill and then *he* hit Max.
16. John hit Bill and then he hit *Max*.
17. Mary had a red *coat* in her closet.
18. Mary had a *red* coat in her closet.

These studies have not necessarily provided new insights into language structure, but they have supported (and in some cases may decide between) alternative linguistic hypotheses. On the other hand, linguistics has had an enormous influence on studies concerned with the nature of the brain. The neurologist *cum* linguist Caplan (3) has stated that

> the most significant steps towards the clarification of the nature of neurolinguistic theory and towards the actual development of theories in this field, have resulted from the introduction of concepts from linguistics . . . into the study of language disturbances. . . . [T]he character of inquiry in linguistics . . . and the specific hypotheses of Transformational Generative grammar regarding levels of representation in the "language code" are relevant to the study of neural mechanisms underlying language and of organically occasioned disorders of language.

Linguistics raises questions for the neurologist and the brain researcher. Early linguistic tests used with aphasia patients to determine language production and perception often depended solely on isolated words and phrases; today aphasic studies are very sophisticated. Tests to determine differential abilities of patients with different lesion sites to produce or understand syntactic subtleties, such as subcategorization constraints versus semantic contrasts, grammatical versus ungrammatical sentences, or different processing of open- and closed-class lexicons by different groups of patients, may lead to new diagnostic tools. The results of such tests also lead to an increased understanding of brain functions.

Modern linguistics provides detailed descriptions of the linguistic units, rules, and components that can be used in brain studies. An understanding of these autonomous parts of the grammar, including the rules of pronunciation, word and sentence formation, and interpretive rules of semantics, is crucial in separating out the linguistic capabilities of the brain from other cognitive abilities. It is also crucial to an understanding of the role of both hemispheres in the processing of both language and nonlanguage. It should lead to greater knowledge of how these complex systems interact with each other and with the world, and how the left and right cerebral hemispheres store (represent) and process linguistic and nonlinguistic knowledge. Research on the brain and on human language will, we hope, one day make it possible for us to relate "noun phrases and neurones" and understand the major brain mechanisms underlying language, its acquisition, and its use.

REFERENCES

1. Arbib, M. A., Caplan, D., and Marshall, J. C., Neurolinguistics in historical perspective. In: *Neural Models of Language Processes* (M. A. Arbib, D. Caplan, and J. C. Marshall, Eds.). Academic Press, New York, 1982: 5–24.
2. Bellugi, U., Poizner, H., and Klima, E. S., Brain organization for language: Clues from sign aphasia. *Human Dev.* (Special issue, D. Kimura, Ed.), 1983, 2: 155–170.
3. Caplan, D., Prospects for neurolinguistic theory. *Cognition*, 1981, 10: 59–64.
4. Chomsky, N., *Language and Mind*, enlarged ed. Harcourt Brace Jovanovich, New York, 1972.
5. Clarke, E., and O'Malley, K., *The Human Brain and Spinal Cord: A Historical Study Illustrated by Writings from Antiquity to the 20th Century*. University of California Press, Berkeley, 1968.
6. Curtiss, S., Language as a cognitive system: Its independence and selective vulnerability. In: *Developmental Placticity: Social Context and Human Development* (E. S. Gollin, Ed.). Academic Press, New York, in press.
7. Curtiss, S., Kempler, D., and Yamada, J., The relationship between language and cognition in development: Theoretical framework and research design. *UCLA Working Papers in Cognitive Linguistics*, 1981, 3: 161–175.
8. Curtiss, S., and Yamada, J., Selectively intact grammatical development in a retarded child. *UCLA Working Papers in Cognitive Linguistics*, 1981, 3: 61–91.
9. Curtiss, S., Yamada, J., and Fromkin, V., How independent is language? On the question of formal parallels between grammar and action. *UCLA Working Papers in Cognitive Linguistics*, 1979, 1: 131–157.
10. Geschwind, N., Specializations of the human brain. *Sci. Am.*, 1979, 206: 180–199.
11. Glass, A., Gazzaniga, M., and Premack, D., Artificial language training in global aphasics. *Neuropsychologia*, 1973, 11: 95–103.
12. Gleason, J. B., Goodglass, H., Green, E., Acherman, N., and Hyde, M. R., The retrieval of syntax in Broca's aphasia. *Brain Lang.*, 1975, 2: 451–71.
13. Gleitman, L., Maturational determinants of language growth. *Cognition*, 1981, 10: 103–114.
14. Karmiloff-Smith, A., The interplay between syntax, semantics, and phonology in language acquisition processes. In: *Recent Advances in the Psychology of Language* (R. N. Campbell and P. T. Smith, Eds.). Plenum Press, New York, 1978: 1–23.
15. Klima, E. S., and Bellugi, U., *The Signs of Language*. Harvard University Press, Cambridge, Mass, 1979.

16. Klima, E. S., Poizner, H., and Bellugi, U., What the hands reveal about the brain: Evidence from American Sign Language. Unpublished manuscript.

17. Levelt, W. J. M., Sinclair, A., and Jarvella, R. J., Causes and functions of linguistic awareness in language acquisition: some introductory remarks. In: *The Child's Conception of Language* (A. Sinclair, R. J. Jarvella, and W. J. M. Levelt, Eds.). Springer-Verlag, Berlin, 1978: 1–14.

18. Marshall, J. C., On the biology of language acquisition. In: *Biological Studies of Mental Processes* (D. Caplan, Ed.). MIT Press, Cambridge, Mass., 1980: 106–148.

19. Marshall, J. C., The new organology. *Behav. Brain Sci.*, 1980, 3: 23–25.

20. Newmeyer, F. J., *Grammatical Theory: Its Limits and Its Possibilities*. University of Chicago Press, Chicago, 1983.

21. Poizner, H., Bellugi, U., and Iragui, V., Apraxia and aphasia in a visual–gestural language. *Am. J. Physiol.*, in press.

22. Poizner, H., Kaplan, E., Bellugi, U., and Padden, C., Hemispheric specialization for nonlinguistic visual–spatial processing in brain damaged signers. *Brain Cog.*, in press.

23. Popova, M., Grammatical elements of speech of preschool children. In: *Studies of Child Language Development* (D. I. Slobin and C. A. Ferguson, Eds.). Holt, Rinehart & Winston, New York, 1973: 269–280.

24. Riese, W., The early history of aphasia. *Bull. Hist. Med.*, 1964, **21**: 322–334.

25. Saidenberg, M. S., and Petitto, L. A., Signing behavior in apes: A critical review. *Cognition*, 1979, **7**: 177–215.

26. Sebeok, T. A., and Umiker-Sebeok, J., *Speaking of Apes: A Two Way Communication with Man*. Plenum Press, New York, 1980.

27. Terrace, II. S., *Nim: A Chimpanzee Who Learned Sign Language*. Knopf, New York, 1979.

28. Tissot, R., Lhermitte, F., and Ducarne, B., État intellectuel des aphasiques. *l'Encephale*, 1963, **52**: 285–320.

29. Yamada, J., The independence of language: A case study. Doctoral dissertation, University of California at Los Angeles, 1983.

30. Young, E. M., *Mind, Brain, and Adaptation in the Nineteenth Century*. Clarendon Press, Oxford, 1970.

31. Zangwill, O. L., Intelligence in aphasia. In: *Disorders of Language* (A. V. S. de Reuck and M. O'Connor, Eds.). Churchill Livingstone, London, 1964: 261–274.

32. Zurif, E., and Blumstein, S., Language and the brain. In: *Linguistic Theory and Psychological Reality* (M. Halle, J. Bresnan, and G. Miller, Eds.). MIT Press, Cambridge, Mass., 1978: 229–246.

EDUCATION AND RECENT NEUROPSYCHOLOGICAL AND COGNITIVE RESEARCH

M. C. WITTROCK, PhD
Department of Education

INTRODUCTION

The development of relations between education and knowledge about cognitive and neural processes is an ancient and delicate art that has influenced teaching since antiquity. In Aristotle's model of the cognitive processes of memory and recollection (2), imagery was the basis for storing or remembering information, and serially ordered associations among images were the bases for recollecting or retrieving information from memory. In ancient Greece and Rome, students, teachers, orators, and statesmen were regularly taught imagery mnemonics to use to remember or recall information when they were giving speeches or taking examinations. Together, Aristotle's basic model of memory and recollection and the applied ancient imagery mnemonics comprised the "ancient art of memory."

The ancient art of memory continued to influence teaching, and perhaps the design and pedagogical use of artwork in educational and religious buildings, such as medieval cathedrals, for nearly two millennia. Paintings, statues, friezes, tapestries, and other art forms, including the writing of stories and parables using vivid imagery, portrayed abstract concepts taught in school and in church in concrete and memorable forms to people, many of whom were illiterate or marginally literate (33). The historian Frances Yates (36) discusses these issues further. Remnants of this ancient art of memory survive in the 20th century outside the interest of most teachers, in a few courses and books on memory training.

Until the last decade or two, much of American pedagogy has relied in large part on a 20th-century behavioristic model of learning that emphasized E. L. Thorndike's theory of stimulus–response (S-R) connections. In this model, neural connections were strengthened between stimuli and responses by repeated, reinforced practice. B. F. Skinner refined the model, incorporated Pavlovian conditioning, and applied it broadly to classroom teaching and to animal learning. Although the fomulation of associations was again the essence of the S-R behavioristic model, as it was for Aristotle, now the associations were between environmental stimuli and behavioral responses, not among serially ordered images. Gone also in this behavioristic model were the concepts of memory, attention, and knowledge acquisition.

Within the last one or two decades, the recent neuropsychological research on the brain, human cognitive and affective thought processes, artificial intelligence, and language has produced findings and models that refine early 20th-century approaches to learning and teaching, and that renew the ancient interest in the study of cognition, its neural substrates, and its educational implications.

The recent neural and cognitive research promises fundamental knowledge about the mental processes involved in areas of interest to educational researchers and teachers such as knowledge acquisition, attention, learning disabilities, and mental retardation. Educational researchers and teachers want to know the cognitive processes people use to comprehend information. Do they use a spatial and holistic process, a verbal–analytic process, to make sense out of instruction? What information-processing strategies do they use to comprehend, remember, and recall information? How can we stimulate these processes to facilitate meaningful learning? They would also like to know and be able to measure how people differ from one another in these processes, so that they can better design and individualize teaching for them.

To follow this reasoning further, as a researcher and a teacher, I would like to know about the mechanisms and processes learners use to attend to information, to select it, and to relate it to their knowledge store. More broadly, I would like to know about and to understand the neural and cognitive processes and strategies used by the brain and the mind to learn, to acquire, and to use knowledge to direct behavior. At the very least, this knowledge would put useful limits on the models and the teaching procedures I devise. More importantly, this scientific knowledge would increase my understanding of human learning and facilitate the development of useful and effective educational pedagogical practices.

In the following sections of this chapter, I will discuss some of the findings of recent cognitive and neural research pertaining to knowledge acquisition, attention, and related areas. Before beginning these discussions, I want to indicate two fundamental concepts that underlie the discussions that follow. The first fundamental assumption is that teaching and instruction can be improved by understanding the cognitive and neural processes of learners and teachers. That seemingly innocuous and common-sense statement has far-reaching implications for revising paradigms of educational research. The second fundamental concept underlying the following discussions is the hypothesis that the brain is an active generator of models, explanations, and knowledge. It is more than a passive recorder of associations among stimuli and responses. It selectively attends to information, relates it to stored knowledge, and generates interpretations that go well beyond the qualities associated with the stimuli. Rather than being an organ that processes stimuli into responses, the brain actively selects and perceives information, interprets it, and generates signals (electronic impulses and chemicals) that produce and control behavior appropriate for the perceived context and effective for attaining goals or ends. The constructed perception of the situation and the generation of effective strategies for adapting behavior are characteristics of the brain and mind that have implications for revising paradigms of educational research, for designing instruction, and for understanding learning from teaching.

A word of caution is needed before beginning the discussion of education and its relation to recent cognitive and neural research. Neural research, cognitive research, and educational research each represent distinctly different levels of related phenomena. Any one of these three levels provides a different set of problems and contexts than does any other level. Knowledge about the brain gives us hypotheses about cognitive processes, but it does not substitute for or replace the need for psychological research. Neither does neural research tell us directly about, or give us "implications" about, teaching methods or curricular innovations. Instead, research from different levels of related phenomena, such as neural, cognitive, and educational research on learning strategies, can lead to an understanding or theory from which hypotheses about teaching and learning can be derived and tested. But findings of neural research cannot be equated to or extrapolated to educational phenomena, and pedagogical problems cannot be reduced to findings of neural research. Taken in relation to one another — that is, by juxtaposing neural, cognitive, and educational research and by looking for complementary findings — cognitive and neural science can provide an understanding of learners' thought processes that contributes to knowledge about learning from instruction and teaching. From this knowledge can come new hypotheses, models, and studies about teaching and instruction.

RESEARCH ON ATTENTION

An important part of recent neural and cognitive research has studied the tonic and phasic arousal and attentional processes in the limbic system, brain stem, and frontal lobes. McGuinness and Pribram (20) present a model of the neuropsychology of attention. Stuss and Benson (27) summarize the current state of knowledge about attentional processes in the frontal lobes.

The recent research on attention indicates that a variety of types of attention exist, including phasic and tonic attention, voluntary and involuntary attention, and selective attention. In several studies at UCLA, Krupski (17) found that learning-disabled and some mentally retarded children showed deficits in voluntary, sustained attention tasks in school, but not in voluntary, short-term attention. Mentally retarded children 9–12 years old were more distractable (16) than were other children, again only in academic settings. One implication that follows from these studies is that a cognitive remedial attentional training program might be effective with some of these children. The reason is that since only voluntary, sustained attention in school settings seems to be implicated in the attentional problem, a cognitive strategy could help to alleviate the attentional component of the problem.

Hallahan and Reeve (13) summarize years of research on children's ability to recall relevant and incidental information. The normal course of development shows a general increase from ages 5 to 15 years in ability to recall relevant information, but with no or little increase in ability to recall incidental information. However, learning-disabled children showed a 2- to 3-year lag in ability to selectively attend to and learn serial memory tasks. Again, attentional and rehearsal strategies might be useful for remediating this lag in the development of attention.

Attentional strategies have been developed and successfully used to remediate some cases of hyperkinetic behavior in children. Hyperkinetic activity may involve a lack of selective attention (4). Douglas *et al.* (11) developed a remedial cognitive training program to teach 7- and 8-year-old hyperactive children to control their impulsive behavior and to attend selectively to tasks. The program, administered over 2 to 3 months, produced gains on the Matching Familiar Figures Test and on measures of organization, planning, and reading achievement. Camp (6) shows related findings with impulsive and aggressive children taught a simple "Think Aloud" program that asks them to say to themselves, (1) "What is my problem?" (2) "How shall I do it?" (3) "Am I following my plan?" (4) "How did I do?" The program produced gains on the Wechsler Intelligence Scale for Children, on a reading achievement test, and on ratings of interpersonal behavior.

These studies indicate one type of educational implication following from neural and cognitive research on attention. The research presents a useful model relevant for looking at learning disabilities or hyperkinetic behavior. The model suggests a different way to conceptualize the problem — in this case as one involving sustained, voluntary attention. The studies that followed from the model led to some progress in teaching young children strategies to use to control (somewhat, at least) their thoughts and behavior, resulting in improved performance in social behavior and in school learning. (See 8 for further discussion of attention and learning disabilities.)

Attentional hypotheses have also resulted in a reconceptionalization of several fundamental concepts in teaching and instruction. Time on task or time to learn has for many years been considered a fundamental variable in explaining classroom learning. Recently, however, several people have studied attention and time to learn. Peterson and Swing (24), for example, found that measures of attention correlated more highly with learning than did measures of time on task.

Brophy (5) summarized a number of studies on rewards given to students in class by teachers. The usual explanation given for these findings was that a reward served as a reinforcer, strengthening the connection between the stimulus or question and the response or answer. However, Brophy concluded that rewards probably cannot and do not work in this fashion. They are given only to some students, and at most, a few times per class, which is not frequent enough to produce learning according to a reinforcement model. Yet many students, including those not rewarded, learn from rewards. He concluded that a reward enhances learning by directing student attention to the material or behavior wanted by the teacher. The students learn by observing the rewarded student and by attending to the type of learning valued by the teacher. The centrally important concept of reinforcement is still useful, but the attentional model gives an understanding of one of the important functions it provides in the classroom.

Wittrock and Lumsdaine (35) applied an attentional model to some of the data on behavioral objectives originally interpreted to facilitate teaching by giving the teacher precise criteria for deciding when to give reinforcement for correct responses.

In the recent literature, behavioral objectives given to learners seem to function by directing their attention toward the concepts considered most important by the teacher.

Wittrock and Lumsdaine (35) also applied an attentional model to the recent data regarding the facilitation of learning produced by questions inserted between paragraphs in text. Instead of providing the occasion for review and rewards, questions inserted in a text seem to direct attention and information processing. Andre (1) reviewed these studies and reached a similar conclusion, although he believes that attention may not be the only cognitive process stimulated by the questions.

Attentional hypotheses, growing in large part from the recent resurgence of interest in neural and cognitive processes, have contributed in fundamentally important ways to the conceptualization and understanding of learning disabilities, hyperactivity, time on task, rewards, behavioral objectives, and inserted questions. In each case, the introduction of a cognitive and neural process has led to testable hypotheses about learning and teaching; the tests of these hypotheses have produced interesting data that have refined our understanding of basic concepts in educational research.

Other cognitive science findings about attentional mechanisms deserve study in future educational research. One of these findings in cognitive science is that the brain has several attentional mechanisms, including a short-term involuntary component that responds to sudden changes in stimuli, to unanticipated events. Reinforced practice, which usually leads to highly predictable outcomes in easy tasks, may not stimulate this attentional mechanism and may lead to boredom and disinterest. Discrepant information, surprises, and unexpected outcomes might better stimulate interest, providing they are not anxiety-arousing. The possibility deserves further study.

Hemispheric differences in the control of attention have also been studied in several experiments. Warm *et al.* (28) used an auditory task to study hemispheric differences in sustained attention. Over the 80-minute attention interval they studied, the right hemisphere showed quick initial but slow subsequent response times in the detection of infrequent signals. The left hemisphere showed slow initial response times, which did not increase across the 80-minute interval. On the other hand, Dimond and Beaumont (9), studying hemispheric differences in a visual sustained-attention task, found that the left hemisphere produced the greater initial number of correct detections of signals, and also showed the greater reduction in correct detections over time. The right hemisphere showed fewer correct detections initially, but remained constant throughout the study. Although the Dimond and Beaumont (9) and Warm *et al.* (28) studies differ in the specific attentional role they assign to each hemisphere, they agree in finding marked hemispheric differences in sustained-attention tasks.

Hemispheric differences also occur in attention to novel stimuli. Goldberg and Costa (12) found that the right hemisphere processes novel stimuli and integrates intermodal and degraded information better than does the left hemisphere, which better processes unimodal stimuli and stores familiar codes. The right hemisphere, then, seems to play an important role in the early stages of processing new information, while the left hemisphere plays an important role in later stages of processing, or in the encoding of familiar information.

Hemispheric differences occur in disorders of attention as well. The right hemisphere is more involved than the left hemisphere in global disorders of attention, particularly of neglect of the contralateral visual half-field (14).

These results on hemispheric differences in attention indicate the specialization of the hemispheres in the mediation of attention. For educational theory, they imply that the control of attention involves understanding the different roles that hemispheric processes play in attending to a variety of short-term and sustained, novel and familiar tasks.

RESEARCH ON KNOWLEDGE ACQUISITION

The recent findings about the cognitive processes involved in knowledge acquisition, memory, and retrieval are leading to new models and empirical studies in educational research (25). From separate lines of work, neural and cognitive research converges upon several cognitive processes that seem to be involved in learning, memory, and knowledge acquisition. The dramatic and popular findings about the hemispheric processes of the brain showed that information could be learned and understood using two different systems: a verbal–analytic system appropriate for propositional and sequential analyses, and a spatial–holistic system appropriate for imagery and for appositional synthesis. From research on cognitive psychology (e.g., 23), dual-coding models of encoding and memory presented closely related conceptions of information processing. Both the neural models and the cognitive psychological models seemed to many educational researchers not totally unlike two-factor models of intelligence that distinguish verbal and spatial processes. Actually, the neural and cognitive models differ substantially from the factor-analytic models and focus upon the type of processing that occurs, more than upon the type of stimuli that are processed.

These models of cognitive processing, especially the models of hemispheric processes, have recently led to a widespread interest in the study of knowledge acquisition, memory, and learning. It is not useful to try to relate the following studies to either the neural or the cognitive models. Instead, the research seems to derive predictions from different specific models, all of which focus on the transformations learners perform when they encode, remember, or acquire knowledge. Only a few of these studies can be mentioned here to illustrate the educational implications of these cognitive and neural models.

Bower and Clark (3) taught college students to remember an ordered list of words by putting them into a story. This simple teaching device enhanced memory of the ordered list of words from 20% to about 90%.

Pressley (26) enhanced story comprehension and memory by teaching children to form mental images of the sentences to be remembered. In other studies, imagery mnemonics, usually fashioned after the ancient imagery techniques discussed earlier, have frequently been used and found to enhance memory and sometimes comprehension among children 9 years of age and older (see 18 for further discussion). When they are effective, the imagery techniques usually focus on teaching the learners to construct interactive images — that is, images that show relations among the parts of the story or among its characters. The image seems to juxtapose and organize the parts of the characters into a memorable whole.

Doctorow *et al.* (10) taught children to compose summaries for each paragraph of a story they read. Across all ability levels and stories, the generation of summaries approximately doubled comprehension and retention in the 450 students in the study who were randomly assigned to the treatments. (See 32 for a model of reading comprehension based on these and related findings.)

In a recently completed study, Wittrock and Alesandrini (34) asked students to read a chapter with high-imagery text from Rachel Carson's book *The Sea Around Us*, generating images in one condition, verbal analogies in another condition, and both (summaries) in a third condition. A measure of spatial–holistic processing, the Street Test, correlated positively with performance in the imagery group, and a measure of verbal–analytic processing, the Similarities subscale of the Wechsler test, correlated positively with learning in the group generating verbal analogies. Both of these measures correlated positively with learning in the group that performed both processes. The summaries treatment and the verbal-analogies treatment each increased retention when compared to the imagery group.

Linden and Wittrock (19) randomly assigned fourth-graders to four different groups. The first two of the four groups were taught to generate verbal and spatial elaborations as they read the stories in their textbooks. The third group was taught by the same teacher using the same stories, but with no instruction or practice on generating verbal or spatial elaborations as they read. The fourth group of students was taught by the regular fourth-grade teacher, using any method she chose. The two generative-teaching conditions enhanced reading comprehension to a mean of 28.6 or higher from a mean of 17.7 for the control group and a mean of 21 for the students' regular teacher. Both mean differences were statistically significant at the .01 level, and the time to learn was held constant across all four groups. The results imply that if the verbal and imaginal thought processes of children are stimulated as they read, their comprehension and retention can be improved with no increase in time to learn. The results also imply that at least some children do not spontaneously use these learning strategies to their best advantage, but that they can be taught to use them effectively. These findings do not test or prove the cognitive and neural models discussed earlier. But they do show some utility of the models for deriving useful and testable implications for classroom teaching.

RELATIONS BETWEEN EDUCATION AND NEURAL AND COGNITIVE SCIENCES

In the preceding sections of this chapter, I have discussed relations between educational research and recent findings about the brain and cognition in two areas: attention and knowledge acquisition. From the research on attentional mechanisms, it seems clear that there are several attentional processes — short-term and long-term, voluntary and involuntary — that mediate and help to explain the effects of questions teachers use in class, objectives they give to students, the correlation between time to learn and amount learned, and even the effects of rewards upon children who observe other children being rewarded in class. An attentional hypothesis explains how these apparently diverse activities may function, at least in part, to mediate learning from teaching. From the recent research on the cognitive processes in knowledge acquisition, it seems likely that people have characteristic analytic and synthetic mechanisms that they use to make sense out of information, to relate it to what they know, and to remember and to understand it. These findings and models have led to recent studies in classroom learning that have taught children to use learning strategies and metacognitive techniques to enhance their memory and their comprehension, often with sizable gains (see 22 and 32 for further discussion).

The recent cognitive and neural research findings and models lead to new ways for examining other difficult and poorly understood educational problems, some of which we have referred to previously. Some cases of hyperactivity seems to involve a long-term voluntary attentional component that occasionally, at least, responds to lengthy and sustained teaching of a metacognitive technique for controlling impulsive behavior. Some learning disabilities and some forms of mental retardation may also be better understood by analysis and measurement of the learners' attentional and knowledge-acquisition processes and learning strategies, and by remedial training that capitalizes on intact functions or remediates deficient and trainable functions. The point is that an understanding of these attentional and learning processes is essential to proper diagnosis and design of effective remedial teaching procedures. Other difficult problems, such as dyslexia, may also become better understood as a result of new knowledge about the perceptual, attentional, and learning strategies involved in reading.

One of the most important areas to profit from the recent models and findings of cognitive and neural science is the study of learning from teaching, including how it is measured and how instruction is designed to facilitate it. Many of the currently used tests of ability, aptitude, and achievement were not designed to measure the attentional processes or strategies learners use to acquire knowledge. An IQ test tells little about the strategies people use well or poorly. Achievement tests and aptitude tests also do not focus on cognitive processes relevant to learning. The recent models of cognitive processes lead to a new type of test, one that measures the attentional, encoding, and learning strategies that people use to remember and understand information. Process-oriented tests should be relevant and useful for understanding individual differences in learning relevant to the presentation of information in the classroom. These tests do not measure achievement, but they do measure the cognitive processes children use to learn.

The design of instruction also seems to profit from the study of cognitive strategies of learning and knowledge acquisition. Osborne and Wittrock (22) and Osborne (21) discuss the cognitive strategies and models elementary school children use to understand DC current flow in a simple circuit consisting of a battery, a light bulb, and two connecting wires. About one-third of the children believe that the current flows only from the battery to the bulb, where all or nearly all of it is used. Another third of the children believe that two currents flow in opposite directions, one from each side of the battery. The clash of the two currents causes the light to glow, they believe. About one-third of the students believes the physicist's model of current flow — that it is in one direction, constant in amplitude throughout the circuit.

When instructors insert ammeters into the circuits and show that the current does not flow as the children using the first and second models predict, the nearly universal rebuttal offered by the students in New Zealand, England, and the United States is that their model would work at home (the real world), although in school strange and difficult events do occur that disagree with their model. The students retain their model and discard the teacher's data as being atypical.

It is clear that teaching only the physicist's model of current flow is not likely to result in learning that transfers to situations out of school. Neither is showing discrepant and supposedly attention-arousing data enough to induce learning. We do not yet know how to solve this teaching problem.

However, the main point is that physicists and science teachers are now examining the models and cognitive processes children use to learn science in schools. In addition, they are viewing science teaching as the generation of a new model or perspective from a preconception. The study of neural and cognitive strategies has contributed to the reconceptualization of the teaching of science, I believe, by calling attention to the children's thought processes and previously acquired models.

In mathematics learning during the last decade, especially in the study of addition and subtraction, children's problem-solving strategies are being identified (see 7). Tests to measure the strategies children use to solve mathematics problems are also being developed. Again, the study of students' thought processes in mathematics has grown, in part at least, from the recent research in cognitive science.

SUMMARY

In my model of generative learning (30, 31, 32), I have presented an interpretation of learning with understanding that is consistent with the recent research discussed earlier and that has utility for reconceptualizing teaching and instruction. The essence of the model is that learning is a generative process. The brain uses attentional and encoding processes to select information, to relate it to stored knowledge, and to construct an interpretation of it. The brain is a model builder. One of its central functions is to generate understanding, to make sense out of stimuli and events, to build models that lead to adaptive problem-solving behavior, and that produce useful predictions.

Within this model, teaching involves knowing the students' cognitive processes, strategies, and previously acquired models, as well as knowing the subject matter. Teachers must help students use their attentional processes and learning strategies to revise or improve their model or concept. In this model, learning is the generation of a new or revised model from an older one and from the instruction and directions provided by the teacher.

In sum, neural and cognitive systems of the learner are restored to prominence in recent studies of instruction and learning. Models of educational research that eliminate the neural and cognitive processes of the learner have serious competition now. They are being successfully challenged by new ways to view learning from teaching that date from antiquity and that, like their historical counterparts, emphasize the active, generative role of the learners' thought processes and their neural substrates.

REFERENCES

1. Andre, T., Does answering higher-level questions while reading facilitate productive learning? *Rev. Ed. Res.*, 1979, **49**: 280–318.
2. Aristotle, On memory and recollection. Appendix to: *On the soul (De Anima); Parva naturalia; and On breath* (W. S. Hett, Tr.). Loeb Classical Library, Harvard University Press, Cambridge, Mass., 1964.
3. Bower, G. H., and Clark, M. C., Narrative stories as mediators for serial learning. *Psychonom. Sci.*, 1969, **14**: 181–182.
4. Brenner, D. A., and Stern, J. A., Attention and distractability during reading in hyperactive boys. *J. Abnorm. Child Psychol.*, 1976, **4**: 381–387.
5. Brophy, J. E., Teacher praise: A functional analysis. *Rev. Ed. Res.*, 1981, **51**: 5–32.
6. Camp, B. W., Two psychoeducational treatment programs for young aggressive boys. In: *Hyperactive Children: The Social Ecology of Identification and Treatment* (C. K. Whalen and B. Henker, Eds.). Academic Press, New York, 1980: 191–219.
7. Carpenter, T. P., Moser, J., and Romberg, T., *Addition and Subtraction: A Developmental Perspective*. Erlbaum, Hillsdale, N.J., 1982.
8. Conners, C. K., Learning disabilities and stimulant drugs in children: Theoretical implications. In: *The Neuropsychology of Learning Disorders* (R. M. Knights and D. J. Bakker, Eds.). University Park Press, Baltimore, 1976: 389–401.
9. Dimond, S. J., and Beaumont, J. G., Differences in the vigilance performance of the right and left hemisphere. *Cortex*, 1973, **9**: 259–265.
10. Doctorow, M. J., Wittrock, M. C., and Marks, C. B., Generative processes in reading comprehension. *J. Ed. Psychol.*, 1978, **70**: 109–118.
11. Douglas, V. I., Parry, P., Martin, P., and Garson, C., Assessment of a cognitive training program for hyperactive children. *J. Abnorm. Child Psychol.*, 1976, **4**: 389–410.
12. Goldberg, E., and Costa, L. D., Hemispheric differences in relationship to the acquisition and use of descriptive systems. *Brain Lang.*, 1981, **14**: 144–173.
13. Hallahan, D. P., and Reeve, R. E., Selective attention and distractibility. In: *Advances in Special Education*, Vol. 1 (B. K. Keogh, Ed.). JAI Press, Greenwich, Conn., 1980: 141–181.
14. Heilman, K. M., and Valenstein, E., *Clinical Neuropsychology*. Oxford University Press, New York, 1979.
15. Kinsbourne, M., The mechanism of hemispheric control of the lateral gradient of attention. In: *Attention and Performance V* (P. M. A. Rabbitt and S. Dornic, Eds.). Academic Press, London, 1975: 81–97.
16. Krupski, A., Are retarded children more distractible? Observational analysis of retarded and nonretarded children's classroom behavior. *Am. J. Ment. Def.*, 1979, **84**: 1–10.

17. Krupski, A., Attention processes: Research, theory, and implications for special education. In: *Advances in Special Education*, Vol. 1 (B. Keogh, Ed.). JAI Press, Greenwich, Conn., 1980: 101–140.

18. Levin, J. R., On functions of pictures in prose. In: *Neuropsychological and Cognitive Processes of Reading* (F. J. Pirozzolo and M. C. Wittrock, Eds.). Academic Press, New York, 1981: 203–228.

19. Linden, M., and Wittrock, M. C., The teaching of reading comprehension according to the model of generative learning. *Read. Res. Q.*, 1981, **17**: 44–57.

20. McGuinness, D., and Pribram, K., The neuropsychology of attention: Emotional and motivational controls. In: *The Brain and Psychology* (M. C. Wittrock, Ed.). Academic Press, New York, 1980: 95–139.

21. Osborne, R., Children's ideas about electric current. *N. Zeal. Sci. Teacher*, 1981, **29**: 12–19.

22. Osborne, R. J., and Wittrock, M. C., Learning science: A generative process. *Sci. Ed.*, 1983, **67**: 489–508.

23. Paivio, A., *Imagery and Verbal Processes*. Holt, Rinehart & Winston, New York, 1971.

24. Peterson, P., and Swing, S., Beyond time on task: Students' reports of their thought processes during direct instruction. *Elem. Sch. J.*, 1982, **82**: 481–491.

25. Pirozzolo, F. J., and Wittrock, M. C. (Eds.)., *Neuropsychological and Cognitive Processes in Reading*. Academic Press, New York, 1981.

26. Pressley, G. M., Mental imagery helps eight-year-olds remember what they read. *J. Ed. Psychol.*, 1976, **68**: 355–359.

27. Stuss, D. T., and Benson, D. F., Neuropsychological studies of the frontal lobes. *Psychol. Bull.*, 1984, **95**: 3–28.

28. Warm, J. S., Richter, D. O., Sprague, R. L., Porter, P. K., and Schumsky, D. A., Listening with a dual brain: Hemispheric asymmetry in sustained attention. *Bull. Psychonom. Soc.*, 1980, **15**: 229–232.

29. Wittrock, M. C., Learning as a generative process. *Ed. Psychologist*, 1974, **11**: 87–95.

30. Wittrock, M. C., Education and the cognitive processes of the brain. In: *Education and the Brain* (J. Chall and A. Mirsky, Eds.). National Society for the Study of Education Yearbook, Chicago, 1978: 61–102.

31. Wittrock, M. C., Learning and the brain. In: *The Brain and Psychology* (M. C. Wittrock, Ed.). Academic Press, New York, 1980: 371–403.

32. Wittrock, M. C., Reading comprehension. In: *Neuropsychological and Cognitive Processes in Reading* (F. J. Pirozzolo and M. C. Wittrock, Eds.). Academic Press, New York, 1981: 229–259.

33. Wittrock, M. C., Beatty, J., Bogen, J. E., Gazzaniga, M. S., Jerison, H. J., Krashen, S. D., Nebes, R. D., and Teyler, T. J., *The Human Brain*. Prentice-Hall, Englewood Cliffs, N.J., 1977.

34. Whittrock, M. C., and Alesandrini, K., Reading Comprehension and the generation of verbal analogies and summaries. In preparation.

35. Wittrock, M. C., and Lumsdain, A. A., Instructional psychology. In: *The Annual Review of Psychology*, Vol. 28 (M. R. Rosenzweig and L. W. Porter, Eds.). Annual Reviews, Palo Alto, Cal., 1977: 417–459.

36. Yates, F., *The Art of Memory*. Routledge & Kegan Paul, London, 1966.

CEREBRAL-LATERALIZATION THEORY AND THE SOCIOLOGY OF KNOWLEDGE

WARREN D. TenHOUTEN, PhD
Department of Sociology

The principal thesis of the sociology of knowledge is that there are modes of thought which cannot be adequately understood as long as their social origins are obscured. It is indeed true that only an individual is capable of thinking. There is no such metaphysical entity as a group mind which thinks over and above the heads of individuals, or whose ideas the individual merely reproduces. Nevertheless it would be false to deduce that all the ideas and sentiments which motivate an individual have their origins in him alone, and can be adequately explained solely on the basis of his own life experience.
—Karl Mannheim, *Ideology and Utopia* (41: 2)

The purpose of this chapter is to discuss the interface between the neuroscientific conception of the dual brain and the social sciences, giving special emphasis to the sociology of knowledge. All disciplines in the social sciences share, as a necessary component, a concern with human thought and reason. They also share a concern for consciousness, in Hegel's (27: 244) sense of "that which thinks, . . . the thinking being." Because the human brain is the organ of thought and reason, an empirical and theoretical understanding of brain functioning creates for every social and behavioral science a potential intersection with neuroscientific theory and method, and provides grounds for modeling and measuring thinking processes. This opportunity for establishing knowledge of the relationships between neurophysiological processes, on the one hand, and behavioral and communicative processes, on the other, has led to rapid expansions of the fields of neuropsychology and neurolinguistics. More recently there have been efforts toward the eventual development of neuropolitics (37, 57, 58), neuroanthropology (1, 35, 47), and neurosociology (9, 28, 63–67).

In using the theory of cerebral lateralization of cognitive functions of the right and left cerebral hemispheres, there is no reduction of the social to the biological. Such a reduction is implicit in sociobiology. But sociobiology does not attempt to explain the development of complex human social organizational and institutional forms, nor does it address the relationship between thought and social structure. The neurosocial can be considered on two levels. First, neurosociology identifies a *field* of inquiry that has as its object relationships between neurophysiological and social structures and processes. Here neurosociology is parallel to neurolinguistics, neuro-psychology, and other interdisciplinary fields that involve both neurophysiology and a social or behavioral science.

The second, and more restricted, use of a term such as neurosociology is metho-dological, such that work in cerebral-lateralization theory provides resources for the *description* and *empirical measurement* of thinking processes. Insofar as thought is an interior aspect of the social, such a level of analysis can be applied to sociological topics.

INDIVIDUAL HEMISPHERICITY

A wide variety of cognitive functions have been found to be predominantly associated with the functioning of the right or left cerebral hemispheres of the human brain. The modes of information processing and, by inference, of thought, of the right and left hemispheres, have been contrasted as "logical–analytic" versus "Ges-talt–synthetic" (39), as "propositional" versus "appositional" (6), and by numerous other terminologies (6). The choice of terms is unimportant. It should be noted, how-ever, that such terminologies have been borrowed by neuroscientists from philosophy, phenomenology, and the social sciences. Distinctions such as analytic versus synthetic antedate contemporary and even classical neuroscience and play a role in the soci-ology of knowledge. The use of such conceptual terminology represents *interpreta-tion* of the inventories of cognitive functions found to be lateralized to the two sides of the brain as representative of two distinctive modes of thought. This interpretative work is analogous to the factor-analytic procedure of naming a factor on the basis of conceptual continuity of variables loading on the same factor.

In an individual with the most usual lateralization, each cerebral hemisphere will contribute in a varying degree to the solution to a problem. This implies a con-cept of "individual hemisphericity," which was defined in Bogen *et al.* (9: 5) as "a tendency for a person to rely more on one hemisphere than the other." Such hemi-sphericity can reflect the influences of sociocultural experience. For example, in a preliterate society with emphasis on spatial reasoning, we could expect a relative right hemisphericity; in a contemporary society with a mass educational system em-phasizing reading, writing, and logical–analytic skills, we could expect a relative left hemisphericity. This conception of individual hemisphericity refers first of all to the direction of cerebral lateralization, so that individuals can be described as directionally right or left in their individual hemisphericity, and groups can be com-pared for central tendency of the ratio of appositionality to propositionality (an "A/P ratio" [9: 50]), or of some other measure such as $(A - P)/(A + P)$.

Here, two additional aspects of individual hemisphericity will be emphasized. First, "lateral differentiation" refers to the extent to which the two hemispheres are specialized, and are flexibly responsive to the specific cognitive demands of the task at hand. And, second, "hemispheric interaction" refers to the extent to which the capacities of the two hemispheres are used together in a productive and creative way.

Direction of Lateralization

The direction of lateralization is reflected, for example, in the relative performances on cognitive tasks that are known to be to some extent lateralized to a single hemisphere. A person who consistently and reliably shows good performance on "left-hemisphere tasks" but poor performance on "right-hemisphere tasks" can be said to be directionally left-lateralized.

In addition to performances on lateralized tests, left-hemisphericity is also reflected in a tendency to *use* one hemisphere more than the other in problem solving. The relative activation of the hemispheres can be measured by the relative desynchronization of the EEG (indicating activation) for channels homologously placed over the two hemispheres (15, 24), and by a tendency to manifest involuntary conjugate lateral eye movements consistently to the right or the left in response to verbal questions: Here right hemisphericity is indicated by a consistent looking to the left; and left hemisphericity, by looking to the right (3, 25).

Lateral Flexibility: Extent of Lateralization

Extent of lateralization is here viewed as a second aspect of individual hemisphericity, which can also be called lateral differentiation. A laterally differentiated person will tend to use the right hemisphere for tasks for which the right hemisphere has an advantage *and* to use the left hemisphere for tasks for which the left hemisphere has an advantage. Some recent work on field-independent and field-dependent cognitive styles has suggested field independence (i.e., psychological differentiation) to be correlated with extent of lateralization. Witkin *et al.* (70) mean by "field dependence" a failure to develop psychological differentiation, which includes the capacity to separate a stimulus from its perceptual context.

A number of recent studies suggest that field-independent persons are not directionally left-lateralized as much as they are laterally differentiated. Thus, field-independent persons will tend to use the hemisphere that has an advantage for the cognitive task at hand. Subjects who show a right-ear dominance in dichotic listening to verbal stimuli are also found to be relatively field-independent (51). Oltman *et al.* (46) found that field-independent subjects are more right-lateralized for a right-hemisphere task: In this experiment, subjects were asked to judge the similarity of pictures of faces compared to composite faces constructed from half-faces and their mirror images. The composites made of left half-faces were generally judged to be more similar in appearance to the original than were the other composites. The field-independent subjects showed the highest bias to the left visual half-field, thus using the right hemisphere more than the left for a "right-hemisphere task."

Witkin *et al.* (71: 20) have hypothesized that a high level of specialization in the psychological domain, as indicated by field independence, will be correlated with specialization for the hemispheres. This statement is qualified as follows: "The emphasis, it should be noted, is on degree of lateralization of different types of processing in the respective sides and not on the dominance of one hemisphere over the other as a generalized 'hemisphericity' tendency."

Studies of two groups of persons shown by some laterality studies to be less strongly lateralized than the rest of the population—females (33) and left-handers (26)—provide additional indirect evidence linking cerebral lateralization and psychological differentiation. If these groups are, as has been hypothesized, lateralized to a lesser extent than are males and right-handers, then they should be relatively field-dependent. Females have been shown to be field-dependent relative to males (70; but cf. 5), and non-right-handers to be field-dependent relative to right-handers (60). While most right-handed persons make most of their speech-related gestures with their right hands (34), field-dependent persons, who presumably process speech more bilaterally, tend to show more bilaterality in their speech-related gestures (61).

DIALECTICAL REASON AND HEMISPHERIC INTERACTION

It has been emphasized that the claim of two modes of thought characterizing the two hemispheres is already an inference well beyond the data. Here I go even further, contending that the productive interaction of the two hemispheres makes possible the emergence of a third aspect of individual hemisphericity, which can be termed the "dialectical" mode of thought. This conception of a dialectical mode of thought presupposes a strong contrasting specialization of the cerebral hemispheres. It can be argued that the two modes of thought of the two hemispheres are not merely quantitatively different, but rather are "real opposites" in the Kantian sense. Kant (32) saw synthetic and analytic reason as constituting a real opposition, so that the two, together, are able to generate a level of thought that goes beyond both the synthetic and the analytic. To say that the level of thought made possible through hemispheric interaction is dialectical implies that the two modes of thought stand in relationships both of complementarity and contradiction, of unity and opposition. The relationships between the two hemispheres have indeed been shown to include mutual antagonism and also complementarity.

Galin and Ornstein (24) claim that each hemisphere possesses its own consciousness and that relations between the hemispheres are ordinarily antagonistic, with persons "switching" from one mode to the other. Levy et al. (38: 69) point out that the disconnected hemispheres of patients with cerebral commissurotomy, working on the same task, are apt to process the same sensory information in qualitatively different ways and to show mutual antagonism. They see an "interference effect" that has contributed to the evolution of lateralization of functions in the human brain. The propensity of the left hemisphere to note analytic details and to describe with language interferes with the perception of the overall Gestalt, leaving the left hemisphere "unable to see the woods for the trees." And Bogen and Bogen (8: 201) state that "certain kinds of left hemisphere activity may directly suppress certain kinds of right hemisphere activity."

The dialectics of hemispheric interaction also imply a complementarity between the hemispheres. This does not mean that mere proficiency is developed in both modes, so that a person can carry out tasks with one and tasks with the other. Dialectical thinking, as complementarity, means rather that both appositional and propositional thought are brought to bear interactively on one problem. In this sense, what is here called dialectical reasoning could also be called "creative" thinking. Bogen and Bogen (8) contend that creative thinking depends on hemispheric interaction made possible by the cerebral commissures, and that cerebral commissurotomy would have the side effect of reducing the creative thought of an initially creative person.

SOME CLASSICAL SOCIOLOGICAL CONCEPTIONS OF THOUGHT

The idea that human reason can be divided into two distinct modes of thought has emerged independently in a wide variety of archaic and classical philosophies, phenomenologies, and social theories. Distinctions such as synthetic–analytic, inductive–deductive, emotional–rational, and spatial–temporal have long been available to scholars investigating the human mind. At the outset of modern sociology, when the relationships between the mind and society became a topic of scientific inquiry, the concept of a duality of mind had long been available.

Auguste Comte (13) saw the new discipline of sociology, which he also named, as an application of rational–scientific principles to the social world. He imagined society to be founded on lawlike, mathematically expressible propositions. There was no place in this social physics for the other side of human intellect — for feelings, desires, and apprehensions. This exclusion of the nonlogical mode of thought as an organizing principle of social order formed the basis of the utopian socialist Saint-Simon's (55) critique of Comte's positivism. Saint-Simon (55: 43) wrote in 1829:

> The exercise of human intellect may be divided into two distinct modes: conception and verification, or invention and method. The intellect discovers, conjectures, and creates with the former; it justifies its foresights, its inspirations and its revelations with the latter. . . .
> To appraise the nature of these two processes of the human intellect, conception and verification, it will be necessary to take into account the situation in which man is found when he uses the one or the other.

Here we see an argument that the two modes of thought characterizing the mind require understanding of the social context in which they are used. Saint-Simon (55: 46) acknowledged the antiquity of the notion of two modes of thought, for he also wrote:

> All philosophical schools have recognized two distinct modes of human reasoning by which an observer may go through a given series of facts. . . . One recalls the image through which Bacon expressed this idea, namely the double ladder. . . . To discover the superiority of analysis over synthesis is . . . to study whether it is better to lower or to raise the pistons of a pump in order to make it work.

These two "modes of human reason" correspond approximately to the appositional and propositional modes of thought of the right and left hemispheres of the brain.

The problem of mind and society has been a basic concern in the three great intellectual traditions that constitute the classical roots of contemporary sociological theory—the Durkheimian, the Marxian, and the Weberian. It is useful to consider selected notions about human reason and its social determinants in each of these traditions. The materials selected are not intended to represent any scholar's work as a whole, but have the more limited purpose of illustrating the uses in sociology to which notions of mind compatible with cerebral-lateralization theory have been independently put.

The Durkheimian Tradition

In the French tradition of the sociology of knowledge, the seminal figure is Émile Durkheim (1858–1917), a founder of both sociology and social anthropology. Durkheim recognized that society is possible only to the extent that it penetrates the consciousness of individuals. He was concerned with the "constitutional duality of human nature" (16: 150). He argued that humans, in every age, have had the self-conception of "being formed of two radically heterogeneous beings: the body and the soul." These two elements of human nature he saw as not only substantially different, but as independent of each other, and standing in an antagonistic relation to each other. He saw this duality as giving rise to two forms of intelligence. The first he called "sensations" and "sensory tendencies." Sensations include images (sensations that survive themselves) and perceptions (conglomerates of sensations and images). This is close in meaning to Kant's empirical sensitivity. The second he called "reason," by which he meant conceptual thought and moral activity. Here the emphasis is on intellectual and rational exchange, communication, and thinking in universal and impersonal terms.

The duality of human nature, such that both sensory and rational forms of intellect exist in a single and identical being, was explained by Durkheim as a particular case of the division of things into the sacred and the profane. The sacred, in Durkheim's scheme, simply means collective representations that have fixed themselves on material objects. Here objects are no longer only of interest to our personal individuality, but are now set apart, externalized and made impersonal through translation into signs. By externally symbolizing objects, individual consciousnesses can communicate; it is this separation of objects that gives them their sacred character. Thus Durkheim (16: 152) was led to this claim:

> The old formula *homo duplex* is therefore verified by the facts. Far from being simple, our inner life has something that is like a double center of gravity. On the one hand is our individuality—and, more particularly, our body in which it is based; on the other is everything in us that expresses something other than ourselves.

A student of Durkheim, Robert Hertz (28), linked this formulation of a duality of consciousness directly to cerebral specialization. Hertz (28: 3) wrote in 1909:

What resemblance more perfect than that between our two hands! And yet what a striking inequality there is!

To the right hand go honours, flattering designations, prerogatives: it acts, orders, and *takes*. The left hand, on the contrary, is despised and reduced to the rôle of a humble auxiliary: by itself it can do nothing; it helps, it supports, it *holds*.

The right hand is the symbol and model of all aristocracies, the left hand of all common people. What are the titles of nobility of the right hand? And whence comes the servitude of the left?

Hertz's approach to a linkage of the right hand (and the left hemisphere) to positions of dominance, and of the left hand (and the right hemisphere) to positions of subdominance, began with a consideration of cerebral-lateralization theory. He wrote (28: 4):

Of all the hypotheses advanced only one seems to have stood up to a factual test: that which links the preponderance of the right hand to the greater development in man of the left cerebral hemisphere, which, as we know, innervates the muscles of the opposite side. . . . As Broca says, "We are right-handed because we are left-brained." The prerogatives of the right hand would then be found on the asymmetrical structure of the nervous centres, of which the cause, whatever it may be, is evidently organic. It is not to be doubted that a regular connection exists between the predominance of the right hand and the superior development of the left part of the brain. But of these two phenomena which is the cause and which is the effect? What is there to prevent us turning Broca's proposition round and saying, "We are left-brained because we are right-handed?"

Hertz had, in spite of the crudity of his neurophysiology, contributed an insight that the appositional mode of thought of the right hemisphere is particularly appropriate for knowledge practices such as witchcraft, sorcery, and the practices of magic — the "left-handed practices." Such practices are, even in a primitive society, apt to be a deviant form of knowing, in opposition to the dominant ideologies or knowledge practices of society and culture.

It was this topic — relating social dominance and subdominance, handedness, and cerebral lateralization — that Hertz introduced to sociology and social anthropology. In his study of the Maori, he had observed restraint of the left hand, even to the point of binding it to the side of the body — with the intention, he reasoned, of suppressing the disturbing and suspect powers of mind that would manifest themselves (e.g., in sorcery, witchcraft, and divination). He contended that the suppression of the left hand among the Maori derived not from its being weak and powerless, but rather because of its power in association with profane, left-handed practices. Thus Hertz linked the modes of thought associated with the right and left hands with the distinction between the sacred and the profane, and in so doing extended and elaborated Durkheim's conception of the duality of human consciousness.

This essay by Hertz, in combination with the study of primitive classification by Durkheim and Mauss (17), has led to the emergence of comparative analyses of dual-symbolic classification systems (45). There exists in many societies a manifest principle of complementary oppositions, a symbolism of right and left. For example, in Needham's (44) description of Nyoro symbolic classification, the right and the left are contrasted as boy–girl, chief–subject, heaven–earth, white–black, good–evil, hard–soft, culture–nature, and so on. It was Hertz's contention that these sorts of classificatory dualities reveal the effects of acting in the world with manual asymmetry, which he linked causally to cognitive and hemispheric asymmetry, and which he saw as producing the collective representations of dual-symbolic classifications.

While many scholars have described and analyzed such classification systems, their relations to thought have not been systematically explored, and Hertz's arguments remain highly speculative. Klein (35) has recently attempted a structural model of "appositional transformation operators" in relation to such classification systems, but the link of these operators to appositional (right-hemisphere) thought remains indirect.

The Marxian Tradition

The sociology of knowledge in the Marxian tradition has focused on the relationship between consciousness and the antagonistic relations of social classes. The conceptions to be reviewed here are not intended to represent a vast literature or even to place it in its historical and intellectual context. I begin with Hegel's (27) metaphorical analysis of the "master" and the "bondsman," according to which the oppressed consciousness of the bondsman is characterized by its subordination to the consciousness of the oppressing master. The oppressed person to some extent internalizes the meaning systems and culture of the oppressor, "housing" the oppressor in an inauthentic dual consciousness (22). Here the oppressed are apt to have a diffuse, magical belief in the power of their oppressors. Freire (22) contends that under this condition, reality is perceived as dense, impenetrable, and submerged in phenomena. Thought here tends not to be verbally elaborated, but rather exists in a "culture of science" (21).

This mentality is seen by Freire as but one moment, one stage of development, in the consciousness of the dominated. This submerged appositionality can be transformed through pedagogy so that the world is no longer seen as a dense and given actuality; rather, through the discovery of the social power of the word (which Freire calls the power to "name the world"), the world is seen as containing problems and contradictions that can be solved through class practices. Here the initial perceptual orientation is supplemented with an active verbalization. The goal is no longer to eliminate the risks of temporality by clutching guaranteed space, but rather to temporalize space. Thus the development of abstraction, of a temporal perspective, and of intensified verbalization, contributes to the transformation of consciousness from a "submerged" appositionality to a "liberating" oppositionality (conscientização, the process of attaining a critical consciousness and taking action against oppressive elements of reality). By analogy, we can interpret this argument to mean a transformation of thought from a right-hemisphere (appositional) mode to an expanded emphasis on the left-hemisphere (propositional) mode, which then makes possible a dialectical mode of thought based on hemispheric interaction.

The notion that social classes differ in their mentalities — the thesis of Freire — is consistent with Parkin's (48) analysis of class inequality and meaning systems. Parkin contends that the groups and social classes in society maintaining positions of power and privilege should have greater access to the means of legitimation. He argues (48: 83) that the social and political definitions of those occupying the dominant positions in society tend to become "objectified and enshrined in the major institutional order, so providing the normative framework of the entire social system." Thus the dominant value system has a moral framework that promotes the endorsement of existing inequality. Among the working class, this leads to a definition of the reward structure in either "deferential" or "aspirational" terms. The dominated classes are hypothesized to have two value systems reflecting different moments or stages in the development of their class consciousness. Parkin describes these as "subordinates" (cf. Freire's "submerged consciousness") and "radical" (cf. Freire's "critical consciousness").

The structuring of cognitive organization by class conflict is also explored in the work of Lukács (40), who saw the process of the rationalization of work as a reificational phenomenon. On the one hand, rationalization requires a precise breakdown of every phase of production into its elements, so that the results of work can be predicted with precision. On the other hand, the specialization of tasks in productive work involves a disassociation as well from the person of the producer. Under these conditions, the human qualities and individual differences of workers come to be viewed as mere sources of error. Gabel (23: 151) argues that such rationalization of production creates a world of reification dominated by a principle of identity — the deterioration of the "axiological contents of existence and the promotion of immediate utilitarian . . . values," in which categories of efficiency come to substitute for moral intentionality. It is argued that the effects of the rationalization of labor, in which the worker must act in concert with machines, transforms the mental experience of the worker such that time and space are reduced to a common denominator. Time is here degraded to the dimension of space and becomes a quantifiable continuum, filled with the reified and mechanically objectified performances of the worker, with the result that the subject of labor must likewise be rationally fragmented.

In elaborating Lukacs' theme, Gabel (23: 8) sees the world of reified consciousness as "the center of a decline of dialectical temporalization with a compensating prevalence of spatial functions." This spatiality enables what Gabel calls a "dialectic of the totality" (i.e., Gestalt), but strips away the "dialectic of the future," according to which structure or Gestalt can be seen in its temporal and developmental context. The working-class consciousness thus is a false consciousness insofar as the primary aspects of valid perception of being in the world — totality and temporality — are broken up, with totality becoming the central category of working-class consciousness.

The reified, *a priori*, and analytic consciousness of the dominant group is thus seen as producing in the subordinate group a form of consciousness that is quite the opposite: It is excessively dereified, concrete (overstructured, stressing the totality and the Gestalt), lacks identification, lacks objectivity, and is characterized by a preponderance of the experience of the "here and now" (23: 157). Here we see a social process hypothesized to contribute to a mode of thought whose characteristics correspond, albeit roughly, to a relative appositionality (right hemisphericity).

The Weberian Tradition

Max Weber's (1864–1920) sociology outlined the emergence of technical–purposive rationality as the dominant form of human reason in the modern world. This instrumental rationality (*Zweckrational*) requires a belief in the legitimate social authority based on formal and legal mechanisms of compliance. Weber emphasized that the process of rationalization is characteristic of Western social development. In particular, modern capitalism was seen as antitraditional to the extent that profits are sought by means of cognitive organization that is both rational and systematic.

The notion of the preeminence of the propositional with the advent of modern society, which Durkheim referred to as "organic solidarity," was seen from a different perspective by Weber. For example, in his study *The Protestant Ethic and the Spirit of Capitalism* (68), he posited a close association between the cognitive structure of the ideal typical historical individual who carried the new Protestant ideology, and the expansion of capitalist enterprise as an economic mode of production. His analysis implicitly opposed two forms of consciousness, which D. Bakan (2) terms "communion" and "agency." "Agency" means one's existence as an individual; and "communion," the individual's membership in a larger collectivity. Bakan (2: 15) explains:

> Agency manifests itself in self-protection, self-assertion, and self-expansion; communion manifests itself in the sense of being at one with other organisms. . . . Agency manifests itself in isolation, alienation, and aloneness; communion in contact, openness, and union. Agency manifests itself in the urge to master; communion in noncontractual cooperation.

What Weber showed, in Bakan's terms, is that there is an intrinsic unity of Protestantism and capitalism, based on the fact that they both involve exaggeration of agency and a simultaneous repression of communion. Weber's analysis suggests that the agentic tendency in human society rose to dominance with the development of the capitalist, industrialized, modern world. The historical individual he described embraced a doctrine of predestination, asceticism, and calling. The doctrine of predestination tended to alienate each individual from other persons: Since there can be no personal relationship with God in a predestined world, the individual is left free to develop will and to function as an agent. Asceticism leads to the discipline of labor; to mastery of the impulses of the body; and to a preoccupation with empiricism and positivism in mathematics, science, and technology. Calling entails the regulation of one's life through vocation, separates work from the use of the products of labor, and separates the accumulation of wealth from the desire for wealth.

Durkheim, Marx, and Weber are seminal figures in classical sociological theory.

The selected concepts from these three intellectual traditions are sufficient to show the importance of thought and reason to any understanding of the social world. It must be emphasized that these conceptions are based on differing and incompatible ontological and epistemological grounds and are not consistent with one another. Yet they all refer, in one way or another, to the social determinants of modes of thought, and to sociohistorical conditions under which one mode of thought or the other will gain priority. By drawing on contemporary neuropsychology and cerebral-lateralization theory, it becomes possible to interpret these modes of thought in terms of the contrasting specialization of the left and right sides of the brain and in terms of the notion of individual hemisphericity. This connection of sociological and biological levels of analysis makes it possible to study the classical problems in sociology of knowledge not just as social philosophy and social thought, but also as a problem for quantitative, empirical, and scientific study.

CONTEMPORARY STUDIES

The economic organization of modern society has required the development of a work force trained in technical and scientific thought. This has been accomplished historically by the development of modern social institutions. Sartre (56) describes in detail the French resistance to the establishment of the factory system and to the inculcation of its supporting mode of thinking. Foucault (18–20) provides parallel descriptions of the historical development of the clinic, prison, and mental asylum for the control of deviants in accordance with the requirements of practical rationality. The key institution in developing the primacy of the propositional habitus of mind in modern society was that of mass education. Education came to mean the full-time training of children in a highly formalized and systematic form of language use (4, 10). New social categories, such as that of the adolescent, were developed to legitimate the full-time attendance of children in schools with the explicit purposes of developing their cognitive capacities. As Musgrove (42) notes, it was no accident that the introduction of the concept of the adolescent by Rousseau in 1762 corresponded with Watts's invention of the steam engine in 1765.

Direction of Lateralization

I have hypothesized that in modern Western society the socially advantaged groups and classes will tend to appropriate the propositional mode of thought, with subdominant groups functioning in a relatively more appositional mode. In a probability survey of adults in one urban and two rural sites in the United States, this hypothesis was supported. It was found that performance on a "right-hemisphere task," Street's Gestalt Completion Test (A) (62) (Figure 1A), and a "left-hemisphere task," the WAIS Similarities Subtest (P) (69), compared by A/P ratios, showed group differences in test performance. Multigroup discriminant-function analysis indicated that samples of Hopi Indians, rural white farmers and their wives, urban black males and females, and urban white males and females could be discriminated on the basis of these ratios. It was found that the A/P ratios, for individuals, were on the average higher for nonwhites than for whites, with Hopis higher than blacks among the nonwhites. Within ethnic groups, rural dwellers had higher A/P ratios than did urban residents (9, 66). A further analysis of the urban sample (63) showed that when ethnicity and sex were controlled, socioeconomic status varied directly with Similarities performance but was unrelated to Street performance (Figure 1B–D).

Figure 1. (A) Two items from the Street Gestalt Completion Test (62); (B) WAIS Similarities (69) mean scores; (C) Street mean scores; (D) "Right Hemisphericity" $(A - P)/(A + P)$ mean scores. (From 63:Figures 1 and 3. Reprinted by permission.)

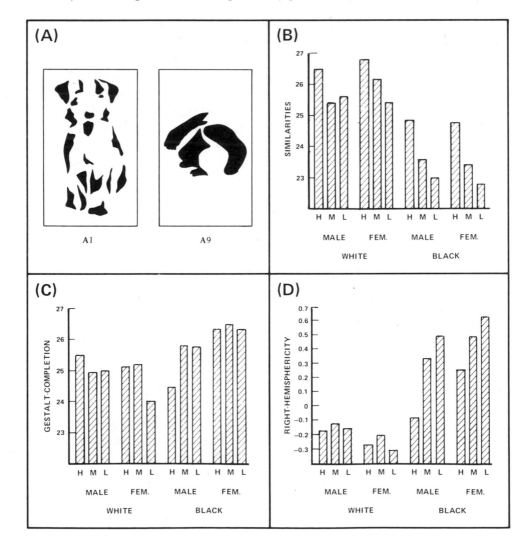

Extent of Lateralization

There are a wide variety of studies indicating that socially subdominant and nonmodern groups and classes are relatively field-dependent. While these studies do not consider the possible neurophysiological concomitants of psychological differentiation, the link between field independence and cerebral lateralization outlined above suggests social and cultural differences an extent of lateralization. Further tests will determine the validity of this conjecture.

Ramirez and Prince-Williams (52) administered a measure of field dependence, the Portable Rod-and-Frame Test, to Anglo, Mexican-American, and Afro-American children, and found the level of field dependence or "field sensitivity" to be higher for the Mexican-American and Afro-American children than for the Anglo. Berry (5) found, for Temne and Eskimo samples, that those members of the society living in urban, Westernized environments were more field-independent (on an Embedded Figures Test) than were those members sampled in their "traditional" settings. Rand (53) compared Jewish children in France, of Moroccan and European descent, and found those with European backgrounds to be more field-independent on an Embedded Figures Test. Similarly, Dershowitz (14) compared Orthodox Jewish and Anglo-Saxon Protestant boys, and found the Protestants to be relatively more field-independent.

Cohen (11) contrasted "analytic" and "relational" cognitive styles, which are close in their meanings to field-independent and field-dependent cognitive styles, respectively. The analytic cognitive style is characterized by a formal model of abstracting information from a situation and by a stimulus-centered orientation to reality, such that parts or attributes have meaning in themselves. The relational cognitive style, in contradistinction, requires a descriptive mode, is self-centered in its reality orientation, and finds meaning in global characteristics of a stimulus. Cohen found that the analytic cognitive style is most typical of children raised in subcultures characterized by formally organized family and friendship groups, while the relational style characterizes children raised in shared-function groups that are less competitive and more cooperative.

These and a host of related cross-cultural studies (see 12), carried out primarily by anthropologists and psychologists, consistently show subdominant racial, ethnic, and cultural groups to be relatively field-dependent, primarily as a result of differing socialization practices. These studies indicate that field dependence is most prevalent in sociocultural settings in which children are maximally subdominant — where discipline is severe and there is pressure toward conformity.

Such socialization practices, along with extended patriarchal structures, emphasis on conformity, and restrictions of emotional expression, have been widely interpreted as aspects of social traditionalism and associated with a cultural preference for continuing traditional social forms as opposed to modern Western forms. It has been pointed out (43) that such contrasting value patterns and institutions are in correspondence with the dichotomies of *Gemeinschaft–Gesellschaft*, mechanical–organic solidarity, and rural–urban life.

Cohen emphasizes that the relational cognitive style, as a culturally specific method of organizing and processing information, can be advantageous in minority-group socialization contexts but not in formal educational settings. In studying race differences in the United States, Hillyard (29) found a distinctive Afro-American cognitive style, based on (1) a view of things as a whole in their environmental contexts, rather than in isolation; (2) a conception of space, time, and number as approximate rather than as exact concepts; (3) an orientation to person rather than things and task requirements; and (4) an emphasis on nonverbal communication. These four orientations can be effective in social and interpersonal settings (36); however, they can be dysfunctional in formal educational settings in which things must be seen in isolation, exact concepts are emphasized, things are emphasized over people, and the system is oriented to the development of clarity and distinctness in language use.

There is considerable evidence that socialization practices and cultural predispositions of nonmodern and subdominant groups and classes contribute to a field-dependent or relational cognitive style. This cognitive style in turn is seen—for example, by Shade (59)—as resulting in a deficit in school success. There is much empirical and theoretical work to be done to clarify the relationships among socialization process, the development of cognitive styles, individual hemisphericity, and successful performance in educational institutions.

Dialectical Reason

The concept of dialectical reason has been utilized in lifespan developmental psychology (54), in the context of a critique of Piaget's (49, 50) theory of cognitive development. According to Piaget, early cognitive development has a dialectical character—shown, for example, in the child's fluidity of switching attention in the initial sensory–motor phases of development, and in attending to two concepts at once in the preoperational level. But, as cognition develops through concrete operations and arrives at formal operations, thought is seen as noncontradictory, and the primitive dialectics of the first two stages are lost. Reigel contends that dialectical operations represent a still higher level of mental development, characterizing the most productive thinking of the mature mind. In dialectical thinking the emphasis is no longer on equilibration, but rather on conflict and contradiction as fundamental to thought. Contradiction contributes to change, to the resolution of old contradictions and the production of new ones.

Studies of humans who have undergone cerebral commissurotomy provide an opportunity for the study of hemispheric interaction and dialectical reason. There is a specific form of creativity that has been shown to be lacking in commissurotomized patients: It is the creative expression of significant symbols, fantasies, and feelings in the form of words. Such expression presumably requires both the right hemisphere's grasp of significant meaning, of symbols, and of the cognitive representation of (negative) emotions, and the left hemisphere's verbal capabilities. A pathological lack of this creative capacity is called "alexithymia." Hoppe (30), in psychiatric interviews with commissurotomized patients, found a quantitative as well as a quali-tative paucity of dreams, fantasies, and symbolizations. Hoppe and Bogen (31) scored 12 commissurotomized patients for Sifneos's measure of alexithymia and found them to be highly alexithymic. The patients also experienced a lack of investment in sub-jective interpersonal relationships and a reduced capacity to engage in productive work. The Hoppe–Bogen result has recently been replicated in a comparison of eight of these patients and a precision-matched control group of eight "normal" subjects (64).

DISCUSSION

The two modes of thought Durkheim saw as characterizing the human mind have parallels in the relationship between self and society. At one pole we find the society within the consicousness of the individual; at the other pole, the individual's consciousness within the society. If these modes of thought are interpreted as ap-positional (right-hemisphere) and propositional (left-hemisphere), then appositional thought can be seen as appropriate for the cognitive representation of the social world within the individual; propositional thought, of the individual within the social world. This distinction of the difference between the appositional and the proposi-tional parallels Bogen's speculation (7) that each hemisphere represents its own other and the world in complementary mappings, such as that the left hemisphere maps the self as a subset of the world, and the right hemisphere maps the world as a subset of the self. Durkheim referred not to the world per se but to the social world.

One interpretation of the difference between the functions of the two hemi-spheres is that they constitute two modes of thought. By seeing these modes of thought as real opposites, in a state of contradiction and complementarity, it can be further inferred that the interaction between the appositional or synthetic mode of the right hemisphere and the propositional or analytic mode of the left hemisphere is able to produce a third mode of thought, the dialectical or creative. Because such concepts have also been utilized in social theory, a link is thereby established between dual-brain theory and social theory, especially the sociology of knowledge. Mannheim's (41) sociology of knowledge has as a basic topic the social processes and structures that shape the thought of the individual thinker. From this perspective, dual-brain theory is useful for the scientific, empirical study of classical problems in the sociology of knowledge, through the actual measurement of brain functioning of individuals in varying social categories, circumstances, and positions, and involved in various social practices.

REFERENCES

1. d'Aquili, E. G., and Laughlin, C. D., Jr., *The Spectrum of Ritual: A Biogenetic Struc-tural Analysis.* Columbia University Press, New York, 1979.
2. Bakan, D., *The Duality of Human Existence: An Essay on Psychology and Religion.* Rand McNally, Chicago, 1966.

3. Bakan, P., Hypnotizability, laterality of eye movements and functional brain asymmetry. *Percept. Mot. Skills*, 1969, **28**: 927–932.

4. Bernstein, B., *Class, Codes and Control*, Vol. 3, *Towards a Theory of Educational Transmission*. Routledge & Kegan Paul, London, 1975.

5. Berry, J. W., Temne and Eskimo perceptual skills. *Int. J. Psychol.*, 1966, **1**: 207–229.

6. Bogen, J. E., The other side of the brain: II. An appositional mind. *Bull. Los Angeles Neurol. Soc.*, 1969, **34**: 135–161.

7. Bogen, J. E., Hemispheric specificity, complementarity, and self-referential mappings. *Proc. Soc. Neurosci.*, 1973, **3**: 341.

8. Bogen, J. E., and Bogen, G. M., The other side of the brain: III. The corpus callosum and creativity. *Bull. Los Angeles Neurol. Soc.*, 1969, **34**: 191–220.

9. Bogen, J. E., DeZure, R., TenHouten, W. D., and Marsh, J. F., The other side of the brain: IV. The A/P ratio. *Bull. Los Angeles Neurol. Soc.*, 1972, **37**: 49–61.

10. Bordeau, P., and Passeron, J. C., *Reproduction in Education, Society and Culture* (R. Nice, Tr.). Sage, Beverly Hills, Calif., 1977.

11. Cohen, R. A., Conceptual styles, cultural conflict and nonverbal tests of intelligence. *Am. Anthrop.*, 1969, **71**: 828–865.

12. Cole, M., Gay, J., Glick, J. A., and Sharp, D. W., *The Cultural Context of Learning and Thinking*. Basic Books, New York, 1971.

13. Comte, A., *The Positive Philosophy of Auguste Comte* (H. Martineau, Tr.). Chapman, London, 1868.

14. Dershowitz, Z., Jewish subcultural patterns and psychological differentiation. *Int. J. Psychol.*, 1971, **6**: 223–231.

15. Donchin, E., Kutas, M., and McCarthy, G., Electrocortical indices of hemispheric utilization. In: *Lateralization in the Nervous System* (S. Harnad *et al.*, Eds.). Academic Press, New York, 1977: 339–384.

16. Durkheim, É., The duality of human nature and its social conditions. In: *Emile Durkheim on Morality and Society* (R. N. Bellah, Ed.; C. Blend, Tr.). University of Chicago Press, Chicago, 1973: 149–163.

17. Durkheim, É., and Mauss, M., *Primitive Classification* (R. Needham, Tr.). University of Chicago Press, Chicago, 1973.

18. Foucault, M., *The Birth of the Clinic: An Archaeology of Medical Perception* (A. M. Sheridan, Tr.). Pantheon Books, New York, 1973.

19. Foucault, M., *Madness and Civilization: A History of Insanity in the Age of Reason* (R. Howard, Tr.). Vintage, New York, 1973.

20. Foucault, M., *Discipline and Punish: The Birth of the Prison* (A. Sheridan, Tr.). Pantheon Books, New York, 1979.

21. Freire, P., The adult literacy process as cultural action for freedom. *Harv. Ed. Rev.*, 1970, **40**: 205–225.

22. Freire, P., *Pedagogy of the Oppressed* (M. S. Ramos, Tr.). Seabury Press, New York, 1974.

23. Gabel, J., *False Consciousness: An Essay on Reification* (M. A. Thompson, Tr.; K. A. Thompson, Asst. Tr.). Harper & Row, New York, 1975.

24. Galin, D., and Ornstein, R., Lateral specialization and cognitive mode: An EEG study. *Psychophysiology*, 1972, **9**: 412–428.

25. Gur, R[aquel]., and Gur., R[uben]., Correlates of conjugate lateral eye movements in man. In: *Lateralization in the Nervous System* (S. Harnad *et al.*, Eds.). Academic Press, New York, 1977: 261–281.

26. Hecaen, H., and Sauguet, J., Cerebral dominance in left-handed subjects. *Cortex*, 1971, **7**: 19–48.

27. Hegel, G. W. F., *The Phenomenology of Mind* (J. B. Baillie, Tr.). Harper & Row, New York, 1967.

28. Hertz, R., *Death and the Right Hand* (R. Needham and C. Needham, Trs.). Cohen & West, Aberdeen, Scotland, 1960: 87–160.

29. Hillyard, A., *Alternatives to IQ Testing: An Approach to the Identification of Gifted Minority Children*. California State Department of Education, Sacramento, 1976.
30. Hoppe, K. D., Split brains and psychoanalysis. *Psychoanal. Q.*, 1977, **46**: 220–244.
31. Hoppe, K. D., and Bogen, J. E., Alexithymia in twelve commissurotomized patients. *Psychother. Psychosom.*, 1977, **28**: 148–155.
32. Kant, I., *Critique of Pure Reason* (F. M. Muller, Tr.). Doubleday, Garden City, N.Y., 1961.
33. Kimura, D., Functional asymmetry of the brain in dichotic listening. *Cortex*, 1967, **3**: 163–178.
34. Kimura, D., Manual activity during speaking. I. Right-handers. *Neuropsychologia*, 1973, **2**: 45–50.
35. Klein, S., Analogy and mysticism and the structure of culture. *Curr. Anthrop.*, 1983, **24**: 151–169.
36. Kogan, N., Educational implications of cognitive style. In: *Psychology and Educational Practice* (G. S. Lesser, Ed.). Scott-Foresman, Glenview, Ill., 1976.
37. Laponce, J. A., *Left and Right: The Topography of Political Perceptions*. University of Toronto Press, Toronto, 1981.
38. Levy, J., Trevarthen, C., and Sperry, R. W., Perception of bilateral chimeric figures following hemispheric deconnection. *Brain*, 1972, **95**: 61–78.
39. Levy-Agresti, J., and Sperry, R. W., Differential perceptual capacities in major and minor hemispheres. *Proc. Natl. Acad. Sci. U.S.A.*, 1968, **61**: 1151.
40. Lukács, G., *History and Class Consciousness: Studies in Marxist Dialectics* (R. Livingstone, Tr.). MIT Press, Cambridge, Mass., 1971.
41. Mannheim, K., *Ideology and Utopia* (L. Wirth and E. Shils, Trs.). Harcourt, Brace & World, New York, 1936.
42. Musgrove, F., *Youth and the Social Order*. Routledge & Kegan Paul, London, 1964.
43. Nedd, A. N. B., and Gruenfeld, L. W., Field dependence–independence and social traditionalism: A comparison of ethnic subcultures of Trinidad. *Int. J. Psychol.*, 1976, **11**: 23–41.
44. Needham, R., Right and left in Nyoro symbolic classification. *Africa*, 1967, **37**: 425–451.
45. Needham, R., Ed., *Right and Left: Essay on Dual Symbolic Classification*. University of Chicago Press, Chicago, 1973.
46. Oltman, P. K., Ehrlichman, H., and Cox, P. W., *Visual Asymmetry in the Perception of Faces and Field Exposure*. EXT RB 76-13, Educational Testing Service, Princeton, N.J., 1976.
47. Paredes, J. A., and Hepburn, M. J., The split brain and the culture-and-cognition paradox. *Curr. Anthrop.*, 1976, **27**: 121–127.
48. Parkin, F., *Class Inequality and Political Order*. Praeger, New York, 1972.
49. Piaget, J., *Judgment and Reasoning in the Child*. Routledge & Kegan Paul, London, 1928.
50. Piaget, J., The stages of intellectual development of the child. *Bull. Menninger Clin.*, 1962, **26**: 120–128.
51. Pizzamiglio, L., Handedness, ear-preference, and field dependence. *Percept. Mot. Skills*, 1974, **38**: 700–702.
52. Ramirez, M., III, and Price-Williams, D., *The Relationship of Culture to Educational Attainment*. Center for Research in Social Change and Economic Development, Rice University, Houston, Tex., 1971.
53. Rand, Y., *Styles cognitifs et personnalité dans une situation de rencontre interculturelle: Étude comparative et analytique*. Doctoral dissertation, The Sorbonne, Paris, 1971.
54. Reigel, K. F., Dialectical operations: The final period of cognitive development. *Human Dev.*, 1973, **16**: 346–370.
55. Saint-Simon, J., *The Doctrine of Saint-Simon: An Exposition* (G. G. Iggers, Tr.). Beacon Press, Boston, 1958.

56. Sartre, J.-P., *Critique of Dialectical Reason* (A. Sheridan-Smith, Tr.; J. Rée, Ed.). NIB, London, 1976.
57. Schubert, G., The evolution of political science: Paradigms of physics, biology, and politics. *Politics and the Life Sciences*, 1983, 1: 97–110.
58. Schubert, G., Psychobiological politics. *Can. J. Pol. Sci.*, 1983, 16: 535–576.
59. Shade, B. J., Afro-American cognitive style: A variable in school success? *Rev. Ed. Res.*, 1982, 52: 219–244.
60. Silverman, A. J., Adevai, G., and McGough, W. E., Some relationships between handedness and perception. *Psychosom. Res.*, 1966, 10: 151–158.
61. Sousa-Posa, J. F., Rohrberg, R., and Mercure, A., Effects of type of information (abstract–concrete) and field dependence on asymmetry of hand movements during speech. *Percept. Mot. Skills*, 1979, 48: 1323–1330.
62. Street, R. F., *A Gestalt Completion Test*. Contributions to Education No. 481, Columbia Teachers College, New York, 1931.
63. TenHouten, W. D., Social dominance and cerebral hemisphericity: Discriminating race, socioeconomic status, and sex groups by performance on two lateralized tests. *Int. J. Neurosci.*, 1980, 10: 223–232.
64. TenHouten, W. D., Hoppe, K. D., Bogen, J. E., and Walter, D. O., Alexithymia and the split brain: Lexical, sentential, and global content analyses. Unpublished manuscript, 1984.
65. TenHouten, W. D., and Kaplan, C. D., *Science and Its Mirror Image: A Theory of Inquiry*. Harper & Row, New York, 1973.
66. TenHouten, W. D., Thompson, A. L., and Walter, D. O., Discriminating social groups by performance on two lateralized tests. *Bull. Los Angeles Neurol. Soc.*, 1976, 41: 99–108.
67. Thompson, A. L., Bogen, J. E., and Marsh, J. F., Cultural hemisphericity: Evidence from cognitive tests. *Int. J. Neurosci.*, 1979, 9: 37–43.
68. Weber, M., *The Protestant Ethic and the Spirit of Capitalism* (T. Parsons, Tr.). Charles Scribner's Sons, New York, 1958.
69. Wechsler, D., *The Measurement of Adult Intelligence*, 2nd ed. Williams & Wilkins, Baltimore, 1941.
70. Witkin, H. A., Dyk, R. B., Faterson, H. F., Goodenough, D. K., and Karp, S. A., *Psychological Differentiation*. Wiley, New York, 1962.
71. Witkin, H. A., Goodenough, D. R., and Oltman, P. K., *Psychological Differentiation: Current Status*. RB-77-17. Educational Testing Service, Princeton, N.J., 1977.

HARMONY OF THE SPHERES AND THE HEMISPHERES: THE ARTS AND HEMISPHERIC SPECIALIZATION

AVRAHAM SCHWEIGER, PhD
Department of Psychology

GENERAL CONSIDERATIONS

A discussion of artistic activity in the context of brain functioning should begin with identifying the objectives of such a pursuit. Thus, at this stage of understanding of the relations of brain and behavior, neuropsychology cannot hope to offer much to artistic practice, either by determining which side of the brain should be used for the creative process or by prescribing how to control such unilateral contribution in the unlikely event that creativity is proven to be associated with just a single hemisphere. There are, however, important aspects of brain–behavior relations that can be gleaned from neuropsychological studies of brain-damaged artists and experimental studies with neurologically intact artists and nonartists (using art stimuli for the independent measure).

Since artistic endeavor differs in some important ways from language functions (see below), it provides a different perspective from which to study brain–behavior relations. Moreover, studies of art and brain can be done together with neurolinguistic investigations, thereby shedding light on the interrelation of these two uniquely human activities. One can understand the ways in which the cerebrum is differentiated and specialized for language and art from studies of brain-damaged artists: What are the necessary, basic cognitive functions that support each, and to what extent can they dissociate from each other following brain lesions? Studies with normals have been limited so far to comparisons of differences between the hemispheres. But even such "crude" differentiation for artistic functions has already provided useful information on, for instance, hemispheric differences in perceiving music between musicians and nonmusicians (6, 33).

Since neuropsychological studies of, for example, philosophical or scientific activities per se are very sparse, and surely such activities may involve creativity, it is of interest to note the special status of the arts* among the other disciplines. It seems that rational and scientific endeavors have not been subjected to the kind of

---

*The word "art" is used in this chapter generically to denote all forms of art, including, among others, music, literature, architecture, painting, and sculpture.

scrutiny that befalls the arts — perhaps because they are deemed to be inextricably involved with language, but not sufficiently different to warrant special attention. The interest in the fine arts by neurologists and neuropsychologists can be attributed, perhaps, to the modular view of cognitive functions and the fundamental presumed differences between linguistic and artistic functions. According to this approach, different modules are subserved by different neuroanatomical substrates. This interest also satisfies the curiosity in the brains and minds of unusual individuals and the need to localize cognitive functions within circumscribed areas of the cortex.

One is reminded of surveys, popular during the 19th and early 20th centuries, that were conducted on the brains of eminent scientists in the best phrenological tradition (e.g., 31). These were, however, studies of brain anatomy, without any attempt to correlate neuroanatomical substrates with specific substructures of the behaviors or activities under study. In contrast, much attention is paid these days to formal properties of the structures of cognitive activities such as language and music, and the underlying neuroanatomical structures are considered but one route to their analysis.

If we study the arts as distinct from language and other cognitive functions, it behooves us to specify the *a priori* reasons that lead to this distinction. For the purpose of the present discussion, artistic activities, both productive and receptive, are viewed as acts of communication, with the work of art being the medium. That is, artists communicate with members of their culture through their art. What distinguishes the work of art from the linguistic medium of communication is the message. Language is used to communicate relatively precise referents in daily discourse (as distinct from literature, poetry, and plays), such as concrete objects, actions, intentions to act, and even emotional states — all conveyed through symbols. Typically, there is no direct, obvious iconic relation between the symbols and their referents (the word "table" itself, as an acoustic unit, does not resemble anything in the physical object we call a table). A work of art, on the other hand, evokes affective responses in the perceiver, thereby communicating them directly. This direct mode of communication can be characterized by referring to Vygotsky's description of animal communication as a "spread of affect" (37). The arts represent, perhaps, the independent development of vestigial forms of communication, originating with phylogenetically earlier, preverbal affective intraspecies exchange.

Furthermore, it is assumed here that, for the artist, producing a work of art serves to articulate heretofore amorphous emotional states. For the perceiver, a meaningful piece of art is one that evokes affective states in the process of giving them forms. Certain harmonic and melodic progressions, or color or word combinations, recreate in the perceiver emotional states by such means as tension and relaxation, surprise, and so forth, which become "objectified" — they are experienced as the work of art. A discussion of the rationale for the foregoing assertion would take us outside the scope of the present chapter. The interested reader can find a demonstration of the relations between forms and emotions in music by Clynes and Nettheim (10) and in the visual arts by Arnheim (3).

There are also similarities between language and the arts, such as the usage by both of conventional surface structures and symbols, and the fact that both change systematically over time and across cultures, reflecting environmental and social influences. But, unlike the language speaker, the artist eschews precise referents, even in so-called representational art, where distinct objects and scenes are depicted. In the latter case (e.g., a Renaissance painting of a well-known Biblical theme), the realistic objects convey emotional messages that transcend the direct story told by the surface arrangement of the figures. Thus, Leonardo da Vinci's mural *The Last Supper* would be nothing but a depiction of a mundane gathering of 13 men for a meal, were it not for the care taken in composing the spatial relations among the figures, their relation to the background, color combination, overall balance, and so on. The resulting painting conveys, among other things, the universal feelings of sorrow and pity with a sense of balance and serenity. Likewise in music, a simple, less than inspiring tune that has a precise referent, such as nationalistic pride (*America*), can turn into masterpieces in the hands of ingenious composers (Beethoven and Charles Ives both wrote sets of variations on this tune).

The differences between language and art cannot be denied, despite some recent attempts to apply linguistic analysis to the structure of tonal music (27) or to argue that the two systems are completely similar structurally from meaning to surface structures (5). This quantitative gap between precise, denotative referents and imprecise, connotative evocation of affect is sufficient, apparently, so that art and language have survived as distinct and parallel systems throughout the written history of humankind. This fact, together with the universality of the arts in all cultures, corroborates the notion of arts as media of affective communication that serve needed functions, different from and complementary to those of language. It should be added here that throughout history art has been serving well-defined affective functions in conjunction with social activities, such as religious ceremonies, rituals, the reinforcement of social hierarchy (through music and decorations), the curing of a variety of ailments (2), and so forth. Only in the last two centuries have we seen the sprouting of institutions dedicated for the exclusive enjoyment of the arts (concert halls and museums).

What follows from the discussion above is that the arts have much to do with emotional communication and that they are universal in the same way language is. As such, and from the modular perspective, it is reasonable to expect that, through functional differentiation in the central nervous system (CNS), different artistic activities will be associated with somewhat different neuroanatomical substrates than language (28). The hope, however, of finding that artistic endeavors are subserved by a reasonably and consistently distinct, precisely localized brain tissue is overly optimistic. First, every form of art embodies multifarious cognitive acts on both the artist's and the perceiver's parts (30). Second, it is quite a different matter to produce art than to enjoy it. Third, we would expect to find quite a difference between the act of perceiving a work of art by an experienced artist and a layperson. Thus, the same perspective that leads us to postulate a distinct neuroanatomical substrate for artistic activities points also to the possibility of diversity in cerebral organization for the various individuals and behaviors involved. The question arises as to the similarities and differences in the cerebral organization for different forms of art, as they all converge on the affective message but through different routes.

The Evidence

Artists with Brain Lesions

We turn now to a review of an illustrative sample of reported cases of brain-damaged artists. No extensive or exhaustive review is intended, and the reader is referred to other sources for more complete case presentations (7, 14, 21, 22, 30). The neurological literature has quite a number of reported cases of brain-damaged musicians, but very few cases of painters or sculptors, and an even smaller number of writers or poets have been reported. Accordingly, this discussion will rely mostly on case studies of musicians.

In the framework of this "neophrenological" perspective, the objectives of investigating such a population of brain-damaged artists are as follows:

1. Delineating specific impairments in the various aspects of the patient's artistic skill, unrelated to any primary perceptual or motor deficits and assuming a high level of premorbid ability. The purpose here is to identify dissociations, if any, among skills that make up artistic performance (e.g., producing a work of art can be impaired but appreciation for art may remain intact). Such dissociation would suggest differential participation of separate brain tissues in the respective artistic activities.

2. Identifying deficits in other cognitive abilities, most notably language, in order to identify any dissociation between the latter skills and the artistic capabilities. As before, the reasoning is that skills that dissociate from each other following a brain lesion are most likely subserved by different anatomical substrates.

3. Relating the patterns above to specific brain areas. The inference, even if somewhat tenuous, is that an impaired skill in a patient is subserved by the damaged tissue; if it can be demonstrated that in another patient the same skill is spared and the lesion is in another location, then this inference gains support.

Next, one can attempt to construct a hierarchy of subskills making up the totality of the activity in question and its relations with other cognitive functions. This can be done by demonstrating in brain-damaged artists which subskills can be impaired without a noticeable effect on other subskills and on the total creative act, and which skills, when impaired, result in partial or complete extinction of any creativity. This last objective requires many patients, and there is always the chance of finding a new patient who exhibits an unusual pattern of dissociation. Therefore, it is difficult to feel confident about any two skills that seem to be mutually necessary, no matter how well they might fit into a theory or intuition, lest a new patient present with these skills dissociated.

Another important, more general, reason for such studies of artists with cerebral lesions is the implication they can have for the relations between thought and language. Consider a patient — say, a composer — who is no longer capable of expressing himself or herself verbally as a result of an aphasiogenic lesion, but who nevertheless continues to produce pieces of music at the premorbid level. Now, if "thought" is taken in the broadest sense to denote any conscious experience, any "abstract mental activity," then one must conclude that this patient does not use language while thinking, even when articulating the fine ("analytical") points of his or her piece. That is, this artist demonstrates wordless thinking. The objection to this last assertion could be that the inability to express oneself verbally does not entail a lack of "inner" speech. With careful testing of comprehension as well as production, however, the neuropsychologist can ascertain that the patient indeed can no longer use language functionally.

MUSICIANS

Cases of musicians with brain lesions have been reported since the 19th century. Even with very uneven reporting, ranging from the anecdotal to the most detailed scientific study, what appears is a melange of dissociations of musical skills from each other and from language. Also, one finds impaired musical abilities with both left-hemisphere (LH) and right-hemisphere (RH) lesions. This comes, however, as no surprise. First, the term "musician" has been applied liberally to practically anyone who plays an instrument, whether or not such a musician has had any training in music and can even read musical notation. Data from musicians of classical music have not been distinguished, for the purposes of making inferences, from musicians of popular music. Therefore, the level of training of patients has been an uncontrolled variable although it must play a role in the evaluation of amusia (impairment in premorbid musical abilities following brain damage). Second, a composer might be a different kind of musician from a performer (although many composers are also performers). A drummer may differ considerably in cerebral organization from a singer. Third, many skills are involved in music performance: finger dexterity; motor coordination; sensitivity to pitch, timbre, rhythm; a sense of timing; and so on. These skills and perceptual sensitivities may involve different anatomical systems.

Thus, Botez and Wertheim (9) reported a case of amusia in a farm boy who played music by ear, but received no formal training in music, and finished only 5 years of elementary school. Following a lesion to the RH, this patient suffered deficits in many aspects of music perception and performance. Cerebral organization for this case would most likely differ from that of a right-handed trained musician, a violinist and conductor of a small ensemble (reported by Blau and Henson [7]), who suffered two (!) RH strokes that left him with severe left hemiplegia. This latter musician showed no signs of amusia on testing.

Impairment in musical abilities may be accompanied by aphasia (due typically to an LH lesion). Conversely, a musician may be rendered aphasic by LH damage without losing his or her musical abilities. The two well-known cases that illustrate the relation of amusia to aphasia are the case of the French composer Ravel, reported by Alajouanine (1), and the case of the Russian composer Shebalin, reported by Luria et al. (29). Ravel became aphasic as a result of an unspecified LH disease.

Whereas his musical sensibilities remained intact — that is, he could detect errors in playing known pieces, recognize his music, and so forth — he could no longer compose or perform music. Shebalin, on the other hand, who was rendered aphasic by an LH stroke, continued to compose music that was judged by other musicians to be of the highest quality, certainly at his premorbid level. We do not know from these reports the precise localization of the respective lesions (except in the case of Shebalin, where the lesion was reported to be in the LH), and, in the absence of standardized testing, even the aphasic symptoms are conveyed somewhat anecdotally. Yet one is struck by the divergence of symptoms, so that no single conclusion concerning hemispheric dominance for music, based on these two composers, is possible.

There are other reports of aphasic musicians who, aside from reading or execution deficits, were not amusic. For example, Head (20) reported several such patients and concluded that production and recognition of timing and melodies are not affected in aphasia. Here, Head was clearly overstating the case. Marin (30) reviewed published cases of amusia, with 87 cases having fairly complete clinical reports. Of these 87 patients, 33 suffered some form of aphasia in addition to their amusia. Another example that will serve to dispel the notion of consistent dissociation of aphasia and amusia is the case in Wertheim and Botez (39) of a professional right-handed violinist who suffered an LH stroke. This musician became aphasic ("receptive" aphasia) and showed impairments in several musical skills, such as recognition of musical styles, pieces, and composers; humming a familiar melody; or taking musical dictation.

On the other hand, there is no shortage of reported cases of brain damaged musicians with amusia following RH lesions. One such case has already been described above (9). Marin (30) reviews other such cases, and Gardner (14: 329) reports a case of a composer with a "right-hemisphere disease" who lost the motivation to compose and who "could no longer conjure up the appropriate atmosphere," all in the presence of intact musical skills. In one of our own unpublished studies (34), we examined a 36-year-old, right-handed woman with an RH infarct who was a former singer in a college choir. This patient showed mild sensory loss on the right side, a mild visual–constructive deficit, and no other disorders. Three months after onset she could not carry a simple tune (*Twinkle Twinkle Little Star*). When a recording of her singing was played back, she identified only about 50% of the errors she made.

The hypothesis of RH dominance for music (e.g., 8) is much weakened by reported cases of musicians with RH lesions and no amusia. One such report has been mentioned above (7), and other patients were described in the same publication. In addition, all the cases of musicians with amusia resulting from LH damage (see above) could be taken to provide counterevidence for an exclusive RH dominance for music.

Finally, I could find no cases of musicians with LH lesions, with no aphasia, but with amusia. Such dissociation, given a right-handed patient with speech shown to be in the LH, if ever demonstrated, would be indeed curious. It would imply that within a single hemisphere, brain tissue can differentiate into complex cognitive functions and become totally independent; in short, the two skills would show complete functional and anatomical modularity.

OTHER ARTISTS

It has been suggested that some painters actually improved their painting styles following brain damage (14). Aesthetic criteria, however, are somewhat subjective. It is also not possible to test painting skills in the same objective fashion in which musical skills can be assessed. Consequently, such claims remain, for the time being, speculative. Nevertheless, it is clear from reports of brain-damaged painters that, following damage to either hemisphere, at least some artists undergo a noticeable change in their style. But, as Gardner (14) points out, it is unclear whether this change is secondary to a "psychological" metamorphosis as a result of the disease and its implications (recall the affective message of art), or whether the change in style merely reflects the primary effect of the lesion. At the moment it is not clear how these two effects can be distinguished from each other, in principle or in practice.

Two often-cited cases of painters who changed style following cortical lesions are those of Raderscheidt and Corinth (both studied by the German neurologist Jung [23]). Both painters suffered RH strokes, so that their initial paintings reflect some left-side neglect. Aside from changes that might be attributable to perceptual changes, the works of these painters following the lesions are remarkable for the increased intensity, reduced facility, and lightness of lines. Jung (23) studied two other painters, both with RH strokes; both continued painting, albeit with some difficulties and initial left-sided neglect.

Examples of painters who were rendered aphasic by LH lesions were reported by Zaimov et al. (41) and Alajouanine (1). In both cases, the artists continued their creative output unhindered by severe aphasia. These painters' art is said to have been at the premorbid level; but, in the case of Z. B. (41), the style was changed, became more intense, and, as mentioned above, appeared better in the opinions of some critics (15). We had the opportunity to examine an artist who does work in mixed media (painting, collage, videotape, and processed films). This artist is right-handed and underwent craniotomy for clipping of a left parietal arteriovenous malformation. Examined a year following surgery, the artist showed no aphasic symptoms and only a mild to moderate dyslexia, consisting of slow, slavish reading, with occasional literal paralexias. To my mind, the postoperative artistic output of this artist was indistinguishable from his premorbid works, this being confirmed also by his own observations.

I have noted that the RH is, at times, important for creative activity, and that there are reports of both musicians and painters with LH lesions who continued to produce their art normally. Is it possible, then, for a writer (or a poet) to sustain LH damage, become aphasic, and continue his or her creative output? From the few reported cases, the answer is no, but perhaps the end of this story is not yet told. Alajouanine (1) sketched the case of Baudelaire, the famous French poet, who was rendered globally aphasic by a stroke; his creative output came to a premature halt at the same time. Reportedly, Baudelaire was still able to read the proofs of his own writing, suggesting that his receptive ability for artistic writing was less affected than his production. In the same article, Alajouanine (1) reported a case of another writer with Broca's aphasia. This patient showed considerable recovery of spoken language and the ability to criticize others' writings, but never returned to his premorbid level of creative writing.

In this section, only brain-damaged artists have been discussed. It should be mentioned that the effects of brain lesions on the perception of art by nonartists is quite a different subject, which, for the sake of simplicity, is totally omitted here. Unfortunately, it is very difficult to operationalize the essential parameters of art objects so that they can be studied systematically with laypeople, let alone with neurological patients who are not artists (see below).

SUMMARY

To summarize the foregoing discussion on brain-damaged artists, it seems that there is no consistent association between the side of lesion and artistic deficits. One inference might be that both hemispheres partake in the creative process. A corollary of this duality notion is the intriguing proposal of Bogen (8) that the corpus callosum mediates this kind of creative, interhemispheric cooperation in the creative process. It would be of interest, therefore, to compare the corpus callosum of artists to that of laypeople. But how is one to explain the continuation of artistic productivity in the face of a devastating lesion to one hemisphere (e.g., 29)?

Another hypothesis would ascribe dominance to one hemisphere, but a different one for different individuals, depending, for example, on the manner of acquiring artistic skills (formal education vs. self-teaching, etc.). Indeed, the occasional complete dissociation of aphasia from amusia supports a more idiosyncratic hemispheric specialization in the brain, at least for music. Whereas the acquisition of language is relatively consistent within a given culture, the same cannot be said of the acquisition of musical skills. This argument presupposes an experiential basis for language lateralization, currently a rather controversial assumption. Even if artistic abilities (or artistic potential, whatever this term means) are genetically determined, the possibility still remains that their phenotypic realization in brain tissue will not assume the same neuronal networks in different individual artists.

A more pessimistic view would be to abandon hope for correlating a complex set of activities, such as artistic expression, with a circumscribed neuroanatomical substrate, and to opt for a purely psychological explanation of aesthetic expression. Such an approach is, in my opinion, not yet justified—not from a lack of sufficient case studies of brain-damaged artists, but rather because it is not yet clear that inferences of hemispheric specialization for any function can be based merely on studies of deficits in that function following localized brain lesions.

It seems that artistic functions (at least music and painting) can be dissociated from language in the brain of an artist. But we do not know that this apparent functional modularity reflects consistent, separate, and distinct neuroanatomical substrates with which each activity is associated. Nevertheless, such dissociation demonstrates the possibility of artistic thought and expression without the linguistic medium.

Experimental Work with Neurologically
Intact Subjects

In this section, only experiments using musical stimuli will be dealt with, as these constitute the bulk of the experimental studies in the area of art. This fact is the result of methodological, rather than conceptual, considerations. To be used in the experimental situation, the stimuli should be carefully controlled. The price for this control, however, is a simplification of the stimulus array. It is inconceivable to imagine an experiment with dichotic listening where even a single movement from the Ninth Symphony of Beethoven is used as the stimulus. Therefore, only a small component is typically used, such as a fraction of a melody, isolated chords, or even single tones. These stimuli, then, are used in experiments that investigate hemispheric specialization for music. But this is not much different from studying hemispheric specialization for the visual arts by projecting lines of different orientations and colors in the two visual fields, which would be absurd. I know of no such studies claiming to probe lateralization for painting (imagine Hubel and Wiesel claiming they discovered the way a Picasso is perceived by cortical cells), whereas numerous studies have been published in which this or that element of sound is used, presumably, to study lateralization for music (e.g., 36).

In light of the foregoing discussion, it comes as no surprise that the experimental literature on music and cerebral specialization is inconsistent at best (cf. 16 and 17 for a good review of the experimental literature). No attempt is made here to review this confusing corpus of studies; I only outline briefly some of the issues and assumptions that have been plaguing this field.

First, there are two distinct, ill-defined populations of subjects: nonmusicians and musicians. Since there is no universally accepted demarcation between them, the groups are divided somewhat arbitrarily along the following criteria: A nonmusician is one who has had no musical lessions in the last 2 to 5 years; a musician is one who has received continuous lessons and is presently playing an instrument. This dichotomy might suffice for a crude division of subjects with little or no exposure to music from subjects with extensive musical experience. What it lacks is any distinction of creativity from the ordinary. Many instrumental musicians are just that — instrumentalists. Consequently, all the literature on music and laterality in normals can tell us little, if anything, concerning hemispheric specialization for creativity in music. At best, the experimental results tell us something about lateralization of perception of a variety of sounds by inexperienced subjects versus subjects with training in musical listening.

The technique commonly used for inferring hemispheric differences in music processing is the dichotic presentation of "music" in one ear, with (1) noise, (2) silence, or (3) different "music" in the other ear. This method was first used by Kimura (26) to identify hemispheric dominance for melody recognition, and she reported a left-ear advantage (LEA), reflecting, presumably, an RH dominance for the task (cf. chapter by Noffsinger, this volume). Since then, several reports have appeared suggesting this kind of RH dominance (18, 25, 42). On the other hand, Bartholomeus

et al. (4) did not find any ear differences when the musical stimuli used were sung melodies. Single tones presented dichotically produced only an initial LEA in reaction times, which disappeared later (24). Sidtis and Bryden (36) found a right-ear advantage (REA) to single, dichotic tones (which, thank goodness, reversed to an LEA by the third block of trials). Finally, Peretz and Morais (32) found both LEA and REA (!) in a group of nonmusicians, depending on the presumed requirement of analytic (REA) or holistic (LEA) processing.

Including trained musicians in the studies added a new, if not entirely clarifying, dimension to the results. For example, Bever and Chiarello (6) reported an LEA for nonmusicians in monotic (!) presentations of notes, but an REA for the same stimuli in musicians. These results, however, were not confirmed by Zattore (42), who found an LEA for dichotic melodies in both musicians and nonmusicians. Bever and Chiarello (6), following the writing of Heinz Werner (38), suggested an "analytical" versus "holistic" distinction in the style of processing music by musicians and nonmusicians, respectively. This distinction, based primarily on the experimenters' *a priori* conception of the task rather than on the subjects' performance, is still currently used (32). Werner (38), however, regarded the sophisticated perceiver as capable of perceiving both the parts ("analytically") and the whole ("holistically"); that is, the perceiver can move back and forth between the two styles in the process of perceptual organization. Thus, both Shanon (35) and Schweiger (33) found that musicians might have dynamic shifts in dominance from left to right, depending on the complexity of the task at hand: The more complex the task, the greater the tendency for LH dominance.

DISCUSSION

What can we infer from the sampled evidence presented above with regard to the modularity of artistic activity and its representation in the brain? To begin with, it appears that at least music and painting can be dissociated from language to some extent. Moreover, there are plenty of reported cases of musicians with lesions who showed selective deficits in some artistic skills while other skills remained intact (cf. 21 for a detailed review of dissociations of reading music from language reading and other skills). Most notably and commonly, one finds a dissociation between production and appreciation of art. For instance, Ravel (1) could not compose after the onset of the lesion, but could appreciate music. The poet reported by Alajouanine (1) is said to have been able to read literature critically but not to write it. This kind of dissociation is found also in language functions. The inference is that different neural substrates subserve the dissociated skills. But we do not yet know which regions subserve the reception or expression of art.

The dissociation of artistic from linguistic skills implies a functional independence of these two domains and the kind of modularity discussed by Fodor (13). From the perspective of art as a medium for affective communication, this may not be surprising. On the other hand, the skilled artist may employ symbols, notations, conventional concepts, and other quasilinguistic means, so that complete dissociation

of art from language, as seen occasionally (e.g., the case of Shebalin above), is not expected. Some experimental evidence supports, in fact, a single hemispheric processing for both language and music in musicians (6). Perhaps different styles of artistic expression involve different degrees of quasi-linguistic aspects, leading to gradations of LH and RH contribution. Take, for example, the emotionally intense but structurally loose first movement of Robert Schumann's Third Symphony and compare it with the tightly structured but emotionally inaccessible *Variations for Orchestra* (Opus 30) of Anton Webern. The former could be thought to express and engage direct affective processes. The latter requires an analytic approach associated often with problem solving. So, through "guilt by association" as it were, Schumann's symphony could engage quite a different neural system from Webern's *Variations*. A similar distinction could be drawn between styles of painting, writing, and so forth.

Or, perhaps, the case of aphasia coupled with amusia represents nothing but a spatial proximity of tissues subserving language and music skills, so that the lesion impinges fortuitously on two adjacent areas that are, in effect, functionally independent, thus causing deficits in both. At the moment we lack the evidence to decide between the alternative interpretations. One way of tackling the art–language relations in the brain is through correlational studies of the severity of impairments in the two respective functions following brain damage. The higher the correlation of symptom severity in the artistic and linguistic skills in a given artistic patient, the higher the probability that the two are anatomically related.

Concerning neuroanatomical localization, we can say that it is impossible to predict, at least in the case of music and painting, whether an LH or an RH lesion will result in impairment of artistic expression and appreciation. From the cases reviewed above, we are left with two unsatisfying inferences: Either both hemispheres are importantly involved in artistic endeavor, or such individual differences exist among cerebral organizations of artists as to defy a simple lesion–symptom correlation. The third possibility (and I think the most likely one) is that both of these inferences are partly responsible for the diverse lesion–symptom combinations we encounter.

Unfortunately, experimental studies shed little light on hemispheric specialization for music, except for supporting the variety of lesion–symptom combinations discussed above. This is due, in part, to the general difficulty of interpreting laterality data: Do they reflect the dominant hemisphere's exclusive performance (with the other hemisphere shuttling the material to be processed across the corpus callosum), or do they reflect relative specialization of the hemisphere, so that one is simply better than the other for the task (40)? Added to this difficulty is the problem of generalizing from studies utilizing stimuli that are far from resembling real art. Again, this issue is not restricted to the field of psychology of art. Generalizing, for example, from a tachistoscopic lexical-decision task to real reading is as problematic as any generalization from the studies mentioned earlier. But since art involves affective messages, the reduction of the art stimulus in the experimental setting is even more detrimental to the essence of the process under study and, *ipso facto*, to subsequent generalizations as well. Perhaps the affective dimension of artistic perception can be simultaneously measured during experimental manipulations of art objects (e.g., by using galvanic skin responses, heart rate, pupillometry, etc.), so that more complex stimuli can be used while monitoring their affective impact on the subject.

Beyond the criticism and limitations outlined here, what emerges from experimental studies is a difference between the cerebral organization for music in musicians and in laypeople. This difference is in terms of the extent to which the two hemispheres contribute to the artistic activity (in musicians the LH may contribute more, whereas in nonmusicians the RH seems more involved). But in light of the clinical evidence discussed above, we cannot be sure that the relative contribution of the LH and RH is consistent from artist to artist.

Concluding Remarks

Suppose one were to take seriously the notion of dual cognitive systems in the cerebrum, with two different modes of "mental" processing, two lexicons, two semi-independent "minds," and, perhaps, two different aesthetic tastes. Additionally, the RH assumes, in this somewhat simplified depiction, the artistic functions, while the LH engages in the analytical, linguistic processes (see 8 for a list of dichotomized adjectives that characterize the hemispheres, and 19 for a case study of a woman who, reportedly, can shift from RH to LH — or LH to RH — modes of functioning at will!). What would be the implications of such an unlikely scenario for the psychology of art?

Many opposing processes can be attributed each to a different hemisphere: For example, the dualism in the philosophies and arts of the Far East can be snugly accommodated by the two hemispheres (e.g., the yin–yang forces in the Chinese tradition), especially since they are considered to be complementary rather than mere opposites. As another example, consider Freud's dualism in mental functions in the form of the pleasure principle versus the reality principle. The artist, according to Freud, attempts to express instinctual, erotic wishes through the socially acceptable art object — wishes the artist cannot otherwise acknowledge. Here the duality of mind enters the picture: The RH might operate according to the pleasure principle, while the LH may function in accordance with the reality principle. In the artist, the corpus callosum allows the RH to transmit its "debased" mental products to the analytic LH for their realization into acceptable forms.

Without espousing the foregoing moral–cerebral dialectics, the possibility still remains that certain unconscious processes go on in the RH while the LH maintains the conscious domain under control. For example, in the artistic process, which involves a novel arrangement of familiar elements to form an affective message, the RH may provide the neural substrate for fresh perspectives or insight, simply because of its different mental *modus operandi*.

But almost any duality may fit the two hemispheres, so that without either supporting evidence or a guiding theory, such anthropomorphizing of the cerebral cortices is very speculative at best. It raises ontological problems concerning how the two hemispheres, residing within the same cranium and subjected to roughly the same experiences, develop two opposing perspectives. An answer that explains this duality on the basis of differences in genetic wiring removes the problem to an earlier stage of development but does not solve it. On the other hand, it is conceivable that in the developmental process, the cortices specialize for different processes, and that within each hemisphere there is additional differentiation. A complex process that draws on several resources (sensory–motor, perceptual, emotional, and intellectual), such as artistic expression, demands participation of both hemispheres, albeit to varying degrees in different individuals.

Future desiderata for the neuropsychology of art include the following: (1) experiments with art stimuli that resemble real art, with special attention to including the affective component in the studies—even at the expense of scientific rigor; (2) more investigations of the artistic expression per se in real time in the context of hemispheric specialization—for example, using real-time indices of hemispheric activation, such as electroencephalography (TenHouten, personal communication), cerebral blood flow, galvanic skin response, and so on (cf. 11 and 12 for discussions on physiological measurements of music performance and perception); (3) longitudinal studies of cerebral organization and changes therein, in artists, gifted children, and laypeople undergoing artistic training, under the assumption that cerebral organization is not completely fixed at birth and can be modified through experience; (4) standardized tests for artistic production and perception (not merely tests of this or that separate skill), so that data from different brain-damaged artists can be compared and meaningful inferences can be made concerning levels of impairment or competence.

REFERENCES

1. Alajouanine, T., Aphasia and artistic realization. *Brain*, 1948, 71: 229–241.
2. Alvin, J., *Music Therapy*. Basic Books, New York, 1975.
3. Arnheim, R., *Art and Visual Perception*. University of California Press, Berkeley, 1974.
4. Bartholomeus, B. N., Doehring, D. G., and Freygood, S. D., Absence of stimulus effects in dichotic singing. *Bull. Psychonom. Soc.*, 1973, 1: 171–172.
5. Bernstein, L., *The Unanswered Question*. Harvard University Press, Cambridge, Mass., 1976.
6. Bever, T. G., and Chiarello, R. J., Cerebral dominance in musicians and nonmusicians. *Science*, 1974, 185: 537–539.
7. Blau, J. N., and Henson, R. A., Neurological disorders in performing musicians. In: *Music and the Brain*. Heinemann, London, 1977: 301–323.
8. Bogen, J., The other side of the brain: II. An appositional mind. *Bull. Los Angeles Neurol. Soc.*, 1969, 34: 135–217.
9. Botez, M. I., and Wertheim, N., Expressive aphasia and amusia following right frontal lesion in a right-handed man. *Brain*, 1959, 82: 186–201.
10. Clynes, M., and Nettheim, N., The living quality of music: Neurobiologic basis of communicating feelings. In: *Music, Mind and Brain* (M. Clynes, Ed.). Plenum Press, New York, 1982: 47–86.

11. Critchley, M., and Henson, R. A., Eds., *Music and the Brain*. Heinemann, London, 1977.
12. Deutsch, D., *The Psychology of Music*. Academic Press, New York, 1982.
13. Fodor, J. A., *The Modularity of Mind*. MIT Press, Cambridge, Mass., 1983.
14. Gardner, H., *Art, Mind and Brain*. Basic Books, New York, 1982.
15. Gardner, H., *The Shattered Mind*. Vintage Books, New York, 1974.
16. Gates, A., and Bradshaw, J. L., Music perception and cerebral asymmetries. *Cortex*, 1977, **39**: 390–401.
17. Gates, A., and Bradshaw, J. L., The role of the cerebral hemispheres in music. *Brain Lang.*, 1977, **4**: 403–431.
18. Goodglass, H., and Calderon, M., Parallel processing of verbal and musical stimuli in right and left hemispheres. *Neuropsychologia*, 1977, **15**: 397–407.
19. Gott, P. S., Hughes, E. C., and Whipple, K., Voluntary control of two lateralized conscious states: Validation by electrical and behavioral studies. *Neuropsychologia*, 1984, **22**: 65–72.
20. Head, H., *Aphasia and Kindred Disorders of Speech, Vol. 1*. Hafner, New York, 1963.
21. Judd, T., Gardner, H., and Geschwind, N., *Alexia without Agraphia in a Composer*. Harvard Project Zero Technical Report, No. 15, 1980.
22. Judd, T., Gardner, H., and Geschwind, N., Alexia without agraphia in a composer. *Brain*, 1983, **106**: 435–457.
23. Jung, R., Neuropsychologie und Neurophysiologie des Kontur— und Formsehens in Zeichnung und Maleri. In: *Psychopathologie Musischer Gestaltungen* (H. H. Wieck, Ed.). F. K. Schattauer, Stuttgart, 1974: 27–88.
24. Kallman, H. J., and Corballis, M. C., Ear asymmetry in reaction time to musical sounds. *Percept. Psychophys.* 1975, **17**: 368–370.
25. Kimura, D., Functional asymmetry of the brain in dichotic listening. *Cortex*, 1967, **3**: 163–178.
26. Kimura, D., Left-right differences in the perception of melodies. *Q. J. Exp. Psychol.*, 1964, **16**: 355–358.
27. Lerdahl, F., and Jackendoff, R., *A Generative Theory of Tonal Music*. MIT Press, Cambridge, Mass., 1983.
28. Luria, A. R., *Higher Cortical Functions in Man*. Basic Books, New York, 1980.
29. Luria, A. R., Tsvetkova, L. S., and Futer, D. S., Aphasia in a composer. *Journal of the Neurological Sciences*, 1965, **2**: 288–292.
30. Marin, O. S. M., Neurological aspects of music perception and performance. In: *The Psychology of Music* (D. Deutsch, Ed.). Academic Press, New York, 1982: 453–477.
31. Meyer, A., The search for a morphological substrate in the brains of eminent persons including musicians: A historical review. In: *Music and the Brain* (M. Critchley and R. A. Henson, Eds.). Heinemann, London, 1977: 255–297.
32. Peretz, I., and Morais, J., Task determinants of ear differences in melody processing. *Brain Cog.*, 1983, **2**: 313–330.
33. Schweiger, A., and Maltzman, I., Behavioral and electrodermal measures of lateralization for music perception in musicians and nonmusicians. *Biological Psychology*, 1985, **20**: 129–145.
34. Schweiger, A., Zaidel, E., and Wechsler, A. F., Cross-aphasia in a dextral fashion designer: Atypical organization or a typical impairment? A case study with CT and PET scans correlates. Paper presented at the International Neuropsychology Society meeting, Aachen, West Germany, June 1984.
35. Shanon, B., Lateralization effects in music decision tasks. *Neuropsychologia*, 1982, **18**: 21–31.
36. Sidtis, J., and Bryden, M. P., Asymmetrical perception of language and music: Evidence for independent processing strategies. *Neuropsychologia*, 1978, **16**: 627–632.

37. Vygotsky, L. S., *Thought and Language*. MIT Press, Cambridge, Mass., 1962.
38. Werner, H., *Comparative Psychology of Mental Development*. Science Editions, New York, 1948.
39. Wertheim, N., and Botez, M. I., Receptive amusia: A clinical analysis. *Brain*, 1961, **84**: 19–30.
40. Zaidel, E., Disconnection syndrome as a model for laterality effects in the normal brain. In: *Cerebral Hemisphere Asymmetry: Method, Theory, and Application*. (J. B. Hellige, Ed.). Praeger, New York, 1983: 95–151.
41. Zaimov, K., Kitov, D., and Kolev, N., Aphasie chez un paintre. *Encephale*, 1969, **68**: 377–417.
42. Zattore, R., Recognition of dichotic melodies by musicians and nonmusicians. *Neuropsychologia* 1979, **17**: 607–617.

IMPLICATIONS OF HEMISPHERIC
SPECIALIZATION FOR PSYCHIATRY

PETER E. TANGUAY, MD
Department of Psychiatry

INTRODUCTION

This chapter was presented 2½ days into the conference on hemispheric specialization. The conference was drawing to a close, and none too soon: Many of us were at the point of hemispheric exhaustion, our left hemispheres riven by disordered thoughts, our right hemispheres alternatively sunk into depression or driven to manic exhaustion. Several cases of hysterical deafness had been reported, involving, curiously enough, only the left ear. Worse, there were some in the audience whose corpus callosum had been rendered functionally nonfunctional: They were, I feared, showing unmistakable signs of dementia praecox, despite their mature ages. If this "state of being talked to" continued, I feared we were all in danger of regressing to a lower stage of brain organization, a stage in which our ability to use logical operations would dissolve and be replaced with "synchretic thinking," "primary process operations," and "holistic thought." What we needed was an understanding of the relationships of hemispheric specialization to our current psychiatric disorders — those that I have just finished listing — and, as the title implies, that is what this chapter is about.

I find hemispheric specialization to be a powerfully seductive model for studying psychopathology. It has the advantage of a seeming simplicity, yet it is broadly applicable to almost any behavior you may wish to think about. As a clinician and a research investigator, I find the model theoretically fascinating and well worthy of use in the everlasting search for a better understanding of the etiology, prevention, and treatment of psychiatric disorders. Many others apparently share this interest, as witnessed by the hundreds of articles that have appeared in the past few years on the subject of the role of hemispheric specialization in psychiatric disorders (40, 47). The disorders to which it has been applied range from schizophrenia and depression to hysterical conversion reaction and psychotic disorders of childhood. You will forgive me if I have caricatured some of the resulting ideas in my introduction. Perhaps I was moved to do this because, although it is an elegant theoretical model, it is not always so easy to use it in the everyday study of patients, as we will see from the contradictory results reported in so many studies.

Rationale for Use of the Model

In 1969, Flor-Henry (14) made what I believe to be one of the first arguments in favor of applying the model of hemispheric specialization to understanding psychopathology. His comments were made in the context of a study of the behavioral and emotional manifestations of focal epilepsy. What he noted was that epileptic patients with schizophrenic-like psychoses had either a bilateral or a left temporal focus, while patients with a right temporal focus were more likely to manifest an affective disorder. This was an argument based on known neurological dysfunction. In the intervening years, however, the rationale for studies of right- and left-brain function in psychiatric patients has largely been based upon a postulated similarity between symptoms of psychiatric disorders and aspects of hemispheric function. Schizophrenia, for example, is a disorder in which incoherence, looseness of associations, and illogicality of thinking may be prominent, and in which there may be a concomitant blunting, flatness, and inappropriateness of affect. The former cannot fail to suggest disturbances in language and cognitive activities such as have been linked to left-hemisphere function, while the latter suggests disturbances in right-hemisphere function, at least insofar as various investigators have postulated that emotional phenomena are linked to the right hemisphere (4, 36). Again, based upon the symptoms of affective disorders, the same could be said for affective disorders and right-hemisphere function.

A recent paper by Callaway and Naghdi (8) extends the rationale even further. Based upon their interpretation of previous electrophysiological studies of schizophrenic individuals (studies that were not themselves designed to investigate hemispheric specialization), they postulate that schizophrenics have a deficiency in information processing that can be described as conscious, serial, and limited in channel capacity. In contrast, those processes that appear to be automatic, unconscious, and parallel appear to be normal or supernormal in schizophrenics. If their postulations are true, one would expect to find a left-hemisphere dysfunction in schizophrenia, with concomitant normal right-hemisphere function.

What I propose to do in this chapter is to present an overview of the research on hemispheric specialization and psychiatric disorders, concluding with a critical look at this work, its shortcomings, and in particular the improvements that are needed in future work.

Schizophrenia

Of all the psychiatric syndromes, schizophrenia has been given by far the most attention by investigators interested in left- and right-hemisphere function. Because of space constraints, my review must be brief. For those interested in greater detail, there are several comprehensive review articles on the subject (40, 47).

Dichotic Studies

With few exceptions, schizophrenics manifest significant performance decrement in dichotic perception (47). These deficits are found for linguistic as well as nonlinguistic stimuli, and they are not worse for the right or left ear. Schizophrenics generally show a right-ear superiority for verbal stimuli, and in the one study by Coulbourn and Lishman (10), which used tone stimuli, they showed a left-ear advantage. As such, they do not differ from normal subjects. When the degree of lateralization is studied (i.e., when measurements are made of the absolute right-ear–left-ear differences in the results), schizophrenics have been found (47) to show greater ear differences than do control subjects, usually because of a decrement in left-ear performance. Interestingly, similar decrements have been reported after damage to the corpus callosum (32, 43), though such damage has not been associated with a decrement in right-ear scores, as is the case with schizophrenics. Others (19, 33) have interpreted these findings as indicative of an exaggerated attentional bias toward the right hemisphere, possibly resulting from left-hemisphere overactivation.

Dichoptic Studies

In one of the first studies in which stimuli were presented to the left or right hemiretina of schizophrenic individuals, Beaumont and Dimond (5) reported that schizophrenics were poorer that control subjects in matching letters presented in the right visual field and in matching shapes and digits presented in the left visual field. They interpreted these findings as indicating that the schizophrenic subjects might have a deficient callosal transfer. In another such study, using dot-location and letter-identification tasks (21), schizophrenics, like normals, were found to have a left-visual-field superiority for matching shapes but a reversed-visual-field superiority (left greater than right) for letter identification in comparison to normal subjects. The author interpreted this as being consistent with a left-hemisphere defect in schizophrenic subjects. Other investigators (34) have failed to replicate these findings, however, and Walker and McGuire (47) have suggested that Gur's results could be interpreted as indicative of slower left-hemisphere processing rather than of a lack of linguistic processing in this hemisphere.

Tactile Evoked Response Studies

In 1981, Jones and Miller (27) reported that early peak latencies in the somatosensory evoked response of schizophrenic subjects were the same, irrespective of whether stimuli were delivered ipsilaterally or contralaterally — a finding at variance with that for normal subjects, whose contralateral responses showed earlier peaks. They suggested that this might be a result of defective callosal transmission, much as if these patients had a "split brain." Their methods have since been criticized by Connolly (9) and by Shagass et al. (41). The latter group found no asymmetries in early peak latencies under similar experimental conditions in either schizophrenic or normal subjects. In contrast to each of the above, Gulman (20) reported somatosensory evoked response findings that he interpreted as indicative of callosal transmission, but only from the left to the right hemisphere.

Computer Tomography (CT) Studies

The earliest brain imaging studies used pneumoencephalographic (PEG) techniques. In general, it was found that schizophrenic subjects, and especially those with severe and chronic symptoms, did have a variety of nonspecific cortical and subcortical abnormalities (24). With the advent of the CT scan, a much more precise estimation of anatomic abnormality became available. In a review of some 25 such studies, Weinberger *et al.* (48) concluded that earlier PEG findings of enlarged ventricles, cortical atrophy, and cerebellar atrophy were indeed correct, and that some patients also exhibited certain unilateral defects. Golden *et al.* (18) reported anterior left-hemisphere atrophy in a subgroup of patients, while Luchins *et al.* (29) have reported that schizophrenics have larger left than right frontal areas and larger right than left occipital areas — a result that is the reverse of what has been reported by Galaburda *et al.* (15) in normal subjects. Tsai *et al.* (45) have reported similar reversals in schizophrenic subjects, though their control population consisted of manic patients and not normals. In contrast, careful blinded studies of CT scans by Andreason *et al.* (1) failed to find significant differences in structural asymmetry in 43 right-handed schizophrenic patients compared to 40 normal controls.

Cerebral Blood Flow Studies

Using the xenon inhalation technique, one can measure regional cerebral blood flow (rCBF) within a specific area of the brain, as well as measure mean blood flow in the right or left hemisphere. One rCBF study reported significant bilateral reductions in frontal blood flow in schizophrenic persons (25) along with significantly increased activity in both temporo-occipital regions. In contrast, Matthew *et al.* (30) found a significant decrease in only the right frontal region.

Gur *et al.* (22) measured the rCBF during resting baseline and during performance of verbal and spatial tasks. Schizophrenic subjects did not differ from normals at rest, but they failed to show the asymmetries in blood flow seen in normals as they performed the tasks. Normals showed a greater increase in blood flow to the left hemisphere during the verbal task and a greater flow to the right hemisphere during the spatial task. In contrast, schizophrenic subjects showed no flow asymmetry for the verbal task and a greater left-hemispheric increase for the spatial task. Gur interpreted these findings as indicating that schizophrenic subjects exhibited left-hemispheric overactivation for spatial tasks.

Most recently, and in contrast to all of the studies described above, Ariel *et al.* (3) (again using verbal and spatial tasks) have reported finding significantly lower rCBF values for all brain regions in schizophrenic subjects, with relatively greater reductions in the grey matter of the anterior of the brain. They interpreted these findings as indicative of bilateral anterior deficits in schizophrenic subjects.

Positron Emission Tomography (PET)
Scan Studies

PET scanning is a new technique, and only two studies using this technique have been reported to date (7, 13). Both reported less frontal activity in schizophrenics, with Buchsbaum also reporting decreases in the left central grey regions (in the area of the caudate nucleus) as well. Both studies had small sample sizes.

AFFECTIVE DISORDERS

Although individuals with affective disorders constitute the second most popular group of patients for hemispheric-specialization studies, the number of such studies is still relatively small when compared to work done with schizophrenics. There have been two approaches to studying the question of hemispheric disorders and affective disorders. The first is to study the incidence of affective symptoms in patients with known brain lesions. The second involves neurobehavioral and brain-imaging studies of patients with affective disorders.

Flor-Henry's finding (14) that depressive symptomatology is primarily found in patients with right-hemisphere focal epilepsy, an example of the first approach, has already been noted. In subsequent work in this vein, Robinson and Price (35) evaluated 103 cases attending a poststroke clinic for depressive disorders. They used structured interviews and questionnaires to insure accuracy of diagnosis. Almost one-third of patients were found to be depressed at initial assessment, and two-thirds of these remained depressed at 7- to 8-month follow-up. Patients with left-hemisphere brain injury were significantly more depressed than patients with right-hemisphere or brain stem infarctions. Patients at highest risk for depression were those with left frontal lesions. A similar study of a smaller number of patients by Lipsey *et al.* (28), in which the neurological appraisal of the location of the lesion was improved by the availability of CT scan data for all patients, again revealed that patients with left anterior brain injury were significantly more depressed than patients without such injury. The severity of the depression was significantly correlated with the proximity of the lesion to the frontal pole.

Jampala and Abrams (26) reported two single case studies of right-handed male patients who developed manic episodes following vascular lesions to one hemisphere. The lesions were verified by means of CT scans. In one instance the lesion was in the right hemisphere, and in the other it was in the left hemisphere.

Coming at the question from the second perspective, a few studies have been attempted to actually measure right- and left-hemisphere function in patients who were depressed. Silberman *et al.* (42), using dichoptically presented stimuli, found that depressed women showed a trend toward right-hemisphere superiority in judging whether tachistoscopically presented letters were the same or different. They suggested that the right hemisphere in these individuals might be compensating for a relative deactivation of the left hemisphere.

Yozawitz *et al.* (49) investigated ear asymmetries to dichotic stimuli (lagged clicks in one experiment and lagged words in another) and found that patients with affective disorders had ear asymmetries similar to those seen in persons with right temporal lesions. In another dichotic experiment, using dichotic sound localization, Sackeim *et al.* (38) reported that a 42-year-old man with a bipolar disorder had results that they interpreted as showing hyperactivation of the right hemisphere during a hypomanic episode and of the left hemisphere during a depressive episode.

Using rCBF techniques, Uytdenhoef *et al.* (46) found that patients with a major depressive disorder had left frontal hypervascularization and right posterior hypovascularization. They interpreted their results as suggesting cerebral dysfunction in both hemispheres in depression. These results contrast with those of Gustafson *et al.* (23), who reported normal rCBF in depressed patients, and Matthew *et al.* (31), who reported low rCBF values in the left hemisphere of depressed patients.

HYSTERICAL NEUROSES

A small number of studies have addressed this question: Do hysterical conversion symptoms tend to be found more on the left or the right side of the body? In one Galin *et al.* (16) reported finding a greater likelihood that sensory or motor conversion symptoms would be present on the left side. Of 42 female patients, the symptoms were on the left in 71% ($p < .008$). These results are not in agreement, however, with those of an earlier study (12), which reported no such lateralization.

DEVELOPMENTAL DISORDERS IN CHILDHOOD

A number of interesting speculations have been made on the role of hemispheric specialization in psychopathology and handicapping conditions in children. Various researchers have attempted to study the role of hemispheric specialization in dyslexia. These studies have been based on suggestion that there is a disconnection of the language areas of the left hemisphere from the auditory and visual input systems of the right hemisphere (17), or on the possibility that there is both a right-hemisphere dyslexia and a left-hemisphere dyslexia, each having quite different characteristics (6). The results of such studies have generally supported the hypothesis of incomplete left-hemisphere speech representation in poor readers. However, as Satz has pointed out (39), numerous methodological and conceptual problems have plagued this research.

More recently, it has been suggested that early infantile autism may involve failure of left-hemisphere language and cognitive systems to develop. One study by Dawson (11), in which patients were given the Halstead–Reitan Neurospsychological Battery, suggested that, as a group, autistic subjects showed a pattern of deficits indicating a significantly greater degree of left-hemisphere dysfunction than a comparison group of neurological patients with bilateral or diffuse brain damage.

On a somewhat similar, but more ambitious plane, two authors have suggested that the development (or mal-development) of hemispheric specialization may play a key role in a range of psychopathology in childhood. Rourke (37) has postulated that there is an ontogenetic progression from the salience of right-hemisphere functions to that of left-hemisphere functions, which is manifest in the manner in which children learn to conceptualize. Failure to develop left-hemisphere systems may result in one set of behavioral disturbances in reading and language, while failure in right-hemisphere development results in handicaps in non-verbal communication and the ability to respond socially. I (44) have postulated that development may be viewed as a process that takes place across a number of important dimensions, including those of holistic and sequential cognitive function. If dissociations in the development of each of these modes occur, they may be manifested as a range of psychopathology we label as early infantile autism, schizophrenia, and language and reading disorders. Study of the latter hypothesis is about to begin in the UCLA Child Psychiatry Clinical Research Center.

Conclusion

Despite the usefulness of hemispheric specialization as a theoretical model for studying psychopathology, it is clear that the literature is filled with inconsistent results. A careful appraisal of this literature does not lead me to the opinion that the concept itself is faulty, but that the methods used to investigate the hypothesis are often wanting. In order to improve such endeavors, I make the following suggestions:

1. Investigators must not assume that the disorders such as schizophrenia or early infantile autism are unitary "diseases." They, and perhaps many other disorders in our present nomenclature, are syndromes and may represent quite different subgroups of illnesses. It would appear, for instance, that the "negative" symptoms of schizophrenia (affective flattening, alogia, etc.) may represent a separate dimension from the "positive" symptoms (prominent delusions, hallucinations, etc.) and may need to be dealt with as such (2). More studies need to be carried out to identify valid subgroups if we are to be able to understand how right- or left-hemisphere dysfunction relates to specific forms of psychopathology.

2. Investigators must deal more effectively with issues of symptom assessment and diagnosis. Structured interviews and valid questionnaires are an absolute necessity for this purpose. Any investigator who fails to comply with this mandate is probably wasting his or her time and grant money.

3. Investigators must find better ways of controlling such important variables as medication effect, subject state, degree of chronicity of psychopathology, and the presence of diffuse and nonspecific brain damage. Medication can be particularly difficult to deal with, since the phenothiazines used with schizophrenic patients may remain active in the body for weeks or even months after they are discontinued. The results of CT or PET scan studies in which subjects are not given a task are almost impossible to interpret, since no one knows what was going on in the subject's mind at the time of the recording.

4. There need to be more basic studies of the various neuropsychological and electrophysiological techniques being used with patients. It may be premature to rush to use the latest technique with patients before we have a truly adequate knowledge of what controls the results. I believe that many of the problems with the research reviewed above can be traced to such premature use.

REFERENCES

1. Andreason, N. C., Dennert, J. W., Olsen, C. A., and Damasio, A. R., Hemispheric asymmetries and schizophrenia. *Am. J. Psychiatry*, 1982, **139**: 427–30.
2. Andreason, N. C., and Olsen, S., Negative v. positive schizophrenia. *Arch. Gen. Psychiatry*, 1982, **39**: 789–793.
3. Ariel, R. N., Golden, C. J., Berg, R. A., Quaife, M. A., Dirksen, J. W., Forsell, T., Wilson, J., and Graber, B., Regional cerebral blood flow in schizophrenics. *Arch. Gen. Psychiatry*, 1983, **40**: 258–263.
4. Bear, D. M., Hemispheric specialization and the neurology of emotion. *Arch. Neurol.*, 1983, **40**: 195–201.
5. Beaumont, J. G., and Dimond, S., Brain disconnection and schizophrenia. *Br. J. Psychiatry*, 1973, **123**: 661–662.
6. Boder, E., School failure — evaluation and treatment. *Pediatrics*, 1976, **58**: 394–403.
7. Buchsbaum, M. S., Ingvar, D. H., Kessler, R., Waters, R. N., Cappelletti, J., von Kammen, D., King, A. C., Johnson, J. L., Manning, R. G., Flynn, R. W., Mann, L. S., Bunney, W. E., and Sokoloff, L., Cerebral glucography with positron tomography: Use in normal subjects and in patients with schizophrenia. *Arch. Gen. Psychiatry*, 1982, **39**: 251–259.
8. Callaway, E., and Naghdi, S., An information processing model for schizophrenia. *Arch. Gen. Psychiatry*, 1982, **39**: 339–347.
9. Connolly, J. F., Correspondence. *Br. J. Psychiatry*, 1982, **140**: 429–430.
10. Coulbourn, C. J., and Lishman, W. A., Lateralization of function and psychotic illness: A left hemisphere defect? In: *Hemispheric Asymmetries of Function in Psychopathology* (J. Gruzelier and P. Flor-Henry, Eds.). Elsevier/North-Holland, New York, 1979: 539–560.
11. Dawson, G., Lateralized brain dysfunction in autism: Evidence from the Halsted–Reitan Neuropsychological Battery. *J. Autism Dev. Disord.*, 1983, **13**: 269–286.
12. Fallik, A., and Sigal, M., Hysteria — the choice of symptom site: A review of 40 cases of conversion hysteria. *Psychother. Psychosom.*, 1971, **19**: 310–318.
13. Farkas, T., Reivich, M., Alavi, A., Breenberg, J. H., Fowler, J. S., MacGregor, R. R., Christman, D. R., and Wolf, A. P., The application of 18-F-deoxy-2-fluoro-D-glucose and positron emission tomography in the study of psychiatric conditions. In: *Cerebral Metabolism and Neural Function* (J. V. Passonneau, R. A. Hawkins, W. D. Lust, and F. A. Welsh, Eds.). Williams & Wilkins, Baltimore, 1980: 403–408.
14. Flor-Henry, P., Psychosis and temporal lobe epilepsy. *Epilepsia*, 1969, **10**: 363–395.
15. Galaburda, A. M., LeMay, M., Kemper, T. I., and Geschwind, N., Right–left asymmetries in the brain. *Science*, 1978, **199**: 852–856.
16. Galin, D., Diamond, R., and Braff, D., Lateralization of conversion symptoms: More frequent on the left. *Am. J. Psychiatry*, 1977, **134**: 578–580.

17. Geschwind, N., The organization of language and the brain. *Science*, 1970, **170**: 940–944.
18. Golden, C. J., Graber, B., Coffman, J., and Berg, R. A., Structural brain deficits in schizophrenia: Identification by computed tomographic scan density measurements. *Arch. Gen. Psychiatry*, 1981, **38**: 1014–1017.
19. Gruzelier, J., and Hammond, V., Lateralized deficits and drug influences on the dichotic listening of schizophrenic patients. *Biol. Psychiatry*, 1980, **15**: 759–779.
20. Gulmann, N. C., Wildschiodtz, G., and Orbaek, K., Alteration of interhemispheric conduction through corpus callosum in chronic schizophrenia. *Biol. Psychiatry*, 1982, **17**: 585–594.
21. Gur, R. E., Left hemisphere dysfunction and overactivation in schizophrenia. *J. Abnorm. Psychol.*, 1978, **87**: 226–238.
22. Gur, R. E., Skolnick, B. E., Gur, R. C., Caroff, S., Riegner, W., Obrist, W. D., Younkin, D., and Reivich, M., Brain function in psychiatric disorders: Regional blood flow in medicated schizophrenics. *Arch. Gen. Psychiatry*, 1983, **40**: 1250–1254.
23. Gustafson, L., Johanson, M., Risberg, J., and Silfverskiold, P., Regional cerebral blood flow in organic dementias, affective disorders and confustional states. In: *Biological Psychiatry 1981: Proceedings of the IIIrd World Congress of Biological Psychiatry* (C. Perris, G. Struwe, and B. Jansson, Eds.). Elsevier/North-Holland, New York, 1981: 276–279.
24. Huber, G., Gross, G., and Schuttler, K., A long-term followup study of schizophrenia: Psychiatric course of illness and prognosis. *Acta Psychiatr. Scand.*, 1975, **52**: 49–57.
25. Ingvar, D. H., Functional landscapes of the dominant hemisphere. *Brain Res.*, 1976, **107**: 181–197.
26. Jampala, V. C., and Abrams, R., Mania secondary to left and right hemisphere damage. *Am. J. Psychiatry*, 1983, **140**: 1197–1199.
27. Jones, G. H., and Miller, J. J., Functional tests of the corpus callosum in schizophrenia. *Br. J. Psychiatry*, 1981, *139*: 553–557.
28. Lipsey, J. R., Robinson, R. G., Pearlson, G. D., Rao, K., and Price, T. R., Mood change following bilateral hemisphere brain injury. *Br. J. Psychiatry*, 1983, **143**: 266–273.
29. Luchins, D. J., Weinberger, D. R., and Wyatt, R. J., Schizophrenia: Evidence for a subgroup with reversed cerebral asymmetry detected by computed tomography. *Am. J. Psychiatry*, 1982, **139**: 753–757.
30. Matthew, R. J., Meyer, J. S., Francis, D., Schoolar, J. C., Weinman, M., and Mortel, K. F., Regional cerebral blood flow in schizophrenia: A preliminary report. *Am. J. Psychiatry*, 1981, **138**: 112–113.
31. Matthew, R. J., Meyer, J. S., Francis, D. J., Semchuk, K. M., Mortel, K., and Claghorn, J. L., Cerebral blood flow in depression. *Am. J. Psychiatry*, 1980, **137**: 1449–1150.
32. Milner, B., Taylor, L., and Sperry, R. W., Lateralized suppression of dichotically presented digits after commissural section in man. *Science*, 1968, **168**: 241–242.
33. Nachshon, I., Hemispheric dysfunctions in schizophrenia. *J. Nerv. Ment. Dis.*, 1980, **168**: 241–242.
34. Pic'l, A., Magaro, P., and Wade, E. A., Hemispheric functioning in paranoid and non-paranoid schizophrenia. *Biol. Psychiatry*, 1979, **14**: 891–903.
35. Robinson, R. G., and Price, T. R., Poststroke depressive disorders: A followup study of 103 patients. *Stroke*, 1982, **13**: 635–640.
36. Ross, E. D., The aprosodias. *Arch. Neurol.*, 1981, **38**: 561–570.
37. Rourke, B. P., Central processing deficiencies in children: Toward a developmental neuropsychological model. *J. Clin. Neuropsychol.*, 1982, **4**: 12–18.
38. Sackeim, H. A., Decina, P., Epstein, D., Bruder, G. E., and Malitz, S., Possible reversed affective lateralization in a case of bipolar disorder. *Am. J. Psychiatry*, 1983, **140**: 1191–1193.

39. Satz, P., Cerebral dominance and reading disability: An old problem revisited. In: *The Neuropsychology of Learning Disorders* (R. M. Knight and D. J. Bakker, Eds.). University Park Press, Baltimore, 1976: 273–294.

40. Seidman, L. J., Schizophrenia and brain dysfunction: An integration of recent neuro-diagnostic findings. *Psychol. Bull.*, 1983, 94: 195–238.

41. Shagass, C., Josiassen, R. C., Roemer, R. A., Straumanis, J. J., and Slepner, S. M., Failure to replicate evoked potential observations suggesting corpus callosum dysfunction in schizophrenia. *Br. J. Psychiatry*, 1983, 142: 471–476.

42. Silberman, E. K., Weingartner, H., Stillman, R., Chen, H. J., and Post, R. M., Altered lateralization of cognitive process in depressed women. *Am. J. Psychiatry*, 1983, 140: 1340–1144.

43. Springer, S. P., Sidtis, J., Wilson, D., and Gazzaniga, M. S., Left ear performance in dichotic listening following commissurotomy. *Neuropsychologia*, 1978, 16: 305–312.

44. Tanguay, P. E., Toward a new system of classification of serious psychopathology in childhood. *J. Am. Acad. Child Psychiatry*, 1984, 23: 373–384.

45. Tsai, L. Y., Nasrallah, H. A., and Jacoby, C. G., Hemispheric asymmetries on computer tomographic scans in schizophrenia and mania. *Arch. Gen. Psychiatry*, 1983, 40: 1286–1289.

46. Uytdenhoef, P., Portelange, P., Jacquy, J., Charles, G., Linkowski, P., and Mendlewicz, J., Regional cerebral blood flow and lateralized hemispheric dysfunction in depression. *Br. J. Psychiatry*, 1983, 143: 128–132.

47. Walker, E., and McGuire, M., Intra- and inter-hemispheric information processing in schizophrenia. *Psychol. Bull.*, 1982, 92: 701–725.

48. Weinberger, D. R., DeLisi, L. E., Perman, G. P., Targum, S., and Wyatt, R. J., Computed tomography in schizophreniform disorder and other acute psychiatric disorders. *Arch. Gen. Psychiatry*, 1982, 39: 778–783.

49. Yozawitz, A., Bruder, G., Sutton, S., Sharpe, L., Gurland, B., Fleiss, J., and Costa, L., Dichotic perception: Evidence for right ear dysfunction in affective psychosis. *Br. J. Psychiatry*, 1979, 135: 224–237.

THE SIGNIFICANCE OF HEMISPHERIC
SPECIALIZATION FOR CLINICAL MEDICINE

D. FRANK BENSON, MD
Department of Neurology

Review of Hemispheric Specialization

The contributions in this volume represent a good cross-section of current thought on the approaches to hemispheric specialization, an up-to-date, state-of-the-art report. While they include quite diverse approaches from a variety of disciplines, the most striking observation in this collection of contributions is the constraint shown by the investigators. Following an initial period of exuberant and rather fanciful postulations concerning the activities of the two hemispheres, a considerable retraction to more solid observations has occurred. The contributions in this volume document, in almost all instances, the potential that is present for misleading information and erroneous observations. Restraint and caution in the analysis of individual hemispheric activity epitomizes this period.

This is not to say, however, that the theories of hemispheric specialization developed in the past few decades are no longer recognized. The observations of the 1950s and 1960s emanated from observations following neurosurgical procedures, specifically hemispherectomy and commissural separation; they clearly demonstrated that each cerebral hemisphere was capable of a mental life, even when the other hemisphere was absent, and that when the two hemispheres were both present but anatomically separated, significant differences in the function of the two hemispheres could be demonstrated. In the ensuing years, a number of different means of studying hemispheric specialization, both in the neurosurgically modified individuals and in the intact brain, have been devised. All of these techniques have significant pitfalls and are easily misinterpreted. The reports in this volume clearly indicate this problem, and the restraint that characterizes many of the contributions demonstrates a maturation of the scientific inquiry into individual hemispheric activity.

Many of the wildest and most fanciful hypotheses that followed the initial observations have been discarded, replaced by considerably more cautious hypotheses. Nonetheless, differences in the function of the two hemispheres are still recognized. Almost without exception, each contribution in this volume demonstrates that careful, well-managed research can and does demonstrate differences in hemispheric function. There is a great need for improved techniques and more sophisticated

hypotheses; both appear probable in the immediate future and promise better understanding of the individual activities carried out by each cerebral hemisphere.

One distinct conclusion seems evident — that the simple right–left dichotomy
is rarely sufficient. There is so much specialized activity within each hemisphere,
often performed by both hemispheres but in a somewhat different manner, that accurate research into hemispheric specialization will demand isolation and investigation of these individual activities. Research of the future must be far more carefully
directed, utilizing more refined research techniques, use of more carefully selected
research subjects, and development of more sophisticated theoretical models.

IMPLICATIONS FOR PHYSICIANS

Is hemispheric specialization actually important for most physicians? Will increased knowledge of the activities that are performed exclusively by one or in a
different manner by the two hemispheres truly affect medical practice? In the vast
majority of instances, the answer to this question is *no*. Most internists, surgeons,
generalists, and others — physicians who deal with general systemic disturbances — are
not likely to be affected by increased knowledge of hemispheric specialization. Activity of the cerebral hemispheres plays little or not part in the medical problems
dealt with by the vast majority of medical physicians.

In contrast, those MDs who work with brain function are likely to be affected
by improved knowledge of hemispheric activity. Thus, some neurologists and neurosurgeons currently use information about hemispheric specialization as an important
part of their practice. Again, many specialists within these fields have little or no
need for knowledge of hemispheric specialization when dealing with more peripheral
conditions such as the extrapyramidal disorders, cerebellar disorders, spinal and nerve
root problems, muscle disorders, and so forth. Only those specialists who work with
brain disorders, particularly those affecting the cortex, are affected by current knowledge of hemispheric specialization. Neurologists and neurosurgeons use this information for the localization of central nervous system problems; however, the art of
cerebral localization has largely been replaced by x-ray computed tomography and
related diagnostic techniques, so that even here, refined knowledge of hemispheric
specialization is not of tremendous concern. The neurosurgeon is concerned with
what a given portion of a given hemisphere performs when determining the extent
and exact localization of brain surgery. Most often, however, the surgeon's hand is
directed by nature; the location of the tumor, the hematoma, or the contusion is
most often the major determining factor. Thus, increased knowledge of hemispheric
specialization has only limited importance even for those physicians whose practice
concerns brain abnormality, and almost none for a majority of practicing physicians.

FUTURE IMPLICATIONS OF HEMISPHERIC SPECIALIZATION

In contrast to general medicine, there are a number of specialty groups that
do utilize hemispheric specialization or would be affected if sufficient information
was available. These groups, both medical and paramedical, consistently deal with

brain function and would be able to make use of improved knowledge of any differences in the function of the two brains. Four such groups will be identified and discussed in an attempt to highlight some of the future implications and hemispheric specialization as they affect medical and paramedical practices.

Psychometry and Other Measurements of Cerebral Function

Most clinical psychologists and all neuropsychologists are acutely aware of right–left differences. The differences are clearly recognized in a number of currently used testing situations (e.g., verbal vs. performance scales of the Wechsler Adult Intelligence Scale). This information has been available for a number of decades and has allowed the clinical psychologist to make reasonably accurate determinations of whether the major clinical problem of a patient involves the right hemisphere or the left hemisphere [20]. Most such formal scales, however, were devised without specific recognition of the separate functioning of the two hemispheres; as such, they were not designed to delineate these differences clearly. Many psychologists have altered the standard tests in one or more ways to achieve better demonstration of hemispheric differences. In addition, innumerable new tests have been designed and used in attempts to highlight hemispheric specialization. Examples of the latter include a number of specialized language tests [11,27], construction activities [2, 13], facial-recognition tests [4, 31], emotional tests [6, 15], tests of melody [12, 24], gesture tests [10, 23], and others. As demonstrations of consistent differences between right-hemisphere-damaged patients and left-hemisphere-damaged patients, none of these tests has been fully successful; this at least partially reflects selection of subjects for testing. It is clear that not all individuals with right-hemisphere damage show abnormality in all tests purported to be "right-hemisphere," and vice versa. The need to localize function within the hemisphere and then compare only damage to homologous brain areas in the two hemispheres is recognized. This subject selection demand poses a considerable problem, one that has not been fully met in most investigations to date. Continuing activity is great in this area, however, and both the tests utilized and the selection of subjects for testing are being improved consistently. The psychologist who measures brain function is strongly influenced by differences in hemispheric specialization, and, as a group, psychologists are actively investigating in this field.

Remedial Education

Theories suggesting that there are significant differences in right-hemisphere and left-hemisphere functions in individuals have been popular in explaining differences in learning in many educational circles. To date, however, investigations in this direction have not produced a great practical influence. The subfield of education that diagnoses and treats those individuals with specific learning disabilities, remedial education, appears to be particularly influenced by differences in the way the hemispheres function. Currently, as in the past, most education is performed in a holistic, unitary fashion; a single teaching method has been given to a broad

spectrum of both normal and abnormal learners. In recent years, there has been a
search for specialized learning techniques to be used on individuals with a learning
disability; again, most such attempts have used a single teaching method across the
entire spectrum of learning-disabled subjects. In all instances, the result has been
a limited success. Some students improve; others do not. Whether the specific technique is successful remains questionable.

It seems probable that both the testing procedures and teaching techniques utilized in learning disabilities would be improved greatly if information concerning
hemispheric specialization could be put into broader use. If the holistic teaching patterns could be replaced by procedures devised for specific types of learning disability, the overall results should be better. This would demand improved testing, tests
specifically designed to probe the individual student's defects and, conversely, to outline the residual strengths. It is not unreasonable to anticipate that these strengths
and weaknesses would often be based on variations of function within each hemisphere. Based on this information, an educational program could be tailored for the
student's particular situation. Teaching techniques would utilize the testing information in order to produce the best possible end product for the learning-disabled child.
While it may offer only a portion of the necessary information, improved knowledge
of hemispheric specialization would appear to be crucially important for specialists
in remedial education.

Psychiatry

Psychiatry, the venerable field of medical psychology, is just emerging from a
prolonged period of hyperspecialization featuring a limited approach to brain function. Most psychiatrists are now aware that the purely dynamic approach to mental
problems provides only a portion of the necessary solution; the future in psychiatry
demands an amalgamation of the dynamics affecting a given psychosocial situation
with the more basic biological problems that influence an individual brain. Better
understanding of the biological bases of mental activity demands a considerably better understanding of many factors. Among these factors, hemispheric specialization
would appear to be a potentially important factor.

Dual-brain (dual-mind) explanations of psychiatric disorder are ancient (34)
but have not proved tenable. More recent suggestions of cerebral asymmetries (22,
25) or cerebral symmetry (19, 33) as explanations of schizophrenia have not been sub-
stantiated by wider observations. Depression as a left-hemisphere malfunction has
been suggested (9, 21) but lacks strong proof. Flor-Henry (8) and followers have
posited significant differences in the psychiatric symptomatology complicating temporal lobe epilepsy, depending on whether the focus is in the right or the left temporal lobe. Others (17, 28), however, have failed to replicate this difference. There
is sufficient suggestion from current studies to warrant serious consideration, but,
to date, evidence of hemispheric specialization as a major factor in psychiatric symptomatology remains unproved (30).

Correlation of the recognized differences in hemispheric function in individual psychiatric patients with their psychosocial dynamic states and with other biological states such as neurotransmitter balance promises a considerably broader field for future psychiatrists, and a great deal more hope for understanding and helping individuals with mental problems. Psychiatric therapy based on variations of individual strengths and weaknesses, utilizing demonstrations of specialized functions, offers a bright new future for both the psychiatrists and their clients.

Rehabilitation Medicine

It seems probable that the most important use of current and future knowledge of hemispheric specialization will involve the relatively new field of rehabilitation medicine, particularly that part dealing with damage to the central nervous system. Brain damage is common, and its residue is an important aspect of contemporary medicine. Individuals being treated for the residual effects of stroke, of brain trauma, and of postneurosurgical states now have a considerable opportunity to recover major functions. The brain does not regenerate, however, and rehabilitation demands substitution for a damaged function by another function through improved and/or altered use of surviving functions. Just as rehabilitation of acquired blindness would demand improved use of both auditory and somesthetic sensory systems as replacements, there are many functions within the brain that can be utilized to substitute for a missing function or can be taught to improve their own function so as to be of greater usefulness for the patient. Rehabilitation of a brain-damaged patient must be oriented toward improving the surviving qualities, not toward attempting to stimulate nonexisting functions. Thus, changes in optometric refraction are of little help in the blindness resulting from brain damage. Similarly, attempts to return aphasics to normal speech or hemiplegics to normal ambulation are limited in success. Appropriate therapy demands a considerable knowledge of the specific activities of various brain areas; hemispheric specialization of these activities is of obvious significance.

While considerable progress has been made in the past few decades, there remains a need for improved techniques in both testing and therapy; differences in function of the two hemispheres (only one of which may be significantly damaged) promise an avenue of great hope in both respects. Only in recent years have neurologists become involved in neurological rehabilitation, and their activity is already manifested by an increased sophistication in the testing of brain-damaged patients for potential rehabilitation. In addition to the improved testing processes, new plans for rehabilitation, based on implementing the surviving capabilities, are being devised.

Within rehabilitation medicine, a number of subspecialty groups are already active and have made some important inroads in the use of hemispheric and intrahemispheric specialization for their therapy techniques. For instance, within the aphasia rehabilitation portion of speech pathology, specialized techniques are being designed for specific types of aphasia and dysarthria. Thus, melodic intonation therapy (1) is advised only for the aphasic with specific language disturbance. The technique has proved effective only for those whose aphasia is nonfluent, who have relatively preserved ability to comprehend, who have difficulty with repetition, and whose oral agility is disturbed. Similarly, AMERIND (26) and VAT (16) are techniques suggested for totally different types of aphasia, those that feature serious problems in language comprehension. In addition, both techniques are appropriate only for initial language therapy, to be followed by other, selected treatment methods. Many additional techniques that focus on specific disabilities are needed to improve aphasia rehabilitation further. At least some of these techniques will utilize features of hemispheric specialization. Many believe that the success of melodic intonation therapy evolves from the stress on the preserved melodic competency of many left-hemisphere-damaged aphasics, and similar uses of other right-hemisphere competencies may be of value in the future of aphasia therapy.

Specific remedial techniques for different types of dysarthria have also been devised. Again, differences based on the anatomically determined source of the dysarthria and, at least in some instances, the hemisphere involved, are of importance in the choice of remedial techniques (5).

The physical medicine portion of rehabilitation medicine increasingly uses knowledge about hemispheric specialization. Differences in motor disability based on combinations of motor paralysis, sensory loss, and unilateral inattention demand considerably different therapy approaches. Recognition (3, 14) and remediation (7) of unilateral inattention are in early stages, but are already of demonstrated usefulness in improving the final stage of a hemiplegic recovery.

A relatively new approach within rehabilitation medicine concerns cognitive therapy. For many years, alterations in damage to cognitive abilities was considered beyond the reach of rehabilitation; in recent years, however, a number of novel therapy techniques have been devised, some of which appear to be helpful. Thus, use of computer teaching techniques (32), programmed learning (18), and the development of relatively noninvolved skills (29) all provide improvements in the cognitive disability that can follow significant brain injury.

As can be noted from this short review, there is both need and opportunity for many new techniques within rehabilitation medicine. The principles underlying these techniques are broad and are just now being developed; the potential for use of information concerning hemispheric specialization in the development of new rehabilitation techniques appears considerable. In fact, it seems quite probable that a great deal of the new knowledge of hemispheric specialization will come from the efforts of specialists in rehabilitation medicine. As they study ways to help their brain-damaged clients, rehabilitation specialists will be increasingly aware of hemispheric differences and will become more dependent upon these differences to bring about the improvements they seek. More than any other branch of medicine, rehabilitation medicine appears strongly influenced by hemispheric differences in function.

The outline above suggests a probable course for the study of hemispheric specialization and the place this knowledge will take within the practice of medicine. It would appear that most new ideas and new approaches will come from specific areas of medicine (such as those discussed above), those that consistently deal with focal brain abnormalities. While the recent spurt in interest in hemispheric specialization largely followed the work of neurosurgeons, it would appear that the next wave of advances in our knowledge and recognition of hemispheric specialization will come from those individuals who deal regularly with brain-injured patients. Specialties such as rehabilitation medicine, neuropsychology, behavioral neurology, organic psychiatry, and remedial education appear to be those that will produce new information on this aspect of brain function.

REFERENCES

1. Albert, M. L., Sparks, R., and Helm, N., Melodic intonation therapy for aphasia. *Arch. Neurol.*, 1973, **29**: 130–131.
2. Arrigoni, G., and De Renzi, E., Constructional apraxia and hemispheric locus of lesion. *Cortex*, 1964, **1**: 170–197.
3. Battersby, W. S., Bender, M. B., and Kahn, R. L., Unilateral spatial agnosia (inattention). *Brain*, 1956, **79**: 68–92.
4. Benton, A. L., and Van Allen, M. W., Impairment in facial recognition in patients with cerebral disease. *Cortex*, 1969, **4**: 344–358.
5. Darley, F. L., Aronson, A. E., and Brown, J. R., *Motor Speech Disorders*. W. B. Saunders, Philadelphia, 1975.
6. De Kosky, S., Heilman, K. M., Bowers, D., and Valenstein, E., Recognition and discrimination of emotional faces and pictures. *Brain Lang.*, 1980, **9**: 206–214.
7. Diller, L., and Weinberg, J., Hemi-inattention in rehabilitation: The evolution of a rational remediation program. In: *Advances in Neurology, Vol. 18, Hemi-Inattention and Hemisphere Specialization* (E. A. Weinstein and R. P. Friedland, Eds.). Raven Press, New York, 1977, 63–82.
8. Flor-Henry, P., Schizophrenic-like reactions and affective psychoses associated with temporal epilepsy: Etiological factors. *Am. J. Psychiatry*, 1969, **126**: 400–403.
9. Gainotti, G., Emotional behavior and hemispheric side of lesion. *Cortex*, 1972, **8**: 41–45.
10. Goodglass, H., and Kaplan, E., Disturbance of gesture and pantomine in aphasia. *Brain*, 1963, **86**(4): 703–720.
11. Goodglass, H., and Kaplan, E., *The Assessment of Aphasia and Related Disorders*. Lea & Febiger, Philadelphia, 1972.
12. Gordon, H. W., and Bogen, J. E., Hemispheric lateralization of singing after intracarotid sodium amylobarbitone. *J. Neurol. Neurosurg. Psychiatry*, 1974, **37**: 727–738.
13. Hécaen, H., and Assal, G. A., Comparison of constructive deficits following right and left hemispheric lesions. *Neuropsychologia*, 1970, **8**: 289–303.
14. Heilman, K. M., Neglect and related disorders. In: *Clinical Neuropsychology* (K. Heilman and E. Valenstein, Eds.). Oxford University Press, New York, 1979: 268–307.
15. Heller, W., and Levy, J., Perception and expression of emotion in right-handers and left-handers. *Neuropsychologia*, 1981, **19**: 263–272.
16. Helm-Estabrooks, N., Fitzpatrick, P. M., and Barresi, B., Visual action therapy for global aphasia. *J. Speech Hear. Disord.*, 1982, **47**: 385–389.
17. Jensen, I., and Larsen, J. K., Mental aspects of temporal lobe epilepsy. *J. Neurol. Neurosurg. Psychiatry*, 1979, **42**: 256–265.
18. La Pointe, L. L., Base-10 programmed stimulation: Task specification, scoring and plotting performance in aphasia therapy. *J. Speech Hear. Disord.*, 1977, **42**: 90–105.

19. Naeser, M. A., Levine, H. L., Benson, D. F., Stuss, D. T., and Weir, W. S., Frontal leukotomy size and hemispheric asymmetries on computerized tomographic scans of schizophrenics with variable recovery. *Arch. Neurol.*, 1981, 38: 30–37.

20. Reitan, R. M., Psychological deficits resulting from cerebral lesions in man. In: *The Frontal Granular Cortex and Behavior* (J. M. Warren and K. Akert, Eds.). McGraw-Hill, New York, 1964: 295–312.

21. Robinson, R. G., and Price, T. R., Post-stroke depressive disorders: A follow-up study of 103 outpatients. *Stroke*, 1982, 13: 635–641.

22. Roemer, R. A., Shagass, C., Straumanis, J. J., and Amadeo, M., Pattern evoked potential measurements suggesting lateralized hemispheric dysfunction in chronic schizophrenics. *Biol. Psychiatry*, 1978, 13: 185–202.

23. Ross, E. D., The aprosodias: Functional–anatomic organization of the affective components of language in the right hemisphere. *Arch. Neurol.*, 1981, 38: 561–569.

24. Ross, E. D., and Mesulam, M.-M., Dominant language functions of the right hemisphere. *Arch. Neurol.*, 1979, 36: 144–148.

25. Schweitzer, L., Becker, E., and Welsh, H., Abnormalities of cerebral lateralization in schizophrenia. *Arch. Gen. Psychiatry*, 1978, 35: 982–985.

26. Skelly, M., Schinsky, L., Smith, R., and Fust, R., American Indian sign (Amerind) as a facilitator of verbalization for the oral verbal apraxic. *J. Speech Hear. Disord.*, 1974, 39: 445–446.

27. Spreen, O., and Benton, A., *Neurosensory Center Comprehensive Examination for Aphasia*. Neuropsychology Laboratory, University of Victoria, Victoria, B.C., Canada, 1969.

28. Stevens, J. R., Interictal clinical manifestations of complex partial seizures. In: *Advances in Neurology*, Vol. 11; *Complex Partial Seizures and Their Treatment* (J. K. Penry and D. D. Daly, Eds.). Raven Press, New York, 1975; 85–112.

29. Taylor, M., Schaeffer, J. N., Blumenthal, F. S., and Grisell, J. L., Perceptual training in patients with left hemiplegia. *Arch. Phys. Med. Rehabil.*, 1971, 52: 163–169.

30. Trimble, M. R., The interictal psychoses of epilepsy. In: *Psychiatric Aspects of Neurologic Disease*, Vol. 2 (D. F. Benson and D. Blumer, Eds.). Grune & Stratton, New York, 1982: 75–91.

31. Tzavaras, A., Hécaen, H., and Le Bras, H., Le problème de la spécificité du déficit de la reconnaissance du visage humain lors des lésions hémisphériques unilaterales. *Neuropsychologia*, 1970, 8: 403–416.

32. Vanderheiden, G. C., Practical application of microcomputers to aid the handicapped. *Computer*, 1981, 00: 54–61.

33. Weinberger, D. R., Torrey, E. F., Neophytides, A. N., Wyatt, R. J., Lateral cerebral ventricular enlargement in chronic schizophrenics. *Arch. Gen. Psychiatry*, 1979, 36: 735–739.

34. Wigan, A. L., *The Duality of the Mind*. Longmans, London, 1844.

ACADEMIC IMPLICATIONS OF
DUAL-BRAIN THEORY

ERAN ZAIDEL, PhD
Department of Psychology

A Paradigm Case for
Brain–Behavior Relations: Convergence

The scientific study of hemispheric specialization is probably unique in the opportunities it provides for the analysis of brain–behavior relations, because each cerebral hemisphere is a clearly demarcated structural and functional system. Structurally, each hemisphere is a distinct anatomical unit supported by its own cytoarchitecture and physiological and neurochemical processes. Moreover, much of the communication between the two structures occurs through a specific, spatially identifiable fiber system — the neocortical commissures — whose properties are amenable to scientific analysis. Indeed, intercommissural communication can serve as a general model for cortico-cortical interactions (i.e., interactions between cortical modules or cell assemblies). This provides a particularly simple paradigm for investigating general principles of intermodular cortico-cortical facilitation, inhibition, and information transfer.

Functionally, each hemisphere seems to be a distinct and complete cognitive system with a characteristic information-processing style. One can therefore systematically study the differences in how the two hemispheres handle perception, cognition, learning, memory, language, intelligence, orientation to the environment, and social interactions, including alterations during development and with maturation. As these behaviors are central to many of the social sciences, the study of hemispheric specialization is of interest to such diverse fields as linguistics, education, psychiatry, sociology, anthropology, and the arts.

From Structure to Function

We believe that the most important contribution of dual-brain theory concerns the interplay between structure and function in mind–brain relations. In modern neuroscience, underlying structure is becoming increasingly important for the analysis of function, particularly of the highest mental functions. Indeed, a breakthrough in modern dual-brain theory occurred when functional questions, such as

"What is the nature of hemispheric specialization?" were replaced by more structural ones, such as "What function does the corpus callosum play?" If functional questions can be translated into structural ones, then the domain of cognitive psychology enters the purview of neuroscience.

For example, an outstanding question in psycholinguistics is the nature of the representation and construction of lexical meaning during reading. One popular model (1) represents the meaning relation between two words encountered in sequence as a spreading semantic activation between two nodes in a lexical semantic network. By restricting the two words to opposite visual fields (and thus opposite hemispheres), the spreading semantic activation can be directed through the corpus callosum, allowing measurement of the time course, informational complexity, and functional components of the meaning relation, providing a functional analysis of callosal transfer is available. In this situation, the shift from function to structure and back is accomplished by conceptualizing the corpus callosum as a channel of communication (4).

NATURE VERSUS NURTURE IN DUAL-BRAIN THEORY

The early emphasis in dual-brain theory on structural–anatomical models that emphasize callosal traffic has recently given way to functional models that allow considerable normal variation. This is best illustrated by Kinsbourne's attentional model of behavioral laterality effects in hemispheric-specialization experiments with normal subjects (3). This model focuses on psychological differences in attentional and expectancy effects, rather than on anatomical connectivity (2). Another example is the move from the view that individual patterns of hemispheric specialization are prescribed at birth to the dynamic view that hemispheric control shifts as a function of experimental parameters, such as secondary hemispheric priming and overloading (see E. Zaidel, Introduction to Biological and Psychological Studies of Hemispheric Specialization, this volume). Other examples of experimental conditions that change the pattern of hemispheric interaction are hypnosis and anxiety.

But it could be premature—indeed, fatal for dual-brain theory—to adopt wholesale functionalism or "psychologism." The examples of experimental modulation of interhemispheric interaction are all limited in scope and subject to structural constraints. Strong individual differences in patterns of hemispheric organization, such as those due to handedness and sex, resist any environmental perturbation (barring massive early brain damage). Similarly, ontogenesis does not seem to exhibit systematic general changes in relative hemispheric specialization, and even deprivation studies do not always result in reorganization of patterns of cerebral activation. Thus, congenital deafness does not seem to modify left-hemisphere specialization in sign language. In short, we believe it is theoretically premature and methodologically costly to abandon the structural approach to dual-brain theory at the present time, however oversimplified it appears.

Modularity

The two cerebral hemispheres represent two separate information-processing modules. Since both are complex cognitive systems, both process information independently and in parallel (hemispheric independence) and their interaction is neither arbitrary nor continuous. We believe that the general rules or mechanisms for hemispheric specialization and interaction are innately specified, in other words, prewired and neuroanatomically specific, that is, localized. The mechanisms are also "encapsulated" in the sense that they are not arbitrarily sensitive to task parameters and set effects, to the individual's neurological and psychological histories, and to his or her beliefs, desires, and other mental states. These are the three criteria of modularity out of Fodor's list of nine that we accept as valid. In short, the cerebral hemispheres are central superprocessing modules, the kind whose existence is denied by Fodor (1a).

A common cognitive psychological criterion for modularity is resource independence, or the absence of interference in dual-task performance. Using this criterion, each central supermodule may be said to contain central submodules. Thus we do not agree with the view that the two cerebral hemispheres are independent resource pools and that each hemisphere has undifferentiated resources where any two tasks interfere with each other (1b). Rather, we think of the mind as a cognitive–cerebral network with a continuous distance metric defined in terms of functional–anatomical connectivity between modules (3). There is structure in the metric. For example, the distance between some module Ax and another Bx in hemisphere x is "shorter" than between Ax and the symmetric contralateral module By in hemisphere y. There exist tasks that involve separate central processing components within one hemisphere which do not interact (6). Central processing modules within a hemisphere may or may not interfere with output or response programming modules in the same hemisphere, depending on the cognitive load of the task (6). When they do interfere, the interference is greater within than across the hemispheres (6). Moreover, the two hemispheres may interfere with each other by inhibition even in the absence of the corpus callosum (6). In short, some submodules within a hemisphere are independent, and some modules across the commissures from each other are not.

INTERHEMISPHERIC INTERACTION

The next major question facing dual-brain theory undoubtedly concerns the problem of interhemispheric cross-callosal interaction. If each hemisphere is an independent cognitive system, how and when do they communicate, what is the nature of the information transmitted, who (or what) controls the transmission, and how often does interhemispheric transfer occur? A possible answer stems from recent data concerning callosal function in animals and humans. The emerging model is of the corpus callosum as a set of communication channels, each with a definite capacity,

rate, and loss determined by anatomical, physiological, and neurochemical properties of the particular callosal fibers involved. For example, a modality-specific mapping of callosal functions assigns visual functions to the posterior part (the splenium)
of the corpus callosum, auditory functions to an area just anterior to the splenium,
and somesthetic functions just anterior to that through the middle part of the callosum (4). More anterior parts may mediate progressively more abstract information. Indeed, individuals may differ in their degree of callosal connectivity in some
callosal regions (channels) but not in others, and this may contribute to individual
differences in cognitive repertoires.

A promising research approach would study the timing and effects of callosal
transfer of different types of information, from simple binary motor decisions (e.g.,
move or do not move the left index finger) through complex categorization decisions
in choice reaction-time experiments and transfer of meaning or abstract rules in con-
cept-formation tests, to transfer of inhibition, activation, and control signals from
one hemisphere to the other in order to coordinate interaction. Such control traffic
may be especially important in mediating compensatory processing in the intact
hemisphere following damage to the other (5).

Prospects and Challenges

Each methodology and population currently available to the study of hemispheric
specialization has its own limitations (see Bogen, "Some Historical and Methodological
Aspects," this volume). None is definitive. Consequently, a systematic, convergent
approach seems most promising at the present time. We need convergence of normal
and deficit states, of physiological and behavioral measures, of monitoring and intervention studies. Heretofore neglected and of special interest is the use of personality
and learning theories in the analysis of reward systems and learning styles of the two
hemispheres.

Much current excitement attaches to methodologies for real-time monitoring
of cerebral activation (EEG, ERP, MEG, PET, rCBF), but these must have a cognitive window of 1 msec before they become cognitively informative and must be
even faster in order to be biochemically informative. Monitoring of cerebral function
would then complement ever-improving methods for imaging brain structure (CT
scans, NMR, etc.). It can be anticipated that the next 50 years will witness a revolutionary improvement in our ability to manipulate and observe the local structure
of brain through benign and reversible lesions. Experiments made possible by such
technological advances will have to be interpreted with far more sophisticated theoretical modeling tools than we presently possess. The development of improved
theories and more general models of brain–behavior relations in hemispheric specialization already offers a true challenge for future research in human neuropsychology.

REFERENCES

1. Collins, A. M., and Loftus, E. F., A spreading-activation theory of semantic process-
     ing. *Psychol. Rev.*, 1975, **82**: 407–428.
1a. Fodor, J. A., *Modularity of Mind*. MIT Press, Cambridge, Mass., 1983.
1b. Herdman, C. M., and Friedman, A., Multiple resources in divided attention: A cross-
     modal test of the independence of hemispheric resources. *J. Exp. Psychol. (Hum.
     Percept.)*, 1985, **11**: 40–49.
2. Kimura, D., Cerebral dominance and the perception of verbal stimuli. *Can. J. Psychol.*,
     1961, **15**: 166–171.
3. Kinsbourne, M., and Hicks, R., Functional cerebral space: A model for overflow, trans-
     fer and interference effects in human performance: A tutorial review. In: *Attention
     and Performance VII* (J. Requin, Ed.). Erlbaum, Hillsdale, N.J., 1978: 345–362.
4. Zaidel, E., Callosal dynamics and right hemisphere language. In: *Two Hemispheres,
     One Brain?* (F. Lepre, M. Ptito, and H. H. Jasper, Eds.). Alan R. Liss, New York,
     in press.
5. Zaidel, E., and Schweiger, A., On wrong hypotheses about the right hemisphere.
     Cognitive Neuropsychology, 1984, **1**: 351–364.
6. Zaidel, E., Letai, D., and White, H., Modules of the brain: A dual task approach to
     hemispheric function. Unpublished manuscript, Department of Psychology, The
     University of California, Los Angeles.

AUTHOR INDEX

Abert, M. L., 143, 148, 153n., 239, 241, 242n.
Abrams, R., 379, 383n.
Acherman, N., 324, 326n.
Ackerman, R. H., 183, 190n.
Adams, R. N., 237, 245n.
Adevai, G., 344, 358n.
Adler, A., 241, 242n.
Aitken, L., 137, 139n.
Ajmone Marsan, C., 264, 273n.
Akelaitis, A. J., 282, 286n., 293, 300n.
Alajouanine, T., 363, 365, 371n.
Alavi, A., 183, 185, 186, 188, 190n., 191n., 192n., 379, 382n.
Albanese, A., 235, 242n.
Albert, M. L., 35, 39n., 389, 391n.
Alesandrini, K., 335, 339n.
Allard, F., 217, 227n.
Allison, R. S., 241, 242n.
Allison, T., 166, 177n.
Alpert, N. M., 183, 190n.
Alsum, P., 77, 93n.
Alvin, J., 361, 371n.
Amadeo, M., 388, 392n.
Amaducci, L., 235, 242n.
Amaral, D. G., 281, 286n.
Ames, L., 104, 113n.
Andermann, F., 237, 243n., 263, 274n.
Andreason, N. C., 378, 380, 382n.
Andre-Balliseaux, G., 13, 25n., 289, 301n.
Andre, T., 333, 338n.
Andrew, R. J., 48, 50, 60n.
Angelergues, R., 34, 40n., 207, 229n.
Ankerhus, J., 240, 246n.
Annett, M., 79, 91n., 100, 104, 106, 112n., 197, 202n.
Apuzzo, M. L. J., 291, 300n.
Aram, D., 106, 107, 115n.
Arbib, M. A., 319, 326n.
Archer, D., 213, 229n.

Archibald, Y., 207, 226n., 290, 302n.
Arena, R., 239, 242n.
Ariel, R. N., 378, 382n.
Aristotle, 329, 338n.
Armstrong, D. M., 24, 25n.
Arnheim, R., 360, 371n.
Arnold, A. P., 48–50, 60n., 84, 91n., 95n.
Aronson, A. E., 266, 273n., 390, 391n.
Arrigoni, G., 387, 391n.
Asarnow, R. F., 174, 176n., 179n.
Ashton, R., 219, 229n.
Assal, G., 33, 34, 39n., 387, 391n.
Augustine, E. A., 249, 260n.
Axelrod, S., 218, 226n.
Ayoub, D. M., 76, 91n.

Baack, J., 83, 91n.
Babb, T. L., 268, 273n.
Bailey, P., 277, 286n.
Bain, F. D., 219, 229n.
Bakan, D., 350, 355n.
Bakan, P., 79, 91n., 343, 356n.
Baron, J. C., 187, 189n.
Barresi, B., 390, 391n.
Barry, C., 218, 226n.
Barth, D. S., 176, 176n.
Bartholomeus, B. N., 368, 371n.
Barton, M. I., 239, 242n.
Baskin, Y., 8, 9, 10n.
Basser, L., 99, 112n.
Battersby, W. S., 390, 391n.
Battig, W. F., 254, 259n.
Baumbach, H. D., 268, 269, 273n.
Bayer, J., 183, 184, 191n.
Baymur, L., 118, 125n.
Bear, D. M., 213, 226n., 264, 270, 273n., 310, 316n., 376, 382n.
Beard, A. W., 265, 275n.
Beatty, J., 176, 176n., 329, 339n.
Beatty, W. W., 77, 91n.

Beaumont, J. G., 48, 60n., 143, 153n., 312, 316n., 333, 338n., 377, 382n.

Becker, E., 388, 392n.

Becker, J. B., 85, 86, 95n.

Beecher, M. D., 52, 62n., 88, 91n., 95n.

Behan, P., 82, 93n., 105, 113n.

Behrens, M. M., 237, 243n.

Bellugi, U., 110, 115n., 311, 316n., 320, 326n., 327n.

Bemporad, B., 34, 41n.

Bender, M. B., 237, 242n., 390, 391n.

Benowitz, L. I., 213, 226n., 310, 316n.

Benson, D. A., 52, 63n.

Benson, D. F., 33, 35, 39n., 170, 179n., 188, 189n., 199, 200, 202n., 216, 226n., 235–237, 239, 241, 242n., 243n., 245n., 264, 273n., 331, 339n., 388, 392n.

Bentin, S., 220, 229n.

Benton, A. L., 34, 35, 39n., 40n., 41n., 148, 153n., 161, 162n., 194, 202n., 239, 242n., 387, 391n., 392n.

Berenbaum, S. A., 79, 91n.

Berg, R. A., 378, 382n., 383n.

Berger, H., 163, 176n.

Bergstrom, M., 188, 192n.

Berko-Gleason, J., 210, 227n.

Berlin, C., 109, 112n., 128–131, 134, 137, 139n., 140n., 216, 226n.

Berlin, H., 109, 112n., 216, 226n.

Berlucchi, G., 35, 39n., 42n., 155n., 289, 300n.

Berndt, R. S., 215, 226n.

Bernstein, B., 351, 356n.

Bernstein, L., 361, 371n.

Berrebi, A. S., 85–87, 95n.

Berry, J. W., 344, 353, 356n.

Bertelson, P., 147, 153n.

Besner, D., 217, 229n.

Bever, T. G., 359, 368, 371n.

Bhargava, M., 87, 90, 94n.

Bingley, T., 104, 112n., 117, 118, 123, 124n.

Bion, P. J., 208, 230n.

Birch, J., 235, 245n.

Birch, M., 101, 115n.

Bishop, D., 118, 123, 124n., 222, 226n.

Bishop, N., 100, 106, 112n.

Blackstock, E., 106, 112n.

Blakemore, C. B., 247, 259n.

Blau, J. N., 362, 363, 364, 371n.

Blume, W. T., 266, 273n., 281, 286n.

Blumenberg, B., 54, 60n.

Blumenthal, F. S., 390, 392n.

Blumer, D., 264, 273n.

Blumstein, S., 129, 139n., 219, 229n., 325, 327n.

Bobrow, D. G., 149, 154n.

Bocca, E., 132, 139n.

Bock, C., 310, 317n.

Boder, E., 312, 316n., 380, 382n.

Bogen, G. M., 289, 298, 300n., 344, 345, 356n.

Bogen, J., 14, 17, 18, 21, 25n., 26n., 29, 30, 35, 36, 38, 39n., 40n., 41n., 43n., 143, 148, 153n., 208, 209, 226n., 282, 284, 285, 286n., 287n., 289, 291–293, 295, 298–300, 300n., 303n., 312, 316n., 329, 339n., 341, 342, 344, 345, 352, 355, 356n., 357n., 358n., 364, 366, 371n., 387, 391n.

Boller, F., 33, 39n., 198, 202n.

Bolozky, S., 147, 148, 154n.

Bonin, G. Von, 65, 67, 73n.

Booth, J. E., 77, 92n.

Bordeau, P., 351, 356n.

Borstein, B., 34, 35, 39n., 42n.

Botez, M. I., 292, 300n., 363, 364, 371n., 373n.

Bottjer, S. W., 48–50, 60n., 84, 91n.

Bousser, M. G., 187, 189n.

Bower, G. H., 334, 338n.

Bowers, D., 123, 124n., 129, 139n., 236, 240, 244n., 391n.

Bradley, D. 153n., 219, 226n.

Bradshaw, J., 35, 40n., 143, 147, 149, 153n.

Bradshaw, J. L., 12, 25n., 48, 53, 61n., 79, 80, 91n., 217–220, 226n., 227n., 233, 242n., 298, 301n., 367, 372n.

Braff, D., 380, 382n.

SUBJECT INDEX

Street's Gestalt Completion Test, 351, 352
Stress, and directional bias, 87
Stroke cases, 30
Structure and function, 393, 394
Sturge–Weber–Dimitri syndrome, 222
Stuttering, 171–174
Subjectivism, 23–25
Superego, 310
Superficial cerebral hemosiderosis, 280
"Surface dyslexia," 223
Sylvian fissure
  evolution, 54
  hemispheric asymmetry, 234
  monkeys, 52
Symbols, 354, 355
Syntactic language, 200, 201, 201n.
Synthetic reason, 344
Syntax
  frontal areas, event-related potentials, 170
  and lateralization, 107–111
  left hemisphere, 107
  right hemisphere, 211, 216, 222, 223, 297, 298
  and song birds, 49
Syrinx, 48, 49, 84

T-maze, sex differences, rodents, 85–87
Tachistoscope studies, 143 152
  Chelsea case, laterality, 109, 110
  fixation point, 146, 147
  and hemispheric specialization, 143–152
  letters and words, 147
  methodological problems, 33, 34, 56, 146, 147
  as model, 56
  right hemisphere, language, 217, 218
  sex differences, 79, 103
Tactile anomia, 298, 299
Tactual perception, 15, 16
Tail posture, rodents, 85–88
Telegrammatic speech, 107
Temporal cortex
  auditory stimuli, PET, 185
  pathological left-handedness, 117–123

Temporal information, 129
Temporal lobe (see also Temporal lobe epilepsy)
  asymmetry, 235
  auditory stimuli, PET, 185
  cognitive stimuli, PET, 186
  dichotic listening studies, 132, 134–138
Temporal lobe epilepsy
  mood and personality, 264, 265
  and psychosis, 263–273, 376
"Temporary hemispherectomy," 32
Testosterone, 75–91
  left-handedness, learning disorders, 82
  masculinization, 76
  turning preferences, rats, 85–87
Testosterone propionate, 85–87
Thai, pitch, 311
Thalamus
  aphasia, PET, 186
  hemispheric asymmetries, 234
Thiopental, 266
Thorndike's theory, 329
Thurstone's visual-closure factors, 214
Timbre recognition
  and language, 201, 201n.
  right hemisphere, methodology, 36–38
Time perception, 20
Timing, language, 200, 201n.
Token test
  language-impaired children, 106
  right hemisphere, 210, 211
Tone bursts, 129, 130
Tone memory/perception
  dichotic listening, 129
  PET measurement, 185
  right hemisphere, methodology, 36–38
Touch effects, 296, 297
Transcortical motor aphasia, 195n., 196n.
Transcortical sensory aphasia, 195n., 196n.
"Transparency hypothesis," 55
Transverse temporal cortex, 185
Triangularis-opercularis area, 66–73
Turner syndrome, 81, 82